STRANGE
BLOOMS

STRANGE BLOOMS

The Curious Lives *and* Adventures *of the* JOHN TRADESCANTS

Jennifer Potter

ATLANTIC BOOKS

LONDON

First published in Great Britain in 2006 by Atlantic Books,
an imprint of Grove Atlantic Ltd.

1 3 5 7 9 8 6 4 2

A CIP catalogue record for this book is available from the British Library.

ISBN 10: 1 84354 334 6
ISBN 13: 978 184354 334 3

Designed by Nicky Barneby @ Barneby Ltd
Set in 12/14.75pt Jenson Classico
Printed in Great Britain by
MPG Books Ltd, Bodmin, Cornwall

Atlantic Books
An imprint of Grove Atlantic Ltd
Ormond House
26–27 Boswell Street
London WC1N 3JZ

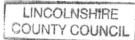

For Chris, Lynn and Robert

'We carry within us the wonders we seek without us.'

Sir Thomas Browne, *Religio Medici* (1643)

Contents

List of Illustrations

Integrated Illustrations

Third picture section

The author and publishers are grateful to the following for permission to reproduce illustrations: pages xxii, 6, 168, plates 21, 22, London Library; pages 16–17, the Marquess of Salisbury; pages 29, 76–7, 87, 150, 182–3, 292–3, 317, plates 3, 6, 7, 8, 9, 19, British Library; pages 45, 228, Royal Horticultural Society, Lindley Library; page 55, plate 24, National Archives; pages 66, 73, 127, 136, 186, 198, 234–5, 250, 339, 371, plates 1, 13, 17, 25,

Museum of Garden History; page 106, Virginia Historical Society; pages 207, 272, plates 10, 11, 12, Ashmolean Museum, Oxford; page 244, plates 14, 20, Canterbury Cathedral Archives; page 362, plates 15, 18, Guildhall Library, City of London; plate 2, Leiden University Library; plates 16, 23, Bodleian Library, University of Oxford.

Acknowledgements

This book would not have happened without the help, advice and encouragement of many people. First, I would like to thank my editor, Angus Mackinnon, for suggesting the idea and for having confidence that I could do it. Any biographer owes a special debt to earlier authors and I am particularly grateful to Prudence Leith-Ross for her interest and help with my researches. I have drawn most heavily on her work with the late Dr John Harvey to identify plants grown and introduced by both Tradescants.

Scholars and specialists were extraordinarily generous in sharing their expertise, none more so than Dr Arthur MacGregor, Senior Assistant Keeper at the Ashmolean Museum, Oxford. I thank him for his encyclopaedic knowledge, exactitude and good humour. His colleagues Dr Jon Whiteley and Kate Heard were both extremely helpful on the portraits and drawings in the museum's collection. I have also benefited enormously from the insights, expertise and enthusiasm of Malgosia Nowak-Kemp at the Oxford University Museum of Natural History; David Sturdy, historian of Lambeth, Oxford and the Tradescants generally; Anne Jennings of the Museum of Garden History; Dr Barrie Juniper, Reader Emeritus in Plant Sciences and Fellow Emeritus of St Catherine's College, Oxford; and historian David Marsh, who shared with me his researches into the Worshipful Company of Gardeners.

For help in appreciating the elder Tradescant's time at Hatfield House, I wish to thank the Dowager Marchioness of Salisbury. Robin Harcourt Williams, Librarian and Archivist to the Marquess of Salisbury, guided me into the archives with great skill and patience, while outdoors, David Beaumont walked me back in time through the Hatfield landscape. At New Hall in Essex, once gardened by Tradescant for the Duke of Buckingham, I am similarly indebted to Sister Mary Magdalene of the Priory of the Resurrection.

Libraries were my home for nearly two years. At the Bodleian Library, Oxford, I would like to thank in particular Dr Bruce Barker-Benfield, Senior Assistant Librarian, and Mike Webb, Head of Cataloguing, Western Manuscripts. Both were generous with their time and knowledge, and helped to turn my visits there into a joy. I pay tribute to the unfailing efficiency and courtesy of staff in the Rare Books, Manuscripts and Maps reading rooms at the British Library, as well as to the staffs of the London Library, the City of London's Guildhall Library, the Huguenot Library at University College London, the Caird Library of the National Maritime Museum and the Lindley Library of the Royal Horticultural Society. My debt is equally great to the many archives and record offices who hold information relating to the Tradescants and their times, and in particular the National Archives at Kew; Magdalen College, Oxford; local record offices in Kent, Northampton and Suffolk; Canterbury Cathedral Archives; the Royal College of Physicians; the London Metropolitan Archives; and the Minet Library in Lambeth, where Jon Newman has accumulated a wealth of knowledge about the Tradescants, generously shared. My thanks go also to Paul Pollak, archivist of the King's School, Canterbury, and to Jane Lingard, whose unpublished MA dissertation for the Courtauld Institute of Art on the houses of Robert Cecil helped to shape my own understanding. Lectures on the Stuart Age at the National Maritime Museum in Greenwich and a study day on early planting by Mark Laird at the Architectural Association, London, gave me many new perspectives.

In planning this book, invaluable suggestions and contacts came from Jan Woudstra, Vanessa Bezemer Sellers, Mavis Batey, David Jacques, and Dr

Brent Elliott, librarian of the Royal Horticultural Society in London, who remained a stalwart source of advice as the book progressed. For translations of Latin letters written during the time of the Civil War, I was lucky to have the help of J. B. Jonas, who took me beyond the letters to an appreciation of character.

My researches in Virginia were made possible by a generous grant from the Authors' Foundation, administered by the Society of Authors. In Virginia itself, I have many contacts to thank, especially local historian Martha W. McCartney, who shared her incomparable knowledge of early settlers and eased my route into the collections of the Library of Virginia and the Rockefeller Library at the Colonial Williamsburg Foundation. Minor Weisiger at the former and Susan Shames at the latter turned my vague questions into concrete references. Martha also introduced me to ethnohistorian Helen C. Rowntree; together we tramped the boardwalks of the Great Dismal Swamp, looking for plants brought back to England by the younger Tradescant. I also enjoyed testing ideas with Dr Thomas E. Davidson of the Jamestown Settlement and with Beverly Straube, curator of the Jamestown Rediscovery Project for the Association for the Preservation of Virginia Antiquities, who gave me many more contacts. Among them was Ivor Noel Hume, who showed me his fine cypress trees by the James River.

Finally, I would like to thank my agent Pat Kavanagh, Clara Farmer and Sarah Norman at Atlantic Books, and all those who helped me to develop this book, especially Jack Klaff for his inspiration and advice at all stages, Robert Petit for his great company, Chris Potter and Lynn Ritchie for shelter and sustenance, and Ros Franey for her continued enthusiasm and support. All errors, gaps, inconsistencies and leaps of faith are, of course, my own.

Note on Sources,
Transliteration and Dates

The notes to each chapter locate unpublished material held in archives and libraries, including Crown copyright material at the National Archives, Kew, and county record offices. I am especially grateful to the Marquess of Salisbury for allowing me to consult and quote from the archives at Hatfield House, and to the following bodies for permission to quote from their material: the Bodleian Library, University of Oxford; the British Library; Canterbury Cathedral Archives; the Diocese of London and the Guildhall Library, City of London; the President and Fellows of Magdalen College, Oxford; the Royal College of Physicians; the Worshipful Company of Coopers and the Worshipful Company of Gardeners.

For reasons of space, the chapter notes give abbreviated titles to published sources. Full titles to many of these appear in the 'Selected Bibliography'.

The list of illustrations identifies the sources for the images in the text and in the plates. My thanks go to Alison Sproston of the London Library and Philip Norman of the Museum of Garden History for their generous help in sourcing many of the images, and to Cressida Annesley of Canterbury Cathedral Archives, Charlotte Brooks of the RHS Lindley Library and Jeremy Smith of the Guildhall Library, City of London.

In quotations, spelling follows the original apart from where I have standardized seventeenth-century usage of 'u' and 'v', and 'j' and 'i', to their modern-day equivalents.

England in the seventeenth century clung to the old Julian calendar, ten days behind the revised Gregorian calendar followed elsewhere in Western Europe. This rarely impinges on the narrative. More problematically, the new year began on 25 March, so 1 February 1616 becomes 1 February 1617 according to today's usage. Wherever possible, I have given dates as if the new year began on 1 January.

Introduction
Of Marvels *and* Monsters

Cradled in tissue paper and shut away in a curator's drawer lie the mortal remains of the Oxford dodo: one skeletal left foot and its dissected head. Neatly sliced along the mesial line, half the skull's covering of dried skin was removed in mid-nineteenth century.[1] Now both parts lie side by side, together with some shavings of skin from the foot that have hardened to a turkey crisp. The dodo looks sad, an impression accentuated by the downward tilt to its jawline and the stubble on its otherwise bald head. No wonder Oxford mathematician Charles Dodgson (better known as Lewis Carroll) fell under its spell as he was writing *Alice's Adventures in Wonderland*.[2]

This same dodo may have been the 'great fowle' kept in a London chamber *c.*1638 and fed pebbles by its keeper to amuse curious visitors such as theologian Sir Hamon L'Estrange, tempted inside by a cloth banner hung in the street.[3] It is certainly all that remains of the stuffed carcass displayed in the astonishing collection of rarities begun by John Tradescant the elder, royal gardener, passionate plant collector, 'painfull [painstaking] industrious searcher, and lover of all natures varieties'.[4] 'Dodar, from the Island *Mauritius*,' stated the collection's first catalogue published by Tradescant's only son John, 'it is not able to flie being so big.'[5]

Such wonders fill this book, which tells the story of the John Tradescants (father and son), whose collection of plants and curiosities opened in

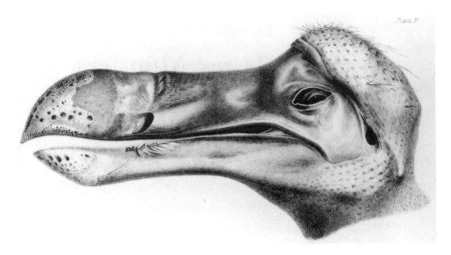

The dissected head of Tradescant's dodo.

London as Britain's first public museum. It is a story of self-definition and cultural innovation, which took the scion of yeoman stock to the gardens of the rich and powerful, even to court. There is danger, too, in wars fought against the French and perilous journeys undertaken to Russia, to the pirate coasts of North Africa and westwards to Virginia. It is also crucially a story of succession between the generations: of a son trained as a gardener to fill his father's shoes and of his determined attempts to match his father's achievements. Had the younger Tradescant's son survived into adulthood (another John, another gardener), he would have carried the struggle into the third generation and so avoided its tragic conclusion.

'Tredeskins Ark' was the name popularly given to the Tradescant collection of plants and rarities at their South Lambeth home on the outskirts of London. From the reign of King Charles I, through the years of civil war and civil government until well into the Restoration, the Ark remained one of the capital's essential sights for any visitor of discernment, applauded by princes, county squires, plant fanatics, ornithologists, foreign dignitaries, fellow travellers and humble schoolteachers. By the 1680s, however, when the collection went on show in Oxford in a splendid new building that drained the university of funds, the name it celebrated was not the Tradescants' but Elias Ashmole's, the wily lawyer and assiduous courtier who had wheedled his way to legal title and successfully wrested control from the younger Tradescant's widow. The metamorphosis of the Tradescant rarities into the founding collection of Oxford's world-renowned Ashmolean Museum provides a bitter sting to the tale.

Yet, remarkably, the Tradescants survived in the popular imagination, celebrated in charming vignettes written by their friends and remembered in a handful of plant names among the many hundreds of plants they helped to introduce. As the centuries passed, they even attracted honours that strictly belonged to others, as if they were the only gardeners of their age, its only plant hunters and collectors. They were not; and their story becomes richer when credit is properly given. Their passionate curiosity took Britain to the frontiers of horticultural knowledge and it is through the example of men like these that Britain became – and remains – a nation of gardeners.

They were more than just gardeners, however, which helps to explain their enduring appeal. The Tradescant story celebrates the triumph of human ingenuity at a time of rapid and profound change when all the old certainties were breaking down – in politics, religion, art and culture, philosophy, even geography. The Tradescants were pioneers (the father, especially) but they were also quintessentially men of their time. How they responded to the risks and opportunities of their lives gives us a privileged glimpse into an extraordinary age, which began in superstition and wonder and ended with the dawning of science.

First and most obviously, the two men stood on the edge of an expanding universe. When the elder Tradescant was busy establishing a name for himself, the Americas were only just beginning to colonize the European imagination. The existence of a fourth continent – unknown before the voyages of Columbus and other late-fifteenth-century seafarers – had thrown Europe into turmoil, overturning accepted habits of thought and challenging the authority of the ancients. If they could get their world map so terribly wrong, what other flaws were waiting to be discovered?

Intellectually, too, thinkers such as Sir Francis Bacon were beginning to develop the ground rules of scientific enquiry. In a bold challenge to the Aristotelian notion that authoritative argument provides the path to truth, Bacon proposed instead a form of scientific testing through controlled experiment. Truth requires evidence from the real world, he believed, and specimens from the natural world – such as those collected by the Tradescants – could begin to play their proper part in the process of investigation.

The science of botany was still in its infancy, however. Not until much later in the century (when Nehemiah Grew published *The Anatomy of Plants* in 1682)[6] would people begin to understand the sexuality of plants. So while a plantsman such as John Tradescant might cultivate new plants through the age-old techniques of selection and grafting, deliberate cross-breeding was out of the question. Even had he grasped the role of pollen in plant reproduction, he would still have faced a mighty psychological and spiritual hurdle. In Tradescant's time, you did not meddle in God's creation. God had made the world in six days and rested on the seventh. He had left no loose ends nor unmade plants for Man to fashion for him.

You do not have to be a gardener to enjoy this book, but it helps if you have a curious spirit. In the early seventeenth century, to be branded 'curious' was a mark of social and intellectual distinction. It meant that you were always pushing at the frontiers of knowledge, in arts and sciences. It also had a very particular use in relation to gardens. To be called a 'curious gardener' placed you in that elite band of men (and a very few women) who set out to collect and grow rare or unusual plants. You were almost certainly in contact with other curious spirits across Europe, such as the Robins in Paris (another father and son, gardeners to the French kings) or, a little later, French florist Pierre Morin, admired by John Evelyn for his rare collection of shells, flowers and insects.[7] Your Dutch contacts might have included the scholarly Johannes de Laet in Leiden; and you would have known roving ambassadors and London-based merchants such as Nicholas Lete with a finger in every plant trade. Despite intermittent European wars, crossing boundaries was something you did all the time.

To be curious, then, was both a state of mind and an aspiration, and few deserved the compliment as much as the elder Tradescant. Born under Queen Elizabeth and in his early thirties when the bookish but bawdy Scottish King James ascended the English throne, Tradescant gardened for some of the most powerful men in the kingdom, among them Robert Cecil (chief minister to King James I); the hated Duke of Buckingham (favourite to two kings); and eventually for King Charles I and Queen Henrietta Maria at one of their minor palaces (Oatlands Palace near Weybridge in Surrey). At the end of his life, his reputation as Britain's premier horticulturalist was rewarded by his appointment as first keeper to the Oxford Physic Garden, England's very first botanic garden.

Throughout his years of maturity, Tradescant was also building up his famous collection of rarities that allowed him to forge a new identity for himself, as self-made man and cultural pioneer. In spirit, his collection linked the *Wunderkammer* of Renaissance princes, which embodied their owners' dominion over nature and culture,[8] with the more rigorously 'scientific' collections of learned societies. Alongside the Tradescant medals, fossils, shells, insects, shoes, weapons, jewels, hats, toothbrushes and every other sort of natural or artificial wonder, even mid-century the collection still displayed objects that today would be dismissed as superstition: feathers from a phoenix, dragon's eggs, a piece of the True Cross, and a coat lined with *Agnus Scythicus*, the famed vegetable lamb from the banks of the Volga that grew like a plant with a stalk attached to its belly and 'died' when it had exhausted the grass within its limited reach. Diversity was the Ark's greatest strength and by opening his doors to the paying public the elder Tradescant shared his marvels with a much wider audience than had ever gained access to such treasures.

Tradescant the younger inherited his father's collection of rarities as well as his job as keeper of the royal gardens, vines and silkworms at Oatlands Palace. What he made of this double legacy is one of the questions *Strange Blooms* sets out to resolve. Although he shared his father's talent for making things grow, these were men of sharply different qualities who lived through very different times. Just four years after the son took on his royal post, King Charles I raised the standard at Nottingham, pitching the country into civil war. Unlike his father, who had sailed with the British fleet to quell the Barbary pirates of the North African coast, and fought alongside his employer, Buckingham, on the French Ile de Ré, Tradescant the younger kept his head down and stayed where he was. London had declared against the king, and for an ex-royal gardener life cannot have been easy. How he fared during the war years we can read in letters to a Dutch friend from the Master of the Watermills, John Morris, who had known the elder Trades-cant and who now kept a watchful and at times reproving eye on the son.

Travel was one passion clearly enjoyed by both father and son. The expe-ditions that the elder Tradescant joined to Russia, North Africa and the Ile de Ré all ended in abject failure, either politically or militarily. But culturally the story was very different. As well as yielding plants and rarities for his col-lection, Tradescant's sixteen-week Russian voyage through storms and fogs into perpetual day has given us an absolute joy: a manuscript diary, wildly spelt and written in a spidery, untutored hand.[9] Yet for all its lack of polish, the diary brilliantly conveys how it feels to venture into the unknown when everything you encounter is wondrous strange: men who hid their heads under their clothes and birds to die for – or at least ones for which Tradescant would happily have paid 5s a skin. His diary shows us, too, a man struggling to find the words to define and communicate the unknown.

North America was another adventure that both Tradescants shared, although this time only the son actually made the crossing. Just ten years after the private Virginia Company had landed its first group of settlers on the riverine swamp that they would name Jamestown in honour of the British king, the elder Tradescant risked half his annual salary on a settlement scheme masterminded by Captain Sam Argall, then sailing back to Virginia to take charge as governor. His passengers should have included the returning Indian princess, Pocahontas (or Mrs John Rolfe, as she then was), but tragically her health failed and she got no further than Gravesend. Tradescant and the princess shared another friend in common: the energetic and flamboyant Captain John Smith, who had landed with that first group of settlers and later bequeathed to Tradescant one quarter of his books, stored in an iron trunk in Lambeth.

People were not Tradescant's only links to the colony across the Atlantic that promised adventurers untold riches, especially those who believed it would lead them through the fabled North-West Passage to the Indies and Cathay. New plants came too, among them the three-petalled Virginian spiderwort eventually named in his honour by Carl Linnaeus as *Tradescantia virginiana*, and trunkfuls of rarities for his collection. Many more were discovered by Tradescant the younger, who visited the now royal colony in 1637 to collect rare flowers, plants and shells.[10] Although its settlements were slowly spreading, much of the land remained unexplored and people still believed that the ocean lay to the west, just beyond the mountains.

No diary of the younger Tradescant's American journeying has survived – perhaps he never kept one – but we can track his footsteps from the plants he brought back: two hundred or so in all,[11] a handful credited to him by name in the great herbal written by his father's friend, John Parkinson.[12] Almost all were bog lovers, like the swamp cypress and the strange, insect-eating pitcher plant (*Sarracenia purpurea*), suggesting that, like most of his compatriots, he did not stray very far from the settled but still swampy lands around the James River. By interrogating anew the documentary evidence, it has been possible to clear up the mystery surrounding the two later journeys that he is supposed to have made to Virginia.

Disentangling the Tradescants' separate contributions to their collection of rarities is rather more difficult. Only one catalogue was ever compiled, by Tradescant the younger with opportunistic help from Elias Ashmole and his friend, Dr Thomas Wharton. (Ashmole astutely paid for its publication, placing Tradescant for ever in his debt.) The outdated titles given to some of the benefactors suggest a greater role for the father, and surviving letters soliciting rarities for both Buckingham and King Charles give us an idea of the wonders he sought. The son has no such supporting evidence, beyond his own claim to have augmented his father's collection with 'continued diligence'.[13]

On their plant skills and interests, we are fortunate in having plant lists from both father and son, and some fascinating differences emerge. Non-gardeners may want to skip lightly over the plant names, but otherwise the gardening content of this book has been written in the firm belief that you can 'read' a whole society through its gardens – politically, socially, morally, even philosophically. Unfolding chapters take us from the embroidered conceits of the Elizabethan court; through the toys, water-jokes, flamboyance and Neoplatonic fantasies of the early Stuarts; to the emergence of plainer, more utilitarian themes during the Commonwealth, uplifted by a strong dose of spirituality; and on to the wildly extravagant French and Italianate flourishes of the Restoration. Dry plant lists confirm the changes taking place, and there are echoes in the gardening writers of the day: these include Sir Hugh Platt's alchemico-horticultural wizardry; John Parkinson's delightful 'speaking garden' written in the language of the King James Bible; Samuel Hartlib's good plain Prussian works of profitable husbandry; Ralph Austen's lyrical spirituality on the lessons to be learnt from orchard trees; and John Evelyn's mannered attempts to produce an encyclopaedic Elysium in words (never finished, of course).

Here, too, you will find the earthiness put back into gardens after the polite attempts of garden historians to sweep the muck and toil out of sight. This is a book for people who like to get their hands dirty, in which dung is measured by the hatful, silkworms nestle between a woman's breasts, only palm trees have sex in the vegetable kingdom and dead dogs are shredded for fertilizer. The Tradescants were gardeners and how they gardened forms a very rich subtext to their story. In the early chapters, we participate in the making of one of England's great gardens – Robert Cecil's Hatfield House, conceived on a dazzlingly ambitious scale. As with any great enterprise, the process is just as illuminating as the finished result and it is heartening to note that even the illustrious Cecil did not always get his plumbing right.

Finally, in tracking their footsteps through England, Europe and Virginia, it is impossible to ignore the companion genius of Shakespeare, who hinted at the fornication of gillyflowers long before the botanists understood how they did it, and who wrote of the same headless race recorded by the elder Tradescant on his way to Archangel. Shakespeare's world was stalked by marvels and monsters, like Prospero's misshapen slave Caliban in his late play, *The Tempest*, first performed at court in 1611 (the same year that Tradescant went to the Low Countries and France, plant-buying for Cecil). Shipwrecked jester Trinculo might well have been Tradescant's scout when he wished he might transport the fishy monster back home. 'A strange fish!' he exclaimed. 'Were I in England now (as once I was) and had but this fish painted, not a holiday fool there but would give a piece of silver. There would this monster make a man; any strange beast there makes a man. When they will not give a doit to relieve a lame beggar, they will lay out ten to see a dead Indian.'[14]

Tradescant liked monsters and he liked marvels too, as did his only son John who trailed after his father's brighter star, like the tail of a comet. Their own garden and orchard at South Lambeth may long ago have disappeared under the concrete and brick of urban development, yet their memory lingers on, growing ever stronger as the strange blooms they loved so much set seed in the rich dark mulch of human desires.

Chapter One

Education *of a* Gardener

John Tradescant's origins – as boy and gardener – remain tantalizingly obscure. The oldest surviving document from Tradescant himself is a letter he wrote in November 1609 to 'Good Mr Trumbull' complaining about the frustrations of travel.[1] Diplomat William Trumbull was just then taking over as English Agent at the Brussels court of the archdukes Albert and his wife, the Infanta Isabella, who ruled over the Catholic Spanish Netherlands through her father, King Philip II of Spain.

The letter does not tell us why Tradescant was travelling to the Low Countries, only that he had become entangled in red tape and that his attempts to buy his way out of trouble had failed. 'I humbly thank your W[orship] for all your Cortisies,' he wrote to the diligent Trumbull, 'but your good Will and labours hath not efected what you desired to dooe for they have put me upon the Rack.' The problem was one of mounting costs with more than a hint of palm-greasing. In total Tradescant's outlay had amounted to 40s, 'besids 24s the pasag to flusshing'[2] – and it seems he had nothing to show for it in return.

The letter is much more revealing about Tradescant the man than it is about his business. Among the neat, carefully phrased letters from other supplicants, it stands out for its blotched and awkward handwriting, haphazard spelling and complete absence of punctuation – even full stops are sorely absent. Its tone of mild pessimism also establishes Tradescant as a man for whom life did not always go as smoothly as his later career might suggest.

This first sighting of Tradescant on Dutch soil is interesting nonetheless because of enduring rumours that the Tradescants were either Dutch or Flemish by birth. It was the peevish antiquary Anthony Wood who first made this claim, in connection with the eventual inheritor of the Tradescant rarities, Elias Ashmole. As a close Oxford acquaintance of Elias Ashmole, Wood was widely believed when he said that Ashmole had acquired the rarities 'of a famous Gardener called Joh. Tredescaut a Dutchman and his Wife'.[3] Although Wood was here referring to the younger Tradescant – demonstrably English-born – the foreign label stuck, along with other invented honours that swelled their reputations (that the elder Tradescant had gardened for Queen Elizabeth, for instance, and that one or the other first brought the pineapple to Britain).[4]

The Dutch theory is attractive on a number of counts. Dutch parentage would help to explain how the elder Tradescant was able to travel freely and easily through the Low Countries unaided, stocking up his master's garden with 'strang and rare' shrubs, roses and flowers.[5] When shopping in the French capital, by contrast, he needed an intermediary to help him find his way about.[6] Tradescant's woeful spelling might provide further evidence of foreign blood, although it could equally point to a relatively humble education in England. There is no suggestion that he knew and used Latin for anything other than plant names, later in life.[7]

A Dutch connection (of blood or training) would also help to explain Tradescant's extraordinary gardening talents and his fondness for the exotic and the strange. Until the sixteenth century at least, gardening in England was much more primitive than on the continent, where France and Italy led the way in matters of style while the Netherlands took the lead in horticultural practice. Dutch ports such as Antwerp provided the gateway through which many coveted rare plants and exotics slipped into Europe, among them the tulips from Turkey and elsewhere that set the Netherlands ablaze with tulip fever in the 1630s.

Against this, neither Tradescant nor any obvious member of his family

appears among the lists of aliens applying for letters of denization or naturalization, nor among the lists of strangers with which a xenophobic England
was periodically obsessed.[8] Records are fallible, of course, but it is remarkable
how many of his foreign-born contacts *do* appear in the lists.[9] In all the bills
and accounts so meticulously kept at Hatfield House, Tradescant's nationality is never specified, unlike 'Henrick Mansfeild a dutchman'[10] who brought
over cherry trees, medlars and walnut trees; or fountain-builder Salomon de
Caus, often referred to simply as 'the Frenchman'. For accounting purposes
John Tradescant was as manifestly English as Mountain Jennings, Cecil's
other gardener and prime earth-mover of his grand new garden.

So any Dutch blood mentioned by Elias Ashmole to Anthony Wood
must have come from earlier generations. Much more likely is the view put
forward by previous biographers that the elder Tradescant was born into a
largely yeoman family that had lived in Suffolk since at least the first quarter
of the sixteenth century. Working on leads unearthed by Mea Allan,[11]
Prudence Leith-Ross diligently tracked members of a family variously
named as Treylnseant, Treyluscant, Tradeskante, Traluscant and Tradescant
around a small area of north-east Suffolk, through wills and fading parish
records of baptisms, marriages and burials.[12] From the mid-1520s, when a
William Treylnseant was living at Wenhaston, some five miles inland from
Walberswick, members of the family moved slowly northwards, settling for
a time at the inland parish of Henstead where Tradescant was one of a
handful of names that appear frequently in the early part of the parish
register, according to a local historian compiling a parochial history of
Suffolk.[13] All the names in fact belong to John Tradescant's immediate
family, for here yeoman Thomas Tradescant fathered many children in the
1550s and 1560s, John's siblings and half-siblings from his father's two
marriages.

Thomas's first wife Elyner, whom he married in 1543, produced perhaps
as many as ten children, although few survived into adulthood and several
died soon after birth (the registers are damaged in places but family wills add
missing names).[14] Elyner herself died in 1564 and that same year Thomas
Tradescant married John's mother, Johane Settaway, who began immediately

to procreate: a first-born John Tradescant, baptized in December 1565 but dead before the end of the month. The following year saw the birth of his brother Nicholas, then shortly afterwards the name 'Tradescant' abruptly vanishes from Henstead's parish register when the family moved again to Corton, a small fishing village four miles beyond Lowestoft perched high on the cliffs above a fast-eroding coastline.

Here at Corton, it seems, the elder John Tradescant was born sometime around 1570 (his dead father would be described as 'Thomas Tradescant of Corton') but, maddeningly, the Corton parish register does not start until 1579 so the chain cannot be guaranteed.[15] Although John Tradescant appears to have moved right away from his Suffolk family roots, his own son John would remember the connection in his will, leaving 5s apiece 'to my two namesakes Robert Tredescant and Thomas Tredescant, of Walberswick in the Countie of Suffolk', and 2s 6d to each of their surviving children. His widow Hester gave them all a further 2s 6d each, describing the two men as 'my late husbands Kinsmen'.[16]

Whether these Suffolk Tradescants came originally from the Low Countries is not recorded. London's Huguenot Library produced one solitary listing for Tradescant: a Catherine Tradescant from Woodbridge in Suffolk, a member of the Walloon congregation of Norwich whose will was listed among those of other 'strangers' proved in the mid-1700s.[17] As the Walloons originated from the French-speaking part of what is now southern and eastern Belgium, this brings us no closer to detecting Dutch or Flemish blood.[18]

Perhaps, after all, the secret of Tradescant's 'Dutchness' lies buried in the Suffolk countryside. Throughout much of the Middle Ages, Suffolk's prosperity flowed from the export of wool to the continent where it was finished by skilled Flemish weavers in the great textile centres of Bruges, Arras and elsewhere.[19] An influx of Flemish settlers to East Anglia – especially during the fourteenth century – brought these cloth-making skills to eastern England, as families were driven out by floods and later by Europe's fomenting religious divisions that pitched Catholics against the growing Protestant tide. After the weavers came the horticulturalists and market gardeners, who settled around Colchester and Norwich in particular, their numbers swelling sharply from the 1570s when the Low Countries began to suffer the economic dislocation of political unrest that would eventually split them into the Protestant north and the Catholic south.[20]

By the time of John Tradescant's birth, the populations of eastern England and the Low Countries were thoroughly interlocked. In a study of English travellers abroad, John Stoye singled out the younger son of a Norfolk family, about 1550, who worked as a merchant's factor in Bruges where he spent the greater part of each year, while his Dutch wife kept house for him in England. After her death he took a second wife with landed estates at Antwerp and with her capital built a large trade between England and the Low Countries. There he stayed until the wars finally brought him home. 'This intimate connection between neighbouring peoples appeared part of the natural order,' commented Stoye.[21]

The trade went the other way just as easily, as evidenced by the correspondence (in Latin) between two men who knew Tradescant well: John Morris, Master of the Watermills in London, writing to his friend Antwerp-born Johannes de Laet. Morris's father was a Dutchman by birth but a free denizen by choice, who had worked for Queen Elizabeth's handsome dancing Chancellor, Sir Christopher Hatton. De Laet, also a free denizen of England, chose instead to return to continental Europe, where he settled in Leiden, although his son Samuel married the daughter of a Dutch merchant who had settled in London.[22] Perhaps the well-travelled John Tradescant would have shared Morris's view that he was a citizen of the world rather than of England.[23] Foreign birth mattered, of course, to those forced by law to pay their taxes twice over, and those who suffered from English prejudice, incipient xenophobia or simply fear of competition. But in John Tradescant's time, nationality was not the only – nor even the most important – way of defining yourself.

There remains the puzzle of where and how the young Tradescant learnt to garden, a journey that would take him from an undistinguished Suffolk coastal village where the rector stored manure in his chancel[24] to the Lord Treasurer's grand new garden at Hatfield House. Sadly, Tradescant's friend,

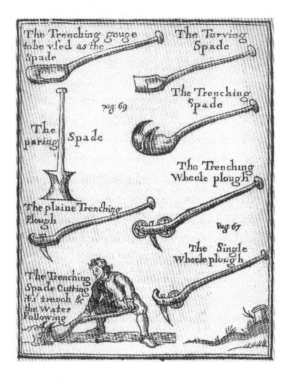

*Spades from a manual
of husbandry by 'lover of
ingenuity', Walter Blith.*

the apothecary and incomparable garden writer John Parkinson, gives us no
clues to Tradescant's early career, merely noting that he was 'sometimes
belonging to the right Honourable Lord Robert Earle of Salisbury, Lord
Treasurer of England in his time, and then unto the right Honourable the
Lord Wotton at Canterbury in Kent, and lastly unto the late Duke of
Buckingham'.[25] How Tradescant came to be Cecil's gardener is passed over
in silence.

Yet Robert Cecil employed only the very best artists and artisans to craft
the properties that were the outward sign of his political power – men who
came with a solid reputation, such as Salomon de Caus, engineer to the
king's eldest son, Prince Henry, or rising stars such as architect Inigo Jones.
John Tradescant's appointment as one of Cecil's named gardeners at Hatfield
suggests he was either known personally to Cecil or had been recommended
by someone of standing.

There are places close to Tradescant's birthplace and further afield in Suffolk where he might have learnt the gardening skills that would carry him to Hatfield and world renown. Less than five miles west of Corton lies Somerleyton Hall, owned by the Jernegan family for nearly three centuries until 1604 when it was bought by the energetic builder and farmer John Wentworth, who sparked local resentment (and a lawsuit) by his enclosure of common land. Wentworth adorned his house and park with fine gardens, woods, fishponds, water gardens, orchards, walks and a plantation of 256 fir trees, reputedly 'the most incomparable piece in the Realm of England' until it was flattened by a hurricane half a century later.[26]

There were even family connections to the place. The Tradescant relatives included a Thomas Tradescant (probably John Tradescant's older half-brother) who was first described as a 'single man' of Somerleyton and later of London. Tradescant's widowed mother took as her second husband a William Stanton whose family held land in Somerleyton.[27] As Wentworth started on his new garden about the time Tradescant went to work for Cecil, this makes the connection unlikely.

An earlier Suffolk garden and therefore more promising as a possible link is Hengrave Hall to the north-west of Bury St Edmunds. The house was built between 1525 and 1538 for Sir Thomas Kytson, a fabulously wealthy wool merchant, merchant adventurer and former sheriff of London who kept a staff in Antwerp.[28] Kytson died in 1540, leaving a second wife, who gave birth to his posthumous son (another Sir Thomas) who embarked on a second round of garden improvements in the late 1570s and 1580s – just when the young Tradescant was setting out on his career as a gardener.

Originally moated (a large fishpond survives, and a formal garden now threatened with weeds), Hengrave Hall was approached by a long straight causeway raised above ditches on either side and lined with a triple avenue.[29] 'It sounds Dutch,' wrote Norman Scarfe in *The Suffolk Landscape*.

And when the builder's son, in 1575, wanted to improve the setting of his house, he got a 'Dutchman gardener' over from Norwich to look at the orchards, gardens and walks, clip the knots, alter the alleys, and re-plant. Three years later, the Queen and Leicester and the entire court were here in late August, and treated to a spectacle 'representing the fayries, as well as might be'.[30]

Kytson's gardens at Hengrave were of a magnificence that foreshadowed Cecil's at Hatfield House. As well as a great and a little park, he had a vineyard or orchard, gardens, a hop ground, a hemp ground, a bowling alley and multiple fishponds. He kept seven boats for the moat and ponds, finishing his waterworks by 1583 when he paid a final bill to 'Martin Plomer, at London, for bringing hoame of the water to all the offices at Hengrave house'.[31] It is possible to imagine Tradescant as a boy-gardener coming to work for just such a Suffolk grandee, perhaps initially apprenticed to one of East Anglia's Dutch gardeners who may conceivably have taken him travelling through the Low Countries and shown him the best places to buy plants.

The Kytsons and Robert Cecil had a friend in common who may have helped the talented young gardener's progress from Suffolk to London and Hatfield: (Sir) Walter Cope, a political figure of some importance and one of Robert Cecil's closest acolytes. Tradescant would later buy trees for Cope in the Low Countries, which could imply a favour returned. From a letter that Cope wrote to Lady Kytson warning her of the dangers of recusancy, Cope was clearly on intimate terms with the family.[32] Before gaining employment with Cecil, Tradescant may even have gardened for Cope at the magnificent new mansion he was building in Kensington around 1605, known originally as Cope's Castle.[33] When John Chamberlain, a chronicler of the times, visited in 1608 he was not allowed to touch a thing, 'not so much as a cherry', as the family was expecting a visit from Queen Anne.[34]

Another possible route to Cecil was through Sir Noel Caron from Bruges, 'Holland Ambassador'[35] at the courts of Queen Elizabeth and King James from 1590 until his death in 1624. Well loved as a philanthropist and founder of an almshouse for poor but honest women, Caron was another keen gardener who sent gifts of fruit to his English counterparts. In 1606 he sent black and red cherries, plums and pears to Robert Cecil, thanking God he had found such a fertile place for his garden, where everything grew in abundance.[36] Caron's much-admired garden, intriguingly, was in South Lambeth where he became one of the major landowners. After Caron's death, John Tradescant would move into one of his properties,[37] founding there his famous garden and proto-museum that was to become popularly known as 'the Ark'. Given this later property link between Tradescant and Sir Noel, the Dutch ambassador remains a possible conduit to Cecil but real evidence is lacking, just as it is for other potential employers.[38] Caron's patronage nonetheless secured advancement for other protégés such as the excitable artist and connoisseur, Balthazar Gerbier, whom he first introduced to English society.[39]

We do at least have the facts of Tradescant's marriage – to vicar's daughter Elizabeth Day of Meopham in Kent. By the time of their marriage Elizabeth's father was long dead from the plague, along with two of her siblings,[40] and her mother was three-times widowed (she would marry again, the year after her daughter).[41] John Tradescant and Elizabeth Day were married in her father's old church of St John, Meopham, on 18 June 1607; he was thirty-seven or so, and she was nearly twenty-one, having been baptized on 22 August 1586. The groom had no obvious connection with the village and apart from his marriage (and a street named Tradescant Drive) has left behind little trace. The bride's 'borrowers' or godparents were Dirreck Harman, Janikin Jesop and Jannikin Garret of London, which may explain where the couple met although there were Garrets living in the village. Wherever they made their first home, Elizabeth Tradescant was back in the largely agricultural village the following year when she gave birth to their only child, who was baptized John after his father on 4 August 1608.

This is a disappointing trail with too many gaps and suppositions to explain how or where Cecil's plantsman acquired his skills. The London-based Company of Gardeners (incorporated in 1605)[42] required an apprenticeship of seven years to cover the many practices involved in 'the trade crafte or misterie of Gardening', including 'planting grafting Setting sowing cutting Arboring Rocking mounting covering fencing and removing of Plantes herbes seedes fruites trees Stockes Settes and of contryving the conveyances to the same belonging'.[43] Even if Tradescant did not serve a formal apprenticeship, someone must have taught him the secrets of his craft, both practical and arcane.

From Tradescant himself, we sense at least that he carried with him on his travels memories of the landscapes and farming practices of East Anglia. (Corton, his probable birthplace, lay close to the Norfolk–Suffolk borders.) When he went plant collecting to Archangel in Russia, he judged Russian sheep to be 'much lik to ther Northfolk sheepe', and the Russian soil of a fine light mould, 'like Norfolke land, without stones'. Their ploughs were like English ones, too, although 'not so neat, muche lik to Essex ploughes withe wheells but the wheells very evill made'. His comments on Russian ships likewise suggest familiarity with a seafaring community, as did his observation on the oily tang of Russian bacon that came, he said, from the 'muche fishe' fed to their hogs.[44]

However circumstantial the evidence of his boyhood might be, the man who would become one of England's most famous gardeners was almost certainly a Suffolk boy with Dutch connections, either inherited or absorbed through the many links between eastern England and the Low Countries. These connections will have helped him on his way, but he must have shown remarkable promise and skill to garden his way into the great Cecil's employment.

Chapter Two

My Lord Treasurer's Gardener

Tradescant's next letter to William Trumbull, the English agent in Brussels, has an altogether more confident ring and leaves no puzzle about its contents. Sent in the autumn of 1610 – the year when Tradescant started working for Robert Cecil at Hatfield House – the letter opens with a flourish. Trumbull is still addressed as 'yr Worshipe' by the more lowly Tradescant, even 'Right Worshippfull', but he is now also 'my honorable good frend'. 'Since I last wase with yr Worshipe,' continued Tradescant in his wild spelling, 'it hathe plessed my Lord tresorur to give me enterteynment and he Spake to me to know wheare the Rarest thing wear then I tould him of Brussell then my Lord said Sirra Remember me and at miccalmas yw shall goe over now since it hathe plesed his Lordshipe to Remember yr Worshipe being theare.'[1]

The 'Lord Treasurer' was Robert Cecil, second son of William Cecil (ennobled as Lord Burghley) who had served Queen Elizabeth as Secretary and later as Lord Treasurer before passing on the political mantle to his younger son. (When Burghley died in 1598, Elizabeth is said to have shown real grief.) Created 1st Earl of Salisbury in 1605, Robert Cecil stood at the centre of a web of connections that would take his humble gardener into a king's employment. For the present, however, it was Tradescant who told Cecil about the rare plants to be found in Brussels, prompting Cecil to remember his earlier dealings with Trumbull, as Tradescant indicates in his letter. When still an embassy secretary, Trumbull had helped Cecil negotiate for tapestries consisting of '2 suites of the Triumphs of Petrarch and the other of Jacob'.[2] He would also prove useful in buying trees for Thomas Howard, 2nd Earl of Arundel and one of the age's greatest art collectors; and he advised the heir to the throne, Prince Henry, on his art collection before the young prince's sudden death in 1612.

Now Cecil wanted plants for his gardens, and it was Tradescant who was doing the bidding, sending Trumbull a long list of plants, together with marginal notes indicating where they might be found as well as further instructions for their safe transportation. From the tone and detail of his letter, it is obvious he had done this before and that Cecil had hired him for just such skills as these. He was less skilled at ordering his thoughts, however, and the requests tumble out, which must have been confusing for poor Trumbull. The plants desired are those on which Tradescant's reputation rests: vines; exotic fruit; beautiful flowers such as roses, narcissi and martagon lilies; any seed that is 'strang' or 'Rare'. From 'Peer [Pierre] the archdukes kitchin gardner' he wanted vines and especially 'the blewe muskadell the Russet grape a greattest quantity of those but of aull other sorts what he hathe'. His Lord was making a vineyard at Hatfield, wrote Tradescant, 'and hathe the frenche men to make it'. The vines growing in the archdukes' kitchen garden were the best he had seen, and so he wanted cuttings and roots, and 'all other Sorts whatsoever he can furnish me withe'.

Also from the archdukes' kitchen gardener he hoped for a rose that he had identified as 'the Rosa incanadine' (the lovely blush-pink alba rose, 'Great Maiden's Blush' now known variously in French as 'Cuisse de Nymphe', 'La Virginale' and 'La Séduisante'). Pierre had given him one the year before, he said, 'but it is dead'. Tradescant also requested a plant of his 'specled Anemone', two or three cherry laurels, a *Viburnum tinus*, the heavily scented but borderline-hardy white clematis (*Clematis flammula*), and two more roses: the evergreen rose, *Rosa sempervirens*, and one he called the thornless rose, 'Rosa Sina Spina'. (John Parkinson described this last rose as being not much bigger than a double Cinnamon rose, called 'the marbled Rose' on account of its veined pink petals.)[3]

While the archdukes' gardener was best for vines, trees and roses, Trades-cant wanted Trumbull to obtain most of his flowers from another source: Mr John Joket, presumably a well-known Brussels nurseryman. Pretty white flowers predominated: a dainty paradise lily, a spring-flowering white pulsatilla, two white irises, a silvery-white star-of-Bethlehem. On the list were also red and white martagon lilies (including the unpleasantly scented *Lilium pomponium* from the French and Italian Alps, a shiny red like sealing wax); red, white and purple hepaticas; colourful crocuses and the autumn-flowering colchicums; a white and a red Persian buttercup; and five different varieties of narcissi. Only one obviously tender plant was requested: the sea lily (*Pancratium illyricum*), a delicate white-flowering bulb from Corsica and Sardinia, but in his accompanying letter Tradescant also requested two or three small grafted orange trees.

Tradescant gave Trumbull clear instructions on how the plants were to be packed. All the trees, shrubs and vines were to be carried in baskets planted about with young roots of 'the best Sorts of gilliflowers' (pinks), especially a rare variety called 'the Infanto', and any other strange varieties. The flower roots he wanted sealed up in a basket or box covered with dry moss or dry sand; and all plants – but particularly the vines – were to be labelled with their names. 'I pray let every severall plant have his name And every severall Vine his name,' he wrote down the spine of the letter. Names were important to a plantsman, especially one who was intent on introducing the best and the newest varieties to his master's garden, although ironically he would later forget the names of the many vines in his own garden.[4]

The only real vagueness concerned payment. 'My Lord I thinke will send over p[aymen]t for to bye them withe,' wrote Tradescant in reference to the orange trees and Mr Joket's flowers – which, considering Trumbull's meagre salary, was perhaps small comfort.[5] Whether Cecil expected to pay for the vines, trees and roses from the archdukes' garden or receive them as a 'gift' was not made clear. Tradescant ended his letter as he began, with a flurry of worships, signing himself 'John tradeskent garner to the Lord Tressurer'.

Trumbull was sent the letter on 21 October 1610 and no doubt set about fulfilling its terms at once. Tradescant may have needed to travel in person to Brussels to help with the commission as his Lordship ordered a payment of £10 to 'John Tradescant the gardener' on 30 October 1610, 'to send over into Flanders to by Vynes to plannt at Hatfeild'.[6]

According to the account books still kept in the family archives at Hatfield House, Tradescant began work as gardener to the Lord Treasurer on 1 January 1610. He received his first payment in November of that year: £37 10s paid in arrears to cover his first three quarters up to Michaelmas, making an annual salary of £50.[7] This was a substantial sum compared to the £10 annual pension paid by Cecil to 'Mr Gerrard the Chirrugeon' (barber-surgeon and apothecary John Gerard),[8] who had gardened for his father at Theobalds. The generous amount suggests that Tradescant was expected to pay for at least some of the garden's upkeep himself, as was common at the time, despite the separate bills he submitted for extraordinary items. It certainly established him as a gardener of rank in Hatfield's hierarchy. For a plantsman such as Tradescant, working for Cecil was one of the most exacting and prestigious jobs open to him. For two generations the Cecils represented the most powerful political dynasty in England, and they gardened in a style entirely fitting to their status.[9]

Robert Cecil, Tradescant's employer, was the intellectually brilliant but physically disconcerting younger son of Lord Burghley and his second wife, the redoubtable Mildred Cooke. As one of his biographers commented: 'Sickly as a baby, a delicate but clever child, he grew up with a definite curvature of the spine which led to the development of a noticeable hump. In adulthood his silent presence could disconcert otherwise bold and blustering men; his eyes especially seemed to probe beyond a superficial truth.'[10] He was also very small with splayed legs, which put him at a considerable disadvantage in an age that read the 'inner man' from outward appearances. Behind his back they called him names like 'Monsieur de Bossu', 'Bossive Robin', 'Microgibbous' and 'bumbasted-legs', and he must have smarted at his father's advice on choosing a wife: 'Make not choice of a dwarf or a fool,' wrote Burghley, 'for from the one thou mayest beget a race of pygmies, the other may be thy daily disgrace.'[11]

Remarkably, Cecil overcame his appearance in the political realm, slipping into his father's shoes as Queen Elizabeth's effective Secretary of State in 1596, two years before Burghley's death, and expertly manoeuvring the peaceful accession to the English throne of James VI of Scotland, for whom he would eventually become Lord Treasurer as well as Chief Secretary. Like his father before him, he would almost literally work himself to death for his sovereign, but a towering sense of public responsibility and acute political acumen were not the only traits father and son shared in common. Robert Cecil also inherited from his father a passion for building and for making fine gardens, fountains and walks. Lord Burghley was the dedicatee of two of the century's most important English books on plants and horticulture: *The Gardeners Labyrinth* by Didymous Mountain (a pseudonym for Thomas Hill), and the famous *Herball* of 1597 written by his garden superintendent, John Gerard.[12] The Bodleian Library in Oxford has a small but charming oil painting of Lord Burghley astride a mule as he inspected his beloved gardens, clutching flowers of honeysuckle and a pink tied into a nosegay. Riding his mule around his garden walks was Burghley's 'greatest disport';[13] and favourite of all his gardens were those of his sumptuous mansion at Theobalds in Hertfordshire, created to accommodate Queen Elizabeth's royal progresses as she descended on her loyal subjects, all but ruining some of them in the process.

One of the most attentive visitors to Theobalds was the German Paul Hentzner, who called at the time of Burghley's funeral in 1598. Finding no one to show him the house, he was at least able to take a tour of the gardens. Entering through one of Theobalds' five classical loggias, he marvelled at the great variety of trees and plants and the 'labyrinths made with a great deal of labour'. A fountain spurted into a basin of white marble, while down the length of the garden ran columns and pyramids of wood, like Hampton Court's heraldic devices. 'After seeing these,' wrote Hentzner in some awe,

we were led by the gardiner into the summer-house, in the lower part of which, built semicircularly, are the twelve Roman emperors in white marble, and a table of

*The magnificent south prospect of
Hatfield House.*

touchstone; the upper part of it is set round with cisterns of lead, into which the water is conveyed through pipes, so that fish may be kept in them, and in summer time they are very convenient for bathing.[14]

Reached by a little bridge was another room for entertainment fitted with an oval table in red marble.

Theobalds came to Robert Cecil on his father's death. More building followed after Queen Elizabeth's death in 1603 when he had to accom- modate two households on the royal progresses, those of King James and of his queen, Anne of Denmark. Soon James – a fanatical huntsman – was casting covetous glances not at the gardens (he would board up the draughty loggia looking west on to the great garden, judging it 'one too many' in the English climate)[15] but at the estate's splendid opportunities for the chase. By 1607, Cecil was left with little choice but to offer Theobalds to his

sovereign, receiving in exchange seventeen manors spread over twelve counties, including the old royal palace of Hatfield House where Princess Elizabeth had spent part of her girlhood.

However saddened he might have been at the loss of Theobalds, Cecil threw himself into the task of creating a house and a garden at Hatfield that would be worthy of a king's visit. Although he could have improved and modernized the old palace, he resolved to build again from scratch.[16] Just before the exchange took place, he visited Hatfield in the company of the Earls of Worcester, Suffolk and Southampton (Shakespeare's old patron), to 'view upon what part of [the] ground I should place my habitation', choosing the highest point of ground to the south-east of the old palace.[17] A puzzling plan made in this year shows the old palace already surrounded by fine gardens – grass parterres, two knots of different design (one geometric, the other based on the fleur-de-lys), a quincunx plantation (perhaps an ornamental orchard), elaborate gateways and changes of levels. Whether these gardens were the ones Cecil took over in 1607, or ones he might have created had he chosen to adapt instead of demolish much of the old palace, is not clear.[18]

As he would later do with the gardens, Robert Cecil brought together several men to build his new mansion at Hatfield, while keeping a close watch himself over all stages of the project. His principal architect was Robert Lyminge, a carpenter by trade, under the supervision of Simon Basil, surveyor of the King's Works. Cecil's agent, Thomas Wilson, was in charge of financial arrangements. Then renowned as a designer of fanciful scenery for court masques, Inigo Jones may have provided his first architectural drawings, for the clock tower and the south front.[19]

With so many craftsmen involved, the building of Hatfield House went ahead at enormous speed – at a time when Cecil was also building at two of his other properties (Cranborne Manor in Dorset and Salisbury House in the Strand), as well as raising in London's West End a grand new market for luxury goods, christened 'Britain's Burse' by James I at its opening in 1609. (Dramatist Ben Jonson wrote an entertainment specially for the opening, in which he depicted his patron Cecil as 'a devotee of expanding overseas trade, novelty luxury imports and mechanical wonders'.[20]) Other courtiers, particularly the Howards, were embarked on similarly ambitious building projects as the great families around the King jostled for influence and prestige. At Hatfield, the family apartments were limited to the ground floor of the east wing, while apartments for the king and queen occupied the first floor linked by a long gallery.

It was a massive enterprise and material piled in from across England and the continent: locally made bricks; recycled stone from the ruins of the former monastery of St Augustine at Canterbury (where John Tradescant would go to work next for Edward, Lord Wotton); and new stone from Normandy, much of it shipped in vessels owned by Dutchmen, then trundled at great expense in small loads along the country's terrible roads. Transport in the early seventeenth century had made few technological advances and the state of the roads in winter was a particular problem.[21]

Building proceeded swiftly through 1608 and 1609, with some changes of plan and a temporary retrenchment as even Cecil began to run out of money. 'Venal though he was,' noted social historian Lawrence Stone, 'he could not squeeze enough out of his official positions to stand the strain, and already his debts must have been approaching the £40,000 level that they were soon to reach.'[22] Amazingly, the gardens were already being laid out around this vast building site, two years or more before Tradescant came to work for Cecil.

By the time they were finished in 1612, there would be two ornamental gardens beneath the principal apartments – a West Garden, overlooked by the queen, and the even grander East Garden given to the king. From his windows on the first floor, the king would have looked over a series of descending terraces ornamented with fountains, flower pots and statues, flanked on either side by espaliered fruit trees. At the bottom was a great water parterre, its boundaries defined by 'a small River, which as it were forms the Compartiments of a large *Parterre*, and rises and secretly loses itself in an Hundred Places, and whose Banks are all Lined or Boarded'.[23] There was also a kitchen garden, a huge orchard, and a vineyard some way to the north.[24]

The man primarily in charge of making the gardens at this stage was Mountain Jennings, who had already worked for Cecil at Theobalds.[25] As early as August 1607, the accounts contain a bill for the 'Expenses of Munton Jenings in going about my Lord's business at Hatfield & to London'. Among other things he charged for 'taking of the plot of the park at Hatfield & other grounds for the enlarging of the same; days diet [food] for himself & man 1/6, man to help carry the chain 1/ a day'.[26] Throughout 1608 and 1609, Jennings received quite considerable amounts for the garden to cover his outlays. From March to the end of September 1609, for instance, he received a total of £198 16s 9d for his work in the garden and for various supplies, including trees, 'prym [privet], osiers, and poles', and 'divers sorts of hearbes'.[27]

Although Jennings remained involved with Hatfield well into John Tradescant's time, around 1609 the search began to find another gardener.

'Bartholomewe the gardner' was approached, but turned the job down on the grounds that he and his wife were too old to move to Hatfield, although he had no objection to spending the occasional month there, 'till my lords garden bee fenished, or to helpe my lord with all the best fruts the lowe contryes can aforde'.[28] In this exchange (between London merchant Robert Bell and Cecil's agent, Thomas Wilson) lies the reasoning perhaps behind Tradescant's appointment: he would bring to Hatfield not just his skills as a gardener but his familiarity with the best the continent had to offer. In the meantime, as Bell reported, he and Bartholomew conferred with Mountain Jennings (judged 'verry suffessent' by the old gardener) and between them they drew up a plot for the gardens 'to bee shewed unto my lord which I thinke will doe verry well, & after may bee chaunged or alltred at my lords pleasure'. A third gardener was also working on various plans for the garden: one Thomas Chaundler, whose appointment does not seem to have been an unqualified success. In January 1610 (the time of Tradescant's arrival), he eventually succeeded in obtaining payment (£4) for the many plans and journeys he had made.[29] More significantly, he also received £55 for work he had carried out in the showpiece East Garden.[30]

Plants were arriving all the time, many as gifts from courtiers and subordinates, and doubtless intended to oil the wheels of state: grapes and 'nectarine plum trees' from Sir Edward Sulyard; fifty orchard trees from the widowed Lady Tresham out of Lyveden New Bield; 400 sycamore trees from the Low Countries sent over by a Cecil relative; 30,000 vines from the wife of the French ambassador; 500 fruit trees from the French queen; and 453 cherry trees from Sir John Tufton.[31] When the trees were not given, they were bought: 500 mulberries from France; cherry trees, medlars, walnut trees and quinces purchased by Mountain Jennings from Dutchman Henrick Mansfeild and carried from Bishopsgate Street to Tower Hill to Durham House and on to Hatfield House.[32]

Much of 1608 was taken up with fencing (especially necessary to keep out the deer from the encircling deerpark), digging foundations for walls, and laying out knots and grass quarters in the ornamental gardens to west and east.[33] Already by the summer of 1609, at least six months before Tradescant's arrival, the Hatfield gardens were taking shape, and a rhythm of creating, maintaining, repairing and extending the different areas was established. Bills for July of that year talk of 'making an end of laying all the grass knots, setting all the borders with pinks, mowing the grass walks, cutting the knots, laying the grass quarters in "colleres", new raking, treading and beating the walks, casting up of brick dust and bringing it in, watering the trees, dressing of pinks, and weeding the walks and quarters'.[34] The following month, the mount was also cut, stones taken out of the knot quarters 'for the planting of Mr Abbats flowers', and more weeders paid, while September in the West Garden saw the need for 'setting and cutting out the earth of one of the quarters, & mending the decayed places of all the rest'.[35]

By December 1609 – the month before Tradescant arrived – holes were being made on both sides of the approach avenue to the house, for the planting of elms.[36] Perhaps the elms did not take or Cecil changed his mind because limes were planted in their place, first a dark narrow avenue through a wood and then – in a sudden expansion of space and light, commensurate with Cecil's status – widening to a forty-foot double avenue at the highest point, giving the approaching visitor a first awed sight of Hatfield's magnificent south front, flanked by fine gardens to east and west and an imposingly green entrance court.[37] Some of the limes reputedly survive to this day, hollowed and decayed, their life extended by pollarding early in the twentieth century. The accounts for March 1610 record customs' charges for 400 lime trees,[38] then in 1612 'Lord General Cecil's man' was paid the huge sum of £140 for bringing over 1,200 lime trees from France; perhaps some found their way into this planting along the approach avenue.[39] All the while, earth-moving continued in the East Garden, 'digging, casting and carrying of earth for the raising of the taras [terrace] walks, and casting up of the good earth on heaps for the planting of the trees and hedges'.[40]

By 1 January 1610, Cecil had a new gardener in place: John Tradescant. From the occasional and modest bills[41] that he submitted before he travelled

to the Low Countries and France in the autumn of 1611 it seems he was
largely in charge of the kitchen gardens at Hatfield, as well as tree-planting
throughout the gardens, and arranging for the importation of trees from the
continent. Although Mountain Jennings continued to take the senior role in
creating their Lord's gardens, by January 1612, Cecil's chief designer Robert
Lyminge was comparing the two men's work in a way that suggested they
were equals in the garden hierarchy.[42]

Robert Lyminge was writing an account of outstanding garden tasks for
Cecil's agent, Thomas Wilson, and ultimately for Lord Salisbury himself.
Mountain Jennings and his men, he said, were well under way with planting
trees and quicksets (hawthorn hedging plants) at the Dell and the river,
although they still needed grafted cherry trees for making the closed walks.
John Tradescant, meanwhile, had been instructed to plant a hedge at the
bottom of the North Walk, and still had to erect trellis around the cross-
walks to keep out the deer until the hedge was grown, and to set up semi-
circular seats.

Lyminge's account then returned to Mountain Jennings, whose men were
busy bringing good earth into the lower part of the East Garden for planting
trees and hedges. Jennings himself had drawn up a plan for the whole
garden, which he would show his lordship. It included a shallow river
issuing from rockwork 'just like that which we saw at the Earl of Exeters, yet
it is not pleasing to the eye, but to be altered into another forme according
to Mountayne Jennings his plot which I thinke will doe better'. (The Earl of
Exeter was Robert Cecil's elder brother, Thomas, who created a much-
admired garden at Wimbledon Manor.)

The focus then switched back to Tradescant, who had staked out the two
triangular walks leading from the house – 'one towards the parsonadge, and
the other answerable to it'. Already they were planting trees there, and
Tradescant would 'take order for the setting of trees and shrubs in the
valleyes, which will doe very well'. No new works would be begun without
Cecil's express approval.

Lyminge asked Wilson to assure their master that not much else could be
done that winter, in view of the short days and the uncertainty of the

weather. In any case, expenses were mounting 'more then was expected'. Among the additional architectural features not included in the original estimates for the gardens were brick walls in the East and West Gardens and nine doorways with pyramid finials; carpenters' bills for rails and balustrades in the lower part of the East Garden; doors and windows for the banqueting house in the West Garden; a pair of great gates for the East Garden and the river by the mill; plumbers' bills for laying pipes to the East and West Garden; and the stone carver's bills for forty-eight stone lions about the house.[43] Lyminge nonetheless ended his account on an optimistic note: 'Now the time serves,' he wrote, 'the bussines shall be forwarded and made substantiall with the best husbandry we can devise.'

Despite Cecil's ambitions for Hatfield House, the king came only once to visit during Cecil's lifetime – in July 1611, and probably only once thereafter: a private visit for the christening of Cecil's grandson in 1616.[44] In the rush to prepare the gardens for the king's first visit, gardeners laboured round the clock on Thursday night and Friday morning at the cost of £1 8s for 'removeinge of diverse things, there against the kinge came to Hatfeild'.[45]

Eight years had passed since the king's first meeting with Cecil after his accession, when one Cecil biographer described the new king as

an awkward, ugly figure dressed in a shabby doublet heavily quilted to protect him from an assassin's dagger, with a straggly beard, a slobbering tongue too big for his mouth, who shambled about fiddling with his codpiece and, throughout the interview, was always leaning against something or someone to support a weight too heavy for his weak, knock-kneed legs. His talk was as unkingly as his looks: a garrulous stream in which out-of-the-way learning and long-winded theories mingled incongruously with homely endearments and jocular familiarities, all uttered in a broad Scottish accent.[46]

At Hatfield, king and gardener would almost certainly never have met, yet on his way up the great staircase to his state apartment, James may have paused at the top beside the carved newel post of a gardener holding a rake, a basket of luscious fruit and a Turk's cap lily, at his feet a pot of flowers. According to Cecil family tradition, the gardener in his doublet and hose and jaunty Jacobean hat is John Tradescant the elder.[47] It could be one of the other gardeners, of course, such as Mountain Jennings, or merely a gardener in the generic sense. But the inclusion of flowers and fruit suggests that this gardener was a grower rather than a digger, and so the gardener's image joins the other favoured players in Cecil's personal iconography as interpreted by John Bucke, his craftsman carver: lions with shields alternating with boys playing musical instruments (bagpipes, cello, recorder, violin, harp), the figures gilded by painter Rowland Bucket (who will later feature as a benefactor to Tradescant's collection of rarities).[48]

'Putti appear everywhere in various guises,' wrote art-historical student, J. B. Lingard,

as anecdotes to the themes of outdoor pursuits, such as gardening and falconry, music, drama . . . and wine. The scheme works like the repertory of the court jester in its juxtaposition of truths and ironies, but it serves to sum up the meaning of a house such as Hatfield: the display and consolidation of status, courtly entertainment, and the taste of the patron.[49]

Hatfield was indeed Cecil's creation and in John Tradescant he had found a plantsman equal to his designs.

Chapter Three

To *the* Low Countries

Cecil's trust in his gardener's skill was amply vindicated by Tradescant's great plant-buying spree through the Low Countries and France in the autumn and winter of 1611 – a journey mapped out by bills of 25 September 1611 (when he received an advance of £6 towards his travel expenses)[1] and 5 January 1612 (when he submitted bills totalling some £140 for trees, shrubs, flowers, shells, freight, expenses and sundry garden items bought on his travels).[2] From his detailed claims for board and lodgings, supper en route, and 'dyet' on board ship during his several journeys by water, it is evident he was away for the months of October, November and part of December at least. The bills cover a period of three and a half months and Tradescant would have wanted to recoup his quite considerable expenses as soon as he could. At least he was paid promptly, just five days after submitting his claims.

Tradescant made his journey into the Low Countries at a time of relative peace. Two years earlier, Spain and the Netherlands had declared a truce in their simmering hostilities, one that would hold for twelve years. Ever since the dismantling of Charlemagne's empire, the Netherlands had been divided into small sovereignties, eventually coming under the control of the dukes of Burgundy and, through death and marriage, into the hands of the Spanish Habsburgs.

Charles I of Spain (who became Holy Roman Emperor as Charles V) passed the Netherlands on to his son, Philip II of Spain, whose centralizing tendencies and ardently repressive Catholicism so enflamed the normally phlegmatic Dutch that in 1568 they revolted against their Spanish masters. The Spanish retaliated with customary cruelty (to Dutch eyes, at least), savagely suppressing the revolt in southern cities such as Antwerp. To the north, rebellion rallied around the standard of William the Silent, Prince of Orange, reared a Catholic but of Protestant parentage. The result was an effective split between the Protestant (largely Calvinist) north and the more Catholic south, which remained under Spanish dominion as the Spanish Netherlands, extending into what is now Belgium and Luxembourg. The split was formalized in 1581, when the seven northern provinces of Holland, Zeeland, Utrecht, Overijssel, Groningen, Gelderland and Friesland joined together as the United Provinces and declared their independence from Spanish rule.

After William the Silent was assassinated by a French Catholic fanatic, his sons Maurits and Frederik Hendrik continued the struggle and the Dutch went on fighting, aided by men and money from England. In retaliation, Philip II of Spain sent over his armada to England in 1588, only to face defeat from a combination of English ingenuity and luck: England's ships were smaller and swifter, her men trained in modern tactics, and the English weather as contrary as ever.

By the time Tradescant travelled into the Low Countries, much of the outright hostility between Spain and England had calmed. Pragmatic peacebroker James I had been on the English throne for eight years and the truce between the Spanish and the Dutch was apparently holding. Philip II of Spain had died and his throne was now occupied by his indolent and ineffectual son, Philip III. Governing the Spanish Netherlands from Brussels were Philip II's son-in-law and daughter, the archdukes Albert and Isabella, whose support for the arts encouraged Flemish painter Peter Paul Rubens back to his family's native Antwerp. Although Rubens and Tradescant were unlikely to have crossed paths on this journey of 1611, Rubens would go on to work for two of Tradescant's future employers: the Duke of Buckingham, whose portrait Rubens painted in Paris when

Tradescant was there with his master; and Charles I, for whom he painted the ceiling to the banqueting hall at Whitehall, where Charles lost his head.

On this journey, however, apart from a night spent in Antwerp and a return visit to Brussels, John Tradescant turned his back on the Catholic south in favour of the northern provinces. Here the burghers had such a well-developed sense of their own horticultural skills that they took as their emblem a fruitful and abundant garden, variously encompassing a Dutch maid, the hat of liberty, and a lion rampant.[3] It was an image reproduced and reinterpreted on seals, coins and engravings such as Willem Buytewech's *Allegory of the Deceitfulness of Spain and the Liberty and Prosperity of the Republic* of 1615. In Buytewech's satirical vision, behatted gardeners diligently tended the flower beds while a lion rampant barred the gate to a two-faced woman (Spain) trailing a leopard and a crouching band of armed men. 'The enclosure had by now become the verdant and well-stocked garden – the *tuin*,' wrote historian Simon Schama, 'that signified the divinely blessed prosperity of the Netherlands and within [which] the Dutch Maid, both comely and vulnerable, was now enthroned.'[4]

In common with most travellers from London to the United Provinces, Tradescant journeyed by water to Gravesend, where he spent the night before boarding the ship that would take him across the narrow seas to the port of Flushing (present-day Vlissingen) at the mouth of the Scheldt estuary. As he charged his employer for three days' expenses in London (2s 6d), he may have worked en route at Cecil's London residence, Salisbury House, between the fashionable south side of the Strand and the Thames.[5] From Gravesend his ship sailed only as far as Ramsgate on the Kent coast, where a 'Contrary wind' forced him to take board and lodging for four more days before he was at last able to continue to Flushing. Some thirty years later, traveller Peter Mundy (an employee of the East India Company) had even less luck; his journey from Gravesend to the Dutch port of Brill (now Brielle) took fifteen days, subjecting him to more life-threatening dangers in its paltry forty-five leagues than twenty-five years spent sailing the globe. 'These are the Chaunces off the world,' he remarked laconically in his journal.[6]

Bad weather was not the only hazard facing travellers who wished to cross

over to the Dutch ports. Still under Spanish rule, the port of Dunkirk was
noted for its piracy, and for many years yet, the sight of an unknown sail
could stir fears of a 'Dunkirker'.[7] But Tradescant's journey passed without
reported incident. At Flushing he paid 3d to go ashore and a further 2d for
a porter to carry his 'Clo[a]k bag', travelling straight on to Middelburg where
he stayed one night before embarking on a ship to Rotterdam. Here he again
paid a porter to carry his bag through the streets and travelled on by water
to Delft where he spent the night and made the first of his many purchases:
a variety of fruit trees including cherries, quinces, medlars, apples, pears and
white currants.[8]

Tradescant kept no record of his travels around the Low Countries and
France although he talked about them to his friend John Parkinson, who
passed on a few brief comments. Of the wild artichoke for instance, which
grew tall and prickly, Parkinson noted that 'John Tradescante assured mee,
hee saw three acres of Land about Brussels planted with this kinde, which
the owner whited like Endive, and then sold them in the winter'.[9] From
Brussels he also brought back a little strawberry that never fruited properly,
despite all his expert care, 'and in seven yeares could never see one berry ripe
on all sides, but still the better part rotten, although it would every yeare
flower abundantly, and beare very large leaves'.[10]

Tradescant's scrupulous bills allow us nonetheless to track his footsteps,
and we can consult the more colourful reports of a handful of other
travellers to the Low Countries, notably Sir William Brereton in 1634, who
took his family across to the Netherlands to consult doctors in Leiden; Peter
Mundy in 1640 (a few years after his visit to Tradescant's own museum of
curiosities in South Lambeth); and diarist John Evelyn in 1641, then a
young man of twenty-one on his way to volunteer his services to the Dutch
cause. Lacking the cachet of France and Italy, the Low Countries rarely
featured on the gentlemanly grand tour and people usually travelled there
for a specific purpose.[11]

Of all these accounts, the most enthusiastic came from Peter Mundy, who
declared himself 'somewhatt affectionated and enclined to the Manner off
the Countrie' – an enthusiasm that John Tradescant would surely have

The pre-eminence of Dutch horticulture.

shared. Noting the difficulty of walking in the Dutch countryside, Mundy concluded that the people sought consolation in 'home delights, as in their streets, houses, roomes, ornamentt, Furniture, little gardeins, Flower potts, in which latter very curious off rare rootes, plantts, Flowers, etts.; incredible prices For tulip rootes. Allsoe Manuffactures and rarieties off Forraigne Countries, off which this place doth a bound and wherin the[y] take delight.'[12] By the time of Mundy's visit, tulip fever had passed its peak but prices were clearly still high.

Like Mundy, Sir William Brereton was struck by the clean, ordered 'daintiness' of Dutch towns with their brick-paved streets, spacious market places, fine churches, and canals ('walled on both sides with freestones') that brought sailing vessels right into the centre of towns; and by the spirit of religious toleration that produced a plethora of churches – Dutch, French,

Arminian, English, Anabaptist and Brownist.[13] In common with many of his contemporaries, Brereton was interested in ways of keeping vagabonds and beggars off the street, noting with admiration the wooden yoke worn as punishment by the wrongdoers of Delft, 'whores, petty larceners, shippers that exact',[14] and the purging of the stews of Amsterdam port, 'wherein of late swarmed the most impudent whores I have heard of, who would if they saw a stranger, come into the middle of the street unto him, pull him by the coat, and invite him unto their house'.[15] He was impressed, too, by the humane treatment of lepers at the Lazaretto outside Rotterdam, 'a dainty fine house, well accommodated with fine gardens and orchards, like a gentleman's house; women to attend them, chamber-pots, and all other necessaries'.[16] While in Amsterdam he prodded and measured a thirty-six-year-old man too fat to walk. 'I never felt horse, nor beast, nor any creature, so thick and fleshy on ribs,' he noted with wonder.[17]

Although they landed at different ports, Brereton and Tradescant made virtually identical journeys around the provinces by boat and wagon, stopping off at Rotterdam, Delft, The Hague, Leiden, Haarlem and Amsterdam. Peter Mundy usefully described the journey from Rotterdam to Amsterdam. Horse-drawn boats set off every hour from Rotterdam, 'precisely att the sound off a little bell, whither they have fraight or Noe', for a cost of three stivers (about 3d) to Delft, where Mundy walked through the town and caught another boat to Amsterdam for two stivers. The boats travelled along canals fed by water drawn up by windmills.

Tradescant also journeyed on to Utrecht (where he bought only a basket) and Vianen. His visits to Rotterdam, Amsterdam and The Hague also produced no purchases, although he may have had other reasons for visiting these towns and cities. Robert Cecil had taken over the running of England's secret service from his father, and foreign intelligence from a man he trusted was always to be welcomed. For Tradescant, there was the added attraction of Dutch horticulture. As the administrative centre of the fledgling republic, The Hague was home to the ruling princes of Orange. Its great courtly gardens still lay in the future, but already in 1610 Prince Frederik Hendrik had sent his steward to investigate the estate of Honselaarsdijk, seven miles to the south-west, which he would purchase the following year after receiving a favourable report on its 'canals, moats, plantations, lower court, orchards, flowers, herbal court, pigeon house and fishing grounds'.[18] Here Frederik Hendrik would plant his gardens with an abundance of rare trees and flowers, demonstrating Holland's lead in matters horticultural. The prince also kept a famous menagerie – visited by Brereton, who saw a 'furious leopard' and a 'young little elephant about three years old'[19] – and decorated his garden grottoes with shells, stones and corals.[20]

At The Hague, Tradescant paid for his dinner but did not claim for an overnight stay. Perhaps like Brereton he stayed as a guest at the 'English house' in Delft (a 'staple' town for English woollen cloth). The house was provided rent-free for English merchants with the added privilege of duty-free food and drink. Brereton was much impressed by its stately dining room, 'dainty bowling-alley within the court', and 'fair, convenient lodgings'.[21] Meals throughout the Netherlands were substantial. He recalled dining with a colonel of the foot regiment and enjoying

royal entertainment, a brave piece of beef, and two curious dainty bag-puddings, the one of suet, flower and almonds, the other with raisins and ordinary spices – an excellent good one; and at [the] latter end of dinner a gammon of Westphalia bacon sliced in great pieces; green leaves here strewed upon the table when covered: here dainty strawberries and cream.[22]

Travelling several decades after Brereton, the naturalist John Ray was horrified by the constant guzzling he observed: 'Generally the *Dutch* men and woman are almost always eating as they travel,' he wrote in some disgust, 'whether it be by Boat, Coach or Wagon'. He cared just as little for the food served up to the common people: ubiquitous salad, meat stewed in 'hotchpots', 'Boil'd Spinage, minc'd and buttered (sometimes also with Currans added)', cod and pickled herrings. While he recommended the novel sandwiches made with thin slices of beef cut from haunches hanging from the rafters and laid upon buttered bread, he passed no comment on the 'Green Cheese, said to be so coloured with the juice of Sheeps Dung. This they scrape upon Bread buttered, and so eat.'[23] As 1s 3d was the most Tradescant paid for a meal in the Low Countries, his fare is likely to have been similarly substantial but not out of the ordinary. He was travelling at Cecil's expense, after all, and meticulously recording every penny spent.

After leaving The Hague, both Tradescant and Brereton then took the wagon to Leiden – a journey of some three hours, passing through trees planted in good order, then an oak wood and parkland, home to both red and fallow deer. After that the land was mostly barren and covered in sand dunes, 'which have been wrought and laid there by the sea'.[24] Approaching Leiden, you saw the windmills first,

whether you slid along the Rijn canals on the tow-barge, taking in the low, cow-grazed meadows through a screen of pipe smoke, or whether you spied the place on horseback, on the road from Leyderdorp of Souterwoude. There they stood, planted atop or just behind the city walls at sentrylike intervals, so many dumb automata, their arms slowly gesticulating in the breeze.[25]

Sir William Brereton found the country around Leiden 'a more pleasant, sweet place than I have met with in Holland', and was especially impressed by 'the daintiest curious gallows that ever I saw'.[26]

Tradescant stayed in Leiden just the one night, paying 1s 6d for bed and board. His plant bill here was disappointingly brief, merely recording £3 spent on 'roots of flowers and Roasses and Shrubs of Strang and Rare' and the payment of a further 26s to a nurseryman called Phalkner (Faulkner?) for 'two pots of gillyflowers 12 sorts in on[e] pot and of Seed gillyflowers plants in on[e] pot'.[27] Although the name was later also applied to the flowers we know as stocks (from the genus *Matthiola*), the gillyflower in Tradescant's time was the July-flowering pink or wild carnation, *Dianthus caryophyllus*, its common name derived from Old French 'gilofre' (itself a corruption of medieval Latin), denoting a strong scent of cloves.

Once a centre of the woollen trade, importing raw wool from England and selling it on as a finished product, Leiden was then enjoying a boost to its fortunes, prompted in part by the city's heroic endurance under siege to the avenging Spanish forces in 1574. Leiden's eventual victory became a symbol of Dutch resistance to Spanish rule, for after months of hunger and disease the city flushed out the besiegers by deliberately breaching the dykes to flood the outlying fields, paralysing the Spanish and allowing rebel forces to sail almost up to the city walls. Populist accounts added a providential storm that turned the siege into 'the national epic par excellence, when sea, wind and polders had fought on the side of the righteous'.[28] 'For this strange preservation,' wrote Brereton in his diary, 'a solemn day of thanks-giving [is] kept yearly in this city.'[29] It still is, more than four centuries later, on 3 October each year.

William the Silent showed his gratitude to the city by founding a university in 1575, the first in any of the northern provinces. Soon it was attracting almost four hundred students a year, more than half from outside the Netherlands, although Sir William Brereton would judge its schools 'very poor, mean things, in comparison of Oxford schools'.[30] Diarist John Evelyn matriculated in 1641 merely by answering questions (in Latin) about his lodgings, name, age, birth and intended faculty. His replies were duly recorded, an oath sworn that he would observe the university's statutes and orders, and after payment of a 'Rix-dollar' he obtained his real purpose: a ticket that exempted him like all other registered students from paying taxes on beer and wine and a few other tolls.[31]

Most students had a higher purpose than cheap beer, however, and the university became especially renowned for its schools of theology, medicine and law. Rembrandt enrolled in 1620 aged fourteen or thereabouts, although he soon abandoned his studies to become apprenticed to a local painter. His father was a local miller and the house where he was born, on the Weddesteeg, looked out over orchards and open fields, at least until the building boom that coincided with Tradescant's visit. 'Calvinism and cloth transformed the city,' wrote Simon Schama about Rembrandt's birthplace, turning 'a gently churchy old market-textile town' into 'a beehive: relentlessly busy, physically congested, humming with economic and cultural energy'.[32]

For a plantsman such as Tradescant, Leiden's real attraction was the physic garden attached to the university's medical school, planted by the great Flemish botanist Clusius (born Charles de l'Ecluse) who had died just two years previously, in 1609. Leiden was not the first botanic garden, of course; that honour belongs to Pisa, founded in 1543, quickly followed by others in Padua, Florence, Bologna and Leipzig, all (like Leiden) attached to their university's medical school because plants were then studied for their therapeutic uses. Clusius's originality was to broaden the focus of his garden from a *hortus medicus* to a real *hortus botanicus* in which medical plants formed only about one-third of the entire collection.[33]

It is tempting to think that Tradescant might have met Clusius on one of his earlier journeys. An introduction to the gardens at Hatfield House by the Dowager Marchioness of Salisbury refers to 'one especially precious plant, the great double anemone, which was a florist's flower and became a cult, as did the tulip. It was grown by Caccine in Italy and given to Tradescant by L'Ecluse [Clusius], gardener to Emperor Maximilian. Hatfield was the first place in England to grow it.'[34] As Clusius died in 1609 and Tradescant most probably started work for Cecil only in 1610, he cannot have received it from him personally for planting at Hatfield, although Clusius may have been the source of its original introduction into England.[35]

Born in Arras, Flanders, in 1526, Charles de l'Ecluse (better known by his Latinized name of Carolus Clusius) studied medicine at Wittenburg in Germany and Montpellier in France, without ever practising as a doctor. 'His main interest,' wrote art-historian Florence Hopper, 'was the quest of the unknown, to discover and observe the phenomena of the plant world in specific and remote regions of Europe as well as to study new plant introductions from all parts of the world.'[36] Much of his botanical writing concentrated on the rare and the exotic. The title of his greatest work (*Rariorum Plantarum Historia*, published in Antwerp in 1601) translates as *An Account of Rare Plants* and it incorporated material from his earlier floras of Spain and Portugal, and of Austria and Hungary. He also wrote the first monograph on the tulip, and gave the first detailed descriptions of plants coming out of the Americas and western Asia.

Clusius did not just observe and describe his precious exotics, he helped bring them into cultivation in the West, growing many of them in his own garden or in those he tended for illustrious patrons such as Emperor Maximilian II in Vienna. As the boundaries of the known world expanded, so did the stock of plants available to the gardens of the West. Along with fellow botanists like Matthias de l'Obel (who gave his name to the genus *Lobelia*), Clusius stood at the centre of an interconnecting web of correspondents (more than three hundred around Europe) intent on exchanging seeds, plants and information about new plants trickling in from the further edges of Europe, North Africa, Turkey and the Ottoman empire, the new American colonies, and the East and West Indies. Perhaps his real interest to gardeners today is that he appreciated plants for themselves, for their curious structure and beauty, and not just their practical uses. In this sense he really was one of the great fathers of the emerging science of botany.[37]

Clusius's appointment as honorary professor of botany at Leiden came at the end of his life. He was in his late sixties when he arrived there in the autumn of 1593 and had in fact originally turned down the offer (like Bartholomew at Hatfield House), pleading age and infirmity.[38] But he had long since left Vienna, disillusioned by imperial employment and the indignity of having his garden torn up and replaced by a riding school on the orders of the new emperor, the Catholic zealot and alchemist Rudolf II.[39] Poor, toothless and suffering from pains in his stomach, Clusius was looking for the status and security that a university post would bring him. He finally accepted the appointment when the authorities agreed to excuse him from lecturing duties. Even so, just as he was setting out for Leiden with the collection of plants he was expected to bring with him, he fell from his horse and dislocated his hip. It was not a very auspicious start.

Helped by an able assistant, however, Delft apothecary Dirck Cluyt, Clusius's garden at Leiden took shape remarkably quickly. In design, it was divided into four quarters or *quadrae*, each in turn subdivided into rectangular beds edged with wood or low earthen dykes and separated by paths of oak bark from the city's tanneries.[40] Plants were grouped logically according to their characteristics, with separate beds devoted to roses, broad-leaved and narrow-leaved irises, plants with flattish flower clusters and so on.

Already when the first inventory was made, the year after Clusius's arrival, his garden was growing over a thousand species, many of them still in pots. A number of the tender species would have succumbed to the terrible winter of 1593–4 and the miserable rains that followed,[41] although some glass protection was provided by the time Sir William Brereton visited in 1634. 'Here, in this little garden, fifty-six beds,' noted Brereton, as methodical as ever, 'all ordinary herbs, roots, and weeds, as well as rare herbs ... tansy, French-wheat, docks, hemlocks, alicampanum, bater-docks, &c. Many roots and plants set in pots, and prosper well.' Brereton came away with an annotated plant list that described 'the nature and quality of the herbs and plants of this garden'.[42]

After much prompting by assistant Dirck Cluyt, first a shed and then a gallery known as the *Ambulacrum* was built along the south side of the garden, where teachers and students could shelter from bad weather and tender plants could be accommodated during the winter.[43] The gallery was erected ten years or so before Tradescant's visit to Leiden. Already its walls displayed a collection of maps, charts, strange animals and plants, curiosities and ethnological material gathered from around the world. Such a combination of botanic garden and collection of curiosities may well have fired Tradescant's imagination and led eventually to his own collection at South Lambeth.

Leiden also boasted another collection of pickled, dried, mummified and otherwise preserved specimens in the anatomy school's museum, which Rembrandt must have frequented in his student years. Its treasures included over a 'yard' of a whale's penis,[44] 'the Entrailes of a Man which is made into a Shirt' and a 'small bone taken from a beaver's penis'.[45] Sir William Brereton devoted a breathless page and a half to the rarities he had admired over and above those in the museum's catalogue, including a 3,000-year-old embalmed pharaoh ('a blackamoor'); the dart of a thunderbolt ('about the length and thickness of your little finger'); and 'the skin's of men and women tanned: a man's much stiffer than a woman's'.[46]

Hard though it may have been for Tradescant to ignore such treasures, he was travelling for his master and after just one night in Leiden he journeyed on by water to Haarlem where his aim was to buy trees, no doubt from the nurseries described by Peter Mundy, who wrote approvingly of Haarlem's 'many pretty groves and woodes, Faire long rancks of Trees with pleasauntt walkes betweene, allso Nurseries off smalle trees, For From hence, they say, Amsterdam and divers other places are supplied with them to Furnish their streetes'.[47]

In Haarlem, Tradescant seems to have visited several nurserymen, as he submitted more than one bill. He spent £4 on 800 tulip bulbs at 10s a hundred (it would be twenty-five years before tulip fever struck in a frenzy of speculation) and was given a 'vine Caled biggare' for free although he was charged 6d for its basket.[48] Possibly from the same source he bought two scythes and one basket with a lock. Then from Cornellis Helin he bought thirty-two early-ripening cherry trees at 4s each to add to the one he had already bought (a little more cheaply) in Delft; one Spanish pear tree; an 'aple quince'; more anemones (clearly a favourite); and sixteen 'province roses'.[49] He also bought 200 lime trees as well as two mulberries, six early-flowering *Daphne mezereum*, six great red currants and two arborvitae trees (*Thuja occidentalis*). From Cornellis Cornellisson in Haarlem he bought forty chequered snake's head fritillaries and the same number of jonquils.

Tradescant was also carrying with him £38 from Cecil's friend Sir Walter Cope, who was to be repaid in trees.[50] The commission was clearly considerable as Tradescant's total purchases for Cecil in Leiden, Haarlem and Delft amounted to less than £34.

After leaving Haarlem, Tradescant spent a few days travelling to Amsterdam, picking up his post but making no further purchases. He then criss-crossed the country, calling in at Utrecht, Vianen, Utrecht again, Haarlem and Leiden, where he loaded up his baskets and pots, and took them on to Delft, then Rotterdam. If he travelled with his purchases, it must have looked like a small forest on the move. Now his main concern must have been to ship his precious cargo to England, which he seems to have done from Brill, another 'cautionary' port held by the English as security for their loan. At Brill, he paid 8s to a servant of Governor Sir Edward Conway for freight, and the Hatfield accounts include a Dutch shippers' bill, recording a further carriage charge of £2 2s.[51]

Tradescant reached Antwerp by 29 October 1611 after a voyage of seven days. He had been away from England for between five and six weeks. Here he called in at Peter van Loor's, a mercantile contact who had already helped Cecil in the purchase of wall hangings, and who advanced Tradescant £60 (to be paid back by the Earl of Salisbury). One of the promissory notes to which Tradescant signed his name was written in Dutch, implying that he had a certain degree of familiarity with the language.[52] After just one day in Antwerp, he set off for Brussels where he stayed three days, shopped again for Cecil, and doubtless got in touch with Trumbull, who would help in arranging the shipment of his further purchases back to England. Now back in the Spanish Netherlands, he was charged 4s for 'the archeduks passport'.

Tradescant's time in Brussels was largely taken up with buying more fruit trees, including seven different kinds of cherry. Two were especially expensive at 12s for a single tree: 'the archduks Cherye', and 'on[e] excedyng great Cherye Called the boores Cherye', which became known as Tradescant's cherry.[53] According to John Parkinson, nurserymen often substituted Tradescant's cherry for the Archduke's cherry because it was much easier to propagate, 'and because it is so faire and good a cherrie that it may be obtruded without much discontent: it is a reasonable good bearer, a faire great berrie, deepe coloured, and a little pointed'.[54]

As well as fruit – bought mostly from John Buret – he purchased more pear trees, a Spanish peach, 500 tulip bulbs, a white apricot, six cherry laurels and fifty small walnut trees. He paid calls on two men who had featured in his letter to William Trumbull of the previous year: Pierre, the archdukes' gardener, from whom he bought ten varieties of vine (at a cost of £1); and florist Mr John Jokket. This time, he bought more martagon lilies, a double hepatica only recently introduced to England, and two different sorts of iris he called 'Irys calsedonye' and 'Irys Susyana'.[55]

All his trees, shrubs and flowers he then had packed into large, padlocked baskets (he even bought two spades for the purpose) and despatched by ship to Flushing, the port where he had first landed. The consignment got no further than Middelburg, however, where it was rescued by Sir John Throckmorton, deputy commander of the English garrison at Flushing.

Tradescant must have again enlisted Trumbull's help, because on 14 November 1611, Throckmorton wrote to Trumbull saying, 'The trees and plants which you sent for the Lord Treasurer, being brought no further than Middelberg by the slothfulness of the shippers, I sent thither to receive them and shipped them into another boat that went for London next day.'[56]

Apart from the usual transport problems, Tradescant's journey into the Netherlands had proved an outstanding success. After Brussels, Paris was next on his itinerary – a slow coach journey of eight and a half days, which cost him just 1s 5d and a further 1s 2d on food.[57] He had plenty of time to plan his future purchases and to anticipate the many difficulties he would face without Trumbull's aid.

Chapter Four

French Exotics

John Tradescant reached Paris sometime in November 1611. This may have been his first venture into France and, after the dainty cleanliness of Protestant Europe, it would have come as something of a shock. Just three years earlier, sharp-eyed scholar Thomas Coryat had described the streets of Paris as 'the durtiest, and so consequently the most stinking of all that ever I saw in any citie in my life'.[1]

On his journey from Calais to the French capital, Coryat was also struck by 'the tokens of what was to him a strange and, above all, a Catholic country'.[2] He was seeing many things for the first time: two monks 'walking together in long black vailes'; and a torturer's wheel, 'whereon the bodies of murderers only are tormented and broken in peeces with certaine yron instruments'.[3] Around Breteuil he noted his first vineyard and a village 'exceedingly ransacked and ruinated' from the country's civil wars. But as the coach rumbled on towards Paris, he marvelled at the richness of the Ile de France with its avenues of walnut trees and the fine country houses of Parisian lawyers.

Despite its unholy stink, Paris in 1611 was a city on the move and Tradescant cannot fail to have been impressed. Politically, it had emerged from the religious strife of the second half of the sixteenth century, when the struggle between Catholics and Protestant Huguenots had produced bloody episodes such as the St Bartholomew's Day Massacre of 1572, in which thousands of Huguenots were slaughtered. The manipulative Catherine de Médicis (wife of Henri II and mother of the next three kings of France) was thought to have had a hand in ordering the massacre. When the last of her sons was assassinated in 1589, the throne passed to the Protestant Henri de Navarre who, as Henri IV, became the first of the Bourbon kings. Abjuring Protestantism, he converted to Roman Catholicism in order to win Paris and reunify his kingdom. 'Paris vaut bien une masse' (Paris is well worth a mass), he reputedly remarked, before finally entering his capital in 1594.

Until his own assassination by a Roman Catholic fanatic in May 1610, Henri IV laid the foundations for a stable, prosperous state, eliminating the national debt, introducing the silk industry to France, encouraging the manufacture of cloth, glassware and tapestries, even bringing over colonies of Dutch and Flemish settlers to drain the marches of Saintonge near La Rochelle. Religious tolerance came with the Edict of Nantes, signed in 1598 and remaining in force until revoked by Louis XIV in 1685. Although it named Roman Catholicism as the state religion, the edict gave Protestants a large measure of religious freedom and created places of safety, among them La Rochelle. 'Those who follow their consciences are of my religion,' declared the French king, 'and I am of the religion of those who are brave and good.'[4]

In Paris, Henri IV (forever honoured as Henri le Grand) continued to beautify his capital like his Valois predecessors, completing Catherine de Médicis' palace of the Tuileries and building the great gallery of the Louvre,[5] then the main royal palace, as well as the Pont Neuf – the first of the city's unencumbered bridges, giving citizens a clear view of the river – and the supremely elegant Place Royale, now the Place des Vosges. He also busied himself in the royal gardens, as Tradescant cannot fail to have noticed. One of his first projects was to restore the Tuileries gardens across a public road from the palace, begun in 1564 but devastated by the civil wars and Henri's own siege of Paris. Here he planted a terrace along the gardens' northern edge, now the Rue de Rivoli, lined with a double row of white mulberries for the rearing of silkworms. Altogether more than fifteen thousand

mulberries were planted in the Tuileries gardens alone, pruned and pol-
larded to produce the new growth on which the silkworms fed.

Among the royal gardeners were Pierre le Nôtre (grandfather of the more
famous André), responsible for re-laying the parterres below the palace
windows; André Tarquin, who looked after the trees; and Claude Mollet,
who designed new gardens for the king to the south of the Louvre and east
of the Tuileries.[6] Also working for the king was a gardener who would
feature as one of Tradescant's most valued contacts in the plant world: Jean
Robin, apothecary and 'arboriste et simpliciste du Roi', a title given to him
by Henri III, and continued by Henri IV and the young Louis XIII – a boy
of just nine years old when his father was murdered. Robin and Tradescant
met during the latter's stay in Paris, probably for the first time. Among the
items that appear on the bill Tradescant submitted to Cecil was 4s for two
fig trees in a basket ('Called the whit fygs') 'withe manye other Rare Shrubs
given me by master Robyns'.[7]

Tradescant needed an intermediary to orientate himself in this booming,
stinking city where the harsh chorus of the city cats kept visitors awake at
night. And so, like others before him, he turned to the English ambassador,
Sir Thomas Edmondes, who lived a coach-ride away in the suburb of St
Germain,[8] paying 'my Lord Imbassettors gardner' 6s 'to goe withe me two
and fro in parrys to by my things'.[9] Hastily posted to Paris to report on the
consequences of Henri IV's assassination, Edmondes was an acolyte of
Cecil's who had previously served as ambassador to the archdukes Albert
and Isabella at Brussels (Trumbull was one of his secretaries). His servants
would be expected to help Cecil's man find what he needed for the
adornment of Hatfield House.

Tradescant's first port of call was probably Jean Robin's own private
garden on one of the islands in the Seine.[10] Some twenty years older than
Tradescant, Robin had been in charge of the royal gardens of the Louvre for
a quarter of a century.[11] By royal decree, he had laid out a small plot for the
growing of simples (medicinal herbs) in 1597 for the Faculty of Medicine.
Although intended originally as a means of boosting his income rather than
a botanic garden in its own right, the Robins' plant collection was

transferred in the 1630s to the Jardin Royal des Plantes Médicinales, cultivated by royal doctor and garden superintendent, Guy de la Brosse.[12]

The parallels between Robin and Tradescant are striking. Both plantsmen with a keen interest in botany, they introduced many plants into their respective countries through their network of contacts, and both had plant-hunting sons who would inherit their gardens and their royal posts. Jean Robin's son Vespasien (born 1579) collected plants around Spain, Italy and the Pyrenees, and in 1603 journeyed as far as Guinea in equatorial West Africa. Vespasien Robin and the younger John Tradescant even died in the same year – 1662.

John Gerard received many plants from the elder Robin, including a pretty chequered snake's head fritillary (he called it a 'checkered Daffodill' or 'Ginny hen flower'), which grew wild around Orléans and Lyons. 'The curious and painfull [painstaking] Herbarist of Paris John Robin, hath sent me many plants thereof for my garden,' wrote Gerard, 'where they prosper as in their owne native countrey.'[13] From further afield came Indian cress – today the common or garden nasturtium but then a great rarity – which 'came first from the Indies into Spaine and those hot regions, and from thence into Fraunce and Flaunders, from whence I have received seede from my loving friend John Robin of Paris'.[14]

In the winter of 1611, when John Tradescant visited their Paris garden, Jean Robin had already published his catalogue of rare plants (in Latin), the *Catalogus Stirpium* (1601) which contained many rare plants from the Orient and Africa, as well as a few from South America and the West Indies. Among its North American introductions was an arborvitae (*Thuja occidentalis*), brought back to France on one of French navigator Jacques Cartier's voyages along the St Lawrence River, when he penetrated deep into Canada in search of the fabled route to Cathay.[15] (Tradescant had just bought two young arborvitae trees in the Low Countries for Cecil.) Robin had also contributed a commentary (again in Latin) to Pierre Vallet's book of the flowers in Henri IV's garden, first published in 1608 and dedicated to Henri's queen, Marie de Médicis.[16] The book's frontispiece looks through a classical arch to the royal flower garden with its ornately planted oblong flower beds and a trellised arbour. Inside are meticulously drawn images of the flowers Tradescant was busy buying around Europe: martagon lilies, crocuses, colchicums, anemones, irises (even the 'Irys Susyana' he had bought in Brussels). Also included are armfuls of tulips, hyacinths and daffodils, although interestingly none of Cecil's favourite gillyflowers. Perhaps this is why they were so often thrown in for free, even here in Paris where his bill to Cecil included 'on[e] pot of gillyflowers Cost nothing'.

Robin himself appears in an engraving in Vallet's book of flowers. His square head, untidy beard and the wispy curls to either side of his high, balding forehead give the impression of a burgher rather than a scholar. 'It is questionable whether either of the Robins was a very good botanist,' wrote American horticulturalist, Marjorie Warner, who suspected them of making false connections between Old and New World varieties in their plant names, giving rise to endless confusion. She nonetheless admitted that 'their zeal and industry in the collection of rarities, and their skill in the care and cultivation of exotics from diverse soils and climates were responsible for the preservation of many of the North American plants introduced in Europe in the first part of the seventeenth century.'[17]

This meeting between Tradescant and Robin cemented ties of friendship and plant exchanging that would continue until the elder Robin's death in 1629. The traffic went both ways, of course. As well as recording many plants received from 'Mounser Robyne' in France,[18] Tradescant sent Robin dried seeds from a berry he had found at Archangel in Russia, 'much like a strabery but of an amber coller'.[19] He may even have given Robin the tree that honours him by name – the black locust or false acacia, *Robinia pseudoacacia*.[20]

Tradescant's plant buying in Paris leant towards the exotic and the tender – plants that might not be expected to survive outdoors through the English winter: pomegranates, orange trees, oleander and myrtle. Cecil's father, Lord Burghley, and Sir Francis Carew of Beddington in Surrey were among the first gardeners to grow oranges in England, and Burghley built one of the first permanent structures to house citrus fruits.[21] John Parkinson's advice on protecting orange trees over the winter was to keep them in square boxes

Chamaris latifolia purpuromolacea   Iris Susiana

Pierre Vallet's 'Iris Susiana', purchased by John Tradescant in Brussels.

that could be carried on hooks or rolled on wheels into houses or a 'close gallerie' for the winter. As an alternative, he suggested planting in the ground against a brick wall, sheltering the plants in winter with boards covered over with 'seare-cloth', 'and by the warmth of a stove, or other such thing, give them some comfort in the colder times'.[22] For bay cherries Parkinson proposed the example of Master James Cole of Highgate, who threw a blanket over them.[23]

While in Paris, Tradescant continued buying fruit: pears, plums, more cherries, Muscat and Lurdlet vines, figs, that pot of gillyflowers thrown in for free, as well as a great hamper of flowers and seeds plus a packet of six books for 10s. His bill for food and lodging in Paris amounted to £1 8s. As he rarely charged more than 2s 6d for a day's expenses, he is likely to have stayed at least a week before hiring a coach to take him to his last plant-buying destination: the Normandy port of Rouen, some eighty-five miles downriver on the Seine.

First, he packed up his trees for the journey home, paying porters to carry them on to the boat and a further 3s to 'the frenche men the kings gardners in onladyng the trees abord the Shipe' – almost certainly men who worked for the Robins. He also gave 3s to the boatmaster who was to bring the trees and other purchases to Rouen, where they were unloaded and heeled into the ground for the duration of his stay. He continued to fret about some precious trees left behind in Paris, even paying a 'Duche man' the considerable amount of £1 4s 'to goe to parrys to enquire after my orrang trees and other trees'.[24]

As one of the main ports for the capital, Rouen offered Tradescant a thriving market in exotics and imported rarities. Here he bought a great 'buffells horne', an 'artyfyshall bird' and a chest of shells containing eight boxes for the hefty price of £12, almost equivalent to three month's salary as the Lord Treasurer's gardener. He also purchased more cherries (this time a variety called 'Biggandres'), mulberries, pears, myrtles, pomegranates, orange trees, double white stock gillyflowers and five different varieties of peach. For the first time he bought cypress trees, 200 at 1s each, plus another 'littill bundall' of six trees. Claude Mollet had used *palissades* of cypress to border

the compartments in his new garden at the Tuileries but they were already
dead by the time of Tradescant's visit, killed off by the severe winter of
1608.[25]

During his time at Rouen, Tradescant cannot fail to have detected signs
of its fluctuating fortunes. Captured by the English in the fifteenth century,
the city saw Joan of Arc burnt at the stake in 1431. Although it became one
of the main cultural centres of France, it had suffered badly during the wars
of religion when it became a Huguenot stronghold. In 1608, Peter Mundy
had come here aged twelve with his father before going on to Bayonne for
two years to learn French. 'There are allsoe many poore people,' he recalled
many years later of his childhood visit to Rouen, 'both men and weomen;
sometimes a man and his wife in stead of horses Drawing small Carrs,
transporting of goods from place to place in thatt Citty.'[26] He also
remembered the river's strange tidal bore and a great bell that he failed to see
'through forgetfulnesse' – he had not yet become the diligent observer of his
later years.

By the time of diarist John Evelyn's visit in 1644, the city had still not
recovered from civil unrest. Its magnificent stone bridge lay in ruins and the
country all around so abounded with wolves that a shepherd had been
'strangled' by a wolf just the day before. Evelyn nonetheless admired the
city's gothic cathedral (built by the English), other fine churches, palaces and
gardens, and a magnificent parliament building. 'The Towne house is also
well built; and so are some gentlemens houses; but the most part of the rest
are of Timber like our Merchants of London in the wodden part of the
Citty,' he wrote.[27]

Perhaps the houses reminded Tradescant how long he had been away.
Now all that remained was to pack up his trees, shrubs, flowers, roots, seeds
and sundry purchases, secure them with padlocks in his hampers and
panniers, and arrange for their shipment back to England. Ever solicitous of
his precious cargo, he gave the boys on the ship 1s 'to be Carfull of the trees'.
For himself, he hired a horse to take him from Rouen to Dieppe where he
kicked his heels for four days, waiting for a ship to take him across the
Channel to Dover. 'This place exceedingly abounds in workemen,' wrote

Evelyn of Dieppe, 'that make and sell curiosities of Ivory and Tortoise shells
... & indeed whatever the East Indys afford of Cabinets, Purcelan, natural
& exotic rarities.'[28]

Once across the Channel, Tradescant went on by horse to Canterbury and
Gravesend for the final journey by water to London, hiring two wherries
(barges) 'to bring the trees to the gardin'. The trees would have reached home
before him. More bills indicate that he stayed in London a further sixteen
days, charging 5s 4d for his lodging and paying additional sums for the
unloading and porterage of trees and pots.[29] Some trees were taken by
wagon to Cecil's London home at Salisbury House while eight loads of trees
were carried to Red Cross Street, and ten porters were hired to carry thirty-
one pots to Petticoat Lane. The same bill recorded a purchase of 1,000
osiers, presumably for Salisbury House.[30]

Tradescant was once more working at Salisbury House in January and
February of the following year, but from another bill he submitted for
garden compost for Hatfield – dated 26 December 1611 – it seems he was
back at Hatfield with his wife and child in time for Christmas.[31] Young
John was then aged three – old enough perhaps to understand a little of his
father's business, especially if he was encouraged to believe that he would one
day follow in his father's footsteps. Even the great Cecil must have rejoiced
at the greening of his garden that resulted from the elder Tradescant's
knowledge of all the best places to look for plants that were strange and rare.

Chapter Five
Waterworks *and* Vines

While John Tradescant was touring the continent buying fruit trees and exotics for Robert Cecil's gardens, work continued on Hatfield's ambitious water features. These were concentrated in the grander East Garden below the king's apartments, which stretched down in a series of terraces to a formal lake or 'water parterre' at the bottom of a slight valley known as the Dell, then fed by a little stream from the main river.

The effect was best described by Frenchman Samuel de Sorbière, who visited Hatfield some fifty years after Tradescant's time.

We Dined in a Hall that looked into a Greenplot with Two Fountains in it, and having Espaliers on the Sides, but a Balister before it, upon which there are Flower Pots and Statues: From this Parterre there is a way down by Two Pair of Stairs, of about Twelve or Fifteen Steps to another, and from the Second to the Third: From this Terrass you have a Prospect of the great Water Parterre I have spoke of, which forms a Fourth; there is a Meadow beyond it, where the Deer range up and down, and abbutting upon a Hill, whose Top ends in a Wood, and there bounds the Horizon to us.[1]

Water gardens on a grand scale started appearing in English gardens towards the end of the sixteenth century, inspired either by personal visits to French or Italian gardens or by engravings such as those of Androuet du Cerceau.[2] Other English examples included Sir Christopher Hatton's geometric fishponds at Holdenby, Sir Francis Carew's resplendent waterworks at Beddington (recently rediscovered), and the Catholic Sir Thomas Tresham's dreamlike water garden at Lyveden, whose bare outline survives to this day. The cruciform house, now a roofless shell, floats above the fat Northamptonshire farmland, spreading its religious message in a stone frieze recounting Christ's Passion. Two snail mounts stand guard over fragmentary canals (once the moat to a formal garden), separated by a raised terrace walk from the orchard, recently replanted with apples, pears, plums, cherries and a central avenue of walnuts. Tradescant must have known this garden well, at least by repute. In 1609, Cecil received a gift of fruit trees from Tresham's widow,[3] having earlier despatched 'Jennings my Gardiner' to Lyveden to view 'one of the fairest Orchards that is in England . . . to pick some such observations as may enable him to spend my money to better purpose'.[4]

Even closer to home, Robert Cecil's father, Lord Burghley, had created a water garden at Theobalds where you could famously row between the shrubs;[5] and among Cecil's improvements to Theobalds, before he was forced to exchange it for Hatfield, was a 'faire square pond' and a river that was 'better than if natural . . . of more pleasure, more profit and more beautiful'.[6] It had crossing fords for deer and places where the heron might feed on shoals of fish. Advising on the work at Theobalds was Cecil's friend, Sir Walter Cope, who paid a special visit there in 1602 to help test the adequacy of the spring water feed. Jennings was apparently confident enough to persuade Sir Walter to keep ten men at work for a week, 'at which time he hath pawned his credit to show sufficient water to make a current river'.[7]

There was also the example – and perhaps the conversation – of Robert Cecil's cousin, Sir Francis Bacon, son of Queen Elizabeth I's Lord Keeper of the Seal, Sir Nicholas Bacon. Francis's and Robert's mothers were sisters who had married the two most powerful men in England, in each case as the second wife. Robert reportedly disliked his cousin, who had failed to advance during Queen Elizabeth's reign, perhaps because of his homosexuality; and although Bacon's standing rose under King James (who shared his sexual tastes), Cecil did nothing to help his relative politically. They had gardens in common, however, and in July 1608 Bacon made a note 'to give directions of a plott to be made to turn ye pond yard into a place of pleasure and speak of this, to my L. of Salsbury'.[8]

Although not published until 1625, Bacon's famous essay, 'Of gardens', echoes the splendour of the Cecil gardens at Theobalds and Hatfield, and their different elements. Princely gardens, said Bacon, should measure not less than thirty acres of ground and contain three distinct parts: a plain 'Greene' at the entrance, a heath or 'desart' at the far end, and in between a square main garden of some twelve acres, surrounded by stately arched hedges hung with birdcages and glinting coloured glass. For ornament he proposed low hedges, clipped pyramids and globes, a fine banqueting house, and a circular mount in the very centre, wide enough for four people to walk abreast. The third part of his plot was a 'Naturall wildnesse' of sweetbriar, honeysuckle and wild vine, close in spirit to the meadow at Hatfield House glimpsed beyond the water parterre.[9]

Bacon also offered words of advice on creating water gardens that clearly came from personal experience, most probably his improvements to the family home of Gorhambury in Hertfordshire, which have now quite disappeared.[10] In the note he made in 1608, reminding himself to talk to Cecil about his gardening plans, he mapped out his ideal water garden. Square and moated, it would be planted with fruit trees and birches, flag irises and lilies, ground-hugging violets and strawberries. On the central island, terraced walks would run alongside a little stream, its water glistening over gravel and fine pebbles. At the heart he imagined a large summerhouse with an upper gallery open to the water, and lower rooms variously described as a 'supping roome', a 'dynyng roome', a 'beddchamber', a 'Cabinett' and a 'Roome for Musike'.

Among his other desiderata were:

An Iland where the fayre hornbeam standes with a stand in it and seats under
   Neath.
An Iland with Rock.
An Iland with a Grott.
An Iland Mounted with flowres in ascents.
An Iland paved and with pictures . . .
An Island with an arbor of Musk roses sett all with double violetts for sent in
   Autumn, some gilovers [gillyflowers] wch likewise dispers sent.
A fayre bridg to ye Middle great
Iland onely, ye rest by bote . . .[11]

As a plan, it was prophetic of what Cecil wanted to achieve at Hatfield.
Hatfield's scheme certainly followed Bacon's principle of perpetual circulation, for Bacon believed that standing water simply made a garden 'un-
wholsome, and full of Flies and Frogs'. He preferred his water to spurt from
gilt or marble fountains (which he said should be cleansed daily by hand to
prevent any gathering 'Mossinesse or Putrefaction'); or gravity-fed from a
higher level into paved bathing pools, 'and then discharged away under
Ground, by some Equalitie of Bores, that it stay little'. The sides and
bottom of such bathing pools could be decorated with images, he proposed,
'And withall Embellished with Coloured Glasse, and such Things of
Lustre; Encompassed also, with fine Railes of Low Statua's'.[12] While dis-
missing garden knots as 'but Toyes', Bacon favoured the tricks and watery
illusions that his secretary, the eccentric Thomas Bushell, would later raise
to an art form in his underground grotto at Enstone.[13]

As Bacon's essay suggests, water might bring a garden to life but it could
also bring plenty of grief. Cecil had already experienced problems of a
technical kind at Theobalds. Baron Waldstein, visiting in 1600, reported
that the raised pools and watermills had already run dry. Two years later,
another visitor, Frederic Gerschow, complained that the 'fine edifice with
waterworks, which formerly rose as high as the roof' was 'at present out of
order'.[14] The waterworks in Hatfield's East Garden were to prove no less of
a problem in their early days.

The task at Hatfield was twofold: first, to design a system of descending fountains for the terraces of the East Garden; and, second, to create a formal 'water parterre' and artificial island down in the valley bottom (now transformed into the much more informally landscaped New Pond) by damming the small stream running through the valley. Work on the fountains does not seem to have started much before 1611, under the intermittent supervision of Mountain Jennings.[15] Actual construction of the conduits and fountains was entrusted to pipemaker Simon Sturtevant. In January 1611, there was a founder's bill for some of the plumbing fitments: stopcocks for the East Garden, the cistern for the terrace, snakes, and the 'Frenchman's roke' (rock).[16] In the same month, Simon Sturtevant signed his name to an estimate for the 1,793 yards of clay pipes sealed with lead, necessary to bring water from springs to the Dell, and a further 1,300 yards from the house, promising 'to finish this pipeworke by the last of Aprill'.[17]

By mid-May of that year – a scant two months before the king's visit in July – a memorandum from Robert Lyminge, John Shawe and Samuel Stillingfleet set out the outstanding work. The new river was still too deep, according to a marginal note, 'and is appointed to be filled up higher to runne more shallow, which wilbe more hansom – Jeninges is here, and undertaketh it'. More promisingly, 'the water is lett in to the workes at the river, which run verye pleasantlye, and the workmen are in hande with the turffinge and perfettinge of the walkes in the iland'. Specifically, in the East Garden 'the tarras walke is levelled and perfitted [perfected], and the little river is indented, and stones and shelles laide in the bottom, and this daye the water runneth in yt'. Tradescant's chestload of shells from Rouen would soon bring added lustre. As a final touch, the temporary hedges on either side of the walks had been removed, and workmen were busy laying turf in their place.[18]

If the river works and island were proceeding as planned, however, the fountains were not. Perhaps, like those at Theobalds, they were running dry or perhaps they just did not look right. Already, by September 1611, Mountain Jennings had submitted a bill for twice altering the rockwork and other urgent tasks required to get the garden ready for the king's visit.[19] So Cecil's agent Thomas Wilson turned to the Huguenot Salomon de Caus, a hydraulic engineer from Normandy who had studied mathematical sciences and was then working in England as mathematics tutor to Henry, Prince of Wales. His portrait casts him as a thickset monkish man, an impression at odds with the flamboyant theatricality of his designs for grottoes and fountains. De Caus would later lay out the gardens of Heidelberg Castle for Prince Henry's sister, Elizabeth Stuart, and her husband Frederick V, the Elector Palatine, whose acceptance of the throne of Bohemia ignited the Thirty Years War, immortalizing Elizabeth as the Winter Queen when the pair were forced into exile at The Hague.

In November of that year, Cecil's agent Thomas Wilson returned from a visit to Hatfield and the next morning, 'so tormented with toothache and cold', sat down to write a long letter to his master, setting out how the fountain problem was to be remedied. De Caus (or 'the Frenchman' as he invariably called him) was further tormenting him with constant changes of plan. 'Every journey brings new designs,' wrote the exasperated Wilson. Despite all the money that had already drained away into the fountains, de Caus's latest plan was to scrap the existing project and start again. He proposed building a new cistern next to the bowling green in the upper part of the East Garden, turning the great open cistern into a fishpond 'to be ready upon all occasions', but dismantling the stone cistern in the riding court and recycling its materials. Water from the new cistern would feed four fountains – one already under construction, two in the quarters of the upper garden and a fourth in the centre of the lower part, each one receiving its water from the fountain above.[20]

Thomas Wilson's letter to Lord Salisbury even included a rough sketch of how the fountains linked together. He went on to describe de Caus's plans for the island, which he illustrated in the shape of a lozenge bisected by a water channel and surrounded by water on all sides. Astride the central channel sat a pavilion or banqueting house, balanced by three further structures: a pump house, a grotto, and a small crenellated building that looks like a viewing tower or a smaller banqueting house. 'At the river,'

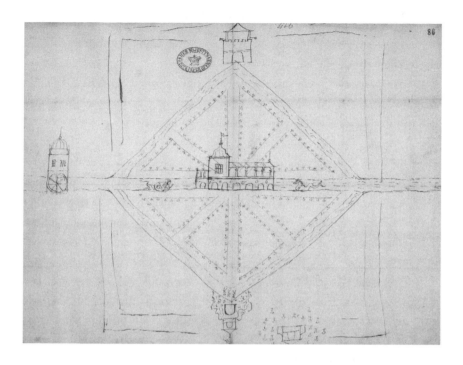

A rough sketch of Salomon de Caus's plan for the water
parterre at Hatfield House.

explained Wilson to Lord Salisbury, 'he meaneth to make a force at the
going out of the water from the island which by the current of the water shall
drive up water to the top of the bank above the dell & so descend into two
fountains.' There is no evidence that any of these garden buildings were ever
erected at Hatfield, although the elaborate waterworks certainly were. Two
men were employed for four weeks each to cast leaves, snakes, and fishes for
the rock and river in the East Garden, and another two men spent two weeks
laying pipes 'for the frenchmans worke'.[21] De Caus may well have recycled
the designs in his other gardens. At Heidelberg for Princess Elizabeth, for
instance, he created a water garden with just such gushing fountains and
fishy creatures[22] and his greatest published work – Les Raisons des forces

movantes – contains similarly fantastical mounts, grottoes and fountains, as well as practical information on how to bring water to fountains over undulating terrain.[23]

Of the parts that were implemented, Cecil cannot fail to have been as delighted by their charming conceits as his fish so clearly were. 'You have also in those Places,' wrote visitor Samuel de Sorbière,

where the River enters into and comes out of the Parterre, open sort of Boxes, with Seats round, where you may see a vast Number of fish pass to and fro in the Water, which is exceeding clear; and they seem to come in Shoals to enjoy all the Pleasures of the Place; and quitting their own Element by jumping sometimes out of the Water, this they do as it were to observe all the things I have describ'd to you.[24]

But the cost of Cecil's waterworks was enormous – £300 for the new cistern alone, plus £100 more for altering the existing pipework. Then there were de Caus's charges (£110) and the expense of the fountains – £112 9s for the grand central fountain, including payments to sculptor Garrett Jonson for the marble basin, to Garrett Christmas for casting the lead figure, and charges for materials such as plaster, wax, resin, oil, solder and lead.[25]

In de Caus's final reckoning, he is clearly labelled as 'the princes Inginer' rather than Cecil's own. The tantalizing possibility exists that he might also have supplied the drawing of an unidentified flower garden, which survives in the Hatfield archives.[26] The plan shows a raised (or sunken?) garden, square in outline with circular beds around the centre, laid out in interlocking curves like the *parterres de broderie* which de Caus would use for the flower gardens of Heidelberg. The intricate scrolls and flowing floral patterns are unmistakably French, of the kind favoured by Henri IV's queen, Marie de Médicis,[27] who sent Cecil fruit trees for Hatfield (plus many more for King James), together with French gardeners to make sure they were properly planted.[28]

Fountains, flower beds and fruit trees were not the only evidence of French influence on Cecil's grand gardens at Hatfield. He also planted a fine vineyard a little over a mile away from the house, on sloping ground to north and south of what is now called the Broadwater. It became one of the garden sights of south-east England. 'I ought not to forget the Vineyard,' wrote Samuel de Sorbière, after describing the great water parterre,

nor the several small Buildings on the side of it, some of which serve for a Retreat to several Sorts of Birds, which are very tame. There are also Arbours or Summer-Houses, like *Turkish* Chiosks, upon some of the Eminences, which have a Gallery round, and are erected in the most Beautiful Places, in order to the Enjoying of the Diversified Prospects of this Charming Country.[29]

Now replanted with evergreens and guarded by crenellated brick walls, the vineyard remains a fine and private place, off-limits to the crowds who flock to the house. Through the grille to its flint-and-brick entrance keep, you can spy its steep terraces dropping down to the water below.

John Evelyn visited in March 1643, finding 'the Garden & Vineyard rarely well water'd and planted'.[30] Pepys came too, one cold day in July – so cold in fact that he had to buy a pair of coarse woollen socks to wear over his thread stockings, 'and after dinner, though weary, I walked all alone to the Vineyard, which is now a very beautiful place again'. Afterwards he met the gardener who showed him the house, the chapel with its 'rare pictures' and 'above all the gardens, such as I never saw in all my life; nor so good flowers nor so great goosburys, as big as nutmegs'.[31]

In Cecil's time, vineyards were a rare sight in southern England. 'There is no wine-growing in this kingdom,' wrote a German visitor in 1592, 'but if you want wine you can purchase the best and most delicious sorts, of various nations, and that on account of the great facility which the sea affords them for barter with other countries.'[32] In fact, vines had been introduced to southern England by the Romans but thereafter their culture was erratic, only an isolated handful struggling through the years of Saxon rule until the arrival of the wine-loving Normans boosted cultivation. The Domesday Book records vineyards at forty or more settlements in south-eastern England (probably an underestimate), all in the hands of Normans or the great monasteries; and numbers continued to grow.[33] Then Henry II's

marriage to Eleanor of Aquitaine netted the wine-rich territories of
Bordeaux and home production suffered, further buffeted by rural
depopulation caused by the Black Death and by Henry VIII's dissolution of
the monasteries. Climate change, too, played a part. The first half of the
sixteenth century was generally mild, then temperatures began to drop and
a 'little ice age' descended on the northern hemisphere, making conditions
even tougher.

Vines travelled to Hatfield from many sources, (including the resourceful
William Trumbull in Brussels), boosted by those brought back by John
Tradescant from Haarlem, Brussels and Paris. One of the first recorded gifts
of grapes came via the good offices of Sir Michael Hicks, Lord Burghley's
former secretary. In a letter to Cecil of 2 October 1609, Hicks wrote
glowingly about the fine ripe grapes of Sir Edward Sulyard, the white
especially, which 'were in my opinion as good as ever I tasted of for the relish
& sweetness: I prayed him to send some to your Lordship to taste of, to the
end, that if you liked of them, you might have some grafts of the same vine'.
Sulyard went one better, promising Cecil half a dozen roots that would bear
fruit in two years' time, as opposed to the three or even four years it might
take a graft. 'Besides,' wrote Hicks, 'he will give your Lordship two nectarine
plum trees of several kinds, when the time of the year is to plant, & anything
else he hath in his garden or orchard.'[34]

From Madame de la Boderie, wife of the French ambassador, Antoine Le
Fevre de la Boderie, came 20,000 vines in early 1611. Thomas Wilson
thought his master should pay at least £50 for them, a sum calculated at eight
crowns the thousand. He had just heard that an additional 10,000 plants were
on their way: 'more than the ground prepared will receive'. The plan was to
'make a nursery of them, set thick together, in some small piece of ground
adjoining, to supply those still which we find defective or dying'.[35]

John Tradescant's letter to Trumbull of 1610, and the bills from his plant-
buying trip to the Low Countries and France, give us some idea of the grape
varieties favoured by Cecil: 'blew muskadell', 'Russet', 'Muscat', 'Vyens
called lurdlet' and 'Biggare'. Half a century later another English king's
gardener would write a small tract, edited by John Evelyn, to encourage the

growing of English vines, with plenty of advice on how to overcome shortcomings in climate and situation.[36] His name was John Rose, gardener to Charles II, who visited the Tradescants' garden in South Lambeth in the company of Elias Ashmole.

In his preface to Rose's little book, John Evelyn describes falling into conversation with him at Essex House, where Rose then gardened for the Duchess of Somerset. The talk turned to the English neglect of their vineyards – much like their neglect of forest trees, a pet subject of Evelyn's – and the diarist was persuaded to put together the gardener's thoughts on growing vines, 'which I so much the more value, as I consider them the native production of his own Experience' rather than the latest fancy of 'some Monsieurs new come over, who thinke we are as much oblig'd to follow their mode of Gardn'ing as we do that of their Garments, till we become in both ridiculous'.[37]

In Rose's view, the vines that best tolerated the English climate were:

1. The small *Black grape*, by some call'd the *Cluster-grape*, a precoce and early ripe fruit.
2. The white *Muscadine* early ripe also, and a well known *grape*.
3. The *Parsly-grape*, so denominated from the shape and indentures of the leafe; it bears somwhat a smaller *raisin* or berrie, but it is of a briske and delicious taste, mature betimes.
4. The *Muscadella* a white *grape*, not so big as the *Muscadine* though as soon ripe.
5. The *Frontiniaq*, both white and red.
6. A new *white Grape*, ripe before the *Muscadins*, which I found in His Majesties Garden in St. James's, with a red wood and a dark green leafe: it ripens as soon in standard as against some Walls, and is a closer bunch than the *Muscadine*.

Cecil's vineyards on either side of the water faced north and south, their terraces tilted to catch the sun. The poverty of the soil meant their roots would stay close to the surface in the approved manner, receiving the 'sweet and benigne showers, dews, and influences' and getting their warmth from the sun, which Rose considered, poetically if a little unscientifically, 'impregnated with a certain *volatile sale*, which produced near the surface of the Earth only, is drunk in by the delicat pores and apertures of the latent rootes'. Look for brambles, said Rose (like the bramble thickets that even now surround the walls of Cecil's vineyard at Hatfield), because this indicates the driest banks and hot stony places where vines do best.[38]

Tradescant was not himself in charge of Cecil's vineyard. That responsibility lay with the Frenchmen he mentioned in his letter to Trumbull of October 1610, later named in the accounts as 'Pier [Pierre] Collin & John Vallett', paid £3 5s and £2 10s a quarter.[39] Cecil also turned to his half-brother's gardener, whom agent Thomas Wilson brought down twice 'to plant vines himself, that I might see the diffrence between the other Frenchmens planting and his'.[40]

Cecil may have liked grapes for the table and to give as princely gifts but there is no evidence he had any interest in making wine. The vineyard served as an ornamental addition to his estate and to his status and like everything else he touched, it became the gold standard 'where *nature* by the *Midwifery of Art*, is delivered of much pleasure'.[41] John Tradescant would naturally turn this to his advantage, when he later sought employment with Charles I as keeper of the gardens, vines and silkworms at Oatlands Palace.

Chapter Six

Muck *and* Mystery

W hen he was not travelling on his master's business, John Tradescant was taking charge of the day-to-day running of the great gardens at Hatfield, in tandem with Mountain Jennings. Payments to Jennings continued until at least September 1612, when he was still working on the East Garden.[1] His charges for regular maintenance slackened off, leaving Tradescant as the principal gardener, with special responsibility for the kitchen garden.

Kitchen gardeners then as now have two main concerns: building up the fertility of the soil, and keeping plants healthy through a constant battle with pests and diseases. Both would have kept Tradescant very busy. Hatfield's soil is not ideal for gardens: an inch or two of sandy, nondescript topsoil lying on top of gravel and heavy clay, although a riddling of flints does at least improve drainage. Tradescant would have needed copious amounts of well-rotted dung and other sources of organic matter to nourish the precious plants he had so tenderly brought back home.

Like all professional gardeners, he would have developed his own recipes for the richest general fertilizers and those needed for particular tasks, taking advice perhaps from the gardening writers of his day but relying just as much on his own experience. As a general fertilizer for kitchen gardens on Hatfield's 'hot sandy or gravelly grounds', John Parkinson recommended

dung from cows rather than horses, being of a 'colder and moister nature';
and although it took longer to compost, 'yet it will outlast it more then twice
so long'.[2]

Other recommended fertilizers were more gruesome, such as this tip from
gardener and author Sir Hugh Platt: 'Dogs and cats applyed to the rootes of
trees before the sap rise, have recovered many olde decaying trees. Shred
them.'[3] As an alternative feed for old trees and vines, Platt offered two quarts
of ox blood (or horse blood as an acceptable substitute) 'tempered with a hat
ful of Pidgions dung', enough to make it up into a 'soft paste', which you
could then apply to the principal roots.[4] For Platt, proof of the fertility of
decaying matter lay with the butchers of London, who used their gardens
expressly to bury 'the bloud, offal, and entrailes of beasts. ... to avoid
offence'.[5]

Puritan fruit-grower Ralph Austen was another who put together a good
list of meaty ingredients for nourishing fruit trees and vines: pigeons' dung,
hens' dung, sheep's dung or 'the like stuffe, that is very *hot*, and *fertill* ... So
also of *Lees of Wine*, the *washing of strong Beere-Barrels*, *Blood of Cattle, dead
Dogges, Carrion*, or the like, laid, or put to the *Roots of Trees*.' To counter-
balance an over-rich soil, by contrast, he recommended replacing some of the
fertile soil with '*sand*, or *cole ashes*, or any *stuffe* that is *barren*'.[6]

While there are as many recipes for compost as there are individual
gardeners, agrarian writer Samuel Hartlib (who would come to know
Tradescant's son well) indicates how local composts reflected local soils and
spoils: sea-mud and 'owse' (ooze) from the marshy ditches of Kent and
Sussex; sea-coal, ashes and horse dung in London; woollen rags in
Hertfordshire and Oxfordshire; malt dust, blood and 'shavings of hornes'
more or less everywhere; green manuring with lupins and tares in Kent; cod
heads and fish in northern New England. Five miles south of Canterbury,
Hartlib knew of a woman 'who saveth in a paile, all the droppings of the
houses, I meane the *urine*, and when the paile is full, sprinckleth it on her
Meadow, which causeth the grasse at first to look yellow, but after a little
time, it growes wonderfully, that many of her neighbours wondered at it,
and were like to accuse her of witch-craft'.[7]

Squeamishness was no virtue when dealing with pests and potential
predators, either. Hatfield's deer were preserved for the chase by building
deer fences around the gardens and paying watchers 6d a night 'for keeping
them out of the garden'.[8] Moles were less fortunate, although the Hatfield
accounts are coyly silent on precisely how they were caught and killed.
Gentlemanly John Evelyn offered a variety of means in his translation of
The French Gardiner. Some gardeners favoured butter pots sunk into the
ground for catching moles, he said. Others preferred a makeshift trap
fashioned out of a two-foot length of wooden pipe, as big as your wrist,
cunningly fixed with small tongues of tin or iron plate at either end, each
one 'fastned to the trunk with a wyre a little slanting at the bottom towards
the middle of the pipe; that so the Mole entering in, and thrusting the tongue
can neither get out at one end or other'. A more foolproof method was
simply to watch the moles working their hills in the early morning and
evening, and to fling them out with a spade. Any that were taken alive
could be buried in an empty butter pot so that their cries would bring other
moles running. And if all else failed, you could destroy them with 'Mole
graines' which he defined as 'a set of sharp Iron points, skewed upon a staffe,
which struck upon the hill when the mole is working, does certainly pierce
him through, amaze, or kill, as you shall finde if you dig immediately
after it'.

Warming to his task, John Evelyn proposed tempting field mice to
drown themselves in water concealed under a layer of oat husks.
Alternatively you could poison them with arsenic or powder of 'Ratts-bane'
mixed with grease, 'but you may by this means endanger your Catts, which
finding and eating the dead mice will not long survive them'. Similarly, to
tempt ants you could hang little boxes pierced with bodkins baited with
arsenic and honey from your fruit trees, taking care not to trap the bees. As
for woodlice, earwigs, and the smaller insects that infest your trees:

you shall place Hoofs of Bullocks, Sheep or Hogs, upon short stakes fixed in the
Ground, or upon the Ozyers which fasten your Palisades, and wall-fruit, and this
Chase will employ two men from Morning break, who must take them gently, but

speedily off, and shake them into a kettle of scalding water, which they are to carry with them; or the other may bruise such as are likely to escape with some instrument of wood.[9]

As one of Hatfield's principal gardeners, Tradescant would have overseen these and all the other routine tasks needed to maintain Cecil's gardens at their peak. The duties are set out in a brief but fascinating note computing the annual expenditure on 'keeping and Maintaining in Repaire' the different areas. Work required in the West Garden, for instance, included 'Cutting mowing Edging the walkes Rowling pruning & Nayling the trees weeding the quartares walkes & bordares with the looking to the nessorie [nursery] below & maintayning all the Headges with pooles & stakes'. In the East Garden, the hedges still needed 'Nurssing up' and the lower garden planting with gooseberries, raspberries, roses, strawberries and flowers.

Specific tasks in the kitchen garden included 'diging dunging sowing & planting of Earbes Rootes hartichokes cabadges & all other Earbes nessicarie for the kichen with the keepping Clene of the gardin & geving Attendance for the sarving of the house with thes Nessicaries'. In the kitchen garden alone, this required the employment of three workmen at 1s 6d a day each, two labourers at 1s a day and six women weeders at 6d. 'Now the Number of working dayes in the yeare may Amount to 293 or thare About Exemting sundayes, Hollidayes which not withstanding Attendance must be geven.' In total, the annual wages bill for maintaining the kitchen garden was estimated at £138 3s 6d.

A similar round of tasks was set out for the vineyard, namely: dressing; dunging; pruning; staking; weeding the vines, borders and walks; and mowing the grass. On the island, the river and streams had to be kept clean, their banks mowed, the walks and alleys edged, the hedges cut and planted where necessary, and the rubbish carried out.[10]

Tradescant's expenses tell us what plants he was growing in the kitchen garden. In April 1612, for instance, he submitted a bill for twenty-four earthenware pans to cover his melons and two water tubs to help in their upkeep. He was also claiming 5s spent on five loads of dung and a total of

19s 6d on various seeds: onion, spinach, marjoram, borage and marigold. The tools he needed included two pairs of garden shears, two garden rakes and twelve bundles of small hazels to mend the garden hedges, priced at 6d the bundle.[11] The following month he bought more seed and tools: four ounces of 'kardus benydctus' seed (known to Parkinson as the 'Blessed Thistle', it was used as a plague remedy and to expel worms),[12] eight ounces of radish seed, a basket of cucumber plants bought in London (together with carriage charges and the cost of his horse in London), and a garden scythe.[13] It was a mundane list after the extravagance of his European travels, but a good kitchen garden was necessary for the smooth running of a great household and valued 'for the many utilities ... to be had from it, both for the Masters profit and pleasure, and the meynies content and nourishment'.[14]

Thomas Wilson, Cecil's agent at Hatfield, would have kept a prudently financial eye on the way Tradescant carried out his duties, but Cecil liked to take personal charge and we know from Tradescant's letter to William Trumbull in Brussels that the great statesman was not above giving 'enterteynment' to his gardener.[15] While we cannot eavesdrop on their conversations, John Evelyn gives us some idea of the gardener's many duties in the instructions he wrote for his own gardener, Jonathan Mosse, who served a six-year apprenticeship at Evelyn's Deptford home in the 1680s.[16] The tone is courteous throughout, as in Evelyn's description of the method to be employed by his Sayes Court gardener, or 'any other with little alteration':

The Gardiner should walke aboute the whole Gardens every Monday-morning duely, not omitting the least corner, and so observe what Flowers or Trees & plants want staking, binding and redressing, watering, or are in danger; and especialy after greate stormes, & high winds and then immediately to reforme, establish, shade, water &c what he finds amisse, before he go about any other work.[17]

The gardener was not to sell any fruit, vegetables or flowers without first gaining permission from his master or mistress; and he was to give his mistress notice 'when any Fruites, Rootes, Flowers, or plants under his care'

'*Skill and pains, bring fruitfull gains*'. *The frontispiece to William Lawson's*
A New Orchard and Garden.

were ready for the still house, and 'to receive her directions'.[18] Only Sunday
was allowed as a free day; and of the seasonal tasks, March was especially
busy when he was to 'Sow Endive, Succory, Chervil, Selleries, purselan
(which you may also continue sowing all the summer to have tender) leeks,
Beetes, parsneps, salsifix, skirrits [a kind of water parsnip], Turneps, &c. and
now Cherish and Earth-up your flowers, and set stakes to the tallest: sow
lettuce'. November and December were to be spent trenching, digging and
muck-spreading; while towards the end of January he was to prune the wall
fruit, 'til the sap rises briskly, especialy finish cutting your Vines'.[19] There
were also months for bringing oranges, lemons and other tender evergreens
outside (May) and for taking them back inside (October).

   Much of the summer was taken up with mowing and rolling on a
rotating basis, so that the grass would be cut 'every 15 dayes, & the gravell
rolled twice every six dayes'. While the gardener was rolling or mowing, 'the

Weder is to sweepe & clense in the same method, and never to be taken from that work 'til she have finished'.[20] The pronoun makes the weeder's sex abundantly clear.[21] Evelyn's timetable also denoted when seeds and root boxes were to be inspected for mould and vermin (every second Saturday) and the beehives checked (daily at noon in hot weather, otherwise once a month). Tools were to be put inside at night and sharpened in wet weather, and dung heaps stirred every quarter. Cypress, box and most evergreen hedges were to be clipped in April and mid-August. Pruning wall fruits and standards was a task for the end of July and the beginning of January, while vines were to be pruned in January '& exuberant branches that hinder the fruite ripning in June'. It was a rigorous schedule and no doubt Robert Cecil was just as exacting in the skill and dedication he demanded from his gardener.

Tradescant's home life would have been subservient to his employment. As he claimed for living expenses while visiting Salisbury House in London, he clearly lived at Hatfield, doubtless in one of the 'gardeners lodgings in the garden', which were reglazed in 1610.[22] Little is known of his wife Elizabeth, beyond the bare details of her birth, marriage and subsequent birthing of a son, their only known child. Elizabeth clearly survived childbirth as otherwise her death would have been recorded in the parish register along with young John's baptism. The records for her home parish of St John at Meopham in Kent record the burial on 18 August 1613 of one 'Elizabeth d. of Wid. Willcocke'. Willcocke was one of her mother's married names, but Elizabeth was a very common name among girls of the time and there were other Willcockes in the parish.

Assuming she returned to Hatfield with her baby son, Elizabeth Tradescant would have run their small household and busied herself with the traditional woman's tasks of brewing, baking, washing, candle-making, distilling, seeing to the dairy as well as all the usual housewifely duties, plus looking after their joint enterprises during her husband's many absences. Concerning relations with her husband, she would have done well to follow the advice of Cambridge-educated East Anglian farmer, Thomas Tusser, whose Tudor best-seller of 1557, A hundredth goode pointes of husbandrie had swollen to *Five hundreth points* by 1573, with the same number thrown in for 'good *huswiferie*'. Expressing himself in excruciating doggerel, Tusser proposed a life of hard work and good cheer, addressing these words to the woman of the house:

> Be lowly not sollen, if ought go amisse,
> what wresting may loose thee, that winne with a kisse.
> Both beare and forebeare now and then as ye may,
> then, wench God a mercie, thy husband will say.[23]

As well as working for Cecil, Tradescant was also busy on his own account. In common with other gardeners of the day, he rented fields from his master – as much as twenty-seven acres of arable land, and thirty-two acres of the old Hatfield Great Wood, which was being divided into enclosures and converted to farmland.[24] At least some of these he would later rent out, as we know from a letter he wrote after he had left Hatfield, addressed to the men who looked after the 2nd Earl's business affairs. Tradescant was behind with his rent on one of the pieces of land he had leased around Hatfield and he was asking Salisbury's agents, cap in hand, to look kindly on his late payment because others had let him down. The letter's faintly wheedling tone echoes that of his earliest surviving despatch to William Trumbull in Brussels. He declares that it was not his fault that his subtenant, Mr Clarke, had failed to pay out £33 of Tradescant's money, or that Clarke had reneged on his promise to collect another £80 owed to him by others in the county, 'but they all have mad bould to keepe my mony and not to pay it'. He went on to praise God that he had not been so 'hardlie pent' that he could not pay his rent on the appointed day 'and I presume that if I had forfetid it my Lord would not take the forfeture'.[25]

Tradescant, it seems, was not very practised as either a landlord or a tenant. A Mr Carter to whom he also owed money (Robert Carter, the Earl's bailiff at Hatfield) had measured the fields for him a couple of years previously and had found that the fields were actually smaller than their rent assumed. Another letter from Tradescant – this time to Captain Thomas

Brett, the Earl's Receiver-General – used this fact to plead for a rent reduction on several of his fields, complaining in passing about the taking of pollards from his land to mend hedges, ploughs and carts. Although his lease made this perfectly lawful, 'they Cut So muche that I greeve to see it'. On top of that, his land at Woodfields had not yet been cleared of trees and he did not know how he might plough, 'but that I prsume of yr worships Justnes for if they Clear not befor our Lady Day as I am now Hindred of this years Season from plowing I shall also be Spoyled for grasing and I knowe my Lord will abat nothing of what I must pay'.[26]

Tradescant would have needed land to pasture his horse; and the reference to ploughing and grassing suggests that he was also farming for profit. In June 1612 he delivered thirty-two trusses of hay 'for the use of the Earl of Salisburye to his groomes', at a charge of 1s a truss.[27] He may also have wanted nursery ground that would allow him to supply trees and plants to his employers and other great houses, much as he had bought from the archdukes' gardener in Brussels. This was how gardens were generally stocked, before nurseries became common. The royal gardener John Rose even used his published manual on vine-growing to promote himself as a plentiful source of his recommended varieties, declaring 'that those who have a desire to Store their Grounds, may receive them of me at very reasonable rates'.[28]

While the joys and frustrations of gardening have remained fairly constant through time, gardening in the early seventeenth century had a spiritual dimension that is largely absent today. For Tradescant and his contemporaries, God still walked the garden and all gardeners could trace their craft back to Adam, even those who championed the new sciences. 'God Almightie first Planted a Garden,' wrote natural philosopher Sir Francis Bacon at the start of his celebrated essay on gardens. 'And indeed, it is the Purest of Humane pleasures. It is the Greatest Refreshment to the Spirits of Man; Without which, Buildings and Pallaces are but Grosse Handy-works.'[29]

For Tradescant's friend, John Parkinson, Adam's God-given knowledge was to be specially prized: his familiarity with the names and natures of all living creatures, and of the purposes of herbs and fruits, whether for 'Meate or Medicine', for use or for delight. 'And that Adam might exercise this knowledge,' wrote Parkinson with a sonority that recalls the King James Bible, 'God planted a Garden for him to live in, (wherein even in his innocency he was to labour and spend his time) which hee stored with the best and choysest Herbes and Fruits the earth could produce.'[30]

As the century progressed, the rising tide of millenarian Puritanism would surge through the writings of men like fruit-grower Ralph Austen, who sought to recreate in England 'another *Canaan, flowing with Milke and hony*' (or more literally with cider, perry and cherry-wines, the products of his Oxford orchard).[31] Closer to Tradescant in time was bluff north country clergyman William Lawson, whose declaration that 'there is no plague so infectious as Popery and Knavery' put him firmly in the Puritan camp. Although he made no mention of Adam by name, the First Gardener was spiritually present in the clergyman's simple words of advice. If you wanted a pleasant and profitable orchard, he said, you should get yourself a good, honest and above all *religious* gardener. 'By religious, I mean (because many think religion but a fashion or custome to goe to Church) maintaining, and cherishing things religious.' Attentive to God's word, honest, charitable in his alms-giving, highly skilled and no 'idle or lazie Lubber' – these were the qualities Lawson valued. 'Such a Gardner as will consciionably, quietly and patiently, travell in your Orchard, God shall crowne the labours of his hands with joyfullnesse, and make the clouds droppe fatnesse upon your Trees; he will provoke your love, and earne his Wages, and fees belonging to his place.'[32]

Lawson's manual on fruit-growing also set out the acceptable limits of man's intervention in the garden and the orchard. For centuries, gardeners had used their art to perfect nature – but only up to a point. It was perfectly acceptable – and even commendable – to propagate vegetatively using the age-old techniques of grafting, inoculation and layering. Tradescant would have been highly skilled at all these operations but for most sixteenth- and seventeenth-century gardeners, such 'improvements' stopped short of tampering with nature herself.

John Parkinson was quite emphatic on this point, refusing to countenance the esoteric gardening tricks put forward by writers such as Sir Hugh Platt (or Plat), an inventor and keen gardener who contributed to a brisk trade in books of 'secrets', offering access to arcane wisdom through a jumble of tips on gardening, alchemy, cooking, home-decorating, cosmetics, physics, healing and outright marvels.[33] Platt's *Floraes Paradise* of 1608 began with instructions on how to construct a philosophical garden 'whose principall fire is the stomacke of the Ostrich', which would apparently allow you to grow tender Indian plants as successfully in England as in Italy or Spain (it is sadly incomprehensible to all but initiates today).[34] The book ended with the delightful entertainment dreamed up by gardener Sir Francis Carew for Queen Elizabeth at Beddington, which involved delaying the fruiting of a cherry tree for a full month by covering the tree with canvas and wetting it when necessary – a method no more arcane than many adopted by today's exhibitors at the Chelsea Flower Show intent on meddling with a plant's natural cycle.[35]

Another of Platt's tiny pocket books, *The Garden of Eden*, mixed gardening advice that would be seen as perfectly reasonable today (such as pinching out herbs to make them grow better, or making sure that seed is not above one year old) with instructions to sow or gather produce according to the cycles of the moon – a belief that was fairly widespread. 'The decrease of the Moone is accounted best to sow in, as the Full to plant roses,' noted tulip-lover Sir Thomas Hanmer, 'but I think it not materiall to observe either.'[36] Platt went much further, however, claiming that the moon's influence might even produce double tulips from single. 'Make Tulipees double in this manner,' he suggested. 'Some think by cutting them at every full Moon before they beare, to make them at length to beare double.'[37]

Although Parkinson dismissed such boasts as 'meere tales and fables',[38] other gardeners were more easily persuaded. Instructions for growing melons penned by the Earl of Essex's gardener (probably John Rose – see Chapter 8), reveal a similarly quaint belief that storing ripe melon seed among dried rose petals would perfume their future fruit.[39] But for Parkinson, scents and colours formed part of the plant's essence 'and one may as well make any plant to grow of what forme you will, as to make it of what sent and colour you will; and if any man can forme plants at his will and pleasure, he can doe as much as God himselfe that created them.'[40]

Parkinson's objections to such tampering were in the first place religious and philosophical. There was a further *scientific* difficulty in that, until the very end of the seventeenth century, the sexuality of plants was not understood. Until Nehemiah Grew began groping towards the true nature of pollen, how plants reproduced was a mystery; only with publication of his Royal Society lectures as *The Anatomy of Plants* in 1682 was the stamen publicly identified as the male sex organ of a flower, and it would take another two centuries for plant reproduction theories to be properly developed and accepted.[41]

Yet while botanists were still struggling towards the truth of sexual reproduction in plants, poets and playwrights were stealing an imaginative march on them. In *The Winter's Tale*, Shakespeare's heroine Perdita scorned the 'streak'd gillyvors' (gillyflowers) as 'nature's bastards', for which she was rebuked by Polixenes, who used a gardener's logic to defend as nature's own the mating of different plant material:

> You see, sweet maid, we marry
> A gentler scion to the wildest stock,
> And make conceive a bark of baser kind
> By bud of nobler race. This is an art
> Which does mend nature – change it rather – but
> The art itself is nature.[42]

The art in question here is that of inoculation – inserting the bud of one plant into the stem of another. This was perfectly acceptable practice for the time. But it took a poet's genius to inject sex into the equation.

Yet for all his rationality and learning, even Parkinson was not entirely emancipated from the old beliefs. Into the lush and fecund Eden that he used as the frontispiece to his great work on the garden of pleasant flowers, Parkinson slipped a Scythian lamb or borametz from fabled Tartary, a 'lamb' that grew like a plant with a stalk attached to its belly. Grazing on the grass it found growing around its single 'foot', yet reproducing by seed like any other plant, this marvellous creature (like the barnacle goose)[43] was an obvious link between the animal and vegetable kingdoms, taken as proof that there were no gaps in the chain of creation and that all created things were secretly linked.[44] It was a theory to which the Tradescants clearly subscribed, for among the exotic fruits listed in their catalogue of rarities was the skin of a 'Boramez, agni scythici'.

Intriguingly, such a 'lamb' actually exists but it is wholly plant, *Cibotium barometz*, a tree fern with pelt-like fur. One can be seen in London's Museum of Garden History at South Lambeth where the Tradescants lie buried in the churchyard. Contrary to its representation in Parkinson, the 'lamb' grows upside down and waves its feet in the air. Sometimes truths are just as strange as fictions.

The Scythian 'lamb' that reputedly bridged the animal and plant kingdoms.

Chapter Seven

Death *of a* Lord

As well as Hatfield House, John Tradescant also gardened at two other properties that Robert Cecil was busy extending and rebuilding: Salisbury House in London and Cranborne Manor in Dorset. To carry out his duties as Lord Treasurer, Cecil needed a fine London residence close to Whitehall and Westminster. At his father's death, Burghley House on the north side of the Strand had passed to his elder brother Thomas and in any case Robert wanted to live on the more fashionable south side with direct access to the River Thames. After living for a time at Cecil House, next door to his brother, he eventually purchased a property from Henry, Lord Herbert, which would form the nucleus of Salisbury House. In the year before her death, Queen Elizabeth had dined with Cecil at his new house, 'where they say there is great variety of entertainment prepared for her, and many rich jewels and presents'.[1]

One of those disturbed by Cecil's Thames-side development was Sir Walter Raleigh, who had lived rent free for twenty years under the queen's protection in property belonging to the Bishop of Durham. As soon as Elizabeth died, Cecil urged the bishop to eject Raleigh and he was 'abruptly and discourteously thrown out into the street'.[2] Cecil further extended his property by applying to Parliament to shift Ivy Lane westwards, branding it as 'verie narrow, foule and solitarie'.[3] This would give him the extended river frontage he so desired, captured by Bohemian artist Wenceslaus Hollar in his riverside view of the three grand houses of Durham, Salisbury and Worcester.

Work in the gardens at Salisbury House included a seat made by 'Jenever the Joiner' and a fountain by 'Poole the Plumer'.[4] It is tempting to think that the 'John Gardener' who was paid for keeping pheasants there in 1609[5] might just possibly have been Tradescant, but there have doubtless been many 'John Gardeners' ever since 'Mayster Jon Gardener' wrote the earliest surviving treatise on English gardening in the fifteenth century.[6] In November 1610, Cecil's London garden was enlarged, the lane repaved with flint and a private walk made with carpenter's work.[7] By the following year, when Tradescant went plant-buying to the Low Countries, the property had two courtyards, a smaller gabled house and a garden loggia. As Hollar's view from the river shows, the impression is one of elongated space, given added emphasis by the trees of the long terrace.

At least some of the trees in Hollar's view may have come back with Tradescant from the Low Countries and France, as around £7 of the freight charges are debited to the Salisbury House accounts.[8] His bills for January and February 1612 record many nights spent in London as he worked on Cecil's garden, arranging the purchase and planting of a variety of hedging plants and materials (sweetbriar, long briar, short thorn and literally thousands of osiers) as well as cherries in tubs, lilacs, white and yellow jasmine, clematis and different coloured roses.[9] Judging from his purchase pf 2,400 nails and 300 hazel poles, he was probably constructing a pergola or series of garden arbours.[10] He also claimed back money for wages paid to the gardeners and labourers; all male, their names read like a roll-call of the English labouring classes: William Robarts, John Hedge, John Coats, Thomas Masse, William Miller, Thomas Byles, Hughe Tedder, John Hoge and Richard Terre (who was paid 2d for two brooms as well as his wages).

The other Cecil property where Tradescant worked, mostly before he went off to the Low Countries, was Cranborne Manor in Dorset, which Cecil had bought in 1599, although it was nine years or so before he began to develop the house and gardens into a delightfully eclectic country house.

Wenceslaus Hollar's engraving
of Salisbury House and its two Thames-side
neighbours (c. 1630).

A Cecil descendant described its fortified medieval walls, tall lattice windows, Jacobean chimneys and sculptured Italian loggias as 'Salisbury's most exquisite architectural bequest to posterity'.[11] Masque-designer and Palladian architect Inigo Jones borrowed its three-arched porch and crenellated tower for the Palace of Fame in his masque, *Britannia Triumphans*.[12]

Far from the noise and stresses of an increasingly crowded London, Cranborne fulfilled the busy courtier's need for a country retreat. Here Cecil might send his family in the dangerous summer months to escape the outbreaks of plague and sweating sickness, which spared no one. His rebuilding plans were also spurred on by King James's obsession with the chase and the magnificent hunting opportunities offered by his Dorset

estate. As at Hatfield, once building began, the pace became frantic, causing one builder to complain that the gardens had been sown too early and were consequently ruined by the continual tramp of builders' carriages.[13]

Once again, Mountain Jennings was despatched 'to survey the garden plott', while John Tradescant was sent down to plant trees in November 1610.[14] Planned as a series of separate gardens,[15] many of its elements remain today and it retains the quieter atmosphere of a family home rather than a showplace, like Hatfield.

While Tradescant was finishing off his garden tasks at Salisbury House in early 1612, Cecil's health was beginning to fail, despite encouraging first reports of his recovery. 'I will begin with the best newes first,' wrote indefatigable correspondent and court observer John Chamberlain on 11 March 1612 to his friend Sir Dudley Carleton in Venice,

that the Lord Treasurer is so well recovered that he walkes dayly in his garden, and yt is thought will shortly remove to Kensington . . . The King and Prince were with him on Sonday, and the Quene every second day the last weeke. His disease proves nothing so daungerous as was suspected, beeing now discovered to be but the scorbut, or (as we terme yt) the scurvy, which is of easie and ordinarie cure yf yt be not too far overpast.[16]

Less than two weeks later, the prognosis was more confusing. 'Within this fortnight,' wrote Chamberlain, 'my Lords disease hath varied (at leastwise in name or opinion) twise or thrise, for first yt was held the scorbut, then the dropsie, and now yt hath got another Greeke name that I have forgotten.'[17]

A cure at Bath was tried on Cecil's insistence, in the company of Sir Walter Cope, Sir Michael Hicks and Cecil's chaplain, 'but as far as I can learne,' wrote the faithful Chamberlain, 'there is more cause of feare then hope . . . and only the vigor of his mind maintaines his weake body . . . Speaches go that he was very yll by the way yesterday and was almost gon once or twise.'[18]

Cecil died on Sunday, 24 May 1612, in the parsonage at Marlborough while travelling home, 'his memorie perfect to the last gaspe'. According to Chamberlain, he 'found so litle goode in the Bath that he made all the haste he could out of that suffocating sulphureous ayre as he called yt, though others thincke he hastened the faster homeward, to countermine his underminers, and (as he termed yt) to cast dust in theyre eyes.' Even had he recovered his health, surmised Chamberlain, he would never have regained his power or credit. 'I never knew so great a man so soone and so generally censured, for mens tongues walke very liberally and freely, but how truly I cannot judge.'[19] One who stayed with him to the end was Sir Walter Cope, to whom Cecil entrusted his papers after he was gone.

His servants would have felt his death keenly and suffered from his rapid fall from grace that saw his reputation daily blackened, 'whether yt be that practises and juglings come more and more to light, or that men love to follow the sway of the multitude'. Chamberlain refrained from giving his own opinion, merely recording that 'they who may best maintain yt, have not forborn to say that he jugled with religion, with the King, Quene, theyre children, with nobilitie, Parlement, with frends, foes, and generally with all'.[20] Cecil had grown ever lonelier in power and became increasingly melancholic after the deaths of his father and his wife. 'The mature Robert Cecil, like the mature Burghley, was a sad man,' commented his descendant, David Cecil. 'Sadder perhaps, because his melancholy was more obsessive.'[21]

Cecil's dying even makes a brief appearance in one of John Tradescant's bills for his garden expenses. Among the vegetable seeds and other mundane items purchased, he added the exceptional item of 4s 'for mowing of the Coorts and East gardyn against the funerall'.[22]

By his own wish, Cecil was buried quietly and privately in Hatfield Church, commemorated by a High Renaissance tomb on which his white marble effigy, staff of office in hand, lies resplendent on a slab of black marble held aloft by matronly figures representing the cardinal virtues of Justice, Prudence, Temperance and Fortitude. Below him lies a macabre effigy of his skeleton awaiting judgment, which in the popular view was singularly cruel, whatever His Maker might have decided. Descendant David Cecil quotes one of the libellous rhymes shouted in London alleyways:

Here lies, thrown for the worms to eat
Little bossive Robin that was so great.
Not Robin Goodfellow or Robin Hood
But Robin th'encloser of Hatfield Wood,
Who seemed as sent from Ugly Fate
To Spoil the Prince and rot the State,
Owning a mind of dismal ends
As trap for foes and tricks for friends.
But now in Hatfield lies the Fox
Who stank while he lived and died of the Pox.[23]

It was not fair but public opinion had raised venomous gossip to an art form, and Cecil was still blamed by many for the death of the popular (and handsome) 2nd Earl of Essex, executed for treason in 1601 after an abortive uprising.[24] Tradescant himself had, of course, benefited from the enclosing of Hatfield Wood by renting land transformed into pasture.

John Tradescant stayed on at Hatfield for at least another two years but much of the satisfaction must have gone out of his employment. Cecil's son and heir William had none of the father's drive or ambition and he never achieved the rank or standing of his father or his grandfather, Lord Burghley. Soon after Robert Cecil's death, the talented artists and craftsmen he had gathered about him began to disperse. His musicians moved on to other noble households or court appointments, and William Cecil's own 'delight in Musick' proved short-lived.[25] The same was undoubtedly true of Hatfield's gardeners. Mountain Jennings was by now working for King James at Theobalds, where he stayed until he died in 1628, planting trees, making walks and trees, tending the nursery;[26] and the story told by Tradescant's estate bills is one of narrowing horizons and increasingly mundane purchases. Intriguingly, he was also receiving a reduced salary: £5 15s a quarter, half the previous amount.[27] Either he was less valued or – a more likely explanation – he was no longer required to fund garden expenditure out of his own pocket.

As well as the trees that he continued to buy in England (fruit trees for the East Garden; more plums, nectarines and cherries, including one 'great Cherytree Caled the arche duks Rathe Ripe' for the huge amount of £5),[28] he was also claiming for sundry seeds and supplies for the kitchen garden: glass cloches to cover the musk melons, a peck of 'Rathe Ripe pease', onion and radish seed, sixpenny nails to secure the pleached and espaliered trees in his Lordship's London garden,[29] and a cheese presse.[30] One of his last actual claims was made halfway through 1614: 'To John Tradescant that he paid for setting a pair of soles upon your Lordships "pompes".'[31] It was surely time to move on.

Chapter Eight

Canterbury Belles

By the summer of 1615, John Tradescant had uprooted himself from Hatfield and taken his family to Canterbury, where he went to work as gardener to Edward, Lord Wotton at St Augustine's Abbey. In social terms, it was a backward step. Although a member of Kent's dozen or so leading families,[1] Lord Wotton lacked the power and influence of Tradescant's other employers. Knighted by Queen Elizabeth and made comptroller of her household in December 1602, he did at least bring some cheer to her last winter. 'The world hath not ben altogether so dull and dead this Christmas as was suspected,' commented John Chamberlain to his friend Ralph Winwood in Paris, surmising that it was because 'the new controller [Wotton] hath put new life into yt by his example, (being allwayes freshly attired and for the most part all in white)'.[2] Wotton's modest advancement continued under James I, who made him a baron early in his reign and later Lord Lieutenant of Kent and a Privy Councillor. He went abroad on diplomatic missions (to France, for instance, to congratulate the young French king on his accession after his father's murder). But he never acquired the viscountcy he so desired and his Catholicism compromised any further public honours.

The appointment was nonetheless appealing to an ambitious gardener and, under Tradescant's skilled hand, the abbey's extensive gardens began to attract attention, aided by the exceptionally fine weather of his first two summers there. 'We have had a long, hot and drie sommer,' wrote John Chamberlain in September 1615, 'and the best and fairest melons and grapes that ever I knew in England'.[3] The fine weather continued long into the following year and by late August 1616, Chamberlain's hosts were bragging of their rare crop of plums. The grain had been long since harvested, noted Chamberlain, all fruits (excepting apples) were plentiful, and it was generally reckoned 'the greatest yeare of apricocks that any man living hath seen in England'.[4] The fine weather was also breeding new agues and sicknesses, however, and by October 1616 Chamberlain's tone was less sanguine, imputing the spreading menace to 'some influence from above, rather than to any naturall reason within our reach, specially yf yt be as we heare that this malignant fever raignes as well all over Fraunce, Spaine and Italie'.[5]

Wotton's gardens at Canterbury were prospering nonetheless as Tradescant filled them with the strange and rare plants that marked him out as a curious gardener. Apothecary John Parkinson paid a visit to 'my very loving and kinde friende John Tradescante, in the garden of the Lord Wotton, whose gardiner he was at that time', where he first saw a strange kind of male mandrake, 'the leaves whereof were of a more grayish greene colour, and somewhat folded together'.[6] Here, too, Parkinson commented on an 'Indian Moly', a Turkish form of wild garlic that had been distributed to his friends by a Naples apothecary, Ferrante Imperato. 'It grew also with John Tradescante at Canterbury,' wrote Parkinson, 'who sent me the head of bulbes to see, and afterwards a roote, to plant it in my Garden.'[7] There was also a wild double-blossomed pomegranate that Parkinson claimed for Tradescant as a new introduction: 'The wilde I think was never seene in England, before John Tradescante ... brought it from the parts beyond the Seas, and planted it in his Lords Garden at Canterbury.'[8]

Here perhaps lies the key to Tradescant's own career move. At Hatfield, he had been very definitely Cecil's man and, on his plant-buying journeys to the Low Countries and France, he had Cecil's shopping list in his pocket. Wotton would allow him much greater freedom to travel further afield, into wild places where he might find strange and wonderful plants growing in their native habitats. A keen fruiterer, he had also come to England's orchard heartland, his wife's home county, where Richard Harris, fruiterer to King Henry VIII, had first planted pippin grafts from France, and cherry and pear grafts from the Low Countries.[9]

In such a closed world of patronage and preferment, it is hardly surprising that Tradescant's appointment at Canterbury reveals a Cecil connection: Robert Cecil had been a previous tenant of the abbey and its ruins, which he used chiefly to plunder stones for his homes and for Britain's Burse, his brand-new shopping centre on the Strand in London. Wotton took over the lease of St Augustine's Abbey from Cecil's son and heir, the 2nd Earl of Salisbury, in the year of Robert Cecil's death, just as he would later take over Salisbury's gardener to bring the gardens to perfection.[10]

It is ironic perhaps that a Catholic (albeit a relatively secret one) should become responsible for one of the oldest monastic sites in the country, which owed its ruin to Henry VIII's break with Rome over his marriage to Catherine of Aragon. Monks had prayed here for nearly a thousand years, ever since Augustine (a Benedictine monk) had arrived at the end of the sixth century on a mission from Pope Gregory in Rome to rekindle Christianity in southern England. When Henry VIII dissolved the abbey in 1538, he took the abbot's lodging for himself, ordering his surveyor James Needham to convert it into a royal posting house where members of his household could break their journeys to and from the coast. Poor Needham was given just two and a half months to prepare a palace fit to receive Henry's fourth wife, the 'Flanders mare' Anne of Cleves, a task that required some 350 craftsmen and many dozens of candles for working through the night. Bad weather thankfully kept her in port an extra two weeks, giving him time to dry out the fresh plaster with charcoal braziers.[11]

The palace found little royal favour and Henry gave orders to demolish the adjacent abbey church, loading the stone on to carts for eventual shipping across the Channel to build the fortifications at Calais (which remained in English hands until 1558) and selling off the rest locally. Within fifteen years, all that remained of the once soaring building were its foundations and small heaps of rubble. The palace and surrounding abbey lands were let to a succession of noblemen: first Lord Cobham,[12] another Lord Warden of the Cinque Ports and Robert Cecil's father-in-law, and later to Cecil himself. Royalty retained the right to stay here when it pleased them (it rarely did) and the lease contained clauses allowing access for the removal of stones.

As Wotton already had a principal seat at Boughton Malherbe, also in Kent, he would have treated St Augustine's as his country home, but unlike Robert Cecil, he put more into the estate than he took out and the place literally blossomed. He may have begun to lay out his new garden before Tradescant moved to Caterbury, but the latter's close collaboration with Mountain Jennings at Hatfield would justify his claim to at least some of the credit. Wotton's sophisticated garden, woven around the abbey ruins, may well be John Tradescant's best-recorded landscape, its spirit captured in a splendidly emblematic map of Canterbury c.1640, and in a detailed description by a military man from Norwich who had stayed in the town in 1635 during a leisurely tour of south-east England.

Canterbury in Tradescant's time was small and compact, tightly girt by Roman and medieval walls, which allowed seven gateways into the city.[13] A river flowed from north to south, and streets were few; even today, it takes just ten minutes or so to cross briskly from Burgate to West Gate along the pedestrianized streets. While modern Canterbury retains its cramped and huddled feel, it was then a city of orchards, gardens, fields and green spaces, its houses strung like beads along the narrow streets and concentrated especially around the towering cathedral, which occupied a large segment of inner city to the north-east. The population was rising, all the same: from about four thousand souls in 1570 to some seven thousand a century later. An influx of aliens, Walloons especially, brought with them new trades such as silk-weaving.[14] Overall, population figures were prevented from rising any further by a combination of low fertility, high infant mortality and a generally high death rate – from tuberculosis, smallpox, influenza and periodic outbreaks of plague, exacerbated by malnutrition and poor sanitation.

St Augustine's Abbey lies directly east of the cathedral, outside the city walls. Around 1640 when the Canterbury map was drawn, the abbey lands extended across thirty acres, at least as large as the cathedral site and dwarfing the city's many other gardens. The cartographer has drawn two entrance gates, the palace, Ethelbert Tower (damaged by an earthquake later in the century), and the wall surrounding the old Privy Garden. The much bigger new garden beyond was laid out pictorially as two orchards and three geometric gardens incorporating circles, squares and triangles: one appears to have a mount at its heart, while another is contained within a border of trees. It is tempting to read this map as a literal representation of how Tradescant's garden looked but that would probably be wrong. The same designs (writ smaller) appear in other gardens of the town, so the 'knots' are probably no more than symbolic representations of reality. Only later – in the eighteenth-century maps of John Rocque, for instance – did map-makers draw gardens as they really were.

A more illuminating guide to Tradescant's Canterbury garden is Lieutenant Hammond, quartered in Norwich, who journeyed around southern England and the Midlands in August and September 1635.[15] In the words of his editor, Hammond was a 'happy, jovial, friendly man of strong church principles, with a marked bent towards ceremonial, pronounced antiquarian tastes, and a dislike of the Celts'. On the Suffolk coast, he fell in with some friends (male and female) and laughingly joined them by the sea, freely enjoying 'their good cheere, which was Wine, Oysters, Musicke, Mirth, &c'. After leaving Faversham in Kent, he attached himself to a large French party led by 'a light and sprightly Madamoiselle' who thought nothing of riding at their head in darkness, but at least their numbers kept their purses safe from footpads. At Canterbury, they stayed at the 'Flower de Luce' posting house, where the French mademoiselle momentarily disconcerted the more strait-laced Englishman by proceeding to undress 'and bed her little, tender, weary'd Corps in our presence'. He quickly recovered himself, reflecting that such behaviour was 'common and familiar amongst them of that Nation', but judging it nonetheless prudent to withdraw. The next morning he left the party to continue on their way to Dover while he enjoyed the cathedral sights, transported by sweet organ

music, a ravishing consort of choristers and a 'snowy Croud' of scholars
from the King's School.

After a thorough examination of the cathedral, he was entertained by
Lady Wotton, a widow by then and in Hammond's eyes a 'bountifull,
generous, and noble Lady'. Her (unnamed) gardener took him round 'the
faire gardens and Orchards, sweet walkes, Labirinth-like wildernesses and
Groves; rare Mounts and Fountaines; all which togeather take up the
encompassing space and circuit of neere 20. or 30. Acres; In most part of
which did those rare demolish'd Buildings sometimes appeare in much
Glory and Splendor'. So, unusually, the gardens incorporated the ruins into
their walks and wildernesses, although in Tradescant's time the planting
would have been tidier than the word 'wilderness' denotes today.

And so the good Hammond tramped around the garden on the heels of
the 'Honest Head Gardiner' who was 'not att all weary'd to march with me
those long walkes, to wheele into those pretty contriv'd wooddy Mazes; to
climb and scale those high Mounts, which I will onely give a touch off'. In
the midst of this 'delicate Garden and Paradice, with the Orchard of delicate
Fruites', he noted in particular 'one sweet and delightfull walke' stretching
a full forty rod (200 metres or so), shaded on both sides by lime trees, and a
'neet and curiously contriv'd Fountaine' at the heart of a sweet garden of
'fragrant and delicious Flowers' close to the main abbey house.

The fountain sounds as fanciful as any by Salomon de Caus: Charon (the
ferryman of the dead) plied his boat on a little green island at the centre of
a basin of 'pure cleere water, knee deep and 4. foot square'. Upon the bank
lay snakes, scorpions and 'strange Fishes, which spout water about the
Ferrimans eares and his Dog's, which is convey'd away by the turning of a
Cocke'. Watery nymphs stood guard at each quarter, one of them lamely
missing one arm, which had been 'disarm'd by the Royall steddy hand of
our gracious Soveraigne, at his Marriage of his Royal Spouse in this City'.[16]
This last detail tells us that the fountain was in place by June 1625 at the
latest, when Charles I first welcomed to England his fifteen-year-old bride,
Henrietta Maria, sister to the French king.[17] By then, Tradescant had
already moved on from Canterbury but the fountain may have been one of

his own improvements for Lord Wotton, drawing on his experience with Salomon de Caus at Hatfield.

When the jovial Lietenant Hammond visited Canterbury some ten years after the royal wedding, he walked as far as the Chapel of St Pancras, Augustine's first church in Canterbury, but made no comment on the kitchen garden. Perhaps the working parts of a garden held no interest for him, unlike reformed pirate Sir Henry Mainwaring who had visited Wotton's garden in 1620 expressly to get Tradescant's tips about growing melons. We know this from a letter Mainwaring had written to Lord Zouche, then Lord Warden of the Cinque Ports. 'This last weeke having some leasure,' wrote Mainwaring, 'I went on Satterday to Canterbury to see my Lord Wotton's Garden and to confer with his Gardner for I doe much desyre that your Lordship should eate a Muske Melon of your own in Dover Castell this year.'[18]

The letter spins a web of extraordinary connections. A keen botanist, plantsman and colonist, Edward Lord Zouche had been a ward of state under the care of Robert Cecil's father, Lord Burghley, and later went to live abroad where he could indulge his passion for plant collecting more cheaply. He met and corresponded with Lord Wotton's half-brother, Sir Henry Wotton, and also with Clusius.[19] Once back in England, he employed the Flemish botanist Matthias de l'Obel as superintendent of his garden at Hackney, a parish rising above the marshes on the outskirts of London, which was then frequented by a number of other aristocrats and rich city merchants attracted by its wholesome air.[20] Here he was said to have 'amused himself with experimental gardening and the science of botany';[21] and according to author Sir Hugh Platt, he successfully transplanted thirty-year-old apple and damson trees.[22] He died in 1625, the year before Edward, Lord Wotton, Tradescant's employer.

Sir Henry Mainwaring was no less interesting: after an early career as a pirate, he received a royal pardon and became one of the most prominent senior naval officers under James I and Charles I, taking part in most naval operations of the time.[23] Early in 1620, the ageing Lord Zouche offered him the post of Lieutenant of Dover Castle and Deputy Warden of the Cinque Ports.[24] His meeting with Tradescant took place soon afterwards, in

March 1620. Mainwaring may even have encouraged the gardener to serve as a gentleman volunteer in the naval expedition under Sir Robert Mansell to quell the pirates of Algiers later that same year. It would in any case have been a fascinating conversation between a plant-hunting gardener and a seasoned pirate turned naval gamekeeper.

The primary subject of their talk – growing melons – was one of intense interest to horticultural enthusiasts as musk melons were still looked on as exotic fruits from generally hotter climates. Even Parkinson admitted in the late 1620s that few gardeners in England had yet developed the skill to grow them properly. He nonetheless put together some rules and orders 'which the best and skilfullest have used'.[25]

According to Parkinson, the best melon seed came from Spain (much better than Turkish seed, in his view), and he listed three main types: sugar melons, pear melons, and the favoured musk melons.

They have beene formerly only eaten by great personages, because the fruit was not only delicate but rare; and therefore divers were brought from France, and since were noursed up by the Kings or Noblemens Gardiners onely, to serve for their Masters delight: but now divers others that have skill and convenience of ground for them, doe plant them and make them more common.[26]

There was no point, said Parkinson, in trying to grow melons naturally, as tender musk melons required all the help they could get. The secret lay in using dung to give the seeds and growing seedlings sufficient heat to compensate for our colder climate; and in watering at times of dry weather, preferably with water that had warmed in the sun for a day or two. A charming illustration of a melon ground appears in John Evelyn's translation of *The French Gardiner* by Nicolas de Bonnefons. This shows raised hotbeds made of horse dung, sheltered by plantation trees and a fine panelled reed fence. 'To this Enclosure you must make a door, which you shall keep under lock and key, that none molest your *Plantation;* and particularly to keep out *Women-kinde* at certaine times, for reasons you may imagine.'[27] (Evelyn considered himself more of an expert than Parkinson, noting in the margin

A *fenced melon ground* from
John Evelyn's *translation* of
The French Gardiner (1672).

to his own copy of *Paradisi in Sole* that April was 'too late by 2 months' to
prepare your hot dung bed.')[28]

Evelyn's lengthy instructions would surely deter all but the most
dedicated from attempting to grow the perfect melon. First the stable dung
in the hotbed had to be trampled like grapes at the wine harvest, then spread
with four inches of compost from the previous year's bed, the earth clapped
hard against the retaining boards around the side. The dung should be
left to heat up and then cooled to tepid, but not allowed to become cold
– this required testing with your fingers. 'The *bed* in perfect temper, and
your *seeds* stepped in good *Wine-Vinegar*, or *Cow-milk* eight and fourty
howers, every *species* apart by themselves: You shall *sowe* them at one *end*
of your bed.' Sowing required making three holes together with your fingers,
'in fashion of a *hens-rump*', and planting three or four seeds in each of
the holes. At night, you had to cover the bed with straw hurdles or woven
mats supported on poles, the gap between bed and covering filled with fresh

dung if it snowed or froze. As soon as the seedlings appeared, you were to cover them with large drinking glasses (or straw hats, in Parkinson's much simpler version), leaving a little air between glass and earth to avoid suffocation.

And so it went on. Seedlings had to be transplanted into special ridged and furrowed beds; cosseted with glass as they gradually acclimatized, and shielded with straw hats to protect the glass from hailstorms; watered with a weak solution of pigeons' dung when they languished; pinched and stopped to allow big fat melons to develop, each one placed on a tile to keep it hot and dry, and to separate it from 'the loathsome *quality* of the *dung*'. After all that fuss, you were well advised to visit your melon plot at least four times a day when your melons were starting to ripen. A good melon should be neither too green nor overripe, vigorous not forced, weighty, firm, dry, and it should 'have the flavor of that pitchy mixture wherewith Seamen dresse their cordage'.[29] Cut open, said Parkinson, a ripe melon was waterish around the seed and pulp but of a good yellow meat. 'The usuall manner to eate them is with pepper and salt, being pared and sliced, and to drowne them in wine, for feare of doing more harme'.[30]

Not all gardeners followed such elaborate rituals, however. Preserved among the Ashmole manuscripts at the Bodleian Library in Oxford are two sets of growing instructions for melons. A one-page note for 'settinge and plantinge of ye melon seede from my lorde of Essex gardner'[31] begins with the instruction to make a bed 'with hott horse dung' and ends with a cautionary note about covering newly planted seeds at night whenever frost threatens. Written in the same neat hand is a much more detailed memorandum entitled *The Melonniere, or the order to dresse and plant the Melon Seedes*.[32] The spidery italic of the title has been misread as Tradescant's scrawl, but none of the individual letters matches the script in his Russian diary and in any case the ink is identical to that used for the 'secretary' hand of the text.[33] The same person undoubtedly wrote the whole paper, using his two different writing styles. It was probably John Rose, who gardened for the 3rd Earl of Essex from around 1640 and who stayed at Essex House until 1661, by which time he was working for the earl's widowed sister, the

Duchess of Somerset.[34] Rose knew Ashmole well, and visited the Tradescant garden in his company in April 1669.

If the method for raising the perfect melon is indeed Rose's, it shows the kind of gardener he was: plain-speaking, independent-minded and distinctly unshowy (especially in comparison to Evelyn's French gardener), preferring his melons to ripen naturally rather than be heated artificially with too much dung, for 'there is nothing healthfull to the persons that shall eat them, and besides [dung] marreth the goodnesse & odoure of the Melon'. Slowly and patiently, he set out the melon-grower's tasks, which included transplanting the seedlings when they had spread three or four leaves, digging up a rootball of earth 'that you hurte them not'; and eventually gathering the melons 'in the morninge before sunne risinge' when 'they smell pleasantly at the butt end, and then they muste be warely kepte from catts who love them greatlye'. The hopeful gardener could also attempt to create 'pompons odoriferous' by putting ripe seed 'amonge rose leaves dryed, or amonge muske, and keepe it so till you will force it'. Alternatively, suggested Essex's gardener, you could force your seeds 'in damaske water, or in some other odoriferous water. By the like meane you maye give them what odoure and savore you will.'[35]

Whatever method you followed, growing melons early and well was considered a gentlemanly skill, which explains why Sir Henry Mainwaring should seek out Wotton's gardener on Lord Zouche's behalf. Horticultural passions ran high, and gardening then (as now) was intensely competitive. A kinsman of gentleman-painter Sir Nathaniel Bacon boasted in a letter that should Bacon visit London from his home at Brome in Suffolk, 'I will shew him melons forwarder then his at Broome'.[36] Bacon would clearly have turned green with envy. Luscious cantaloupe melons even found their way into one of his most celebrated paintings, now in the Tate Gallery's London collection: *Cookmaid with still life of vegetables and fruit*, painted in the early 1620s in characteristic Low-Countries style.[37] There is an intriguing Tradescant connection, too. A close relative of Sir Francis Bacon, Sir Nathaniel Bacon is listed as a benefactor to Tradescant's collection of rarities, presumably for his gift of a 'small Landskip drawn by Sir Nath: Bacon', still among the Tradescant rarities at Oxford's Ashmolean Museum.[38]

In his *Cookmaid* painting, the comely maiden – bosom bared and hair uncapped – cradles a melon in her lap; another lies cut open on the table beside her to reveal its seeds. Heaped around her are exotic vegetables from the New World and some from the Old, all grown to perfection but showing realistic touches of botrytis (powdery mould) and pecking by birds: marrows, squashes, pumpkins, ornamental gourds, runner beans, black and white grapes, brown-skinned onions and new-fangled white turnips. A basket of fruit overspills with peaches, plums, pears, figs and apples; cherries and plums lie heaped on a cabbage leaf stripped from one of the giant exhibition specimens that take up a good quarter of the canvas. Glimpsed behind the cookmaid is a hotbed of the kind recommended by Parkinson, Evelyn and the Earl of Essex's gardener. Tradescant would doubtless have shown just such a pile of dung to Sir Henry Mainwaring when he came to call at St Augustine's Abbey.

While the elder Tradescant busied himself with his lord's garden, he prepared the ground for his family's continuing rise in social status by giving his son the classical education he himself lacked. The school he chose was on the doorstep: the King's School, Canterbury, in the old almonry buildings at the north-western corner of the cathedral precincts. The boy joined the school as a King's scholar in late 1619, aged eleven, and stayed for the customary four years until 1623, when his father entered service with the Duke of Buckingham. He probably attended as a day boy, although boarding was an option – in 1570, a joiner had been paid £5 to make 20 'bedsteads in ye Mynt for ye scholers'.[39]

At the school that many claim to be England's oldest,[40] scholars such as Tradescant received a generous £4 a year to cover their food and education, and an annual Christmas allowance of purple cloth to make new gowns. Although the fifty scholarships were intended for poor boys, most were in fact the sons of gentry, their numbers augmented by 'commoners' who paid for their education. Each quarter, the younger Tradescant had to sign for his allowance and already his handwriting was neater than his father's.[41] He must have received some schooling before he went to the King's School, as to gain admittance he had to prove competence in reading and writing, and to know by heart the words to the Lord's Prayer, the Angelus, the Apostles' Creed and the Ten Commandments.

Here at Canterbury, the boy would have learnt Latin (the international language of botanists as well as clerics), grammar, spelling, mathematics, astronomy, music and perhaps some Greek and Hebrew. A recent history of the school describes the regime set out in its founding statutes: boys learnt English in the bottom class; began Latin in the second where they also studied books such as Aesop's *Fables*; progressed to more Latin in the third; and then, in later classes, learnt how to write Latin verse and speeches, eventually conversing easily in Latin 'so far as is possible for boys'.[42] Even among themselves, the boys were supposed to speak only Latin or Greek, and to avoid any 'lowness' in their games. There were lighter moments, too – school plays at Christmas (an earlier scholar was playwright and spy Christopher Marlowe, son of a Canterbury shoemaker) and sports days when prizes were awarded for races against other boys.[43]

Many of the younger Tradescant's contemporaries went on to become Anglican clergymen, or retired to their Kentish estates to live the life of country squires. A near-contemporary was Anglo-Saxon enthusiast William Somner, who wrote a famous book about the antiquities of Canterbury, which he dedicated to anti-Puritan Archbishop William Laud.[44] As events would later prove, the young Tradescant was no scholar at heart but his schooling gave him at least enough Latin to construct appropriate names for the strange new plants he would find on his travels.

Chapter Nine
A Virginian Adventure

Unlike his son John, the elder Tradescant never crossed the Atlantic in search of plants from the New World, so the North American varieties that passed through his hands came to him from other sources: merchants, sea captains, botanists, adventurers who knew of his fascination for the marvellous and the strange. And he forged close associations with two men who typified the glory-seeking vigour of the age: Captains John Smith and Samuel Argall. The first remembered him in his will, suggesting a friendship that celebrated their shared interest in travel and exploration. The second took his money in a plantation venture that fared no better than Tradescant's earlier attempt to make his capital work for him. Through these two men he participated in one of the most thrilling adventures of the age: the exploration and colonization of the unknown lands opening up across the seas.

There is little doubt that the discovery of the New World turned the old one inside out, eventually freeing the Western imagination from the straitjacket of scholastic thought laid down by ancient Greek and Roman authorities. When Italian-born Christopher Columbus sailed across the Atlantic in 1492 under the flag of the Spanish monarchs Ferdinand and Isabella, he was looking for a route to the fabulous Indies and never quite believed that the islands he stumbled across belonged to the Caribbean.

Fired by similar ambitions, Genoese barber-surgeon John Cabot (real name Giovanni Caboto) set off from the English port of Bristol just five years later on a voyage to Asia. Unfortunately North America stood in his way and he landed instead on the continent's north-eastern seaboard.

While these journeys failed to produce their desired outcomes, their geographic discoveries exposed the flaws of traditional thought. If the ancients could make such basic miscalculations in their world geography, how could one accept without question their categorical certainties in other spheres of human knowledge? Medieval bestiaries might happily accommodate barnacle geese and vegetable lambs, but what were they to make of an anteater or an armadillo? The shock waves inevitably posed a threat to the authority of the Bible, requiring all the sophistry of theologians to explain away Europe's ignorance of America. 'It was as though the creation was a jig-saw puzzle,' wrote John Prest in his engaging study of botanic gardens. 'In the Garden of Eden, Adam and Eve had been introduced to the completed picture. When they sinned, God had put some of the pieces away in a cupboard – an American cupboard – to be released when mankind improved, or he saw fit.'[1]

Yet for all the upset caused by the discovery of this brave new world across the Atlantic, England was slow to capitalize on Cabot's 'prior discovery' claims and nearly three-quarters of a century would elapse before Queen Elizabeth I granted a patent to discover and settle the 'heathen and barbarous' lands in America not possessed by Christian people – first to Sir Humphrey Gilbert and then (after Gilbert was drowned at sea) to his half-brother, Sir Walter Raleigh.[2] A favourite of the queen until he married one of her ladies-in-waiting without her knowledge or consent, Raleigh characterized Elizabethan attitudes to colonization in which trade, plunder and settlement were inextricably mixed.[3] Although he never himself set foot on Virginian soil (its boundaries initially stretched from Florida right up to Canada), Raleigh was one of the leading promoters of early attempts to settle the Virginian coast at Roanoke Island, including the 'lost colony' of 1587 whose mysterious fate haunted later colonists.[4] When its leader, John White, sailed back to England for supplies, he left behind his daughter and granddaughter, Virginia Dare, the first English child born to would-be colonists. Bad weather, the Spanish Armada and resurgent Anglo–Spanish hostilities conspired to delay him and, on White's eventual return three years later, all trace of the settlers had disappeared, apart from the word 'Croatoan' carved on a palisade. After this debacle, Raleigh turned his energies towards fighting the Spanish and the quest for the fabled gold of El Dorado, the failure of which would eventually lead to his execution.

An enthusiastic chronicler of the English voyages of 1580s and 1590s was Richard Hakluyt, who did much to articulate the early goals of colonization so that men like John Tradescant clamoured to take part in the adventure. For Hakluyt, the reasons for looking westwards to the New World were many and varied, touching on trade (safeguarding the overseas market for English cloth), maritime expansion (building up England's merchant and marine navy), social policy (as a safety valve for vagrants, criminals and orphans in a country perceived as becoming overpopulated), religion (as a refuge for Puritans and religious exiles), foreign policy (anti-Spain, as ever) and pure self-interest (settlements in North America could prey on Spanish silver ships).[5] But the Stuart crown was far too preoccupied with its Ulster plantations, and the task of forging an internal empire from the multiple kingdoms of the British Isles, to give much practical support to any overseas colonization. The early Stuart kings looked to Virginia for what they might take out of it in taxes and financial gain, rather than as part of a coherent vision for expanding British influence overseas.

This left the field wide open to private enterprise and it was the private Virginia Company that promoted the first permanent settlement of Virginia, backed by wealthy London merchants and a wide range of like-minded adventurers who at some point crossed paths with Tradescant. These included his former employer, Robert Cecil; collector and courtier, Sir Walter Cope; melon-devotee Edward Lord Zouche; Sir Dudley Digges, who would take Tradescant with him on a diplomatic mission to Archangel on the Russian coast; and wealthy merchant Nicholas Lete, whom John Gerard had described as being 'greatly in love with rare and faire flowers and plants, for which he doth carefully send into Syria, having a servant there at Aleppo, and in many other countries'.[6] Gerard himself invested £25, the same sum as Tradescant, bequeathing the interest and any profits that might arise to two of his grandchildren.[7] A passion for rare plants and for the colonization of the New World were natural bedfellows, it seems; the Company of Gardeners was among the London livery companies investing in the Virginia Company in its first ten years.[8]

Set up by royal charter in 1606, the Virginia Company sent its first group of 104 settlers (the actual number is disputed) across the Atlantic in December of that same year in three ships under the overall command of Captain Christopher Newport – the *Susan Constant*, the *Godspeed* and the *Discovery*.[9] The journey around the Canary Isles to the West Indies and then up the coast to Virginia took four months, the first spent stormbound in English waters. The Company's instructions to the settlers underlined the economic forces driving the enterprise:[10] they were to establish a safe port on a navigable river as far inland as possible to evade attack from the Spanish but still able to take the fifty-ton barques necessary for trade. If they had a choice of tributaries, they should 'make Choise of that which bendeth most towards the North-west for that way shall You soonest find the Other Sea'.[11] They should also look for a river springing out of lakes rather than mountains, as this, too, might help them reach the Pacific Ocean and China.

The Company also laid down how the colonists should establish their settlement: contemporaneously clearing, fortifying and building a store-house for victuals; preparing the ground, sowing and planting; exploring the river and prospecting for minerals. Only after the public buildings had been erected should they work on their private houses, neatly aligned in a way that would become quintessentially American. 'Lastly and Cheifly,' said the Company, remembering the nobler motives of colonization, 'the way to prosper and to Obtain Good Success is to make yourselves all of one mind for the Good of your Country & your own and to Serve and fear God the Giver of all Goodness for every Plantation which our heavenly father hath not planted shall be rooted out.' The first colonists included only one preacher, however, so serious proselytizing would have to wait.[12]

Among that first group of settlers was Captain John Smith, then in his late twenties but already with a colourful (and no doubt colourfully

embellished) life history. Having sought his fortune in his teens fighting for
the French army and then for the insurgents in the Low Countries, he set
off for Italy and a string of adventures that included being thrown overboard
as a Huguenot, rescue by a pirate, the killing of three Turks in single combat
while serving under the archduke of Austria (a feat that earned him the
reward of his own coat of arms from a grateful Zsigmond Báthory, Prince
of Transylvania), further battles and slavery in Constantinople, followed by
wanderings to Morocco and his eventual return home in 1605.[13]

    Although myth-making was part of his character, at least some of his
story was true as Smith bequeathed his treasured grant of arms from
Zsigmond Báthory to Thomas Packer, one of the king's Privy Seal clerks.
His last will, written shortly before his death in 1631, also named John
Tradescant as one of three men who were to share his library.[14] The books
were kept in a trunk bound with iron bars at the Lambeth home of his
friend, Richard Hinde or Hynde, son of a salter. Half the books were to go
to Thomas Packer's son (another Thomas) who was to get first choice, while
the other half was to be shared between Hinde and 'Master John Tredeskyn',
whose friendship with Smith goes otherwise unrecorded. One possible
survival is a hand-coloured manuscript of William Strachey's *The Historie of
Travaile into Virginia-Britannia* of 1612, now among the Ashmole collection
of manuscripts in the Bodleian Library.[15]

    As might be expected from his eventful past, Smith was quick to resent
authority and the long sea journey to Virginia was clearly a trial. After
challenging Captain Newport's leadership, he was locked up and nearly
hanged in the Caribbean, reaching the North American coast in chains.
When the sealed box containing the Virginia Company's list of nominees to
form the first governing council was finally opened on arrival, John Smith's
name was found to be among them. Only after the preacher's intercession
was he eventually allowed to take his place. The council's first leader was an
obvious if unfortunate choice: Edward Maria Wingfield, the only senior
member of the Virginia Company willing to risk his own life in the venture,
but a poor decision-maker for all that.

    The settlers' muted rapture at the sight of the lush Virginian coast after

1. John Tradescant the elder portrayed in the museum catalogue eventually published by his son in 1656.

2. Leiden's hortus botanicus in 1610, the year before John Tradescant went plant-buying to the Low Countries and France for Robert Cecil.

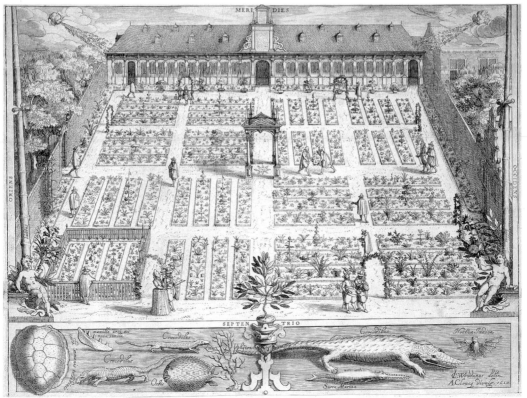

3. Robert Cecil, 1st Earl of Salisbury and
John Tradescant's earliest recorded employer.

5. John Tradescant's great rose daffodil (no. 6)
in John Parkinson's Paradisi in Sole,
Paradisus Terrestris.

4. Tradescant's good friend, royal apothecary
John Parkinson.

6. Captain Samuel Argall, John Tradescant's co-investor in Virginia, trading for food with the natives.

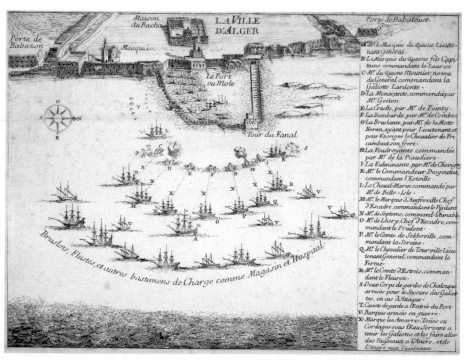

7. The port of Algiers c.1620, where Tradescant sailed with the British fleet to quell the Barbary pirates.

8. Queen Henrietta Maria, the French wife of King Charles I who employed both Tradescants at Oatlands Palace.

9. An early orangerie for overwintering exotics, including Queen Henrietta Maria's precious orange trees.

weeks at sea is well captured by George Percy, eighth son of the Earl of Northumberland, who here describes their first entry into Chesapeake Bay on 26 April 1607. 'There wee landed and discovered a little way, but wee could find nothing worth the speaking of, but faire meddowes and goodly tall Trees, with such Fresh-waters running through the woods, as I was almost ravished at the first sight thereof.' Inevitably the small band of raw Englishmen were apprehensive as well as enraptured and that night, as they returned to their ship, 'there came the Savages creeping upon all foure, from the Hills like Beares, with their Bowes in their mouthes'.[16] A skirmish ensued in which a captain and a sailor were hurt.

Further explorations confirmed both the Edenic nature of the landscape and the unpredictability of its inhabitants.[17] Two days after landing, the exploration party passed over beds of mussels and oysters, which 'lay on the ground as thicke as stones: wee opened some, and found in many of them Pearles'. Later they were entertained in a 'very kindly' fashion by the Indians (as the native Americans of Virginia continue to call themselves today) who first greeted them by laying their faces to the ground, making a doleful noise, and scratching the earth with their nails. 'We did thinke that they had beene at their Idolatry,' commented Percy. Invited to eat, the settlers sat on mats, smoking tobacco 'which they tooke in a pipe made artificially of earthe as ours are, but far bigger, with the bowle fashioned together with a piece of fine copper'. They were then entertained to a dance: 'one of the Savages standing in the midst singing, beating one hand against another, all the rest dancing about him, shouting, howling, and stamping against the ground, with many Anticke tricks and faces, making noise like so many Wolves or Devils'.[18]

As their explorations continued, Percy dutifully noted the good and fruitful soil, excellent timber, abundant vines 'in bignesse of a mans thigh', the turkey eggs, squirrels, rabbits, and birds in extraordinary colours: crimson, watchet (pale blue), yellow, green, and murry (a rich dark red). Plenty and strangeness were the watchwords. Among the woods were beech, oak, cedar, cypress, walnut, sassafras, vines, 'and other Trees unknowne'. Fruits included 'Strawberries, Mulberries, Rasberries and Fruites unknowne.' Wildlife was equally abundant: 'great plentie of fish of all kindes', giant sturgeon, plentiful red and fallow deer, bears, foxes, otters, beavers, muskrats, 'and wild beasts unknowne'.[19]

John Tradescant's son John would journey through just such a landscape thirty years later when he came to the colony in search of plants, shells and rarities. Perhaps like Percy and his companions before him, he would follow a path into the woods, 'desirous to knowe whither it would bring vs; wee traced along some foure miles, all the way as wee went, ... the ground all flowing over with faire flowers of sundry colours and kindes, as though it had beene in any Garden or Orchard in England'.[20] John Smith expanded the list of native trees, fruits and plants to include elm, ash, black walnut, white poplar, damson-like cherries, a few bitter crab apples and persimmons bearing fruit 'like a medler; it is first greene then yellow, and red when it is ripe: if it be not ripe it will drawe a mans mouth awrie, with much torment, but when it is ripe, it is delicious as an Apricock'. He noted, too, 'Many hearbes in the spring time there are commonly dispersed throughout the woods, good for brothes and sallets [salads], as Violets, Purslin, Sorrell, etc. Besides many we used whose names we know not.'[21]

By mid-May, the settlers had begun to erect the fort at the site they would name Jamestown in the king's honour. Wingfield as leader must assume responsibility for this unhappy choice. The anchorage was good and its inland location would keep the Spanish at bay. But the land was also swampy, infested with mosquitoes, ill suited to growing crops and poorly supplied with drinking water. To overcome the lack of freshwater springs, the settlers dug wells that became brackish if dug too deep and contaminated by human filth if dug too shallow.

In June, Captain Newport returned to England, leaving the hundred or so settlers 'verie bare and scantie of victualls'. The tone of Percy's narrative changed and in the unbearable heat of summer the litany of deaths began: John Asbie of the 'bloudie Flixe', George Flowre of the 'swelling', Gentleman William Bruster of a 'wound given by the Savages', Jerome Alikock of a wound, Francis Midwinter and Corporal Edward Moris 'suddenly'. More names followed in quick succession, no causes given. 'Our men were destroyed with cruell diseases, as Swellings, Flixes, Burning Fevers, and by warres, and some departed suddenly, but for the most part they died of meere famine. There were never Englishmen left in a forreigne Countrey in such miserie as wee were in this new discovered Virginia.'[22]

By the autumn of that first year, fully half their number had died. The settlers' worsening plight brought a change in leadership but as the cool of autumn returned it seemed the worst was over. Disease subsided, their crops of peas, corn and beans began to mature, and friendly relations were established with the native population who could so easily have wiped them out.[23] They had yet to face the rigours of a Virginian winter, however. 'In the year 1607 was an extraordinary frost in most of Europe,' wrote Captain John Smith, 'and this frost was founde as extreame in Virginia.'[24] The beginnings of a seven-year drought compounded their hardships and further shrank the sparse supplies of the native population.[25]

Despite his troubled relations with the Virginia Company back home, Smith was moving into the limelight, although he had not yet taken over as president. (That would happen in September 1608, the year of the younger Tradescant's birth.) For all his faults Smith had the necessary qualities of energy, resourcefulness and decisiveness to lead the dwindling group of survivors through conditions of extreme hardship. Although prickly and hard to get on with, he was not averse to 'mixing on equal terms with carpenters, common soldiers, and even the "naked savages", so long as they did not cross him too overtly'.[26]

That first December, while exploring the Chickahominy River area, Smith was captured by Indians and taken before their paramount chief, Powhatan who threatened him with death. His life was spared by the intervention of Powhatan's daughter, ten- or eleven-year-old Pocahontas (real name Matoaka), who laid her own head on the block. That, at least, is the version Smith reworked for his *Generall Historie of Virginia* published many years later,[27] although the girl makes no appearance in his first account when he preferred to take the credit himself.[28] In fact the story is suspect on many levels: as ethnohistorian Helen Rountree has convincingly argued, despite the girl's high spirits and the favour she enjoyed from her father, she was very unlikely to have been present at such an occasion, and Powhatan was far more likely to have been feasting his foreign captive than threatening his life.[29] There can be little doubt, however, that genuine affection grew up between the swashbuckling settler and the chief's daughter, who strode into Jamestown Fort and summoned the boys to join her in cartwheels 'naked as she was all the Fort over'.[30] In Smith's writings, she appears as a guardian spirit, braving the 'darke night' and 'irksome woods' to warn him of imminent dangers. '*James*towne with her wild traine she as freely frequented, as her fathers habitation,' he wrote of her later, and it is surely significant that after Smith's departure there followed a 'long and troublesome warre' between the settlers and her father, Powhatan.[31]

Smith described Powhatan as the chief ruler of the area, holding sway over many kings or governors. 'He is of parsonage a tall well proportioned man, with a sower looke, his head somewhat gray, his beard so thinne that it seemeth none at al, his age neare 60; of a very able and hardy body to endure any labour.' Constantly attended by a guard of forty or fifty of the tallest men from his nation, Powhatan had – according to Smith – 'as many women as he will', bestowing them on those who best deserved them once he had wearied of them. Succession passed not to his children but to his brothers and after that to his sisters, the line passing through the heirs (male and female) of the eldest sister. 'It is strange to see with what great feare and adoration all these people doe obay this Powhatan,' commented Smith.[32]

In Britain, the great chief's name is forever linked to John Tradescant through 'Powhatan's mantle', a deerskin cloak or hanging that still takes pride of place in the Tradescant collection of rarities at Oxford's Ashmolean Museum. In a design created by thousands of tiny white marginella shells, a human figure stands flanked by two animals in profile, scattered around with thirty-four shell circles of varying sizes.[33] As we shall see later, the mantle most probably came into the Tradescants' hands sometime between 1634 and July 1638, when it was described by a young German visitor as 'the robe of the king of Virginia'.[34] Only later (in the museum catalogue of 1656) was it specifically identified as '*Pohatan*, King of *Virginia's* habit all embroidered with shells, or Roanoke'.[35]

Powhatan did indeed give a mantle to Captain Newport in 1608 during a farcical coronation ceremony when a bemused and at times startled Powhatan was forcibly 'crowned' at the behest of the Virginia Company. Captain Newport had arrived back in the colony bearing gifts from King James – an English bed and furniture, a basin and ewer, a scarlet cloak and a copper crown – and wanted Powhatan to come to Jamestown to receive them. Powhatan refused, insisting that the Englishmen should come to him as he was a king too, and in any case he would not 'bite at such a baite'. Newport sent his gifts by water and came himself by land but they had 'fowle trouble' getting Powhatan to kneel to receive his crown, 'he neither knowing the maiestie, nor meaning of a Crowne, nor bending of the knee'. At last, weary of trying to explain the coronation customs of the Old World, they leant heavily on Powhatan's shoulders and as soon as he stooped a little, Newport clapped the crown on his head. At a pistol signal from the coronation party, the cannons on the ships in the river let off such a 'volly of shot' that Powhatan leapt to his feet in 'horrible feare'. When he calmed down, he remembered himself enough to 'congratulate their kindnesse' (the account is John Smith's) and gave Captain Newport some gifts in return: his old shoes and his mantle – both presumably intended for the English king, and a 'heape of wheat eares' (about seven or eight bushels) for the settlers.[36]

Like much else in Virginia's early history, the tale is probably better than the truth, at least as far as the provenance of the mantle goes. Twenty-five years separate this crowning from the cloak's appearance at Lambeth, and although it might have come from the royal collection or as a gift from John Smith (also present at the crowning), any documentary proof is lacking. It is far more likely that a different ceremonial cloak came to the Tradescants in the 1630s, around the time of the younger Tradescant's visit to the colony – a story taken up in Chapter 21.

Smith remained in Virginia until the autumn of 1609 when he was badly hurt in a gunpowder explosion 'which tore his flesh from his bodie and thighs'.[37] The injury forced him back to England, so he escaped the cruel winter known as the 'starving time', when one settler reportedly ate his wife[38] and those colonists who did not flee to the Indians were compelled 'to devoure those Hogges, Dogges, and horses that weere then in the colony, together with rats, mice, snakes or what vermin or carrion soever we could light on'.[39]

Smith's quarrel with the Virginia Company erupted into open warfare and he took his revenge by writing their name out of the books that he continued to publish about the colony to which he never returned, turning his attentions to New England instead. He died in June 1631 and was buried inside the church of St Sepulchre, London, by which time John Tradescant was living in Lambeth close to another beneficiary of John Smith's books, Richard Hinde. It seems likely that all three would have met to hear Smith's tales of Virginia and the new world opening up across the Atlantic.

About the time of Smith's departure, another sea captain was beginning to make his mark in Virginia: Captain Samuel Argall, who would also count John Tradescant among his associates. Sent originally to Jamestown to trade on behalf of a Mr Cornelis and to fish for sturgeon,[40] Argall returned to Virginia in 1610 with Lord Delaware, the new governor whose arrival prevented the colonists abandoning Jamestown after the horrors of the starving time. Argall's skilful seamanship was credited with pioneering a new direct route across the Atlantic, which cut the voyage to as little as fifty-one days and avoided Spanish galleons in the Caribbean.

Despite the later criticisms of his conduct, Argall had his admirers who favoured his hard-line approach to discipline and colonization. He continued Smith's exploration northwards along the coast, turning his hand to shipbuilding and Indian trade. It was on a trading expedition up the Potomac that he tricked Powhatan's daughter, Pocahontas, on to his ship and carried her off to Jamestown.[41] As negotiations for her release dragged on she grew ever closer to her captors and fell in love with widowed planter John Rolfe, who confessed his own love for her in a tortured letter to acting governor Sir Thomas Dale in which he recognized the perils of 'marrying strange wives' and wondered aloud if his 'love' was the work of the devil.[42] But her conversion to Christianity proved their saving grace, and after taking the name Rebecca, she married her planter in 1614. No one asked about her

first Indian husband, a 'pryvate Captayne called Kocoum',[43] who simply
faded from the story.

With their eye fixed firmly on a propaganda coup, the Virginia Company
arranged for Mr and Mrs John Rolfe and their baby son Thomas to
accompany Sir Thomas Dale back to England in May 1616,[44] contributing
£4 a week towards their maintenance. Tradescant had been working for
Lord Wotton at Canterbury since the previous year at least, and he would
have followed their progress with interest. Despite the initial dismay that
had greeted news of the couple's marriage, the visit was a social triumph.
Smith himself helped to fan the flames of interest, later including in his
general history of Virginia a letter he had supposedly written at the time to
Queen Anne, although this may have been a simple literary device as no
original has ever come to light. 'During this time,' he wrote of his erstwhile
friend, 'the Lady Rebecca, alias Pocahontas, daughter to Powhatan, by the
diligent care of Master John Rolfe her husband and his friends, was taught
to speake such English as might well bee understood, well instructed in
Christianitie, and was become very formall and civill after our English
manner; shee had also by him a childe which she loved most dearely.'

The Rolfes stayed at Brentford where Captain Smith came to call 'with
divers of my friends'. The meeting began awkwardly. The young Pocahontas
had believed Smith killed in the explosion and he had clearly sent her no word
of his recovery in the intervening years. 'After a modest salutation,' wrote
Smith, 'without any word, she turned about, obscured her face, as not seem-
ing well contented; and in that humour her husband, with divers others, we
all left her two or three houres.' When the meeting reconvened, the Lady
Rebecca reminded Smith of the many courtesies she had shown him, and of
his promise to her father of mutual support. 'You called him father being in
his land a stranger,' she said. Now she would call Smith father, 'and you shall
call mee childe, and so I will bee for ever and ever your Countrieman'.[45]

She was at court for Ben Johnson's Twelfth Night masque in January
1617, as John Chamberlain dutifully noted in a letter to his friend Sir
Dudley Carleton: 'The Virginian woman Poca-huntas, with her father
counsaillor hath ben with the King and graciously used, and both she and

Simon van de Passe's
engraved portrait of Pocahontas,
Mrs John Rolfe.

her assistant well placed at the maske.'[46] As seating at a court masque mirrored social standing, Rebecca Rolfe was highly favoured indeed. Also present was the newly created Earl of Buckingham, George Villiers (Tradescant's future employer), who danced with the queen.

All was apparently going well. Simon van de Passe engraved her portrait and copies sold hotly. She is dressed as a Jacobean woman of rank in tall hat and brocaded overgarment, her neck stiffly gartered with a fine lace ruff, flat and starchy. A single pearl drop earring draws attention to her softly waved hair, while in her long fingers she twirls a feathered fan, her wrist encased in a heavy cuff trimmed with more lace. You wonder how she can move under all that heavy finery, but the expression that shines from her strong, handsome features is one of self-possession.[47]

When the time came for the Rolfes to return to Virginia, for Pocahontas it was 'sore against her will'.[48] There seems little truth in the story that Pocahontas' health had begun to suffer; rather that her death was 'unexpected' as Smith recorded in his history. John Chamberlain sent his friend news of her fate. 'The Virginian woman (whose picture I sent you) died this last weeke at Gravesend as she was returning homeward.'[49] Even brusquer was the burial record for St George's Church, Gravesend, which noted that on 21 March (1617) 'Rebecca Wroth wyffe of Thomas Wroth gent A Virginia Lady borne was buried in the Chauncell.' The original church burnt down in 1727, destroying any contemporary memorial to her. Today a garden named in her honour blooms around the rebuilt church, watched over by her statue, a replica of the one unveiled in Jamestown by the governor of Virginia.

John Smith's sadness is evident from the account he supposedly wrote for Queen Anne.[50] During his brief stay in London, he said, the courtiers and acquaintances who had gone with him to visit the Lady Rebecca generally concluded that 'God had a great hand in her conversion, and they have seene many English Ladies worse favoured, proportioned and behavioured'. One wonders whether Tradescant yet counted among Smith's friends to be included in the visit to Brentford. But he had in any case another connection with the returning princess, which might equally have gained him an entrée to her society. The captain who was to take the Lady Rebecca back to Virginia on his 'good ship' the George was none other than Samuel Argall, with whom Tradescant had just struck a deal to invest in a new Virginian venture.

Argall was then returning to the colony with a dual mission: to take over as lieutenant-governor in charge of the settlement, and to start a plantation of his own.[51] For this he had the backing of five associates, all either family members or men with Kentish connections. Among the five was John Tradescant, then at Canterbury. He could easily have made the relatively short journey to Gravesend, to say Godspeed to his investment and to catch a glimpse of the 'Indian Princess' whom John Smith had described as 'the very nomparell' of Powhatan's kingdom.[52]

The Virginian adventure that Tradescant co-sponsored is recorded in a fat leather-bound volume of state colonial papers relating to America and West Indies.[53] The volume covers the years 1622 to 1623 although the list itself is dated 12 February 1616/17. It names Captain Samuel Argall and his five associates 'allowed severall Bills of Adventure for transport of 24 persons at their charge'. Among the investors, Captain Argall was venturing the largest sum of money (£100), and Tradescant and Canterbury Member of Parliament Sir William Lovelace the least (£25 each). The other three investors (all relatives of either Argall or Lovelace) advanced £50 each. As the only person named without either a title or an 'Esquire' after his name, Tradescant was clearly in good company.

To Tradescant, £25 represented an enormous sum, half the salary Robert Cecil had paid him for keeping the gardens at Hatfield. Such an investment shows him willing to risk his own hard-earned money in pursuit of his passions and it also indicates the kind of man he liked and trusted. Argall and Smith sound remarkably similar: doers rather than dreamers, who valued hard work and determination above rank or popularity. It was, all the same, a brave investment. Despite the fanfare about Virginia's potential, spread abroad by John Smith and other pamphleteers, the settlement was not producing the quick returns that had been promised. In fact, for small investors, it was barely producing any returns at all.

From the beginning, the Virginia Company's principal method of financing was through joint-stock funds, which pooled investors' resources and spread the risks. Investors bought shares of £12 10s each, which were to be invested and reinvested over the following years until 1616, when there was to be a final dividend giving investors a grant of land and the return of their capital with profit. That was the theory, anyway, but there were no funds to be divided in 1616, although the Company did declare a dividend of land – not the wild 500 acres suggested in the heady early days but a more modest fifty acres, with perhaps more to follow.[54] For some years there had been no hope of raising more money by subscription so the Company had relied increasingly on the Virginia lottery for finance, its winning tickets entitling the lucky gambler to an exchange for shares in Virginia joint-stock. (The lottery was finally outlawed by King James as a public nuisance.) From 1618, the system of 'headrights' became increasingly popular, by which adventurers were invited to buy shares either for their own use or for tenants, receiving fifty acres per head for each person sent to the colony.[55]

Unlike the New England Puritans, settlers went to Virginia primarily for reasons of commerce and gain. At first, however, they struggled to find economically viable products. Early exports had concentrated on natural resources like black walnut, pitch, tar and sassafras root. Encouraged by King James, the settlers persevered with silkworm cultivation using native mulberry trees. The Virginia Company despatched several books on silk production in the early 1620s,[56] together with Richard Surflet's translation of a French treatise on agriculture and horticulture by Charles Estienne and Jean Liebault, *Maison Rustique, or, the Countrey Farme*.[57] This last work contained one of the earliest accounts in English on how to cultivate tobacco, which John Rolfe had begun to plant in Virginia with seed imported from Trinidad and South America, much sweeter than the bitter-tasting Indian weed.

The crop quickly caught on, much to the disgust of King James who hated smoking so much he published a diatribe against the habit. Reputedly sick after his first pipe, James warned that smoking not only led to depravity but was 'a custom lothsome to the eye, hatefull to the Nose, harmefull to the braine, dangerous to the Lungs, and in the black stinkinge fume thereof, neerest resembling the horrible Stigian fumes of the pit that is bottomeless'.[58] His opposition later eased as the royal finances drew benefit from the taxes and duties levied on the crop. In Tradescant's time, tobacco was taken as a palliative, although not a cure, for 'pains of the head, rheumes, aches in any part of the body' – even migraines, apparently; and herbals still gave details on how it should be smoked: 'The drie leaves are used to be taken in a pipe set on fire and suckt into the stomacke, and thrust forth againe at the nosthrils.'[59]

Soon tobacco was replacing all other crops in Virginia, even food, thereby contributing in the short term to a further worsening of conditions. When Captain Argall arrived back in Jamestown in 1617, he found 'but five or six houses, the Church downe, the Palizado's broken, the Bridge in pieces, the Well of fresh water spoiled; . . . the Colonie dispersed all about, planting Tobacco'.[60] With support from his backers, Tradescant included, Argall had arrived in the colony to found a new kind of settlement. The difference was control, for instead of simply investing in the general activities of the Virginia Company, Tradescant and his fellow associates were backing a specific plantation which the vigorous Argall would oversee on the ground. Another seasoned Virginia hand adopting the same tactic was Ralph Hamor and between them they were pointing the way to the future.[61] But Argall was also returning to public duty in Virginia and it was said he neglected the colony's affairs for his own private business. Argall, it seems, was attracted to the area west of Jamestown where he established his settlement known as 'Pasapheigh, alias Argall's towne' on land assigned for the support of the governor.[62] This proved to be a mistake, as after he had slipped away from the colony in some disgrace, the new governor (George Yeardley) proceeded to extract 'petty rente' from the men who had settled there to make them acknowledge the Governor's prior claim 'and that they had bene wrongfully seated by Capt. Argall upon that lande'.[63]

'Argall's Towne' is clearly shown west of 'Blockhouse Jamestown' on a detailed chart of the James River (known originally as the Powhatan River) compiled by Johannes Vingboons, a chartmaker employed by the Dutch West India Company.[64] As a settlement it proved a disastrous investment however. The settlers placed there by Captain Argall had moved elsewhere by March 1620,[65] and the Virginia Company in its instructions to Governor Yeardley expressly denied Argall's claim, 'directly forbidding that a charter of Land granted to Captain Samuel Argall and his associates bearing Date the twentieth of March, 1616/1617, be entered in your Records or otherwise at all respected for as much as the same was obtained by slight and cunning'.[66] With the claim denied and Argall out of the colony, John Tradescant must have lost his entire investment.

After he left the colony, Argall's reputation for probity continued to plummet and in 1622 he was embroiled in a series of court trials based on financial claims arising from the expedition in March 1618 of the Neptune, under his command. Fitted out by a group of wealthy adventurers including Lord Delaware and his wife, Lady Cecily, and Tradescant's future employer, George Villiers, the Neptune was chartered by the Virginia Company to bring Lord Delaware back to the colony. Delaware died on the voyage to

Virginia, where his body was taken for burial and his stores offloaded. Argall was then accused of helping himself to Lord Delaware's goods and selling them for his own profit while pretending 'that the same was for the good of the Lady de la Ware'.[67]

Argall nonetheless continued in the king's service, taking part – like John Tradescant – in an expedition to the Mediterranean against the Barbary pirates. Knighted by King James at Rochester, Argall later captained the vessel in which the Earl of Essex attacked Cadiz, a mission that also ended in dismal failure, and he died shortly afterwards. In his will he left £20 apiece to his 'three loving sisters' to buy themselves a piece of plate 'in remembrance of my love' and showed special favour to two married women: chandler's wife Anne Percivall and Kentish widow Judith Buckhurst. Unlike Captain John Smith, however, he left nothing to John Tradescant.[68]

The Virginia Company, meanwhile, struggled on, renewing its efforts to expand the colony and to encourage diversification into other crops and industries, this last without much success as tobacco offered quick, short-term profits. Jamestown was beginning to flourish as a settlement but in March 1622, Powhatan's brother and successor Opechancanough struck back at the settlers' creeping invasion with a well-planned uprising that left a quarter – maybe even a third – of their number dead at the end of a single day. Although Jamestown itself was spared, the uprising sparked the Company's final demise. After sending commissioners to investigate at first-hand, King James revoked its charter and dissolved the Company in 1624, turning Virginia into a royal colony.

The elder John Tradescant's last official contact with Virginia came in 1623, when Company records indicated the carriage on board the *Abigail* of a letter 'from George Sandys to Mr John Tradesicant at my Lord Wottons house',[69] contents unknown. As Sandys was then the Company's treasurer in Virginia, it is possible that the letter concerned Tradescant's investment in Argall's plantation venture. Sandys was a cultivated man who spent much of his time in the colony translating Ovid's *Metamorphoses*, so it would be cheering to think that he included in his letter some mention of Virginia's extraordinary flora. Sandys was also much concerned with the colony's attempts to create a silk industry, and by the same ship he wrote to Virginia merchant John Ferrar, touching on the French and Walloon vine-dressers who had settled around Elizabeth City and were then 'employed about silkworms'.[70] Perhaps Sandys was seeking Tradescant's horticultural help. He may even have sent Tradescant some plants with his letter – he was, after all, writing to the man who introduced the Virginian spiderwort into English gardens.

The plant named after Tradescant came to him from Virginia: *Tradescantia virginiana*, known in his time as 'Tradescant's Spiderwort' and given its Latin name a century or so later by Swedish botanist Carl Linnaeus, the father of modern plant naming. Writing in 1629, John Parkinson explained that Tradescant had 'first received it of a friend, that brought it out of Virginia, thinking it to bee the Silke Grasse that groweth there, and hath imparted hereof, as of many other things, both to me and others.'[71] Thomas Johnson confirmed the plant's provenance, calling it *Phalangium Ephemerum Virginianum* and in common English, the 'Soone-fading Spiderwort of Virginia, or *Tradescant's* Spiderwort, for that M. *John Tradescant* first procured it from Virginia'.[72]

Chapter Ten

A Muscovy Rose

Buried among the Ashmole manuscripts at Oxford's Bodleian Library is a sea-stained, ink-spattered diary of a journey to Russia written on stiff greying paper. Entitled A *viag of Ambasad undertaken by the Right honnorabl* Sr *Dudlie Diggs In the year* 1618, it runs to just twelve double-sided pages, bound together with many other manuscripts into a handsome folio volume.[1] For nearly two centuries, its authorship lay undetected. W. H. Black, compiler of the Ashmole manuscripts catalogue, called it this 'curious narrative of the voyage round the North Cape to Archangel', which started with a list of the principals involved in the diplomatic mission and continued with observations on the weather and on the commercial, agricultural and domestic state of Russia at the time of Digges's journey. 'It is written in a rude hand,' was Black's scholarly verdict, 'and by a person unskilled in composition.'[2]

The diary's authorship might have remained a mystery, but for Dr Joseph von Hamel, a member of the Imperial Academy of Sciences at St Petersburg, who came to England with Tsar Alexander in 1814[3] and was present at Oxford when the tsar received an honorary doctorate from the university.[4] Intending to write an account of the early naval and commercial exchanges between Russia and England, he applied himself to Russian papers at Oxford's Ashmolean Museum and the Bodleian Library. Among the puzzles in his head – as he himself described – was the name and location of a

Russian island where John Tradescant had apparently seen an abundance of white hellebores (since identified as the false helleborine, *Veratrum album*) – so abundant, in fact, that 'a good ship might be loaden with the rootes hereof, which hee saw in an Island there'. The reference came from John Parkinson, who credited the sighting to 'that worthy, curious, and diligent searcher and preserver of all natures rarities and varieties, my very good friend, John Tradescante, often heretofore remembred'.[5]

And so Dr Hamel struggled with the manuscript's ink blots, spidery handwriting and almost complete absence of punctuation until he came to the description of shrubs that the writer had seen when Digges's mission reached the Russian port of Archangel. There it was in a listing of plants, after currants and an abundance of roses seen growing on the islands of the Dvina delta: 'helebros albus enoug to load a shipe'. As Hamel himself wrote many years later, 'It was as if a sudden flash of light discovered to me that, in the *brochure* on which I had laid my hands, I saw a MS. of Tradescant.'[6] His quiver of excitement remains potent to this day. Parkinson must have heard the reference to the ship from his friend; perhaps he was even privileged to read the diary that Dr Hamel was now holding, the only sustained piece of Tradescant's writing known to have survived in which he described the many curious sights of his Russian journey.

It was probably through his employer Lord Wotton that Tradescant met Sir Dudley Digges and attached himself to the mission in an undisclosed capacity.[7] Described in the *Dictionary of National Biography* as a 'diplomatist and judge', Digges had recently built himself a fine house at Chilham, just over five miles from Canterbury. There is no evidence to confirm suggestions that Tradescant may himself have helped Digges with his garden;[8] but just as Sir Henry Mainwaring had visited Canterbury to consult Tradescant on Lord Zouche's behalf, it is possible that Digges may have sought his help too, at least informally. Despite their difference in status, they shared a common interest in Virginia and in foreign lands generally. Knighted at Whitehall in 1607, and a shareholder in both the East India and the Muscovy Companies, Digges was obsessed with finding the North-West Passage and in 1612 co-founded a company for trading by that route. But as the journey to Russia would prove, he was a poor traveller and an even worse ambassador.

English trade with Russia had arisen in the mid-sixteenth century out of the failure to find the north-eastern route to Cathay and the Indies through the Arctic seas above Europe's northern cape. Two shiploads of merchant explorers (including expedition leader Sir Hugh Willoughby) had perished in Lapland's frozen wastes, where they had tried to bivouac during the winter after storms had blown their ships badly off course. Travelling in the third ship, the expedition's pilot Richard Chancellor eventually reached Moscow where he opened negotiations between Russia's Ivan IV (known in the West as Ivan the Terrible) and England's Edward VI. And so the Muscovy Company was founded in February 1555 to develop commerce with Russia and to explore overland routes to the East. Like the later Virginia Company, it ran on joint-stock funds, which spread the risks among its investors and allowed non-merchants to take advantage of opening markets.

Under Ivan and his successors, English merchants enjoyed special privileges, including the right to duty-free trade, although the Dutch were soon nudging their elbows, and conditions in this 'rude and barbarous kingdom' were tough indeed. English agents found themselves trapped in an environment where 'the harsh, frigid climate, the long and difficult travel between the ports and the commercial centers, and the animosity of the natives all conspired to make trading an ordeal not to be undertaken by the fainthearted'. The verdict comes from American academic Geraldine Phipps, in a monograph on Tradescant's contemporary, English merchant-diplomat Sir John Merrick, who was well liked by the Russians.[9] Those who travelled with him found themselves immeasurably depressed by 'the tedium of those endless northern journeys'.[10]

When Tradescant journeyed to Archangel with Digges's mission, Russia was ruled by the first of the Romanovs, Mikhail Feodorovich, great-nephew of Anastasia Romanov, wife of Ivan the Terrible. Then at war with Poland, Mikhail desperately wanted an English alliance or at the very least a large loan to buy arms and ammunition. England, on the other hand, was still looking to open trade routes to the riches of the East, especially along the Volga to

Persia (after the Turks had cut off the route from Russia to Persia in 1580)[11] and overland to China through Siberia. In the protracted negotiations that followed, each side hoped to use the wants and ambitions of the other as leverage but unfortunately they were playing for different stakes. The Russians looked on trade as politics while to the English trade was simply trade. King James had no intention of sending an army to Russia, and although he would happily countenance a loan, he was not the kind of man to go digging into his own pockets. Any money would have to be raised by the merchants who would benefit from the opening of new trade routes. The Muscovy Company, however, was then in dire financial straits through a combination of trade disruption, competition with the Dutch and sheer financial mismanagement.[12]

In September 1617, the English ambassador Sir John Merrick returned to London with Tsar Mikhail's two ambassadors, Stefan Ivanovich Volinksky and Mark Ivanosin Pozdeev, who kicked their heels at court, surrounded by their entourage, offering 'a source of amusement, bewilderment, and annoyance to the officials required to attend them at formal functions. The public appearances of these exotic foreigners and their strange customs were curious spectacles relished by many English observers.'[13]

Eventually, after months of stalled negotiations, James redeclared the Anglo-Russian friendship in suitably vague terms but declined to sign either a defensive or an offensive pact with Mikhail. He did, however, agree to send an English ambassador back to Russia bearing 100,000 roubles (£60,000) towards the loan, contingent on the Russian concession to allow English merchants to cross Russian soil into Persia. The near-bankrupt Muscovy Company then set about trying to raise this money as a joint venture with the East India Company, although at best only half the sum was ever raised. Sir Dudley Digges – a member of both companies – was chosen as ambassador and entrusted with an immediate £10,000 towards the loan, while an additional £20,000 was to be transferred from Hamburg.

On 3 June 1618, according to Tradescant's narrative,[14] the party weighed anchor at Gravesend and sailed down the Thames to Tilbury Hope in the *Diana* out of Newcastle under its Master, Mr Swanley of Limehouse, with part-owner Mr Nelson also on board. Digges's entourage included six king's gentlemen: Arthur Nowell, Thomas Finche, Thomas Woodward, Adam Cooke, a Mr Fante, and Henry Wyeld, each attended by a manservant. Other followers included an interpreter (George Brigges); a chaplain (Richard James, who stayed on in Russia to produce the first Anglo-Russian dictionary); and Digges's secretary, Thomas Leak. Also in Digges's entourage, given no particular function, were Jesse De Quester of Filpot Lane, London; Captain Gilbert and his son; a Scott by the name of Carr; and thirteen 'Wustershir men', among them 'on[e] Jonns an Coplie'.[15]

The Russian ambassadors were travelling in the same convoy, which numbered seven ships in total. Tradescant observed them from a distance throughout the journey. On St Peter's Day, Digges sent over fresh victuals: 'on[e] quarter of mutton, half a littill porker, and 3 live pullet'. This gift was in addition to the 'two small salmons and 9 gallons of Carnary Sack' delivered to the Russians at Newcastle. 'The curtiseys hathe passed a yet witheout requittall,' noted Tradescant with a hint of disapproval.

As with any other sea journey of the time, the problem for Digges was getting started. Leaving Gravesend on 3 June, they took forty-three days to travel a distance of 2,040 nautical miles, reaching Archangel on 16 July.[16] After taking refuge from the weather at Queenborough Port on the Isle of Sheppey, they sailed slowly up the North Sea coast, battling contrary winds 'whear all our landmen fell sick, and my Lord himselfe for 4 daies very sick'. Along the way they sought shelter at Tynemouth haven, making a further stop in Newcastle where Tradescant and a companion went ashore to buy provisions: beef and mutton and 'many other nesesaryes'. In an echo from his continental journeys, Tradescant shows himself a canny judge of prices, buying 'ii salmons for 5s. the cupple and sum for 4s. the cupple, whiche at London would have bin worth £2 10s'. That night they dined 'with many dishes' at the town's best inn, paying only 8d apiece for their wine, 'whiche in London I think 2s. the peece would have hardli matched it'. They clearly went to bed well pleased, rejoining the ship the next day with some £17 worth of provisions.

An hour after they reached the *Diana*, however, the wind changed and, 'being so full in our teethe', the vice admiral determined to put into port but as 'my Lord and myself [were] most against it', they remained out at sea, their judgement being proved right when the wind changed in their favour. Assuming that Tradescant had voiced his opinion, this suggests that whatever his private reasons for undertaking the voyage, others valued his seamanship. Indeed, throughout the voyage Tradescant reveals himself as an experienced seaman, perfectly at home with latitudes and wind directions (although he sometimes confuses the days and dates of the month, and even the month itself).

More gifts arrived before they finally left the northern shores of England: three salmon and a hogshead of beer from local dignitaries. But as they sailed up the Scottish coast, preparing to cross over to Norway, a storm blew up that raged for several days. 'In which 4 dayes my Lord Ambassittor was exstreem sick, in so much that all they in the ship mad question of his life, partli by sea sickness and partli by over muche coller [anger], that he was purswaded to be set on land or not to live.' Seasickness was not something that afflicted Tradescant, it seems. But they were now midway between Scotland and Norway, and Elsinore lay some 110 leagues to the south-east. As the wind began to calm, 'we perswaded him [the captain] to hould on his coorce. And on Thursday his lordship, after the calme, reseved sume meate, which in 4 days before he hade refused.' The next day he even had a little sleep, 'the Great God be blessed for it'.

By Friday, 26 June, the wind was blowing fair and their people were well recovered. Taken up with watching over his lord's sickness, Tradescant got no sleep but by then they had crossed latitude 60 degrees and were entering the white nights of the Arctic. 'This was the first plas whear darknes seases for the night,' noted Tradescant in his diary. 'Thear you mought have wrought or wrot at midnight,' which perhaps he was doing even then. Certainly, the ink-changes in his diary show that he kept his record almost daily (this was not a fair copy made after the event), and his handwriting grows wilder with the storms.

On the penultimate day of June, Tradescant was rewarded with his first exotic sighting: a strange bird that flew on to the ship in the night, 'which was taken alive and put to my costody, but dyed within two dayes after being

60 leags from the shore, whos like I yet never sawe, whos case I have reserved. This was in 66 degrees in the latitud.' So Tradescant had already started his habit of collecting the outlandish and the strange, and knew enough about collecting to record where he had found the unknown bird. As they were still only off the coast of Norway, it was unlikely to be the 'Gorara or Colymbus from *Muscovy*' later recorded in the Ark's catalogue,[17] although its beak or head might have survived among the 'thirty other severall forrain sorts, not found in any Author'.[18]

There followed a short interlude in which a Mr Decrass came aboard, seeking counsel about whether to send his small sailing boat to Greenland so late in the year. He was sent on his way with two bottles of the ambassador's wine, one of sack and one of claret – the right present for people of his sort, judged Tradescant, but perhaps too generous 'by reson of our long voyag'. The good wine he had enjoyed in Newcastle was becoming a tantalizing memory, perhaps. That night, they saw the sun shining to the north 'about an howr hyghe', and the next day many whales, despite the 'extreeme fogge', which meant that they had sailed 'witheout the light of sune 5 dayes'.

But on a Monday morning almost five weeks after leaving England, they sighted the snow-covered North Cape, 'whear we felt the ayre very could, the land being highe land, all ilands, with many bayes amonst the lande'. There were other ships, too, including a man-of-war belonging to the Danish king, whose demands to stop and have their passes checked they boldly brushed aside, saying their boat was stowed and that in any case 'we had an Inglishe Ambassator abord'. The Russian ambassadors' ship did likewise and they sailed on, close by the coast of Wardhouse (modern-day Vardöhuus) where the king had a castle commanding Lapland, home to many Danes as well as Lapps. Tradescant had no desire to live there himself, and he declared that even if he were offered the whole kingdom, 'I had rather be a portter in London, for the snow is never of the ground wholly, but liethe in great packes conttinnewally'. Nor did he like the white nights, complaining that 'the sun shinethe there continnewally when it is no foggs whiche most tims it is'.

Other travellers shared Tradescant's dislike of these forbidding treeless wastes. Some twenty-five years later, the tireless Peter Mundy travelled by sea from Danzig (Polish Gdańsk) through the Baltic, then up around the North Cape and down to Archangel. Like Tradescant before him, he looked out at the islands of Vardö and shuddered. 'For From the Cape hither, beeing about 120 Miles, there was not a tree or bush to bee seene. I thincke itt to bee the uncomffortablest country and most inconvenientt For the liffe of Man off any other part off the world thatt is inhabited, yeilding little or Nothing Fitting For his sustenance or Comffortt.'[19]

Now that they were heading south again, Tradescant was relieved to have a fair wind, and after they had passed Cross Island (so named from its numerous wooden crosses, which were ruthlessly cut down for fuel by ships' crews)[20] the snows were beginning to abate 'and the nature of the coaste to change from russet to a greener coller, the inland being full of shrubby trees, and furthr of we moughte perseve great woods, but all this way no kind of grayne'. They were also visited by two men in a small boat laden with freshly salted fish; Digges bought a very large fish for 4s, the price Tradescant had paid for two in Newcastle.

Tradescant then turned a cool eye on the two men, noting that the elder was aged about fifty, one-eyed and 'hard favored', while the younger, half his age, was 'well favored' and 'well limbed'. Both were clad in sheepskins, the fur side turned inwards, and both wore crucifixes about their necks 'very arttifityally made' in contrast to their boat, which was small and neat, and reminded him of a Dutch boat he called a 'scuts'. 'I have seene manie in Ingland of ther profetion worse fationed,' he concluded, perhaps even then scouting for the Nordic garments he would later display at the Ark, which included a Russian vest; a 'Greinland-habit'; a 'Match-coat from *Greenland* of the Intrails of Fishes', boots from Lapland, Greenland, Muscovy and Russia; 'Shooes to walk on Snow without sinking'; Russian stockings without heels; Russian shoes shod with iron; and the splendid 'Duke of *Muscovy's* vest wrought with gold upon the breast and armes'.[21] (He would also put on display a tiny Russian abacus, miscatalogued by his son as 'Beads strung upon stiff wyers, and set in four-square frames wherewith the Indians cast account'.)[22]

More wildlife was sighted as they sailed down into the White Sea on the final leg of their voyage: first a great white fish, twice the size of a porpoise, 'being all over as white as snowe' and apparently a great destroyer of salmon. Peter Mundy saw one too, 'a Fish much bigger then a grampus, milk white',[23] offering this as a possible explanation for the naming of the White Sea: 'For otherwise itt mightt bee called the blacke or Red Sea by the colour off the water'. Dr Hamel thought the fish must have been a white dolphin, sometimes confused with the beluga of the Volga and the Caspian Sea.[24] Mundy's editor opted instead for a white whale. The next day, when they were just three leagues from the shore, many small birds came aboard. 'I have thre of ther skins,' declared Tradescant proudly, 'whiche were caut by my self and the rest of the company. They did much resemble the maner of our Inglishe linnets but far lesser.'

And so they reached the bar across the harbour's mouth at Archangel, where they lay becalmed for a day before crossing it with only a foot's draught to spare. Russian soldiers gave an immediate welcome to their own returning ambassadors, ignoring the English party; but as they reached the mouth of the Dvina River, the 'Grand Prestave'[25] came to salute them with boatloads of soldiers. In true ambassadorial style, Sir Dudley Digges was entertained in his cabin with a 'banket of sweetemeats, the agent and the rest of the Inglishe marchants having had the like entterteynment just before his coming'. As the grandee took his leave, there was a mutual exchange of ceremonial shot, giving Tradescant a poor opinion of Russian guns and soldierly skills. He was much more impressed by the fresh stores supplied by the English agent, however: 'on[e] good bullock, 2 sheep, 10 hens, 2 fesants, 6 pattriges, non lik the Inglishe'. Life on board ship must at times have resembled Noah's Ark.

That night they were visited by a boatful of 'Sammoyets', nomads from northern Siberia, 'a misserable people of small grouth' who gave rise, in Tradescant's opinion, to the myth of a headless race, 'for they have short necks and commonly wear ther clothes over head and shoulders'. His words echo Othello's tales to Desdemona about the many sights and adventures of his travels, when he talks to her of

> ... antres vast and deserts idle,
> Rough quarries, rocks and hills, whose heads touch heaven, ...
> And of the Cannibals, that each other eat;
> The Anthropophagi, and men whose heads
> Do grow beneath their shoulders.[26]

The Sammoyets who came aboard that night were indistinguishable men from women, 'because they all wear clothes like mene and be all clad in skins of beasts packed very curouslie together, stokins and all'. Peter Mundy encountered them, too, and from his wider knowledge of different peoples compared them to Tartars and Malays living on islands in the Straits of Malacca. 'They eatt all Manner off Trash,' he added, 'as gutts, garbage, etts., sometymes Raw, sometymes halffe roasted, a very strange wild beastly people, somewhatt like to those aboutt Cape Bona Esperance.' Mundy tells us that they were polygamous and neither Christians nor Turks, 'butt observe a certayne religion, having preists off their owne'.[27]

Twice that night they weighed anchor because of the tides – the first lasting just two hours before the ebb, and then a 'long flud like ours'. As soon as he could after anchoring, Tradescant asked for a boat to take him ashore, anxious to explore the flora and fauna at first-hand. His initial descriptions are hesitant, revealing the difficulties of describing new plants and wildlife without a developed taxonomy. There were first of all berries, one rather like an English strawberry 'but of another fation of leaf. I have brought some of them home with me,' he said, together with a variety of moss and fruit-bearing shrubs 'suche as I have never seene the like'. On that first trip ashore, he also found a piece of snakeskin, and disturbed five birds he wanted so much he would have given 5s for one of their skins; the mature birds were 'great to the bignes of a fesant, the wings whit, the bodies green, the tayll blewe or dove coller'.

Their final mooring was 'befor the Inglishe house', the Muscovy Company's outpost in Archangel, which had moved from its original site on Rose Island to the new wooden town springing up around the monastery of St Michael.[28] Here they went ashore with all the pomp they could muster.

The lodgings reserved for the English ambassador and his party belonged to two Dutchmen and an Englishman called Wilkinson. The houses were built of whole tree trunks laid on top of each other, the gaps packed with moss. But as the bedsteads were poor, said Tradescant, they were 'content to lay our bodi on the ground'.

Continuing his explorations, Tradescant was carried in an imperial boat from island to island, 'to see what things growe upon them', enthusing over the single roses 'wondros sweet' and many other plants which he resolved to take home with him. Such beauty stood in stark contrast to what Tradescant saw as the 'basness of the people', singling out for special scorn a local commander who ate their coarse cakes with relish, thinking them a great banquet when they were but 'sower creame and otmeall pasties very poorli made'. The faint sneer recalls the German Paul Hentzer's jibe at the English view of foreigners: 'If they see a foreigner very well made, or particularly handsome, they will say, "It is a pity he is not an Englishman".'[29]

Tradescant's descriptions of Archangel itself are curiously slight, suggesting that he was too focused on his botanizing to pay the usual traveller's attention to the sights of the town and the manners of its inhabitants. We get a far better idea of its turreted churches and castle, its windmills, tame bears[30] and 'pretty handsom shew' from Mundy, who visited Archangel some four years after fire had destroyed its monastery and town, but much rebuilding had already taken place.[31] The town stood in the Dvina estuary where the river divided into two great branches; on the far bank was the monastery of St Nicholas, and the surrounding country was reputedly a 'vast wast with great wildernesses, woods, Marishes'.[32]

Mundy took time to observe the Archangel churches, built of wood and graced by 'pretty towers, with spires covered with boards [shingles] Finely contrived, cutt and placed one over another, making a handsom shew, as in some places with us slate is used'. Adjoining towers housed the church bells, 'which are strucken by cords tied to their Clappers'. Foreigners, however, were not allowed inside Russian churches, 'which by reportt is after the greekish manner'; nor were they allowed to buy the painted icons that Mundy so coveted. Not even the Russian servants of Archangel's English and Dutch merchants could be bribed into buying one on his behalf, for fear of death by burning, although the ones he did manage to glimpse he found disappointing, of 'no greatt worckmanshipp' and painted in the manner of 'antientt pictures after the old Fashion'.[33]

Tradescant stayed in Archangel a little under three weeks, returning with the *Diana*, which set sail for England again on 5 August 1618. On the first night of their return journey, they anchored off Rose Island, the site of the original English factory but now forlornly guarded by some ten soldiers who lived in a 'littill souldgers house' on the island's only high point. Here they bought grass for their sheep and Tradescant made a final botanizing excursion, gathering 'of all suche things as I could find thear growing, whiche wear 4 sorts of berries, which I brought awaye with me of every sortt'. He leaves us, too, with a haunting image of the wild, low-lying island with its long bank of dry white sand, 'the land being eyther woods or meddow, but seldom eyther mowne or fed'.

The journey home took seven weeks. Tradescant's account details the many storms, changing winds, sudden gusts, occasional becalmings, snow, fogs, and 'much rayne' in a steady voice, although once they would have perished had the gusting wind continued. God's name is invoked several times, usually in gratitude. When they reached Cross Island, the decks were leaking from constant rain, 'whiche for my own part I felt for it rayned doune thourow all my clothes and beds to the spoyll of them all'. After eight weeks of constant daylight, he welcomed the return of '3 howers night' with evident relief; later he recorded how the sun shining through rain clouds had a great circle around it, 'even as hathe the moone in raynie time'. They sighted whales, grampuses, several Dutch or Flemish boats and were once given chase, but then to his obvious relief – after a full month without view of land – Tradescant was walking with another man on the deck when he saw a glimmer of coastline, 'whiche was present[ly] approved by the wholle company, which land was to the southward of Baffam Ness, part of the cuntrie of Scotland'.

It would take another nine days before they reached St Katherine's dock near the Tower of London 'whear, God be thanked, we ended our viage having no on[e] man sick, God be thanked'. He had come home safely and, in a final sitting, he set out a list of 'Things by me observed', determined to record his impressions and observations before memory wiped the slate. The list is fascinating not just for its insights into life in northern Russia but for what it tells us about Tradescant the man, whose interests were cast far more widely than the plants he went to Russia to collect.

He was first of all interested in how ordinary people lived in an agricultural economy – the crops they grew (rye, wheat, white oats, barley oats, and peas) and their times of sowing and harvest; the houses they built for themselves and their means of heating and sleeping (on bedsteads, he thought, with bedding of bear and other skins unlike the beds of foreign traders, which were boarded like English ones but 'of a mean fation'); their meat, bread, beer, mead, carts, horses, homesteads. And he was not merely interested in how things looked (the habitual preoccupation of the tourist) but in how they were made. Russian houses, for instance, were constructed from long trunks of fir cut in half, glassed with a substance he called 'slude'; and the flattish roofs were made from boards laid lengthwise down the roof on overlapping strips of birch bark 'as broad [as] a yearing calf or broader and 3 yards long', in order to keep out 'the wet and rayne and snowe'. Their stoves he heartily applauded, especially the way they were used to cook meat, 'whiche is so well don that it givethe great content to all strangers'.

Their meat and bread generally he considered 'resonable go[o]d'. Both wheaten and rye breads were as plentiful as in most parts of England, but never baked very well, and Russian loaves came in 'many foollishe fatyons' – some, for instance, were so small one could swallow a whole loaf in two mouthfuls. Others were forced into a large doughnut (a shape he compared rather laboriously to a horseshoe, only round instead of open-ended). The brown rye bread that he ate at the Dutch and English houses was better, he admitted, than any he had been served in England. On the subject of Russian alcohol (beer and mead) he seems something of a connoisseur, considering most Russian beer 'of an ill tast' apart from one he drank at the English house – brewed by a Russian – which he declared better than any he had tasted in England both for strength and savour. For their best mead he had only praise, considering it an 'excelent drinke, mad of ther hony, which is the best honny of the world'.

In several of his descriptions, Tradescant shows himself well acquainted with English farming communities, especially those in East Anglia (Norfolk and Essex), which he may have known as a boy. Russian carts he judged little, long and narrow, 'muche like them of Stafordshir', their wheels made of two pieces of slit fir, thick at the middle and tapering towards the edge. Hens and cocks were small, as were their pigs. He found their horses well shaped, short-kneed and well jointed, and from Captain Gilbert (long a resident in Russia) he learnt of the stamina of Tartar horses, much like Barbary horses 'but of the best use of any in the knowne world'.

Although Tradescant had little to say about town architecture, he remarked on the way the Russians used timber for paving (the trees were simply cut in half as the inhabitants lacked saws and planes), and on their palisaded homesteads in which dwellings for cows, sheep, horses and people faced into a central timber-paved yard, 'muche like cloysters heer in Ingland'. A practical man himself, he admired the feats of carpentry achieved with only rudimentary tools: 'And yet yu shall see things don beyond any mans judgment onli withe a hatchet and a chisell and a draing [drawing] knife and withe much speed'. Of course, the wood was remarkably soft, he could not help adding as a possible explanation. And he took a close look at the twelve-foot-high wooden fences dividing neighbour from neighbour, held together with mortice joints.

He noted, too, how the country houses stood on artificial mounds, further protected beyond their palisades by dams of tree trunks, seven or eight feet high, designed to hold back the floodwaters from thawing ice, which also cast up huge boulders on riverbanks. Through all this detail, you can imagine him striding around the farmsteads, interpreter in tow, examining, questioning, trusting only what he saw at first-hand or learnt from a reliable source, among whom he definitely did not include Johnson the Dutchman, who told him the country grew both tulips and narcissi but who was 'always dru[n]ke once in the day'.

Only after he had recorded all his agricultural impressions did Tradescant

The briar rose from John Gerard's
Herball, said to resemble
the Muscovy rose.

turn his attention to Archangel's trees and plants, which were surely his
motive for travel. Again, he faced the difficulty of naming or at least
describing unfamiliar species and varieties, although many also grew in
Britain. But as the German-Russian botanist Franz Josef Ruprecht pointed
out in a study of plants found near Archangel and its islands in 1841,
Tradescant lived before the time of the great botanists and naturalists such
as Robert Morison, John Ray, Leonard Plukenet, and James Petiver, 'and
could have derived little from anyone except Turner and Gerard. Being little
skilled in Latin, he had hardly consulted the works of Lobel or Clusius.'[34]
Careful observation had to take the place of scholarly identifications.

   Describing the country as '5 parts ... woods and unprofitable grounds',
he had seen four different kinds of fir trees (which Dr Hamel identified as
Scots pine, Siberian spruce, Siberian larch and Siberian fir) and huge birch
trees, which yielded a 'fine coolle kind of drink' in the springtime, when
juice was collected from incisions made in the bark. He devoted much
attention to a little tree with very pliant wood much used by Flemish,

Dutch, Hamburger and Russian coopers – especially for their great casks of caviar – and by English merchants who took the wood to Greenland for making barrels. The gardener in him questioned the name of wild cherry given by the English to one of the trees (botanists have confirmed it as *Prunus padus*, the bird cherry). 'I canot beleeve it is of that kind,' said Tradescant stubbornly, although it was like a cherry in leaf and bore a blackish berry, a little smaller than a *Sorbus*, 'but was not ripe at my being theare'. If a twig were placed in the ground, he observed, it would take root, and so he had brought some back with him, 'which I hope will growe, for all the unfit season of the yeare they be very willing to grow'.

Among the shrubs he noted were white, black and red currants, 'far greatter than ever I have seen in this cuntrie', which he attributed to the vigour of the Russian summer, so quick that plants blossomed and ripened into perfect fruit. He also found a low-growing berry much like an amber strawberry (most probably the cloudberry, *Rubus chamaemorus*), used locally as a cure for scurvy. Comparing its leaves to our 'avince' (*Geum rivale*, a pretty herbaceous plant still grown in gardens today), he dried a few berries to procure seed, sending some to 'Robiens of Parris', the French king's gardener.

And then there were the wild roses, 'single, in a great abundance', spread over four or five acres on Rose Island – a magnificent sight. Tradescant compared them to the cinnamon rose, adding that those 'who have the sence of smelling say they be marvelus sweete'. This is the only purely personal detail he revealed about himself; Tradescant was a gardener who had no sense of smell, a fact he confirmed later in his diary when he mentioned the stench of fish oil from the Dutch boats, 'which stinkethe so filthily that it is redy to poyson all those that go by. But being deprived of that sence it ofended me not.'

How he must have longed to smell the roses and the pinks he found growing wild on Rose Island, comparable to the best English sorts, 'with the edges of the leaves deeplie cut or jaged very finely'. Some of the roses he brought back to England, hoping they would thrive with him, and they very probably did – one of the plants listed as growing in his Lambeth garden in 1634 was *Rosa Muscovitica*[35] and it was still growing there in 1656: the 'Muscovie

Rose'.[36] Not a name in use today, it has been tentatively identified with *Rosa acicularis*, which, according to a botanist visiting towards the end of the nineteenth century, was not unlike R. *cinnamomea*. 'I was much struck with the uniformity of the briars of the neighbourhood of Archangel and other parts of Northern Russia,' wrote G. S. Boulger in *The Journal of Botany*, 'and the specimens of these which I bought home are typical *Rosa acicularis* of Lindley.'[37]

On Rose Island, Tradescant found another plant he could not name, one he likened to hedge mercury, which has since been identified as Lapland cornel, *Cornus suecica*. The fruits, he said, made a very fine show, having three leaves at the top of every stem and a berry in every leaf about the size of a hawthorn's but brighter red, all three berries growing close together. He took up many roots to bring home but then suffered a double calamity. First, as fresh water was scarce, the plants were watered with salt water 'but was mad beleeve it was freshe'. Watering for the early plant collectors was ever a problem; one thinks of Captain Bligh (buried a few paces from the Tradescants in the churchyard of St Mary, Lambeth), who sparked a mutiny on the *Bounty* when he watered his precious breadfruits before his men. Even without the watering fiasco, 'the Boys in the ship, before I peseved it, [did] eat of the berries, except sume of them com up amongst the earthe by chance.' One hopes the plants survived the journey after all Tradescant's trouble, even if many were also native to Britain.

Further plant sightings included three or four 'whorts' (cowberries, cranberries and bilberries, perhaps); angelica (*Archangelica officinalis*, a common plant of the Dvina delta);[38] lysimachia; a potentilla; a little saxifrage; a giant sorrel 'half the heyght of a man'; and the purple cranesbill of Muscovy, its large purply-blue flowers tending towards red. 'Brought to us by Mr John Tradescant', said Parkinson in his great herbal of 1640 and, as far as he knew, not described in any prior publication 'although we have had it long time in our Gardens'.[39]

Finally, Tradescant made a careful note of the trees and plants he heard about but did not see for himself: oak, elm, ash, apple, pear and cherries in the interior, much as in England 'but the frut les and not so plesant'. From the Volga, he received reports of a plant with fennel-like leaves known as

'God's tree', which was described to him as 'pasing sweet and of great vertues'. According to Hamel, this was a literal translation of the Russian (*Boshige derewo*) for southernwood, *Artemisia abrotanum*, which was then very common in England, a connection Tradescant missed but then he had not seen the plant for himself.[40] And there were the tulips and narcissi reported by the drunken Dutchman, which were unlikely to have bloomed in Archangel itself. Peter Mundy (who noted the extraordinary amount of angelica growing in the fields, as well as many wild flowers and long grasses) saw some gardens of the 'common sort' about the town, but only cabbages growing there.[41]

Although he had finished with plants, Tradescant's observations continued for several more pages, starting with a description of five different sorts of boats so precise in its attention to purpose and construction that it reads like an official report but enlivened with vigorous language – like the oily, stinking sealskins 'blowne out like a blader' to rid them of their grease; and the thirty men launching a barge with such a racket you might think the 'wholl toune had bin together by the ears'. (Six Englishmen could have done the job just as well, he could not help remarking, himself included.) He must surely have grown up among a boat-building community to have noticed the barge hulls secured not with iron nails or wooden dowels but sewn together with bark, caulked at the seams with fine moss then resined and tarred; and the little boat like a Thames wherry, used to carry hogs, sheep, fish, hens and wildfowl to market, made of three or four deal boards finely cleft and then hewed, never more than two boards deep and again sewn together with bark. As for the oval, flat-bottomed boats used for loading ships in the harbour, they 'weare good for the East Indian Company', he judged, despite having no protection from the elements. Perhaps the Company – co-sponsors of the loan to Tsar Mikhail – had asked him to report on trading opportunities.

Tradescant gives us sharp visual touches, too, like the dragons and birds used to decorate the barge prows, hung with fringed cloth and bells 'that make a noyse withe the winde'. And for the 'great persons of the land' was reserved a kind of houseboat to travel up and down the river with a 'fine littill borded house' in the poop or – better still – a house in the middle, 'prettili bult with prtti windowes in them' and painted red, blue or green, 'but the greattest all red which I judge is of greatest state'.

Here Tradescant's diary came to an abrupt end, the final half-page filled with confused jottings – most probably in a different hand – about astrological gardening, Abraham's wife after Sarah (Keturah), the difference between the Julian and Gregorian calendars, and the 'golden number', phi. As for the rest of the diary, despite W. H. Black's dismissive verdict on its crude composition and rude handwriting, it is a model of careful observation. Tradescant's Russian journey may have yielded no great botanical discoveries but as a fellow botanist approvingly observed, he had 'recorded some two dozen wild plants from his own observation, a short but interesting list'.[42] Of course, his rough approximations of unfamiliar plants could not match the detailed descriptions of trained apothecaries such as John Parkinson or Thomas Johnson who in any case had the benefit of quiet study and long acquaintance with many of the plants' growing habits – see, for instance, Parkinson's painstaking portrait of Tradescant's Muscovy cranesbill. No, John Tradescant's achievements lay elsewhere – in the curiosity that drove him to make uncomfortable, even perilous journeys in search of strange plants and novelties of every description, and in his practical gardening skills that allowed so many of them to flourish in their new home.

As a diplomatic mission, however, Sir Dudley Digges's voyage to Archangel was a complete failure. While Tradescant botanized in the vicinity, Digges stayed at Archangel for two weeks before setting out southwards on his journey to Moscow with the loan intended for Tsar Mikhail. He had not gone far when he stopped again and, without a word of explanation to the Russian officials accompanying him, scuttled back to Archangel.[43] On 2 September 1618, he set sail for England, leaving behind several of his party with 20,000 roubles of the loan for the Russian tsar. The rest he took home with him.

The English were apparently as mystified as the Russians by Digges's sudden volte-face. Writing to George Villiers, then Marquess of Buckingham, he later complained of his treatment at the hands of certain Russian officials, and suggested he feared for his own personal safety. Polish troops were massing near Moscow and it was known he was carrying a large amount of money intended for the tsar.[44] It seems his nervousness was unfounded, as the men he sent on to the tsar's court reached Moscow safely in January 1619, after an admittedly difficult journey through the Russian winter. But by then it was too late. The Russian government refused to deal with the envoys, who were not the men they were expecting, and Digges's substitute was not granted an audience by the tsar until the following March. By the time Tsar Mikhail condescended to receive the money intended as a loan, Russia and Poland were no longer at war, having signed a peace treaty almost three months earlier. It is unlikely that the loan was ever repaid, and the Russians were in no mind to extend the Muscovy Company's trading privileges by allowing their merchants to cross Russia into Persia. So while English gardens may have benefited from the expedition, the Muscovy Company was badly out of pocket.

Chapter Eleven

Pirates *of the* Mediterranean

Botany can be a dangerous profession for a man determined to travel in pursuit of his passion. We next hear of Tradescant sailing into the Mediterranean with the British fleet to crush the Barbary pirates of Algiers – another dismal political failure redeemed by the treasures Tradescant brought back from his Mediterranean foray. Among them was the 'Argier Apricocke', its yellow fruit smaller than any other 'but as sweete and delicate as any of them', according to John Parkinson, who tells us that 'this with many other sorts John Tradescante brought with him returning from the Argier voyage, whither hee went voluntary with the Fleete, that went against the Pyrates in the yeare 1620.'[1]

The pirates of the North African coast were a mixed crew of many nationalities who threatened Europe's fragile peace and disrupted its favourite occupation: the business of trade and making money. If it seems odd that Tradescant should attach himself to a military expedition – rather like a modern-day plant hunter hitching a ride to Iraq – the public and private spheres were then not so carefully divided and casual volunteering was nothing out of the ordinary. As a young man, even gentlemanly John Evelyn had rushed across the Channel to join the Dutch in their siege of Gennep, arriving when the battle was already won. After ten days of baking daytime heat and nightly river mists, he declared himself 'pretty well satisfied' with the confusion of armies, and left.² Tradescant at least saw action with the fleet, as he was clearly listed with other 'gentleman volunteers' on the pinnace *Mercury*, serving under Captain Phineas Pett.³

In early Tudor times, English trade had flourished in the Mediterranean, even to its eastern shores, known as the Levant.⁴ As Turkish maritime power increased, trade faltered and ceased completely from 1550 to the early 1570s. But after Spain and other Catholic forces destroyed the Turkish fleet at the battle of Lepanto in 1571, English ships ventured back into the Mediterranean; and as Anglo-Spanish relations drifted towards war, ties between England and the Ottoman empire grew closer. Queen Elizabeth gave a charter and monopoly privileges to a new joint-stock company, the Levant Company, and sent an ambassador to Constantinople, paid for by the 'Turkey merchants' who became synonymous with luxury and wealth, founded on their rich trade in carpets, cloths, silks, oils, sweet wines, currants and Eastern spices.

Like many diplomats posted abroad, the English ambassador would play a key role in bringing plants back into England. When London herbalist and barber-surgeon John Gerard was gardening for Queen Elizabeth's Lord Treasurer, Lord Burghley, he described the route taken by the red lily of Constantinople from the wilds of Turkey into his own garden at Holborn:

This plant groweth wilde in the fieldes and mountaines, many daies journeis beyonde Constantinople, whither it is brought by the poore pesants to be solde, for the decking up of gardens. From thence it was sent among other bulbs of rare and daintie flowers, by master *Harbran* ambassador there, unto my honorable good Lord and master, the Lord Treasurer of England, who bestowed them upon me for my garden.⁵

Plants were also flowing courtesy of plant-loving London merchants such as Nicholas Lete of the Levant Company and John de Franqueville. Parkinson mentions both of them in connection with the double yellow rose from Turkey, 'which first was procured to be brought into England, by Master Nicholas Lete, a worthy Merchant of London, and a great lover of flowers, from Constantinople, which (as wee heare) was first brought thither from Syria'. But Lete's yellow rose quickly died, as did all those he gave to others, and 'afterwards it was sent to Master John de Franqueville, a Merchant also of London, and a great lover of all rare plants, as well as flowers, from which is sprung the greatest store, that is now flourishing in this Kingdome'.[6] The Jerusalem artichoke almost certainly came to England via John de Franqueville's garden; botanist John Goodyer describes receiving two small roots in 1617 from 'Master *Franquevill* of London, no bigger than hens egges: the one I planted, and the other I gave to a friend, mine bought mee a pecke of rootes'. The account appeared in Thomas Johnson's revised edition of John Gerard's *Herball* accompanied by a stern warning that whether the roots were boiled, stewed or baked in pies, they 'cause a filthie loathsome stinking winde within the bodie, thereby causing the belly to bee pained and tormented, and are a meat more fit for swine, than men'.[7]

Both Lete and de Franqueville were well known to John Gerard himself, who mentioned them with love and gratitude in his own *Herball* of 1597. It was Lete who sent Gerard a yellow variety of clove gillyflower from Poland 'which before that time was never seene nor heard of in these countries'.[8] Lete's Syrian factor in Aleppo also sent his master three pounds of cotton seeds, although Gerard could only entrust their success to the Lord. When he himself planted some cotton seeds, they grew 'very frankly' at first but then perished 'by reason of the colde frostes that overtooke [them] in the time of flowring'.[9]

Keen to obtain Mediterranean plants directly, Gerard despatched one of his assistants, William Marshall, as a ship's surgeon aboard the *Hercules*, to scout for new varieties. Marshall brought back seeds of the spreading plane tree which he found 'growing in Lepantae, hard by the sea side, at the entrance into the towne, a port of Morea [the Peloponnese], being a part of Greece, and from thence brought one of those rough buttons, being the fruite thereof'. Gerard rightly warned against its choking dust (pollen). Among its varied uses, he suggested that the fruit of the plane tree drunk with wine 'helpeth the bitings of mad dogs and serpents, and mixed with hogs grease, it maketh a good ointment against burning and scalding'.[10]

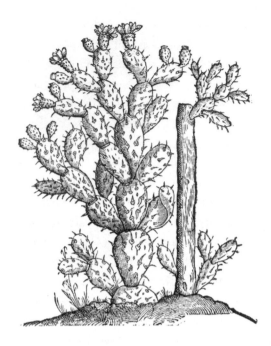

The prickly Indian fig tree,
a Mediterranean novelty for
British gardeners.

Another Mediterranean plant brought back by Marshall for Gerard was the Prickly Indian fig tree or *Ficus indica*, a 'strange and admirable plant', which Gerard described as being a 'multiplication of leaves' covered in whitish prickles, producing figlike fruit 'stuffed full of a red pulpe and juice, staining the hands of them that touch it, as do the Mulberies, with a bloudy or sanguine colour'. As well as growing in the East and West Indies and Virginia, said Gerard, 'It groweth also at Saint Crux and other places of Barbarie, & also in an Iland of the Mediterranean sea called Zante,' about a day and a night's sailing with a 'meane winde' from the port of Petrasse [Pátrai] in Morea, 'where my servant *William Marshall* before remembred, did see not onely great store of those trees made of leaves, but also divers other rounde bodied plants, of a woody substance'. Marshall obligingly brought many of them home 'in tubs of earth, very fresh and greene for my garden, where they flourished at the impression heerof'. Medically, however, Gerard had no idea what to do with the plant, although he prudently included a report from those who had eaten liberally of the fruits 'that it hath changed their urine to the colour of bloud, who at the sight thereof have stoode in great doubt of their life'.[11]

Hostilities between England and Spain checked the direct introduction of Spanish plants into England for a time, but then the accession of James I to the English throne increased the likelihood of a lasting peace and plant hunters once again crossed into Spanish territory. John Parkinson supported Dutch botanist Wilhelm Boel on a plant-hunting trip through the western Mediterranean in 1607 and 1608. Boel brought back more than two hundred different sorts of seeds, 'besides divers other rare plants, dried and laid betweene papers, whereof the seeds were not ripe'. Parkinson planted all his seeds, 'and by sowing them saw the faces of a great many excellent plants'. But his joy was short-lived, as 'many of them came not to maturitie with me, and most of the other whereof I gathered ripe seed one yeare, by unkindly yeares that fell afterwards, have perished likewise'.[12]

While Parkinson may have lacked the skills and the technology to overwinter Boel's tender importations, he was still able to boast of the many Spanish plants that flourished in his London garden at Long Acre, like Spanish broom and the great double yellow Spanish bastard daffodil, which he proudly called 'Parkinsons Daffodill', for 'I thinke none ever had this kinde before my selfe, nor did I my selfe ever see it before the year 1618, for it is of mine own raising and flowring in my Garden.'[13] Among the twenty-one varieties of auricula he was able to describe from first-hand experience was one he called the Spaniard's blush, 'being of a duskie blush colour, resembling the blush of a Spaniard, whose tawney skinne cannot declare so pure a blush as the English can'.[14]

Plant hunters may have benefited from the lull in hostilities between European powers, but merchant vessels at sea were under increasing threat from pirates, as privateers of all nations – deprived of the opportunity to attack 'enemy' ships – threw in their lot with the outright pirates operating out of the Barbary ports of North Africa: Algiers, Tunis, Tripoli and Moroccan Salé.[15] Although nominally owing allegiance to the Turkish sultan, these North African regencies existed as virtual pirate states, their numbers swelled by Moors thrown out of Catholic Spain who nursed their own grievances against Christendom. It was an explosive mix, especially as the pirates were lumped together as 'Turks' and therefore Moslems, even though they included a number of renegade Christians, captives-turned-pirates and simple freebooters attracted by the rich pickings and open markets of the Barbary coast. Among them were many English who – as German traveller Paul Hentzner remarked – made 'good sailors and better pirates, cunning, treacherous, and thievish'.[16]

One man in particular hated piracy in any form: King James I of England. He equated pirates with the bullies who had blighted his Scottish childhood, tugging and pulling at his strings before he could stand up for himself. Mention of piracy would send him into a rage and he was proud of hanging English pirates – as many as nineteen in a row dangled from Wapping Pier, late in December 1608.[17] The Barbary pirates offered the additional provocation of religion, and James had already expressed his hatred of the Turk in an epic poem celebrating the Christian naval victory at Lepanto.[18] (One Spanish participant in the battle was Miguel de Cervantes, creator of Don Quixote, who was later carried off as a slave to Algiers and endured five years of captivity before he was ransomed by his impoverished family.)

By the second decade of James's reign, the problem of piracy was growing more serious. Not just ships were at risk: whole coastal towns panicked at the sudden appearance of pirate fleets. Instead of hanging pirates, James tried a different approach, offering pardons to woo privateers away from piracy. One who responded was the man who had visited Tradescant at Canterbury to talk about melons, Sir Henry Mainwaring. After he had turned against piracy, Mainwaring wrote a short discourse on his former calling which he presented to the king as a thank-you for his own pardon, signing the dedication 'Your Majesty's new Creature'.[19] Widely circulated among leading figures of the day, it called for the suppression of pirates on the Barbary coast and provided much useful information on pirate habits and fortifications. From it we learn, for instance, that the inner harbour of Algiers was protected by a mole and 'great store of singular good Ordnance' commanding the whole road[20] or anchorage, 'which is very dangerous if the wind come Northerly'. Mainwaring may also have inspired the May date for the British raid on Algiers, remarking that 'Generally not any Pirates do stir in the Straits from the beginning or middest of May till towards the last of September.'[21]

Mainwaring was not Tradescant's only link to the Algiers expedition, however. His employer, Edward, Lord Wotton, was one of a fourteen-man commission asked in 1617 to advise the king on how to tackle the Barbary pirates. Another member was the Lord Keeper, Sir Francis Bacon; and among the many merchant representatives brought into its deliberations was plant-loving Nicholas Lete of the Levant Company. Tradescant's old friend and Virginian co-investor, Samuel Argall, captained one of the merchant ships sent into the Mediterranean, and belonged to the expedition's inner war cabinet.[22] And a prime mover behind the whole expedition was the king's favourite and Tradescant's next employer: George Villiers, still only a marquess (his dukedom came after his Spanish escapade of 1623), who took command of the navy as Lord High Admiral in 1619, replacing the 'corrupt and supine' Earl of Nottingham.[23]

In his determination to act against the Barbary pirates, James was keen to bring other powers into the action – Spain and the United Provinces especially, whose uneasy truce was still holding but whose relations were driven by suspicion. Not surprisingly, negotiations dragged on interminably, and in the end the English fleet went ahead alone with little more than separate expressions of goodwill and assurances of cooperation from the other powers.

The man appointed in July 1620 to lead the fleet against Algiers was Sir Robert Mansell, whose long career in the navy spanned a time of notorious corruption. Granted the office of Treasurer of the Navy in 1604, he made a fortune when he finally sold it on being appointed Vice Admiral of England in 1618. The action at Algiers certainly did not go well for him and he afterwards turned away from the navy to the manufacture of glass, for which he had bought the monopoly. 'To judge from his performance on this occasion,' wrote historian Christopher Lloyd, he 'must be regarded as one of the most inept admirals in history.' To be fair, however, Mansell was operating under hopelessly conflicting instructions: to root out the Algerine pirates without endangering His Majesty's ships, and to redeem Christian slaves without attacking the city of Algiers itself, for fear of offending potential allies in any future conflict with England's then ally, Spain. Not surprisingly, Mansell spent much of his time aimlessly cruising about, 'awaiting clarification of such impossible instructions'.[24]

The fleet of six royal warships and twelve smaller merchant ships set off from Plymouth Sound on 12 October 1620 on a voyage that would last a full year.[25] As many as a quarter of the sailors may have been press-ganged into joining the force.[26] Tradescant was not yet among them; his ship, the *Mercury*, was still at Ratcliff shipyard along with its sister ship, the *Spy*. Both had been commissioned especially for the Algiers expedition from Master Shipwright Phineas Pett, who would also captain the *Mercury* to the Barbary coast.

Born into a virtual dynasty of shipbuilders and one of the best shipwrights of his day, Captain Pett had good royal connections[27] but also stood accused in two major fraud and naval mismanagement scandals. Although the king cleared him of the earlier charge, which involved selling for private gain the cargo of a ship fitted out entirely at the state's expense, in collusion with his 'very good friends' Sir Robert Mansell and Sir John Trevor, it seems likely that the charges were well founded and that all three had set out to defraud the state.[28] Even on the commission to build two ships for the Algiers expedition, Pett had tried to boost his profits by unilaterally increasing their size 'upon some hopes of thanks and reward', as he said himself somewhat disingenuously in his autobiography. The trick did not work, however, and the merchants who were footing the bill refused to pay for the extra tonnage, leaving Pett with debts of £700 (or so he claimed); 'notwithstanding I was forced to hasten the business and to keep extraordinary numbers of workmen at great rates, and in a place where the provision and materials were nightly stolen and embezzled to my utter undoing.'[29]

While Pett was still finishing off his two ships at Ratcliff on the Thames, the main fleet made its way down the Iberian peninsula, reaching Gibraltar at the end of October, then sailing along the Spanish coast and stopping briefly at Malaga and Alicante to take on provisions. After 'being fitted with Wine, Water, and other such necessaryes', they sailed across to the North African coast, dropping anchor at Algiers on 27 November where they attempted to press their demands: the restitution of some 150 English ships captured during the previous five years, together with their cargoes and all the English subjects then living in the town, whether slaves, renegades, boys or freemen. Negotiations dragged on for ten days or so, with endless toings and froings and English complaints about the 'perfidious and fickle' Turks.[30] In the end, all that the English gained for their pains were 'some 40. poore captives, which [the Turks] pretended was all they had in the towne', although even some of these may have been snatched back and locked up again. Acceding to Algerine demands that a consul should stay behind, Mansell had an ordinary seaman dressed up for the part who went ashore to see what he could do to help the English captives left behind.[31] By 8 December, the fleet had set sail for Majorca.

Launched in the middle of October, Pett's two pinnaces, the *Mercury* and the *Spy*, were ready to sail by Christmas, when Tradescant would have joined them with the rest of the crew. The pilot came on board, together with Sir John Ferne (captain of one of Mansell's merchant ships) and Pett's wife, who just that summer had given birth to their eleventh (and last) child.[32] By New Year's Day, the pilot and Pett's wife had departed, but it was the middle of the month before the voyage proper began, and on 8 February 1621 they anchored in Malaga roads with the two supply ships they were accompanying into the Mediterranean. Pett's autobiography passed over the next seven and a half months in silence, presumably because even he was unable to gloss over the combination of incompetence and sheer bad luck that dogged his 'very good friend' Mansell's fleet on its return to Algiers.

The fleet proper meanwhile had been sailing between Majorca, Alicante and Malaga, taking on provisions and offloading their many sick men. They made occasional forays against pirate ships, invariably without success. On Christmas night, for instance, they chased eight or nine Turkish ships 'and made divers shot at them, but by reason it was a darke night, and that they sayled better then our ships, they escaped us', wrote sailor John Button in his journal.[33] News from home was no better. When Mansell's fleet anchored at Alicante on 31 December 1620, they were greeted by 'great joyes, triumphs, and solemne processions in the cittie'. The inhabitants were celebrating the overthrow of the king and queen of Bohemia (King James's daughter, Elizabeth Stuart, and her husband), driven from Bohemia by the Catholic forces of the Holy Roman Emperor after reigning for less than a year. It was a joy the English most definitely did not share.

At last the fleet met up with Pett's long-awaited pinnaces; the *Mercury* with Tradescant on board had a burden of 240 tons, sixty-five men and '20 peeces of Brasse ordnance', while the *Spy* was smaller at 160 tons, fifty-five men and eighteen brass guns.[34] Tradescant's pinnace was heavier and better armed than several merchant ships in Mansell's fleet and clearly part of the fighting force, rather than simply a supply ship as has sometimes been supposed.

As the attack on Algiers did not take place until mid-May, Tradescant had nearly three months to botanize in the Mediterranean while the *Mercury* tramped up and down with the rest of the fleet, following Mansell's orders. On 9 March, the *Mercury* sailed for Tétouan on the Moroccan coast, then on to Malaga, where the fleet took on 'some Beereage, Wine, some Wood and Water'. Most probably towards the end of April he visited the island of Formentera, which lies just to the south of Ibiza, as Thomas Johnson records seeing a small red-flowered trefoil he called the 'Rough Starrie headed Trefoile' in 'the garden of Mr. *Tradescant*, who did first bring plants hereof from Fermentera a small Island in the Mediterranean Sea'.[35] According to one member of the expedition, the island was empty of people 'but affoordeth wood in greate aboundance, very easey to be gotten, for yt groweth downe to the sea shore of which the whole ffleete tooke in great store. There is uppon this illand wild hogge and wild asses.'[36]

Another Tradescant introduction from the Mediterranean was a wild pomegranate tree, which bore flowers 'farre more beautiful then those of the tame or manured sort,' in Parkinson's view, 'because they are double, and as large as a double Province Rose, or rather more double, of an excellent bright crimson colour, tending to a silken carnation'. The garden varieties were plentiful in Spain, Portugal, Italy and other warm countries, he said, while English gardeners could preserve them only with great care.[37]

Spring is a magnificent time in the Mediterranean and among the many plants Tradescant saw growing wild in great abundance was the 'Corne Flagge' or gladiolus. 'They grow in France and Italy,' John Parkinson tells us, and about Constantinople, 'being (as is said) first sent from thence. John Tradescante assured mee, that hee saw many acres of ground in Barbary spread over with them.'[38] Tradescant also had time to step ashore on to Spanish soil as he later talked about Spanish onions to Parkinson, who described them as 'both long and flat, very sweete, and eaten by many like an apple, but as John Tradescante saith, who hath beene in Spaine, that the Spaniards themselves doe not eate them so familiarly', preferring our own white onions, 'which they have there more plentifully then their sweete Onions'.[39] Among the plants listed in Tradescant's first plant catalogue of 1634 were several other Mediterranean natives that he may have brought back from his Barbary adventure, among them four rock roses (Cistus), two Smilax, a turpentine tree (Pistacia terebinthus), and perhaps a sweet yellow restharrow (Ononis speciosa).[40]

By the end of April, the fleet had reached Majorca, where they took on more supplies and made their final preparations for the forthcoming attack on Algiers. 'The town of Maiorke is large and well fortified,' wrote one of the participants in his journal, 'the people industrious both men, women and children given to labour, loving and courteous to strangers: here we found all manner of victuals in plenty and at easie rates. Their chiefe Marchandise are Oyle, Wood, and Cheese, wherof the countrey affordeth plenty.'[41]

On 16 May, the fleet set sail for Algiers, 'the wind Easterly a small breath'. Reaching Algiers five days later, they dropped anchor in strict formation. In the middle, closest to the mole, were the six warships and Argall's Golden Phoenix. Their plan was to torch the pirate ships in the harbour by sending in two small ships captured from the Turks and packed with assorted 'fire-workes': dry wood, pitch, resin, tar, and brimstone. Grappling irons would hook the fireboats on to the Algerine ships, while three brigantines were fitted with 'fire-bals, buckets of wildefire, and fire pikes to make their fire-workes fast unto the ships'. Seven further rescue boats were to take to the water, 'well filled with armed men', to protect the attackers. The weather was unkind, however. Three nights running, the attack was aborted when the wind dropped or changed. On the fourth night, after 'a great showre of raine' the wind veered round to the right direction and the deadly flotilla set off once more 'but comming within lesse then Musket shot of the Moulds head it fell calme'. Even worse, the English lost the element of surprise 'by reason of the brightnesse of the moone'. The attack went ahead all the same 'but wanting winde to nourish and disperse the fire', the 'fireworks' had no effect whatsoever. Six men were killed outright, another four or five would later die of their injuries, and thirteen were slightly hurt. No wonder Phineas Pett chose to remain silent about the fleet's achievements.

Adding further insult, the next day four pirate vessels slipped into the harbour, having eluded the six English ships posted by the mole expressly to prevent this. Two nights later, the English drove ashore a Turkish vessel with 130 aboard, including twelve Christian captives. All drowned apart from a dozen Turks who made their way safely to land. This they learnt from two Genoese captives who swam out to the fleet, which now stood out to sea. The captives also told them that, had they waited, they could have captured more pirate ships that had slipped into port but now the Turks had strung a boom across the harbour, making further entry impossible.

It was altogether a humiliating failure. By early June the fleet had sailed away from the Barbary coast once more, heading for Spain. Four of the royal warships and five of the merchant ships returned home, leaving Mansell and his remaining fleet starved of victuals but still with orders to patrol the Mediterranean. International relations – especially between Catholics and Protestants – were deteriorating as the twelve-year truce between the United Provinces and Spain came to an end. The English fleet might be needed closer to home and so in September it was finally recalled, by which time Mansell had already turned home in advance of his orders.

Mansell had precious little to show for his year at sea, apart from a few rescued Christian captives and the occasional captured prize, including a ship from Leghorn (Livorno in Italy) carrying Jewish merchants and a 'Flemming' bound for trade with Algiers, 'laden with Venice cloth, Legorne dishes, and divers other commodities: there was also found in her two or three thousand pound in ready money'.[42] But the seas were no safer, as John Chamberlain indicated to Sir Dudley Carleton in a letter of October 1621. Travellers still needed God's help to 'escape the pirats who are strong and busie abroad ... Yt seemes our fleet set out against them the last yeare did little goode, and went neither to Gravesend, nor Ostend, nor to no end.'[43]

Captain Phineas Pett arrived back in England in late September, 'and the 20th day at night, I came safe to my house at Chatham, finding my wife and children all in good health, for which mercy of God I gave God thanks, as did also my whole family'.[44] Tradescant may have come home earlier, transferring to one of the ships that left the Mediterranean in July. He would have fretted about getting his plants back safely and Wotton must have wanted his gardener back home. One imagines he returned to Canterbury with his head full of Moorish gardens like the rose-entwined crystal fountains of the Paradise Gardens east of Fez, seen by traveller John Leo[45], or the fruit gardens of Tagodast with their enormous quinces and vine-draped bowers, 'the Grapes whereof being red, are for their bignesse called in the language of that people, *Hennes egs*'.[46] And when he looked on the pirate stronghold of Algiers, he might – like Leo – have seen its beauty as well as its fortifications. 'In the Suburbs are many Gardens replenished with all kinds of fruit,'[47] wrote Leo, including, no doubt, the sweet and delicate apricot, which Tradescant so proudly brought home with him.

Although he does not yet seem to have been collecting rarities in any systematic sense, Tradescant may also have packed a few Mediterranean items into his bags such as shoes from Spain, North Africa and Turkey; a Spanish toothpick; some 'Barbary Spurres pointed sharp like a Bodkin'; a Spanish tambourine; and various small Turkish objects, including a leather travelling bucket and a 'Hand of Jet usually given to children, in *Turky*, to preserve them from Witchcraft'.[48] His collection of rarities would also include some historical items such as an iron manacle supposedly taken from the Spanish fleet of 1588 and sixteenth-century medals of Philip II of Spain. And among the benefactors to his collection appear the names of Sir John Trevor and 'Mr Pette', who must surely be the *Mercury's* captain, Phineas Pett.

Chapter Twelve

Trunks *and* Treasures

Tradescant stayed with Wotton at Canterbury for a period of between five and nine years. As a gardener he was marking time: apart from visits from his friend Parkinson and Sir Henry Mainwaring, Tradescant's achievements in the garden went unremarked. But he clearly remained visible to the rich and powerful. While Wotton's star was slowly fading (he would die in 1626, having retired to Boughton Malherbe after exclusion from the Privy Council on the grounds of his Catholicism), his gardener continued to rise in the world and we next find him working for King James's all-powerful favourite George Villiers, by now 1st Duke of Buckingham and Lord Admiral of England. Naval connections may even have brought Tradescant to Buckingham's notice and Buckingham was accustomed to getting what he wanted, in the private no less than in the public sphere.

The first record of Tradescant's change of employment appears in the personal account book kept by Buckingham's Treasurer, (Sir) Sackville Crowe.[1] Tradescant is performing for the duke the same service that recommended him to Robert Cecil: journeying into the Low Countries to buy trees. 'Paide to John Tradescant by his L[ordshi]ps order for his journey into the Lowe Countries for his charges and Trees bought for his L[ordshi]p there: £124.14,' reads the entry among other expenses paid from

Buckingham's private purse in the months up to March 1624, following Buckingham's madcap (but unsuccessful) journey to Spain with Prince Charles to woo the Spanish infanta for the prince.

It was an intriguing appointment that saw Tradescant move away from the garden to a much more personal role within the duke's household. Then in his mid-fifties, Tradescant found himself for the second time in his life working for the most powerful man in England after the king, but in most other respects his employers could not have been more different. While Cecil had surmounted physical shortcomings to inherit his father's position, Buckingham owed everything to his long-legged charm and sophisticated French gloss, acquired during an extended stay in Blois and Angers while he was in his late teens.[2]

The second son of his father's second marriage, Buckingham was born in August 1592 at Brooksby Hall in Leicestershire, where his ancestors had 'chiefly continued about the space of four hundred yeers, rather without obscurity, then with any great luster',[3] according to his first biographer, the ever-diplomatic Sir Henry Wotton. Buckingham was in his early twenties when he caught the king's eye in 1614 on one of James's progresses through Northamptonshire. From then on his rise was meteoric as he quickly supplanted the king's previous favourite, Robert Carr, created Earl of Somerset the year before.

James had married his Danish queen Anne in 1587 (their first few months of marriage were spent at Elsinore where 'the pervasive mood was alcoholic')[4] and although he did not much care for women, he did his duty when required and fathered a number of children. All his favourites were men, starting with his much elder kinsman, Esmé Stuart, 6th Sieur d'Aubigny, who had arrived at the Scottish court when James was just thirteen. Timorous and bullied by his tutors and the Scottish lords who jostled for position around the 'cradle king', James had immediately succumbed to d'Aubigny's French dazzle.[5] This early experience set the template for his later male relationships with one significant difference: after d'Aubigny, it was James who would become the wise and generous 'uncle' towards his younger favourites. 'Dear Dad and Gossip' is how Buckingham addressed the king in his letters, which are remarkable for their vigour if marred, inevitably, by their ingratiating tone.

Cupbearer, knight, gentleman of the bedchamber, master of the horse, baron, viscount, Lord Lieutenant of Buckinghamshire, earl, privy councillor, marquess, Lord Admiral of England and finally the reward of a dukedom while still in Madrid with Prince Charles – Buckingham was 'the first duke for nearly a century to have no trace of royal blood in his veins'.[6] Within ten years of springing to the king's notice he straddled the kingdom like one of the Barbary mares he so astutely introduced into the royal stables, able to tug the king's head this way and that, and mostly getting what he wanted. Although he became the most hated man in England, feared for the very real power he wielded, he exerted enormous charm on those close to him[7] and cut an undeniably elegant figure on the dance floor. The chaplain to the new Venetian ambassador described a court masque in January 1618 when the king, naturally quick-tempered, upbraided his courtiers for their slowness at taking up the dance.

Upon this, the Marquis of Buckingham, his Majesty's favourite, immediately sprang forward, cutting a score of lofty and very minute capers, with so much grace and agility that he not only appeased the ire of his angry lord, but rendered himself the admiration and delight of everybody. The other masquers, thus encouraged, continued to exhibit their prowess one after another, with various ladies, also finishing with capers and lifting their goddesses from the ground. We counted thirty-four capers as cut by one cavalier in succession, but none came up to the exquisite manner of the marquis.[8]

Whatever the physical nature of Buckingham's relationship to his sovereign, James had allowed – even encouraged – his favourite to marry, approving his choice of Katherine Manners, the plain but spirited and enormously wealthy daughter of the Earl of Rutland, once she had renounced her Roman Catholicism. They were eventually married in May 1620, the year after the death of Queen Anne, and James showered Kate with real kindnesses, watching over her like a father when she sickened with

George Villiers,
Duke of Buckingham.

smallpox after the birth of the couple's first daughter; and sending her presents of dried plums and grapes, a box of violet cakes and some chickens.[9] It was by all accounts a happy marriage, despite Katherine's temper and Buckingham's frequent absences on his master's business.

Unlike Robert Cecil and Lord Burghley before him, Buckingham has not come down to us as a great plant lover (trees excepted). He did like houses and property in grand settings, however, and by the time Tradescant went to work for him he had four, all of which Tradescant would have known well. First came Burley-on-the-Hill in Rutland, which had passed by inheritance to Lucy Harington, Countess of Bedford, a great gardener in her own right who is associated with fine gardens at Twickenham Park (once Sir Francis Bacon's), Woburn Abbey and Moor Park in Hertfordshire. Badly in debt, the countess sold Burley to Buckingham for £14,000 plus the transfer to her of one of his Warwickshire properties, which effectively doubled the purchase price.[10] When diarist John Evelyn visited in the 1650s, he said Burley was 'worthily reckon'd among the noblest seates in England, situate on the brow of an hill, built *a la modern* neere a Park Waled in, & a fine Wood at the descent'.[11]

Buckingham's next property was Wallingford House in London where the Admiralty now stands on Whitehall, a prime location he bought from William Knollys, Viscount Wallingford, for the knock-down price of £3,000, reputedly as part of a deal to secure the freedom of Wallingford's sister-in-law, the Countess of Somerset. Following her marriage to the Earl of Somerset (the king's favourite before Buckingham), she had been imprisoned in the Tower along with her husband for the murder of Sir Thomas Overbury, who had threatened to stand in their way. 'Some think the deliverie of the Lord of Somerset and his Lady out of the Towre was part of the bargain,' confided the ever-watchful John Chamberlain to his friend Sir Dudley Carleton at The Hague.[12]

Buckingham's other London property also came to him as part of a faintly underhand deal – the much grander York House (previously Norwich Place) on the fashionable riverside of the Strand, giving easy access to Whitehall and the king. Then owned by the archbishops of York, it had traditionally been leased to successive Lord Chancellors or Keepers of the Great Seal and was currently let to Sir Francis Bacon.[13] Born in the house during his father's tenure as keeper, Bacon had taken out a twenty-one-year lease in 1617 when he became Lord Chancellor but his political star had burnt brightly for just three years before it expired with an enormous bang when – despite Buckingham's support – he was found guilty of taking bribes in the sale of patents and monopolies. Thrown out of office for life, fined a massive £40,000, imprisoned for a short time in the Tower and banished from court, he could have no possible use for such a grand riverside residence. Or so Buckingham thought, and conveniently offered to take it off his hands. Bacon, however, was enormously fond of the place and needed considerable persuasion before he agreed to surrender the remainder of his lease to Buckingham for £1,300.

All that remains of Buckingham's grand London house is the watergate by master mason Nicholas Stone, a close associate of Inigo Jones. Now marooned in a small public park and flanked incongruously with municipal bamboo, it marks the Thames' northern shoreline before the nineteenth-century embankment shifted the river southwards. Through its rusticated arch, Buckingham (and perhaps also his gardener) often alighted for journeys to Whitehall or further upstream to Chelsea and Richmond, paying his waterman anything from 5s to £1 or £2 and once as much as £10 for the short trip to Somerset House.[14]

Buckingham's fourth property was New Hall in Essex, which gave him a palatial country retreat close enough to London for occasional grand entertaining. One of Henry VIII's 'greate' houses[15] and later modernized by the Earl of Sussex, New Hall cost Buckingham £20,000, considered at the time a great bargain as it came with much land and annual rents. The house alone had 'cost £14,000 the building, which is now altering and translating according to the moderne fashion by the direction of Innigo Jones the Kings surveyor'.[16] Since providing masques and architectural drawings for Robert Cecil, Jones had made a second journey to Italy (in 1613–14) with the Earl of Arundel, bringing back the classical proportions and monumentality of antique Rome and the Italian Renaissance to an England reared on medieval gothic.

Once again, Buckingham stood at the vanguard of English taste, driving his avenues in the French style across the gently undulating Essex countryside. The best description comes to us from John Evelyn's visit during the Commonwealth when he wrote glowingly of the

garden a faire plot, & the whole seate well accommodated with water; but above all the Sweete & faire avenue planted with stately Lime-trees in 4 rowes for neere a mile in length: It has 3 descents which is the onely fault, & may be reformed. There is another faire walk of the same at the Mall & wildernesse, with a Tenis-Court,[17] & a pleasant Terrace towards the Park, which was well stored with deere, & ponds.[18]

It was an image that recurred in *Sylva*, Evelyn's great work on trees written to encourage the planting of oaks for the navy (Buckingham would surely have approved) when he hoped that more country gentlemen's estates should be 'crown'd and incircl'd with such stately rows of *Limes, Firs, Elms* and other ample, shady and venerable *Trees* as adorn *New-Hall* in *Essex*.[19]

Even today, in New Hall's reincarnation as an independent Catholic boarding school for girls, the effect is stately and impressive, although the approach has been much shortened, and the original avenue long since replaced with just a single avenue of lime trees inside an outer flanking of young oaks and other sheltering trees. The three 'descents' criticized by Evelyn are mere bumps in the terrain, which he wanted flattened to intensify the approaching visitor's sense of awe. As the avenue trees matured they would in any case have obscured the full extent of the house and its imposing gateway (now demolished) into the courtyard.

Trees were, in fact, Buckingham's passion and they came to Buckingham from all quarters: 'one thousand timber trees of Oake' from King James's woods in Kent, to which Charles I later added another 500;[20] 1,000 walnut trees from the Earl of Northumberland, for which his man was given £20 and a further £25 paid for their carriage to Burley;[21] fir tree seeds by the thousands chivvied out of John, Earl of Mar, by his cousin Thomas, Earl of Kellie, with further instructions from the king to 'send one to Burleigh with 4 or 5 thousand of them, with the like instructions of time, place, and maner of setting and preserving them'.[22] In an undated letter to his king addressed as usual to 'Dear Dad and Gossip', Buckingham enthused about another wood he had found, which he was determined to include with the rest, 'and two hundred acres of meadowland, with broome closes and plentiful springs running through them, so that I hope Newhall Park shall be nothing inferior to Burlie'.[23]

The same letter contained a curious reference to Mountain Jennings, Tradescant's fellow gardener at Hatfield, who was then gardening for the king at Theobalds. After thanking James for his excellent 'melons, pears, sugared beans, and assurance of better fruit planted in your bosom than ever grew in paradise', Buckingham told him about a plan he was hatching to get Mr Jennings to plant some trees for the king, referring to the gardener as 'the fittest man we could have chosen for this business'. Something clearly went wrong, for in the accounts for 1624, against the record of £50 paid to 'Jenninges the Housekeep at Theobalds for the setting of those Trees wch my Lord sent the king', Sackville Crowe has written in the margin that 'This my Lord would not have comaunded againe though it were for the [king's] use'.[24]

It has always been assumed that, as Tradescant went tree-buying for Cecil and Buckingham, he must also have overseen the planting of avenues and other trees at New Hall and Burley, but Sackville Crowe's account book suggests otherwise. True, Crowe's accounts relate to Buckingham's private purse rather than to his estates, so they cover extraordinary items and not regular household payments such as wages. Nevertheless, late in 1624 – when Tradescant was already recorded as working for the duke – two other 'Gardiners', named as Robert Phippes and Richard Harris, received significant payments for providing trees (in one entry, specifically elms) and taking them to New Hall: first £200, then a further £100 on 27 November, then £75 15s to Harris alone, and a final sum of £250 'Paide to Harris and Phippes in full for the Trees brought and sent to Newhall between Micha[elma]s and Christmas'.[25] While the accounts do not say whether Phippes and Harris actually planted the trees as well, Sackville Crowe makes two claims for journeys he undertook himself to Newhall in connection with the trees, the second time staying '6 daies to overlook ye setting of the trees'. It is inconceivable that Crowe would have done this if the experienced Tradescant had been on hand to supervise the work, so Tradescant, it seems, was moving beyond his station as a gardener, although that was how he continued to be publicly described.[26]

Of all Buckingham's properties, the most sumptuous was his London riverside residence, York House, which he redesigned to house his growing art collection, and used for entertaining on a grand scale. In charge of works was the duke's art adviser, Balthazar Gerbier, the 'excitable little adventurer' with his 'astonished protuberant eyes' and 'full, petulant mouth'.[27] Born in Middelburg of French Huguenot parents,[28] Gerbier had come to England in 1616 with the help of the Dutch ambassador, Sir Noel Caron, and entered Buckingham's service. Although contemporaries viewed his career with 'a mixture of irritation and odium'[29] – and Gerbier's own talents as an artist were not of the first rank – as a connoisseur and art custodian he amply repaid Buckingham's trust.

Buckingham had already started his improvements to York House when the lease was legally transferred late in 1624, and the frantic rebuilding must have reminded Tradescant of Hatfield House. Gerbier himself described how 'there hath been much daubing and breaking through old rotten decayed Walls', even before the purchase was completed, and rooms had to be quickly prepared for foreign princes and ambassadors, 'so as on a suddain, all the Butterises that upheld that rotten Wall were thrown down, the Seelings of Roomes supported with Iron-bolts, Belconies clapt up in the old Wall, daubed over with finishing Morter'.[30] Not surprisingly, the moral that Gerbier drew from this experience was never to begin building on a piece of ground before it was properly purchased, and he tellingly went on to write a guide designed to help gentlemen avoid being swindled by their builders.[31] He was nonetheless proud of the increasing splendour of York House, where he was keeper of Buckingham's art collection. 'The surveyor Inigo Jones has been at York House to see the house, and he was like one surprised and abashed,' wrote Gerbier to Buckingham from Gravesend. 'It would only require me to get the reversion of his place to be an eye-sore to him, for he is very jealous of it.'[32]

The gardens, too, received the best that money could buy. The Parliamentarian Sir Thomas Wentworth described for a friend's benefit 'a goodly statue of stone, set up in the garden before the new building, bigger than the life, of a Samson with a Philistine between his legs, knocking his brains out with the jawbone of an ass'.[33] In fact, the statue was a magnificent mannerist composition by the Flemish-born Italian sculptor Giambologna, given originally to Prince Charles when he and Buckingham were in Spain to woo the infanta. After the prince's ardour cooled, he gave the statue to Buckingham to adorn the gardens of York House, where it was known rather strangely as *Cain and Abel*. Henry Peacham much admired it in the new chapter on antiquities that he added to his celebrated guide to princely behaviour, *The Compleat Gentleman*, considering that the York House garden 'will bee renowned so long as *John de Bologna's Cain* and *Abel* stand erected there, a peece of wondrous Art and Workemanship'.[34] The Giambologna now adorns the new sculpture gallery at London's Victoria and Albert

Museum while the fountain that originally accompanied it reputedly rests in the gardens of Aranjuez, once the summer residence of Spanish kings.

These four properties – in London, Essex and Rutland – would all have become familiar to John Tradescant as he travelled between them on the duke's business. The one letter from him, preserved among the nation's state papers (see Chapter 13) was written from New Hall in July 1625 and it seems reasonable to assume that he made this his base. His son John was then approaching seventeen and was in all probability already being trained to work alongside his father, just as he would train his own son John to work with him in the Lambeth garden. Whether the elder Tradescant's wife was still alive, we do not know, nor is it possible to chart his progress in the duke's gardens as it had been at Hatfield.

Tradescant was in any case taking on more intimate responsibilities within the duke's household as confirmed by his next entry in Buckingham's private accounts. Once again it relates to a foreign journey, this time made by Buckingham to France to bring back Prince Charles's eventual bride, the fifteen-year-old French princess Henrietta Maria, sister to the king of France, Louis XIII.

After the Spanish match had fallen through, the choice of a bride for the future king of England had narrowed to the French princess, a Catholic like the Spanish infanta, who would therefore need papal dispensation to marry a Protestant. Negotiations for the marriage, and for a treaty of friendship between England and France, had dragged on through most of 1624, embroiled in the political and religious fallout resulting from the eviction from Bohemia of Frederick and Elizabeth, King James's son-in-law and daughter. By mid-March 1625, everything was ready. Buckingham was about to set off for Paris where he would stand proxy for Charles at a French wedding ceremony, then bring England's new queen back across the Channel. Indeed, a number of his coaches had already left for Dover, bearing part of the magnificent wardrobe he would need for such a ceremonial occasion. In addition to twenty-seven embroidered suits richly laced with 'silk and silver plusches', Buckingham intended to enter Paris resplendent in a suit made of rich white satin and burnt velvet, 'sett all over both suite and cloak with Diamonds the value whereof is thought to be fourscore thousand pounds besids a feather made with great Diamonds'. Diamonds also studded his sword, girdle, hatband and spurs. For the wedding itself, he planned to wear a suit of 'purple satten Imbroidred all over with ritch orient pearle the Cloak made after the Spanish fashion with all things suitable the value whereof will be 20,000 *l*'.[35]

Before Buckingham could set off for Paris, word came that James was seriously ill at Theobalds. Buckingham rushed to the king's side as did his mother, the Countess of Buckingham. Both ministered to James – it was even rumoured their plasters and 'posset-drinks' hastened his end – but on 27 March 1625 the king died. 'The corps was brought from Tiballs [Theobalds] on Monday night and passed through Smithfeild about nine a clocke,' wrote an older, sadder Chamberlain, 'so through Holbourn, Chauncerie-lane, and the Strand to Denmarke House, where yt reposes till the tenth of the next moneth apointed for the funerall ... The shew wold have ben solemne but that yt was marred by fowle weather, so that there was nothing to be seen but coaches and torch.'[36] The funeral was held on 7 May, 'the greatest indeed that ever was knowne in England', with black mourning distributed to more than nine thousand individuals and a magnificent hearse 'wherein Inigo Jones the survayer, did his part'. Despite all the pomp, 'the order was very confused and disorderly; the whole charge is said to arise to above 50,000*li*.'[37]

By the time Buckingham was able to leave for Paris to escort Charles's bride back to England, the short wedding ceremony had already taken place in front of Notre Dame Cathedral, the Duc de Chevreuse standing proxy for Charles instead of Buckingham. Buckingham journeyed with just three gentlemen in his retinue: the Earl of Montgomery, 'Mr Secretarie Moulton' (Sir Albert Morton, the newly appointed Secretary of State) and Sir George Goring. They sailed from Dover, liberally tipping everyone: the soldiers at the fort, the ship's master, the pilot, the ship's company, the French pilot, the boatmen of Boulogne who had the privilege 'to bringe all Straungers on Shoare', and the French postmaster's wife and daughter in memory of their 'good usage' on the abortive Spanish trip.[38] To save time, they travelled mostly by horseback, hiring just twenty horses at each stage so they were taking relatively few servants. (The original plan had allowed for at least 250 members of the household, including twenty-two watermen dressed in 'skycollored taffaty all guilded with anchorage and my Lords Armes'.[39]) Buckingham's fine clothes travelled separately – in the good care of John Tradescant, who was advanced £20 'for his journey to Paris with my Lords stuff & Trunkes etc'.[40] Inside the trunks was doubtless the resplendent, diamond-spattered white suit, as one of Buckingham's recorded expenses was £125 for four suits 'and for the lining for his L[ordshi]ps white embroidered suite'.[41]

Buckingham travelled to Paris by way of Abbeville and Amiens, paying for horses, guides, servants, dinners, ostlers and overnight stays, and distributing largesse as he went – to the poor, to the duke's servant who brought a present of fish, and £50 'To the Companies of the Towne that gave his L[ordshi]p a volley of shott at his L[ordshi]ps coming and parting'. In Paris, where Buckingham stayed at the Duc de Chevreuse's magnificent hôtel, the duke's spending was once again directed towards making a good show and enjoying himself in French courtly society – paying for barbers, needles and white silk pasteboard (used in millinery), several sorts of ribbon, powder for his head, and giving £100 for the king's musicians 'that plaid to his L[ordshi]p at the Duke of Shevereux his house the 22th of May'. Intent on educating his lordship's taste, Balthazar Gerbier had previously told him to observe how the French – and especially the Duc de Chevreuse – displayed their paintings, putting the principal piece over the chimney. 'For all their bravery,' said Gerbier, 'there is still magnificence in gold.'[42]

After he had delivered the duke's trunks, Tradescant stayed on in the French capital to buy trees and flowers, renewing his friendship with the Robins with whom he had sporadically exchanged plants and seeds in the fourteen years since he had visited Paris for Cecil. Jean Robin was now an old man but Vespasien was still active in the service of the French king. Sackville Crowe recorded that Tradescant was given £100 for 'the buying of Trees flowers &c'. He appears in the accounts sandwiched between an English friar (given £50 by his lordship's order) and the great Flemish painter Peter Paul Rubens, paid £500 'for drawing his L[ordshi]ps picture on horsback'. A further £20 was given 'to the Kings Gardiners for divers Plantes presented his Grace by John Tradescant'.[43]

One place Tradescant would almost certainly have visited to buy trees and flowers for Buckingham was the nursery of René Morin, who was in business from at least 1619,[44] and whose fame would later be eclipsed by his younger brother Pierre, known as Pierre the younger or Pierre III. (Confusingly, both René's father and his eldest brother were also called Pierre, and all three brothers were noted florists and collectors.) Pierre Morin the father had gained a reputation as a gardener from about 1575, and after his death in 1617 his large plot of ground in the rue de Thorigny was shared between his three sons.[45] Like Jean Robin before him, René Morin published a plant list, *Catalogus plantarum horti Renati Morini inscriptarum ordine alphabetico* (1621),[46] and both he and his younger brother traded in plants. A specialist in cyclamens, René was particularly interested in shrubs, woody plants, herbaceous perennials, foliage plants and bulbs above all, including among his stock many fashionable hyacinths, grape hyacinths, narcissi, anemones, crown imperials and tulips, 'among which the new species from China were said to be of surpassing beauty'.[47] He shared with Tradescant an interest in North American exotics, and it is probably from this time that the two started to exchange plants.

Tradescant must also have met the younger Pierre, who was connected by marriage to Guy de la Brosse, the royal physician and gardener credited with the eventual founding of the Parisian Jardin des Plantes.[48] Pierre established his own nursery and garden south of the Seine in the Faubourg St Germain, close to La Charité hospital. This is the address he gave in his plant catalogues, which date from mid-century,[49] but his oval garden was already well enough established in 1644 to welcome the diarist and virtuoso John Evelyn, who so admired its design that he later copied it at his Deptford garden, Sayes Court, on the south bank of the Thames. Evelyn described Morin's garden as 'an exact Oval figure planted with Cypresse, cutt flat & set as even as a Wall . . . The Tulips, Anemonies, Ranunculus, Crocus's &c being of the most exquisite' – so rare, in fact, that they 'constantly drew all the

Virtuosi of that kind to his house during the season; even Persons of the most illustrious quality'.[50] Evelyn also admired Morin's extraordinary collection of curiosities, returning for a second visit in 1651.[51]

A sketch of Morin's garden survives in a small leather-bound notebook kept by Richard Symonds in 1649, devoted to the ecclesiastical sights of Paris and its immediate suburbs. Coats of arms and inscriptions were his chief interests, but he also sketched statues, fountains (a fine satyr clutching a dolphin in the Luxembourg Gardens, for instance) and garden plans, occasionally jotting down brief descriptions. He was so taken with Morin's garden that he gave it a double-page spread, picking out the oval beds in green and adding a key to identify the planting. This included: boxes of orange trees, myrtle and phillyrea; tall cypresses used as accent plants; rare tulips, flowers and herbs in the box-edged beds; and green walks of 'Alaternus' (presumably Italian buckthorn, *Rhamnus alaternus*). There were also seed beds to one side and 'od places wherein loosely grow, all Green trees rudely like a wood'.[52] Of course, when Tradescant visited Paris with Buckingham in the summer of 1625, this garden may not yet have taken shape. But he cannot have passed over an opportunity to talk plants and curiosities with men whose careers and interests so closely paralleled his own.

Over the years, Tradescant and his son continued to exchange plants with the Robins and the Morins, even recording the plants received between 1629 and 1633 at the back of Tradescant's own copy of John Parkinson's *Paradisi in Sole Paradisus Terrestris*, now preserved at the Bodleian Library in Oxford.[53] From Morin in 1629, for instance, came a double green anemone, two sorts of double white anemones (including one described as 'thrice fayre'), and several ranunculi (among them the 'Great whyt Renuncculus single'). The Robins were even more generous, sending at various times during the year a tulip, a scarlet lobelia (*Lobelia cardinalis*) and an aster; two irises (including a tiny dwarf Juno iris from the Levant called *Iris persica*); ten different varieties of anemone; and a single rose identified as the Austrian copper rose, *Rosa foetida* 'Bicolor', its petals nasturtium-bright orange on one side reversing to yellow. (Jean Robin died in April that year, so these may have come from his son Vespasien.) Two years later it was René Morin who was the more generous, sending one ranunculus, three narcissi, a yellow flower tentatively identified as the evergreen *Helichrysum stoechas;* and one of the first geraniums to enter Europe from its native South Africa, *Pelargonium triste,* bearing pale star-shaped flowers streaked brownish-purple and sweetly scented at night. (No plants that year are credited to Robin.)

Buckingham stayed in Paris for a week, enjoying an endless round of dancing and festivities but managing also to squeeze in some serious talk with Cardinal Richelieu, confidant to the Queen Mother and chief minister to the French king. He was liberal to the poor and the musicians who had entertained him, including a harpist and a lute player, and he generously rewarded his old fencing and dancing masters whose skills had helped him to advance at court. When he came to leave, he began tipping in earnest, paying out skilfully graded sums to the doorkeepers to the king's chambers and the king's cabinet; to his guard, archers, trumpeters and drummers; to the king's coachmen, footmen and hunting guards; to the hunting grooms of the king's stables and to the retainers of the queen, the Queen Regnant and the Queen Mother; and the huge sum of £500 'to him that brought the Kings Present'.[54]

As there is no separate entry in the accounts for Tradescant's lodging, it seems likely that he would have been accommodated along with the rest of Buckingham's retinue at the Duke de Chevreuse's residence; later, when collecting rarities for Buckingham, he would remember Chevreuse's famous collection and in particular the 'strang fowlls', which his own master (and perhaps he himself) had 'partlie seene'.[55]

On the return journey, Sackville Crowe took charge of Buckingham's trunks, leaving Tradescant free to look after the trees and flowers he had bought in Paris. He may have left the main party and taken them straight home to one or other of Buckingham's properties, thereby missing the meeting of Charles and Henrietta Maria on English soil.[56] By all accounts, it was a nightmarish time for Charles, who had lodged in Canterbury to await his bride, staying at St Augustine's Abbey, the home of Tradescant's former employer Edward, Lord Wotton. Henrietta Maria was delayed first by her mother's illness at Amiens and then by storms; the captain entrusted with bringing her across the Channel was Tradescant's old acquaintance, Phineas Pett. Charles and his court meanwhile kicked their heels in Canterbury, spending their days in conversation and their nights in dancing.[57] It was doubtless during this time that one of Lord Wotton's fountain nymphs lost an arm, as later described by the jovial Lieutenant Hammond. At last, on 12 June, a queasy Henrietta Maria reached Dover and was carried to the town on a litter, then travelled by coach to Dover Castle, which Buckingham had prepared for her at great expense in his role as Lord Warden of the Cinque Ports (a post he had bought from the ageing Lord Zouche the previous year). But the French party turned up their noses at English hospitality; 'Le château est un vieux bâtiment fait à l'antique,' commented the Comte de Tillières, 'où la reine fut assez mal logée pirement meublée' [The castle is an old building done in the old style, where the queen's lodging was poor and its furnishings even worse].[58]

Early the next day, Charles set off for Dover where he dined with the queen, then brought her back to Canterbury by coach, causing the first marital upset by refusing to allow one of Henrietta Maria's attendants to sit with them for the journey. Contemporary accounts reported a warm welcome for the young queen despite her Catholicism, which gave rise to much unease. 'From *Barrome* Downe the King and Queene came the same night to the Citie of *Canterburie*, all the wayes whereupon they rode being strewed with greene rushes, Roses, and the choicest flowers that could be gotten, and the trees loaden with people of all sorts, who with shouts and acclamations gave them a continuall welcome.'[59] There were speeches (which probably bored the king and of which the queen would scarcely have understood one word), then they spent the night together at Canterbury. The occasion is caught by Endymion Porter, one of the grooms of the Bedchamber, who wrote lovingly to his wife the next day in his beautifully rounded hand: 'This last night the king and queene did lie together here att Conterburie, Long maye they do soe, and have as manie children as wee are like to have.'[60]

Buckingham's fine clothes were hauled to Canterbury, then on to Gravesend, where they were embarked on a barge for carriage home: one barge for the servants and another for the trunks. The royal party came in by barge, too, receiving a royal salute from the guns of the Tower of London, 'which did so thunder and rattle in the aire, that nothing could be heard for the terror of the noice'.[61]

That same year (1625), John Tradescant made at least one more journey with Buckingham to the Low Countries, as recorded in Sackville Crowe's account book. (He may also have been the unnamed gardener given £100 to 'goe into Fraunce'.[62]) The purpose of Buckingham's Dutch trip was twofold: to seal an anti-Habsburg alliance with the United Provinces, Denmark and any other countries that could be persuaded to sign the treaty (in the event, none did); and to try to pawn the crown jewels to raise money for Charles – an attempt that raised a paltry £18,355. 15s. 6d from the money lenders of The Hague.[63]

Buckingham's party (which included Lord Holland, his nephew Lord Feilding, and his gardener) crossed over to Holland from Harwich at the beginning of November, taking wagons on to Brill and then small boats to The Hague, where Buckingham stayed with the ambassador, Sir Dudley Carleton, and they were entertained by the Prince of Orange. Here they would also have called on the exiled King and Queen of Bohemia, Charles' sister. Buckingham found time to visit Leiden, where he spent £450 on a collection of exquisite Arabic manuscripts,[64] and where Tradescant presumably spent the £150 he was given for trees.[65]

This is the last appearance that Tradescant makes by name in Sackville Crowe's accounts, although he went with Buckingham to relieve the Huguenots of La Rochelle in 1627 and was most probably still in his service when Buckingham set out on his fatal last trip to Portsmouth the following year. Other gardeners appear in his lordship's private accounts, but none by name. Crowe records £20 given to the 'french Gardiner for the payment of his debtes and for travelling charges', and £5 'Given to the Gardinir of Wallingford house by his L[ordshi]p order complayning that he was not paid'.[66] (This last is reminiscent of an earlier payment 'Given to the Gardiner of the Springe garden a Suite of his L[ordshi]ps cloth, and 5l. in money by an olde promise made by his L[ordshi]p'.[67])

As Tradescant was still being described as the duke's gardener when he set off for La Rochelle, in all probability he remained in overall charge of the duke's gardens. Nevertheless he was branching out in other ways and Buckingham rewarded him with the grandly titled office of yeoman garnetter at Whitehall, overseeing the royal granary. Such lucrative offices depended on patronage, and the way in which they were peremptorily granted and withdrawn caused enormous resentment. The man ousted from the garnetter's post to make way for Tradescant (James Heydon) later petitioned the king for the right to buy a compensatory monopoly: taxing aliens for salted herrings brought into the country, for which he was prepared to pay £50 a year for twenty-one years.[68] Not all monopoly offices were cash cows, however. The previous year, the same James Heydon had petitioned the Secretary of State to complain not only of his ousting by John Tradescant, but of the poor value of the replacement office he had bought: the right to scrap iron, discarded cannons and bullets lying about His Majesty's ports, which proved to be worth much less than the £200 he had offered to the king.[69]

For once, John Tradescant's activities outside the world of gardening were flourishing and as his next venture showed, he was turning his employment with Buckingham to good account. The man who took his lordship's trunks to Paris was also the man who would help him amass treasures of a different kind.

Chapter Thirteen

A Passion for Strangeness

John Tradescant's European journeyings had clearly stirred his curiosity about the natural world and strengthened his passion for the rare, the strange, the exotic and the outlandish. Buckingham's wealth and natural acquisitiveness would enable him to turn curiosity into collecting, ostensibly for his master but almost certainly on his own account, too.

Buckingham already collected paintings, sculptures, tapestries and other works of art by the yard, employing his own scout in Balthazar Gerbier, who toured the art capitals of Europe, his pockets stuffed with cash supplied from the ducal purse by Sackville Crowe, tracking down suitable prizes and negotiating their purchase on Buckingham's behalf. In November 1624, for instance, Gerbier wrote to Buckingham from Boulogne to report progress on his negotiations and to whet his master's appetite with prospective purchases: tapestries to a design by Raphael, 'rich with gold and silver and silk', worth perhaps £15,000 and presently on the road from Antwerp to Paris; more paintings in Paris, including three Raphaels, a Michelangelo, and a Tintoretto of a naked figure, so beautiful 'that flint as cold as ice might fall in love with it'.

In the same letter (written when stormy seas prevented him crossing over to England to talk to Buckingham in person) Gerbier made a dig at Tradescant, who must have earned himself a doleful reputation for his apologies. 'I will not do as John Tredescant,' said Gerbier slyly, 'who asks pardon at the beginning; for as your Excellency well replied to him at Newhall, that, for him who has an evil purpose to offend, asking pardon first is not enough: but at the end, on my knees, my lord, I ask pardon, if my ignorant zeal has made me slip into any fault.'[1] Tradescant clearly lacked a courtier's easy graces but perhaps Gerbier was also worried that Tradescant's interest in rarities might take him into territory that Gerbier considered very much his own.

He need not have worried, for Tradescant's passion was directed towards the wonders not of art but of the natural world, especially the flora and fauna of North America and West Africa. He set out his requests in a letter written on Buckingham's behalf to Edward Nicholas, then Secretary to the Navy and therefore a functionary of Buckingham's in his role as Lord Admiral of England, asking merchants to supply him with all manner of rare beasts, birds and plants.[2] Still preserved among the state papers of the Stuart Crown (and attributed in a pencilled note on the reverse to '*the celebrated John Tradescant*'), the letter begins rather grandly:

Noble Sir,

I Have Bin Comanded By my Lord to let yr worshipe understand that it is His Graces Plesure that ye should In His Name Deall withe All Marchants from All Places But Espetially the Virginie & Bermewde & Newfound Land men that when they [go] Into those parts that they will take Care to furnishe His Grace Withe All Maner of Beasts & fowels & Birds Alyve. Or If Not Withe Heads Horns Beaks Clawes Skins fethers flyes or seeds plants trees or shrubs. Also from [West African] Gine or Binne or Senego turkeye.

Tradescant then mentioned two collectors by name: Sir Thomas Rowe (Roe), ambassador at Constantinople, and Captain Roger North, whom he linked 'to ther New Plantation towards the Amasonians'. More places and objects followed in a jumble: '& Also from the East Indes withe Shells Stones Bones Egge Shells with What Cannot Com Alive'. Remembering the 'strang fowlls' glimpsed at the Duc de Chevreuse's apartments in Paris, he slipped in a request for a 'payer or two' of young Dutch storks 'Withe Divers kinds of Ruffes Whiche they theare Call Campanies', then ran immediately into his final salutation:

This having mad Bould to present my Lords Comand I Desire ye furtherance yr asured servant to be Comanded till He is

Newhall this 31 Day July 1625   John Tradescant

Written more neatly than his Archangel diary, Tradescant's letter has minimal punctuation and no paragraphs; thoughts follow on without logic or spacing, all squashed together yet leaving one third of the page blank. In a more untidy hand he added a more detailed wish-list addressed specifically to 'the marchants of the Ginne [Guinea] Company & the Gouldcost [Gold Coast] Mr humfrie Slainy, Captaine Crispe & Mr Clobery & Mr Johne Wood Capemarchant'.

Letter and list together give us a fascinating insight into Tradescant as a collector: size and strangeness are his chief criteria. Like a tourist describing the marvels he wishes to see, everything must be 'the Bigest that canbe Gotten': the heads of a sea cow (the manatee or dugong) and a river horse (hippopotamus); an elephant's head 'with the teethe in it very larg'; 'the Greatest sorts of Shellfishes Shelles of Great flying fishes & Sucking fishes with what els strang'.

That word again – strange, it sparkles like the shiny stones he was seeking along with the strange sorts of 'fowelles & Birds skines & Beakes, Leggs & phetheres thatbe Rare or Not knowne to us' and the 'strang fishes skines of those parts'. Lacking a vocabulary to name or codify the unknown, he can only pile on the words to communicate the objects of his desire, like the many different sorts of 'serpents & snakes skines & Espetially of that sort that hathe a Combe on his head Lyke a Cock'. The proto-anthropologist within him also seeks West African clothes, weapons and long ivory flutes, while the gardener (and experienced plant collector) puts in a request for 'All sorts of ther fruts Dried As ther tree Beanes Littill Red & Black in ther Cods

Strange fishes from the western coast of Africa.

with what flower & seed Canbe Gotten the flowers layd Betwin paper leaves
In a Book Dried'. Tradescant's sense of wonder is compressed into his final
request for 'Any thing that is strang'. While the earliest Roanoke settlers
reported that native Americans were swiftly disarmed by the 'glasses, kniues,
babies [dolls], and other trifles, which wee thougt they deligted in',[3]
Tradescant experienced a contrary dazzlement at the shimmering wonders of
the natural world.

   As he explained to Nicholas, he was soliciting such treasures not on his
own behalf but for his master Buckingham, who up until then had
concentrated on art and antiquities.[4] Aside from their art collections,
English princes and courtiers had come slowly to the Faustian craze for
collecting natural and artificial rarities that had swept much of Europe,
spawning the *Wunderkammer* of Habsburg rulers such as Emperor Rudolf II,
or the encyclopaedic collections of a Francesco I de' Medici.[5] In England, by
contrast, most displays of natural curiosities had been of the showground

variety, exploiting the gullible and those who liked 'To gaze at trifles, and toyes not worthy the viewing'.[6] But even in England, scholarly collectors or virtuosi had begun to put together cabinets that jostled the wonders of art and nature with the artefacts of newly discovered peoples and continents – the very same sights that had caught Tradescant's eye on his journey to Archangel. As Gerbier had helped to form the duke's taste in art, so would Tradescant direct him in the collection of curiosities, drawing on the models he had seen in England and Europe.

One early English collection that Tradescant would almost certainly have visited belonged to Robert Cecil's associate, Sir Walter Cope. From the end of the sixteenth century, Cope's collection was one of London's sights for gentlemen travellers, immortalized by Swiss medical student Thomas Platter, who paid a visit in 1599 accompanied by 'Herr Lobelus, a London physician' – presumably the great botanist, Matthias de l'Obel or Lobel, later botanist to James I. Wide-eyed with astonishment, Platter followed Cope into an apartment 'stuffed with queer foreign objects in every corner'. Among the noteworthy objects he described were many that would have appealed to Tradescant in their strangeness and beauty: outlandish beasts and fishes vying for attention with man-made treasures and nature's deformities, the weird, the unexpected and the simply fantastical. They included in no particular order (like the collection itself): a petrified thunderbolt; an embalmed child; the bauble and bells of Henry VIII's fool; seals from Queen Elizabeth and the Turkish emperor; flies that glowed at night in Virginia instead of lights, 'since there is often no day there for over a month'; the twisted horn of a bull seal; shoes from many strange lands; the horn and tail of a rhinoceros ('a large animal like an elephant'); a horn that had grown around an Englishwoman's forehead; a pelican's beak ('the Egyptian bird that kills its young, and afterwards tears open its breast and bathes them in its own blood, until they have come to life'); a torpedo fish, which petrified and numbed the hand of anyone who touched it; and a long narrow Indian canoe suspended from the ceiling. Platter gave up compiling a detailed inventory when he reached number fifty on his list, merely adding that Cope 'possessed besides many old heathen coins, fine pictures, all kinds of corals and sea-plants in abundance. There are also other people in London interested in curios, but this gentleman is superior to them for strange objects, because of the Indian voyage he carried out with such zeal. In one house on the Thames bridge I also beheld a large live camel.'[7]

The Cecils, too, were great collectors: Lord Burghley had collected maps, and 'Seaven ould Mappes of divers Countrees' were recorded in an inventory of 1612 as 'given to Jo. Traesc.'.[8] Perhaps he had heard talk of Lord Burghley's own *Wunderkammer*, which included among its treasures a *Handstein*[9] sent from Germany by magus Dr John Dee's notorious medium, Edward Kelley. As well as collecting paintings, like Buckingham, Robert Cecil had enjoyed mechanical curiosities, reputedly enlivening his dinner table with a tame parrot given to him by Sir John Gilbert. 'He must be kept very warm,' advised Gilbert, 'and after he hath filled himself he will set in a gentlewoman's ruff all day.'[10] King James I had a similar love of strange creatures, and so pined to own a flying Virginian squirrel that Shakespeare's patron, the Earl of Southampton, wrote to Cecil to see whether he could obtain one for the king. 'I would not have troubled you with this,' said Southampton, 'but that you know so well how hee is affected to these toyes.'[11]

Tradescant would also have seen a number of foreign *cabinets de curiosités* on his travels, not least the gallery or *Ambulacrum* beside the botanic garden at Leiden and the famed collection of rarities in the public anatomy hall of Leiden's university where dissections took place on a revolving table in a converted chapel. In summer, when the weather was too hot for dissecting corpses, skeletons were exhibited instead.[12] 'In addition to various animals, ranging from a ferret to a horse, the rearticulated skeletons of a number of notorious criminals could be seen,' writes Dr Arthur MacGregor of Oxford's Ashmolean Museum. 'These included the remains of a sheep-stealer from Haarlem and of a woman strangled for theft.' One could also admire an ass's skeleton ridden by a woman who had killed her own daughter, and, astride an ox, the skeleton of a man executed for stealing cattle.[13] An engraving of 1610 included a skeletal Adam and Eve with a (non-skeletal) snake slithering through the tree of the knowledge of good and evil. A woman onlooker is shown inspecting a human skin draped like hosiery over her companion's arm. The times did not yet allow for female squeamishness.

Catalogues and inventories for the Leiden anatomy hall pick out many objects of the type that Tradescant specifically sought from the merchants of the Guinea Company and the Gold Coast: the skin and horn of a rhinoceros head, the head of a seahorse, the snout of strange fishes and the bills of strange birds, the 'bristly Skin of a Brasilian Beast' and the 'Horn of an Outlandish Ox', a coral tree from the East Indies, and a great 'Bloud-stone' from Arabia.[14] Guided by the anatomy-servant, visitors to the anatomy theatre would be overwhelmed by the sheer scale and multiplicity of objects on display – in the entrance hall, hanging from the beams and walls of the anatomy chamber itself, stuffed into little chambers and the growing number of cupboards needed to house the skeletons, rarities, prints, instruments and books that continued to swell the collection.

In Paris, too, were cabinets that would have inspired Tradescant's tastes. Admittedly the royal collections had declined since their brilliance under François I; there was a collection at Fontainebleau and a rather modest 'cabinet de singularitez' at the Tuileries Palace. At the end of his reign, Henri IV had entrusted traveller Jean Mocquet with the task of bringing back plants and rarities from his travels, and although Mocquet dutifully journeyed to the Holy Land and Syria, Henri's assassination brought the plan to a halt. Setting off in 1614 to travel round the world, Mocquet got no further than Spain and his only outcome was a book of his travels published in 1617, *Voyages en Afrique, Asie, Indes Orientales et Occidentales*.[15] The Salle des Antiques next to the Galérie at the Louvre had been finished by 1609 but there was not a great deal in it, and many of France's most avid collectors lived outside Paris (Gaston d'Orléans at Blois, Nicolas-Claude Fabri de Peiresc at Aix, and apothecary Paul Contant at Poitiers).

At least Tradescant had the example of the 'curious' Morin brothers, all three of whom were known to collect shells, corals and marine life as well as flowers.[16] Tradescant would have visited René and almost certainly the other two brothers when he went to Paris with Buckingham in 1625. John Evelyn accorded the younger Pierre Morin the highest praise in 1644, noting how he had passed from being 'an ordinary Gardner' to become one of the most 'skillfull & Curious Persons of France' for his rare collection of shells, flowers and insects. Morin lived in a 'kind of Hermitage at one side of his Garden', explained Evelyn,

where his Collection of Purselan, of Currall, whereof one is carved in a large Crucifix, is greately esteemed: besids his bookes of Prints, those of Alberts [Durer], Van Leydens, Calot, &c. But the very greatest curiosity which I esteemd, for being very ingenious and particular, was his collection of all the Sorts of Insects, especialy of Buter flys ... These he spreads, & so medicates, that no corruption invading them he keepes in drawers, so plac'd that they present you with a most surprizing & delightfull tapissry.[17]

Seven years later, Evelyn paid Morin the compliment of a second visit, this time singling out for special mention his Red Sea crabs. 'He had aboundance of incomparable shells, at least 1000 sorts which furnish'd a Cabinet of greate price, & a very curious collection of Scarabies & Insects, of which he was compiling a natural historie; also the pictures of his Choice flowers & plants in miniature.'[18] Evelyn clearly respected Morin as a fellow virtuoso who intended to publish the fruits of his research: here indeed was no 'ordinary Gardner' in Evelyn's scheme of values.

All these collections would have given Tradescant a clear idea of the kind of treasures he should seek, and Buckingham's naval connections allowed him to reach out wherever ships were trading and exploring. In a world greased by patronage, Tradescant knew that attaching Buckingham's name to a shopping list of treasures would almost certainly guarantee their acquisition. Even merchants and sea captains might find their fortunes dependent on Buckingham's goodwill. Just the following year, Humphrey Slaney (one of the merchants mentioned by name in Tradescant's letter) would petition Buckingham for the return of £850 worth of his goods, which had been taken by pirates to the Barbary port of Salé and later captured by the king's fleet from two Dutch ships and brought into the Thames.[19] Another of the men mentioned by name in the letter was Sir

Thomas Roe, England's ambassador at Constantinople, who tried to obtain Turkish marbles and relics for Buckingham. Roe even bribed Turkish officials to help secure sculptures from the city's Gold Gate but local outcry forced him to give up his plans.[20]

While Tradescant solicited rarities from 'All Marchants from All Places', his detailed list was aimed specifically at merchants and captains trading with Guinea and the Gold Coast, which then included the whole coastal region from Senegal down to the mouth of the Congo in what is now Zaire.[21] English merchants had been trying to gain a toehold in the Portuguese-dominated West African trade since the previous century but, without a base on the coast, their efforts were no more than sporadic. Quarrels with the Portuguese over privateering led the English effectively to abandon the Guinea trade for some years from 1571. But the outbreak of war with Spain in 1585 brought them back, and soon a group of merchants from London and the West Country obtained a patent granting them a ten-year monopoly of English trade with the region. By 1625, the leading English merchants involved in the West African trade included all the men Tradescant mentioned by name in his letter: Humphrey Slaney, William Cloberry, John Wood and Nicholas Crispe.[22]

Early travellers[23] to the West African coast brought back tales of strange and luscious fruits, like those seen by merchant William Finch in Sierra Leone in 1607, including what was surely one of the first English descriptions of a banana: 'They have certain Fruits growing six or eight together on a Bunch, each as long and big as a Man's Finger, of a brown, yellowish Colour, and somewhat downy, containing within the Rind a certain pulpy Substance of pleasant Taste.'[24]

Even stranger were the birds, like the turkey-sized 'Comb-Bird' of Senegal, its grey feathers streaked black and white: 'They have large Wings, which they use but little, perhaps because their Strength is not pro-portionable to their Bulk. They walk as gravely as *Spaniards*, carrying their Heads lofty, which is covered . . . with a Kind of soft Hair about four or five Inches long. This hair hangs down on each Side, and is frizzled at the End, which has given Occasion to the Name.'[25] Other birds seen in West Africa

included one with four wings; another called the Ha! Ha! Bird ('good to
eat, and remarkable for its repeating, distinctly and articulately, the syllables
Ha! Ha! so clearly that you take it for the Voice of a Man'); and an
apparently legless bird that hung motionless from trees with the aid of two
strings, 'in Colour, so like a dead, or withered Leaf, that he can hardly be
discovered'.[26] (In fact, the legs had probably been removed by local traders,
as happened to the first birds of paradise to reach European collections.)

The West African water creatures, too, were just as Tradescant desired:
the great sea cow or manatee, timid despite its great bulk, up to eighteen feet
long and five feet in diameter. 'It is round from the Head to the Navel, and
then flatten by Degrees, forming a Tail, which resembles, in Shape, a Baker's
shovel.'[27] The torpedo or numb fish received minute inspection, starting
with the eyes and ending with the brain.[28] Here, too, were swordfishes, sea
tortoises, crocodiles and the river horse or hippopotamus, when fully grown
'about a Third bigger than a large Ox, whom he resembles in some Parts, as
he does the Horse in others'.[29]

Such were the wondrous creatures that Tradescant solicited, apparently
on his master's behalf, and one imagines that merchants sent in the beasts,
birds, fishes and assorted body parts as requested. Immediately on receipt of
Tradescant's letter, Secretary Nicholas noted in the margin: 'Letters to be
written to the marchants of Gynny according to this now delivered to me by
Mr Carey.' One merchant wrote to his factor overseas, requesting '2 or 3
Apes', but forgot to add the 'r' in 'or', so it looked like 203. Eighty were sent
at once, and the rest promised on the next ship.[30]

The records are strangely silent on whether Buckingham's 'collection' ever
had a separate existence, or whether he simply allowed Tradescant to use his
name. Certainly no detailed reports have come to us of the wonders seen in
any Buckingham cabinet. French physician Pierre Borel would later list it –
along with Tradescant's collection and a possible third collection 'à la maison
des oiseaux' (at the house of the birds) – in a gazetteer of European cabinets de
curiosités published in 1649.[31] But Borel's list was out of date on several
important collections that had been long dispersed by the time his book
appeared, so we cannot trust him as a reliable source.[32] The great

Buckingham art collection lasted only to the civil war, when the 2nd Duke sold some two hundred paintings in Antwerp in 1648, while other paintings passed into English hands.[33]

It is tempting to think that many of the strange beasts and birds sent to Buckingham found their way to Tradescant's own collection at South Lambeth; the names of 'George Duke of Buckingham' and 'Lady Katharine Dutchess of Buck.' appear immediately after King Charles and Queen Henrietta Maria in the list of benefactors to the collection in 1656.[34] In his will, Buckingham had instructed his wife Kate to look after the servants not mentioned by name so she may have continued her late husband's generosity towards his gardener.[35]

Yet despite Tradescant's fervent entreaties to the merchants of Guinea and the West African coast, the museum catalogue of 1656 lists relatively few items specifically from 'Ginny': just rabbits, the 'Foot of a Ginny Dogge', bows and arrows, a 'Ginny Drum made of one piece' (still surviving in the Ashmolean collection), three sorts of knives, bracelets, a lantern, drinking cups made of birch, and plates made of rushes. Ivory spoons and an ivory horn may also have come from the West African littoral, as well as unidentified plumes or parts of birds, like the 'Feathers of divers curious and strange forraign Birds'.[36] The Tradescants did, indeed, show a hippopotamus, and several of the birds and fishes described by early travellers to West Africa, so perhaps the catalogue simply failed to locate specimens precisely.

If nothing else, the contacts Tradescant made using Buckingham's name allowed him to develop good relations with merchants such as Humphrey Slaney whose treasured goods would continue to come to him after the duke's death. At the back of his copy of Parkinson's *Paradisi in Sole*, he noted the receipt of two precious plants in 1629: an oriental plane tree (*Platanus orientalis*), and the smoke tree, *Cotinus coggygria*, that grows wild from southern Europe to central China. Neither was a new introduction; Gerard had listed the plane tree in his garden catalogues of 1596 and 1599,[37] but it would prove a valuable addition to Tradescant's garden where it was later joined by the occidental plane tree brought back from Virginia by

Tradescant's son. Their chance mating would produce the London plane tree, *Platanus × hispanica*, which has become a stalwart of the capital's streets and parks. As both parents were growing with the Tradescants in the mid-1650s, the union could have happened in Lambeth, although the first to recognize the London plane as a new variety was Jacob Bobart the younger at the Oxford Physic Garden.[38]

In the spring of 1627, however, Tradescant's thoughts would have been far away from his garden. Now in his late fifties, he was about to embark on his last foreign mission with Buckingham, one with far more serious implications than a wedding journey to Paris with his master's trunks. This time his employer was taking him to war and we can only assume that he willingly accepted the challenge.

Chapter Fourteen

To *the* Aid *of the* Huguenots

The campaign in which Tradescant became embroiled was sparked by
Europe's simmering religious animosity, exacerbated by the perennial
hostility between the English and the French. As Lord Admiral of England,
Buckingham was responding to appeals for help from French Huguenots in
their stronghold at La Rochelle on France's south-western coast, where they
feared assault from the Catholic forces of Cardinal Richelieu, Louis XIII's
chief minister. Married to the French king's sister, King Charles I of England
was effectively going to war with his brother-in-law.

For Buckingham, taking his gardener to war made perfect sense. Skilled at
transforming parks into gardens with terraces, raised walks and sunken
plumbing to feed the fountains, Tradescant would bring to the enterprise his
engineering skills in digging trenches and raising defensive earthworks to protect Buckingham's troops. Soon formal gardens would themselves adopt the
outward forms of military design, incorporating bastions, waterworks and
ramparts to bring interest and complexity to otherwise dull landscapes.[1]
Buckingham was simply initiating that process in reverse – putting his
gardener's skills to work for his military aims, just as he turned to his art adviser, Balthazar Gerbier, for help in designing mines.[2] Gerbier had even received
early training in the 'Framing of Warlike Engines', along with the other gentlemanly skills of writing, drawing, mathematics, geometry and architecture.

The engineer's role in warfare was becoming ever more critical, especially in the kind of siege situation that Buckingham would face in his French campaign. Old-style city walls (tall and thin) offered scant protection against metal cannonballs; instead defenders needed solid, sloping bastions and star-shaped defences that kept the besieging enemy always in sight. From the attackers' point of view, sieges 'became a matter of digging passageways and building mounds of earth to protect soldiers. Warfare was won less by wounding enemies than engineering the landscape to favor the objectives of one army over another.'[3] Sadly for Buckingham and his engineers (Tradescant included), the engineering of earthworks contributed to some of the greatest mishaps of the campaign.

Buckingham's expedition to the Ile de Ré off the coast of La Rochelle is a story of early promise and valour turned sour by inexperience and indecision. Europe's powers were engaged in complicated manoeuvrings for supremacy, and although the fundamental divide was between the largely Catholic South and the largely Protestant North, and between the Habsburgs and everyone else, alliances were constantly shifting. At least Buckingham's objectives in taking his fleet to relieve the Protestant Huguenots of La Rochelle were relatively clear: to check the power of Cardinal Richelieu; to deal a blow to French naval ambitions; and to win popularity for himself.[4] For this last to work, he needed to lead the expedition in person, yet such was the public's distrust that most people assumed he would cede command at the last moment. Fittingly for a man dedicated to appearances, Buckingham declared his intentions through his wardrobe, a hint picked up by the Florentine resident who carefully reported 'the military costume which he wears, with an immense collar and magnificent plume of feathers in his hat'.[5]

The duke's steady preparations for war are evident in Sir Sackville Crowe's meticulous accounts, as transparent as any diary,[6] starting in spring 1627 with the purchase, sewing and washing of linens and cambrics for himself and his pages, at a cost of several thousand pounds. A host of clothing-related bills followed to pay for new outfits and trimmings supplied by his mercer, draper, hosier, milliner, furrier, haberdasher, embroiderer, upholster, gilder, goldsmith, jeweller, cutler, shoemaker and spurrier, all separately listed. He paid the enormous sum of £1,080 6s to Captain Benjamin Henshaw, described as 'Silkman', and spent £28 on gold and silver buttons. He was also buying outfits for his attendants, including twenty pairs of shoes, stockings and shirts for his labourers. As this was war, he wisely paid £50 to his apothecary, Edward Taylor, and a lesser amount to his surgeon, Walter Preiste.[7] Although in good health and fine spirits, he took to his bed for several days beforehand to gather his strength.[8]

In contrast to earlier adventures, the duke understandably spent little on entertainment and leisure, apart from music, making several payments to musicians and for musical instruments. He bought a new case for his harp and spent £49 at his bookseller's. In a flash of extravagance he paid Mr Walsingham Grisly £367 8s 6d for the Earl of Bristol's silver perfuming pan; and returned the £13 he had borrowed from Mr Edward Clark at the gaming tables. He no longer lost at tennis.

As the time to leave approached, more military matters crowded into the accounts with further payments to his saddler, tentmaker, trunkmaker, pewterer, brass worker, lantern man, locksmith, gunsmith (for three pairs of new French pistols and repairs to others), cutler, armourer, wax chandler, tallow chandler, glassman and bottleman. Nearly £50 went to the purser of his flagship, the *Triumph*. He bought seven banners for his trumpeters as well as drums and sticks. The provisions listed give some idea of the diet enjoyed by the duke and those who shared his table: wine, salted meats, poultry, quail, fish, tongue, pullets, fruit, pickles, confectionery, oranges and lemons. A payment to the French cook suggests that he came too, although by the end of the campaign he would have few ingredients left to prepare.

All Buckingham's equipment had to be carted off to Portsmouth, where his army was gathering and where in June 1627 King Charles inspected the fleet before it finally set sail at the end of the month. A sentimental note creeps into the duke's accounts with the purchase of an engraved crystal cross for his sister, the Countess of Denbigh. The final entry of all, before he left for war, was for £200 'Delivered to my Ladie Dutchess of Buckingham by his L[ordshi]ps command in new Gold in the little chamber at Whitehall'.[9]

On 20 June, Buckingham took up quarters on the *Triumph*. Of the hundred or so ships in his fleet, forty were royal and the rest commandeered merchantmen. As one of Buckingham's personal company, John Tradescant was most probably quartered with him on the flagship where he would have found himself in strange company. With money for the navy desperately short, the sailors were intermittently mutinous, and the men forcibly impressed to serve as foot soldiers were 'poor rogues and beggars' sent without shoes, money or clothes.[10] The complaint echoes Falstaff's words of self-condemnation in Shakespeare's *Henry IV, Part I*. The epitome of a corrupt recruiting captain, Falstaff approached only wealthy householders whom he then allowed to buy themselves out of service, replacing their numbers with 'slaves as ragged as Lazarus in the painted cloth ... and such as indeed were never soldiers, but discarded unjust serving-men, younger sons to younger brothers, revolted tapsters and ostlers trade-fallen, the cankers of a calm world and a long peace'.[11]

A manuscript listing Tradescant's fellows in Buckingham's retinue paints them as misfits, adventurers and incompetents, with a few shining exceptions. The list named eight men belonging to Buckingham's council or cabinet: a German count; two violent papists; a Scottish doctor of divinity; a doctor of physick; Ashburnham, the duke's kinsman; Howard, Earl of Suffolk; and Ffrancisco, the duke's Italian major domo. An even motlier crew followed in their wake, men apparently 'now Employed and much Entrusted'. They included a well-known pirate; a young knight who had 'lost his estate foolishly'; a young sea captain, 'half papist half protestant'; two saved from hanging by the duke; and a man named Dawson, 'so infamous for swearing hee is sayd to gett a serjant major-shipp by it'. Four were specifically named as engineers: one of the men saved from hanging, together with Rudde-Keene, 'a Cheefe-Ingeneere never but a simple ovrseer of pioneers before'; Audly-Rowe, 'a prime Ingeneere, but soe unknowen a one, as hee cast up the trench the wronge waye'; and John Tradescant, described as 'the Dukes gardiner now an Ingeneere and best of all this true and most Deservinge'.[12] It surely cannot have been hard to shine in such company.

By 10 July most of the fleet had anchored off La Rochelle on France's south-western coast; storms and chasing after piratical Dunkirkers had delayed their crossing. But now they encountered the first of their real problems: cautious of accepting English help against their own king, the Rochellois played for time. They were fasting and could not speak; they needed to bring in their harvest; they should consult other Huguenot congregations throughout France. Their excuses continued to multiply. While the townsfolk vacillated about whether to accept the English offer of men and supplies to repel a threatened attack by Richelieu's forces, Buckingham sailed across the narrow channel to the Ile de Ré, a low-lying island of sandy coasts, dunes, salt marshes, maritime pines and holm oaks less than three miles off the French coast (to which it is now joined by an arcing toll bridge), garrisoned by at least 1,500 French infantry under the command of Marshal Toiras.[13]

The confusion of their landing gave the English a foretaste of what was to come, for despite Buckingham's undoubted valour he lacked the experience to know when to press his advantage. By the time the main English force began to disembark, the French horse and infantry were lurking behind sandhills and then bravely attacked. The English meanwhile, 'to whom (after their tossinge in the shipps) noe ground seemd Terra firma enough, (especially such as was only loose dust and quicksand,)'[14] joined battle with the French soldiers and, after a short sharp fight, put them to flight. Marshal Toiras and his surviving forces retreated to the main town of St Martin where they shut themselves away in the unfinished citadel, which 'squatted like a huge petrified starfish at the water's edge'.[15] Had Buckingham followed at Toiras's heels, he might have swept the French forces off the island but instead he delayed, courteously allowing the French to bury their dead and wasting precious time. Over the next few days, he skirted the island's second fort and took possession of the town of La Flotte, then St Martin itself, but the French forces remained secure behind the citadel's solid walls.

This is not, of course, the story of Buckingham's campaign but rather of Tradescant's experience of warfare on foreign soil, and a poor soil it was, hard and rocky where they needed to dig their trenches and treacherously

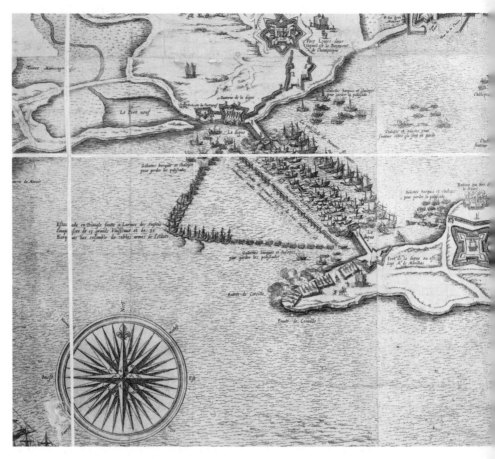

La Rochelle in May 1628, besieged by the forces of the French king.

muddy where they wanted to flee. Salt from the salt pans was one of the
island's main commodities, plus a 'certaine smalle wine', but otherwise it
produced very little. 'For those of our men who went forth, eyther to get
timber, corne, fuell, or any forage besides sower and unripe grapes, and the
shreddes of vine stalkes, found little provision,'[16] wrote Lord Herbert,
whose eyewitness account of the expedition was published in Latin in the
1650s and then in English more than two centuries later.

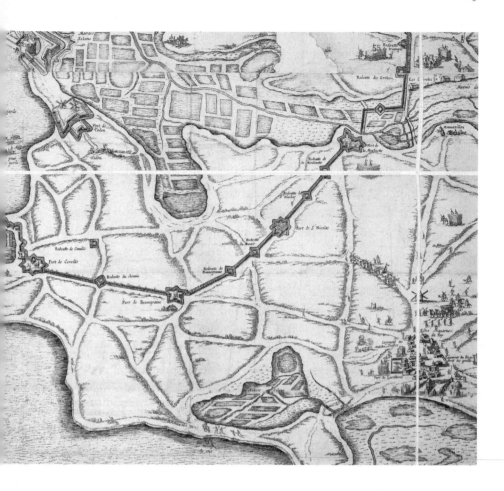

As the English waited for reinforcements (2,000 troops were promised from England and the same number from Ireland), Buckingham rejected the option of taking the citadel by force, deciding instead to starve its defenders into submission. This required two lines of defensive action: patrolling the seas to stop the landing of French supplies and providing protective shelter for the English army camped around the citadel walls. Their first engineering mistake was to dig their trenches so far from the walls that the

French were able to push their own defences outwards.[17] Only after five or six weeks did the English move closer in. Not surprisingly, Buckingham despaired of his engineers' lack of experience and wrote to his Secretary of State, requesting more skilled men and in particular 'Cornelis, the Dutch engineer' to join him in Ré. He wanted Cornelis to bring with him the 'fireworks left behind' and asked also for 'vessels, munition, stores, pickaxes, shovels, and other tools for work in trenches'.[18] Unlike most of his fellows, Tradescant at least knew how to dig trenches and raise earthworks even if he lacked the military training to know where they should be dug.

As a few small boats succeeded in slipping through the English blockade to bring supplies to the beleaguered French, Buckingham ordered the construction of floating moles in a half-moon around the seaward side of the citadel but, once again, his engineering solutions proved woefully inadequate. The first was put together from 'the keeles and bottoms of shipps: this beinge fastened with Anchors, and 7 great peeces of Ordenance [cannon] placed on top of it, with Gabions [baskets filled with stones] to defende them' but it proved too weak to withstand the battering of wind and waves. Next, Buckingham stretched a line of masts and long pieces of timber fastened with cable between 'the Cittadell and the Continent' – presumably mainland France – but that too came to nothing. Lastly, after failing to make a floating barrier of ships tied together and loaded with empty barrels, 'our seamen did sinke some lesser shipps, loden with great stones, neare the Porte, but not eyther in such quantity or number as that all passage was shutte up from the Enemy'.[19]

In the waiting game that followed, enlivened by occasional skirmishes, Tradescant found time to indulge his favourite pastime: he went botanizing on the island noted for its Mediterranean-type flora where today hollyhocks self-seed in the cracks and crevices of the island's small towns. We know of at least two plants he brought back, neither particularly showy or rare, but as a plantsman Tradescant delighted in the infinite variety of even humble plants that others dismissed as weeds. One was the white or common sea wormwood (*Artemisia maritima*), which apothecary Thomas Johnson said grew 'with Mr *Parkinson* and others, and (as I remember) it was first sent over from the Isle of Rees by Mr. John Tradescant'.[20] The taste was a 'little bitterish', he said, and the smell 'not unpleasant'. John Gerard had included it in the first edition of his Herball, maintaining that 'These Woormwoods do growe upon the raised grounds in the salt marshes neere vnto the sea, in most places of England; which being brought into gardens doth there flourish as in his naturall place, and retaineth his smell, taste, and naturall qualitie.' Johnson disagreed, adding: 'I have not heard that the later growes wilde in any place with us in England.'[21]

As for its virtues, both authors agreed it was effective at killing worms in the belly and guts, especially if mixed with rhubarb (Gerard) or boiled with rice (Johnson). Johnson also recommended a number of other uses for it: as an insect repellent in chests, presses and wardrobes; as fodder to make coastal-grazing cattle grow 'fat and lusty very quickly'; as a poultice of leaves pounded with figs, saltpetre and 'the meal of Darnel' to ease dropsy; and drunk with wine, as an antidote to poisons, especially hemlock.

The other plant Tradescant bought back with him from France was the sea stock gillyflower (Matthiola sinuata), which John Parkinson tells us was first 'brought out of the Isle of Ree by Rochel by Mr. Iohn Tradescant when the Duke of Buckingham was sent with supplies for Monsieur Subise'. Like the wormwood, it was not as showy as its garden cousins, so Parkinson included it not in his 'Garden of all sorts of Pleasant Flowers' but in his more robustly masculine herbal of 1640, Theatrum Botanicum, along with several other gillyflowers deemed 'of lesse beauty and durability'. Its leaves were handsome enough, soft and whitish, cut into deep dents 'like the knagges of a Bucks horne, which make it seeme the more beautifull'. Tradescant might just have caught the last of its flowers, 'of a pale blewish purple colour, almost like unto a Dove or Crane colour',[22] and would certainly have watched the seed pods ripening into August.

Conditions were hard enough for Buckingham's army camped in the open, but that year torrential rains added to their miseries. 'The Autumne now growinge on,' wrote Lord Herbert, 'the earth was so moystned with frequent raines that the souldgers on eyther side had no ground but myre to do their duties in.' While this was 'incomodious' to the French soldiers in

Creeping sea wormwood,
brought back by John Tradescant
from the Ile de Ré.

the citadel – who had huts and planks with which to cover themselves –
it was

altogeather greevious to us; who, beinge of a more tender and delicate constitution,
did hardly indure to watch in durty places and the open Ayre. Hence were
ingenderd ill habitts of their bodies, which had theire conclusion in Catarrhs,
diseases of the lunges, Burninge feavers and Disenteries: our number herupon were
so dimminished that they could scarsly bee made up againe by supplies sent
afterwards both from England and Ireland.[23]

Herbert's account is confirmed by a soldier's journal, which described the
water-filled trenches and the sickness spreading through their exhausted
army, 'having neither good Lodging but in the Trenches nor meat but that
which stunck nor drinck but water, all ye provision of wine in the Iland
being spent'.[24] Yet neither side allowed the strains of warfare to diminish the
courtesies of their relations. When Buckingham heard that Toiras, the
French garrison commander, was enquiring whether any melons were kept

on the island, he personally sent him over a dozen. Toiras rewarded Buckingham's messenger with twenty crowns, 'and the next day sent 6 bottles of Citron flower water and 12 little boxes of powder de Cipres'.[25]

By the beginning of September, the Rochellois at last accepted Buckingham's offer of support, made seven weeks previously. Over two thousand troops arrived from Ireland and the English prospects were improving, but not enough to guarantee victory. Sir Edward Conway wrote to Mr Secretary Coke from La Rochelle, telling him that 'the place to sustain a siege requires 8,000 or 10,000 . . . Now that succours are come to us from Ireland we begin to approach, the ground we work is rocky, our number small, the trenches with every rain full of water.'[26] The same message was sent to Buckingham's Secretary of the Navy, Edward Nicholas by William Bold, the Duchess of Buckingham's steward, newly arrived in Ré from England: 'the winter comes on apace, the men endure much wet in the trenches, and John Tradescant is one of their best engineers; "pity our misery!"'.[27] Yet the French forces in the citadel were suffering too and would have capitulated but for Buckingham's delay in defining terms. The night before their intended surrender, a French fleet of small boats laden with men and supplies broke through Buckingham's defences, and the English awoke to jeering soldiers inside the citadel showing 'flagons of wine, Turkeys, Capons, Neats tonges, and other provisions on the toppe of their pikes'.[28]

Buckingham made a final desperate assault on the citadel but as the ladders used to scale the walls were too short, his men could only climb to the top and there, 'castinge their threatninge eies aboute, they remained unmoveable till they were shott and tumbled doune'.[29] One final engineering disaster awaited them, which, in terms of casualties, represented perhaps the greatest failure of all. Buckingham had already prepared the ground for a possible retreat from the Ile de Loix, a marshy islet some way west of St Martin reached by a narrow causeway that could be walked at most by five or six men abreast. Here he had ordered the construction of earthworks to protect his men but 'most preposterously' (the exasperation was Herbert's) these were raised at the far end of the causeway so that 'neyther on the one side we could conveniently fight nor hansomly retyre on the other; what therefore in both kinds might have advanced our designes proved hurtfull in every way'.[30]

The English marched in no kind of order to the dyke, for having 'layd aside their courage, a kinde of secure rashness invaded them'. Around them lay mud, salt pans and 'a kinde of drowned Cuntrey'. The French attacked. The English were routed. Some tried running on to the dyke, which continued for about three hundred paces to a bridge of small ships joined together and passable only at low tide. The French ran after them on to the dyke and 'cast our men on eyther side into the ditches and saltpitts adjoyninge'. Those who fell into the water and mud were easily picked off by French pikes, while those who made it to the bridge found neither rails nor fences to steady them. The result was predictable pandemonium. 'One might observe these thrustinge forward, and others puttinge them backe, untill their weapons fallinge out of their hands, and grapled together, they fell arme in arme into the sea.' Any soldier who made it to the far side then stumbled upon 'that preposterous and perverse fortification . . . but neyther so high nore firme as it could eyther defend our men or keepe backe an enemy, which afterward proved much to our disadvantage'.[31]

Somehow in all this confusion, the English officers managed to rally those men who had crossed over to the far side and they pushed the French back across the causeway, until gathering darkness called a halt to their pursuit and the English were able to embark into their ships as quickly as possible. More than five hundred had been killed in the final retreat and many more drowned.[32] In total, out of 7,833 men who took part in Buckingham's campaign (including the 1,899 who joined as reinforcements), only 2,989 returned safely.[33] In another of the cruel ironies that dogged the campaign, Buckingham set sail for home on the day that the promised reinforcements from England lost sight of the English coast. Buckingham had achieved none of his aims and was returning even more hated than before.

John Tradescant was lucky to be alive, when more than six out of ten of his master's army were dead. Despite the personal commendations he had won, he cannot have looked back with any relish at the contribution made by his fellow engineers. In botanical terms, however, he had the consolation of the plants he was bringing back to England, humble as they were, and after he had followed Buckingham from Portsmouth to Plymouth, he was rewarded with a rogue strawberry generally known as the 'Plymouth Strawberry'. Ever alert, he found it in the garden of a Plymouth woman whose daughter had gathered the roots and planted them instead of common strawberries, 'but she finding the fruit not to answer her expectation, intended to throw it away: which labor he spared her, in taking it and bestowing it among the lovers of such varieties, in whose gardens it is yet preserved'.[34]

The story has come to us from Thomas Johnson, who must have heard it from Tradescant himself when he visited his garden at Lambeth. Nearly three centuries later, the celebrated gardener E. A. Bowles planted it at Myddelton House, Enfield, in his 'lunatic asylum' devoted to botanical misfits and curiosities. 'It is certainly wrong in the head if ever a plant was,' wrote Bowles, 'for it is just an ordinary wild Strawberry in every way until it blossoms, then every portion of the flower is seen to have been changed into leafy structures; the petals are little green leaves, even the anthers and carpels are replaced by tufts of tubular leaves',[35] which go on to produce strange red fruits like spiky hedgehogs. After sightings in Hyde Park, Hampstead and Cambridge, the Plymouth strawberry became a botanical dodo, disappearing for many years until it turned up unexpectedly in the garden of Gloucestershire clergyman Canon Ellacombe, who passed it on to Bowles.

Tradescant's own Plymouth strawberry plant or its successors went with him to South Lambeth, where it survived into the plant list put together by his son and published with the museum catalogue of 1656.

The Duke of Buckingham was not so long-lived. The year after the disastrous expedition to the Ile de Ré saw him back in Portsmouth, preparing another expeditionary force to go to the aid of the Huguenots. His unpopularity had increased even more, if that were possible, although his king remained devoted to him. That summer, a London mob had hacked to death Buckingham's astrologer, John Lambe, while in

Portsmouth, mutinous crowds demanding pay had tried to drag the duke himself from his coach.[36]

On 23 August 1628, as his pregnant duchess remained in her bed at the Greyhound Inn, the duke received a false report from the Count de Soubise that La Rochelle had been relieved. After a hasty breakfast, he hurried to tell King Charles the good news, but never reached his coach. Disaffected lieutenant John Felton, a veteran of the Ile de Ré campaign, stepped forward from the crush and stabbed him through the chest. Alarmed by the shouting, Kate Buckingham looked out of her window to see her dying husband laid out on a table.

Charles was at prayer when the news of Buckingham's death reached him. He

continued unmoved, and without the least change in his countenance, till prayers were ended; when he suddenly departed to his chamber, and threw himself upon his bed, lamenting with much passion and with abundance of tears the loss he had of an excellent servant and the horrid manner in which he had been deprived of him; and he continued in this melancholic . . . discomposure of mind many days.[37]

For the second time in his career, death had robbed John Tradescant of a powerful employer who had helped him advance professionally and socially. As for assassin John Felton, he had sewn a confession into his hat, not expecting to survive the immediate aftermath of Buckingham's slaying. The subsequent investigation discounted any idea that he might have conspired with others to commit the deed. Felton acted alone, they decided, believing that he was ridding the country of a great evil. Convinced at the end that his action was inspired not by God but by the Devil, Felton was hanged at Tyburn, his body dumped in a cart and taken to Portsmouth where it hung in chains outside the city walls.

A second expedition went to La Rochelle where its exploding mines, among them no doubt those designed by Balthazar Gerbier, failed to penetrate the French sea defences. 'I did also contrive some Mines,' wrote Gerbier in his autobiography, 'which were to have blown up the Dycke at

Rochell, for all which I never so much as touched a penny of the Kings, nor of the Duke of *Buckinghams* monies.'[38] You can almost hear the whine in his voice as he sought to counter accusations of self-interest and betrayal.

It was all in vain. The Huguenot stronghold capitulated in October 1628 and within two years England had signed peace treaties with France and Spain. By then John Tradescant had embarked on a new career that would bring him lasting fame. Instead of travelling the world in search of rarities, he would now summon the world to his door in an outlying suburb of London, where a man might in one day behold more curiosities gathered together than if he had spent a lifetime in travel.[39]

Chapter Fifteen

Lambeth Walks

The place Tradescant chose to gather together his remarkable collection of plants, natural treasures and man-made wonders was South Lambeth, some three miles south-west of London Bridge, then London's only permanent crossing point and a worthy sight in itself. The Venetian Horatio Busino described how the two banks of the river were connected by 'a very noble stone bridge of nineteen very lofty arches, on each side of which are convenient houses and shops, so that it has rather the air of a long suburb than a handsome structure such as a bridge'.[1]

Today, the nearest bridge is at Vauxhall. Traffic crossing the Thames here thunders around the vast one-way system of Vauxhall Cross before heading east towards the A2 and Kent, swinging round to the new Covent Garden Market at Nine Elms, or turning southwards down South Lambeth Road to Stockwell, Clapham and Brixton through acres of urban hinterland: the cramped mean streets of Victorian speculative building infilled with pubs, hotels, service businesses, drab cafés and the corner shops so necessary to modern city living.

If you head south from the river, you will pass a small park showing signs of urban decay, pausing perhaps to admire its ancient plane trees, then a vast builders' warehouse promising to supply 'all your landscape needs'. Soon you will reach a cluster of largely Portuguese tapas bars where the old South

Lambeth Road survives as a dog-leg beside the new. One of these bars marks
the site of Tradescant's former home. While the area shows the inevitable
strains of multiple occupation (abandoned shopping trolleys, mattresses and
council rubbish bins overspilling into the street), a love of plants survives
even here in the yuccas, box hedges, roses and bay trees planted in the
occasional front garden. And back from the main road, in one of the tiny
gardens allowed by the late nineteenth-century developers in what is now
Tradescant Road, is a eucalyptus tree from a continent as yet undiscovered
in Tradescant's time, named after the imaginary Terra Australis Incognita of
ancient maps that apparently stretched down to the South Pole.

In the late 1620s, when Tradescant moved in with his family and his
precious rarities (the exact date is uncertain), South Lambeth was still open
country, which began almost as soon as you crossed the river, leaving behind
the stews of Southwark, the theatres and bull- and bear-baiting rings of
Bankside and the tenemented ribbon development along the Thames's
southern bank. The northern part of Lambeth was an area of marshland
punctuated by windmills and chequered with ditches that drained off the
water into the Thames.[2] ('Lambeth' is a Saxon name, meaning either a quay
from which lambs were shipped or – more probably – a muddy harbour.)
Further south, the old turnpike roads cut across the meadows, pastures and
market gardens of the central plain before rising up to the southern hills and
leading on towards Croydon.

Winding country lanes reinforced the rural aspect, and as John Gerard
attested in his Herball of 1597 you could find here an abundance of herbs
and simples such as those gathered and sold by the herbswomen of
Cheapside Market.[3] In his southern rambles, for instance, Gerard spotted
wild rocket growing close to where Tradescant would settle, 'as yee go from
Lambithe bridge to the village of Lambithe, under a small bridge that you
must passe over hard by the Thames side'.[4] Following his admirably precise
directions, you might also find hedgehog grasses growing in watery ditches
'as you may see in going from Paris garden Bridge to Saint Georges fields';[5]
willowherb and yellow loosestrife in the 'moist meadowes' between
Lambeth and Battersea and under the archbishop's wall at Lambeth;[6]

dropworts growing 'between the plowed lands in the moist and wet furrowes of a fielde belonging to Battersey by London ... and about the Bishop of Londons House at Fulham'.[7]

The space and better air of the Lambeth countryside made perfect sense for a man seeking to establish a garden on the outskirts of London. Already in Tradescant's time Lambeth was home to a burgeoning community of market gardeners, including many Dutch gardeners who had moved here around 1600, when the 'Art of Gardening' had begun to creep 'into Sandwich, and Surrey, Fulham, and other places'.[8] Fifty years later there were still old men in Surrey who could remember the arrival of the first gardeners 'to plant Cabages, Colleflowers, and to sowe Turneps, Carrets, and Parsnips, to sowe [early-ripe] Pease, all which at that time were great rarities, we having few, or none in England, but what came from Holland and Flaunders'.[9]

Another early Lambeth gardener was Dr Simon Forman, Queen Elizabeth's astrologer and quack doctor, who planted roses in his garden at Lambeth Marsh and practised his arcane form of astrological gardening.[10] Later gardens would include Cuper's Garden and the Spring Gardens admired by John Evelyn that metamorphosed into the renowned Vauxhall pleasure gardens much enjoyed by Pepys, although Sir Roger de Coverley would have been happier 'if there were more Nightingales and fewer Strumpets'.[11]

In an observant aside on early gardening practice, the Horatio Busino noted that much of the ground around London was far too gravelly for growing vegetables, a problem the market gardeners had solved by digging up the gravel (which they sold for ship's ballast, road repairs and for making mortar) and filling the holes with the 'filth of the city, which serves as excellent manure, rich and black as thick ink'.[12] The filled holes were then enclosed by palings, deep ditches or soft mud mixed with rotting straw and thatched with rye straw.[13] The Gardeners' Company, too, would claim to have 'cleansed the City of all dung and noisomeness'. Even into the next century fastidious eaters would claim that asparagus grown by London gardeners in beds of dung was 'of a Colour unnatural, and a Taste so strong and unsavoury'.[14]

For Tradescant, hoping to attract visitors to his collection, Lambeth had

the added advantage of good transport links to the fashionable world. Just
a mile or so away from his house was the horse ferry between Lambeth
Palace and Whitehall, an ancient crossing leased out by the archbishops of
Canterbury who retained the right to travel free, along with their servants,
goods and chattels.[15] The river was London's principal artery for the
transport of people and goods; in Queen Elizabeth's day, as many as 2,000
'wherries' or light river boats plied for trade from the many water stairs
leading down to the river.[16] Traveller Thomas Platter admired their
charming upholstery and embroidered cushions, although the river below
the bridge was very low when the tide was out and he considered it
dangerous to pass through.[17] Many other travellers felt the same, preferring
to bypass the bridge on foot.

Horatio Busino paints an even more Venetian picture of river travel in
early-Stuart London:

The river ebbs and flows so rapidly that under the bridge between the arches any
mill might be kept at work, the tide turning every six hours with great strength, the
difference between high and low water mark amounting to from ten to twelve feet.
Notwithstanding this the wherries shoot along so lightly as to surprise everyone.
These wherries look like so many mutilated gondolas, without prows or felzi
[canopies], though they have seats aft with sundry convenient cushions. They row
like galley oarsmen, each with extremely long oars, and are very dexterous at
steering clear of each other. There are also long covered barges like Bucentors
[Venetian ceremonial barges], very handsome, especially those of the king and other
noblemen and gentlemen, pulling six or eight oars and which really fly over the
water.[18]

The South Lambeth property that gained popular fame as 'Tradescant's
Ark' had belonged to the Dutch ambassador, Sir Noel Caron, whom
Tradescant must have known when he worked for Cecil and who may well
have helped to engineer his early success. Caron had died (still in his post) in
December 1624 and there were difficulties over his will, which took some
years to resolve. As a foreign-born alien granted letters of denization by the

Crown,[19] Caron was allowed to bequeath his English property only to 'the issue of his own boddy begotten'.[20] His will was declared invalid and when his heirs launched lawsuits to try to recover his English properties, the matter was referred to the Privy Council.

Caron was one of South Lambeth's main landowners, holding most of the freehold land in the Manor of Vauxhall (or Faux Hall as it was then written). At the beginning of the century, he had bought a 'great howse' with a dairy and some seventy acres of land where he built himself a fine new mansion surrounded by gardens and parkland studded with trees. In April 1610, Lewis Frederick, Prince of Wirtemberg, on a visit to England went after dinner 'to see the resident Ambassador of the States, Mr Carron, who lives out of the city, opposite Westminster, in a very fine house of his own, well furnished, and with beautiful gardens round about: it is called South Lambeth (*Sudlambet*)'.[21] A plan of 'Faux Hall Manour' drawn by Thomas Hill in 1681[22] shows Caron's splendid turreted mansion ('Carroone house') flanked by avenues of trees, its park stretching north-eastwards towards where the Oval cricket ground is today.

Tradescant's property abutted Caron's southern boundary. Caron had added it to his estate in 1618 along with several other pieces of land purchased from Sir William and Katherine Foster. Before Caron's time, the plot had comprised in 1592 a 'messuage [dwelling house and holding], barn, orchard, garden, outhouses and ground' then owned and occupied by Lawrence Pallmer.[23] At some point Caron divided this plot into two: Tradescant would occupy one portion and in due course Elias Ashmole would take up residence in the other, rather larger portion. Their respective properties are shown on Hill's 1681 survey, by which time Ashmole had also leased the Tradescants' old house.[24] Determining where the boundaries between their two properties lay, as well as the location of both Tradescant's garden and his orchard, has given rise to lingering confusion, but historian David Sturdy is surely correct when he says that Tradescant's garden ran eastwards from the house while his orchard occupied the three-acre Walnut Tree Close.[25] This last site was marked on Hill's survey by spiky trees but not the flowers or glasshouses shown on some other properties. The whole block was developed in the

1880s and, according to Sturdy, the Tradescants' house lay on the site of the
present numbers 113 to 119 South Lambeth Road. Their main garden, covering just under an acre, occupied most of the present Meadow Road, while
the orchard and field ran southwards, occupying much of the present
Tradescant and Walberswick Roads. Four scattered fields of two to nine acres
made up the rest of the Tradescant farm property.

Tradescant almost certainly moved into the house in late 1628 or 1629,[26]
after Buckingham's death but before the dispute over Caron's will was settled.
Eventually, out of respect for Caron (who, as an Anglophile and charitable
founder of almshouses, was much loved in his adopted country) the Privy
Council advised that it was 'honourable and just' to sell his lands and dis-
tribute the proceeds among his kin. For reasons that are no longer clear,[27] the
properties Caron had acquired from the Fosters (including that occupied by
Tradescant) escheated or reverted to the Dean and Chapter of Christ Church,
Canterbury, as Lords of the Manor of Vauxhall. Tradescant therefore had a
number of possible introductions to his South Lambeth home: as an early
protégé of Caron's (unproven); through Balthazar Gerbier's known links to the
Dutch ambassador (unlikely); as an ex-employee of the Duke of Buckingham,
whose interests were promoted by the king through the Privy Council; or
through his own Canterbury connections acquired while working for
Edward, Lord Wotton, at St Augustine's Abbey. Tradescant never owned the
freehold to his South Lambeth properties; sometime after Caron's will was
settled, the head lessee of the Vauxhall escheat was Thomas Bartholomew,
who was therefore the Tradescants' landlord.[28]

Tradescant worked hard and quickly to get his garden established,
whether he was gardening from scratch (as David Sturdy maintains)[29] or
planting in an already established garden (as Prudence Leith-Ross prefers).[30]
According to the lists he kept in the back pages of his own copy of John
Parkinson's Paradisi in Sole,[31] he added a few new plants for the first three
years from 1629, which largely record Tradescant's debts to his French
contacts, the Robins and the Morins. From an unidentified source came four
more roses 'whearof [nurseryman] Mr Tuggy Hathe two', one strange vine,
one red 'Honnysoccle' and 'Two Irisses without Name'.

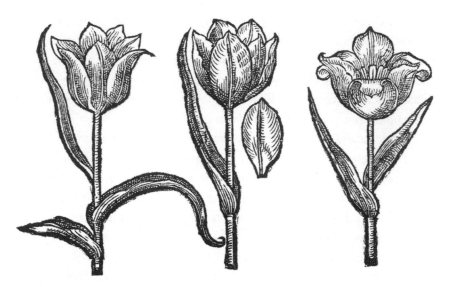

Three new tulips added by Thomas Johnson to John Gerard's Herball *(1633).*

Tradescant's interests spread beyond the 'florist's flowers' so beloved by the Frenchmen, however. Other contacts sent him trees and shrubs that gave his garden body and structure: the oriental plane tree and the smoke bush from merchant Humphrey Slaney; young slips of the Mediterranean strawberry tree (*Arbutus unedo*) and a gum-producing tragacantha; a shrubby evergreen from the Mediterranean or the Canaries, moon trefoil (*Medicago arborea*), of borderline hardiness. For those who can coax it into flower, it bears dense racemes of yellow flowers from late spring to early autumn but it did not survive into Tradescant's garden list of 1634 (see later) so he probably had no luck with it.

In 1630 Tradescant recorded just a consignment of bulbs and flowering plants from Sir Peter Wyche (then English ambassador at Constantinople) including one daffodil, one cyclamen, four ranunculi, two tulips and four sorts of anemones. The following year numbers again increased slightly, with more offerings from René Morin, including the sad geranium. Several other contacts (named as 'LW', 'TS', 'Mr Colfe', and 'W. Win') despatched tulips (among them one 'Tulipe Beau withowt a Circle' and 'more good tulipes unknowne'); while from Brussels came six hyacinths and three named narcissi.

By 1632, Tradescant's garden was ready to receive a large number of new plants; he made eighty-seven separate entries at the back of Parkinson's garden book covering more than one hundred different varieties (from Brussells came '16 tulipes', for instance). At least nineteen plants were new to England, coming in almost equal numbers from southern Europe and the Mediterranean, and from the eastern seaboard of North America. New North American varieties that would go on to become garden favourites included the pretty foam flower (*Tiarella cordifolia*); the pale-yellow Canada goldenrod (*Solidago canadensis*); the Atamasco lily (*Zephyranthes atamasco*); and a primrose-yellow cone flower (*Rudbeckia laciniata*), cousin to the ever-popular black-eyed Susan. He also imported to Britain the poison ivy, *Rhus radicans* – which still featured in the garden list of 1656 – and *Eupatorium ageratoides*, now classed as a weed. From central and southern Europe came two rock roses; *Eleagnus angustifolia*; the snowy mespilus, *Amelanchier ovalis*; and the resinous mastic tree, *Pistacia lentiscus*. Two of his new introductions that year stand out as particularly exotic: a rosette-shaped bromeliad from Central and South America and the West Indies (*Bromelia karatas*); and a clump of bamboo-like giant reed, *Arundo donax*, from southern Europe.

Tradescant clearly felt his garden was sufficiently advanced to receive a visit from apothecary Thomas Johnson, who was then embarked on the massive task of revising John Gerard's *Herball*. Many new plants had entered the country in the intervening three and a half decades and Gerard's original contained many errors and passages lifted uncritically from earlier authors. (This was how books got written. Only later would plagiarism become a sin.) Johnson's tone towards Tradescant is respectful and admiring, although not as warm as John Parkinson's; the elder Tradescant was thirty years his senior, after all. But he still calls him 'my kinde friend'[32] and refers to him as 'that great Treasurer of natures rareities'.[33]

We know the month of Johnson's visit from his entry on the sad geranium that Tradescant had received from René Morin in 1631: 'There is of late brought into this kingdome,' wrote Johnson, 'and to our knowledge, by the industry of Mr. John Tradescant, another more rare and no lesse beautifull than any of the former; and he had it by the name of *Geranium Indicum noctù odoratum*: this hath not yet beene written of by any that I know.' Unable to include an illustration because he had forgotten to make a drawing during his visit, Johnson nonetheless carefully described its flowers, each consisting of 'five round pointed leaves [petals] of a yellowish colour, with a large blacke purple spot in the middle of each leafe, as if it were painted, which gives the floure a great deale of beauty, and it also hath a good smell. I did see it in floure about the end of July, 1632, being the first time that it floured with the owner thereof.'[34]

Tradescant will have walked around the garden with Johnson, pointing out any varieties he thought might usefully go into the revised *Herball*. One of the plants Johnson mentions by name is 'Pistolochia' (today *Aristolochia*) from Virginia, more commonly known as Virginian snakeroot or snakeweed. Likening it to a variety described by Clusius, Johnson says it

grew with Mr. John Tradescant at South-Lambeth, An. 1632, was agreeable in all points, but here and there one of the lower leaves were somewhat broader and rounder pointed than the rest: the floure was long, red, crooked, and a little hairie, and it did not open the top, or shew the inner side, which I judge was by reason of the coldnesse and unseasonablenesse of the later part of the Sommer when it floured.[35]

Other plants specially noted by Johnson included 'Tradescants Narcisse, from Master John Tradescant of South-Lambeth', a double yellow daffodil described as the 'largest and stateliest of all the rest';[36] a ladies' slipper orchid native to northern parts of Europe and England;[37] two sorts of laburnums;[38] the prickly strawberry Tradescant had found in Plymouth;[39] the young plane trees sent to him by Humphrey Slaney;[40] and a horse chestnut that John Gerard had reported growing in Italy and sundry places in the East.[41] Despite popular belief, there is no evidence that Tradescant introduced this tree to Britain; a native of the wild border region between

Greece and Albania, it was introduced into western Europe in 1576 and to the British Isles early in the seventeenth century.[42]

Several times Johnson linked Tradescant's garden with that of nurseryman Ralph Tuggie of Westminster. Tuggie, who died in the spring of 1633, specialized in carnations and was clearly the leading nurseryman of his day.[43] Anyone seeking carnations, said Johnson, should repair to his widow's garden 'which in the excellencie and variete of these delights exceedeth all that I have seene; as also hee himselfe whilest he lived exceeded most, if not all of his time, in his care, industry, and skill in raising, encreasing, and preserving of these plants and some others'.[44] Both Tradescant and Tuggie grew two North American starworts or asters, which Johnson called the shrubby starwort and the small shrubby starwort. The former he judged particularly useful because 'it floures in October and November when as few other floures are to be found'.[45] It is still called Aster tradescantii today.

Johnson also admired a spring-flowering gentian of an 'exquisite blew' found growing in 'most of our choice Gardens. As with Mr. Parkinson, Master Tradescant, and Master Tuggye, &c'.[46] Both Tradescant and Tuggie had 'very great varieties' of auriculas, one of the most treasured of the florists' flowers that showed astonishing variety in both leaf and flower. According to Johnson, the petals might be 'either smooth and greene, or else gray and hoary, againe they are smooth about the edges, or snipt more or lesse; The floures some are fairer then othersome, and their colours are so various, that it is hard to find words to expresse them, but they may be refer'd to whites, reds, yellowes, and purples'.[47]

Tradescant's own notes of his garden are recorded in his plant list of 1634, Plantarvm in Horto Iohannem Tradescanti nascentium Catalogus. Only one copy is known to have survived, among botanist John Goodyer's papers at Magdalen College, Oxford, bound into a small leather-backed volume with several other short works, including Hugh Platt's Floraes Paradise of 1608 and Thomas Johnson's botanising journeys into Kent and Hampstead Heath of 1632.[48] In the Latin title Tradescant's name is grammatically wrong (it should be 'Johannis' not 'Johannem'), suggesting this copy was a printer's proof, although the fault could equally lie with Tradescant himself.

From the list we know that Tradescant planted his garden with more than 770 separate varieties (both genus and species), which would almost certainly have been laid out in order beds according to plant families, as in the botanic gardens he had admired in Europe. Like his French contacts, he was particularly strong on flowering bulbs and herbaceous plants: anemones, auriculas, narcissi, tulips, crocuses and colchicums, geraniums, hyacinths, irises and lilies. In season, his garden would have been a riot of colour and smells despite its regimented appearance. He could also offer visitors twenty-seven different varieties of rose, including two introductions to England: Rosa virginiana, and the Muscovy rose he named Rosa Muscovitica which he had doubtless brought back with him from Archangel. And he had a fine collection of rock roses (Cistus), including several not seen before in England. Many more fruits grew in his orchard: nearly 170 different varieties, including apples, pears, plums, cherries, apricots, nectarines, peaches and vines.

Fellow plant enthusiasts would have admired the new plants coming into English gardens. Not counting the introductions recorded in his copy of Parkinson's Paradisi in Sole, these included the false acacia from North America (eventually named Robinia pseudoacacia after the Robins of Paris) and the Persian lilac, Syringa x persica. Among other plants making their first documented appearance in an English garden were two asters; three plants he named after himself (an auricula, a narcissus and a trifolium); a Virginian geranium; two cardamines; a variety of meadow rue (Thalictrum); a walnut; several rock roses; false Solomon's seal (Smilacina racemosa); and the parsley-leafed vine, Vitis vinifera var. 'Apiifolia'.

Of course, John Tradescant was not the first English gardener to introduce new plants to his garden, nor was he the first to catalogue the plants growing there. Nearly forty years earlier, John Gerard had produced a catalogue listing his plants in Latin and in English, which he revised in 1599.[49] The two men were in touch with much the same plant-exchanging fraternity of curious gardeners and merchants so their gardens naturally had many plants in common. Both Gerard and Tradescant list an Epimedium, for instance, which they may have received from the same source, for as Gerard tells us in his *Herball*, 'This rare and strange plant was sent to me from the French Kings Herbarist, *Robinus*, dwelling in Paris at the signe of the blacke head, in the streete called D*u bout du* Monde, in English, The end of the world.'[50]

Both men also grew potatoes, which Gerard had received as tubers from Virginia and 'which growe and prosper in my garden'.[51] By the time Tradescant's plant list appeared, they were losing their novelty value, however. In a barbed aside on changing tastes, Parkinson remarked that 'The Potato's of Canada are by reason of their great increasing, growne to be so common here with us at London, that even the most vulgar begin to despise them, whereas when they were first received among us, they were dainties for a Queene.'[52]

Comparing the two catalogues today is complicated by the many different names then in use, and by the system of binomial plant names (genus followed by species), which was not developed until the eighteenth century.[53] Compounding the problems, both Gerard and Tradescant resorted to catch-all listings, such as Tradescant's tulip varieties listed simply as 'Num. 50. diversae flamulae'. Even so, the many correspondences are clear and the majority of species overlap between the two lists, even if named varieties often differ. Both men were growing plants that we still consider exotics such as the spiky yucca and the pomegranate from southern Europe. Both men listed tender plants that could not survive an English winter outdoors – *Canna indica* from South America, for instance, and the cactus *Opuntia vulgaris*, then called *Ficus indica*. Gerard wrote of this last plant in his *Herball* that it had never yet borne fruit in England, 'although I have bestowed great paines and cost in keeping it from the injurie of our cold climate'.[54]

Gerard had some trees apparently not growing with Tradescant, including lime, yew, three varieties of sorbus and the sweet gum (*Liquidambar styraciflua*). He also had a few exotics not found in Lambeth (such as aloe, the castor oil plant and the marvel of Peru), more obvious 'simples' or apothecary plants, and a number of ferns, which, as a group, appear to be completely absent from Tradescant's list, although both gardeners stocked a large variety of grasses.

Gerard's list contained some plants that failed to thrive with him. One plant that he includes, *Sabdariffa*, identified by B. D. Jackson as *Hibiscus sabdariffa*, he described in his *Herball* as being 'most impacient of our cold clymate, in so much that when I had with great industrie nourished up some plants from the seede, and kept them unto the middest of Maie; notwithstanding one colde night chauncing among many, hath destroied them all'.[55]

Tradescant similarly grew a number of plants not found in Gerard's garden. As well as the many North American varieties and the new introductions, these included the strawberry tree; the horse chestnut; the smoke tree; the giant reed; two laburnums (*Laburnum anagyroides* and *L. alpinum*); three varieties of box (presumably banished by Gerard because he hated its 'evill and lothsome smell');[56] and a lemon tree. Tradescant's catalogue also extended to classic orchard fruits such as apples and pears, although Gerard could at least boast fifteen varieties of cherry and thirty of plums.

Among Tradescant's contemporaries, even a few dedicated 'amateurs' were so passionate about their plants that they, too, kept meticulous records. The Revd Walter Stonehouse neatly wrote down the names of hundreds of plants growing in his Yorkshire rectory at Darfield in a tiny vellum-bound volume. He also drew a plan showing the ornamental design of his flower beds and plotted the contents of his orchard; many of the fruits overlap with those in Tradescant's orchard so perhaps they came from Lambeth as the men must have known each other well.[57]

At South Lambeth, Tradescant could also hope to entice visitors with his collection of rarities. Already at Thomas Johnson's visit in 1632 some of the curiosities were on display, as he included in his revised *Herball* an illustration of 'Indian Morrice Bells' that could be seen 'amongst many other varieties' with Mr John Tradescant at South Lambeth. As Johnson explained, these were made from the shells of a poisonous West Indian fruit ('especially in some of the Islands of the Canibals') into which small stones had been inserted in place of the kernel. Threaded on string and dried in the sun, they were worn for dances like a Morris dancer's bells, 'Which ratling sound doth much delight them, because it setteth forth the distinction of sounds, for they tune them and mix them with great ones and little ones, in such sort as we doe chimes or bells'.[58]

Johnson was a privileged visitor; it would be a year before another visitor recorded his own impressions of the whole collection. By then Tradescant had advanced to the crowning appointment of his career, socially at least: gardening for his sovereign, King Charles I and Queen Henrietta Maria at Oatlands Palace, near Weybridge in Surrey. As Tradescant was then aged sixty, it was a remarkable testament to his energy and skill, and also to King Charles's sense of responsibility towards the faithful followers of his murdered friend, the Duke of Buckingham. Or perhaps Charles simply wanted to give his French wife one of the best gardeners England had to offer.

Chapter Sixteen
Queen's Silk

Tradescant went to work for his king in 1630, on Lady Day (the feast of the Annunciation, 25 March), which was then the start of the new calendar year. His appointment as keeper of the royal gardens, vines and silkworms at Oatlands Palace in Surrey was confirmed by a royal warrant of 20 August 1630 to 'our trustie and welbeloved John Tradescant'. Backdated to the start of his employment, the warrant awarded him an annual salary of £100. This was twice the amount Robert Cecil had paid him but the king explicitly required him to provide all materials as well as labour.[1] He was taking over from the previous keeper, 'John Bonnall deceased' (usually written John or Jean Bonoeil), an expert on silkworms rather than gardens who had written a treatise on silk production recommended by Prussian agricultural reformer, Samuel Hartlib.[2]

Tradescant's salary was not excessive. In a similar career move some twelve years earlier, Mountain Jennings (already paid as keeper of the royal gardens at Theobalds) had received an additional royal warrant, granting him £50 'for making a place for the silkworms, and for providing mulberry leaves'. As well as 'feeding heeding and keeping' the royal silkworms, Tradescant would incur charges in overseeing the basic gardening and husbandry tasks spelt out by the warrant, namely 'digging dressing weeding supporting and keeping our Vines and vineyards there, and other works and charges

Oatlands Palace from the south in a sketch by Anthonis van den Wyngaerde (1559).

incident to the keeping of our said gardens and vineyards and the walks thereunto belonging'.[3] Any improvements to the garden requiring building works would be charged separately.

How much time Tradescant actually spent at Oatlands is not known. He was certainly allocated quarters at the palace alongside other royal servants as payment was made in 1636 to two carpenters for 'cutting a doorway and pinning in a new dorecase att John Tredeskins lodging'.[4] It seems likely that he divided his time between the palace and his own house in South Lambeth, helped by his gardener son John, who was now in his early twenties.

Close to the Thames at Weybridge and a convenient river journey from Lambeth, Oatlands was one of string of minor palaces and properties that King Charles had settled on Queen Henrietta Maria as part of her jointure on marriage.[5] It had first come into royal hands in the 1530s when a covetous King Henry VIII had acquired it from a wealthy family of London goldsmiths turned country squires, intending to create a vast hunting tract across Surrey heathland that would join Oatlands to his palace at Nonsuch.[6] Building works began while Henry was married to Jane Seymour. Work stopped at her death and was then completed in a hurry to receive his Flemish bride, Anne of Cleves, whose marriage was over before she had time to visit. Oatlands welcomed instead Henry's fifth wife, the ill-fated Catherine Howard, whom he married at the palace on 28 July 1540, but their union did not survive the revelations of her 'unlawful, licentious and voluptuous life'[7] and she was beheaded some eighteen months later.

Thereafter, the royal occupation of Oatlands was sporadic. Used chiefly as a staging post for royal progresses around the country (dictated as much by Tudor sanitation as royal pleasure), it was also valued by Queen Elizabeth for its excellent hunting. When plague threatened other royal residences at the start of his reign, King James had arranged for his eldest son – the nine-year-old Prince Henry – to take up residence at Oatlands with his sister, Princess Elizabeth, and seventy servants, a number that had doubled by the end of that year.[8]

Oatlands mansion house and park were especially favoured by Queen Anne who thought the air of Oatlands did her good, and James plainly relished its plentiful opportunities for the chase. During his reign, the palace made brief but frequent appearances in state papers when king and court removed here for short stays, or money was disbursed for its upkeep and enlargement. In 1609, for instance, Keeper Sir John Trevor (a close associate of shipbuilder and sea captain, Phineas Pett) received £900 'for purchase of lands for enlarging Oatlands Park, to those who agree to sell their estates'; and later that same year an order was given to fell and enclose a grove within the park, 'for breeding the King's pheasants there'.[9]

Visits continued throughout Charles I's reign; and Henrietta Maria gave birth to their eighth child and fourth son here in 1640, although she does not seem to have lavished on it the same degree of care and attention she gave to her more favoured residences such as Somerset House, Greenwich and later Wimbledon Palace. By the time Tradescant came to work for the queen at Oatlands, her marriage to Charles had overcome its early difficulties (reputedly exacerbated by Buckingham) and settled into one of lasting affection. Until she became embroiled in the struggles between king and Parliament, Henrietta Maria appears as a joyful if essentially frivolous exponent of seventeenth-century French manners, an innocent at heart who gathered around her the lighter elements of court society. On a maying expedition into the countryside, for instance, she packed her fearsome train of courtiers into 150 coaches and was always first to spring out of her coach when a bush was spied 'with its beautiful load of white and pearly blossoms', gathering a sprig for her hat.[10] Of her first-born son, she wrote to her friend Mamie St George, 'He is so ugly, that I am ashamed of him, but his size and fatness supply the want of beauty.' In the next breath she asked her friend to send her 'a dozen pairs of sweet chamois gloves, and also . . . one of doeskin; a game of *joucheries*, one of *poule* and the rules of any species of games now in vogue'.[11]

Henrietta Maria doubtless inherited her love of flowers from her mother, Marie de Médicis, to whom Pierre Vallet had dedicated his great book of flowers.[12] In a complementary tribute, John Parkinson dedicated his book on the pleasure garden to Henrietta Maria, later calling it his 'Feminine' work in contrast to his more 'Manlike' herbal, *Theatrum Botanicum*, which he dedicated to Charles I.[13] Tradescant would have known the French Queen Mother, by reputation at least, through his Parisian contacts, the Robins and the Morins, and he may just possibly have been the gardener mentioned in a letter that Henrietta Maria sent to her mother early in Tradescant's appointment. 'As I am sending this man into France to get some fruit-trees and some flowers,' wrote the young queen, 'I most humbly entreat your majesty to be pleased to assist him with your power, if by chance any one should do him wrong and hinder him; you will do me much honour.'[14] Queen Henrietta Maria liked to surround herself with her own countrymen, however, gardeners included, but the letter does at least confirm the close interest she took in her gardens.

As Oatlands Palace was pulled down after the civil war, little remains of the rambling Tudor palace where John Tradescant took up his last substantive appointment. The men who surveyed the property for

Parliament after the troubles have left behind the clearest record,[15] which springs to life when their words are set against sketches by Anthonis van den Wyngaerde executed a century or so earlier.[16] In Wyngaerde's panoramic view, a densely wooded park extends to left and right of the palace, and beyond it can be seen the winding Thames. A distant Windsor castle rises out of woodland, while a cart pulled by three horses trundles along the dirt road that runs alongside the south wall.

The parliamentary commissioners brought a more measured eye to their task, describing the palace's 'divers large & faire structures of excellent brick building' set around three courts: the Great and Middle Courts, both turfed, and the Innermost Court, paved in rough freestone. Serjeant Painter John de Critz (a Fleming who reappears later in the Tradescants' story) was responsible for painting and gilding a huge dial (twenty-four feet in compass) at the entrance to the house, ornamented with the royal initials (J and A) on the sides and a crown at the top. A similar dial adorned the Inner Court, 'conteyning in it the seven planetts and twelve signes [of the Zodiac] with each guilded', also painted with the 'fower quarters of the yeare with shippes hilles dales &c'.[17]

Inside the palace, rooms were mostly panelled and floors either wooden-boarded or matted. Generally only two storeys high, the palace complex was adorned 'with severall Turretts Llanthorns & spacious Gatehouses & standing round severall large & fayre Courts it is no lesse delectable then in it selfe every way usefull'.[18] High-chimneyed in typical Tudor style and squeezed within its squarely enclosing walls, the palace was graced with later additions by architect Inigo Jones, Surveyor of the King's Works and inventor of court entertainments for both James I and Charles I.

This was the third time that Inigo Jones and John Tradescant had crossed paths professionally, for Jones had also worked for Robert Cecil and Buckingham. Jones's royal appointment dated from 1615 when he took over from Simon Basil as Surveyor to the King's Works (he had earlier worked as Surveyor to Henry, Prince of Wales). Already for Queen Anne at Oatlands he had taken down an old brick gate at the end of her gallery, 'mureing upp the walls there, and making two other gates, as also in making the greate gate there with other woorkes'.[19] Surviving drawings for the great gate reveal its exquisite design, reworking themes Jones had learnt from Italian Renaissance architect Sebastiano Serlio. It led into Oatlands' newly created vineyard and 'the long privey walke addioyning'. Artist Paul van Somer had included it in the background to his portrait of Queen Anne, no doubt consciously projecting her artistic modernity.[20]

Among other garden works undertaken at this time, the green above the vineyard was levelled to make a new walled garden, the ground 'being trenched very deepe to kill the Fferne Rootes',[21] and Jones designed for Queen Anne a building that Tradescant would come to know intimately: the silkworm house, which bore witness to King James's continuing obsession with creating an indigenous silk industry. Although no drawings have survived, the royal accounts of Keeper Sir John Trevor give some idea of its magnificence. Marke Barnes the joiner was paid for 'wainscotting of the Silkewormehouse with ovall and arched pannills', which also incorporated a 'wroughte freeze', and he was paid extra for the 'double woorke of the portall being made like on both sides'. Carpenter William Portington received £28 for 'all the tymber boordes nayles and carpentry' required to construct shelving for the silkworms. Glazier George Locksmith primed and painted the stairs and doors, while other craftsmen carved mantels and jambs for the chimney, and painted the late queen's arms on to glass (she died in March 1619, soon after her silkworm house was completed).[22]

Creating a silk industry in Britain was one of King James's enduring enthusiasms, which owed much to the example of France, where Huguenot Olivier de Serres had written a treatise on the culture of silkworms that came to the notice of Henri IV. Soon regarded as an expert on the white mulberry tree, de Serres was commissioned to provide mulberry trees for the French royal parks including Fontainebleau and the Tuileries. An English version of de Serres's treatise appeared in 1607 dedicated to King James, with an additional English gloss from its translator, Nicholas Geffe.[23] That same year, King James wrote to the deputy lieutenants of his counties, requiring landowners to purchase and plant 10,000 mulberry trees each, which were to be delivered to purchasers in March or April the following year at a cost of 6s the hundred. He also drew their attention to the treatise on growing mulberry trees and tending the silkworms.[24] William Stallenge received a twenty-one-year licence to print the treatise and another licence to import mulberry seeds.[25] As Geffe had remarked in his English addendum to de Serres's treatise, mulberry trees would need to come from 'beyond the Seas' to satisfy demand. 'My purpose is and I will so project,' he went on, 'that within five yeeres to furnish *England* with ten millions of white Mulberrie plant or upwards which may be generally dispersed, for the good and benefit of the whole kingdome.'[26]

State papers reported intermittent progress: in August 1609, for instance, Frenchman Francis de Verton, Sieur de la Forest, was said to have travelled some 1,100 miles throughout the Midlands and eastern counties of England, taking with him a travelling show of silk spinners at work and distributing 100,000 mulberry trees. Defending himself against rumours that he could not fulfil his orders, he claimed to have half a million trees in his nursery back in France.[27] In July 1614, Tradescant's predecessor at Oatlands was granted (with survivorship) the office of keeping silkworms at the royal palaces of Whitehall and Greenwich,[28] while four years later a groom of the royal chamber requested payment of his expenses 'whilst travelling about with the King's silkworms the past three months, withersoever His Majesty went'.[29]

But despite all James's exhortations, England never saw a flourishing silk industry. There was confusion first of all over which sort of mulberry trees to plant: the more delicate white mulberry reputedly preferred by the silkworms, or the hardier black mulberries, better suited to the English climate although apparently less palatable to the worms. Geffe's translation of de Serres's original treatise suggested that the different varieties of tree produced different kinds of silk: 'grosse, strong, and heavie' from the black as opposed to 'fine, weake, and light' from the white.[30] While he advised against mixing the worms' feed to combine their separate virtues, Geffe maintained that either sort was acceptable but gave the advantage to the white for anyone planting afresh.[31] John Parkinson was less certain, noting that 'some are confident that the leaves of the blacke will doe as much good as the white: but that respect must be had to change your seede, because therein lyeth the greatest mysterie'. He declined to pronounce on how this might be done, however, referring his readers instead to an (unnamed) tract.[32]

By the mid-1650s, Samuel Hartlib deplored the continued English deficiency in keeping silkworms, pointing to a 'Mr Moriney in Paris' who had a large book on the 'seeding' of insects (surely Pierre Morin, whose interest in entomology had been noted by Evelyn). Hartlib was convinced that raising silkworms was easy, child's play even: 'the special businesse is to be carefull in feeding them, and keeping them sweet.' He could point to the shining success of 'divers *Ladies, Gentlewomen, Scholars, Citizens* &c' who had 'nursed up divers worms to perfection, though they have had little skill in the managing of them . . . I am informed that one near *Charing-Crosse* maketh a good living by them: also another by *Ratliff-Crosse;* yea, even in *Cheshire* at *Duckenfield* they thrive & prosper.'[33]

Yet however down-to-earth the English tried to make the whole business of rearing silkworms to produce fine silks, the French professed to take infinitely greater pains. It is hard to imagine the practical Tradescant paying too much heed to the regime outlined in the 1616 English printing of *Maison rustique, or, The Countrey Farme,* which derived much of its information on silkworms from Olivier de Serres. The tone is remarkably tender towards 'these prettie creatures' whose upkeep on a farm was properly the housewife's responsibility, along with that of the honey bee. Good ventilation, temperature control and rigorous hygiene were of critical importance. Windows should be glazed or covered with paper of 'fine Linnen Cloth' to protect the worms from inclement weather or predatory birds, and no vermin, crickets, lizards or rats allowed to 'kill and spoyle these little things'. The interior of the silkworm house should contain pillared partitions to which should be fastened boards or hurdles 'sprinkled with a little vineger, and rubbed with sweet hearbes, because they love sweet smels'.

According to *Maison Rustique,* the task of caring for silkworms began as soon as spring was drawing close. Mulberry trees should be dunged 'during the new Moone of March' and the breeding 'seed' or eggs chosen by bathing them in wine and selecting the heavier ones that sank to the bottom. After bathing in white wine, the eggs should be warmed near a fire and then 'betwixt two pillowes stuffed with feathers ... or betwixt the breasts of women (provided that they have not their termes at that time)'. As they began to hatch, the worms should be taken away with mulberry leaves and placed upon the boards 'that have been rubbed over with Wormewood or Sothernewood, or some such like hearbe'. Good smells remained important throughout their short lives and the silkworm house should be 'perfumed with Frankincense, Garlicke, Onions, Larde, or broyled Sawsages, that you may minister matter of pleasure unto these little creatures: and againe, if they be weake and sicke, these smells refresh and recover them'.[34] In his earlier treatise, de Serres even went so far as to instruct the silkworm keeper to 'drinke a little wine earlie in the morning before he goes to worke' to preserve the worms 'from all stench, specially from the naughtie breath of folks'.[35]

It was also the keeper's task to make sure the worms were properly fed: twice a day until their second 'change or drousines', then three times a day until their fourth change and after that as many as five or six times a day 'for then you must spare no foode, but rather cloying them, to fill and satiate their appetite, hasting them by much eating to perfect their taske'.[36] The silkworm house should be swept daily, its floor sprinkled with vinegar and strewn with sweet-smelling herbs and the silkworm shelves cleaned every two to three days. After about nine weeks (in England), the bodies of the worms would turn amber, signalling that silk production was about to start, and then the shelves should be provided with arched branches of rosemary, lavender, oak, chestnut or broom to give the worms a resting place while they spun their silk. The keeper had also to remain vigilant against disease, stopping draughts and using smoke-free coals sprinkled with a little malmsey wine, aqua vitae, frankincense or the much-favoured sliced sausages. Rosewater was the prescribed remedy for any silkworms suffering from sunstroke, and a few days' starvation for any that had overeaten. Once the worms had produced their silk, a final task was to select which worms to keep for breeding: fat ones were best, and more females than males. Their sex could be distinguished by staring into their eyes 'for the females have thinner eyes, and not altogether so blacke, as the males'.[37]

Despite Hartlib's claim that silk production was child's play, Tradescant would surely have employed an under-keeper to carry out the day-to-day tasks of caring for the royal silkworms at Oatlands Palace. As well as looking after the vineyard, he also had overall charge of the several gardens at Oatlands. By the time of the parliamentary survey in 1650 these included the Great Garden, the Long Garden, the King's Privy Garden, the Queen's Privy Garden, and the New (French) Garden.[38] The surveyors made a careful count of the orchard trees, noting 162 wall fruits and 314 other fruit trees. They also picked out two garden features: the Great Garden's 'faire and handsome Cisterne or fountaine' and, in the Long Garden, 'A close Walke of one hundred yards in length arched & very neatly ordered'. This last was almost certainly the garden arbour designed by Inigo Jones[39] and installed under Tradescant's supervision in 1632, a stately wooden structure fourteen feet wide and of the same height that extended for 263 feet along a series of ten-foot-bays or panels, twenty-six in all. Two carpenters were required to construct the frame, Reynold Butler and Bartholomew Rogers, who charged by the bay (an inclusive sum for timber and workmanship) and who also erected a new wooden fence around the garden, six feet high 'with round Toppes'. Another new fence went up around the vineyard.[40]

Through Exchequer accounts for Oatlands, it is possible to establish the rhythm of Tradescant's royal employment, and to compare the relatively modest expenditure on Oatlands with the other royal palaces listed, such as Theobalds, Hampton Court, Greenwich, Eltham, and London properties including the Tower of London, Whitehall, the old palace at Westminster and Denmark House.[41] The elder Tradescant's time as gardener saw two main periods of activity: the building of the arbour in 1632; and the construction of a new bowling green and orange garden in the autumn of 1634. These last two were covered by separate royal warrants. The first, dated 23 September 1634, granted to 'our Servant John Tredescant Keeper of our Gardens at Oatelands the sume of one hundred Pounds ... for the making of a Bowling greene at Oatelands, and for workmanshipp and materialls for the same according to our directton and Command'.[42] One week later, another warrant granted an additional £450 to Henry Wicks, His Majesty's paymaster, to fund the creation of a new orange garden, and for walling Tradescant's new bowling green.[43] As specified in the royal warrant, these works included

the inclosing of a peece of ground with a Brickewall containing five and twenty roods or thereabouts adjoining to our Gardens at Oatelands intended for the keeping of Orange trees in winter and making of a Shedd in length about two hundred threescore and too foote with a Colehouse adjoyning thereunto. As also for the inclosing of a peece of ground for a Bowling greene there, with Rayles Posts Lattices and Painters worke.

Bricklayer William Dodson built a wall with buttresses around the new orange garden while carpenter Bartholomew Rogers set up posts, pales and rails around the bowling green. He also made a new roller and set up 'a doorcase and doore in the wall betweene the privy Garden and Orrenge Garden'.[44]

The parliamentary surveyors who visited Oatlands made no mention of its orange garden or valuable orange trees[45] and in fact paid far more attention to Queen Henrietta Maria's much-loved palace at Wimbledon, the beautiful old country house of the Cecils. Charles had bought it for her the year after Tradescant's death and here André Mollet of the French dynasty of royal gardeners laid out a fine garden to complement Inigo Jones's extensive architectural alterations.

The parliamentary survey of Wimbledon is an absolute delight. Carried out in 1649 by the same four surveyors who visited Oatlands (Hugh Hindley, John Inwood, John Wale and John Webb), it devoted seven detailed pages to the house and eleven to the gardens.[46] In the orange garden house, for instance, 'now standing in squared boxes fitted for ye purpose', were 'fortie two orange trees bearing fayre & large Oringes' (valued at £420 altogether), one lemon tree (value £20) 'bearing greate and very large Lemmons' and a pomecitron tree, a kind of citrus known to the Romans.

Outside in the orange garden were six pomegranate trees, eighteen more
orange trees, which had not yet fruited, intricate knots, two apricot trees,
one cypress, fourteen laurels, a bay tree and two long galleries or walks much
like the one Inigo Jones had designed for Oatlands. The surveyors'
enchantment is evident as they paced the different garden areas, measuring,
counting, putting a value on beauty and rarity, scrupulously noting the white
marble Diana fountain, the mermaid fountain, the birdcage fountain, the
various garden houses (summerhouses, banqueting houses, plain garden
houses and 'one little shadow or summer house, covered with blew slate &
ridged with lead & fitted for resting places, with Maze and wilderness'). In
the upper garden were 131 lime trees and 68 shrubs of good growth, plus
cherry trees, fruit trees, wall fruits and box borders. After passing through
the 'hartichoke garden' and the 'Phesant Garden', the surveyors came to the
vineyard garden, by then apparently turned into an orchard with 507 fruit
trees of diverse sorts (the number has been added later: did they need to
conduct several counts?), 144 lime trees and more than 350 espaliered and
'special' wall fruits including apricots, peaches, pears, plums, May cherries
and Bon Chrétien pears. In the same garden were two little shadow houses
and 'two rollers of stone with very large and handsome frames of Iron',
worth £16 the pair.

After Wimbledon, the surveyors went on to appraise another royal palace
at Richmond where they examined a circular knot in the privy garden,
noting its box quarters planted with flowers, and the white-painted seats
encircling a yew tree at its heart.[47] Alleys of rose trees emphasized the
garden's formality. Even more handsome as a centrepiece was the birdcage
for turtle-doves in the great orchard: 'this Cage is of a round modle walled
in the Bottome foure foote high, posted with pillars of wood and wyred
round & Turretted overhead & covered also wth wyre & also with blew
slate'.[48] Its declared value was £10, equivalent to just one of Wimbledon's
fruit-bearing orange trees.

The splendour of Wimbledon and Richmond suggests that it is possible
to make too much of the Tradescants as royal gardeners. Despite the epitaph
on their tombstone, celebrating their fame as 'Gardiners to the Rose and Lily

Queen' (the Tudor rose allied to the French lily by Henrietta Maria's marriage to Charles), Frenchman André Mollet had far greater claim to the title. As well as designing the showcase gardens she loved, he also worked for the Prince of Orange and later for Queen Christina of Sweden, to whom he dedicated *Le Jardin de Plaisirs* in 1651.[49]

Mollet's book on the pleasure garden is a blueprint for the French style that he was helping to champion across Europe. In its grand garden plans, individual trees have been reduced to small identical lollipops marching out across the landscape in a rigorous geometry designed to impress, while individual flowers appear as stitches in a scrolling tapestry of feathers, escutcheons, vases and shells. Mollet boasted in his foreword to the reader that France now had the most beautiful gardens of anywhere in the world, in terms of the artifice that man can bring to them (*'quant a l'artifice que l'homme y peut apporter'*). Harmony decreed that flowers should be separated by size into taller shrubs such as roses and Spanish gorse, and the shorter, rarer bulbs and herbaceous flowers such as pinks, double gillyflowers, crown imperials, martagon lilies, tulips, anemones, ranunculi, auriculas and irises. All were favourites of curious flower collectors, but now the single flower was subservient to the overall design. A garden had become a form of horticultural wallpaper and it is easy to imagine how a passionate plant lover like Tradescant might begin to feel overtaken by fashion.

In any event, after the new orange garden of 1634 Tradescant oversaw no major new developments at Oatlands requiring additional finance. Most improvements were internal, such as 'furring and boarding the floores in the Queenes Bedchamber and presence Chamber',[50] and the construction of a new balcony in Queen Henrietta Maria's withdrawing chamber in 1635–6.[51] That same year, repairs were undertaken to bays around the Bowling Green, a brick wall in the vineyard was taken down and Serjeant Painter John de Critz painted part of Oatlands' 'Lanthorne' with 'Sky cullour in oyle'. The following year (1636–7), a black marble fountain appeared in the accounts, and painter Thomas Preston was paid for various works including 'priming stopping and painting white lead in oyle the old Tymberworke of the Somer gallery in the Queenes privy Garden'[52] – routine maintenance that suggests the elder Tradescant's attention was occupied elsewhere. Indeed, one great advantage of his royal post was that it allowed him time to devote to his own interests, and he had his own orchard and garden to think of, as well as his swelling collection of curiosities that sought to encompass the whole of God's creation, as manifested in the wonders of nature and art.

Chapter Seventeen

Tradescant's Orchard

Fruit was Tradescant's overriding passion, as it was for many of his countrymen. Ever since he travelled through the Low Countries and France for Robert Cecil, his name has been associated with much of England's best. Of plums, his friend John Parkinson wrote in 1629 that 'the choysest for goodnesse, and rarest for knowledge, are to be had of my very good friend Master John Tradescante, who hath wonderfully laboured to obtaine all the rarest fruits hee can heare off in any place of Christendome, Turky, yea or the whole world.' As well as obtaining stock for his employers, Tradescant also supplied young trees to London's burgeoning nursery trade, such as 'Master John Millen, dwelling in Olde streete, who from Iohn Tradescante and all others that have good fruit, hath stored himselfe with the best only, and he can sufficiently furnish any'.[1]

The story of how French and Dutch stock came to enrich home-grown fruit production is told in *The Husbandman's fruitfull Orchard* of 1609, written by an experienced fruit-grower identified only as 'N.F.'. Credit for England's abundance is given to King Henry VIII's fruiterer, 'one Richard Harris of London, borne in Ireland', who brought French pippin grafts back to England together with cherry and pear grafts from the Low Countries, then 'tooke a peece of ground belonging to the King, in the parrish of Tenham in Kent, being about the quantitie of seaven score acres'. Here he made the mother of all orchards, 'planting therein all those foraigne grafts' so that now, '(thankes bee to God) divers Gentlemen & others, taking delight in grafting (being a matter so necessary and beneficial in a Comon-wealth) have planted many Orchards, fetching the grafts out of that Orchard, which Harris planted called the New-garden'. And now because England was growing 'such fine and serviceable fruit', she had no more need of 'any foraigne fruite' and was able to serve other places.[2]

In Elizabethan times, London had three fruiterers all recommended by John Gerard: Vincent Pointer of Twickenham, introduced as 'a most cunning and curious graffer and planter of all manner of rare fruites'; Henry Banbury of Tothill Street, Westminster, described as another 'excellent graffer and painfull planter'; and the 'diligent and most affectionate lover of plants Master Warner' who had a nursery in Horsleydown, Bermondsey.[3] Gerard added a cryptic warning to 'beware the Bag and Bottle' – a notorious public house, perhaps, or an unscrupulous rival. Cheating of customers was a common enough complaint according to Parkinson 'for it is an inherent qualitie almost hereditarie with most of them, to sell any man an ordinary fruit for whatsoever rare fruit he shall aske for: so little are they to be trusted'.[4]

By Tradescant's time, John Millen had taken over as London's premier supplier of fruit trees to the public,[5] while Tradescant's great contribution was to scour the nurseries and orchards of Europe, bringing back new varieties to improve English stock. Already an impressive range of fruits was available in England. In *Paradisi in Sole*, Parkinson provided separate descriptions for thirty-six named cherries, fifty-eight different apples, sixty-one plums, more than sixty-five pears, and twenty-one peaches apart from the many to which 'wee can give no especiall name; and therefore I passe them over in silence'.[6] Samuel Hartlib would soon claim an incredible 500 pear varieties, although his mathematics was surely the product of double or even triple counting.[7]

In 1634, when Tradescant compiled his plant list and catalogue of fruits,[8] he was generally growing around half to two-thirds of the varieties known to Parkinson for each type of fruit and he could boast a white nectarine that

Parkinson knew of but had not seen.[9] Many of Tradescant's fruits were indeed extremely rare, including the 'white diapred plum of Malta, scarce knowne to any in our Land but John Tradescante', which Parkinson described as 'a very good plum, and striped all over like diaper'.[10] Other fruits in Parkinson's lists were even stranger, such as the black and bobbly 'great 16 ounce peare' (the number of black fruits generally is remarkable); the long white grape which Parkinson described as 'like unto a Pigeons egge, or as it were pointed pendent like a Pearle';[11] and the 'Cameleon or strange changeable Cherry', named by Parkinson himself 'not only because it beareth usually both blossomes, greene and ripe fruit at one time thereupon, but that the fruit will be of many formes; some round, some as it were square, and some bunched forth on one side or another, abiding constant in no fashion.'[12] It was just the sort of fruit to appeal to John Tradescant, who naturally included it in his garden, perhaps given to him by Parkinson. Tradescant also grew six named vines (the parsley-leaved vine, the Frontenac vine, the 'great blew Grape', the potbaker grape, the raisin grape and the currant grape), with 'divers others'. In fact, according to Parkinson, Tradescant grew around twenty different vine varieties but 'hee never knew how or by what name to call them'.[13]

The fruits that are named by Parkinson evoke an age when diversity rather than standardization was king. Some celebrated the town or county where the fruits flourished first: pears from Warwick, Lewes, Worcester, Norwich, Windsor, Petworth and Arundel, for instance.[14] Then there was the 'ten pound peare, or the hundred pound peare', which was in fact 'the best Bon Chretien of Syon, so called, because the grafts cost the Master so much the fetching by the messengers expences, when he brought nothing else'.[15] Many more names proudly announced oddities of form, like the 'Urinall Cherrie', long and round; and the many varieties of apple: the gillyflower apple ('a fine apple, and finely spotted'),[16] the Cowsnout, the Crows egge, the 'womans breast apple' ('a great apple'), and the 'Cats head apple', which 'tooke the name of the likeness'. Disappointingly, the paradise apple was 'light and spongy, and of a bitterish sweet taste, not to be commended'. By contrast, 'sops in wine' was 'so named both of the pleasantnesse of the fruit, and beautie of the apple'[17] (similar to John Tradescant's 'Sack and Sugar', perhaps), while several French names indicated continued foreign imports, among them Pome de Rambures, Pome de Capanda, Pome de Calual and Donime Couadis. The rarest of these fruits were cherished for the table as well as the orchard. As Parkinson observed, 'The best sorts of Apples serve at the last course for the table, in most mens houses of account, where, if there grow any rare or excellent fruit, it is then set forth to be seene and tasted.'[18]

But did Tradescant supply fruit trees to the general public? When Thomas Johnson visited South Lambeth in 1632, he made no mention of Tradescant's orchard, quoting instead just two authorities on fruit: 'my two friends Mr. *John Parkinson*, and Mr *John Millen*, the one to furnish you with the history, and the other with the things themselves, if you desire them'.[19] The same message (about cherries) he repeated for plums, apricots, gooseberries, apples and pears. 'Most of the best peares,' he claimed, 'are at this time to be had with Mr. *John Millin* in Old-street, in whose nursery are to be found the choisest fruits this kingdom yields.'[20] At no point did he propose Tradescant as a general fruiterer.

Of course, when Johnson visited South Lambeth, Tradescant may not have built up enough new orchard stock for sale. We know that his son would go on to supply fruit trees and plants more widely, but Johnson's silence remains puzzling nonetheless, given the huge variety of fruits Tradescant included in his plant list of 1634, just a year or two after Johnson's visit. Either Johnson was not overly impressed by Tradescant's orchard, or (a more likely explanation) Tradescant supplied plants to a fairly narrow range of friends, nurserymen, contacts and other curious gardeners. His plant list was compiled primarily for information and only indirectly for the purposes of trade.[21]

The puzzle surrounding Tradescant's operation as a nurseryman is compounded by a tantalizing collection of sixty-six watercolours of garden fruits and one rogue lily, found among the Ashmole manuscripts at Oxford's Bodleian Library.[22] Known generally as 'Tradescant's Orchard', the collection depicts many luscious varieties of fruit grown in Stuart orchards:

cherries, plums, damsons, apricots, nectarines, peaches, pears, grapes, and
single varieties of strawberry, gooseberry, date, quince and hazelnut.
Interleaved with blank pages, the fruits are arranged by type and roughly by
ripening date. Colours are vibrant and strong, especially the bright reds
shading into yellow. Here, too, are creamy-white cherries, velvety black
plums, mottled brown peaches, and a Jerusalem pear striped cream and
green like a melon. Among the cartoon insects and birds lurking in the
foliage you will find a dangling spider, a bright lilac butterfly, an exotic
lizard, a fat robin sitting on a plum, a frog with bulging eyes, and a tiny
squirrel eating a giant hazelnut.

Physical analysis of paper, watermarks and handwriting by Dr Bruce
Barker-Benfield of the Bodleian Library tentatively dates the collection to
the 1620s or 1630s, just when Tradescant was building up his orchard at
South Lambeth.[23] Sometime later that century – by which time it was
missing several pages – the manuscript came into the hands of Tradescant's
neighbour Elias Ashmole, who bound the remaining folios into a handsome
book between covers of polished brown leather, now mottled and speckled
with age. Ashmole's coat of arms appears on the spine and on the two brass
clasps. He also wrote a table of contents, giving page numbers for the fruits
illustrated.[24] And he may have added the red martagon lily opposite the first
page of contents, which looks out of place among the fruit.

Tradition has long linked the collection to the Tradescants because of a
comment scrawled against one of the plums: 'The Amber plum which J.T.
as I take it brought out of France and groweth at Hatfield ripe Septem the
8'. (Parkinson described this waxy yellow plum as having a 'sowre unpleasant
taste' while admitting that he may have been fed the wrong plum by
mistake.)[25] The same hand wrote captions to all but one of the watercolours,
providing names and ripening dates, sometimes added in a different ink.
The script is a clumsy italic, incorporating occasional letters from the
'secretary' hand used for business – but according to Dr Barker-Benfield, 'the
script is *not* that of the elder John Tradescant'.[26] Nor does the inclusion of
the popular 'Tradescant cherry' or Ashmole's subsequent ownership
necessarily prove a link to the Tradescants, despite the claim made in the

original Bodleian catalogue that the book was 'undoubtedly made by or for SIR [sic] JOHN TRADESCANT, or one of his family'.

So who commissioned the watercolours, and why? The Hatfield reference suggested to Oxford scholar R. T. Gunther that the fruits were painted as a guide for visitors to Hatfield's great orchards,[27] possibly by gentleman artist Alexander Marshal whose *Florilegium* is now in the royal collection at Windsor Castle.[28] Although Marshal stayed for a time at Lambeth with Tradescant's son and painted on vellum a book of their choicest flowers and plants,[29] only one illustration in 'Tradescant's Orchard' (of the red gooseberry) bears any resemblance to his style; like the other pages, it is painted on paper not vellum. And despite their liveliness and charm, these watercolours have none of the exquisite beauty of other contemporary natural history compendia mixing flowers, fruit, insects and birds, such as works by Georg Hoefnagel and Crispin de Passe the elder.[30] The style here is crude and the wildlife seems to have strayed in from a pattern book, with little regard for proportion or climate. Had Cecil wanted to compile an illustrated guide to his orchard, he had many better artists working for him.

All the evidence points to a much more practical purpose for the collection, perhaps as a very early example of a sales catalogue designed to tempt prospective purchasers with its colourful fruits and touches of real life (here leaves turn brown and a snail eats a fallen cherry).[31] Well thumbed and missing a number of pages, the collection was intended for consultation in the orchard rather than quiet study in a library, and its compiler provided precise ripening dates to help customers in their choices. Such information would have been particularly useful for wealthy landowners wishing to plant fruit that would ripen as they progressed around their several properties. But there are problems with this interpretation, even before trying to link it to the Tradescants. At least one of the ripening dates indicates a much warmer climate than England, even allowing for the ten-day difference between the new-style Gregorian calendar used in Europe and the old-style Julian calendar still in use in England. Parkinson gives early August as the ripening date for the 'red primordian Plumme', not 12 July as here.[32] Either the caption-writer got his dates wrong, or he had watched the fruit ripen in southern Europe.

As to whether Tradescant commissioned the fruit paintings or used them to promote sales of his own fruit, the case remains at best unproven. For each category of fruit, roughly half the painted varieties also appear in Tradescant's plant list of 1634,[33] slightly more for cherries and fewer for peaches. There is a far better correlation between the watercolours and Parkinson's (longer) list of fruits in *Paradisi in Sole*, and also with the fruits Parkinson chose to illustrate.[34] All the plums and *all* the cherries so gaily painted in 'Tradescant's Orchard' are found in Parkinson, for instance, with only slight variations in name. Visually, these two works are also similar in style and in the case of the burlet grape, Parkinson's engraving is virtually identical to the outline of the corresponding watercolour in 'Tradescant's Orchard'. This does at least tie the collection very firmly to the English fruit market, despite the foreign ripening dates. And it suggests fruit seller John Millen as another possible compiler or user of the illustrated catalogue, with his documented links to both Parkinson and Tradescant.

Whatever its provenance, 'Tradescant's Orchard' helps to paint an extraordinarily rich picture of fruit-growing in Stuart times, and Parkinson's praise puts the elder John Tradescant right at its heart. Stuart orchards must have been a splendid sight, planted to one side of a south-facing flower garden (if Parkinson's advice on layout were followed), providing shelter but not too much shadow. The tenderest fruits (apricots, peaches, nectarines, early cherries) would have been planted against south-facing walls; plums and quinces against east-, north- and west-facing walls, and the orchard fruits all mixed in together 'without regard of measure or difference, as Peares among Apples, and Plums among Cherries promiscuously; but some keepe both a distance and a division for every sort, without intermingling'.[35] Parkinson's own preferred planting pattern was the quincunx, allowing a gap of sixteen to twenty feet between trees in all directions. This he believed would create the most graceful orchard, especially when the trees were allowed to arch and interlace together. Taller pear trees should be placed as shelter to the north and east. Within them,

10. John Tradescant the elder, attributed to Emanuel de Critz.

11. John Tradescant the younger, attributed to Thomas de Critz.

12. The younger Tradescant's second wife, Hester, with her stepchildren, John and Frances.

13. Two plants brought back by John Tradescant the younger from his Virginian journey of 1637: the tulip tree (Liriodendron tulipifera) and a wild red columbine (Aquilegia canadensis).

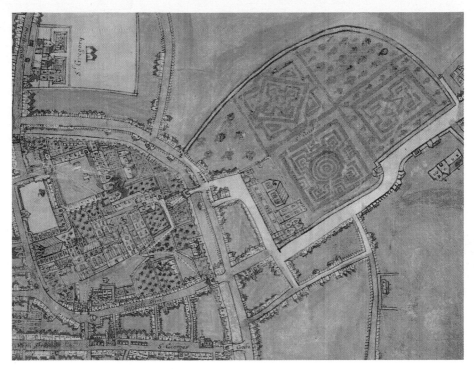

14. Canterbury Cathedral (left) and, outside the city walls, St Augustine's Abbey, gardened by John Tradescant the elder for several years from 1615.

15. A Victorian watercolour of Elias Ashmole's Turret House, adjoining the Tradescant property in South Lambeth, shortly before it was sold for redevelopment.

The Tradescant Cherry
June the 21

16. The Tradescant cherry from a collection of early seventeenth-century
watercolours of fruit known as 'Tradescant's Orchard'.

your best direction is to set Damsons, Bulleis [a kind of plum], and your taler growing Plums on the outside, and your lower Plums, Cherries, and Apples on the inside ... Thus may you also plant Apples among Plums and Cherries ... Other sorts of fruit trees you may mixe among these, if you please, as Filberds, Cornellian Cherries in standerds, and Medlars: but Service trees, Baye trees, and others of that high sort, must be set to guard the rest.[36]

As an experienced fruit-grower, Tradescant would have been skilled in propagating fruit through grafting (inserting a shoot or scion of the desired variety into a tough rootstock) and inoculation, a technique practised in the South but virtually unknown in the North, which involved inserting a bud instead of a whole sprig from one tree into another.[37] He would have pruned his wall fruit every year in late autumn or early winter, taking care not to dislodge the buds whose growth he wished to encourage. He doubtless developed his own special compost and manure to revive ailing trees (Parkinson's recommendation was to 'take a good quantite of oxe or horse bloud, mixe therewith a reasonable quantitie of sheepe or pigeons dung, which being laid to the roote, will by the often raines and much watering recover it selfe, if there bee anie possibilitie, but this must bee done in Januarie or Februarie at the furthest'.)[38] He would have kept a vigilant eye on the caterpillars, ants, earwigs, snails, moles, and birds intent on spoiling both his pleasure and his profits, perhaps heeding Parkinson's advice to arm himself with a 'birding or fowling peece' to help 'lessen their number, and make the rest more quiet: or a mill with a clacke to scarre them away'.[39]

Of all the other ills that might befall his orchard, he would have spotted the first signs of canker in his trees, cutting away the affected wood and dressing the wound with his own well-tried remedy, 'vinegar or Cowes pisse' perhaps, or 'Cowes dung and urine'.[40] And when the time came to harvest his fruits, he would have found both a market and a way of transporting the fruits that would save them from harm, packing them in dry hogsheads lined at both ends with the finest, sweetest straw, giving them air but not moisture, the cherries poured gently into broad sieves that could be stacked one upon the other for carriage to market.[41]

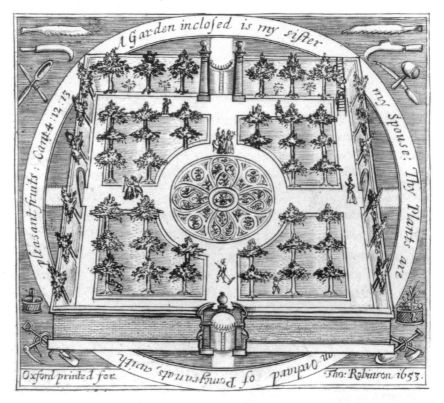

Profits and spiritual pleasures intermingle in the frontispiece to Ralph Austen's
A Treatise of Fruit-Trees *(1653).*

An orchard provided many other pleasures too, and he would quite
possibly have gained from it the spiritual satisfaction that was to become
such a feature of Puritan gardening in the troubled years that followed. One
of the age's most eloquent spokesmen was Hartlib protégé Ralph Austen,
who established an orchard, nursery and cider business in Oxford, where he
had settled by the mid-1640s.[42] Profits and pleasures were Austen's guiding
principles; indeed, the two are shown graphically shaking hands on the
frontispiece to his best-known work, A *Treatise of Fruit-Trees*, which he
dedicated to Hartlib.[43]

Like the current heir to the British throne, Ralph Austen was a man who talked to trees. 'Fruit-trees discover many things of God,' he wrote in simple prose that defies mockery, 'and many things of ourselves, and concerning our duty to God. We enquire of, and discourse with Fruit-trees when wee consider, and meditate of them, when we search out their vertues and perfections which God hath put into them, when we pry into their natures, and properties, *that is speaking to them*.'[44] He developed this theme in *The Spirituall use of an Orchard*, meditating on his observations from nature. The fact that grafts of very different materials do not thrive, for instance, he applied to human friendship, love and marriage. 'This should teach all who intend to enter into the state of *Marriage*, to looke well to their choice, that it be upon good grounds, and not for worldly advantages in the first place, as most do, and match a *Soule to the Earth*, betweene which there's no *likenesse*, nor proportion.'[45]

A true plantsman such as Tradescant must surely have shared Austen's delight in the pleasures an orchard can bring to the senses: to the ear (in birdsong and the gentle motion of boughs and leaves); to touch (in their cooling fruits and cool fresh airs); to the eye (by 'decent formes' of trees, *allées*, walks, seats and arbours, and by the 'curious colours' of blossoms, leaves and fruits); to taste (from ripe and raw fruits and the drinks and dishes made from them); but not, poor man, to smell, though others could enjoy the scent of blossoms and leaves, and of freshly dug earth.[46]

Now reaching the end of his life, Tradescant could also look back with quiet satisfaction to the part he had played in enriching the orchards of England. Whatever its provenance, the plumply ripening fruit and teeming wildlife of 'Tradescant's Orchard' gives us a privileged glimpse into a very Stuart Eden.

Chapter Eighteen

The Lambeth Ark

To reach John Tradescant's treasured collection at South Lambeth, you crossed the ditch running alongside the road by a small bridge and passed through an enormous arch made from the ribs of a whale[1] into a courtyard, where there was also 'a very ingenious little boat of bark'.[2] From here you could pass straight into the garden containing 'all kinds of foreign plants, which are to be found in a special little book which Mr. Tradescant has had printed about them' – his plant list of 1634.[3] The rarities themselves would have to wait more than twenty years before they too were ordered and catalogued into a printed list, a comment perhaps on where the elder Tradescant's true affinities lay.[4]

No detailed description has come to us of how the rarities were displayed: whether in the house or in a special garden building[5] like Morin's hermitage in Paris or the *Ambulacrum* at Leiden's botanic garden. On balance, a slightly better case can be made for locating the rarities in an upper room of the house itself, which was certainly large enough to accommodate the collection.[6] In later legal wrangles between Elias Ashmole and the widowed Hester Tradescant, she was reported to have 'fetched downe' a Queen Elizabeth milled shilling from the 'Clossitt of rarityes' that Tradescant had 'kept in a roome in his house in South Lambeth'.[7]

A visitor in the early 1660s, the Amsterdam-born artist William

Schellinks, described alighting from the Thames boat 'past the Spring Gardens at a place called John the Diskin [his spelling was even more wildly erratic than Tradescant's], where one can see in a large long room a collection of rare antique curiosities, costumes of various nationals and strange weapons, also fishes, plants, horns, shells'.[8] It sounds very like the room occupied by the Museum Wormianum, a contemporary Danish collection put together by Ole Worm, Professor of Medicine, who organized the objects in his catalogue according to a hierarchical taxonomy rising from inanimate stones and minerals through plants and animals to human anatomy and cultural artefacts.[9] Tradescant's collection was more of a jumble, however, and to make any sense of it you would have needed the services of its keeper, whose dramatic delivery was legendary.[10]

In a fitting coincidence, the earliest surviving description of John Tradescant's collection was by fellow traveller and East India Company employee Peter Mundy, who had just arrived back from India in 1634, four years or so before he made the journey to Archangel described in Chapter 10. Unlike William Schellinks, who delayed his visit to the Tradescants until his last full day in London, Mundy hurried there almost at once, having been invited with one other friend by a Mr Thomas Barlowe, who had travelled back with him from India aboard the *Mary*. The three men spent the whole day together examining ('and that superficially')

such as hee had gathered together, as beasts, fowle, fishes, serpents, wormes (reall, although dead and dryed), pretious stones and other Armes, Coines, shells, fethers, etts. of sundrey Nations, Countries, forme, Coullours; also diverse Curiosities in Carvinge, painteinge, etts., as 80 faces carved on a Cherry stone, Pictures to bee seene by a Celinder which otherwise appeare like confused blotts, Medalls of Sondrey sorts, etts. Moreover, a little garden with divers outlandish herbes and flowers, whereof some that I had not seene elsewhere but in India, being supplied by Noblemen, Gentlemen, Sea Commaunders, etts. with such Toyes as they could bringe or procure from other parts.[11]

Mundy was delighted; despite the many sights he had seen in his years of travel, he declared himself 'almost perswaded a Man might in one daye behold and collecte into one place more Curiosities then hee should see if hee spent all his life in Travell'. Although he went on to visit Sir Henry Moody's collection of optical marvels at his house in the Strand[12] and the Tower of London, where he marvelled at a massive unicorn's horn ('about 1½ yards in length and 2 or 2½ Inches diameter att the bigger end'), Tradescant's rarities quite properly took first place. Two other visitors who came at around this time must have given Tradescant quiet satisfaction: Viscount Cranborne and his brother Robert, sons of the 2nd Earl of Salisbury and grandsons of his former employer, Robert Cecil. The trip cost them 9s in 'going by water and for seeing John Tradeskins Antiquities'.[13]

One of the more assiduous visitors to the Ark was young German student Georg Christoph Stirn, who came in July 1638 and diligently recorded the objects that caught his eye.[14] His list is remarkable for what it reveals about perceptions as well as content. Despite his education, Stirn made none of today's distinctions between the real and the mythic, paying equal attention to the wonders of nature and those fashioned by the hand or brain of man; here on apparently contiguous display were 'the hand of a mermaid, the hand of a mummy, a very natural wax hand under glass'. The 'robe of the King of Virginia' (see Chapter 9) was squeezed between 'some very light wood from Africa' and 'a few goblets of agate'. Stirn's litany of outlandish beasts and birds ran the gamut from the merely exotic ('a salamander, a chameleon, a pelican, a remora,[15] a lanhado from Africa') to the simply fabulous: a barnacle goose introduced as 'a goose which has grown in Scotland on a tree'. John Gerard had ended his *Herball* with just such a creature, which he hailed as 'one of the marvels of this land (we may say of the world)'.[16] Their shells grew on trees, he explained,

in the north parts of Scotland, & the Ilands adjacent, ... wherein are conteined little living creatures: which shels in time of maturite doe open, and out of them grow those little living things; which falling into the water, doe become foules, whom we call Barnakles; in the north of England, Brant Geese, and in Lancashire, tree Geese: but the other that do fall upon the land, perish and come to nothing.

While including Gerard's text in his revised edition of the Herball, Thomas Johnson nonetheless introduced a note of realism by declaring that barnacle geese hatched from eggs like any other birds, a discovery he credited to 'some Hollanders' making a third attempt to find a passage to China.[17]

Stirn's inventory of other marvels seen at Lambeth reflects Tradescant's own obsession with size ('a bat as large as a pigeon, a human bone weighing 42 pounds') and his fondness for foreign boots and shoes, as well as the century's taste for the gruesome (a piece of human flesh on a bone and the poisoned arrows used by West Indian executioners; Peter Mundy invariably noted and even sketched outlandish methods of executions encountered on his travels). The cult of celebrity was alive even then, for among the precious objects on display was 'a beautiful present from the Duke of Buckingham' (a bejewelled feather reminiscent of his splendid French wardrobe for the wedding festivities in Paris) and a scourge reputedly used by Holy Roman Emperor, Charles V. Christian relics remained popular and Tradescant's collection could apparently boast (without qualification) 'a small piece of wood from the cross of Christ'.

The spirit behind Tradescant's collection is clearly one of curiosity and wonder: here are the wondrously strange birds, beasts and fishes he sought from the sea captains adventuring to the coasts of Africa and America, the East and West Indies and all points in between. Here too are the curious clothes and artefacts that distinguish the Turk from the Jew, the Christian from the Moslem, the Barbary Arab from the Greenlander. While Tradescant sought 'the Bigest that can be Gotten' in his natural history specimens, he was equally in thrall to the miniaturist talents that could render 'the passion of Christ carved very daintily on a plumstone'. In its very breadth and equivalence lies the essence of Tradescant's collection. Although later naturalists such as John Ray and ornithologist and ichthyologist Francis Willughby might inspect the rarities for purposes of identification, John Tradescant collected them for the sheer joy of collecting, seduced by the

Inside the Museum
Wormianum *of* Danish *collector,*
Ole Worm.

MUSEI
WORMIANI
HISTORIA

LUGD · BATAVORUM
EX OFFICINA ELSEVIRIANA
Acad Typog. 1655.

merchant adventurers whose brave voyages sparked the beginnings of global consumerism. The Latin inscription that appears under his portrait in *Musaeum Tradescantianum* quite fittingly refers to his Lambeth 'storehouse' near London ('in Reconditorio Lambethiano prope Londinum') where he mingled the wonders of nature with variations on the exotic trinkets he would have seen displayed at Britain's Burse on the Strand: bracelets from Guinea, tobacco pipes from Brazil, a cow's tail from Arabia, a variety of China dishes, a rich vest from the great Mogull.[18]

Tradescants (or Tredeskins) Rarities was the name they used themselves for their collection. Only later was it called more popularly 'Tradeskins Ark', celebrated in verse (which has survived) and also, doubtless, in bawdy song (which has not). The contexts are not always flattering. Royalist poet Robert Herrick slipped Tradescant's shells into a poem about female ugliness[19] (the two must have met when Herrick was Buckingham's chaplain on the Ile de Ré expedition).[20] Another royalist poet, John Cleveland, invoked 'natures whimsey, one that out-vies / *Tredeskin* and his ark of Novelties' in a poem of 1651, poking political fun at dissenting preacher and Parliamentarian, Sir Thomas Martin.[21] Just after the Restoration, Tradescant's Ark took a brief bow in a little book by Thomas Powell, extolling human wit and ingenuity in mechanical arts and inventions such as clocks, spheres, artificial motions, spinning and weaving, music, shipping and the taming of wild beasts. Tradescant appeared in the final section on 'certain pretty Knacks and extravagancies of Art', which paraded miniature marvels like ivory ants and an ox-drawn wagon made of glass that could be hidden under a fly. Many more such examples could be found in 'the Archives of sundry Princes and private persons' and specifically in 'John Tredeskin's Ark in *Lambeth*'.[22]

The biblical reference is apt. Alhough the 'Ark' was most probably intended to evoke the cramped inclusiveness of Tradescant's enterprise, the man himself has something of the patriarch about him. Bearded and wreathed in honour, he stares back at us from the museum catalogue prepared after his lifetime, his expression coolly appraising but not unkind. In Christian thought, Noah provided an allegory of salvation and he also 'carried the ancient knowledge of nature' that descended from Adam to Seth and then to Enoch.[23] The reminder comes from the catalogue to an exhibition exploring biblical metaphors of knowledge in early modern Europe – an exhibition hosted by Oxford's Bodleian Library where so many fragments of Tradescant's story lie gathered. 'Applied as a metaphor, the Ark allowed contemporary collectors to become Noahs,' wrote authors Jim Bennett and Scott Mandelbrote. 'Their collections came to represent new Arks, in which learning could be expanded and completed.'[24] John Tradescant was still at the first – the collecting – stage and had not yet moved on to sort, classify and decode his collection. But his celebrated gardening skills meant that he, like Noah, carried the ancient knowledge of nature, able to demonstrate how plants from around the world might be encouraged 'with proper care, [to] thrive in this kingdom'.[25]

He was also a social innovator who, by his vigour and example, changed the nature of collecting, which had started out as an essentially aristocratic occupation. Henry Peacham had first included it among the necessary accomplishments for men of refinement in the second edition of *The Compleat Gentleman* (1634), for which he wrote an enthusiastic new chapter on collecting statues, medals and sundry antiquities.

The pleasure of [collections] is best knowne to such as have seene them abroad in *France, Spaine, and Italy*, where the Gardens and Galleries of great men are beautified and set forth to admiration with these kinds of ornaments. And indeed the possession of such rarities, by reason of their dead costlinesse, doth properly belong to Princes, or rather to princely minds.[26]

Yet Tradescant was not a prince, nor even by birth a gentleman: he was a gardener and a self-made man who had bettered himself socially by his own efforts and, most spectacularly, through his collections of plants and rarities. His example showed that it was possible for 'middling sort' of men to create new identities for themselves and to earn the social respect of their peers.[27] Thomas Johnson frequently referred to him as 'Master', a courtesy title given to 'whosoever studieth in the Universities, who professeth the liberall sciences, and to be short, who can live idly, and without manuall labour, and will beare the Port, charge, and countenance of a Gentleman, he shall bee called Master: For that is the title that men give to Esquires, and other Gentlemen'.[28]

It is often said that both Tradescants sealed their wills with a coat of arms, thereby claiming official (and perhaps spurious) recognition for their rise to gentlemanly status.[29] This is not true. The seal on the elder Tradescant's will bears the imprint of an emperor's head chosen from among his own rarities, no doubt.[30] The way in which the son would lay claim to a status he quite possibly did not enjoy raises some intriguing questions later on.

Without resorting to any official seal of approval for his enhanced status, Tradescant the elder brought the collecting habit closer to ordinary people by throwing open his doors to anyone who could pay the entrance fee. Gentlemen had always shown their *cabinets de curiosités* to friends, family and social equals but Tradescant (whose collection equalled or surpassed theirs in its riches) adopted the showman's practice of charging a fee for sight of his marvels, much as Trinculo had thought of doing with the dead-drunk Caliban. Of course he was almost certainly not alone in this: Peter Mundy mentioned a similar collection of rarities owned by a 'Mr Job Best ... dwellinge att Rattcliffe', who may have allowed access to his collection on much the same terms.[31] Tradescant's collection was the better known and better regarded, however, and by charging an entrance fee he was once again leading by example.

The actual fee was most probably set at 6d per person, less than the 8d Tradescant had spent on wine at Newcastle's best inn on his way to Muscovy, but still affordable only to those who had money to spare on enjoyment. Around the time of the younger Tradescant's death, Westmorland antiquary and Member of Parliament Sir Daniel Fleming (an ardent royalist) spent a total of 7s 6d taking four people to visit the Ark: 2s for a boat there and back, 1s for a coach from Whitehall, 2s entrance ('given for ye sight there unto 4'), and a further 2s 6d 'spent at Jo. a Tradeskins'.[32] It is distinctly possible that he spent this last amount buying plants: he had a fine garden at Rydal Hall, where he built a stone summerhouse or 'grot' overlooking the lower of Rydal's two waterfalls, and liked his home so much that he commissioned three prospects of house, garden, grotto and vale.[33] He may even have taken inspiration from 'a small Landskip drawn by Sir Nath: Bacon' seen at the Ark.[34]

Did the king and queen come to visit? Later commentators made wild claims, just as some raised Tradescant's status to 'Sir John'. Normandy-born scholar and Lambeth Palace librarian Dr A.C. Ducarel (who lived for a time at Tradescant's South Lambeth house) informed a fellow botany enthusiast that Tradescant

lived in a great house at South Lambeth, where there is reason to think his museum was frequently visited by persons of rank, who became benefactors thereto: among these were King Charles the First (to whom he was gardener), Henrietta Maria his Queen, Archbishop Laud, George Duke of Buckingham, Robert and William Cecil, Earls of Salisbury, and many other persons of distinction.[35]

As several of these people were dead by the time Tradescant opened his Lambeth doors, the benefactors have clearly been mixed in with the visitors but the generally cautious Prudence Leith-Ross thought a royal visit likely. Its most probable date, in her view, was the autumn of 1635 when the king instructed the keeper of the Hampton Court wardrobe, William Smithsby, to 'deliver unto John Tredeskyn' various items of royal clothing, namely 'King Henry the Eight his Capp, his hawking Bagg and Spurres'. A second warrant followed six weeks later, specifying 'King Henry the Eight his cap, his stirrups Henry 7th his gloves and combcase'.[36] Not all these items found their way into the catalogue of 1656, although it did include Henry VIII's hawking hoods and gloves (both listed twice), stirrups, and 'dogs-coller', as well as Edward the Confessor's knit-gloves, Anne Boleyn's 'Night-vayle embroidered with silver' and her 'silke knit-gloves'.[37] Smithsby was still in charge of the wardrobe at Hampton Court at the time of Charles's execution, and among the goods inventoried for sale was 'One hawkeing glove of Henry ye 8th' (sold for 2s) and 'Six combe cases yt were Henry ye 8th' (sold for 7s).[38] Perhaps the sale included items that should by rights have gone to John Tradescant.

The king had a proven link to Tradescant as a collector, asking his Oatlands gardener to perform much the same scouting role as Tradescant had for the Duke of Buckingham. Three years into Tradescant's royal appointment, a letter was read out from Secretary of State Francis Windebank to the court of the East India Company, signalling 'His Majesties pleasure, that the Company should write for such varieties as are expressed in a paper thereinclosed, and being returned to deliver them to John Tredescant to bee reserved by him for His Majesties Service'.[39] The matter was put into the hands of Andrew Ellam, bookkeeper to the East India Company, who was required to send the paper 'by their next shippe to their severall ffactories, that such things as may bee had may bee returned for England, according to his Majesties pleasure'. A similar request was made three months later, without naming Tradescant, requiring Arab and Persian manuscript books for the king's pleasure.[40]

The paper asking for 'varieties' has not survived so we do not know whether the king wanted plants, exotic beasts, birds and fishes, or cultural artefacts. But it does throw up an interesting question: was the king seeking 'varieties' for himself or might the approach to scattered merchants help to explain how Tradescant built up such a fine collection of plants and rarities? Prudence Leith-Ross deduced from the letter that Tradescant was by this time in charge of the king's cabinet of rarities, but in fact that post was already filled, by Dutch artist Abraham van der Doort, whom Charles had inherited after the death of his brother, Prince Henry, along with Henry's own collection.

The harried van der Doort remained in his post until he hanged himself in 1640, frustrated by missing medals, obstructive colleagues, his own poor command of English, and perhaps even jealousy that 'the kinge had designd some other man to keepe his pictures, which hee had not done'.[41] His inventories meticulously recorded the state and provenance of objects in the king's collection, including the 'round ould shuting ordinary Box in a worme eaten rotton frame, the Picture of king Henry the 8th, imboast in one Cullor of wax' given to the king by 'Mr Surveyor', Inigo Jones.[42] As in many princely cabinets, pictures predominated; Charles's collection contained no sign of any exotic beasts or stuffed birds that might have made the slow journey back from the East Indies, and just a sprinkling of objects that might overlap with Tradescant's collection: a sea compass under glass; a little iron anchor; a musical instrument given by Sir Henry Wotton, kept in a case of crimson velvet laced with silver lace; a 'spurr Royall'; an East Indian idol given to the king by van der Doort himself; a tiny jewel weighing less than an ounce carved with sacrificial oxen above a flaming altar. Whatever rarities were delivered on the king's behalf into John Tradescant's hands from the East India Company's factories may quite possibly have stayed there.

Chapter Nineteen
Family Matters

Through all these years of his father's triumphs, John Tradescant the son has stayed quietly in the shadows. School records tell us that he left the King's School, Canterbury, at fourteen in 1623, the same year that his father joined the Duke of Buckingham's service. The customary four years of schooling had not turned him into a scholar, although it gave him at least the rudiments of Latin for the future naming of botanical species.

At fourteen, he would have gone straight to work. Many younger boys would have begun their apprenticeships much earlier. As gardening was his birthright (his choice too, no doubt), the boy would almost certainly have gone to work alongside his father, learning the many skills involved in the ancient craft of gardening and perhaps standing in for his father on the latter's absences abroad.

We hear nothing more of John the son until his marriage on 29 February 1628 (at the relatively young age of nineteen)[1] to Jane Hurte at St Gregory by St Paul, an ancient City church adjoining London's great cathedral. The wedding took place some six months before Buckingham's assassination and it seems probable that the couple moved to South Lambeth with the elder Tradescant when the house was ready. The marriage would bring Tradescant two children. The first was a daughter, Frances, described as 'about nineteen' at her marriage in January 1645, which – if correct – would mean she was

Jane's daughter from a previous marriage. This could explain Frances's uneasy place within the Tradescant household as she grew older, but the girl's age at marriage was provided by her stepmother, John's second wife, and is quite possibly wrong.[2] The couple's son – another John – was born five and a half years into the marriage and was baptized at the parish church of St Mary, Lambeth, on 4 November 1633, where he is described as 'John the sonne of John Tredeskin'.[3]

A little over a year after the birth of his son, on 19 December 1634, the younger Tradescant was admitted and sworn a freeman of the Company of Gardeners,[4] paying 2s 6d and freely promising 10s more.[5] The records show that he chose to join by redemption (that is, by paying a fee). A more usual route was to serve an indentured apprenticeship of seven years to a freeman of the Company.[6] Shortly before Tradescant, for instance, the new freemen included 'John Hinche junior apprentice to his father now Master', and soon after him came Leonard Girle (destined to become one of London's leading nurserymen), 'bound to Richard Roland for 7 years from Michaelmas past'.[7] As Tradescant's father was not a member of the Company, the son's induction into the art of gardening did not constitute a formal apprenticeship, nor is there any evidence that he served a formal apprenticeship with anyone else. His joining when he did tells us something about how gardening in London was changing, and perhaps also about how Tradescant the younger sought to carve out his own future within it.

From medieval times, most forms of commercial life in London were governed by craft guilds or 'mysteries' (no sanctity was implied; the word comes from the French *métier* meaning trade or profession),[8] which were tightly woven into the City's economic and political fabric. Guilds controlled entry into a craft, through apprenticeships and training, and attempted to outlaw competition from non-members. In this sense they combined the functions of trading standards authorities and closed shops. They were also benevolent fraternities, looking after the interests of members and their communities, and they promised a degree of political power for those who climbed up through their ranks, especially the elite freemen privileged to wear the guild's special uniform or 'livery'.[9]

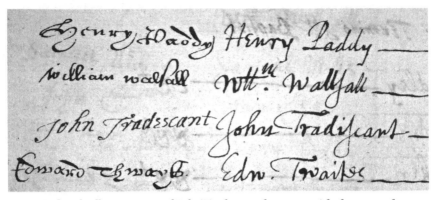

The schoolboy signature of John Tradescant the younger (the boys signed in the left-hand column).

While the Gardeners today enjoy their rightful place in the pecking order of London livery companies (ranked sixty-sixth out of more than a hundred companies), in John Tradescant's day they did not even scrape into the lists. Contemporary listings first paraded the twelve great companies (the Mercers, Grocers, Drapers, Fishmongers, Goldsmiths, Skinners, Merchant Tailors, Haberdashers, Salters, Ironmongers, Vintners, and Clothworkers) followed by the ten merchant adventuring companies (including the 'Turkie Merchants' and the 'Merchants of Virginia'), and then by some fifty other guilds and mysteries covering all possible trades from the Brown-bakers to the Wool-packers. The Fruiters appeared some two-thirds down the list, displaying a naked Adam and Eve on their coat of arms, and a serpent coiled temptingly around a fruit-laden tree.[10] Of the Gardeners, however, there was simply no trace.

Historian David Marsh attributes their exclusion to the way the gardeners attempted to bypass the City authorities during their formative years by appealing directly to King James, instead of first seeking the approval of the City's Court of Aldermen as guilds were supposed to do. In effect, the upstart Company of Gardeners was attempting to bully its way into control of London's plant and market garden trade, which the City authorities naturally resisted. Relations between the wealthy City and a perennially cash-starved sovereign were often fraught and the Gardeners picked the wrong side, as they would later discover to their cost. Indeed, Marsh goes even further to suggest that the Gardeners may have been a court-inspired foundation in the first place.[11]

After existing for several centuries as an informal fellowship, the Company received its first royal charter from King James I by Letters Patent dated 18 September 1605, giving it control over gardeners in the City of London and within a six-mile compass.[12] No one living within this area was allowed to practise the 'trade crafte or misterie' of gardening without first gaining admission to the Company and submitting to its ordinances – a prohibition that naturally extended to the Tradescants in South Lambeth.[13]

Eleven years later, James increased the Company's powers and privileges, forbidding any person not a member of the Company from selling garden produce except at those places where 'foreigners' (meaning those who were not freemen of the City) sold their wares.[14] This second charter also gave the Company powers to search London's markets and examine 'all manner of plants stocks sets trees seeds slips roots flowers herbs and other things that shall be sold', seizing and burning any 'unwholesome dry rotten deceitful and unprofitable' wares. In June 1632, the Company's virtual closed shop was backed by a warrant issued by the Recorder of London, requiring the apprehension of anyone practising the trade of gardening in contempt of the Company's charters. Then in December 1634 – just two weeks before John Tradescant became a freeman of the Company – King Charles issued a royal proclamation, calling on mayors, sheriffs, justices of the peace and other officers to put their weight behind the Company in its efforts to control the nursery trade. Charles decreed that 'no person or persons whatsoever whether Denizen or Stranger not having served as Apprentice or Apprentices to a Freeman of the said Company by the space of Seven years and not having been by them admitted into their Society do henceforth presume to take upon him or them the Art or Science of Gardening'.[15] The king further commanded that no one should oppose the Company in its powers to burn or destroy any 'dead unwholesome and corrupt plants' seized at market or anywhere else, and that members of the Company should be free to sell their produce at any time 'in any of our Markets' without disturbance or molestation from anyone.

For the elder Tradescant, the Company of Gardeners brought no real benefits to his work as a gardener or to his plant exchange with other curious gardeners, especially as it lacked the prestige of the great livery companies. Other distinguished court appointees and craftsmen flourished in their careers without the protection of a guild, such as Serjeant Painter John de Critz. But for the younger Tradescant, self-interest might have propelled him into the Company's fold, alerted perhaps by his father's connection with Oatlands of the king's intention to back the Company in its struggle for control over the sale of London's produce. Becoming a freeman would at least ensure his continued livelihood into the future, especially if he planned to expand his father's show garden into more of a nurseryman's operation.

Any plans he might have nurtured to develop the South Lambeth garden were soon disrupted, however, by the death of his wife, Jane. The page that should have noted her death is missing from the parish register but the churchwardens noted the payment of 12s for the burial of 'Jane the wife of John Tradeskin' on 1 June 1635.[16] As she was the first of the Tradescant family to be buried at Lambeth, her funeral charges were the highest to cover the initial opening of the ground. No record survives of the cause of Jane's death; the following year was a bad one for plague, when deaths in London rose sharply, especially in the autumn months. One effect of her death can perhaps be read in Tradescant's poor payment record with the Company of Gardeners. After joining, he paid two quarters' dues for 1634 and one the next year, then nothing at all until around 1650, when a new sequence of records begins after the upheavals of the civil war.[17] Either he was a desultory payer like many of his fellows or his plans were overturned and he no longer needed the Company's protection in the intervening years.

Living in the house of his widowed father, the younger Tradescant was now left with two small children, a boy aged nineteen months and a girl aged between seven and nine years. From the evidence of family wills, theirs was not a family of extended kinship so the children probably stayed at Lambeth under the care of family servants. Impermanence was a fact of early modern life and as Lawrence Stone remarked in his classic study of the family, sex and marriage, 'None could reasonably expect to remain together for very long, a fact which fundamentally affected all human relationships. Death was a part of life, and was realistically treated as such.'[18]

The younger Tradescant was approaching twenty-seven years of age and his father was an old man of sixty-five or so, who nonetheless showed little sign of slackening his pace. The elder's three parallel careers – as royal gardener, gardener on his own account and proprietor of London's most celebrated marvels – would have kept the son extremely busy at a time when most men in his situation would have already walked into their fathers' shoes. His flirtation with the Company of Gardeners suggests that he was at least ready to branch out on his own. But he had to stand aside one more time while his ageing father again took centre stage.

Chapter Twenty

A **Physick** *for the* **Dying**

Plant-collecting John Tradescant was the obvious choice for the final appointment of his career: as supervising gardener to the physic garden attached to Oxford University, Britain's first botanic garden, founded in 1621 although not actually planted for at least another decade.[1] Contrary to the accepted view that death robbed Oxford of his services, it seems he may have lived just long enough to make a start, at least.

Oxford don John Prest has likened the botanic garden to an encyclopaedia, its order beds for different plant families laid out to be 'read' like the pages of a book whose gradual 'printing' provoked enormous excitement. 'Each new plant from the farthest corners of the world was awaited with expectation, and received with enthusiasm, identified, and named.'[2] Initially at least there was also a biblical link to the Garden of Eden. First the search for Eden had been literal and geographic, and when no real garden was found, 'men began to think, instead, in terms of bringing the scattered pieces of the creation together into a Botanic Garden, or new Garden of Eden'.[3]

The Physic Garden or *hortus medicus* generally had a more specific purpose: to teach medical students how to identify and use plants, following the example of the monks of medieval monasteries, who had long cultivated plants for healing. Unlike its European forebears at Pisa, Padua, Montpellier and Leiden, however, the impetus for Oxford's Physic Garden was more horticultural than medical, and its foundation reflected 'partly, if not primarily ... the aristocratic taste for gardening which became manifest at the end of the sixteenth century, and which was fuelled by enthusiasm for accumulating collections of plants emanating from the voyages of explorers and colonists'.[4] Indeed, the garden's first incumbent professor of botany – Robert Morison, appointed only in 1669 – devoted himself almost exclusively to taxonomic botany, despite his medical training.

The Oxford garden owed its existence to the generosity of Henry, Lord Danvers, subsequently Earl of Danby, who gave the university £250 in 1621 to acquire five acres of meadow ground between Magdalen College and the River Cherwell.[5] Construction was very protracted and it was a decade before the garden was enclosed by a high wall interset with three imposing gateways. The main entrance gate is usually attributed to master stonemason and sculptor Nicholas Stone, who had designed the watergate at Buckingham's grand London residence, York House. Another inspiration was Inigo Jones's great gate for Oatlands Palace, although Jones himself was highly critical of the result at Oxford, attributing its design not to Stone but to 'sum mathematitians of Oxford that desined for a gate for ye garden of simples, lamly'.[6] (His main quarrel was that they misunderstood architecture as a disciplined art.) Other garden buildings would follow, including a 'conservatory for evergreens', sometime after Tradescant's death.[7]

As the water meadows were prone to flooding, the ground had to be raised with additional soil before any planting could take place. 'In the year 1633,' wrote Oxford historian Anthony Wood, 'all the wall being finisht, and soon after the floor raised, which cost the Earl 5000 £. and more, he caused to be planted therein divers Simples for the advancement of the Faculty of Medicine.' According to Wood, the earl had 'settled a Gardener, John Tredesken, Senior' to tend the garden but deferred appointing a professor because 'the Garden could not be soon enough furnished with Simples, and they with a maturity'.[8] Danby's overtures to Tradescant were not confirmed until November 1636, when Tradescant carried a letter to Dr Frewen, President of Magdalen College, stating among other things that 'Mr

Great dragons and small dragons, used in physic as a plague remedy.

John Tredeskine is willinge to persever in his worke with some assurance of Estate'.⁹ Although the letter is not entirely clear, Danby appears to be thanking Frewen for promising to make a further grant to complete the 'newe Garden' – perhaps of land that could be planted for his own profit by the gardener (Tradescant). Danby himself had to 'add divers thinges for the finishinge of that worke', so the garden was clearly started but not yet finished.

It was not until the following year, after Magdalen College had renewed the lease of the land to the university, that any deal was concluded, Lord Danby having come to 'some reasonable good termes of agreement with John Tradescant of West . . .[?] designed for ye gardiner, viz. for a yearly stipend of 50 *li*. by ye yeare or thereabouts'.¹⁰ Most histories of the garden suggest that Tradescant cannot have started to plant the garden because 'not longe after, viz. in the yere 1638 about Easter, ye saide John Tradescant died'.[11] But historian David Sturdy has unearthed an employee, fifty-year-old Thomas Bayler, who registered with the university on 28 April 1637 in his capacity as 'Serviens mri Johis Tredescan Universit oxo Hortul' (servant of Master John Tredescant, gardener to Oxford University).[12] Bayler is listed as a 'serviens' not a 'hortulanus', so he was in all probability a manservant rather than a labouring gardener. Tradescant was not the sort to employ such a man speculatively, so it seems that he had at least one full growing season to begin planting the garden, which by Loggan's plan of 1675 was laid out in four quarters, incorporating order beds laid out in simple geometric designs.

As the younger Tradescant later demonstrated a keen interest in simples, it is tempting to imagine that he might have helped to plan the garden with his father. He cannot have given much practical help, however, as sometime in 1637 he sailed to Virginia in search of rare plants and shells, leaving behind his two motherless children.

In any event, Tradescant would not live to see the Oxford garden fully planted. He must have known he was dying early in January 1638 when he made his will, 'being sicklie in bodie but perfect in mynde – thanks be to God'. For a man who had spent a lifetime collecting plants and rarities from all corners of the known world, it was a very short will in which he described himself simply as 'Gardyner'. After rendering his soul to the Almighty and his body to the earth for burial in the parish 'where it shall please God to call me out of this world', he left to his son John the lease on his South Lambeth property and another in Woodham Water, Essex, and then made provision for his two grandchildren, Frances and John, treating them equally despite the difference in their sexes. They were to receive the leases on two other properties in and around London, one in Long Acre (close to his friend Parkinson, no doubt) and another in Covent Garden, Middlesex, the profits to be 'equallie devided betweene them after our Ladie-day now next comeing'. They were also to receive equal shares in £150 held by Lord Goring and £17 held by his brother-in-law, Alexander Norman. If either child were to die before marrying or reaching the age of twenty-one, the

other was to inherit instead. All the 'rest and residue' of his 'goods &
chattells' he left to his only son John, with one proviso: 'That if hee shall
desire to p[ar]te with or sell my Cabinett that hee shall first offer ye same to
ye Prince'. Perhaps he already suspected that his son was not driven by the
same collecting passions as himself, or perhaps he was simply being
prudent.[13]

Tradescant appointed his 'trustie & welbeloved' friend, John Whistler
Esquire, as overseer of his will, and as executors he chose his brother-in-law
Alexander Norman (a London cooper by profession who had married his
wife's sister, Dorcas) and his friend William Ward, previously steward to
Buckingham at New Hall, where the two must have met. A fellow plant
enthusiast, Ward had taken over Tradescant's post as garnetter at the
Whitehall Granary; he was known also to Parkinson who had much
admired a tamarisk tree growing at his Essex property, 'very beautifull and
rare, not to be seene in this Land I thinke, but with Mr William Ward.'[14]
Ward and Parkinson also discussed fruit, and specifically the striped
Jerusalem pear, its bark striated red, green and yellow like the fruit itself and
'of a very good taste: being baked also, it is as red as the best Warden, wherof
Master William Ward of Essex hath assured mee, who is the chiefe keeper
of the Kings Granary at Whitehall'.[15]

The three witnesses to Tradescant's will also tell us something about the
man himself: wealthy South Lambeth neighbour John Lardner;[16] Arnall
Cornelius, who may have been a neighbour of Alexander Norman in the
Tower Hill precinct of the parish of St Botolph without Aldgate, where
Cornelius had two houses;[17] and Welshman Edward Morgan, another keen
plantsman and botanist described by Hartlib as 'one of the best Herbarists
for English plants' who, by 1651, was busy raising a 'Publick Botanical
Garden neare the booling greene or alley at Westminster'.[18] In signing his
will, the dying man spelt his name John Treadeskant.

An unknown British artist painted Tradescant tightly swaddled on his
deathbed against red velvet drapes, tufts of grey hair protruding from his
nightcap and tasselled neckcloth, a black bow tied beneath his full beard.[19]
Sr. John Tradescant Senr. lately deceas'd reads the italic caption. The exact date

of his death is lost as the parish registers leap more than a year from June 1637 to August 1638.[20] His will was proved on 2 May and the date of his funeral is usually given as 17 April 1638, when the great bell of St Mary, Lambeth, would have tolled in mourning and the parish black cloth would have covered his hearse as it made its way slowly northwards past open fields, gardens and the imposing avenues of Caron House, over the ditch and on to the King's High Way, bringing the solemn procession to the doors of the church, close by the archbishop's palace and the horse ferry. The great bell and the black cloth cost his estate 5s 4d, 1s more than the fourth bell and the black cloth would have done; the cost of dying naturally reflected wealth and status, as did everything in life.[21]

St Mary, Lambeth may have clung to the old ways of hanging garlands in church. 'Cypresse Garlands are of great account at funeralls amongst the gentiler sort,' wrote William Coles, 'but Rosemary and bayes are used by the Commons both at Funeralls and Weddings.' As evergreens, their purpose was to remind us 'that the remembrance of the present solemnity might not dye presently, but be kept in minde for many yeares'.[22]

Among his mourners would have come many of London's surviving elite of curious gardeners: John Parkinson; apothecary Thomas Johnson; Master of the Watermills, John Morris; Edward Morgan; William Ward; colleagues; neighbours from South Lambeth and fellow parishioners. With his son still away in Virginia, the only family member present was most likely his brother-in-law, Alexander Norman. Both his wife and his daughter-in-law were dead, and his two grandchildren were aged just four and around nine. Out in the churchyard his body was the second to be laid to rest in the family plot, after his son's wife Jane.

Obtaining money owed by the royal coffers was notoriously difficult but Ward and Norman managed to collect Tradescant's last payment for his work at Oatlands by the end of that year – on Christmas Eve in fact, when a book of royal payments recorded an order 'dated 16th day of June 1638 to Alexander Norman and Willm Ward Executors to John Tradescant late Keeper of His Majesties Gardens at Oatelands the some of £50 parcell of his Allowance of £100 per Annum for keeping the Vyne and Vineyards

Gardens etc there payable quarterly and due for halfe a year ended at our Lady day last 1638'.²³

The younger Tradescant was never a contender for his father's Oxford post, it seems. Danby appointed in his stead the eccentric Brunswick-born Jacob Bobart, a former soldier and giant of a man ('his son in respect of him but a shrimp') who sported a long flowing beard, which he tagged with silver one Whitsuntide, drawing 'much Company in the Phisick-Garden'.²⁴ He also walked a pet goat instead of a dog and understood Latin 'pretty well'. Bobart was considered an excellent gardener and the garden acquired a good reputation (it was especially famed for its topiary figures) but the catalogue of more than 1,400 plants that he brought out anonymously in 1648 was much plainer than Tradescant's earlier list. Listed first in Latin, then in English, the plants included many wild and common garden plants, among them the 'simples' of a physic garden, as well as quite ordinary vegetables (cabbages, parsnips, long-rooted turnips) and modest numbers of orna-mental varieties (seven auriculas, nine anemones, nine irises, twenty-one roses and just five different cherries compared with Tradescant's fifteen). Of course there were some exotics, too, including a yucca, pomegranate, orange, pomecitron, olive and an Indian fig, and a number of plants described as Virginian. Two plants commemorated Tradescant: 'Tradescants spiderwort' (*Tradescantia*) and 'Tradescants Tree Primerose'.²⁵ But in its early days at least, Oxford's Physic Garden was not a storehouse of rarities, an impression confirmed by John Evelyn at his first recorded visit in 1654. 'Hence we went to the *Physick* Garden, where the Sensitive (& humble) plant was shew'd us for a great wonder,' he wrote in his diary. 'There Grew Canes, Olive Trees, Rhubarb, but no extraordinary curiosities, besides very good fruit, which when the Ladys had tasted, we return'd in Coach to our Lodging.'²⁶

Although Bobart may have usurped Tradescant's place as Oxford's founding gardener, it was John Tradescant whose legacy was the more enduring. England had indeed lost one of her great gardeners who combined a rare passion for plants with the nurturing skills to coax them into life, even when their habits and habitats were unknown. Strangeness was his delight in all God's kingdoms, whether animal, vegetable or mineral, and in the arts and industry of men. As gardener, traveller, storekeeper and self-made man, he helped to put English gardens on the world map just as he welcomed the world's infinite variety into his own garden at Lambeth. His role, like Adam's, was to dress the garden and to keep it, and now the question was: would his gardener son carry on his great work into the next generation?

Chapter Twenty-One
Sweet Virginia

Modesty was one of the younger Tradescant's virtues, according to gardening rector Walter Stonehouse, who knew both Tradescants well enough to pen anagrammatic verses for their museum catalogue when it eventually appeared.[1] The impression he gives of Tradescant the younger is of a man ever conscious of walking in his father's footsteps, who found himself wanting whenever their talents were compared. In one respect at least the younger man very literally trod where his father had never gone: he alone crossed the Atlantic to the New World in search of plants and rarities, bearing letters of commendation from the king.[2]

While there is no evidence of a royal warrant for his journey, Tradescant's presence in the colony merited the attention of Secretary Sir Joseph Williamson, an inveterate hoarder, who recorded it in a three-page note relating to Virginian affairs. Only two events are listed for 1637: 'Sir J. Harvey Gov[ernor] there. & John Tredescant was there to gather up all rarityes of Flowers, plants, shells &c.'[3] Williamson's jottings dart around chronologically so it is not possible to date Tradescant's entry into the colony with any certainty. The link with Governor Harvey is interesting nonetheless, and as it may explain how Tradescant came to Virginia it is worth taking a brief detour into the politics of Harvey's governorship.

Harvey was another controversial governor who succeeded in alienating his governing council to the point of outright revolt.[4] After arriving in the colony as a sea captain in the early 1620s, he became closely allied to the hardliners who favoured a return to military laws, receiving a knighthood for his eagerness to serve the king. By 1629 he was governor and set about fostering commercial ventures that would find profitable markets in England. Within a couple of years he had fallen out with many on his council, and was complaining to the authorities in England about the expense of office. By choice, it seems, he used his own house as the meeting place for official business and, after three years in office, had received nothing towards the entertainment of his guests.[5]

Tradescant would certainly have enjoyed a taste of that hospitality, as did Dutchman David de Vries who sailed to English Virginia a few years before him from nearby New Netherland, hoping to buy corn.[6] The Dutchman's experiences give us some idea of the conditions Tradescant faced when he himself made the journey westwards. On his way up the James River, de Vries and his companions stopped at the home of 'a great merchant, named Mr. Menifit' (council member George Menefie, Jamestown's official merchant) where they were entertained to dinner. They also found time to admire his two-acre garden 'full of Provence roses, apple, pear, and cherry trees, the various fruits of Holland, with different kinds of sweet-smelling herbs, such as rosemary, sage, marjoram, and thyme. Around the house were plenty of peach-trees, which were hardly in blossom.'[7] Life for the settler elite had improved considerably since the days when they reputedly ate their wives.

At Menefie's house word came that the governor wanted to see them, so they left their host and in two hours had sailed up to Jamestown 'where the governor stood upon the beach, with some halberdeers and musketeers, to welcome us. On my setting foot upon the land, he came up to me, and bid me heartily welcome. He then proceeded with me to his house, where he bid me welcome with a Venice glass of sack.' More hospitality followed: an invitation to dine with the governor, and to spend the night at his house. When de Vries sailed for home, a week or so later, Harvey sent him away with half a dozen live goats and a ram, a present to the Dutch governor, having heard there were no goats at Fort Amsterdam.

Although shocked by the English passion for gambling ('they lose their servants in gambling with each other'), de Vries judged English Virginia a

fine country; altogether a beautiful flat land, full of all kinds of fine large trees – oak, hickory, chestnut, ash, cypress, and cedar, and other kinds. There come here yearly, between thirty and forty ships of various sizes, from two hundred lasts and upwards, mounting twenty-eight, twenty-four, and nineteen guns, which come here to load tobacco, and carry it to England.[8]

Politically, however, Virginia was riven by disagreements. Harvey's governing council complained of his autocratic manner and his support for the Catholic Lord Baltimore, who had been given a royal charter for Maryland (named in honour of Queen Henrietta Maria) on lands to the north and east of Potomac River.[9] Although Virginians were decidedly royalist in outlook (and would later mostly take the king's side against Parliament), they considered the territory a rightful part of Virginia. Secretary of the Council, William Claiborne,[10] was especially incensed as Maryland's land claim extended to Kent Island where he had established a trading base and was conducting a lucrative trade in beaver furs with the Susquehannock Indians. His backer for a time was merchant adventurer William Clobery,[11] already known to the Tradescants over the Guinea trade. Open warfare was inevitable when Governor Harvey backed an edict from Maryland's first governor, Leonard Calvert, banning Virginian traders from Maryland waters. The fallout from this conflict between Harvey and Claiborne may even have had repercussions for the Tradescants, as we shall see.

At first, Virginia's rebellious council succeeded in ousting Harvey from office and forcing his recall to London but their victory was short-lived. Once back in England, Sir John had his escort locked up in the Fleet prison and prepared a spirited defence, alleging a conspiracy against his leadership and labelling Claiborne and the others as insurgents.[12] They, in turn, accused Harvey of being a Catholic-lover and a philanderer. Wherever the truth lay, it was perhaps inevitable that an autocratic king could in no way countenance mutiny against one of his chosen officers and on 11 December 1635, at a meeting presided over by King Charles, the Privy Council reinstated Harvey as governor of Virginia.[13]

Harvey's return to Virginia did not go smoothly, however. After his reinstatement was formally ratified in April 1636, he asked the king for a ship, planning to ease his mounting debts and defray the costs of his voyage (which he had guaranteed out of his own pocket) by taking with him '100 passengers for Virginia, more than 20 being gentlemen of quality'.[14] The younger Tradescant may even have been one of the intended passengers, arranged through his father's royal connections at Oatlands Palace.[15] But the *Black George* proved so leaky that 'all in her have undergone divers hazards of perishing' and Harvey was forced to abandon ship at Portsmouth. Leaving behind his goods and most of his company, he then made his own way to Virginia on a smaller ship, arriving back in the colony on 18 January 1637.[16]

It was now twelve years since Virginia had been reconstituted as a Crown colony. From the start of his reign, King Charles had declared it was not his intention to 'take away or impeach the particular interest of any private planter or adventurer, nor to alter the same otherwise than should be necessary for the good of the public'.[17] Troubled at home by an upsurge of religious fundamentalism, Charles gave no more practical support to transatlantic colonization than his father had done. Royal interest remained narrowly focused on fiscal benefits to the Crown. But life for the settlers was beginning to ease from the earliest pioneering days and the immigrant population had started its inexorable rise: from 1,232 (non-native) souls in 1625 (of whom 952 were males and 280 women, among them 23 blacks of both sexes), to 3,000 in 1630, and 8,000 in 1640.[18]

Most of the towns and plantations were still grouped around the James River, although the original four corporations were subdivided into eight shires or counties: James City, Henrico, Charles City, Elizabeth City, Warwick River, Warrisquyoake, Charles River and Accomac.[19] The interior was still largely unexplored, and well into the middle of the century maps continued to promise an ocean lying just beyond the (Appalachian) mountains to the west, which would open up the fabled route to China. The route's existence was one of the colony's greatest selling points; all the planters had to do was 'to make a further Discovery into the Country West and by South up above the Fall, and over the Hills', apparently 'confident upon what they have learned from the Indians, to find a way to a West or South Sea by land or rivers, & to discover a way to China and East Indies or unto some other sea that shal carry them thither'.[20] They clearly hoped the discovery would deliver up the East Indian trade and make them all rich.

As he contemplated the voyage westwards across the Atlantic, Tradescant could expect to spend between five and seven weeks at sea (less on the return, when prevailing winds cut the return journey to between twenty and thirty days).[21] A one-way journey cost £6, plus extra charges for freight.[22] He would have been well advised to consult John Smith's list of 'necessaries' for private families or single men preparing for the crossing and to pack in his trunks one Monmouth cap, three suits (of 'Canvase', 'Frize' and 'Cloth'),[23] three pairs of Irish stockings, four pairs of shoes and garters. For the sea voyage he was advised to take enough coarse canvas for a two-man bed at sea and a thick rug to cover them during the voyage, as well as canvas to make a bed and bolster in Virginia, and a pair of canvas sheets. Conditions on board ship were primitive and in an early outburst of consumer indignation, complaints against the victualler of the George of London, Cape merchant Robert Page, reached as high as the Privy Council.[24] To supplement the shipboard diet, Smith recommended that travellers should take sugar, spice and fruit for the voyage (at an estimated cost of 12s 6d for six men at sea), and a store of basic victuals to last a full year: eight bushels of meal, two bushels each of peas and oatmeal, a gallon each of brandy and oil, and two gallons of vinegar.

As plant hunting might take Tradescant into wild territory, he would probably have taken Smith's recommended arms for one man (or two men sharing), shown here with their estimated costs:

1 Armor compleat, light. 17s.

1 long peece five foot and a halfe, neere Musket bore. 1ſ. 2s.

1 Sword. 5s.

1 Belt. 1s.

1 Bandilier. 1s. 6d.

20 pound of powder. 18s.

60 pound of shot or Lead, Pistoll and Goose shot. 5s.[25]

The best time to travel was during the winter. The English settlers considered the summer months of June through to August particularly unhealthy, especially for new arrivals who tended 'to die during these months, like cats and dogs, whence they call it the (sickly) season. When they have this sickness, they want to sleep all the time, but they must be preventing from sleeping by force, as they die if they get asleep.'[26]

Tradescant would have landed at Jamestown where ships entering the colony were required to unload, despite the decayed state of the storehouse there,[27] and where Harvey would have made him as welcome as he had earlier done the Dutchman David de Vries. Here he would no doubt have made his base, enjoying Harvey's hospitality throughout his time in the colony, either as a house guest or at least a frequent visitor. Harvey's house remained 'the rendezvous of all sorts of strangers, who have any occasion of resort thither upon any businesse'.[28] As Harvey himself had complained to the Lords Commissioners of the Plantations back in London, he might as well be called the 'host' as the 'Governor' of Virginia and if he did not receive some 'speedie remedie and releife ... not onlie my creditt but my hart will breake'.[29] Overall, however, conditions at Jamestown had markedly improved since the early days of settlement and, by April 1638, Harvey's faithful supporter, Secretary Richard Kemp, could report to his counterpart in England that 'People of late are more given to affect good buildings; scarce any inhabitant but hath his garden and orchard planted; most endeavour the raising of stocks of cattle or hogs; the savages ever awake to do them injuries in the streightest times of peace'.[30]

Jamestown today is quietly atmospheric, its archaeology exposed in places where the original fort awaits rediscovery, reburied elsewhere to aid its long-term preservation.[31] Beyond the remnants of the fort and town, a circular drive loops through vestiges of secondary forest, where walnut, beech and loblolly pines cluster among groves of oak and hickory. The open water of the James River is never far away. A narrow causeway connects the 'island' of historic Jamestown to mainland Virginia and the site of the Jamestown Settlement museum with its recreated stockade, Indian village and replica ships that made the first crossing in 1606–7. Heading north-east, the Colonial Parkway tunnels underneath the tourist hub of Colonial Williamsburg, giving drivers a taste of soaring forest either side as it connects Jamestown to Yorktown and the York River (called the Charles River in Tradescant's day) where Powhatan made his chief settlement at Werowocomo, until forced further inland to escape the Europeans' continued expansion.[32]

Powhatan was long dead by the time Tradescant came to Virginia (he died the year after his daughter, Pocahontas), succeeded by his half-brothers or blood relatives through his mother's line: first Opitchapam, and then Opechancanough who led the uprisings against the English settlers in 1622 and again in 1644. Tradescant's visit fell in a period of relative calm but the wider Indian presence would have kept him mostly within the area of English settlement, as plotted by the land claims and patents granted by the Virginian authorities. Just a few years before his visit, the English were still mostly concentrated along the margins of the James River (north and south), with smaller clusters south of the York River and along the west-facing coast of the Eastern Shore beyond Chesapeake Bay.[33] Settlers were creeping further afield all the time, of course; and within days of Governor Harvey's return to the colony, he thoroughly incensed his Council by granting a patent (on the king's express orders) to Charles's favourite, Henry Lord Maltravers, covering a huge tract of land south of the James River stretching into what is now North Carolina.[34]

Tradescant was not, of course, the first visitor to the colony to take an interest in its plants. Ever since Raleigh's attempts to colonize Roanoke, would-be settlers had assessed the commercial potential of New World flora. Thomas Hariot reported on such 'marchantable commodities' as sassafras ('a kinde of wood of most pleasand and sweete smel; and of most rare vertues in physick for the cure of many diseases'), sweet gums and 'many other Apothecary drugges', as well as native dyes, crops, roots, fruits, berries, fowl, fish and trees.[35] Eight medical men were among the colonists who arrived in Jamestown during the first year of settlement, among them two physicians, four surgeons and two apothecaries.[36] One of the physicians was the German Johannes Fleischer, a skilled botanist trained in philosophy and medicine. He lasted less than a year, dying in Jamestown in midsummer 1608. His epitaph underlines the dangers of his profession: 'he surveyed what the German soil produced in terms of plants; what in America flourished, he viewed, too, and thereby perished.'[37] Another medico-botanist was Dr Lawrence Bohun who arrived in June 1610 and stayed until the following spring, experimenting with native plants and herbs as he sought remedies for the distresses of the Old World and the New.[38]

During the settlement's first quarter-century, Virginian plants were regularly reaching the gardens of Britain and Europe – witness the elder Tradescant's plant catalogue of 1634 and the many North American plants added to the blank pages at the back of his copy of Parkinson's garden of pleasant flowers.[39] Among the Virginian plants he grew at Lambeth was a yellow aster introduced 'by the meanes of Master *George Gibbes* Chirurgion of *Bathe*, who brought in his returne from thence, a number of seeds and plants hee gathered there himselfe, and flowred fully only with M. Tradescant'.[40] (Even John Parkinson had not been able to coax it into flower.) Gibbs served a seven-year apprenticeship as an apothecary in Bath before sailing to Virginia as a ship's surgeon.[41] Quite possibly he was the source of the Virginian seeds that Parkinson received from a 'Mr. Morrice' and dated 18 March 1636/37.[42] 'Morrice' is surely John Morris, Master of the Watermills, whose interest in Virginian plants generally and in Tradescant's plant expedition in particular is explored more fully in the next chapter. Tradescant himself is another possible source of the seeds, assuming he had managed to send some back by ship to his father (a good friend of John Morris). A number of the plants appeared in his museum catalogue of 1656 (including ones he definitely brought back himself from Virginia) but it is unlikely he could have got them home in time.

Whoever provided the seeds, the smudged and crumpled lists of 'desiderata' and the actual importations that survive today illuminate the kind of difficulties John Tradescant would have faced as he hunted for strange plants in a strange land. First of all, there was the problem of identification. Although experienced as a gardener, he had no real training in botany, so the 'wish-lists' he must have carried with him could only be approximate. One list among the Goodyer papers in Oxford included several plants Tradescant did in fact bring back, including 'Ciprasse nuttes or young trees', a maidenhair fern and a columbine.[43] Its compiler also sought Indian plants with no domestic equivalent, such as 'Musquaspen' (described as a 'small roote of a fingers bignes as red as blood wherewth they dye their mattes') and 'Poconas' ('a small roote in the mountaines which they use for swellinges and so painte their faces'). Many of the descriptions were undeniably vague, such as the request for a 'small lowe tree whose white flower is like a small hedge Honysuckle'[44] and a 'plante that beares a Scarlet flower', ending with the catch-all 'any other herbe or seede growing there allthough you thinck we have the same in England for we finde most thinges to diffarr'.

Then there was the added hoop of language. True, Tradescant might have taken with him a rudimentary dictionary, such as one included by his father's friend John Smith in A Map of Virginia of 1612, which started with the helpful question: Ka ka torawincs yowo (what call you this)?[45] More useful was William Strachey's list of more than eight hundred Algonquian words spoken by the Indians living around the Powhatan/James River, intended for anyone wishing to learn 'how to confer, and how to truck and Trade with the People'.[46] Invaluable for a collector such as Tradescant were its translations of plants and trees (including grapes, groundnuts, 'Gynny wheat', mulberry, walnut, rose, peas, 'blew berries of the bignes of grapes very pleasant', chestnut, groundnut, 'a Flower of a fine thing' and the 'Gum that yssueth out of a certaine tree called the Virginia maple'), as well as words for sundry animals, beasts, birds, snakes, fish, and shells. It would also give him a basic vocabulary for practical things such as spades, barrels and a canoe, and for the usual travellers' complaints ('my leggs ake', 'I understand you not' or the slightly more hopeful 'I understand you a little but not much'.) It would even help him in his dealings with native women, should he care to make use of the Indian words for 'a womans breast', 'a womans Secret' and mutual declarations of love.[47] But for many of his encounters with the local population, he would surely have needed the services of an interpreter and a guide.

We have no definite idea of where Tradescant travelled in Virginia as he has left behind no diary and few eastern Virginian records survived the burning of Virginia's state court building during the civil war. From the two hundred or so plants he is said to have brought back from the colony,[48] a handful found their way into the herbal then being compiled by his father's friend, John Parkinson, who added drawings and tentative descriptions wherever possible.[49] From these few plants, it is possible to plot the terrain Tradescant must have crossed.[50]

Out of eleven plants definitely attributed to Tradescant by Parkinson, the great majority thrive in damp woods and thickets alongside the streams and woodland fringes of North America's temperate eastern seaboard. All can be found in the areas immediately north of Jamestown (now James City County) and south across the James River (now Surry County). One plant in particular confirms that Tradescant need not have strayed very far from Jamestown in his search for botanical rarities: the swamp or bald cypress (*Taxodium distichum*),[51] which has the most restricted range in Virginia of all Tradescant's plants. Happiest when growing with its feet underwater for much of the year, it will not tolerate the brackish water found downriver from Jamestown towards Chesapeake Bay. Tradescant most probably found it west of Jamestown, on either side of the river (so in James City or Surry Counties). Today there is a fine stand growing in sheltered waters close to the causeway to Jamestown Island, and another further west on the modern development known as 'First Colony'.[52] As there are more cypress swamps to the south-east (in Isle of Wight County), it is just possible that Tradescant may have crossed the James River looking for plants there. This area was only just beginning to be settled around the time of his departure from Virginia,[53] however, and nothing in his character suggests he had the necessary verve to stray very far into the wild.

Of the other plants Parkinson credits to Tradescant, several can be found all over present-day Virginia: American bur-reed (probably *Sparganiun americanum* – Parkinson called it the 'great branched Burre Reede of Virginia'),[54] which thrives on muddy or peaty shores and shallow waters; the American sycamore or buttonwood tree (*Platanus occidentalis*),[55] common to the rich soils bordering lakes and streams from New England down to Florida and westwards to Texas and Nebraska, and growing in all but two mountain counties of Virginia; an 'early red Columbine of *Virginia*', its flowers 'of a sad reddish colour' shading into yellow;[56] and an evergreen climber that Parkinson called the 'sweete yellow climing *Virginian* Jasmine', since identified as *Gelsemium sempervirens*.[57] Adopted as the state flower of South Carolina, 'Carolina jessamine' grows from Florida to Texas and north to Arkansas and southern Virginia. 'Smelling very sweete', according to Parkinson, it is a rampant climber, 'spreading very farre upon the trees, or any thing standeth next to it'. Having raised one himself from Tradescant's seed, Parkinson was not entirely happy at its classification 'but that Master Tradescant is confident to call it a Jasmine, and therefore I am content to put it with the rest to give him content'. However, he went on, a little testily, 'I would be further informed of it my selfe, before I would certainly give my consent.' Parkinson might happily admit the success of the younger Tradescant's efforts but he was not prepared to bow to him botanically.

More common in the piedmont than the coastal plain (but still a feature of woodlands in the Jamestown and Yorktown areas) was American spikenard (*Aralia racemosa*), which Tradescant found growing 'with the spike of flowers and seed at the toppes of the stalkes', according to Parkinson, who likened it to 'the great Turky Garlicke with a twined head'.[58] A pungently sweet tonic herb, it was then widely used by North American Indians who may have introduced it to him. Tradescant was also able to describe for Parkinson the sassafras tree with its figlike leaves and thick grey bark, although he does not seem to have brought back any specimens. 'The flowers are small and yellow made of threds very like to the Male Cornel tree as Master John Tradescant saith and the fruite small blackish berries, set in small cups upon long footstalkes many clustring together.'[59] Moving on through drier woods and higher ground to the west or south, he would have found a 'Noble Liverwort', *Hepatica americana*;[60] and a 'goodly *Virginia* grasse with a joynted spike', which Parkinson grouped with others growing on hills and woods in Germany and Italy. 'The last came from *Virginia*,' he wrote, 'and Master John Tradescant the younger brought it from thence also, with a number of other seedes and rare plants.'[61]

Two plants among his introductions prefer moist woods and slightly cooler conditions (but again he may have found these in James City and Surry Counties): the American bladder nut (*Staphylea trifolia*);[62] and a 'Forraine or strange Maidenhaire' (the delicate fern, *Adiantum pedatum*, called by Parkinson *Adiantum fruticosum Americanum*).[63] Even weirder was the carnivorous pitcher plant, *Sarracenia purpurea*, an inhabitant of sphagnum bogs, which Parkinson called the 'hollow leafed strange plant of Clusius'. 'This strange plant hath such strange leaves, as the like are seldome seene in any other that we know growing, . . . each by it selfe, being small below, and growing great upward, with a belly as it were bunching forth, and a bowing backe, hollow at the upper end, with a peece thereon like a flappe, and like unto the flower of Aristolochia.' The plant he described had been sent to Clusius from Paris, hence its name, 'But of late Master John Tradescant the younger, found this very plant in *Virginia*, having his toppe thereon, which he brought home, and groweth with him.'[64] Although not common, it can still be found in bogs in James City and Surry Counties; and while there is no record of its use by Powhatan Indians, the Iroquois to the north were still using it in both a love potion and a fever remedy early in the twentieth century.[65]

Two more trees were later credited to Tradescant as new introductions to Britain: first, the red maple, *Acer rubrum*, still common to all counties of Virginia, whether on the coastal plain or in the mountains. A century after Tradescant's visit, Philip Miller of the Chelsea Physic Garden would link the man to the tree, then called the Virginian flowering maple and 'rais'd from

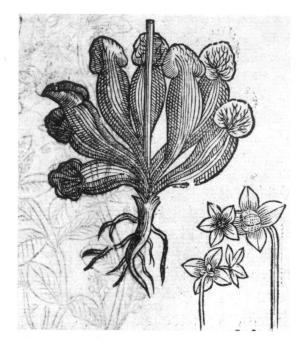

The 'hollow leafed strange plant', Sarracenia purpurea, brought back from Virginia by John Tradescant the younger.

Seeds which were brought from *Virginia* many Years since by Mr. *John Tradescant*, in his Garden at *South Lambeth* near *Vaux-hall*, and since, in the Gardens of the Bishop of *London* at *Fulham*, where it has flower'd for several Years, and produces ripe Seeds, from whence several Trees have been rais'd'.[66]

And finally, Tradescant was credited with the introduction of the tulip tree (*Liriodendron tulipifera*) which thrives in deep, rich and rather moist soils on slopes and beside streams. In Virginia today it can still be found growing wild around swamps and streams and is sometimes used as an avenue tree. As the strange, creamy-green cup-shaped flowers first appear on trees that are at least ten years old, Parkinson would not have witnessed any flowering of the tree grown from Tradescant's seed. The attribution comes in *Sylva*, John

Evelyn's discourse on forest trees in which he notes that 'They have a *Poplar* in *Virginia* of a very peculiar shap'd *leaf*, as if the point of it were cut off, which grows very well with the *curious* amongst us to a considerable stature. I conceive it was first brought over by *John Tradescant* under the name of the *Tulip-tree*, but is not that I find taken notice of in any of our *Herbals*; I wish we had more of them.'[67]

Even if Tradescant did not travel great distances in his search for plants, he would have needed to find a way to negotiate the many creeks and waterways feeding into the James and York Rivers. Despite John Smith's claim that the Indians had cleared the forest floor for brushwood, allowing a man to gallop his horse through the woods, Tradescant would have found it easier to travel by water – by Indian canoe, flatboat, scow, pinnace or some other small sailing craft. If he ventured as far as Lower Norfolk County, he may even have used one of the first public ferries, launched as a private enterprise in 1636 by Adam Thoroughgood. A skiff ferried passengers between what are now the cities of Norfolk and Portsmouth, west of Virginia Beach. It proved so popular that within a few months it was taken over by the county and supported by a levy of £6 on each taxable person in the county.[68]

He would barely have encountered any roads. These would remain wretched for a century at least, 'mere expanses of sand and mudholes, or only narrow trails', which generally followed high ground along the ridges between streams, so that even later plant hunters found conditions arduous. Had Tradescant attempted to ride into the interior, he would have needed good saddlebags to carry all his provisions, clothes and any bedding he took with him, stuffing 'every crevice of the saddle pockets' with

the slips and roots and seeds gathered along the way. Thickets and swamps must be explored on foot; only the scantiest of supplies could be taken – it was needful to rely on the produce of stream and forest or the donations of friendly Indians. There could be no wholesale gathering but only the taking of small samples that might be tucked away in coat pockets or bundled on the back. The total risk of such journeyings was great; the returns uncertain.[69]

Although he is unlikely to have ventured into the Great Dismal Swamp on Virginia's southern borders with what is now North Carolina, Tradescant may have experienced similarly unpleasant conditions to those reported a century later by naturalist William Byrd II, sent with a small party to survey the borders between the two states.[70] Despite the many botanical treats uncovered (including a *Yucca filamentosa*, which Tradescant first introduced to England in his museum catalogue of 1656), surveying the Great Dismal Swamp was a misery. Byrd believed its thickets were so overgrown that no beast, bird or even reptile could survive towards the centre.

The surveyors pursued their work with all diligence, but still found the soil of the Dismal so spongy that the water oozed up into every footstep they took. To their sorrow, too, they found the reeds and briers more firmly interwoven than they did the day before. But the greatest grievance was from large cypresses which the wind had blown down and heaped upon one another. On the limbs of most of them grew sharp snags, pointing every way like so many pikes, that required much pains and caution to avoid.[71]

The cypresses that caused Byrd such grief were the very same species that Tradescant had brought back to England.

For all the success of his plant hunting, Tradescant would also have scouted for shells, dried carcases and body parts of local fauna, and ethnological material such as clothing, utensils and weapons. The museum catalogue of 1656 included many such items: 'Indian Crowns made of divers sorts of feathers'; 'Black Indian girdles made of Wampam peek, the best sort'; 'Virginian purses imbroidered with Roanoake'; a 'Match-coat of *Virginia* made of Racoune-skins' and another (or was it two?) from Virginia-Canada, of feathers and deerskins; six sorts of 'Tamahack' and assorted bows, arrows, quivers and darts. Among the natural history specimens were Virginian muskrats, a 'Wilde Catt' and fox, 'Beavers skin, teeth and testicles', rattlesnakes, three sorts of Virginian hummingbirds, 'a black bird with red shoulders and pinions', two sorts of bitterns, bats, and another unidentified 'Red and blew Bird'.[72] Sea captains and travellers had been bringing such booty back to England since the early days of colonization but Tradescant would surely have traded in person with the Indians who came to Jamestown. If he had gone looking for shells and fossils himself, he need not have travelled very far. As the Reverend John Clayton would later report to the Royal Society, 'The Back-bone of a Whale, and as I remember, they told me of some of the Ribs, were digg'd out of the Side of a Hill, several Yards deep in the Ground, about four Miles distant from *James Town*, and the River.'[73] Clayton also found perfect fossilized teeth, at least two or three inches long, among the looser banks of shells and earth.

The greatest Indian prize displayed at Lambeth was undoubtedly the cloak attributed to Powhatan, paramount chief in the days of Captain John Smith and now remembered chiefly as Pocahontas's father. The mantle has already been glimpsed in Chapter 9. Made from four tanned hides of the white-tailed deer sewn together with sinew thread and decorated with more than 17,000 individually stitched marine shell beads, it is one of the most iconic native American artefacts outside North America. The shell decorations show a human figure (front view) flanked by two animals in profile – possibly a white-tailed deer and a mountain lion – set among thirty-four roundlets of different sizes.[74] It seems the cloak reached the Tradescants at Lambeth sometime after 1634 and before the summer of 1638, so up to twenty years after the great chief's death. The painstaking Peter Mundy omitted it from his list of marvels seen in 1634,[75] giving the honour of first recorded sighting to German student Georg Christoph Stirn who – in July 1638 – listed 'the robe of the king of Virginia' among the wondrous objects he had seen in South Lambeth.[76] The Powhatan connection was made much later – in the museum catalogue of 1656 – and like so much else about the 'cloak', Powhatan's ownership is now disputed.

Experts are not even sure that it *is* a cloak. Dr Tom Davidson, senior curator at the Jamestown Settlement, maintains that the mantle works as a cloak for a man six feet tall. Alternative interpretations point to a ritual wall hanging, possibly acquired as loot by English colonists after the uprising of 1622 from a Virginian Algonquian temple where the chief's family kept the remains of their dead.[77] Another theory – not mutually exclusive – is that

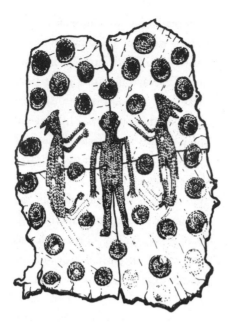

'Powhatan's mantle' in the Ashmolean
Museum, Oxford.

the shell circles symbolically represent the paramount chief's power over lesser social districts.[78] Uncertainty surrounds even the precise shell species used for decoration. While they are generally recognized as belonging to the marginella family, they have been variously identified as a Caribbean species, a Virginia coastal species and (by Gary Coovert and Helen C. Rountree) as fossil shells, *Prunum limatulum* from the York or James Rivers.

Compounding the confusion is the possible sighting of just such a princely decorated cloak further north in Maryland by a Jesuit priest who was so impressed that he included it in his annual report for 1639 to the Society's General in Rome, noting that the only way you could distinguish a chief from the common people was by some badge, 'either a collar made of a rude jewel, or a belt, or a cloak, oftentimes ornamented with shells in circular rows'.[79] But these annual letters (written in Latin) from the Maryland and other missions were usually sent to London first, where they were collated and edited by a member of the Jesuit provincial who could have added the cloak detail himself, after seeing the mantle on show at the

Tradescants' museum.[80] So the Maryland 'sighting' may actually have originated in London.

There remains the question of how the mantle found its way to South Lambeth. Of course the younger Tradescant could have brought it home himself, as we know from John Morris that he was back in England by June 1638, the month before its first confirmed sighting.[81] To acquire such an important item he would have needed an intermediary, someone with access to high-status native goods and connections stretching back to earlier decades. A number of Virginia's elite planter families present themselves as possible candidates, among them the Wyatts, Wests, Yeardleys and Ferrars,[82] but one other name constantly crops up in the network of connections surrounding the cloak's journey from Virginia to the Tradescants at Lambeth: the colony's leading Indian trader William Claiborne, then in dispute with his own governor as well as the authorities of Maryland over his trading activities on Kent Island. The Marylanders were convinced that Kent Island belonged to them just as Claiborne was equally convinced of his own prior claim and he manfully held out until Maryland governor Leonard Calvert used the stick of armed invasion and the carrot of land to force the Kent Islanders into submission.[83]

While Tradescant was in Virginia, Claiborne made the reverse crossing across the Atlantic to argue his case in person before the king who referred the matter to the Lords Commissioners for Foreign Plantations. They gave their verdict in April 1638 (as Tradescant Senior lay dying at Lambeth), declaring that Lord Baltimore's patent extended to Kent Island and that Claiborne's commission was only a 'Licence under ye Signet of Scotland to trade with the Indians of America in such places where the said Trade had not been formerly granted by his Ma[jes]ty to any other'.[84] So Claiborne had lost, even though his licence was apparently obtained before Baltimore's patent.[85]

Given the dates of his visit to England, Claiborne could have brought over the cloak himself and presented it to the elder Tradescant before his final sickness. While the evidence tracking its progress from Virginia to Lambeth is entirely circumstantial (and the Maryland sighting is far from conclusive), Claiborne was Virginia's premier Indian trader and of all the possible sources for the cloak, he is the only one to appear (as 'Captain Cleborne') among the Tradescants' principal benefactors honoured in their museum catalogue of 1656.[86]

Tradescant was back in England by early June at the latest and eased himself immediately into his father's old job at Oatlands Palace.[87] Even if news of his father's approaching death had cut short his stay in the colony, he would have needed time to pack his precious roots, seeds and assorted rarities, using perhaps threads of native silk grass to protect them on the long return voyage. We know from Parkinson that he brought back the swamp cypress as seed, which 'doe spring very bravely' when planted in English soil.[88] As for living plants, he would have learnt how to transport them safely from his father or perhaps he was familiar with the method proposed by tulip aficionado Sir Thomas Hanmer on 'HOW TO PACKE up ROOTES and SEND them to REMOTE PLACES'. This involved despatching fibrous roots tied with moist moss or grass and all other kinds 'dry without earth in papers, and soe boxt up that they shake not, nor have any heavy thing to presse them hard together, and thus they may bee convey'd safely very farr'.[89]

John Tradescant is supposed to have made two more journeys to Virginia, in 1642 and 1654. For both years, his name appears among the land patents granted to other settlers who claimed to have paid his passage out to Virginia. This was the so-called 'headrights' system of land distribution, designed to encourage immigration into the colony, which became the principal basis for title to Virginian land in the seventeenth century. Under a process dating back to the old Virginia Company's great charter, any person who paid his own way to Virginia was granted fifty acres of land 'for his own personal adventure', and similar amounts for each person whose passage he paid.[90] The claim was not necessarily made immediately on arrival in the colony: one settler was awarded land for the transportation of three wives 'who, it is safe to conclude, were successive'.[91] So a patent's date may not represent the year of entry; and despite legal checks, the system was open to all kinds of abuse. Settlers who travelled back and forth to England made repeated claims to the benefit of themselves or their friends, which seems to have been perfectly acceptable although multiple claims for sailors entering the colony must have raised eyebrows: Sarah Law received 300 acres for importing John Good – probably a sailor – as many as six times.[92]

The first person to claim 'headrights' for transporting John Tradescant to the colony was Bertram Hobert or Obert, who on 10 October 1642 put in a claim for 650 acres on the north side of the Charles River 'in Peanpetanke Creek, near land of Mr. Vaus, etc. and E. into the great creek from the Oystershell banck'.[93] The claim was based on the transportation of thirteen people: 'Bertram Hobert, himselfe twice, Sarah his wife, Francis Pepper, Francis, Negro, Tho. Austin, his wife & 2 children, John Tredescant, Jon Eyres, Edward Goldborne, Tho. Bawcocke'. It has always been assumed that Hobert's claim represented a second journey for Tradescant as well, but close scrutiny of the facts reveals a different story.

Bertram Hobert or Obert first enters Virginian records in May 1640 as an attendant of Sir John Harvey, whom Harvey wished to thank with the gift of 'one milch cow called goulding'.[94] Born an alien (most probably of French or Dutch origin),[95] Hobert had by then served Harvey for nearly six months and was about to accompany him back to England 'in the good ship the Planter of London'. Back in England, explained Harvey for the record, Hobert was 'to attend me also to the Bath, & so to continue with me until the end of November next ensuing paying for his passage forth and back to Virginia'. Harvey also wished to thank Hobert for the 'gift and delivery of a negro woman servt called ffranke & a youth called ffrancis pepper who hath one year to serve me'. For all these services – and for Hobert's 'usefulness unto me in respect of my Lameness' and his 'willingnes to do me his best service now in my time of great necessity & suffering' – Harvey wished to give Hobert the cow from his herd of neat cattle on James Island 'to enjoy forever with her increase for the releif of his wife who he leaveth in much sorrow for his departure'. The deed of gift also promised Hobert the choice of another cow, should the first one die.

Harvey was by then reaching his lowest ebb, and his gratitude towards Hobert is palpable. Replaced as governor by Sir Francis Wyatt, physically ill and deeply in debt, he had also been ordered by the court to appoint an agent to dispose of his house, lands and personal property to pay off his creditors, retaining just a life interest in the house where he had entertained so many guests at his own expense. He was also allowed eight cows, four breeding sows and his furniture.[96] By late 1641 he had returned to England and would later claim in his will (drawn up in 1646) that people in Virginia owed him £2,000, plus the £5,000 he claimed he was due in governor's back-pay.[97]

Hobert, we can assume, travelled to England with Harvey, then returned to Virginia in time to register his land claim, paying for the two servants (Frank and Francis Pepper) whose names appear in the land patent, and making the second of his own Virginian journeys for which he claimed land. While it is perfectly possible that Hobert might have met Tradescant in England through royalist or Huguenot circles, it is inconceivable that Tradescant should have made a second journey to the New World without setting off a single echo in the 'chatter' of the times. One person who would certainly have remarked on any further Virginian forays was John Morris, who recorded the younger Tradescant's movements throughout the 1640s but never mentioned a second journey to the colony.[98] Nor did any of the wide circle of 'intelligencers' surrounding agricultural reformer Samuel Hartlib – not even Dr Robert Child, who acted as the medium of a seed exchange between Tradescant and the son of New England governor John Winthrop in 1645.[99]

The most probable conclusion is that Hobert's claim relates to Tradescant's known journey of 1637–8, when his passage might even have been paid by Sir John Harvey as a financial ploy to increase his land holdings. But now that Harvey's career in the colony was obviously finished, he may have given or traded the headright to the faithful Hobert, who went on to become a successful citizen of Virginia. After the grant of his first land patent, Hobert/Obert and his descendants make frequent appearances in the early records of Virginia, producing children, marrying, making wills, reporting on crop damage, acquiring and assigning more land. On 26 March 1656, for instance, he acquired a further 773 acres[100] of fertile, level and well-watered land reaching down to Rappahannock Creek.

Even more doubtful is Tradescant's so-called third journey of 1654, when his name appears on another land patent claimed by William Lea. Again, it is inconceivable that contemporary records should remain silent if Tradescant had returned again to the colony. Tradescant would surely have mentioned it himself in the preface he wrote for the museum catalogue to Tradescant's rarities, begun in 1652 and not published until 1656.[101] In this, his only published writing to survive, Tradescant blames the long delay on a catalogue of disasters including lawsuits, sickness, the unavailability of his engraver and a death in his immediate family, but he gives no hint of a new Virginian journey that would have amply compensated for any delay.

In fact, on closer examination, this second land claim of 6 February 1654 looks plainly fraudulent. Lea was claiming 500 acres in Charles City County, south of the James River and west of an Indian swamp called Ohoreek, a claim based on the transport of ten people: 'John Trediskin, John Aires, Bertrum Obert, Thomas Austen, his wife, John Austin, Richard Austin, Edward Golbourn, Jane Glinn, William Lea'.[102] Apart from Glinn and Lea himself, all these people had already appeared (under variant spellings) in Bertram Obert's list of 1642. 'As abuse of the system increased,' wrote historian W. Stitt Robinson, 'headright lists sometimes included fictitious names or in some cases names copied from old records.'[103] And that is surely what William Lea has done here. It is highly improbable that all these people would journey a second time from England to Virginia at the same person's expense, or even that they would all still be alive twelve years after the original grant. Nor is it likely that settler Bertram Hobert would have given away any new land rights to a third party.

William Lea did not even keep the land for very long. The following year he assigned it to John Rutherford and Mycum Curry, presumably for a fair profit.[104] He was a speculator, not a settler, and Jane Glinn was quite possibly his accomplice. He was not to know that more than 350 years later, one of the names he 'borrowed' would continue to excite such interest.

But even if the younger Tradescant did visit Virginia only once, this does not detract from his achievements as a collector. He made the perilous crossing to a colony that was growing more civilized but where life was still dangerous for incomers fresh from Europe and he accomplished his mission

successfully. Of the two hundred or so new plants he brought back, a few
(documented by Parkinson and others) became notable additions to English
parks and gardens, among them the swamp cypress, the tulip tree and the
later progeny of the American sycamore. He was adding, too, to the
Tradescant storehouse of rarities at Lambeth and at last seemed ready to
make his own way in the world.

Chapter Twenty-Two

Of Cabbages *and* Kings

Parkinson was not the only person to remark on the younger John Tradescant's return from Virginia. Also watching from a distance was the elder Tradescant's old friend John Morris, who had inherited a lucrative business supplying water to much of London from his father, Dutchman and free denizen Peter Morris.[1] With homes near his watermills at London Bridge and a suburban retreat at Isleworth, across the Thames from Richmond and Sheen, Morris belonged to the European elite of wealthy men of letters whose curiosity embraced botany and rare plants as well as more bookish pursuits such as philosophy and philology. Latin allowed these scholars to correspond with each other across national barriers, making them truly 'citizens of the world'.[2]

Although not a scholar himself, the elder Tradescant had always been held in the greatest respect by men like Morris and his friend Antwerp-born Johannes de Laet, a director of the Dutch West-India Company who had lived in London for a time before returning to the Netherlands and settling in Leiden. Throughout the years of civil unrest and war in England, Morris and de Laet corresponded in Latin, exchanging their thoughts on plants, books, people and the political situation. Morris was working on a biography of English adventurer and mercenary Sir John Hawkwood (never published),[3] while de Laet was preparing an Anglo-Saxon dictionary; he would also publish works on Brazilian plants and an edition of Vitrivius' *De Architectura*. Both men wrote dedicatory poems published in Parkinson's herbal, *Theatrum Botanicum*, and were linked to other English botanists and plantsmen such as Thomas Johnson.[4]

A hypochondriac by nature and ever watchful of his health (bad digestion, stomach troubles and kidney stones were among his complaints), Morris was a moderate Puritan and equally moderate Parliamentarian who became increasingly disturbed by the violence unleashed by the civil war. His letters take the temperature of the times and allow us to track the younger Tradescant as he tried to adapt to changing circumstances. In June 1638, soon after de Laet's return to Leiden following a visit to London, Morris wrote to his friend to tell him the sad news of the elder Tradescant's death.

Our Tradescant passed away, alas, soon after you left, then his son came back from Virginia where he had gone to seek plants with letters of commendation from the King. From there, I hear he brought 200 plants until now unseen in our part of the world. I have not yet been to visit him as he has taken his father's place and is completely shut off in his 'palace'.

Morris would become increasingly disillusioned by the younger Tradescant's capabilities but here he predicts for him a great botanical future, 'for although I allow that he is unschooled and obviously uncivilized, he is nonetheless extremely skilled in gardening matters'.[5]

In fact, John Tradescant went to work at Oatlands long before his appointment was officially sealed. Only on 12 November 1639 did his name appear among a batch of five assorted warrants authorizing royal payments, including an allowance of £100 a year 'unto John Tridiscant keeper of his Majesties gardens at Oatlands payable quarterly from Midsomer 1638 during his Majesties pleasure, in the place of John Tridiscant his father deceased'.[6] He clearly spent most of that first summer in the queen's service, for in Morris's next letter to de Laet (of 4 September 1638), he wrote:

I have been to Lambeth two or three times to squeeze out of John Tradescant that catalogue of Virginian plants you were asking about on another occasion. When an opportunity of meeting him arises (for he is still far from here in the Queen's palace) I will question him about those rarer plants which are to be collected for you and I don't give up hope altogether. I fear only that some of them not accustomed to our soil or our skies may have been missed out from the published catalogue.[7]

By October, he told de Laet that he had still 'not yet met Tradescant but Parkinson makes me hope that in any case, very many of those exotic plants you desire will be found in the more elegant of our native gardens, so I don't doubt that I will be able to send them to you, together with anemones, irises and some bulbs; we must only await an opportune moment to get hold of them'.[8]

Despite being so busy at Oatlands, John Tradescant found time to marry for a second time that year, to Hester Pookes who described herself in her allegation for a marriage licence as a twenty-five-year-old spinster of St Bride's Parish, London, which meant she was old enough to give her own consent to her marriage.[9] Evidence of a later portrait suggests that she subtracted some five years from her real age, however, making her about the same age as her husband.[10] As a widower with two young children and a job that kept him often away, Tradescant would have needed another pair of capable hands to help run the home and the collection of rarities. The couple were married on 1 October 1638 in the old City church of St Nicholas Cole Abbey,[11] towards the west end of Knight-Riders Street close to the Thames. London chronicler John Stow described it as 'a proper church, somewhat ancient, as appeareth by the waies raised thereabout, so that men are forced to descend into the body of the Church'. Cold Abbey was another of its names, 'as standing in a cold place, as Cold Harbor, and such like'.[12]

Of all the women in the Tradescants' story, Hester is the only one to gain her own voice, which became increasingly shrill in later life. She also had a face, appearing in a number of family portraits now in the Ashmolean Museum, Oxford, including one painted around the time of her marriage in which she appears in a wide-brimmed black hat and black dress underneath a large white lawn collar, neatly edged with double strips of a lustrous fabric. The most sympathetic of all her portraits, it shows her as a handsome, self-possessed woman, dark-haired and dark-eyed, a touch unsettling in the intensity of her gaze. She was evidently a good match.

Hester's pedigree remains uncertain, however. After looking into her complicated relations, art historian Rachel Poole[13] concluded that she was the granddaughter of a French tailor from Valenciennes, John Pookes (Poux or Powkes), who came to England around 1560 and settled in the precincts of St Martin-le-Grand where there was a flourishing 'stranger' community.[14] Hester was certainly related to the tailor and his wife (another Hester, also called Paschina Oblaert, from Bruges) as she named several of their descendants as kin in her will, but Tradescant's bride was not the daughter of their eldest son as identified by Poole.[15] Parish records have so far failed to reveal precisely who her parents were, despite extensive sleuthing by art historian Mary Edmond,[16] although the records do establish a crucial link between the Pookses of St Martin-le-Grand and two families of court painters known to John Tradescant and his father.

The link occurred through the two marriages of the tailor's daughter, Sara Pooks, whose children the Tradescants would later acknowledge as Hester's 'cousins'. A son of Sara's first marriage was Cornelius de Neve, who painted portraits of George Villiers, Duke of Buckingham, and Elias Ashmole, and to whom was once attributed the posthumous portrait of the elder Tradescant garlanded with flowers, shells, fruit and plainer vegetables (parsnips, turnips and onions).[17] Sara's second marriage (as his second wife) was to Antwerp-born John de Critz the elder, Serjeant Painter to King James and now to Charles I.[18] Three of the sons from his first marriage all became painters: John de Critz II (who succeeded his father to the office of Serjeant Painter), Thomas and Emanuel. Old John de Critz had worked for Robert Cecil at Hatfield House and a 'John decreets' (probably the son) appeared in the royal accounts for Oatlands Palace in the mid-1630s.[19] It was doubtless through this Oatlands connection that John Tradescant met his future wife.

The link between the Tradescants and the de Critzes produced a number of family portraits attributed at various times to both Thomas and Emanuel de Critz, although the earliest family group of Hester Tradescant and her two stepchildren was painted by another (unidentified) artist. All three subjects are wearing clothes richly coloured and trimmed with lace. 'They are presented to us in the height of their prosperity,' writes Rachel Poole, 'when they were rich, well known, and much considered and their museum a centre of interest to friends and scholars.'[20] But the artist has caught a disturbing detail that gains significance only with hindsight. In reaching out to touch the shoulder of her stepson, Hester seems to exclude the girl standing between them, whose later marriage to a man nearly three times her age continues to puzzle.

Hester and John Tradescant began married life in a state of some financial ease. As well as Tradescant's generous Oatlands salary, the household benefited from entrance fees to the collection of rarities and money from plant sales. John Morris had obtained plants from the elder Tradescant, although whether he paid for them or received them as gifts is not clear. In November 1638, for instance, John Morris told de Laet 'from that one plant received from John Tradescant senior two years ago I now possess sixteen, granted too that I have given away six or seven others to friends'.[21] The following January, Morris promised to prepare for his friend 'plants of unusual colours from John Tradescant that are most suitable for the time of year', implying a bulk order for which the younger Tradescant would surely have charged. Morris specifically promised exotic irises and hyacinths, 'at least however many that have not perished in our little gardens'.[22]

As well as tending his garden at Lambeth, Tradescant was entering into the life of the parish, which provided an increasingly important focus for family life.[23] Participation in parish affairs involved obligations as well as rewards, and it seems the younger Tradescant played a more active role in the church than his father, making a voluntary contribution of 2s 6d towards a decent gilt cup and two silver flagons for the communion table,[24] contributing 2s for the relief of distressed Protestants in Ireland,[25] and assuming parish office as a surveyor of highways (in 1649) and as a collector for the poor (in 1657).[26]

In the early years of his employment, he was also kept busy at Oatlands where he would have witnessed the thatching with reeds of a brick 'snowe well' in the park and the construction of a new five-inch-square brick drain taking waste water into the valley.[27] This was a newfangled icehouse built to provide ice for preparing summer desserts and for cooling wines. Its dimensions exactly match one of the earliest recorded icehouses built at Greenwich in 1619: sixteen feet in diameter and thirty feet deep.[28] How food might be frozen to keep it fresh was only just beginning to be understood. John Aubrey even attributed Sir Francis Bacon's death in 1626 to the experimental stuffing of a chicken with snow to keep it fresh, an experiment that proved strangely fatal. Feeling suddenly unwell, Bacon was taken to Lord Arundel's house in nearby Highgate and put in a damp bed, from which he caught such a chill that he died several days later.[29]

Also during Tradescant's first year at Oatlands, George Portman was paid for decorating the wall in the Privy Garden's open gallery with eight of the queen's houses. They were painted French-fashion 'in Landskipp in oyle and underneathe a leaning place aboute three foote high painted with devisions of marble and the Ceelinge with Cloudes and sky colour'.[30] Inigo Jones's designs for the wall show blank compartments framed by a narrow decorative border, incorporating a female bust (the queen?) in a cartouche, swags and grotesque masks.[31] Nearly a decade later the wall was much admired by Sir Thomas Herbert (then effectively King Charles I's gaoler), who accompanied the king under armed guard on his slow journey southwards, after the Scots had 'sold' him back to the forces of Parliament. In a brief memoir, Herbert remembered Oatlands as

a large and beautiful House of the Queen's upon the River of *Thames*; where, upon the Plaister'd Wall in the Stone-Gallery, respecting the Gardens, were very curiously pourtray'd that Royal Edifice (with *Pontefract Castle, Havering, Eltham, Nonsuch,* and some other Palaces assigned to her Majesty) in like manner as you see at *Fontainbleau,* of several stately Houses of the *French* Kings.[32]

Like all gardens, those at Oatlands revealed much about their owners' tastes and habits. While Queen Henrietta Maria liked her gardens for show,

Charles used them for health and recreation, as Herbert's memoir revealed. Throughout their journey southwards, the king made use of the bowling greens, groves and walks of the houses where they stayed, or rode out to neighbouring houses if there were none to hand.[33] During his short stay at Oatlands (in mid-August 1647) he would have enjoyed the bowling green built by the elder Tradescant and now restored by his son, who would later submit a claim for amending the walks in the vineyard garden and other garden works at Oatlands, '& for repairing the Bowling Greene there'.[34] After his flight to the Isle of Wight, Charles was incarcerated in Carisbrooke Castle where the governor converted the barbican 'for his Majesty's Solace and Recreation ... into a Bowling-green, scarce to be equalled, and at one side build a pretty Summer-House, for Retirement'.[35]

Show and spectacle were at the heart of other court entertainments and especially the masques that had already featured prominently in the Jacobean court. Adored by Queen Anne (although the bookish King James was often bored by them) they were elevated to new heights by Charles and Henrietta Maria who – scandalously, to some – took part in the action themselves.[36] Show was their very purpose: what you saw mattered more than poetry, or drama. Each followed a predictable sequence: an anti-masque in which order and harmony were disrupted by vice; a middle section in which evils and vices were banished by heroic virtues in the guise of king and queen; and a climax in which the actors danced with the audience, bringing the courtiers into the resolution of conflict and demonstrating the triumph of divine-right monarchy.[37] The architect of the spectacle was royal surveyor Inigo Jones, who collaborated first with playwright Ben Jonson and, after they quarrelled, with William Davenant. Their *Britannia Triumphans* of 1638 can be read as Charles's justification for the notorious 'ship money' tax, proposing a theatrical resolution to the kingdom's threatened chaos.

In the very last masque of Charles's rule, *Salmacida spolia* of 1640, as the rebellious Scots gathered on the border to invade England, a pregnant Henrietta Maria floated down from the heavens on a mechanical cloud, illuminated with 'lightsome Rayes' and 'environed with her martiall Ladies' dressed 'in Amazonian habits of carnation, embroidered with silver, with plumed Helmes, Bandrickes with Antique swords hanging by their sides, all as rich as might be, but the strangenes of the Habits was most admired'.[38] As spectacle it was – like all Jones's productions – truly astonishing, but as an act of self-delusion it was pure madness. 'In the weeks of crisis,' wrote Roy Strong, 'with an empty exchequer and an appalling political situation, Charles still rehearsed the masque daily, his faith in the efficacy of such spectacles even at that late hour still apparently unshattered.'[39]

The garden naturally found its place in Stuart masques within the realm of order and cosmic harmony, opposed to the chaos of tempests, wild forests and flaming hells. One Ben Jonson masque first staged in 1631 (*Loves Triumph, through Callipolis*) ended in a richly ornate Italianate garden of the kind favoured by Henrietta Maria. 'The masque closed with a simple allegory,' observed Strong. 'Within this peaceful garden representing the State of England, a palm tree, the emblem of peace, arose bearing the British crown, while round its trunk were entwined the lily and the rose.'[40]

Tradescant was more concerned with the day-to-day realities of keeping a garden in good order than with its rarefied Neoplatonic ideal, and he continued to juggle royal duties with his other responsibilities. By the summer of 1639, as the king and queen went back and forwards to Oatlands,[41] Morris was at last able to send his friend de Laet Tradescant's long-awaited catalogue of Virginian plants – completed, it seems, with help from Morris himself and advice from Parkinson. 'The dried plants have been inspected,' wrote Morris, 'and at the same time examined carefully but there are still many seeds remaining which do not yet reveal what sort they will be.'[42] Morris's next letter (of August 1639) returned to the subject of exotic hyacinths and irises, of which 'Tradescant and Parkinson only have very few ... and those who have more, have only single specimens: for they do not tolerate our weather and our soil to the extent that they produce seed'. Morris's opinion of Tradescant's competence was hardly helped by an unfortunate mix-up over some distinctly coloured anemones, which Morris had asked to be put aside for him but somehow Tradescant had allowed their marker stickers to be 'greatly muddled up' by his labourers or the 'carelessness of the little women weeding through them'.[43]

The summer of 1640 was a busy time for Tradescant as the pregnant Queen Henrietta Maria chose Oatlands for the birth of her eighth child, Prince Henry, who was christened in a private ceremony there on 21 July. 'The Queen was never better nor so well of any of her children as of this,' was the official verdict.[44] Even the Venetian ambassador was caught up in festivities, informing the Doge and the Venetian senate:

All the ministers and those of Spain in particular lighted bonfires at this happy event, and I also did not fail in my duty, and further performed the proper offices with the king, which were received most graciously. The day after to-morrow I shall go to Oatlands, where the queen is, to do what friendship requires and express the solicitude with which your Excellencies regard the happy events of this House.[45]

In the country, the mood was getting darker. Charles and the Scots had gone to war over Charles's attempts to introduce religious uniformity across his kingdoms. Desperately short of money, the king reconvened Parliament after a gap of eleven years, but religious differences were threatening to frac-ture the country's shared Protestant culture. In the king's camp were his hated archbishop of Canterbury, William Laud, and others attracted to Arminism, a form of high Anglicanism that emphasized free will and which many equat-ed with popery. Opposing them were the Puritans, a name invented by their enemies; they called themselves 'the godly' and lived at a high level of spirit-ual intensity, determined to strip the Church of ritual and hierarchy. Whatever side they favoured, the people at large fretted, like the moderate Puritan John Morris who – as early as July 1640 – wrote to his friend warn-ing of the dangerous political situation. His letter ended with a plaint that the mimosa de Laet had sent him did not grow, despite all his care.[46] By October, he was afraid that civil war was inevitable. Yet while chaos threat-ened the kingdom, he could still put together his thoughts on how to grow slender-leaved anemones, which Tradescant had promised him but which did not flourish in London, 'I believe because of the smoke of the coal'.[47]

John Tradescant's own conduct throughout the civil war years suggests a man determined to survive rather than one driven by principle or passion. Unlike his own father, he did not take up arms on his employer's behalf, nor did he follow fellow botanist Thomas Johnson or Hester's kinsman, John de Critz II, into the royalist camp. Both lost their lives in the king's service: the younger de Critz at Oxford[48] and apothecary Johnson at the siege of Basing House where he died of fever following a wound to his shoulder.[49] As far as we know, Tradescant simply stayed at his royal post as long as he could. In the summer of 1641 the queen spent much time at Oatlands, where she would have kept her gardener busy tending the walks, the gardens and her beloved orange trees. She was still there in September, when plague and smallpox raged in London, Westminster and the suburbs, and the 'sickness' had travelled the fifteen miles to Oatlands.[50]

By then, the amateur painter Alexander Marshal was staying at South Lambeth with the Tradescants, from whose house he sent greetings to a friend in Northamptonshire, saying that 'since the Queen has been at Oatlands I have been there every week'.[51] He also passed on greetings from his host, John Tradescant, and a Dutch portrait painter, John Baptist Gaspars, who was quite possibly staying with them, too. It was probably during this visit that Marshal was painting the flowers in Tradescant's garden for one of the treasures of the Tradescant collection, 'A Booke of Mr. TRADESCANT's choicest Flowers and Plants, exquisitely limned in vellum, by Mr. Alex: Marshall'.[52] The Tradescant Florilegium has since disappeared although two volumes of a similar work by Marshal (executed on paper) belong to the Royal Collection at Windsor Castle, and the British Museum has an exquisite group of watercolours by Marshal (this time on vellum) of costly flowers tied with ribbons into bunches of threes: gorgeous 'broken' tulips, feathered and flamed in their markings, anemones and a few other flowers.[53] The approaching civil war might have lowered people's spirits but it did not lessen their appreciation of such rare beauty. Even the practical Samuel Hartlib was a fan of Marshal's work. 'Dr Merricke knows a very ingenious Man that is imploied about extracting colours out of diverse plants,' he recorded in his notes. 'The same Man is a most exquisite Painter for the lively drawing of Plants and Insects. Hee has drawn the choicest flowers of John Traduskens garden.'[54]

Then in August 1642 the inevitable happened, as John Morris had feared: the king raised his standard at Nottingham and civil war broke out. For some months the royal household had been preparing for this outcome, and Tradescant must have known his tenure of the Oatlands post was in jeopardy. The docket confirming his appointment awarded him an annual salary 'during His Majesties pleasure' and now His Majesty had other things on this mind. Already custody of Oatlands had passed to royal servant Thomas Jermyn, effectively removing the palace from the royal accounts,[55] and Queen Henrietta Maria had travelled to the Low Countries to raise money for the royal cause by pawning the Crown Jewels and enlisting Catholic support. In The Hague she stayed with the exiled Queen of Bohemia, Charles's sister Elizabeth. On the sea journey over to Holland, one of the baggage ships sank and the maids lost all their clothes.[56] Whether Tradescant continued to work regularly at Oatlands and draw his annual salary is doubtful. The survey of Oatlands carried out for Parliament in June 1650 described the palace's 'five severall Gardens . . . all which may be made very usefull and proffitable to the whole house if ordered and preserved as they ought to be',[57] suggesting little more than a caretaker regime during the troubles.

Life in London, which declared for Parliament, cannot have been easy for anyone, regardless of political or religious views. Even before the declaration of war, Morris had described for his friend de Laet the peculiar weather of the previous winter, which he interpreted as a divine warning.[58] 'Good God!' he wrote. 'What winds, rain, next floods and finally very severe frost. And meanwhile, something you may wonder at even more, pure summer in mid-January. Or is it here the finger of God, who is telling us to be wise – or die?' Plants continued to occupy Morris's thoughts, but of Tradescant he had begun to despair. 'Hope of Tradescant is in vain,' he wrote to de Laet in April 1642, 'he is altogether not taking after his father, nor does he have in him one single vein of his father's testicle etc.'[59] The reference (to words used by the Latin Stoic and satirist, Aulus Persius Flaccus) demonstrates the extent of Morris's exasperation. By October, Morris reported that soldiers were swarming everywhere. He had bought muskets for protection and asked his friend to send him some 'horsemens pistols' from Holland.[60]

There was looting by soldiers in his suburban retreat at Isleworth. Fearing trouble, he had already removed his wife and family to the relative safety of their City home near London Bridge, and made sure that his precious library was safe.[61] As he told de Laet, the victorious king's forces had marched as far as Turnham Green just west of the capital but were then forced to withdraw. The king spent the night at Hampton Court before making his way via Oatlands and Reading to Oxford.

Londoners responded to the royalist threat by indulging in a frenzy of trench-digging and fortification. William Lithgow, a Scot who visited London in early 1643, wrote in praise of the

daily musters and showes of all sorts of *Londoners* here ... marching to the fields and outworks, (as Merchants, Silke-men, Macers, Shopkeepers, &c.) with great alacritie, carrying on their shoulders yron Mattocks, and wooden shovels, with roaring Drummes, flying collours, and girded swords; most companies being also interlarded with Ladies, women, and girles: two and two carrying baskets for to advance with the labour, where divers wrought till they fell sick of their pains.

Shortly before leaving London, Lithgow set out on a 'wearisome dayes journey' of 'eighteen Kentish myles' around the string of trenches and forts which by then ringed the city to the north and south of the Thames. He started at Wapping, close to the river, where he found a 'seven angled Fort, erected of turffe, sand, watles, and earthen worke, (as all the rest are composed of the like) having nine Port holes, and as many cannons'.[62] Further protection came from a palisade of sharp wooden stakes around the top, pointing outwards. Along the trenches he marched, past Whitechapel, Mile End Green, Shoreditch and Kingsland, Hoxton and Finsbury Fields, up to Islington, Holborn Fields, and back down again by St Giles Fields, Tyburn and Marylebone to the river at Chelsea. Crossing over by boat to the Surrey side at Lambeth (where the ferry was kept on the Middlesex side at night, to avert a surprise attack, and guards were posted to check the passes of people crossing by day),[63] he visited the forts at Nine Elms and Vauxhall (close to the Tradescants at South Lambeth), and at St Georges's Fields, which he considered the 'rarest and fairest … reared after the moderne modell of an impregnant Citadale'.[64]

Lambeth was particularly dangerous for a royalist. Lambeth Palace (home to Archbishop William Laud) was attacked by apprentices, and later turned into a prison for royalists where many died, especially in the autumn of 1645.[65] Soldiers guarding the prison caused a commotion one Sunday at Tradescant's church of St Mary, Lambeth in a curious incident that left one parishioner dead and another wounded. The Tradescants would almost certainly have been among the congregation. According to one version of events, the parish officers rebuked a soldier 'who sat with his hat on during divine service'. Driven from the church by watermen pelting them with stones, the soldiers fired back in self-defence.[66] In a contradictory version, the soldiers broke into the church, tore the common prayer book to pieces, 'pulled the surplice off the minister's back, and committed other outrages to the great terror of the people, till the watermen came to their rescue'. Whatever the real truth, the incident reflected concern over the rector, Daniel Featley, who trod a perilous path between the Calvinists and the king and was subsequently deprived of his living, dying in 1645.[67]

Potentially just as perilous, on a purely personal level, was the marriage of John Tradescant's young daughter Frances to her widowed great-uncle, Alexander Norman. He had previously married the elder Tradescant's wife's sister, Dorcas, soon after the death of her first husband (also a cooper).[68] Frances and Alexander were married at the City church of St Bartholomew the Less on 28 January 1645,[69] the day after Hester Tradescant had lodged the marriage allegation naming 'Alexander Norman, of St Botolph, Aldgate, Citizen & Cooper of London, Widower, 56, & Frances Tradescant, dau. of John Tradescant, of South Lambeth, Gent., who consents, about 19, his consent attested by his wife Hester Tradescant; at Little St Bartholomew, or St Mary Magdalen, Old Fish Street.'[70] In fact, if Frances was born after John's marriage to Jane, she would have been just seventeen, not nineteen, making the discrepancy in ages even more shocking. A search of the records for other marriages celebrated around this time reveals no such differences in age.

Parents still exercised considerable control over their children's choice of

London's civil war fortifications: Captain Eyre's sketch of the quadrant
fort at Vauxhall (1643).

a mate and in difficult times the economics of a marriage would carry far
more weight than romantic attachment. But Alexander Norman was not
even a good economic match. A cooper by profession, Norman rented a
house for £6 a year in the East Smithfield precinct of St Botolph without
Aldgate, lying just outside the City walls close to Tower Hill.[71] Once the site
of a fine abbey and a plague burial ground, the area had become crowded
with garden plots and small tenements, interspersed with more attractive

buildings like the brick-and-timber almshouses built by the Merchant Tailors at the west end of Hogg Street. John Stow remembered a farm where he had 'fetched many a halfe-penny worth of milke' still hot from the cow. The ditch outside the City walls used to be regularly cleansed of filth and mud, 'But now of later time, the same Ditch is inclosed, and the bankes thereof let out for Garden plots, Carpenters yards, Bowling Allies, and divers houses thereon builded, whereby the City wall is hidden, the Ditch

filled up, a small Channell left, and that very shallow.' At least Norman's
work was close to hand: he was master of a business supplying casks to the
Ordnance, then housed with its many workhouses and 'faire and large Store-
houses for Armour, and habiliments of warre' on the site of the old
Monastery of St Clare in the Minories.[72] But despite his several apprentices,
Norman's 'allowance' as a cooper was only £3 a quarter – compared with
John Tradescant's £25 for the equivalent period – although his bills certainly
brought him additional payments.[73]

One of the best things that can be said about Frances's husband is that the
elder Tradescant had trusted him enough to appoint him as one of his two
executors, although the sum of £17 described in his will as being 'in ye hands
of my brother in law Alexander Norman' quite possibly represented a debt.
Norman's first marriage to Frances's great-aunt had brought him his cooper-
age business, and it seems he was about to prosper again by his second
marriage into the Tradescant clan.[74] After marrying Frances, Norman
continued to play an active part in the affairs of his guild, the Company of
Coopers, rising through the ranks to become younger warden, but then his
progress was mysteriously checked, unlike most of his fellows who were voted
almost unanimously into higher office.[75] He died in 1657 and was buried in
St. Botolph, Aldgate, in early September,[76] owing his father-in-law at least
'fourscore pounds or thereabouts' plus interest on the principal. It was a
marriage that cannot have brought the young Frances Tradescant much joy.
In his own will, John Tradescant forgave his widowed daughter her late
husband's debts but left her only £10, a sum that compares very meanly with
the £100 he left to a friend's widow. Hester did not mention her stepdaugh-
ter at all when she came to draw up a will. Either Frances was dead by then or
feuding between daughter and stepmother lay at the root of Frances's strange
marriage to a man who had once been married to her grandfather's sister-
in-law.[77]

With Frances gone from the house, Thomas de Critz painted a portrait
of her brother John handing his stepmother a jewel shaped like a dangling
flower.[78] The painting's date – 1645 – is written on the back, and the
subjects' ages inscribed on the canvas: the boy is twelve and 'Sr John

Tradescant his Second Wife' is aged thirty-seven, although she looks younger. This is the portrait that gives the lie to the age she declared at her marriage. Rachel Poole describes the painting as being 'peacefully domestic in feeling' as the boy gazes up at his stepmother with 'pretty deference'.[79] It seems close in date to another painting also now attributed to Thomas de Critz in which John Tradescant stands beside a heap of exotic shells with a bulbous-nosed and bearded Roger Friend, captioned 'his friend Zythepsa of Lambeth' ('Zythepsa' is Greek for brewer, which perhaps explains the nose).[80] The painting implies that Friend has given Tradescant the shells for his collection, although his name does not appear in the list of benefactors. 'In both pictures,' comments Poole, 'there is the same glimpse of evening sky in the background, and the same predominance of grey in the dresses.'[81] Their mood is calm but sombre, reflecting the Tradescants' determination to weather the turbulence of the times, perhaps.

Morris continued to mention Tradescant in his letters to de Laet, consulting him over a yucca along with nurseryman Ralph Tuggie's widow and others who 'take pleasure in such exotic plants';[82] and making enquiries for a friend of de Laet's in connection with a seed catalogue. 'I have already met Tradescant, Parkinson and other friends learned in botanical matters about that,' he wrote in February 1646, 'and they have freely promised me their co-operation.'[83] But four months later, he wrote again to de Laet complaining about

how obviously sparse the crop of botanists has recently become, with Johnson and Parkinson dead, and now that skilful young man who gardened for Lord Newport before the civil war forced into exile because of his 'popery'. Tradescant himself lives almost in exile from the profession, having virtually given up these studies to maintain a trade with the Canary Islands. The best and only hope left to us is the Duke of Buckingham's young man, a skilled enough gardener but completely ignorant of letters.[84]

That Johnson had died after the siege of Basing House is well known (another royalist at the siege was Inigo Jones, who escaped in a blanket) but

Parkinson's death is usually given as 1650 and it seems strange that Morris should get this wrong, as they were often in contact.

What trade Tradescant was conducting with the Spanish-dominated Canary Islands is another puzzle. London had harboured Canary merchants since the days of Henry VIII at least, and the Canary Islands provided a key staging post in Elizabethan Captain John Hawkins's attempt to break into the transatlantic slave trade, shipping black slaves from West Africa to Spanish colonists in the West Indies.[85] Now a timber trade was opening up between New England and the Canaries, the Azores, the West Indies and England, which may have interested Tradescant. Or perhaps he was trading in the Canary Islands' staple products of sugar from the plantations and a purple dye called orchil derived from lichen that at times turned the islands purple. Tradescant displayed it in his collection of curiosities, along with three dozen or so 'materialls of dyers and painters', from lapis lazuli to charcoal black and cochineal red.[86] Through his wife's connections, he would have a good market for his product but he does not seem to have used his trade with the Canaries to augment his collection of foreign rarities in any systematic way.

Throughout the war years, Tradescant seems to have kept his collection of rarities open to the paying public as he struggled to keep afloat financially, like everyone else dependent on the public purse. In September 1647 he was already contemplating the compilation of a catalogue, as reported by foreign visitor Rasmus Bartholin to the noted Danish collector, Ole Worm. While admitting to grudging admiration for 'Mr Tredoscus's collection of rarities', Bartholin unctuously added to Worm that he would have been moved

to even greater admiration if I had not been convinced that your own well-stocked collection is far ahead of his, although I did not have your museum catalogue to hand, and have not been able to see the last edition. I cannot deny that he possesses wonderful objects in the form of natural curiosities brought home from India and he has promised to have a list of them printed.[87]

Worm's own view of Tradescant's capabilities was more forthright. When his son Willum visited England in 1652, Ole Worm wrote to him saying, 'concerning Tradescant, I have heard that he was an idiot'.[88]

The king's execution on 30 January 1649 brought the old order to its brutal end. His scaffold was erected outside Inigo Jones's Banqueting House on Whitehall, the setting for royal masques until the preservation of Rubens's painted ceiling required a change of venue. Morris wrote to de Laet of his shock, fearing that the country would go to ruin. Disgusted with everything, he asked his friend for consolation, but plants could still occupy their correspondence – in this case, the humble English sea cabbage.[89] De Laet had scribbled its name, *Brassica Angliae minima*, across his friend's letter announcing the king's death. Morris's next letter began:

I have put off writing to you until now for the sole reason of making further enquiries about that 'Brassica Anglia' which appears under that name neither in John Gerard, nor in Johnson, nor in Parkinson. I cannot imagine it is anything other than the name implies, an English sea cabbage. I have since written off to my London gardener and to our most skilful triumvirate in matters of plants: Tradescant, Morgan and Blackburn.[90]

So Tradescant had been rehabilitated in Morris's eyes to the ranks of the skilful, his name now linked to Edward Morgan (witness to old Tradescant's will and the 'very Skillfull *Botanist*'[91] admired by John Evelyn) and the unknown Blackburn.

It was the last time Morris would mention Tradescant in his letters to de Laet, although he continued to write about the political situation (expressing the commonly held view that with Cromwell preparing to go to Ireland, 'the monarchy has been changed, not abolished')[92] and about plants, commenting on orchids and the arrival of a new gardener, as well as promising to send more plants to his friend. He probably never fullfilled that promise. In December 1649, de Laet died at The Hague from a sudden stroke. Morris wrote to de Laet's son Johannes, expressing his deep sympathy and proposing that Johannes should take over the correspondence in his father's place. As usual, Morris had written on the letter, 'Leave this with Mr Cruzo, merchant at his house in Bishopstate streete nigh the Black Bull Inne, to be transmitted as above.'[93]

If the wealthy John Morris feared that he would hardly find the means to support his family or his studies after the king's execution, life must have been doubly hard for John Tradescant, whose fortunes had been linked to royal patronage. Proposals to ease his financial worries began to surface in the intelligence reports of Hartlib's *Ephemerides* as early as 1649, when Tradescant apparently offered to sell his collection of rarities for the same annuity he had received from the king for gardening at Oatlands – £100 (the figure of £1,000 pounds had been crossed out) – 'and to perfect the Garding of it. This might bee added to the University of Cambridge by which meanes with the additions they might out-strip Oxford in their bookish-Library.'[94] The sale's financial logic was the subject of another note by Dr Robert Child (the intermediary between Tradescant and John Winthrop Jnr in New England): 'Hee offers to sell all for a hundred lb. a year which is really worth above a thousand lb. But then the advantage is that his son being brought up to looke to the Botanical Garden and Plant's the charge of keeping one of purpose to attend those businesses is clearly saved.'[95] So old Tradescant was right to suspect that his son might want to part with his precious collection, although with the king dead and the young Prince Charles plotting with the Scots to crush the new republican government, the younger Tradescant could hardly be expected to offer the rarities to the prince, as stipulated by his father's will.

The transaction was not to cover the plant collection, it seems, as young John Tradescant III was already being trained as a gardener to follow in the footsteps of his father and grandfather. Selling the rarities was therefore compatible with another proposal that surfaced in Hartlib's jottings: the offer by Hatton Garden physician, Dr George Bate, to give £400 to endow a botanical garden, 'which they designe to bee John Tradesken, or the Ld. Arundel house over the waters'.[96] Nothing seems to have come of this proposal, although Tradescant dedicated his museum catalogue to the College of Physicians, suggesting a possible obligation. The college, however, could afford neither to stock a garden nor to pay gardeners' wages, making an institutional link unlikely. (The college eventually signed an agreement with Oxford University to maintain the Physic Garden there for an annual grant of £150.)[97]

The rival site was in Lambeth Marsh, on former meadowland close by the river. It was sold in 1634 to Lord Arundel who leased it to his employee Abraham Boydell Cuper, and either Abraham or his son opened it as a public pleasure garden known as Cuper's or Cupid's Garden.[98] John Aubrey wrote of the gardens in his *Natural History of Surrey*: 'Near the Bank Side lyes a very pleasant Garden, in which are fine Walks, well kept in good Order, known by the Name of CUPIDS GARDEN.' Aubrey remarked on the gardens' arbours, walks and 'mangled Statues', which had once formed part of Arundel's famed collection of statuary brought over from Italy.[99]

The execution of King Charles I put an end to Tradescant's royal career. Although he would live to see the monarchy restored, he was not granted (and probably did not seek) further royal office. The man who became famous as Charles II's gardener was John Rose, another colleague and fellow liveryman in the Company of Gardeners, who wrote the guide to English vine-growing at John Evelyn's suggestion.[100]

Oatlands Palace did not long survive the creation of the Commonwealth. Although the parliamentary surveyors charged with its valuation considered that the houses and buildings 'are generally in very good repair and not fitt to be demolished or taken downe', they entered no annual rental value and put a valuation instead on materials only: £4,023 18s. This sum was to cover the Tudor palace (half fairy tale, half rabbit warren) with its litany of separate chambers for king, queen, named courtiers and staff ('the Queens Cabbinet Roome, the Queens Closet, the Queens Chappell Gallery ... the Queenes Christall roome ... the Queenes Coffer roome, the Queens withdrawing roome, the Queen's privy Chamber ... the Queen's bedchamber ... the Queen's backstaires'); the two graceful gatehouses, turreted at each corner; the bakehouse, buttery, tiled hay barn, stables for upwards of twenty horses; the 'five several gardens' with their espaliered fruit trees, and the handsome fountain in the Long Garden. Oatlands Park was valued separately: an annual value of £166 for the land, £13 for its thirteen fallow deer, and £493 2s for more than two thousand trees beyond those marked out for the navy's use, mainly decayed pollards or very young spring wood.[101]

Like several other royal palaces, Oatlands was assigned as security for soldiers' overdue pay. It was sold for £4,933 18s to Robert Turbridge of St Martin-in-the-Fields as agent for sixteen named officers, quartermasters and troopers of the Parliamentary Army to whom pay and expenses were still owed.[102] In 1653, the palace was pulled down and some of the bricks bought to construct the locks on the Wey Navigation. Left standing was Inigo Jones's magnificent gateway, which the Earl of Lincoln later moved to the terrace near his mansion, Oatlands House, as part of the design for the gardens produced by William Kent.[103] After the estate was sold for development, the gateway was eventually broken up and the pieces were turned into a rockery at the Pelican public house in Addlestone, until rescued by the Walton and Weybridge History Society and put on display in the Elmbridge Museum, Weybridge. Another original Tudor gateway – to the stables from the south courtyard – survives in a modern housing estate, trapped within a warren of pedestrian walkways and streets bearing names like Tudor Walk, West Palace Gardens and Catherine Howard Court.

A few items from the gardens at Oatlands found their way with other works of art into the inventories and valuations of the king's goods prepared for Parliament to prevent embezzlement and to facilitate the sale of goods not wanted by the state. These included three lead cisterns; a clock and two dials; two stone sundials with a wooden seat (sold for £2 0s 6d); and 'severall Oring Trees' (in fact 'about three score'), which were valued at £20 but eventually sold for just £5.[104] Their buyer had found himself a bargain. Unearthed during twentieth-century excavations of Oatlands Palace was another reminder of the Tradescants' service as royal gardeners: a handful of cherry stones found in the palace garderobe or lavatory, of date and variety unknown.[105] DNA testing may one day tell us whether these were indeed cherries grown in the time of either Tradescant.

Chapter Twenty-Three

The Useful Gardener

John Morris may have entertained all sorts of reservations about the younger Tradescant's manners, learning, managerial competence, even his ability to control his women weeders, but he had no doubts about his gardening skills. And it is as a gardener that Tradescant projects himself in one of the most accomplished of the family portraits, attributed to Hester's kinsman Thomas de Critz, in which the younger Tradescant leans on his spade against a vista of parkland trees, dressed in a black cap and white shirt beneath an open coat edged with grey fleece.[1] 'It is an impressive picture,' writes Rachel Poole.

The solitary rugged figure, his shaggy unfastened dress, the spade suggesting the most primitive toil, together make an appeal almost startling in its unusualness. Whatever its precise date – which must fall between 1645 and 1656 – this fine picture is original in conception: to a high degree instinct with understanding and feeling for character, and not less with the power to render it with sympathy and courage.[2]

There is also a sadness to the painting that indicates it may have been painted in the late 1640s, after Tradescant had lost his royal post, or in the early 1650s when he suffered a family tragedy; the expression in the gardener's 'tired and baggy brown eyes' is undeniably melancholic.[3] Despite the painting's claim to represent *Sr John Tradescant Jnr in his garden*, the backdrop is almost certainly imaginary.

Gardens were inevitably changing in response to the violence and social upheavals of the civil war, which was rapidly transforming the world inhabited by the younger Tradescant. Of course, some vestiges of the old order remained, especially in the provinces far away from the seats of power. During the Commonwealth years, a disappointed royalist such as Sir Thomas Hanmer could happily retire to his family estate at Bettisfield in Flintshire to cultivate his tulips and to plant his gentleman's garden with anemones, primroses, cowslips, gillyflowers and auriculas in much the old way.[4] And flowers could still transcend politics, as when Hanmer sent 'a very great mother-root of Agate Hamner' (his most famous tulip) to Parliamentarian Major General John Lambert at Wimbledon, where he lived in Queen Henrietta Maria's confiscated palace.[5]

The new watchword in gardening was not so much 'rarity' as 'utility', exemplified by the Prussian émigré and social reformer Samuel Hartlib who first travelled to England in the mid-1620s and settled there from the 1630s, an exile from Europe's Thirty Years War.[6] A near contemporary of the younger Tradescant, Hartlib was deeply influenced by the Utopian writings of Sir Francis Bacon, believing, like Bacon, that empirical investigation and its wider dissemination might pave the way to universal improvement and peace. Once settled in London, Hartlib cultivated a vast network of mainly Protestant contacts across northern and central Europe, dedicated to exchanging political news as well as scientific ideas and innovations, an 'intelligencer' role that would later be taken over by the Royal Society. Bee-keeping and the rearing of silkworms were among Hartlib's passions, and husbandry the subject of his most ardent tub-thumping. Among the authors whose work he promoted was Surrey farmer Sir Richard Weston, whom he described as 'a Papist but of a free and communicative disposition and one of the greatest husbandmen in all England'.[7] *Samuel Hartlib His Legacie* was, in fact, an expanded version of Weston's own discourse on Flemish husbandry, written as a legacy to his sons.[8]

Hartlib certainly knew of Tradescant, whose name appeared several times in his notebook jottings, and he would surely have paid a personal visit to Tradescant's South Lambeth garden, pausing to admire the rarities that also often featured in his notes. Hartlib's curiosity had a strong scientific bent, compelling him to note for instance that the 'Unicorns horne is of a sea-fish (and no Land-beast) which is caught in Green-land'.[9] Although he was appreciative of beauty, he was more concerned to pass on observations of a practical nature. In *Universal Husbandry Improved*, for instance, he noted that some plants from hot regions could thrive in colder climates, as proved by apricots, peaches, flax, yucca and, apparently rhubarb, which Parkinson had said came originally from the East Indies. More specifically he talked of the 'great *Spanish* Cane (much used by Weavers and Vintners)', which 'Master *John Tradeskin*, brought from the Western-Isle, and it flourisheth well in his Garden, and groweth great and tall'. The giant reed (*Arundo donax*) had, in fact, grown at South Lambeth since 1632, but the point of Hartlib's story was 'that things brought out of a hot Countrey do flourish with us,'[10] not when and by whom they might have been introduced into Britain.

And what of Tradescant himself – how did he manage to adapt his garden to the new political climate of Commonwealth England? The answer lies in the plant list finally published with his museum catalogue in 1656.[11] Although direct comparisons are hampered by double entries and shifting, pre-Linnaean plant names, it represents an extraordinary expansion on the elder Tradescant's list of 1634.[12] According to one count, the number of different varieties had more than doubled, from the elder Tradescant's 768 to a massive 1,701 plants under his son.[13] Of even more interest is how the garden had changed in the intervening twenty years.

Overall, in his choice of plants for the Lambeth garden, Tradescant was opting for plants that could be used by physicians and apothecaries rather than simply admired by other 'curious' gardeners.[14] Yes, he was still growing all his father's favourite flowers and for whole groups he simply copied out his father's lists with one or two additions, most obviously with anemones, auriculas, rock roses, crocuses, irises and daffodils. Under 'Narcissus', for instance, he repeated in the same order the twenty-eight varieties listed by his father (including 'Wilmots double Daffodill', 'Tradescant's great rose Daffodill' and several plants that are now not considered daffodils at all, such as the Atamasco lily from Florida), slipping into the list one he had received from the Morins: the Cape tulip or blood lily, *Haemanthus coccineus*. He also had all his father's twenty-seven old roses (among them the 'Moscovie Rose' and *Rosa virginiana*), again with just a few additions including two very simple forms, the single musk rose (*Rosa moschata*) and the single dog rose (R. *canina*).

Like his father, too, he claimed to grow a 'great variety of gallant Tulips', providing a list of thirty individual names, only three of them included in Sir Thomas Hanmer's far more extensive record.[15] In general, however, Tradescant had simply maintained his father's stocks of decorative 'florist flowers' without attempting to keep pace with the many new varieties appearing in the gardens of the curious, or breeding new varieties himself.

He was nonetheless continuing to introduce new ornamental plants on a fairly small scale. More than twenty plants were labelled 'Morini', indicating that they came from the Morins (probably Pierre) in Paris. These included ferns, the southern swamp lily (*Crinum americanum*), a new variety of crown imperial, a foxglove with burnt-orange flowers, a variegated giant reed, Italian lords and ladies (*Arum italicum*), blue-eyed grass (*Sisyrinchium graminoides*), the sweetly scented yellow jasmine from Madeira and the Canaries (*Jasminum odoratissimum*), and the March lily (*Amaryllis belladonna*) from the south-western Cape, also known as the naked lady. From the Morins, too, came peppers and beefsteak tomatoes (he called them 'love apples', *Pomum amoris fructu, Phoeiceo rubro, Morini*) and two real exotics that would have tested all his skills as a gardener: the Turk's cap cactus from the West Indies (*Melocactus intortus*), of a beauty verging on the grotesque; and the prickly custard apple from Barbados.

Both these last two would have required protection from anything approaching winter frosts. They joined his father's stable of tender plants, which he had skilfully kept alive and perhaps propagated, including the 'lesser Indian Figge' (another cactus, from the *Opuntia* family); oranges, lemons and the borderline-hardy pomegranate, *Punica granatum*; and great showy Angels' trumpets (*Brugmansia*). He was adding tender exotics of his own, such as *Aloe vera* from Spain, a liquorice from Brazil and the marvel of Peru (*Mirabilis jalapa*) from the tropical Americas.

To overwinter tender perennials, the Tradescants must have built some form of shelter at South Lambeth. 'All that are curious in plants have a roome purposely for this use adjoyning to their garden,' wrote Sir Thomas Hanmer mid-century, 'where not only tender flowers are put in wynter, but also delicate trees & shrubs, such as the Orenge, Lemmon, Pomegranate, Mirtle, Jasmyne and the like, and many sorts of Greenes.'[16] Heating was a problem, as the fumes from stoves were known to be harmful to plants. John Evelyn's solution was to

have a large Pan of Coales throughly kindled, & free of the leaste Smoake or *nidorous* smell . . .; and then placing it upon a *Hand-barrow*, have two men carrie it gently about the Conservatory, & betweene the Ranges for an hower at a tyme, & then set it downe, at one extreame, distant from any tree . . . This don constantly morning & evening, whilst the rigour of the season continues, you will find [it] preferable to all stoves, or artificiall warmings whatsover.[17]

Tradescant gave Virginia, New England and Barbados as the source of many plants new to his catalogue since his father's time, including a guava and a 'caribbee palm' from Barbados; the '*Virginian Jucca with shorter and narrower leaves*' (*Yucca filamentosa*); an amaranthus from New England; and all his own introductions from Virginia. Among this last group were the trees to which he proudly gave his name: the red maple, introduced as '*Tradescant's Virginian Maple*', followed by '*his other Virginian maple*', quite possibly the plane tree, *Platanus occidentalis*; the tulip tree, here introduced as '*Tradescant's white Virginia Poplar*'; and the swamp cypress which he called '*Tradescant's Virginian Cypresse*'.[18] Of all the plants that we know he brought back from North America, one that did not appear to have survived was Carolina jessamine, unless he had accepted Parkinson's doubts about its classification and now called it something else.

On the whole, however, Tradescant's success with even tender exotics was extraordinary at a time when he was adding a huge variety of new plants.

Taking his cue from Hartlib, he too was switching his prime focus from
rarity to utility, as shown by what happened to the *Ranunculus* family of
plants in his collection. He still had his father's great showy Persian
buttercups from the eastern Mediterranean, North Africa and south-west
Asia, among them the splendidly named 'Drape de argentine' and a *'double
Asian Crowfoot with a blood-red flower'*. He even received from Morin in Paris
a new Portuguese variety with violet-scented, shining yellow flowers. At the
same time, he almost doubled his collection by introducing humbler
members of the family (not all of them classed with buttercups today) of
interest to botanists, medical herbalists, apothecaries and doctors of physic.
These included the *'yellow rough-headed Crowfoot of Fallow field'*, water
crowfoot, ivy-leaved water crowfoot, meadow crowfoot, and the bane of any
temperate gardener trying to work a damp, heavy soil: creeping buttercup,
R. *repens*.[19]

Weeds and 'worts' were the new watchwords. A close comparison
between the catalogues of 1656 and 1634 reveals not just the addition of
common varieties to their showier siblings, but whole new classes of herbs
and simples ignored by the elder Tradescant: plants such as bishop's weed,
stinking bean trefoil, dill, anise, parsley, hoary cress, silverweed, mugwort,
spleenwort, stinking black horehound, burdock, goosefoot, fireweed,
common twayblade, Good King Henry, bryony, shepherd's purse, treacle
mustard, cannabis, motherwort, caraway, horsetail, chervil, honeywort,
germander speedwell, chamomile, herb Christopher, poison hemlock,
meadow thistle, basil thyme, costmary, navelwort, greater dodder, ivy-leaved
toadflax, dog's mercury, wild carrot, small teasel, bittersweet, dwarf elder,
cancerwort, eyebright, horseshoe vetch, meadowsweet, fenugreek, fumitory,
hedge woundwort, lady's bedstraw, needle furze, dyer's woad, duckweed,
rupturewort, butcher's broom, patience dock (he called it 'Monks Rubarbe'),
alexanders, starry swine's succory, pepperwort, masterwort, hedge mustard,
the dead nettles, common nipplewort, common dock, lovage, laserwort,
liverwort, flax, perennial ryegrass, moonwort, dyer's rocket, hairy willowherb, crested cow-wheat, sweet clover, lemon balm, annual mercury, bird's
nest orchid, creeping Jenny, Jack-go-to-bed-at-noon, common basil, wild

clary, corn salad, sainfoin, marsh woundwort, pellitory of the wall, feverfew, Venus' comb or shepherd's needle (both names current, then as now), thoroughwax or hare's ears, creeping cinquefoil, wood sorrel, hog's fennel, mouse-ear hawkweed, little hogweed, water smartweed, floating-leaf pondweed, sand plantain, lungwort, rib grass, charlock, spiked rampion, sundew, madder, arrowhead, corn spurry, summer and winter savory, scammony, groundsel, thyme, sawwort, ragwort, sowthistle, flixweed, deadly carrot, tower mustard, common cattail and rough cockleburr.

It was a fine list, organized by Latin names and giving common ones wherever possible, many of which are much the same today. Either Tradescant had become a real expert at naming his weeds and wild flowers or he received help, most probably from his cataloguer Elias Ashmole whose ability to soak up facts and arrange them into classification systems was becoming legendary. Ashmole had also taken up simpling, defined as the art of recognizing and gathering medicinal plants, and he counted Jacob Bobart the elder of the Oxford Physic Garden among his friends.[20] In the same year that Tradescant brought out his catalogue, 'herbarist' William Coles published an introduction to simpling dedicated to Ashmole ('the most Exquisite Lover of Plants') even though the two had not yet met.[21] He went on to praise Ashmole's famous support for all those dedicated to advancing learning of any kind, and flattered him for his addiction to the 'exquisite formes, and wonderfull varieties of those vegetable Creatures'.

Coles was interested in herbs from the standpoint of healing rather than horticulture. 'I am no Gardiner,' he declared craftily, 'nor no Gardiners Sonne, yet I hope the Gardiners will not be angry with me, if I set downe a few Directions for the more convenient placing of Plants in a Garden.'[22] Perhaps this explains why Tradescant (both a gardener and a gardener's son) was not listed among Coles's mentors who included John Parkinson's fierce critic, Dr William How,[23] 'Master Morgan the Gardiner at Westminster', and 'Master Robert' (corrected to Bobart) of Oxford's Physic Garden. In his much larger herbal published the following year, Coles gave a passing nod to Tradescant's gardening skills, noting that two rare forms of 'the Savine-Tree or Bush' (the juniper, *Juniperus sabina*) were to be found 'in some of our

more curious Gardens, as in that of John Tradescants Garden at Lambeth',
suggesting that Coles had at least visited South Lambeth by then.[24]

Tradescant may not have known what cures to effect with the herbs he
was growing, but the garden's new emphasis on healing herbs supports some
informal connection at least with Dr Bate and the physicians. He may even
have sold his weeds in the London herb markets if he was growing them in
sufficient quantities. One of his new plants was the insectivorous sundew
(Drosera rotundifolia) used to make a bright yellow cordial, rosa solis, which
had long been esteemed as a tonic and aphrodisiac before it became a
popular drink. Sir Hugh Platt's recipe in Delightes for Ladies involved soaking
a gallon of the herb for twenty days in a gallon of good 'Aqua Composita'
together with sliced dates, bruised spices (cinnamon, ginger and cloves), fine
sugar, and red rose petals. Ambergris, musk, gum amber, powdered coral
and pearl, and fine gold leaf were added extras, recalling the aureum potabile
(drinkable gold) of the alchemists, who numbered Ashmole among their
fraternity.[25]

As well as herbs and weeds, Tradescant planted many more food crops
than his father had done and found room for the new exotic crops like
rhubarb and tobacco, adding an occasional new variety to his father's range
of soft fruits. In other areas, too, the younger Tradescant was developing the
garden, planting mosses and ferns for the first time (the fern varieties
identified include the royal fern, male fern, maidenhair, adder's tongue,
hart's tongue, rustyback, deer fern and bracken).

He was also extending the range of trees, always problematic in a flower
garden. His father had grown relatively few (apart from fruits in his orchard),
concentrating on rarer or more ornamental species such as the Italian cypress;
the false acacia; and the 'Turpentine tree', Pistacia terebinthus, still rare enough
for Hartlib to remark on one seen at 'Mr Cupid the Earl of Arundels
Gardiner' in his Southwark garden.[26] The younger Tradescant planted many
more, not just his new introductions from Virginia but the common trees of
the English landscape – beech, birch, hornbeam, common oak, limes, black-
thorn, white and black poplars, mountain ash and the wild service tree. They
would have to fight for space with the new ornamental shrubs coming into

Peas and beans from John Parkinson's 'The Kitchen Garden' in
Paradisi In Sole (1629).

the garden, such as Persian lilac (Melia azedarach), a pink-flowered rhododendron from the mountains of Europe (Rhododendron hirsutum), and varieties of
shrubs that are now classics of the temperate garden – berberis, viburnum and
the spindle tree (Euonymus europaeus). And he was still growing his father's sun-
seeking bulbs and flowers, including his favourite pinks and gillyflowers,
geraniums, peonies, hyacinths, wallflowers, lilies, daylilies and sweet williams.

Altogether, the younger Tradescant's plant catalogue represented an
extraordinary degree of skill in putting together and maintaining such a
catholic range of plants. Bobart at Oxford could match him for simples,
perhaps, but his garden lacked many of the tender exotics and star
performers collected by both Tradescants over many years. Only his father's
orchard fruits were missing, presumably because he was running the orchard
as a nursery business and therefore planting stock in considerable quantities
rather than single specimens.

One customer in the late 1650s was Lord Hatton of Kirby Hall, once
Comptroller of the Household to Charles I, whom Tradescant would have
known through their royal connections. After Hatton had spent the early
Commonwealth years on the continent, he devoted himself passionately to
his gardens on his return, making a note to ask his man 'if he have procured
the plants from John Tradescant he undertooke to gett & have sent them to
Kirby. To desire him to gett from thence the sweet leafed Maple & the large
leafed Laurus tinus. To mind him of the White Mulberry trees he promised
me & desire to helpe me to 6 ordinary mulberry trees.' Hatton's list then set
out his request for '200 Apples 200 Peares 100 Cherries 100 Plumms 100
for Peaches & Nectorins'. Beside the list he has scribbled, 'A larger
proportion of stocks then last yeare', suggesting a steady trade from South
Lambeth to Kirby.[27] Hatton wanted cherries 'Most fleshy & less watery',
plums 'Dry firm the skin' and the 'Red streaked Apple'. Tradescant was not
Lord Hatton's only London supplier. In 1659 and 1660, he was also buying
or receiving plants from Mr (Edward) Morgan; the Walkers (senior and
junior) at St. James's; the head gardeners at Leicester House and Newport
House; and presumably John Rose, as he kept lists of his tulips and sent a
man to record the plants flowering with Rose in July 1658.[28]

Aside from apples (listed simply as '*very many sorts of choice Apple trees*'), the younger Tradescant found space for soft fruits such as grapes, currants, gooseberries, strawberries and blackberries, and for nut trees traditionally grown with fruit (hazel, filberts and walnuts among them). As well as the unnamed apples, his garden included some fruit trees like medlars (surprisingly absent from his father's list), cherries, and a '*purging Indian Plumme*'. It is tempting to suggest that the illustrated fruit list known as 'Tradescant's Orchard' (see Chapter 17) might relate to his nursery business as opposed to his show garden, but its tentative dating puts it a little earlier and he would surely have got his ripening dates right.

Tradescant's sale of orchard trees fits well with the spirit of the age, which laid such stress on gardening's productive virtues. Samuel Hartlib even devised a scheme for reducing poverty by the universal planting of fruit trees.[29] His idea, set out in a short pamphlet, was for a new law requiring citizens to plant twenty apples, pears, walnuts or quinces for every piece of land producing £5 rental a year, under the control of newly appointed tree wardens. Communities should likewise fence and plant commons and wastes, giving the produce 'to the poor, and necessitous people of every Town'.[30] He saw a clear health gain, claiming that apples were good for 'hot stomacks' and 'tempering melancholy humours'; pears were rather 'cold' and 'binding', good for the 'bloody flux' and as a digestive aid; walnuts by contrast were used in antidotes against the plague and the biting of venomous beasts; while quinces were good for just about everything else. And to the obvious economic and social benefits, he added the spiritual pleasures (like his protégé, Ralph Austen) 'when one may behold the waste and wilde places abounding with fruitfull trees (*like the Garden of God*) keeping their order, and distance: each one offering the weary traveller some little collation to quench his thirst, and refresh his spirits; inviting him to rest under their shadow, and to taste of their delicates, and to spare his purse'.[31]

Tradescant was a man at the crossroads, looking back to the 'curious' gardening of his father's generation and forward to scientific horticulture and the experiments of the Royal Society. Others might later use his garden and his natural history specimens to further their own scientific researches but Tradescant was a gardener, pure and simple. He could make things grow, even if his manners were rough and boorish and his conversation not learned enough for gentleman scholars such as John Morris or John Evelyn, who paid a perfunctory visit to Tradescant's rarities in September 1657 (shortly after visiting a famous rope-dancer, and the hairy woman, Barbara Ursler) but had nothing to say of either Tradescant the man or his Lambeth garden.[32]

These were troubled times, of course, and Tradescant belonged to the 'lost generation' of men whose advancement was checked by the turmoil of civil war and the new political realities of the Commonwealth. There were other routes to financial prosperity, however, and these years also witnessed the rise of commercial nurseries that survived through several generations of the same family.[33] Many were founded by men Tradescant would have known through the Company of Gardeners, which sprang back to life in 1650 with the restoration of parliamentary rule. In November of that same year Tradescant was admitted to livery and became an Assistant, one of two dozen or so senior members appointed to assist the Company's Master and two Wardens. He was no more assiduous at paying his dues than before, leaving his sixpenny quarterage fees unpaid for several years then paying for as many as seventeen quarters in arrears.[34]

Had Tradescant joined one of the great companies like the Mercers or the Grocers, the privileges of livery would have given him voting rights in City elections and a ceremonial role on grand civic occasions. Horatio Busino, chaplain to the Venetian ambassador, was dazzled by a procession of Grocers honouring the election of one of their number as Lord Mayor in 1617. 'Their gowns resemble those of a Doctor of Laws or the Doge, the sleeves being very wide in the shoulder and trimmed with various materials, such as plush, velvet, martens' fur, foynes [ferret or weasel] and a very beautiful kind of astrakhan, while some wear sables.'[35] While the Gardeners did not yet play a public role in City affairs, Tradescant's admission into livery nonetheless signified that he was counted among the seniors of his profession. Like his fellows, he would have been expected to give the

Company 6s 8d 'towards the buyinge of some plate and other necessaries for the use of the Companie', as well as 3s 4d to the clerk and 1s to the beadle.[36] According to the rules, the Company's treasures were locked away in a 'substantial chest' with several locks, their keys distributed among the Master and the two Wardens who were all to be present whenever the chest was opened.[37]

The last year in which Tradescant appeared in the Company's records was 1661–2. Master for that year was his rival for the endowment of a physic garden, Bodwin Cuper of Cuper's (or Cupid's) Garden in Lambeth.[38] Among the assistants was Leonard Girle or Gurle, who built up one of London's largest nurseries in Whitechapel (between Brick Lane and Greatorex Street), famous for fruit trees, ornamental trees, shrubs and seeds.[39] Tradescant's fellow liverymen included John Rose, still listed for Essex House but just appointed gardener to King Charles II at St James's Park;[40] and Christopher Gray of Fulham whose namesake would later introduce many North American plants and employ pioneer naturalist and botanical artist Mark Catesby in the family nursery. There is every sign that John Tradescant wanted his own son to continue the gardening tradition in just the same way, taking the family name to a third generation of great gardeners, but in this ambition he was to be cruelly thwarted.

Chapter Twenty-Four

A Snake *in* Eden

In mid-June 1650, the Tradescants received a visit at South Lambeth that would profoundly affect the fate of their precious collection of rarities. Elias Ashmole, then aged thirty-three, a lawyer and a recent translator of alchemical texts, took his second wife Lady Manwaring (a wealthy woman twenty years his senior) and his friend Dr Thomas Wharton to view the rarities and probably the garden. No details of the visit have survived, nor do we know whether Ashmole – at this early stage – coveted the rarities for himself. Only the fact of their visit is certain, recorded among the notes Ashmole intended for an (unwritten) autobiography: 'My selfe, wife & Dr: Wharton, went to visit Mr: John Tradescant at South Lambeth.'[1]

As events would later prove, the unsophisticated gardener was no match for the wily Ashmole, even though parentage had given Tradescant the slight edge. Born the only child of a Lichfield saddler, soldier and improvident family man, Ashmole was already making a name for himself as a virtuoso and acquirer of knowledge (Evelyn believed him 'Industrious' rather than truly original)[2] whose interests embraced the old magic and the new sciences – astrology, alchemy and magic cures on the one hand, but also chemistry, natural philosophy and botany on the other. Like Tradescant too, no doubt, he was an ardent royalist and they shared a keen interest in plants. Ashmole had recently taken up simpling and believed in the curative properties of plants. Otherwise, one imagines they had little in common.

On matters of wealth and status, Ashmole's second marriage had put him slightly ahead. Married the first time for love (again to a much older woman), Ashmole had quite deliberately courted Lady Manwaring for her money; her lands and jointures brought him 'the best elixir that he enjoyed, which was the foundation of his riches, wherewith he purchased books, rarities and other things'.[3] As he himself commented sometime before this second marriage, 'It pleased God to put me in mind that I was now placed in the Condition I alwaies desired, which was, that I might be enabled to live to my selfe & Studies, without being forced to take paines for a livelyhood in the world.'[4] By today's standards, his courtship of the wealthy widow (three times married already, infatuated with him and quite possibly suffering from the pox)[5] is tainted with opportunism; aside from its obvious financial benefits, the marriage was in all other respects a disaster.

Ashmole's physical appearance matched his moral ambiguities: here was a man adept at manipulating his public image and putting his best face forward. In later portraits (one by Hester Tradescant's kinsman, Cornelius de Neve, and another magnificently framed by the master woodcarver Grinling Gibbons) he appears with the trappings and self-congratulatory smirk of a distinguished courtier. An earlier engraving by fellow royalist William Faithorne has probably caught a good likeness of Ashmole in his thirties, when he first met Tradescant. Carefully positioned within a stonework niche with masonic overtones, he stands (head and shoulders only) on a pedestal atop a plinth of books draped with a blank apron that suggests hidden mysteries.

But Ashmole's face is arresting enough: searching eager eyes and an expression (according to his biographer, C. H. Josten) 'of a highly intelligent and sensitive man, combining practical abilities and determination with a good measure of speculative powers and introspection'.[6] Swearing was one of his bad habits, to the extent that he worried he might fall foul of Puritan morality and a new law proscribing profanity and cursing.[7] In a vain attempt to reverse his premature baldness, he daily smeared ointment on his head;

and he disputed the judgement of his friend, the Parliamentarian William Lilly, that his hair was 'a kinde of red or sandy colour', preferring to describe it rather as 'faire light browne'.[8] Not shown in Faithorne's engraving was Ashmole's facial scar (from falling into a fire grate as a baby) or the ring he habitually wore in his left ear, hidden by shoulder-length curls that drew the eye away from his balding crown.[9]

After his first visit to South Lambeth, Ashmole busied himself with family affairs (he and his wife were embroiled in bitter property disputes with her brother and her eldest son; another son so feared the prospect of his mother's remarriage that he had tried to murder Ashmole in his bed). He continued his hermetic education, publishing in 1652 a collection of alchemical writings, *Theatrum Chemicum Britannicum*,[10] which placed his interest in botany and gardens in an alchemical context. As Ashmole himself explained, the quest for the philosopher's stone had four different goals: mineral, vegetable, magical or prospective and angelical. Alongside the mineral stone able to turn base metals into gold, the alchemists sought the vegetable stone, which would help them perfectly to know

the Nature of Man, Beasts, Foules, Fishes, together with all kinds of Trees, Plants, Flowers, &c., and how to produce and make them Grow, Flourish & beare Fruit; how to encrease them in Colour and Smell, and when and where we please, and all this not onely at an instant, Experimenti gratia, but Daily, Monethly, Yearly, at any Time, at any Season; yea, in the depth of Winter.[11]

Here at least was a definite point of contact between Ashmole and Tradescant, which might in time account for the growing bond between them.

Soon after his Lambeth visit, Ashmole attempted his first magical experiment: ridding his house of insects and other pests by casting lead images of flies, fleas, caterpillars and toads.[12] News of the experiment's apparent success reached Samuel Hartlib, who recorded that Ashmole had 'contrived an Astrological or Magical Remedy from the last great conjunction with Saturne etc wherby hee [hath] driven away all fleas out of

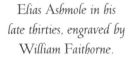

Elias Ashmole in his
late thirties, engraved by
William Faithorne.

his house etc which Dr Child promised to learne more fully from him'.[13]
Ashmole must also have told Hartlib about the visit he later made to
botanist and medical practitioner John Goodyer in Petersfield, 'absolutely
the chiefest Botanicus in all England or Europe in Mr. Ashmoales
judgment'. As Ashmole took along his alchemical mentor, William
Backhouse, the conversation would naturally have turned to sympathetic
cures. 'Hee hath an excellent Garden,' wrote Hartlib about John Goodyer,
'and all kind of Exotick Plants whatsoever. Amongst other Mr Ashmoale
(who is very wel acquainted with him) related an Irish Plant which he hath,
which doth purge when one weares it in ones pocket.'[14] Such a cure would
appeal to the health-conscious Elias Ashmole, who rid himself of stomach
ache (caused by drinking water after eating venison at an astrologers' feast)
by holding a piece of bryony root in his hand. 'Within a quarter of an

houre,' he recorded, 'my stomack was freed of that great oppression, which nothing which I tooke from Dr: Wharton could doe before.'[15]

As Ashmole's studies and reputation advanced, relations with his second wife were coming under increasing strain. Even his most sympathetic biographer admitted that Ashmole's 'notions of matrimonial fidelity were not so strict as to exclude the contemplation of occasional peccadilloes'.[16] An imbalance in years and in affection was partly to blame for their estrangement, and Lady Manwaring's increasing loneliness. Ashmole's astrologer friend, William Lilly, described her as 'a lady very handsome, and of a goodly structure. Low, merry, and chearfull, but accidentally very much Saturnine'; he also called her 'ferox', 'furibunda', 'tetrica', 'laboriosa' and 'a person of great Animosity'.[17] In February 1652, Ashmole asked the stars whether it would be good for his wife to have an unnamed woman companion to board with her.[18] Then, on 11 May 1652, at a little past seven in the morning, his wife posed the question: whether she 'shall have any disgrace by going to Mr. Tradescants to live'.[19] The arrangement was startling. Ashmole was already renting a house in Blackfriars, so why Lady Manwaring (or Mary Ashmole, as she now was) should have proposed going to live with the Tradescants is a puzzle. Had Ashmole planted the idea, or had it really originated with his wife? The 'disgrace' posited by the question could be social (implying their difference in status) or marital (by broadcasting her desire to live away from home). The Tradescants did at least have plenty of space for house guests, accommodating Alexander Marshal and perhaps also Flemish portrait painter John Gaspars at a time when Tradescant's daughter Frances still lived in the house.[20]

The stars must have given a favourable reply as three days later Ashmole's wife arrived at 'Mr Tradescants' in the evening, followed shortly by Ashmole himself, who noted on 28 May 1652 that 'I & my wife Tabled this Summer at Mr Tredescants', although he continued renting his house in Blackfriars.[21] For Ashmole it was a happy move because while he was staying with the Tradescants he and his friend Dr Thomas Wharton joined forces with Tradescant to catalogue his collection of rarities and the many hundreds of plants in his garden. It was a task long overdue: already in 1648 Hartlib had noted that 'Tradusken should bee induced to make an exact Catalogue of all his Museum'[22] and presumably suggested this to him. Just as Tradescant had dithered and delayed over his catalogue of Virginian plants (which contained no more than 200 items), so he needed the energy and cataloguing skills of a voracious virtuoso such as Elias Ashmole, for whom naming was claiming mastery over a subject in the same way that maps staked out territory on the ground.

Although not published for several years, the catalogue was largely completed by September 1652. As Ashmole was out of London from August of that year, they must have started work as soon as he and his wife went to 'table' at South Lambeth. Addressing 'the Ingenious Reader' in his only published writing to survive, Tradescant himself related the project's history. 'About three years agoe,' he explained, '(by the perswasion of some *friends*) I was resolved to take a *Catalogue* of those *Rarities* and *Curiosities* which my *Father* had scedulously *collected*, and my *selfe* with continued diligence have *augmented*, & hitherto *preserved* together.' Tradescant's 'friends' had moreover persuaded him that enumerating the rarities would bring honour to the nation and '*a benefit to such ingenious persons as would become further enquirers into the various modes of Natures admirable workes, and the curious Imitators thereof*'. Here speaks Ashmole the educator and born taxonomist, surely, adding a serious purpose to Tradescant's much-vaunted collection that offered '*more for variety than any one place known in Europe could afford*'.

'I readily yeilded to the *thing* so urged,' confided Tradescant to the reader, 'and with the assistance of two worthy *friends* (well acquainted with my design,) we then began it, and many *examinations* of the *materialls* themselves, & their *agreements* with several Authors *compared*, a *Draught* was made, which they gave into my hands to examine over.'[23]

As the three pored over their specimens and scholarly authorities, they brought order into the collection by dividing it broadly into objects of nature and art. First came birds, beasts and fishes from around the world, named in English and given their provenance where known. Brazil supplied many bird parts and fishes. Whole birds and four-footed beasts came especially from Virginia, many quite possibly brought back by Tradescant himself. A number of specimens came also from the West Indies, Scotland, Turkey and West Africa. Other places mentioned ranged from Jerusalem, Mauritius, the East Indies, Arabia and India to the royal gardens at St James's, Westminster, which supplied a dead emu. Doubtless under Ashmole's guidance, the three cataloguers consulted bookish authorities where they could and they would have relied on Dr Wharton's skills as an anatomist, much of it gained from his dissections of animals and fish. (Izaac Walton praised his great learning and experience, and included his dissection of a monstrous fish in later editions of *The Compleat Angler*.)[24] The items had never been properly logged and a number of entries remained distinctly vague, such as 'Sixteen severall strange beaks of Birds from the East India's' and 'Twenty severall sorts of clawes of other strange birds, not found described by Authors'. The discipline of natural history was in its infancy and here was too much strangeness. Both Tradescant's helpers slipped their own contributions into the text: Dr Wharton under his initials (he gave the head and bones of a civet, and a 'Phocaena's' fish head), while Ashmole gave another bird, 'The Gorara or Colymbus taken upon the *Thames* and given by *Elias Ashmole, Esq*'.[25]

The next four sections (written in Latin) covered shells, insects, minerals and 'Outlandish Fruits'. Tradescant grouped them together as '*Materia Medica*', making a joke against himself perhaps when he suggested that 'Encroachers upon that faculty, may try how they can crack such shels'. Despite the Latin he had learnt at school, he would have needed all Ashmole's scholarship and Dr Wharton's medical training to catalogue the many snakes, fossils, rocks, crystals, stones, gems and petrified matter, all by their Latin names. In fact Wharton was probably the leading authority for many of these items. An expert on human glands[26] – Wharton's duct is named after him, and Wharton's jelly in the umbilical cord – he was one of the few physicians brave enough to stay in London during the terrible plague years of 1665 and 1666. All three men would have contributed to discussions about the exotic fruits, which included bananas, coconuts from the Maldives, a pineapple, mangos and mangosteens, pine cones, seeds, roots and gums. Perhaps Hester Tradescant took an interest in the vegetable and mineral dyes that her painterly cousins would have used to mix blacks, yel-lows, reds, blues and white, including the dazzling lapis lazuli.

The rest of the collection was devoted to 'Artificialls, as Utensills, Householdstuffe, Habits, Instruments of Warre used by severall Nations, rare curiosities of Art, &c'. These were listed in English, apart from the coins, which would have given special pleasure to Ashmole, who was building up a fine collection of his own. As the catalogue progressed, descriptions became vaguer; either Ashmole was losing interest or the three were hurried in their task. Among the items they examined were works of exquisite delicacy ('flea chains' of silver and gold, 300 links to a single inch; a cherry stone perfectly cut with St George and the dragon on one side and eighty-eight emperors' faces on the other), mixed in with the ethnological items adored by the elder Tradescant and early travellers like Peter Mundy: the Indian 'morris-bells' made of shells and fruits, seen by Thomas Johnson; a stone circumcision knife; a 'Brazen-ball to warme the Nunnes hands'.

Shoes came from across the world, showing how cultures adapted to weather. (Missing, of course, were the cultures such as 'Ginny' where shoes were little worn.) Perhaps the 'Russia stockens without heels' came back with the elder Tradescant from Archangel, while his son would surely have sourced many of the Virginian items himself. Here, too, were treasures from the history of naval exploration: a trunnion from Captain Drake's ship; the knife that supposedly killed Henry Hudson on his search for the North-West Passage (in fact he was cast adrift by a mutinous crew and never seen again); a canoe and the picture of an Indian with his bow and dart, dating from the year of Martin Frobisher's first voyage (1576). Among the cultural artefacts and utensils were objects that resonated with personal histories, like the inch-long letter case 'taken in the Isle of Ree with a Letter in it, which was swallowed by a Woman, and found'.[27] Perhaps the scaling ladders came from the same campaign, when their inadequate height forced Buckingham's final retreat from the citadel of St Martin. Few items, by contrast, looked forward to the development of scientific disciplines: just a handful of surgical instruments and 'Severall sorts of Magnifying glasses: Triangular, Prismes, Cylinders'. Apart from the boots worn by Queen Henrietta Maria's

famous dwarf, Sir Jeffrey Hudson (given into her service by the
Buckinghams, who served him up in a pie), the collection was largely bare
of the medical curiosities that obsessed educated men such as John Evelyn
and even Ashmole himself. The final 'utensil' is pure fairground: 'A steel-
glasse that showes a long face on one side, and a broad on the other'.

Right at the end of the catalogue – after the long list of plants examined
in the previous chapter – Tradescant included a list of principal benefactors.
The names and in many cases their outdated titles confirm the
overwhelming impression that most of the collection was put together by
the elder Tradescant, despite his son's contrary claims. All the old employers
are here: King Charles and Queen Henrietta Maria; Robert Cecil and his
son, William; Lady Wotton; the Duke of Buckingham and various members
of his family (wife, sister, daughter); Sir Dudley Digges who led the
diplomatic mission to Muscovy. Here, too, are many whose lives intersected
with the elder Tradescant and whose gifts pay tribute to the respect in which
he was held.[28] Those who gave items to Tradescant's son probably included
merchant James Bovey or Boovy; Richard Ligon who spent several years in
Barbados; and (Sir) Thomas Herbert, who accompanied King Charles I on
his slow journey southwards towards the end of the first civil war. Herbert
knew the Tradescants well, later informing Elias Ashmole that he had been
'sundry times at Mr. Tredescons, (to whom I gave severall things I collected
in my Travailes.) & was much delighted with his gardens'.[29] There was even
speculation that Herbert – who travelled to Mauritius – may have donated
the dodo, but Victorian scholar H. E. Strickland was surely right when he
said that 'had the garrulous Sir Thomas actually killed, skinned, and
brought home a Dodo, he would not have failed to record such an exploit
in his Travels'.[30]

One benefactor who may have known either or both Tradescants was the
strange Thomas Bushell, secretary to Sir Francis Bacon, who had
entertained King Charles and Queen Henrietta Maria in his underground
grotto at Enstone in Oxfordshire. They were apparently entranced by his
fantastic waterworks, which included joke fountains that 'sportively wet any
persons within it' and a 'Cistern of stone, with five spouts of water issuing out of a

ball of *brass, in which a small* Spaniel *hunts a* Duck, *both diving after one another, and having their motion from the water*.[31] According to Ashmole's friend John Aubrey, the queen gave Bushell an entire mummy from Egypt but 'the dampnesse of the place haz spoyled it with mouldinesse'. After spending the civil war years on Lundy Island, Bushell crossed swords with Cromwell and the Parliamentarians, going to ground in a house in Lambeth Marsh, where he hung the long gallery 'all with black, and had some death's heads and bones painted'. At opposite ends of the room were his couch in a gothic niche and a pallet bed on which lay 'an emaciated dead man stretched out'. As for Bushell himself, Aubrey found him 'a handsome proper gentleman when I sawe him at his house aforesayd at Lambith. He was about 70 but I should have not guessed him hardly 60. He had a perfect healthy constitution; fresh, ruddy face; hawk-nosed, and was temperate.'[32]

Bushell's taste for the other-worldly would have appealed to both Ashmole and Tradescant. While still working on the catalogue, Ashmole took time off to visit Maidstone assizes 'to heare the Witches tryed, & tooke Mr: Tredescant with me'.[33] The two men were clearly growing closer, and Ashmole was introducing the other man to interests of his own. The date Ashmole gave for this visit was 2 August 1652. If correct, they would have missed the star trial of the previous Friday when the 'chief Actresse', Anne Ashby (alias 'Cobler'), 'fell into an extasie before the Bench, and swell'd into a monstrous and vast bigness, screeching and crying out very dolefully; and being recovered, and demanded if the Divell at that time had possessed her, she replyed she knew not that, but she said that the spirit Rug came out of her mouth like a Mouse'.[34] At the end of the trial, six witches were condemned to death by hanging, having confessed that the devil had given them a bit of flesh, which 'whensoever they should touch, they should thereby affect their desires'. The flesh was found in a patch of grass, as indicated, and described as being 'of a sinnewy substance, and scorched'. After judgment, three of the women pleaded they were pregnant 'not by any man, but by the Divell'. Ashmole and Tradescant must have attended subsequent trials of others caught up in the affair, accused of having bewitched 'nine children, besides a man and a woman' and of having caused the loss of '500 pounds worth of Cattel' and of 'much Corn at Sea wrack'd, by Witchcraft'.[35]

Another interest that the social-climbing Ashmole may have communicated to Tradescant was genealogy and specifically the right to bear arms as proof of gentlemanly status. Ashmole's own interest may have been sparked by his parents' difference in status, and during the civil war years he asked the stars whether he would 'obtain a coat of arms', which came to him eventually with the discovery of his grandfather's armorial seal.[36] Perhaps he put the same thoughts into his host's head, as by the time the catalogue was published the younger Tradescant had acquired a coat of arms which he emblazoned across the frontispiece: three fleur-de-lys on a wavy diagonal known in the archaic language of chivalry as a 'bend wavy'. He used the same arms to seal his will.[37] The fleur-de-lys appears in another coat of arms on the family tomb erected by Hester Tradescant, and on an outside wall to their South Lambeth home where it was described by a later occupant as displaying 'three fleurs de lys, impaled with a lion passant'.[38] The lion brings an intriguing echo of the Dutch emblem (see Chapter 3) and was perhaps added by Hester, although she used her husband's arms to seal her will.[39]

Whether Tradescant ever properly registered his coat of arms is another matter. His father had never used arms, so where had they come from? English society may have been fluid enough to allow men to become gentlemen 'by adding field to field, by prospering in trade, by service to the Crown or to a great man in public or household office',[40] but proof was also required that coats of arms were legitimate. Periodic 'visitations' around the counties by Garter and Clarenceux Kings of Arms tested the validity of claimed pedigrees and armorial displays. These could be bought quite legitimately. At the time, the test of being a gentleman was simply one 'who is so commonly taken, and reputed', and if necessary, 'a King of Heralds shall give him for money armes newly made, and invented with the Creast and all'.[41]

Tradescant was increasingly described as a 'gentleman' in official records, so the public acceptance of his acquired rank is not in doubt. Yet no trace

has been found at the College of Arms of any Tradescant arms. When his
relative, Robert Tradescant of Walberswick in Suffolk, applied for his arms
to be registered in 1664, he was specifically rejected as 'no gent' and his name
ignominiously published with nineteen others found 'Presumptuously and
without any good ground or Authority to have usurped the Armes Name
and Title of Gentleman'.[42] As for John Tradescant, he would have needed
help from a man with Ashmole's connections to trace or acquire arms for
himself. Given Ashmole's later role as Windsor Herald, it is hard to imagine
he would have countenanced an outright fraud, so the legitimacy of the
Tradescant arms must remain an open question.

Ashmole himself did not stay tabled with the Tradescants for very long.
Soon after the witches' trial, he was again on his way, leaving his wife behind
at Lambeth while he set out (on 13 August 1652) for Berkshire and his
birthplace at Lichfield, then travelling on to Gawsworth in Cheshire where
he stayed with the rector, Henry Newcome, the husband of his first wife's
younger sister. It was the first time the men had met and Newcome was
delighted with his 'very cordial friend and relation'. Ashmole stayed with
them about a month 'and went daily a simpling in the mountains and
mosses about us'.[43]

The news from London was bad, however. First Dr Wharton fell sick of
a 'violent and dangerous Feaver', which took him close to death and lasted
almost a year. Then – on 11 September 1652 – came the death of John
Tradescant's only son John, not yet nineteen years old and already trained to
follow the honoured profession of his father and grandfather. He was buried
four days later in the churchyard of St Mary, Lambeth next to his mother
and grandfather. Although death was ever present in seventeenth-century
London, the loss must have devastated his father. 'Presently thereupon my
onely Sonne dyed,' wrote Tradescant to explain the long delay in publishing
his catalogue, 'one of my Friends fell very sick for about a yeare [Dr Wharton],
and my other Friend [Ashmole] by unhappy Law-suits much disturbed. Upon
these accidents that first Draught lay neglected in my hands another year.'[44]

Perhaps a clue to Tradescant's state of mind is contained in another
portrait of him attributed to Hester's relative Thomas de Critz in which he

drapes a black cloak over his lace-edged white shirt, one arm resting on a ledge beside a human skull sprouting gingery moss in place of human hair.[45] He looks haunted, as if he has not slept for days, and he does not quite meet the viewer's eye. As befits a gardener, the artist has given prominence to his hand, which holds the cloak in place. Pink and fleshy, it is the hand of an overseer rather than a labourer; its physicality matched by the wildness of his bushy hair spreading almost to his shoulders.

Now owned by the National Portrait Gallery in London, the portrait once belonged to writer and virtuoso Horace Walpole,[46] another gothic aficionado, who associated the skull with the old alchemical remedy, powder of sympathy, which reputedly cured wounds at a distance by associative magic. Earthy in smell and taste, skull moss was supposed to be scraped from a cadaver of someone who had died a violent death. London druggists established a brisk trade with Ireland, where hanged criminals were left on the gibbet until they fell to pieces.[47] Skulls and skull moss were also used to cure diseases of the head, specifically epilepsy.[48] The father of microscopy, Dr Robert Hooke, noted in his diary the opinion of a woman acquaintance that 'a soveraine remedy for the falling sickness [epilepsy] was made out of the mosse of a mans skull'.[49] By including the skull in his portrait, might Tradescant be telling us that his son died from both a wound and fits, which today we would interpret as tetanus contracted from an infected wound, still a very real danger for gardeners? Or should the skull and its alchemical associations rather be read as a sign of Ashmole's growing influence over the bereft father?

While Tradescant grieved for his son, Ashmole was much taken up with lawsuits – involving first his wife's relatives and then his wife herself, who had gone back to stay with the Tradescants soon after their son's death, remaining with them until the following January.[50] In the summer of 1654, she again left her husband 'to lodge at a Mr Witts' and launched a suit against Ashmole in Chancery, claiming it had become improper or impossible for her to live with him. According to Ashmole's biographer, no record of the legal proceedings has been found, although Lady Manwaring's outpourings to the court are known to have covered more than 800 sheets of paper.[51] The suit dragged on for three years and ended in victory for Ashmole. Lilly considered his friend to have been 'unjustly provoaked', while repeatedly attempting to persuade his wife to return. Tradescant, meanwhile, had to contend with one more delay to the catalogue: 'the prefixed Pictures were not ready, and I found my kinde friend Mr Hollar then engaged for about tenne Moneths, for whose hand to finish the Plates, I was necessarily constrained to stay untill this time.'[52]

His chosen artist was Prague-born Wenceslaus Hollar,[53] engraver of Stuart London, an almost exact contemporary whom he would have known through his wife's connections and who went on to produce many engravings for Elias Ashmole, including those for his most famous book on the history of the Order of the Garter.[54] Hollar was now back in London after self-imposed exile following the civil war, when he had served in a royalist regiment and been taken prisoner at the siege of Basing House where so many of the Tradescant connections converged. John Aubrey tells us that Hollar was 'very short-sighted, and did worke so curiously that the curiosity of his worke is not to be judged without a magnifying glasse'.[55] He also had a daughter who was one of the 'greatest beauties' Aubrey had ever seen.

John Tradescant finally published his museum catalogue in 1656. Samuel Hartlib immediately took notice, musing whether an inventory by Danish collector Ole Worm might not 'fitly bee Englished and with the Latin also printed and added to Traduoken'.[56] The year and perhaps the event is commemorated in another husband-and-wife portrait attributed to Emanuel de Critz in which Hester Tradescant hands her husband a sprig of myrtle, the traditional emblem of love and fidelity.[57] The couple have clearly aged, although Tradescant's beard and unruly hair remain a rich dark brown. Hester is the real casualty. The attractive woman of her marriage portrait has given way to an ageing crone, albeit one richly dressed in a silky yellow fabric, her broad white collar fastened with a square brooch and a dangle of pearly embroidery.[58]

Publication of the catalogue did at least ensure a lasting memorial to the Tradescants' achievements as collectors, celebrated in anagrams and dedicatory verses by the Revd Walter Stonehouse, a fellow gardening fanatic

who had died the previous year. Stonehouse's royalist sympathies had lost
him his living as rector of Darfield in Yorkshire, and his horticultural spirit
was broken when he eventually returned home in 1652 after the civil war,
only to find that few of his plants had survived. 'I have no hope of a new
colony,' he had written rather pathetically in his plant catalogue.[59] His poem
in praise of the elder Tradescant showed no such weariness of spirit:

> . . . CAN Death oppress
> Such HONEST ART as this, or make it less?
> No: Fame shall still record it, and expose
> Industrious care to all eternity.
> The body may, and must: ARTES CANNOT DIE.

He added a final 'e' to 'John Tradescante' to make the anagram work.

For Tradescant the son ('Heire of thy Fathers goods, and his good parts'),
Stonehouse's chosen anagram was 'Cannot hide Arts', suggesting that he
remained in awe of his father's accomplishments:

> . . .Whilst thou conceal'st thine own, and do'st deplore
> Thy want, compar'd with his, thou shew'st them more.
> Modesty clouds not worth; but hate diverts,
> And shames base envy, ARTS he CANNOT HIDE
> That has them. Light through every chink is spy'd.

Did Ashmole experience 'base envy' – not towards Tradescant the man
but towards the collection he had inherited from his father? While his
original offer to catalogue the rarities with Wharton had most probably
arisen from disinterested scholarship, now – with the boy Tradescant dead
– the collection lacked an obvious inheritor. Ashmole made a calculated
move which he would later use in court proceedings to prove the justice of
his claim. He undertook to pay the catalogue's publication costs, thereby
putting the other man in his debt; and the unwary Tradescant played straight
into his hand by accepting the offer. It is possible that Thomas Wharton

knew of this plan and disapproved. Ashmole and Wharton fell out badly about this time and were not reconciled until 1669, when Ashmole noted that their friendship began to be renewed after having been 'discontinued for many yeares, by reason of his unhandsome & unfreindly dealing with me'.[60]

How Ashmole gained legal title to the rarities must be deduced from the two different versions of events put forward in the subsequent wrangle over their ownership. With his only son dead and his daughter out of the house (she was widowed the year after the catalogue's publication but apparently was never considered a possible inheritor), Tradescant will have discussed the collection's fate with his wife Hester. The idea that it might go to the University of Oxford was certainly current. 'John Tradescant hath no roomes for his Rarities but Oxford hath roome enough,' noted Samuel Hartlib early in 1657.[61] Likewise John Evelyn recorded his impressions of a visit to South Lambeth that September, adding that 'other innumerable things' were 'printed in his Catalogue by Mr. Ashmole, to whom after the death of the widdow, they are bequeathe'd: & by him designd a Gift to Oxford'.[62] This last information can only have been added after Tradescant's death in 1662, however, when Hester became his widow.

According to Ashmole's story, as set out in his legal pleadings when he moved to have his claim recognized, it was Hester who first told him that John Tradescant intended to give the collection to him, in view of his 'former paines, care and charge' in producing the catalogue, and because they knew how much he valued it. At Tradescant's request, a scrivener drew up a deed of gift on 14 December 1659, which Tradescant apparently approved and signed, declaring in the presence of his wife that 'he well liked the same, and soe did the said Hester his wife'. In effect, while giving the rarities to Ashmole, the deed allowed the Tradescants to enjoy their 'keeping and use' until the death of the surviving partner; but in holding the collection in trust for Ashmole, they were to preserve it 'without spoil'. Although apparently not written into the deed, Ashmole also agreed to pay £100 to Mary Edmonds, widow of South Lambeth victualler Robert Edmonds and daughter of Tradescant's 'loving freind', Edward Harper, or to her surviving children, within six months of receiving the rarities.

Hester's version of the story was very different, however. As she later argued in her defence, her husband had come home drunk in the company of Ashmole and four strangers ('distempered' was the word she used). Ashmole 'did then produce a writing which without reading' he asked her 'to put her hand as witnes thereunto, which shee inadvisedly did'. She had no idea who directed the scrivener to draw up the deed, she said, nor whether her husband approved of the draft. Only when the deed was sealed and handed to Ashmole before witnesses, together with 'a Queene Elizabethe milled shillinge' in token of the gifted collection, did she begin to suspect that the deed of gift 'might be prejudice to her'.

Both accounts then briefly converge: Ashmole gave the signed deed to Hester, in his version so that she could keep it until he would 'call for it'. Hester's account was more forthright. Once she held the deed in her hands, 'shee tould her said husband that shee thought hee would not have suffered himselfe to bee so much abused and threw the said writing to him'. Ashmole had then intervened, saying, 'I pray you take it and consider thereof, and if you like it not, I will not have it for a world.' The next morning (still according to Hester) the full implications of the deed hit home. Prompted by his wife, Tradescant read it more carefully and declared it was 'contrary to his intencon': in private hands, the collection could be too easily 'imbezilled and made away'. He then attempted to cancel the deed by breaking off the seal and 'razing out his name in the endorsement'. He would have burnt it, she said, if she had not persuaded him to keep it to show 'how ill' Ashmole had treated him. He was apparently so offended by Ashmole's 'contrivance' that he swore Ashmole should 'never have a groate of his'.[63]

The truth about what really happened between Elias Ashmole and John Tradescant in all probability lay somewhere between these two accounts. It seems highly likely that Ashmole would have used his growing influence over Tradescant to secure his signature without Hester's full knowledge or consent. She was obviously the stronger partner in the marriage (if a little unstable, even then) and is unlikely to have fallen under Ashmole's influence to quite the same extent as her 'unpolished' husband. Ashmole may well have presented himself to Tradescant as a conduit to Oxford University but this did not form part of the legal agreement. The deed as written gave the collection to Ashmole outright, without any guarantee as to what he might do with it, and as such it clearly went against the couple's intentions and their interests. Although they could enjoy the rarities for both their lifetimes, the deed had turned them into little more than keepers of their own collection, which they now held in trust for Ashmole, unable legally to sell or trade a single item. Whether he had obtained Tradescant's signature by getting him drunk or simply tying him up with words, he had performed a masterly trick on them both – and as a lawyer, he knew it was legally binding.

For a time, however, life at South Lambeth returned to normal. The Tradescants continued to show 'their' rarities, believing that they had successfully repelled Ashmole's attempt to usurp control. Even children came to view the collection, thereby adding to London's educational advantage which schoolteacher Charles Hoole attributed to 'the variety of objects which daily present themselves to them, or may easily be seen once a year, by walking to Mr. *John Tradescants*, or the like houses or gardens, where rarities are kept'.[64] Hoole was particularly impressed by the printed catalogue brought out by 'that ingenuous Gentleman'.

In 1660, Charles II was restored to the throne and Tradescant apparently rushed out another edition of the catalogue, newly dedicated 'TO THE SACRED MAJESTY OF CHARLES the II' from 'I Iis Majesties most obedient and most Loyal Subject'.[65] Now in his fifties, the former Oatlands gardener does not seem to have pursued any further royal career, unlike Ashmole, who speedily insinuated himself into royal favour, gaining an audience with the king just two weeks after Charles II's joyous entry into London and securing the post of Windsor Herald two days after that.[66] King and courtier shared an interest in chemistry, coins and medical curiosities. It was Ashmole who showed Charles conjoined twin girls, 'dryed and preserved with Spices'; and a pickled foetus cut from a woman's belly, bottled and preserved from putrefaction by royal physician Dr Edward Warner, 'the flesh not so much as rumpled, but plump as it was when taken out of ye wombe'.[67]

The Restoration brought one more legal irritant to the Tradescants in the form of a threatened summons from Master of the Revels, Sir Henry Herbert, who was flexing his muscles in an attempt to regain the powers – and the income – he had enjoyed under the two previous monarchs.[68] Before the Puritans had extinguished public merrymaking, Herbert had not only overseen the royal masques so relished by Charles I and Queen Henrietta Maria but had also extended his jurisdiction to licensing every other kind of show, 'whether natural, or artificial; whether of trick, or ingenuity'. Crucially, these included the showing of strange beasts such as elephants, beavers, camels and 'an outlandish creature, called a *Possum*'. Most of these were live animals, it is true, but as artificial shows and waxworks also fell within his remit, Herbert now tried to argue that the stuffed specimens on display in Tradescant's collection constituted a public performance. On 4 May 1661, Herbert therefore notified his officer of the revels, Mr Ralph Nutting, of information received 'that John Traduskyn does make shew of several strange Creatures without Authority from his Majesties office of the Revells. These are therefore in His Majesties name to will and require you to bring before me the said John Traduskyn to answer for the said contempt.'[69]

Tradescant was duly served with a warrant accusing him of 'a contemptuous practice' by showing his rarities and thereby invading the rights of the Master of the Revels. Tradescant complained to the king, who responded swiftly – so swiftly, in fact, that one wonders whether Ashmole had intervened on Tradescant's behalf, just as Hester Tradescant would later perform a kindness for Ashmole, despite their legal wrangling. Perhaps the catalogue's new dedication to Charles was part of the pleading. Sometime in the following month (the actual day is left blank), the king issued his own warrant in response to Tradescant's complaint, declaring himself satisfied that the fact was not only 'of very harmelesse import', nor was it

prejudicial to any person but that it hath been practised & continued, uninterruptedly, by him and his Father, with the Allowance or good Liking (at Least) of Our Progenitors, for many yeares past. Our expresse pleasure & Comand is, That the said Tredeskyn bee suffered, freely & quietly to proceed, as formerly, in entertaining & receaving all persons, whose Curiosity shall invite them to the delight of seeing his rare and ingenious Colecons of Art & Nature.[70]

The king then ordered the original warrant to be withdrawn and the case dropped. Herbert had failed and Tradescant was free – with royal encouragement – to show his rarities to the curious public.

The law was keeping Tradescant busy, that year. In May he was summonsed to appear as a witness to a special inquiry sitting at the Queen's Arms Tavern in Southwark to tell them what he knew about a recent riot.[71] He was also one of a group of nineteen citizens from 'gents.' like himself to basket-makers and watermen accused of having 'wilfully … refused to pay their assessment for poor relief … to the grave damage of all parishioners, and inhabitants, in evil example and against the peace'. It was all a mistake, however; Tradescant and eleven others were exonerated by the Surrey Quarter Sessions sitting at Kingston.[72]

The fate of his rarities continued to prey on Tradescant's mind. Just before his tiff with the Master of the Revels, he drew up his last will and testament while he was still – unusually for the times –'of perfect health, minde, and memorie'. After commending his soul to God and his body to the earth, where it was to be decently buried as close to his father and to his son as possible for a sum not exceeding £20, he asked for any outstanding debts to be settled and then set out his bequests. To his daughter, the now widowed Frances Norman, he left £10 while at the same time forgiving her the debt of some £80, plus interest, which he had 'long since lent her late deceased husband'. To receive her bequest, however, Frances and any new husband ('if she shall be then againe married') had to give his executrix (her stepmother, Hester) 'a generall release for the same', suggesting that she would get even this small legacy only if she made no trouble. Although married daughters often received only token bequests in family wills, having already received a property settlement on marriage, the language used is coldly legalistic in marked contrast to the warmth of his next bequests. To his namesakes Robert and Thomas Tredescant of Walberswick in Suffolk, he left 5s each 'in remembrance of my love', and 2s 6d to each of their children living at the time of his death. Once again, he asked for £100 to be paid to 'Mrs Marie Edmonds, the daughter of my loving freind Edward Harper' after the death of his own wife, Hester; and if Marie were to die first, he wanted the £100 to be divided equally between her four children, who were also his godchildren: Hester, John, Leonard and Elizabeth Edmonds. As the children's names suggest, the bond between the two families was very close. And to Hester's widowed 'cozen', Katherine King, he left (after his wife's death) 'the Little House commonly called the Welshmans house situate in South Lambeth aforesaid together with that Little Piece of Ground now enclosed thereunto adjoyning; and to her heirs and assignes for ever'. One wonders what Frances Norman thought of that.

Hester was to get everything else, apart from 'Rings and small tokens of my Love', which he asked her to bestow among his other friends and kindred, leaving her to decide 'how manie and to whome shee shall think deserving'. As for the rarities, his will left no doubt about his wishes: 'Item, I give, devize, and bequeath my Closet of Rarities to my dearly beloved wife Hester Tredescant during her naturall Life, and after decease I give and bequeath the same to the Universities of Oxford or Cambridge, to which of them shee shall think fitt at her decease.'[73] So Hester was to be given control over big decisions as well as small, and this bequest replaced a previous will in which he had apparently left the collection to the king, after his wife's death, fearing that some 'private person' might again try to purloin the rarities.[74]

Making plain his intentions in this way was surely his reason for writing his last will while still in good health, marshalling for good measure a number of upstanding citizens to witness the act. These included fellow parishioners John Scaldwell (John Scaldwell junior and senior were both churchwardens in the early 1650s), Fulke Bignall (one of the church's most active members);[75] and 'Notary Publique' Richard Hoare. He also appointed two 'Overseers' to his will, giving them 40s each: Mark Cottle,[76] soon to be appointed Registrar of the Prerogative Court of Canterbury (the most prestigious of the Church courts involved with proving wills), and Dr Thomas Nurse of the Royal College of Physicians who practised in

Westminster. With such an impressive line of defence, Tradescant must have believed that the fate of his rarities was secure.

Despite his apparent good health, John Tradescant had only one more year to live. He died on 22 April 1662 and was buried in the family grave three days later.[77] He was fifty-three years old, young by today's standards but closer to the century's norm. His funeral would have been attended by friends, family, neighbours and fellow liverymen of the Company of Gardeners, dressed in their finery, no doubt. Attending the funerals of fellow liverymen and their wives was one of the duties set out in the Company's rules, once they had been lawfully summoned by the Beadle.[78] The Company's clerk recorded Tradescant's passing in the list of liverymen for 1661–2, writing 'dead' against his name.[79]

The bereaved widow set about erecting a monumental tomb to her husband and his family in the churchyard. By November, she had secured the agreement of the church authorities after giving the churchwardens the magnificent sum of £50 'to be kept as a Stocke for ye Use of ye poor of ye Parish'.[80] Signing their 'free Consent' to her request were more than a dozen parishioners, almost all of whom had served the church as churchwardens, collectors for the poor, or highway surveyors. (They included John Scaldwell, witness to Tradescant's will, and Boyden Cuper from the Company of Gardeners.)

The tomb she commissioned was strikingly original – so original, in fact, that Samuel Pepys made a note to obtain an engraving of it from shoemaker and book collector, John Bagford. Drawings of the tomb are now preserved among his papers in the library of Magdalene College, Cambridge.[81] Carved in stone were ruins, broken columns, a crocodile, shells, pyramids, a hydra and skull, and trees curving round the corners – a fitting memorial to her collector husband and his father. The south end displayed the new coat of arms, three fleurs-de-lys on a bend wavy, impaled by a lion passant. By the time permission for the memorial was granted, however, the fate of the Tradescant rarities themselves was looking distinctly uncertain.

Chapter Twenty-Five

ᴀ Death *by* Drowning

S traightaway, Ashmole pounced, determined to prove his eventual title to
the collection. Within twenty-two days of John Tradescant's death, he
had filed a Bill of Complaint at the Court of Chancery 'against Mrs
Tredescant, for the Rarities her Husband had settled on me'.[1] Chancery was
one of two courts of equity (the other was Exchequer) specializing in
wrangles over property, trusts, marriage settlements, wills, tithes, frauds and
business disputes; it could order the performance of a contract although not
award damages. Hester swore her reply on 1 July 1662 but justice moved
slowly, then as now, and in the meantime Hester continued to show the
Tradescant rarities.

Ashmole's complaint to Chancery was heard nearly two years later by the
Lord Chancellor, the Earl of Clarendon, on 18 May 1664.[2] Appearing as
counsel for Elias Ashmole were two of the leading advocates of the day, Sir
John Glynne and Sir John Maynard. Both powerful lawyers on the
parliamentary side, they had switched allegiance just in time to regain high
office at the Restoration and were swiftly appointed King's Serjeants.[3] From
helping to secure the impeachment and execution of the old king's trusted
adviser, the Earl of Stafford, they now took part in the state treason trials
that exacted revenge on the king's enemies. Pepys had watched them ride
together in the cavalcade at Charles II's coronation, gleeful that Glynne's

horse had fallen on him 'and is like to kill him' (it did not) – a just and timely fate for a rogue, in Pepys' view, and one that people wished also for his companion.[4] Yet however universally they were despised for their shifting political loyalties, no one disputed their immense advocacy skills. In securing their services, Ashmole was arming himself with the legal equivalent of a great cannon.

Little is known of Hester Tradescant's defence team, a Mr Gillingham and Keeke Eydon, but in the matter of witnesses she more than held her own. Ashmole called five witnesses, including his 'most intire freind', physician and fellow alchemist Dr William Currer;[5] and Elizabeth Dugdale, the future third Mrs Ashmole and daughter of his good friend, antiquarian (Sir) William Dugdale. (Lady Manwaring, it should be said, was not yet dead.) Hester produced eight witnesses in all, including Mary Edmonds, the family friend given £100 by John Tradescant in his will and perhaps also by the deed of gift; her 'cousin' Katherine King; two of the witnesses to her husband's will, notary public Richard Hoare and leading Lambeth churchman Foulke Bignal. She also called two artists: her kinsman, Cornelius de Neve, who had painted Ashmole that February,[6] and the Bohemian engraver of the Tradescant portraits, Wenceslaus Hollar.[7] (That Hollar should brave the wrath of a powerful patron such as Ashmole was typical. John Aubrey described him as a 'very friendly good-natured man as could be, but shiftlesse as to the world, and died not rich'.[8]) The testimony of the witnesses was read out in court, as was John Tradescant's will.

In the absence of full transcripts for Chancery proceedings, three sets of court notes and a fat volume of court judgments give a flavour of the day.[9] On Hester's behalf, Gillingham argued that 'the pretended deed [was] gained by a surprise and afterwards cancelled'. Glynne countered for Ashmole by declaring that Hester's answer was 'scandalous all over'. The deed had been sealed 'upon mature consideracon' but then Mrs Tradescant had got her hands on it and burnt it, 'after which Mr Tredescant offered to seale another deed'. Counsel for Hester argued that the deed was revocable and had in fact been revoked by Tradescant's last will, giving the rarities to his wife for her lifetime and then to one of the universities, because it was better they should go 'to a publique use and not to his own private use'. Ashmole's counsel counter-attacked by stressing the pains he had taken in making the catalogue, and painting Hester as a more than willing party to the original gift. No one mentioned Hester's claim that Ashmole had plied her husband with drink, at least not in open court. Nor did either party acknowledge Dr Thomas Wharton's help in compiling the catalogue.

After hearing all the arguments, the Lord Chancellor summarized the case before proceeding to judgment. It was clear from the outset where his sympathies lay. He began by defining John Tradescant's 'many rarities & Antiquities consisting of bookes Coynes Medalls Stones Pictures Mechanicks & other things of that Nature' which he kept in a room in his house at Lambeth and which he called his 'Clossitt of rarityes'. The plaintiff – Ashmole – having composed a catalogue of the collection 'att his owne charge', which was 'published in a printed booke' called *Musaeum Tradescantianum*, had gone to Mr Tradescant's house sometime in December 1659, where he was entertained by Tradescant and his wife 'with great professions of kindness'. It was Hester Tradescant herself who had told him of her husband's resolve to give him the rarities, 'knowinge the great Esteeme & value' he put on them. Afterwards, Mr Tradescant said that he was willing to make the gift 'in Consideracon of [Ashmole's] said fformer paines in making the said Booke' but with certain conditions: 'that hee & the Defendant his wife might enjoy the same during their lives' and that after their deaths Ashmole should give £100 to Mary Edmonds if she were then living or to her children if she were dead. He then asked his scrivener to draw up a deed to this effect, granting Ashmole 'all his rarities or Curiosities of what Sort soever whither naturall or Artificiall in his said Clossett or in or about his said house'. He and his wife were to have the use of them during their lives and to keep them 'without spoyle or Imbessellment'.

The deed was then sealed and approved by John Tradescant 'freely & willingly', and it was Hester herself who had fetched down a 'Queene Elizabeth milled Shillinge out of the said Clossett' to stand token for the whole collection. In the end, it was not thought necessary to 'Clogge the deed' with the payment of the £100 to Mrs Edmonds or her children so that

Hester Tradescant in later life.

it might better appear to be 'a free & generous gift', made out of Tradescant's 'entire Affecon & singular Esteeme' for Ashmole, who he did not doubt would 'preserve & augment the said rarityes for posterity'. There was even a perfectly plausible reason behind Hester's desire to keep the deed after it had been signed and approved: not anger at its contents but rather her wish to clarify with friends 'whither her enjoyment of the Rarityes during her life were not prejudiced by her beinge witness to the said Deed'. Ashmole left it with her willingly, not doubting her 'preservacon both of the said rarities & of the deed in regard shee herselfe had been instrumentall to gaine them' for his benefit. But since her husband's death – still according to the Lord Chancellor in his summing up – she had the rarities in her possession and threatened to destroy or dispose of them other than as set out in the deed, denying that her husband had ever made such a deed 'and hath in truth, burnt or cancelled the same', claiming to be the sole inheritor to the rarities, as her husband's executrix.

The judgment was leading to its obvious conclusion. Not only had

Ashmole composed the catalogue at his expense, but he had promised to pay
£100 to Mrs Edmonds or her children. The deed was gained, determined
the Lord Chancellor, after long debate and hearing the 'prooffes' on both
sides, 'without any fraud or undue means'. Hester Tradescant had failed to
prove 'undue carriage' in the way the deed was obtained, which his lordship
declared was 'fairly gained & well executed & with the Defendants consent
& was made upon good & valuable consideracon & with Intention to be
irrevoakable'.

It was therefore ordered and decreed that the plaintiff, Ashmole, was to

have & enjoy all & Singular the said Bookes Coynes medalls Stones Pictures
Mechanicks & Antiquities & all & sundry other 'Rarytiies & Curiosities of what
sort or kind soever – whither naturall or artificall & whatsoever was graunted by
the said deed as itt now stands good in court which were in the said John
Tredescants said Clossitt or in or about his said house att South Lambeth the said
sixteenth day of December 1659 when the said deed was executed.

For Hester, the order must have been devastating. Not only did it cover
the rarities in her house, but it quite possibly extended to the exotics in her
garden. Although she could enjoy the rarities during her remaining lifetime
(she was then just a little over fifty), she was now merely keeping them in
trust for Ashmole, unable to dispose of a single item. The judgment also
required her to submit to an intrusive inspection by Sir Edward Bysse and
William Dugdale who were to catalogue the collection 'and to certifie the
particulars that are wantinge, if any bee'. She faced further examination
about the rarities, because of her alleged obstruction during the case, and she
was ordered to restore to the closet any items that appeared to be 'wanting
or imbessled'. She was also ordered to give some security that she would
safeguard the rarities according to the letter of the deed.

Aided no doubt by his powerful advocates, Ashmole's victory was total.
The court had believed his version of events: that John and Hester
Tradescant were willing signatories to the deed and only later changed their
minds, by which time in law it was too late. Even today, a deed of gift cannot

be revoked unless it contains a specific clause allowing this. Although the original deed was never produced in court (it had been allegedly burnt or otherwise destroyed by the Tradescants), neither side suggested that it had contained such a clause. Ashmole simply had to prove that he had obtained the deed fairly, and the court believed that he had.

Given the absolute nature of her defeat, it seems foolhardy of Hester to have continued trading in rarities as she did, unless she restricted herself to items acquired after her husband's death. One of her buyers was William Courten, grandson of wealthy London merchant Sir William Courten, the original colonizer of Barbados and a contemporary of the elder Tradescant. A 'William Curteene Esq' had already appeared among the Tradescant benefactors, probably the father of Hester's collector who was not born until 1642. This youngest Courten (who also called himself William Charleton to avoid family creditors) amassed a huge collection of artificial and natural curiosities that impressed John Evelyn as 'one of the most perfect assemblages of rarities that can be anywhere seen'.[10] By the time of his death it was reputedly worth £50,000 and he willed it to (Sir) Hans Sloane, the eventual founder of the British Museum, on condition that he kept the collection 'intire'.[11]

Courten was buying curiosities from Hester Tradescant in June, July and September 1667, as little as three years after the hearing in Chancery. Written in a charming mix of English and Italian (his father had exiled himself to Italy), Courten's pocket account book details among his purchases from Hester a Virginian woodpecker (2s 6d), a jet box with small sheers (5s), two eggs of the 'soland goose' (5s), 'La tetta dun Heron with its top' (2s 6d), Barbados cotton and a sponge (1s each). Other items were listed entirely in Italian, including *cristallo che rapresenta il diamante del Duca di Toscana* (5s); *carta d'India gialla, carta d'India rossa, characteri Indiani* all 1s each; and four items worth 10s each: *1 rostro d'un uccello; 1 cosa d'Illnorio d. dar sorella, 1 pittura in Ambra dal sorella data,* and *Piume di fenice.* Hester threw in several items for nothing: a linnet's egg, a sparrowhawk's egg and one *Ostreea impetrita.*[12]

Yet despite their bitter legal dispute, relations between Ashmole and Hester Tradescant were sufficiently cordial for Ashmole to turn to her for help when his precious library in the Middle Temple was threatened by London's great fire in 1666. 'The dreadfull fire of London began,' he noted for 2 September, and the following day despatched a great number of books and other objects from his chamber to her house at South Lambeth.[13] Had he delayed one more day, he would not have found a spare boat, barge, coach or cart at the Temple, where the streets were choked with people trying to rescue their belongings as the fire was 'flaming into the very Temple'.[14] In the event, Ashmole panicked unnecessarily as the fire destroyed only one building in the Middle Temple, not his. Hester looked after Ashmole's books for over a month, until the afternoon of 11 October when he noted that 'my first Boat-full of Bookes, which were carried to Mrs: Tredescants: 3 Sept: were brought back to the Temple'.[15] The rest followed one week later. (Ironically, Ashmole's Middle Temple chambers were destroyed in another fire, which broke out in the room next to his, the year after Hester Tradescant's death. His losses included a 'Collection of neere 9000 Coynes & Medalls ancient & Moderne, being the Gather of 32 yeares' and 'Divers valuable Peices of Antiquity, & sundry Curiosities of Art and Nature.'[16])

Throughout this time, it seems that the widow Tradescant kept her South Lambeth garden and collection open to visitors. The Minet Library at Lambeth has an unidentified advertisement among its cuttings, given a date of 1667, announcing 'That the Rarities and Curiosities (late Mr. Tredescant's) with several valuable additions, are still remaining at his house in south-Lambeth, where (as formerly) they are now to be seen'.[17] Ashmole – now married to Elizabeth Dugdale after Lady Manwaring's death on 1 April 1668 – visited with 'Mr Rose the Kings Gardner' before going on 'to Capt: Forsters at South Lambeth'.[18] As a fellow liveryman of John Tradescant's at the Company of Gardeners, Rose may well have known the garden already. His visit suggests it was still worthy of interest, although it was slipping out of the top rank. With the monarchy's restoration, gardening had left behind the plainer, utilitarian tones of Cromwell's England to embrace the whims and fancies of continental Europe.

By the 1690s, Tradescant's garden had dropped out of sight completely while Captain Foster's (presumably the one seen by Ashmole and Rose) remained among those celebrated in and around London. 'Captain Foster's garden at Lambeth has many curiosities in it,' wrote a visitor in 1691. 'His greenhouse is full of fresh and flourishing plants, and before it is the finest striped holly hedge that perhaps is in England.' He also had myrtles ('not the greatest but of the most fanciful shapes that are any where else'), a good choice of flowers, a glass beehive, a great variety of Virginian and other birds, and – no doubt of special interest to vine-grower John Rose – 'a framed walk of timber covered with vines, which, with others, running on most of his walls without prejudice to his lower trees, yield him a deal of wine'.[19] (The same author praised John Evelyn's Deptford villa, especially its walks and holly hedges, noting that it had 'a pretty little greenhouse, with an indifferent stock in it'.)

Another probable visitor to the Tradescants' Lambeth house and garden was Count Lorenzo Magalotti, 'the most learned and eminent character of the court of Ferdinand II of Tuscany'.[20] In 1668 and 1669 he accompanied the hereditary Prince of Tuscany around Spain, Portugal, England and Holland. In London, after visiting a hydraulic machine beyond Lambeth Palace at Vauxhall, His Highness's party went on to 'India House', situated 'on this side of the water' and full of 'rare and curious things, both animal and vegetable'. Many of the animals and curiosities came from India, we are told, 'and are kept here to gratify the curiosity of the public'. The label 'Indian' was not always used to imply a precise geography and the items they particularly admired were surely from Tradescant's rarities. They included sycamore trees from the banks of the Nile; several species of bird including birds of paradise, 'exquisitely beautiful' on account of their red and flesh-coloured feathers and very long tail; and nightingales from Virginia. There were also 'different sorts of animals, terrestrial and aquatic, curious for the magnitude of their bodies and the symmetry of their parts', and a strange rough-skinned fish, the size of a sea calf, its head long and deformed 'with a horrid looking mouth, in which are two rows of teeth, both upper and under, in shape like those of a saw'.[21]

The Italian visitors were less dazzled by English gardens, however, and perhaps also by Tradescant's own. On a different occasion, the Grand Duke set out from Lambeth Palace 'to see sundry gardens, in which, as is generally the case in England, if we except the disposition and arrangement of the parterres, there is little to be admired, as they cannot preserve from the rigour of the climate those trees which add so much to the beauty of the Italian garden'.[22]

While Hester Tradescant was keeping open house and garden, her relations with the inheritor of the rarities were about to become very much worse when, in September 1674, Ashmole consulted the stars to find out whether he should buy 'the house of Mrs. Blackamore'[23] – the next-door property at South Lambeth. In fact, the two houses were actually adjoining; only by moving in with Hester again could he get any closer. Taking his brother-in-law to view 'the great rarities in John Tredeskin's study'[24] was one thing, but now Ashmole could visit almost at will. The stars clearly considered it a good move because on 2 October 1674 he recorded the time ('11H. 30. A.M.') at which 'I & my wife first entred my House at South Lambeth',[25] noting just three days later that 'This night Mrs: Tredescant was in danger of being robbed, but most strangely prevented'. Whether he went to her aid or merely observed from afar is not made clear.

For Hester, having a spy on her doorstep must have been intolerable, especially as Ashmole chose this moment to serve her with a writ of execution relating back to the original court decision of ten years earlier.[26] Now she faced an imminent inspection by the two-man commission appointed to undertake an inventory of the rarities, both fellow heralds of Ashmole at the College of Arms and one now Ashmole's father-in-law, Sir William Dugdale. Perhaps she *had* traded away items from the original collection and feared discovery, or perhaps she could simply take the strain no longer. Hester snapped and told him he could take the rarities away, claiming (in front of a small crowd of neighbours) that he had robbed her of her 'Closet of Rarities, & cheated me of my Estate'.

Ashmole remonstrated with her (or so he later claimed), calling on her friends and neighbours to intervene, but Hester would have none of it. If he did not take the rarities away at once, she would throw them into the street. That, at least, was the account later written by Ashmole, which he forced

Hester to sign in the presence of witnesses.[27] In fact, his own notes tell a quieter story, indicating that the rarities came to him in two lots: first on 26 November 1674, when 'Mrs: Tredescant being willing to deliver up the Rarities to me, I caried severall of them to my House'; while five days later (on 1 December) he recorded that 'I began to remove the Rest of the Rarities to my house at Southlambeth'.[28]

Whatever his legal rights, Ashmole's persecution of the ageing widow is one of the shabbiest chapters in the Tradescant story. Nor did relations between them improve now that he had installed Tradescant's cabinet in his own attic. The submission that he forced Hester to sign in front of witnesses, her kinswoman Katherine King and King's nephew Thomas de Critz[29] among them, presents her as a shrill, unbalanced scandalmonger, but from her point of view Ashmole had indeed stripped her of her most precious inheritance. 'Bee it knowne unto all Persons,' began her abject recantation, 'that I Hester Tredescant of South Lambeth in the County of Surrey widdow doe acknowledge & Confess in the presence of Mr: Justice Dawling and other the Wittnesses hereunder subscribed, that I have very much wronged Elias Ashmole of the same place Esquire by severall fals scandalous & defamatory Speeches Reports, & otherwise tending to the diminution and blemishing of his Reputation & good Name.'

Ashmole had then set out her particular slanders. Three related to their boundary wall, a common cause of friction between neighbours, even today. First, she had apparently reported to several people that Ashmole had made a door from his garden into her orchard, by which he might come into her house 'as soone as the breath was out of my Body, & take away my Goods', when there was, 'in truth', no such door. Second, she had wrongly accused him of stealing 250 feet of her garden when he replaced their shared fence with a wall, presumably by siting it one foot into her garden for its entire 250-foot length. Now she was forced to admit that the wall had in fact been 'lyned out in the presence of my Cosen Blake the Plummer, whome my Landlord Mr: Bartholomoew had impowred on his behalfe so to doe'. Third, she had 'caused a great heape of Earth & Rubbish, to be layd against his Garden wall, so high, that on the sixt day of August last in the night, by

the helpe thereof it is strongly presumed that Theives got over the same &
robd the said Mr: Ashmole of 32 Cocks & Hens'. Even when ordered to
remove it, she had refused, saying that 'it should lye there in spight of his
Teeth', and so for six weeks or more he 'lay in continuall feare of having his
house broken open every night'.

As well as forcing her to admit his version of how the Tradescant rarities
came to his house (in which she even helped him to remove some of them
herself), Ashmole also required Hester to retract her statement that she had
made him promise 'to bestow the said Rarities on the University of Oxford',
either when she delivered them to him or at any time since. This last
'slander' is curious, especially as Ashmole had already opened negotiations
with Oxford about giving the rarities a home. He clearly wanted to claim
the 'gift' as his own, without any hint of coercion from the collection's
previous owner.

The submission ends with her humiliating apology, by which she admits
that all the particular slanders 'and many like false & scandalous Reports &
Words, as I have unadvisedly & rashly spoken against him without any
Provocation of his in words or deedes, so I am really and heartily sorry that
I have so greatly wronged him therein'. In the presence of the judge and the
witnesses, therefore, she 'asked him publique forgiveness for the same: And
doe herby voluntarily & freely promise the said Mr: Ashmole that noe
manner of Rubish or Earth shalbe layd against his said Garden Wall, and
that hence forth I will not say or doe anything against him or his wife, that
may tend to the damage reproach or disreputation of them or either of
them.'

Ashmole had achieved what he wanted: possession of the Tradescant
rarities and silence from Tradescant's widow, the one irritant to the quiet
enjoyment of what were now his treasures. The next time Hester appeared
in his jottings is the laconic entry recording her death, three days after he had
gathered some peony roots, which he may have wanted to help cure his
wife's repeated miscarriages. For 4 April 1678, he wrote '11 H:30' A.M. my
wife told me Mrs: Tredescant was found drowned in her Pond. She was
drowned the day before about noone as appeared by some Circumstances.'[30]

From the hostile evidence of Ashmole's lawsuits, suicide while the balance of her mind was disturbed seems the most likely cause of Hester's drowning, but her burial in sacred ground suggests that contemporaries took a gentler view. Perhaps like Hamlet's Ophelia, she was found to have drowned herself in her own defence and was therefore, as a gentlewoman, deemed worthy of Christian burial. She was interred on 6 April 1678, 'in a Vault in Lambeth Church yard, where her husband & his son John had been formerly layd'.[31] The words are Ashmole's, who probably attended the funeral together with the many neighbours and friends who had witnessed their increasingly acrimonious disputes. Now Hester would share the flamboyant tomb she had commissioned to commemorate the two gardening Tradescants with her stepson and her husband's first wife.

Hester's will, drawn up more than ten years previously when she was 'weake in bodie but of good sound and perfect minde and memorie', paints a much more sympathetic portrait of her than the raging scold she had become.[32] Her main beneficiaries – her two 'kinswomen', spinster Sarah de Critz and the widowed Katherine King – had already been named as heirs to her lands, tenements, property and 'personall estate', so here she was following her dead husband's instructions to bestow rings and token bequests to friends, neighbours and family. These small but individually determined mementos included 2s 6d apiece to John Tradescant's kinsmen Thomas and Robert Tredescant, 'sometime of walderwicke in the countie of Suffolke', and their children; 5s to her kinswoman Ester Sampford and lesser sums to Ester's children and grandchildren; 5s to her 'kinsman', painter Cornelius de Neve; £10 to be shared between her 'goddaughter Murrey and her children that I Christened'; 20s each to her goddaughter Ester Grace, and to Grace and Elizabeth Hall, but 40s to Joane Christmas. Money to buy rings (20s each) she left to Mistress Weyman and 'Goodwife Nightingal', 40s to public notary Richard Hoare, and £10 to another neighbour 'to buy her a piece of plate'. To the poor of Lambeth she left £5, to be distributed at the discretion of her executrices, her kinswomen Sarah and Katherine, who were to receive the residue of her personal estate. As overseers of her will, she appointed her 'good friends' Mark Cottle Esquire and Mr Thomas Southwood, gentleman. To these two and to Cottle's wife, Elizabeth, she left £5 apiece 'to buy them Rings in Remembrance of me'. Frances Norman, previously Tradescant, received nothing, although she might have died in the six and a half years that separated the writing of her father's and her stepmother's wills. Aside from this one lacuna, Hester's will portrays her as a woman with a wide network of family and neighbourly connections.

Ashmole moved as swiftly as ever. Before the month was out, he had 'removed the Pictures from Mr Tredescants House, to myne'.[33] These were probably the Tradescant family portraits, which he could argue were among the 'Pictures' repeatedly included with Tradescant's rarities in the Chancery hearing of 1664. He also promptly paid the £100 to Mary Edmonds that had been one of Tradescant's conditions to the gift, although not apparently written into the eventual deed.[34] As Tradescant had also left her £100 in his will (assuming the deed of gift to have been revoked), to be paid after Hester's death, one wonders whether she was paid twice. Then, in March 1679, Ashmole reunited for a time the two South Lambeth properties, by obtaining a lease on the house next door from Hester's old landlord, Mr Bartholomew, thereby laying claim to the Tradescants' garden of rare plants and simples as well as their cabinet of curiosities.

He used old John Tradescant's own copy of Parkinson's *Paradisi in Sole, Paradisus Terrestris* to record the 'Trees found in Mrs Tredescants Ground when it came into my possession'. It contains just thirty trees or shrubs, a threadbare list compared to the garden's earlier riches, and it is hard to imagine that the garden had been reduced to this. Among trees identified by Ashmole were two varieties of plane trees, the Robins' false acacia (*Robinia pseudoacacia*), a 'Lotus Arbor' (*Celtis australis*) from the Mediterranean, a horse chestnut, a common lime, viburnums, a sycamore, a Judas tree (*Cercis siliquastrum*), a stag's horn sumach, a lilac, a strawberry tree (*Arbutus unedo*) and the maritime pine (*Pinus pinaster*).[35] He failed to spot the red maple and swamp cypress noted much later by Philip Miller, or the tulip tree linked to Tradescant by John Evelyn.[36]

Even in death Ashmole could not leave Hester Tradescant alone. Perhaps

Hester's will had inflamed his acquisitiveness and convinced him that she had cheated him out of his rightful property, because he now filed a complaint in Chancery against her executrices, 'Sarah de Creets Spinster and Katherine King widdow both late of South Lambeth in the County of Surrey and now of Greenewich in the County of Kent'. Despite his earlier assertion that Hester had delivered over to him 'the Rest of the Rarities', Ashmole now claimed that she had evaded the full examination of her collection by delivering up to him just a portion of his entitlement. And before a proper investigation could take place, she had 'departed this life possessed of all the said Raretyes but such as shee delivered as aforesaid unto your orators possession or also shee had disposed of the same to some other use or person'.

Ashmole wanted Hester's executrices to restore to him the missing rarities that he believed were rightfully his or – and this seems to have been the driving force behind his latest litigation – to compensate him out of the late Mistress Tradescant's 'very greate parsonall Estate consisting of moneys plate Jewells goods household Stuffe Bonds Bills Mortgages and other goods and Chattels'. In his complaint he returned several times to her great wealth, which seems to have taken him by surprise and a share of which he now wanted to claim. He was not thinking only of himself, he declared; he intended giving all the Tradescant rarities and antiquities to the University of Oxford, 'who are now buildinge a faire Musaeum to preserve them in'. Concealing the rarities from him was also 'disappointing the University of Oxford of enjoying the benefitt of your orator.'

Although the two women were his principal targets, his fertile brain conjured up a whole family conspiracy and he accused them of 'Combyning and Confederating themselves with Thomas de Creetz their Nephew and with Grace de Creets their sister and with diverse other persons to your orator unknowne', whose names he nevertheless wanted attached to the complaint when they did become known. As evidence of the women's cheating, he said that they had recently delivered to him two cabinets, one of medals and the other of rarities. Although the medals cabinet should have contained coins to the value of more than £200, including 'diverse gold

Coynes and Meddalls both ancient and Modern', the one he received contained 'onely a few gold Meddalls and those worth not above five pounds'.

In their defence, the sisters repeated Hester's assertion that the deed of gift had been 'but fraudulently obtained by the Complainant from the said John Tredescant in a Surreptitious manner and when the said John Tredescant was in drincke'. Hester had tried to have the deed 'soo surreptitiously gotten' overthrown, and had enjoyed the rarities until a little before her death, when she had delivered or had caused to be delivered to the complainant (or somebody entrusted by him to receive them) 'all such Rarities as by the said pretended Deed did belong to him'. Any rarities that she had kept belonged to a 'Latter Colleccone', put together by Hester herself after her husband's death. And since Hester's death, in response to Ashmole's demands, they had delivered to him 'severall things and rarityes to buy their peace and quiettnes'.

Unlike Hester Tradescant, however, the sisters refused to give way any further to Ashmole's bully-boy tactics, claiming that he was now promoting his complaint 'for vexacon & molestacon of these Defendants who are women unable to Struggle with him'. The only rarities still in their hands were from Hester's later collection and not worth any more than £5, for which sum they were prepared to sell them to him.[37]

Whether Ashmole accepted their taunt is not known, as there is no record of the case ever coming to court. By 1686 both women were dead and even Elias Ashmole would have found it difficult to pursue mostly unnamed and unsubstantiated confederates.

Chapter Twenty-Six

The Ark Comes *to* Rest

O nce Ashmole had taken the rarities into his attic, he closed his doors to the paying public, admitting only gentlemen, scholars, distinguished visitors and friends, rather in the manner of the lordly owners of the old *cabinets de curiosités*. John Evelyn described returning in July 1678 from 'Mr. Elias Ashmoles Library & Curiosities at *Lambeth*' where he had gone with his wife and 'deare friend', Mrs Godolphin. 'He has divers MSS,' wrote Evelyn, 'but most of them *Astrological*, to which study he is addicted, though I believe not learned; but very Industrious, as his history of the Order of the Gartir shews.' Ashmole showed Evelyn a toad in amber, and Evelyn admired the fine prospect from the turret, 'it being so neere Lond: & yet not discovering any house about the Country'.[1]

Evelyn gave a rather different account of this meeting in a short memoir of his friend, Mrs Godolphin, in which he told Ashmole to 'leave off yr Giberish, & *tell* us our Fortunes'. He particularly wanted to know whether the pregnant Mrs Godolphin would give birth to a boy. 'Yes indeede, shall she,' replied Ashmole, 'a *brave Child*,' although he later communicated a more fearful message to Evelyn's wife. Mrs Godolphin was delivered of a boy as predicted but died of a fever shortly afterwards. Evelyn remained unconvinced by Ashmole's performance, however, commenting that 'as to Mr *Ashmole*; (who was willing to be thought a profound *Artist*) I believe him as much a *Conjurer* as my-selfe'.[2]

Another friend admitted to Ashmole's sanctum was Izaak Walton, author of *The Compleat Angler*, first published in 1653 and still in print today. Walton was well into his seventies when he visited Ashmole at Lambeth before bringing out the fifth edition of his angling classic. He was there to marvel at the 'many strange Creatures to be now seen (many collected by John Tredescant, and others added by my friend *Elias Ashmole* Esq; who now keeps them carefully and methodically at his house near to *Lambeth* near *London*)'. His list of fishy marvels is indeed enticing:

You may there see the Hog-fish, the Dog-fish, the Dolphin, the Cony-Fish, the Parrot-fish, the Shark, the Poyson-fish, sword-fish, and not only other incredible fish! but you may there see the Salamander, several sorts of Barnacles, of Solan Geese, the bird of Paradise, such sorts of Snakes, and such birds-nests, and of so various forms, and so wonderfully made, as may beget wonder and amusement in any beholder; and so many hundred of other rarities in that Collection, as will make the other wonders I spake of, the less incredible; for, you may note, that the waters are natures store-house, in which she locks up her wonders.[3]

Walton's amazed enthusiasm links him firmly to the elder Tradescant who looked at the world with 'wonder and amusement' and sought to capture nature's splendours for his own storehouse at Lambeth. Others were moving beyond the stage of collecting and cataloguing wonders to a more scientific appraisal of their relationships to each other. Naturalist John Ray and his collaborator Francis Willughby typified this new approach, using the dried birds in 'Tradescants Cabinet' to extend their understanding of exotic, non-European species. Ray referred to their visits several times in his translation and enlargement of Willughby's work on ornithology, published in 1678 several years after Willughby's early death at the age of thirty-seven.[4] As they appear to have visited together, they must have gone to Lambeth when the collection was still with Hester Tradescant, but their approach looks forward to Ashmole's new regime and especially to the collection's eventual transfer to Oxford.

The stuffed birds and body parts that interested them most were the 'Indian Mockbird', another dried 'red Indian bird', the 'red-breasted Indian Blackbird', a penguin and the dodo. 'We have seen this Bird dried, or its skin stuft in Tradescants Cabinet,' wrote Ray of the dodo, who also described a dodo's leg he had seen at Leiden, cut off at the knee: 'It was not very long,' began his meticulous account, 'from the knee to the bending of the foot being but little more than four inches; but of a great thickness, so that it was almost four inches in compass, and covered with thick-set scales.' (He also could not help remarking that the flesh was so fat and copious that three or four dodos were sometimes enough 'to fill an hundred Seamens bellies', but not very tasty if they were 'old, or not well boyled'.)[5] The penguin that they saw in 'Tradescants Cabinet at Lambeth' was also dried, although Danish scholar and collector, Ole Worm, had apparently kept a live one in his house for several months. 'It would swallow an entire Herring at once, and sometimes three successively before it was satisfied,' reported Ray.[6]

The point of the new emphasis on precise description – as typified by Ray and Willughby – was to aid positive identification. That the Tradescants contributed to the general confusion is clear from Ray's description of the Indian mockbird or 'Caerulus Indicus', which he had seen dried in 'Tradescants Cabinet'. After detailing its size and plumage, Ray wondered whether Tradescant had not simply added the epithet 'Indian' to another bird already described.[7]

Science was putting a stop to some long-cherished fancies – that birds of paradise had no feet, for example, 'a thing not long since believed by learned men and great Naturalists', according to Willughby and Ray. 'This errour once admitted, the other fictions of idle brains' quite naturally followed: 'viz. that they lived upon the coelestial dew; that they flew perpetually without any intermission, and took no rest but on high in the Air, their Wings being spread; that they were never taken alive, but only when they fell down dead upon the ground'. The authors then quoted an eyewitness account – from Johannes de Laet, Tradescant's old acquaintance and the correspondent of John Morris – who had two such birds of different kinds, and had 'seen many others, all which had feet, and those truly for the bulk of their bodies sufficiently great, and very strong Legs'.[8]

Evelyn, Willughby and Ray were all Fellows of the fledgling Royal Society, founded in 1660 as a 'Colledge for the Promoting of Physico-Mathematicall Experimentall Learning'. Inspired in part by Francis Bacon and enthusiastically supported by Charles II, it became known as the Royal Society of London for Improving Natural Knowledge, holding weekly meetings to witness experiments and discuss scientific topics. Even before the Society's official incorporation in 1662, Ashmole was among a list of forty people 'judged willing and fit to joyne with them in their designe, who if they should desire it, might be admitted before any other'.[9] He was elected on 2 January 1661, attended his first meeting a week later and was formally admitted on 15 January. His great interest in the old doctrines of alchemy and astrology meant, however, that he did not play as active a role as he normally sought in gatherings of learned men but he was often in their company and a number of Fellows visited him at South Lambeth, among them Robert Hooke, first curator of experiments and one of the Society's secretaries, who came with others in April 1677. 'Saw tradeskants raritys in Garret,' wrote Hooke in his diary. 'Saw Dees and Kellys and many other Books and manuscripts about chymistry, conjurations, magick, &c. [He] made me exceeding welcome.'[10]

The Society rapidly set about acquiring a library and a 'Repository' of scientifically interesting specimens. Had Ashmole wished merely to increase scientific knowledge with his rarites, he might have considered giving them to the Society, which had bought a rival collection in 1666 for the knock-down price of £100.[11] This was Robert Hubert's collection of 'Rarities of Nature', which – like the Tradescants' – had been open to the paying public every day, with special exhibits shown for an extra fee to 'more curious' persons on specified days of the week ('strange Fruits and Excrescents' could be seen on Wednesdays and Saturdays, for instance). Divided into animal and vegetable rarities, the collection was strongest on fish although it also boasted beasts, birds (including a 'Legge of a *Dodo* a great heavy bird that cannot fly'), serpents, insects or flies, exotic vegetables (and some oddly

17. John Tradescant the younger in
his museum catalogue of 1656.

18. The Lambeth Ark (left) where the Tradescants lived and
showed their precious collection of rarities.

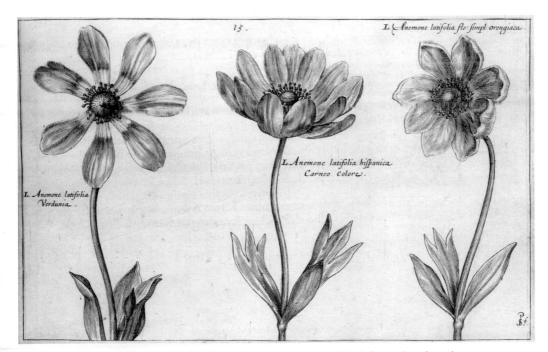

15.

L: Anemone latifolia flo: simpl: orengiaca.

L Anemone latifolia hispanica
Carneo Colore.

L. Anemone latifolia
Verdunia.

19. The younger Tradescant's nursery trade included distinctly coloured
anemones supplied to other curious gardeners.

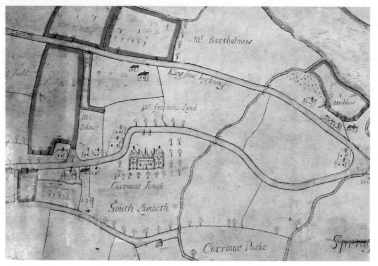

20. The Tradescants' South Lambeth house and garden in 1681, to the left of 'Carroone House'. Adjacent are Elias Ashmole's larger property and the Tradescants' orchard.

21 and 22. Typical items from the Tradescant's rarities, jostling the wonders of nature and man: Russian clothes and weapons (sketched by Peter Mundy on his journey to Archangel) and a bird of paradise in flight.

23. An Indian village engraved from a watercolour by early colonist John White, before the younger Tradescant's journey to Virginia in 1637.

24. The original will seals and signatures
of the John Tradescants, father and son,
revealing the dubious coat of arms adopted
by the younger Tradescant.

25. The Tradescants' ornately carved tomb at
St Mary, Lambeth, erected by Hester
Tradescant to honour the travels and strange
passions of her husband and father-in-law.

shaped, like the lemon representing the secret parts of a hermaphrodite), sea plants, metals and minerals, and 'things of strange Operation', like stones that smelt of violets when dropped into water or turned to dust when tossed into the fire.[12]

Once the Society took it over, its 'purpose' became theoretically more serious. Hooke himself disdainfully asserted that 'the use of such a Collection is not for Divertisement, and Wonder, and Gazing, as 'tis for the most part thought and esteemed, and like Pictures for Children to admire and be pleased with, but for the serious and diligent study of the most able Proficient in Natural Philosophy'.[13] Yet for all Hooke's grand designs, haphazard donations from merchants, travellers and Fellows continued to shift the Repository's focus back to that of the old *cabinets de curiosités*.

Ashmole in any case had no intention of allowing 'his' collection of rarities to sink within a common enterprise. The memorial he planned was to his own industry, intelligence and achievements, conceived on a staggeringly ambitious scale. Even before Hester's death, when the rarities were to become his in fact as well as in law, he opened discussions with Oxford University (his old alma mater from the civil war days, when he joined Brasenose College) about giving them the rarities, '& to propose the building of some large Roome, which may have Chimnies, to keepe those things aired that will stand in neede of it'.[14] Ashmole had always imagined the collection sited in its own purpose-built chambers and his practical mind was already contemplating the correct atmospheric conditions. Negotiations went ahead, and by 1677 (the year before Hester's death) the university was proposing to erect a building to house 'John Tredeskins raritys', with a lecture room and a 'labratory annext' for a lecture in 'Philosophicall History' to be read by Dr Robert Plot, author of *The Natural History of Oxford-shire* (and a practising alchemist).[15] Construction brought its own problems; in pulling down houses to make way for the new building, they dug too close to the 'Exeter Boghouse' and caused a foul-smelling flood.[16]

Architectural credit for the fine new building goes to master mason Thomas Wood, although its design has also been attributed to architect Sir Christopher Wren, founder member and a president of the Royal Society for which he had produced an unused design for a similar building.[17] By the time Ashmole's building was ready in 1683, it had cost Oxford a sobering £4,540, exhausting the university's funds and putting a stop even to basic book-buying for several years. Dr Robert Plot was to become the museum's first keeper and the university's first professor of chemistry, anticipating an endowment from Ashmole that in fact never materialized.[18]

Ashmole went to Oxford in August 1682 'to see the building prepared to receive my Rarities'[19] and on his return drafted rules for the museum as well as proposals for the Ashmolean professorship in natural history and chemistry. Both were to perpetuate his name, as the first proposition made clear: 'That there shalbe setled at Oxford a Professor of Naturall History & Chemistry, which with the Musaeum, shalbe called Ashmolean, the Lecture to be first read by Doctor Plot.' Rarities from the 'Phisick & Anatomy Schoole' were to be brought to the new museum (apart from those needed for teaching), together with 'all such Rarities as shalbe hereafter given to or bestowed upon the University'. No books or rarities were to be lent or taken out of the museum 'upon any pretence whatsoever'; and Sundays and holidays excepted, the rarities were to be open to the public daily, from 8 to 11 a.m. and again from 2 to 5 p.m. in summer or 2 to 4 p.m. in winter. Various provisions followed about the professorship that Ashmole was proposing, whose appointment would remain in his gift or that of his widow; and as a consequence of endowing the professorship, Mr Ashmole 'shalbe acknolwedged a Benefactor and Founder, & that all Honors & Respects done or fit to be done to such Benefactor & Founder, shalbe paid & allowed to him'.[20]

Ashmole began packing up his rarities in February 1683, helped by Dr Plot, who wrote to a fellow naturalist in York that he had been 'all this week at Mr Ashmoles packing & boxing up his donation, which amounts to 26 Boxes some of them 5. others 4. long, a yard over & two foot deep, all filld'.[21] Others were also watching the progress of the rarities to Oxford. Anthony Wood recorded in his diary for 20 March 1683 the arrival of 'Twelve Cart-loads of Tredeskyns rarities' from Ashmole in London (soon followed by 'mad Custos', Dr Plot);[22] while Sir Daniel Fleming in Westmorland was informed by a correspondent that 'John Tredeskins Rarities are come downe from London by water. The Elaboratory (which Some call the Knick-knack-atory) is almost finish'd & ready to receive them.'[23]

Ashmole himself remained at home, troubled by gout, attending neither the royal opening of the museum (in the presence of the Duke and Duchess of York and the Lady Anne, later Queen Anne) nor the reception for the university. He sent instead a dignified and flatteringly youthful portrait of himself by John Riley to hang in its Grinling Gibbons frame in the large, first-floor room. Wearing a gold chain and medal from the Prince Elector of Brandenburg, Ashmole as painted by Riley rests his right hand on the crowning achievement of his published career: a history of the Order of the Garter, sumptuously bound and surrounded by the kingly and princely honours he had received in return. Properly wigged, honoured and applauded, he would have looked down graciously on the outlandish collection largely put together by the elder Tradescant.

Although grudgingly prepared to admit the Tradescants' original ownership of the collection, he was claiming to himself all the munificence of his gift. As he wrote in May of that year to the Vice-Chancellor of his 'honored mother the University of Oxford', he had long wished to provide some testimony of his duty and filial respect, 'and when Mr: Tredescants Collection of Rarities came to my hands, tho I was tempted to part with them for a very considerable Sum of money, and was also press't by honourable Persons to consigne them to another Society [the Royal Society, perhaps?] I firmly resolv'd to deposite them no where but with You.'[24] The letter does him no credit today, especially his suggestion that he could have made a handsome profit from the collection, which had come to him gratis (apart from the £100 he paid to Mary Edmonds as a debt of conscience, perhaps). In the same letter he formally presented the collection to the university, while reserving for himself and persons appointed by him the custody of it during his lifetime.

In case anyone should need reminding that it was he – Elias Ashmole – who was the owner and donor of the extraordinary wonders on display, the preamble to Ashmole's statutes, orders and rules for the museum swept the Tradescants aside, crediting the entire collection's conception to Ashmole's own character, energy and dedication. 'Because the knowledge of Nature is very necessarie to humaine life, health, & the conveniences thereof,' he began, and because that knowledge required the inspection of particular objects that are

extraordinary in their Fabrick, or usefull in Medicine, or applyed to Manufacture or Trade: I Elias Ashmole, out of my affection to this sort of Learning, wherein my selfe have taken, & still doe take the greatest delight; for which cause alsoe, I have amass'd together great variety of naturall Concretes & Bodies, & bestowed them on the University of Oxford, wherein my selfe have been a Student, & of which I have the honor to be a Member.[25]

As a piece of self-promotion, it was breathless in its arrogation of the Tradescants' collecting role. Ironically, however, the collection as a whole fared better with Ashmole as the driving force instead of the vacillating gardener or his increasingly unbalanced wife, who might conceivably have traded away its treasures. The younger Tradescant had neither the clout nor the determination to bully Oxford into building a separate museum, where the collection stayed intact until well into the nineteenth century. Had Tradescant given his rarities to Oxford without Ashmole's intervention, they would doubtless have been distributed haphazardly around the university, quickly losing any integrity as an historic collection. Even so, Ashmole's failure to endow the promised professorship meant that his museum never developed into the dynamic centre for scientific experiment and research that the university had hoped. Although he was not solely to blame for this, Ashmole was – in the words of a recent history of the university – 'interested in the museum almost exclusively as a monument to his lifelong preoccupations and a testament to his largesse. Thus, despite his earlier pledge to support a broader vision in which the edifice was only the first step in fostering scientific life at Oxford, Ashmole resisted repeated solicitations that would have furthered such a goal.'[26] Such a development would also have been a fitting and lasting legacy to the elder Tradescant, whose passion for the rare, the strange and the outlandish had put him in the vanguard of an earlier generation.

Tradescant's rarities could at least enjoy a fine new home. An early visitor to the Ashmolean Museum described the walls of the first-floor room 'all hung round with John Tradescant's rarities, and several others of Mr. Ashmol's own gathering'. The room where Dr Plot read his lectures on chemistry was 'very spacious and high, curiously wainscoted', while the cold basement – well furnished with furnaces – was 'very convenient for all the operations in chymistry'.[27] But without Ashmole's endowment, the grasping Plot was disappointed in his expectations of a generous salary and so he read his lectures only to those who paid to study chemistry with him, seeking further to enrich himself through an elaborate scheme to market an alchemical elixir called 'the alkahest'.[28] The rift between Ashmole and Plot grew ever wider, until Ashmole complained openly that 'Plot does no good in his station but totally neglects it, wandering abroad where he pleases'.[29]

Ashmole lived on until 1692, increasingly plagued by minor and more serious ailments: gout, vertigo, fits of toothache, boils on his throat and groin, diabetes perhaps, and strangury (a blockage or irritation of the bladder). Sometimes the cure provoked new symptoms, like the crushed black snails he applied to his gouty foot which sparked a prolonged inflammation.[30] He probably took solace from his garden, which he had always enjoyed, planting the walls with fruit trees soon after he had moved to Lambeth and sending seed to his father-in-law, Sir William Dugdale, who had requested 'Roman-Lettice', 'that kinde of Larkesheele, which is used in Sallets', and the large 'July-flower' (gillyflower).[31] For a time he also enjoyed the Tradescants' garden next door after he had leased the house from landlord Mr Bartholomew in 1679. It doubtless furnished him with exotics to impress his visitors or to give to others, like the orange tree ('a great Raritie') that he presented to the wife of a Chancery official.[32] He soon sublet at least the front part of the Tradescants' house, incorporating some of the remaining parts into the offices for his own house.[33] In December 1681 he tried to rid the two houses of rats by casting rat talismans, including one he placed in 'the door-sill going from Mrs Tradescants kitchen into the passage going into the da[i]ry house', and another 'in the middle of the passage going to my apple-chambers in the old building of Mr. Tradescants house'.[34]

Despite his worsening health, Ashmole maintained his gardening contacts: Jacob Bobart the younger of the Oxford Physic Garden drank a glass of wine with him in London, and Charles Hatton praised his baking pear as the best he had ever seen 'for largeness, firmeness, and good tast'. Grafted on to dwarf rootstock, 'It is in shape and colour like ye Spanish Bon Christien. He calles it ye Ashmole peare.'[35] To a Mr Woolrich (probably John Worlidge, author of one of the century's most delightful books on the art of gardening) he communicated the 'Secret of raising flowers from a Virgin earth', raising the intriguing possibility that he applied his alchemical knowledge to gardening, unless he was simply experimenting with earth that had never been dug before.[36] His house, meanwhile, grew larger and grander as he added new rooms, garden walls and a stable for his coach and horses. He also bought a farm of nineteen and a half acres known as Plummer's Farm – also in South Lambeth – for his wife's jointure.[37]

He saw in two more reigns: that of James II, after Charles's death in 1685, and the 'glorious revolution' of 1688, which replaced James with his eldest daughter Mary and her husband, Prince William of Orange, sparking a whole new gardening vogue for Dutch formality. Ashmole's health was by now in steady decline and a coterie of friends and colleagues tried to conceal from him a burglary of coins, medals and small valuables from his Oxford museum, on the grounds that he was 'very weake, & crasie in mind as well as bodie'.[38]

Ashmole died at his South Lambeth home on 18 or 19 May 1692 aged seventy-five and was buried, like the Tradescants, at St Mary, Lambeth, inside the church at the altar end of the south aisle.[39] 'Soon after Mr. Ashmole's Death,' wrote Anthony Wood of his friend, 'his Widow Elizabeth, who seemed to have had a great Love and Fondness for her husband, (which was sometimes before Company expressed) married a lusty Man called John Reynolds ... but had no Issue by him.'[40] 'Mistris Ashmole is maried to a stone-cutter of Lambeth,' wrote gossipy John Aubrey to Wood, 'so I hope she will now at last put a memoriall for her first Husband.'[41] This she did – a black marble tombstone bearing the arms of Ashmole impaling those of Dugdale, surmounted by Ashmole's mercury crest. After Elizabeth's death, the stonecutter Reynolds inherited Ashmole's Lambeth house, which then passed to his subsequent widow.

With Ashmole gone, John Aubrey made a respectful journey to Lambeth, stopping off to mourn his 'worthy Friend and old Acquaintance' at the church of St Mary and continuing southwards towards Stockwell. 'At *South Lambeth*, the farthest House was the House where *John Tredescant* liv'd, and shew'd his choice Collection of Rarities; where he had a Garden stor'd with choice Plants.' One of those remembered by Aubrey was the balm of Gilead tree, which grew also with Edmund Wyld Esquire at Houghton Conquest in Bedfordshire,

till in the hard Winter the Mice kill'd it. I do not hear of any other now in *England*. The House and Garden Elias *Ashmole* bought; as also the Rarities, which he gave to the *Musaeum* at *Oxford*. Very few rare Plants are now remaining here: only a very fair Horse-Chess-Nut Tree, some *Pine-Trees*, and *Fumack-Trees*, *Phylerea's*, &c. and at the Entrance into the Gate, over the Bridge of the Mote, are two vast Ribs of a *Whale*.[42]

The Tradescants' house continued to mark the boundary between gardened land and open fields until well into the eighteenth century, as drawn by John Rocque for his map of the environs of London in 1746. In 1750 the bridging of the Thames at Westminster brought development closer and the city spread rapidly southwards. While Ashmole's house – known as Turret House – developed into a fine gentleman's residence, its gardens extended to incorporate Tradescant's orchard, and its south-facing façade celebrated in watercolours that record its elegant circular lawn and stately cedars of Lebanon,[43] the next-door property sank into decline. William Watson, Fellow of the Royal Society, visited in mid-century with a Dr Mitchell and reported on the garden's sorry state to the Royal Society, having been for 'many Years totally neglected, and the House belonging to it empty and ruin'd'.[44] Yet even though the garden was 'quite cover'd with Weeds, there remain among them manifest Footsteps of its Founder'. The flowering plants he listed were Italian borage, solomon's seal, one of the

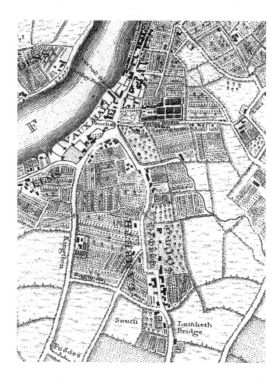

John Rocque's map of the
environs of London (1746):
the Tradescant-Ashmole
properties survive just to
the north east of South
Lambeth Bridge.

birthworts (Aristolochia clematitis), and the weird purple-flowering voodoo lily that briefly stinks of rotting meat. There may have been others, he remarked, flourishing at different times of the year. Watson also noted a great buckthorn in the orchard, and two strawberry trees (Arbutus unedo) 'the largest I have seen', which must have survived the severe winters of 1729 and 1740 'when most of their kind were kill'd throughout England'. Among Watson's audience at the Royal Society that day was the antiquarian Revd. William Stukeley, who recorded Watson's agreeable surprise to find, 'after so long a neglect and utter disreguard [sic], many curious plants of Tredescant's growing among the weeds, and still struggling to maintain the honor of their planter'.[45]

Philip Miller, curator at the Chelsea Physic Garden, reported the same story of botanical survival in the face of neglect when he remarked on the swamp cypress still surviving in the Lambeth garden, more than a century after the younger Tradescant had brought back seeds from Virginia. It was still in 'great Health and Vigour' despite the 'many Hooks' driven into the trunk 'to fasten Cords thereto for Drying of Clothes'. [46]

A later occupant of Tradescant's house and garden was the Lambeth Palace librarian and public servant, Dr Andrew Coltée Ducarel, who wrote a reply to his friend William Watson some twenty-five years later. Ducarel sought to correct Watson's confusion about the extent of the Tradescant garden, which he believed much larger than Watson had supposed. 'Bounded on the West by the road, on the East by a deep ditch (still extant) it certainly extended a good way towards the North, and took in not only my orchard and garden, but also those of two or three of my next neighbours; and some ancient mulberry trees, planted in a line towards the North, seem to confirm this conjecture.'[47]

Writing nearly a century and a half after the elder Tradescant's death, Ducarel credited him (a little over-generously, perhaps) with being 'the earliest collector (in this kingdom) of every thing that was curious in Natural History', among which he specifically included minerals, birds, fishes and insects. As well as coins and medals, Tradescant had 'a great variety of uncommon rarities', while the catalogue published by his son enumerated the many plants, shrubs and trees growing in his garden. 'Some of these plants are (as I am informed), if not totally extinct, at least become very uncommon, even at this time ... And this able man, by his great industry, made it manifest (in the very infancy of Botany), that there is scarce any plant extant in the world that will not, with proper care, thrive in this kingdom.'[48]

The Tradescants' star was clearly in the ascendant. Yet unlike Frenchman Pierre Morin, neither Tradescant appears in the surviving fragments of John Evelyn's great encyclopaedic (but unfinished) work on gardening, *Elysium Britannicum*, which grew into an enormous 'Heap as to fill some Thousand Pages' of densely packed drafts, rewrites and projects.[49] Evelyn appreciated the scholarly, the rare and the curious; and had the Tradescants left behind a literary legacy more substantial than a manuscript diary or a published catalogue, they might have better earned his respect. Others were more appreciative of the Tradescants' contribution as plantsmen and pioneering collectors. In a work published in 1790, botanist and writer Richard Pulteney included brief biographies of them as key early figures that had helped to establish botany in England. Pulteney's professional judgement was surely right when he said that despite not having

contributed materially to amplify what is more especially meant by English botany, or the discovery and illustration of the plants spontaneously growing in *England*, [the Tradescants stood] too high not to demand an honourable notice; since they contributed at an early period, by their garden and museum, to raise a curiosity that was eminently useful to the progress and improvement of natural history in general.

(Pulteney also had a dig at Ashmole, saying that the younger Tradescant had bequeathed the museum to him by a deed of gift. 'It afterwards became part of the *Ashmolean museum*, and the name of TRADESCANT unjustly sunk in that of *Ashmole*.')[50]

Both Tradescants also appeared in the second edition of the Revd. J. Granger's biographical history of England of 1775, which had started out as a (now hilarious) attempt to develop a systematic approach to biography by compiling 'a Methodical Catalogue of British Heads'. According to Granger's system, subjects could be divided into twelve separate classes from royalty in Class 1 down to the mixed bag in Class 12: people of both sexes, generally from the 'lowest Order', who were remarkable for just one circumstance, 'such as lived to a great Age, deformed Persons, Convicts, &c.' Tradescant appeared far down the list in Class 10 along with other 'Painters, Artificers, Mechanics, and all of inferior Professions' not included elsewhere. It was not a snub. Others in his class included Inigo Jones, Nicholas Stone, Sir Balthazar Gerbier and Wenceslaus Hollar. John Parkinson, John Gerard, John Evelyn and Elias Ashmole were in the class above (among physicians, poets, and 'other ingenious Persons' who had distinguished themselves by their writings) but so, too, was Jacob Bobart the elder, while in the class below (just one notch above the convicts and elderly persons) were the 'Ladies, and others, of the Female Sex, according to their Rank'.[51]

As for the Tradescants, Granger garbled the facts of their lives a little, as ever, and continued the process of hyperbole that obscures their very real achievements, writing of the elder Tradescant that he was

the first man, in this kingdom, that distinguished himself as a collector of natural and artificial curiosities, and was followed by his son in the same pursuit. He, as Parkinson informs us, introduced a considerable number of exotic plants into England, and made it appear that, with due care and cultivation, almost any vegetable of the known world may be taught to thrive in this climate.[52]

As their posthumous reputation grew, so the Tradescants attracted all manner of spurious titles, honours and credit that really belonged to others. Mountain Jennings's role at Hatfield was largely subsumed into his fellow gardener's fame and other early collectors of plants and curiosities were largely forgotten. Father and son were invariably thrown together, blurring their very distinct achievements and virtues. Yet there were differences, as we can see from the two provenances given to the fragment of the True Cross displayed in their museum.

John Parkinson first told the story of this sacred relic in his herbal, classifying it with 'Strange and Outlandish Plantes' among his 'Last Tribe' of spices, drugs, other fruit and strange trees from the East or West Indies. The wood was from the aloe tree, said Parkinson, very rare in Europe until the Venetians brought some from Cairo and the East Indies. He had seen a 'great peece' of it 'with Master *Tradescant* the elder before he dyed . . . and of the best sort, as bigge and as long as a mans legge, without any knot therein, which as he said our King *Charles* gave him with his owne hands'. It was venerated by many as a great relic, said Parkinson, and was therefore 'fetched away againe from [Tradescant's] Sonne, to be kept as a monument or rellicke still'. Parkinson then added dryly that if all the pieces of the True Cross scattered around the world were gathered together in one place, they would make 'many cart loads full'.[53]

Elias Ashmole told a very different version, however, in which it was Queen Henrietta Maria who delivered a much smaller piece (now shrunk to some six inches long) to the younger Tradescant for safekeeping at the start of the civil war. When she later asked him to send it on to her in France, he detained a small piece, 'which casually had been broken from it'. Tradescant gave a piece to Ashmole, who could not resist passing on a fragment to the Right Honourable Henry, Earl of Norwich and Earl Marshall of England.[54] (Strangely, the museum catalogue of 1656 contains no reference to the cross, although it was seen by Georg Stirn in 1638 and reappeared again in an Ashmolean catalogue of c.1684–90.[55] Perhaps Ashmole kept the whole piece and later gave 'his' fragment to the museum.)

It is, of course, possible to reconcile the two versions, with King Charles taking back the relic and giving it his wife, who later passed a piece of it to her Oatlands gardener for safekeeping. Put side by side, however, the two versions call into question the younger Tradescant's fitness to succeed his father as a collector. Not only did Charles ask for the return of the original relic, but the fragment broken from the piece entrusted to Tradescant by the queen suggests on his part carelessness at best and theft at worst. It seems the younger Tradescant failed his father as a collector and entrepreneur, even if he proved a worthy successor as a gardener and plant hunter.

While time was maintaining – even enhancing – the Tradescants' reputation, their family tomb was faring less well. 'This once beautiful monument hath suffered so much by the weather,' wrote Ducarel in 1773, 'that no idea can now, on inspection, be formed of the North and South sides.'[56] Happily, the drawings preserved in the Pepys Library at Cambridge could remedy this defect; the tomb was repaired about this time and fully restored by public subscription in 1853.[57] Among the six committee members overseeing the restoration were the rector of Lambeth, the keeper of the Ashmolean Museum and Sir William Hooker of the Royal Gardens at Kew. But the names recorded on the tomb were muddled (they still are) with the younger Tradescant's first wife Jane (buried in 1635) confusingly given in marriage to his father, so the tomb appears to commemorate two married couples (John and Jane, John and Hester) and their adolescent son and grandson, John.

The Tradescants' house became a boys' school, which survived well into

Victorian times until it was demolished and the land sold to builder Frederick Snelling in 1879.[58] The following year, Ashmole's old house went up for sale, described in the sale catalogue as a 'comfortable Family Residence' with coach house and stabling, lawns, pleasure grounds, kitchen garden and paddock spread over four acres and fourteen perches. The pleasure grounds were extensive and well timbered, boasting lawns 'planted with Choice Shrubs, Flower Garden with Grotto and Summer House, capital Kitchen Garden, Greenhouse, and Two Vineries heated with Hot Water, Furnace House, Gardener's Shed, Tool House and Closet'. Compounding the mix-up between the two adjacent properties, the sale brochure for Ashmole's old house grandly proclaimed that here had lived

Sir John Tradescant, his Son and Grandson – they were Gardeners successively to Queen Elizabeth, James I., and Charles I. – were men of great energy and travelled over the then known world, and to this spot brought the various plants they had collected, and many curiosities ... In the Paddock is a Mulberry Tree, supposed to be one of the first brought into this country.[59]

Despite the house agent's historical inflation, the estate was destined for development, and potential roads were superimposed on the stately lawns and curving carriage drive. The sale realized a little over £16,000,[60] and by 1893 when the large-scale Ordnance Survey map for London's outlying districts was revised, the two properties, together with their gardens and Tradescant's orchard, had been replaced by some 130 terraced houses, including those fronting on to South Lambeth Road.[61] The new streets on Ashmole's old property were named Tradescant Street (now Road) and Walberswick Street in honour of his neighbour, while Tradescant's house bordered on to what is now Meadow Place. A wartime edition of the *Surrey Mirror* noted that the precise spot where Ashmole's Turret House had once stood was then occupied by 'Mr Challis's tea shop', nearly opposite the Tate Branch Library in South Lambeth Road.[62] Today, the tapas bars along this stretch of the South Lambeth Road indicate a highly localized Portuguese community.

Tradescant's famous 'Clossitt of rarityes' at the Ashmolean Museum also enjoyed mixed fortunes. Not all the perishable specimens survived. Some fell victim to neglect by keepers and visitors. A German visitor in 1710 complained that the keeper was 'always lounging about in the inns' and that 'the people impetuously handle everything in the usual English fashion . . . even the women are allowed up here for sixpence; they run here and there, grabbing at everything and taking no rebuff from the Sub-Custos'.[63] Other objects simply decayed or were eaten by pests, a fact of life – and death – which Ashmole's original statutes had foreseen, permitting the keeper to remove and substitute any item that 'growes old & perishing'. He also wanted the rarer items 'apt to putrefie & decay with tyme' to be painted 'in a faire Velome Folio Booke, either with water colors, or at least design'd in black & white, by some good Master'.[64] (Sadly, no such fine volume ever seems to have been kept.)

By the time Tradescant's old house in Lambeth was pulled down, many of the rarities it once contained had been dispersed around the museums of Oxford – geological and zoological specimens to what is now the Oxford University Museum of Natural History; books, coins and manuscripts to the Bodleian Library; ethnological items destined for the Pitt Rivers Museum. The remaining antiquities were housed along with paintings and sculpture in the new Ashmolean Museum, making way for the Museum of the History of Science in the original building. Tradescant's rarities survive in a single small room of the new Ashmolean, reached through a panelled antechamber and corridor displaying many of the Tradescant portraits that Ashmole took from their house after Hester Tradescant's death by drowning. The collection's centrepiece remains Powhatan's mantle, displayed beneath the garlanded portrait of John Tradescant the elder. Some items not associated with the Tradescants have found their way into this sanctum, including Guy Fawke's lantern and an iron-plated hat, worn for Richard Bradshaw's own protection as the chief judge at the trial of King Charles I.

Contrary to popular myth, Tradescant's dodo was never deliberately thrown on the fire, thereby undergoing a second ritual extinction, nor were its head and foot saved by chance from the flames. The myth grew out of a mistranslation of the original Latin explaining its fate: that it was withdrawn from display at the museum's annual visitation or inspection, and only the enduring parts kept. 'There was no fire, no destruction, no act of vandalism, but an attempt to preserve what could be preserved.'[65] In any event, the dodo rose again from the (mythical) flames, reincarnated in Alice's wonderland by Oxford mathematician Charles Dodgson as one of the queer-looking party that fell into the pool created by Alice's tears: 'a Duck and a Dodo, a Lory and an Eaglet' and many other 'curious creatures',[66] which would have been quite at home among Tradescant's marvellous monsters, joining perhaps the Senegalese 'Comb-birds', which walked as gravely as Spaniards.

The dodo's head and left foot are now locked away with other precious specimens of the Oxford University Museum of Natural History in the room that saw the great evolution debate of 1860 between Church and science on Darwin's new theories of evolution. (By most contemporary accounts the scientists won, despite the recent rearguard actions of creationists.) Shut away in cupboards elsewhere in the museum are other Tradescant specimens that even today reflect their collector's passion for bigness (an elephant's massive limb bone), exoticism (a blackened crocodile's head, heavy as a petrified log, its leathery skin sewn together with string beneath the jaw), and nature's freaks (a four-horned sheep's head, complete with mangy pelt, or the three-clawed hoof of an elk). Here too are nature's marvels such as the dried bladder fish with one glass eye, open-mouthed like the tortured figure in Edvard Munch's *The Scream*; and a dried West Indian plectognath fish, its skin patterned all over with hexagons.

Remodelled and restored in the mid-eighteenth and nineteenth centuries, the church of St Mary, Lambeth sank into decline after the last war, and in 1972 services were discontinued.[67] The churchyard all but disappeared under weeds, and the church itself was shuttered and boarded. Its renaissance was inspired by John and Rosemary Nicholson, who came to the dying church looking for the Tradescant tombs. Fired into action by the threat of demolition, announced in 1976, they campaigned to resurrect the church as the world's first Museum of Garden History. The following year

saw the formation of a Friends group and of the Tradescant Trust, with the
Ashmolean Museum's then director, Sir David Piper, as its first trustee.
Slowly, enough money was raised to put a roof over the church, clean the
building and clear the churchyard. The first exhibition opened in 1981,
celebrating the 350th anniversary of the death of Tradescant's old friend and
Virginian pioneer, Captain John Smith. Two years later, HM Queen
Elizabeth the Queen Mother opened a knot garden in the churchyard
designed by the then Marchioness of Salisbury – the Tradescant Trust's first
president and married to a descendant of the elder Tradescant's first known
employer, Robert Cecil.

The garden was planted with old-fashioned shrubs, roses, herbaceous
perennials, annuals and bulbs that Tradescant would have known and loved:
variegated holly, myrtle, rosemary, germander, a variegated sea buckthorn
and *Tradescantia*, his famed Virginian spiderwort. Among the species roses
and their later cultivars were the white rose of York, the crimson apothecary's
rose and the milk-white musk rose.

Inside the church you would look in vain for Ashmole's black marble
tombstone with its proud Latin boast: *sed durante Musaeo Ashmoleano Oxon.
nunquam moriturus*, ('as long as the Ashmolean Museum at Oxford endures,
he will never die').The Museum of Garden History has commandeered the
side chapel for office space, temporarily covering over the tombs on the floor
in an act of poetic justice or cultural vandalism, depending on your point of
view. Outside, however, the Tradescants lie once more in a garden planted
with old-fashioned flowers, close to Captain William Bligh of the *Bounty*.
The story has come full circle and the collectors have become the centrepiece
of another's collection.

This seems perfectly right, for it is as collectors that the Tradescants
created their most enduring legacy. Plants were their especial passion, of
course. The elder Tradescant loved anything rare, new, quirky or different,
from the lunatic strawberry he discovered at Plymouth to the 'wondrous
sweet' roses he described so eloquently on his Russian journey. His son
broadened the collection to include more workaday plants but he, too, had
an eye for novelties, as witness his Virginian introductions. Their combined

Tradescant's famed Virginian spiderwort,
Tradescantia virginiana.

interests and skills help to explain the continuing British fascination with the raw stuff of a garden – its plants – as opposed to the passing fancies of design. Each age refashions Eden in its own image but here were two men who magically wed Noah's natural knowledge and wisdom to Adam's dogged determination to clear the weeds and make God's garden grow.

Yet the Tradescants speak to non-gardeners just as strongly because they loved all of God's creation, not simply its living plants. Their eclectic collection jostled objects as diverse as the testicles of a beaver, the 'robe of the King of *Virginia*', the hand of a mermaid and 'the passion of Christ carved very daintily on a plumstone'.[68] To Tradescant the father goes the credit for pioneering the collection, using the names of his illustrious employers to call for rarities from around the known world and the rarer, bigger, or stranger the better. Here was a true original, a self-made man who trod his own path, which others followed.

For Tradescant the son life was undoubtedly more difficult as he struggled to emerge from his father's shadow at a time of great civil disorder.

Although he continued his father's social rise, gaining riches and setting the seal on his family's gentlemanly status, he lacked the scientific bent to turn curiosity into scholarship. Yet by delivering the Tradescant collection into the hands of the wilier Elias Ashmole, he assured its continued survival. For this we remain for ever in his debt; and in documenting the entire collection of Tradescant plants and rarities, he proved himself worthy of his father's mantle at the end.

To edge her knot garden in the Lambeth churchyard where the Tradescants lie buried, Lady Salisbury used dwarf box, *Buxus sempervirens* 'Suffruticosa'. Known as French or Dutch box in the elder Tradescant's day, this was an exciting new introduction, which – according to his old friend John Parkinson – was 'onely received into the Gardens of those that are curious'.[69]

In the spring of 2003, the low box hedge was all but flattened by the amorous attentions of a frustrated and lonely adolescent fox. Although Queen Anne is said to have hated the plant's musty smell, it can seemingly drive a fox wild. Disaster threatened, until the young fox was found dead on the lawns of nearby Lambeth Palace – a victim, some may say, of the strange passion that plants have excited down the centuries in beast and man.

Notes

Introduction, Of Marvels and Monsters

1. H. E. Strickland and A. G. Melville, *The Dodo and its Kindred* (London, 1848), pp. 32–3.

2. See Arturo Valledor de Lozoya, 'An unnoticed painting of a white dodo', *Journal of the History of Collections*, 15, 2 (2003), p. 210, n. 45.

3. Simon Wilkin (ed.), *Sir Thomas Browne's Works* (4 vols, London, 1835), vol. 2, p. 174.

4. John Parkinson, *Paradisi in Sole, Paradisus Terrestris* (London, 1629), p. 152.

5. John Tradescant, *Musaeum Tradescantianum* (London, 1656), p. 4.

6. Nehemiah Grew, *The Anatomy of Plants* (London, 1682).

7. John Evelyn, *The Diary of John Evelyn*, ed. E. S. de Beer (6 vols, Oxford, Clarendon Press, 1955), vol. 2, p. 132.

8. See Marjorie Swann, *Curiosities and Texts* (Philadelphia, University of Pennsylvania Press, 2001).

9. Bodleian Library, MS Ashmole 824, Part XVI, fols 175r.–186v.

10. National Archives, CO 1/1 fol., 30r.

11. J. A. F. Bekkers, *Correspondence of John Morris with Johannes de Laet, 1634–1649* (Assen, Van Gorcum & Comp., N.V., 1970), pp. 2–3.

12. John Parkinson, *Theatrum Botanicum* (London, 1640).

13. Tradescant, *Musaeum Tradescantianum*, introduction.

14. William Shakespeare, *The Tempest*, Act II, Scene ii (London, The Arden Shakespeare, 1999), ed. Virginia Mason Vaughan and Alden T. Vaughan, p. 208.

Chapter One, Education of a Gardener

1. British Library, Additional MS 72338 (Trumbull Papers, vol. 98), fol. 108.

2. Situated on the Scheldt estuary, Flushing (Vlissingen) was one of the main ports for travel between England and the Netherlands.

3. Anthony Wood, *Athenae Oxonienses*, 2nd edn (2 vol, Oxford, 1721), vol. 2, column 888. The reference is absent from the first edition of 1691.

4. See, for instance, Mea Allan, *The Tradescants* (London, Michael Joseph, 1964), p. 144, and Jeanette Winterson, *Sexing the Cherry* (London, Bloomsbury, 1989).

5. Hatfield House Archives, Bills 58/3, General 11/25, and Bills 67b.

6. Hatfield House Archives, General 11/25.

7. See his personal copy of Parkinson's *Paradisi in Sole, Paradisus Terrestris*, now in the Bodleian Library, Oxford (Antiq.c.E.1629.1).

8. See William Page, *Letters of Denization and Acts of Naturalization* (Lymington, Huguenot Society of London, vol. 8, 1893); William A. Shaw, *Letters of Denization and Acts of Naturalization* (Lymington, Huguenot Society of London, vol. 18, 1911); and William Durrant Cooper (ed.), *Lists of Foreign Protestants and Aliens* (London, Camden Society, 1862), Camden Society, old series, vol. 82. Aliens could acquire the privileges of native-born subjects by obtaining an Act of Naturalization through Parliament (used chiefly for the children of Englishmen born abroad) or by applying to the Crown for a Letter of Denization.

9. The lists include Johannes de Laet; Serjeant Painter John de Critz; the Brussels-born children of William Trumbull; and grotto-builder Isaac de Caus.

10. Hatfield House Archives, The Building of Hatfield House, p. 129.

11. Allan, *The Tradescants*, pp. 17-25.

12. Prudence Leith-Ross, *The John Tradescants* (London, Peter Owen, 1984), pp. 22-4.

13. British Library, Additional MS 19,081, fol. 32. Other deeds summarised (fols 39, 40r. and v.) mention a Thomas Tredestant of Henstede (John Tradescant's presumed father) and Thomas Tradescant of London, yeoman, son of Thomas Tradescant of Corton. The latter was almost certainly the elder Tradescant's father.

14. The children's names include Margaret (b. and d. 1544), Nicholas, Agnes, Thomas (twice), Johne, Elyner, Marjorie (b. and d. 1561), and William.

15. See *The Register Book of the Parish of Corton, 1579–1783*, and microfilmed parish registers for Henstead parish.

16. National Archives, PROB 11/308 and PROB 11/356.

17. William John Charles Moens, *The Walloons and Their Church at Norwich: Their History and Registers, 1565–1832* (Huguenot Society of London, 1888), p. 198.

18. Books of English surnames consulted include P. H. Reaney, *A Dictionary of English Surnames*, 3rd edn, ed. R.M. Wilson (London, Routledge, 1991).

19. See Nigel Heard, *Wool: East Anglia's Golden Fleece* (Lavenham, Suffolk, Terence Dalton Ltd., 1970).

20. Nigel Goose, 'The Dutch in Colchester in the 16th and 17th centuries', in Randolph Vigne and Charles Littleton (eds), *From Strangers to Citizens* (Brighton, Huguenot Society of Great Britain and Ireland and Sussex Academic Press, 2001), pp. 88–9.

21. John Stoye, *English Travellers Abroad*, revised edn (New Haven and London, Yale University Press, 1989), pp. 171–2.

22. J. A. F. Bekkers, *Correspondence of John Morris* (Assen, Van Gorcum & Comp., NV, 1970), pp. xii–xix.

23. Ibid., p. 36, letter of 23 May 1640.

24. See M. R. Soanes and D. R. Butcher, *A History of St Bartholomew's Church, Corton* (Corton, Suffolk, revised edn, 1997), pp. 3–4.

25. Parkinson, *Paradisi in Sole*, p. 152.

26. Suffolk Record Office (Lowestoft), *A Perfect Survey of the Manor of Somerleyton House*; written survey: 194/A11/11 (and transcript). See also Tom Williamson, *Suffolk's Gardens & Parks* (Macclesfield, Windgather Press, 2000), pp. 16–19 and 29.

27. Leith-Ross, *The John Tradescants*, pp. 22–3.

28. Nikolaus Pevsner described Hengrave Hall as 'one of the most important and externally one of the most impressive houses of the later years of Henry VIII' in *The Buildings of England: Suffolk*, 2nd edn, rev. Enid Radcliffe (Harmondsworth, Penguin, 1974), p. 263.

29. John Gage, *The History and Antiquities of Hengrave* (London, 1822), pp. 16–17.

30. Norman Scarfe, *The Suffolk Landscape*, revised edn (Bury St Edmunds, Suffolk, Alastair Press, 1987), p. 225. Recently returned to public access, the Hengrave Hall Manuscripts in the University of Cambridge Library may yield futher information.

31. Gage, *The Histories and Antiquities of Hengrave*, pp. 17–18

32. Ibid., pp. 181–2.

33. See G. S. H. F. Strangways, *The Home of the Hollands, 1605–1820* (London, John Murray, 1937), pp. 5–8. Cope briefly owned most of North Kensington.

34. Norman Egbert McClure (ed.), *The Letters of John Chamberlain* (2 vols, Philadelphia, American Philosophical Society, Memoirs 12, 1939), vol. 1, p. 258, letter of 7 July 1608.

35. Page, *Letters of Denization*, p. 65.

36. Historical Manuscripts Commission 9, *Calendar of the Manuscripts of the most Honourable the Marquis of Salisbury*, Part 18 (London, HMSO, 1940), p. 210, letter of 25 July 1606.

37. Canterbury Cathedral Archives, DCc-ChAnt/F.63.

38. Other possible employers put forward include Henry Brooke at Cobham Hall, Lord Burghley at Theobalds and Sir Henry Fanshawe at Ware in Hertfordshire.

39. Sir Balthazar Gerbier Kt, *A Manifestation* (London, 1651), p. 6.

40. The parish register for 23 April 1593 starkly records the family drama: 'Jeames Day,

Samuell his s. & Sara his d. were buried (Diing of the plauge) between St. Bartholomews Day and Michaellmasse Day'.

41. Leith-Ross, *The John Tradescants*, pp. 24–5. Gertrude Day's subsequent husbands were John Forrerd, [Richard] Wilcockes and George Lance.

42. See Melvyn Barnes, *Root and Branch* (London, Worshipful Company of Gardeners, 1994).

43. Guildhall Library, MS 28953, fol. 2.

44. Bodleian Library, MS Ashmole 824, Part XVI, fols 175–186.

Chapter Two, My Lord Treasurer's Gardener

1. British Library, Additional MS 72,339, fol. 147–8.

2. Robert Hill, 'Ambassadors and Art Collecting in Early Stuart Britain', *Journal of the History of Collections*, 15, 2 (2003), pp. 211–28.

3. John Parkinson, *Paradisi in Sole, Paradisus Terrestris* (London, 1629), p. 416.

4. Ibid., p. 563.

5. Hill, 'Ambassadors and Art collecting' p. 212.

6. Hatfield House Archives, The Building of Hatfield House, p. 136.

7. Hatfield House Archives, Accounts 160/1, fol. 106r.

8. Ibid., fol. 62v.

9. See Pauline Croft (ed.), *Patronage, Culture and Power* (New Haven and London, Yale University Press, 2002), and especially the chapter by Paula Henderson, 'A shared passion: the Cecils and their gardens', pp. 99–120.

10. Alan Haynes, *Robert Cecil Earl of Salisbury* (London, Peter Owen, 1989), p. 11.

11. Louis B. Wright (ed.), *Advice to a Son* (Ithaca, Cornell University Press for the Folger Shakespeare Library, 1962), p. 10.

12. Didymous Mountain, *The Gardeners Labyrinth* (London, 1577); and John Gerard, *The Herball* (London, 1597).

13. A. G. R. Smith (ed.), *The 'Anonymous Life' of William Cecil*, Studies in British History, vol. 20 (Lewiston, NY, Lampeter, 1990), quoted in Henderson, 'A shared passion', p. 99.

14. Paul Hentzner, *A Journey into England in the Year 1598*, ed. Horace Walpole (London, Strawberry Hill, 1757), pp. 54–5.

15. Malcolm Airs, '"Pomp or Glory": The Influence of Theobalds', in Croft (ed.), *Patronage, Culture and Power*, p. 10.

16. For a discussion of the building of Hatfield House, see Lawrence Stone, *Family and Fortune* (Oxford, Clarendon Press, 1973), pp. 62–91.

17. Letter from the Earl of Salisbury to Sir Thomas Lake, 15 April 1607, in Hatfield House Archives, The Building of Hatfield House, p. 1.

18. Plan of old palace, Hatfield House Archives, Cecil Papers Maps, Supp. 24.

19. Stone, *Family and Fortune*, p. 80.

20. Pauline Croft in her introduction to *Patronage, Culture and Power*, p. xv.

21. Stone, *Family and Fortune*, pp. 69–71.

22. Ibid., p. 76.

23. Samuel de Sorbière, A *Voyage to England* (London, 1709), pp. 64–5.

24. Stone, *Family and Fortune*, p. 88.

25. See Jennings's bill of November 1606 for cherries, plums, apricots and peach trees bought for the new privy garden at Theobalds, Hatfield House Archives, Bills 12.

26. Hatfield House Archives, The Building of Hatfield House, p. 192.

27. Ibid., p. 123.

28. Ibid., p. 24, Robert Bell to Thomas Wilson, 26 September 1609.

29. Ibid., p. 34, Thomas Wilson to Mr Howghton, 6 January 1610.

30. Ibid., pp. 34, 128 and 152.

31. Ibid., pp. 28, 29, 36 and 226.

32. Ibid., pp. 129 and 249.

33. Hatfield House Archives, Hatfield House & Gardens, p. 319. Watchers were employed at 6d the night to keep the deer out of the garden.

34. Ibid., p. 319. Brick dust was used to colour the earth in embroidered parterres.

35. Hatfield House Archives, The Building of Hatfield House, p. 220.

36. Ibid., p. 222, December 1609.

37. Dowsing the South Court garden by Edward Fawcett in June and July 1991 suggested a formal layout of paths, oblong flower beds, stone statue bases and stepped banks but detailed archive evidence is lacking.

38. Hatfield House Archives, The Building of Hatfield House, p. 224.

39. Hatfield House Archives, Hatfield House & Gardens, p. 321.

40. Hatfield House Archives, The Building of Hatfield House, p. 223.

41. Ibid., p. 188. 'John Tradescant's bill, for compass for the kitchen garden £2 1s 4d'.

42. Ibid., pp. 94–5, January 1612.

43. Ibid., pp. 182–7.

44. Claire Gapper, John Newman and Annabel Ricketts, 'Hatfield: a house for a Lord Treasurer', in Croft (ed.), *Patronage, Culture and Power*, p. 87.

45. Hatfield House Archives, The Building of Hatfield House, p. 148.

46. David Cecil, *The Cecils of Hatfield House* (London, Constable, 1973), p. 129.

47. Information kindly supplied by the Dowager Marchioness of Salisbury.

48. John Tradescant, *Musaeum Tradescantianum:* (London, 1656), p 183.

49. J. B. Lingard, 'The Houses of Robert Cecil, First Earl of Salisbury, 1595–1612', unpublished MA dissertation, Courtauld Institute of Art, 1981, p. 51.

Chapter Three, To the Low Countries

1. Hatfield House Archives, The Building of Hatfield House, p. 140.
2. Hatfield House Archives, General 11/25 and Bills 58/2, 58/3, 58/31, 59/-.
3. For a fascinating discussion of the emerging Dutch nation, see Simon Schama, The Embarrassment of Riches (London, Collins, 1987), pp. 69–93. The 'hat of liberty' alludes to the practice of shaving slaves' heads when they were about to be freed.
4. Ibid., p. 71.
5. Hatfield House Archives, General 11/25.
6. Peter Mundy, The Travels of Peter Mundy, vol. 4, ed. Lieut. Col. Sir Richard Carnac Temple (London, Hakluyt Society, 1925), 2nd series, no. 55, p. 61.
7. Sir William Brereton, Travels in Holland, ed. Edward Hawkins (Manchester, Chetham Society, vol. 1, 1844), p. 4.
8. Hatfield House Archives, Bills 58/2.
9. John Parkinson, Paradisi in Sole, Paradisus Terrestris, (London, 1629,) p. 520.
10. Ibid., p. 528.
11. See John Walter Stoye, English Travellers Abroad, revised edn (New Haven and London, Yale University Press, 1989), pp. 171–211.
12. Mundy, The Travels of Peter Mundy, vol. 4, pp. 60–81.
13. Brereton, Travels in Holland, p. 7.
14. Ibid., pp. 19–20.
15. Ibid., p. 55.
16. Ibid., p. 10.
17. Ibid., p. 51.
18. Quoted in Vanessa Bezemer Sellers, Courtly Gardens in Holland (Woodbridge, Garden Art Press, 2001), p. 17.
19. Brereton, Travels in Holland, p. 31.
20. Brereton went on to visit Frederik Hendrik's brand-new garden of Ter Nieuburch, laid out in the 1630s, long after Tradescant's journey.
21. Brereton, Travels in Holland, p. 19.
22. Ibid., p. 33.
23. John Ray, Observations (London, 1673), pp. 50–1.
24. Brereton, Travels in Holland, p. 38.
25. Simon Schama, Rembrandt's Eyes (London, Allen Lane/Penguin Press, 1999) p. 195.
26. Brereton, Travels in Holland, p. 38.
27. Hatfield House Archives, Bills 58/3.
28. Schama, The Embarrassment of Riches, p. 27.
29. Brereton, Travels in Holland, p. 47.

30. Ibid. p. 40.

31. John Evelyn, *The Diary of John Evelyn*, ed. E. S. de Beer (6 vols, Oxford, Clarendon Press, 2000), vol. 2, p. 52, 28 August 1641.

32. Schama, *Rembrandt's Eyes*, p. 200.

33. Much of the background on Clusius and his Leiden garden comes from L. Tjon Sie Fat and E. de Jong (eds), *The Authentic Garden* (Leiden, Clusius Foundation, 1991)

34. The Marchioness of Salisbury, *The Gardens at Hatfield House* (London, St. George's Press, 1989), p. 3.

35. From the internet (http://brunelleschi.imss.fi.it), website of the Institute and Museum of the History of Science, Florence, Italy. 'One of the most renowned gardens of late sixteenth–century Florence, the Caccini were celebrated for their rare plants. In 1607, the Flemish botanist Carolus Clusius (Charles l'Ecluse), to whom Caccini was wont to send seeds from his garden, stood in wonder before a bed of anemones that had arrived from Constantinople. '

36. Florence Hopper, 'Clusius' world, the meeting of science and art', in Tjon Sie Fat and de Jong (eds), *The Authentic Garden*, pp. 13–36.

37. Tjon Sie Fat, 'Clusius' garden: a reconstruction', in Tjon Sie Fat and de Jong (eds), *The Authentic Garden*, pp. 3–12.

38. Clusius was not the university's first choice. They had originally approached the great botanical scholar, Bernardus Paludanus.

39. For a highly entertaining account of Clusius at Leiden, see Mike Dash, *Tulipomania* (London, Victor Gollancz, 1999), pp. 51–72.

40. For a detailed description of Clusius's garden and its reconstruction see Tjon Sie Fat, 'Clusius' garden', in Tjon Sie Fat and de Jong (eds), *The Authentic Garden*.

41. Dash, *Tulipomania*, p. 60.

42. Brereton, *Travels in Holland*, p. 42.

43. Erik de Jong, 'Nature and art, the Leiden Hortus as "Musaeum"' in Tjon Sie Fat and de Jong (eds), *The Authentic Garden*, pp. 37–60.

44. From 1531 to the end of the seventeenth century, whales had mysteriously beached on the Dutch coast on more than forty occasions. See Schama, *The Embarrassment of Riches*, p. 133.

45. *Catalogue of all the Chiefest Rarities* (Leiden, 1691), quoted in Schama, *The Embarrassment of Riches*, p. 132.

46. Brereton, *Travels in Holland*, pp. 41–2.

47. Mundy, *The Travels of Peter Mundy*, vol. 4, p. 65.

48. Hatfield House Archives, Bills 58/2.

49. Hatfield House Archives, Bills 58/3.

50. Hatfield House Archives, Bills 58/3.

51. Hatfield House Archives, General 11/25 and Bills 69.

52. Hatfield House Archives, Bills 67b. A rough translation kindly supplied by Robin Harcourt Williams, archivist to the Marquess of Salisbury, reads: 'I the undersigned am borrowing hereby, against a guarantee, the sum of forty pounds sterling by order of Sir Peter van Loor, to be paid [?] by my Lord the Earl of Salisbury, [in witness of which] this has been written and signed in Antwerp on 29 Octob. and hereof two similar receipts have been made [signature?] this is the second. John Tradescant.' Van Loor was a useful source of credit for courtiers making purchases abroad. An endorsement to Hatfield House Archives, Bills 58/31, suggests that Tradescant received £60 from Peter van Loor 'uppon two bills of exchange'.

53. Hatfield House Archives, Bills 58/2.

54. Parkinson, *Paradisi in Sole*, p. 574.

55. Hatfield House Archives, Bills 58/2.

56. Historical Manuscripts Commission 75, Downshire MSS, vol. 3 (1938), p. 182.

57. Hatfield House Archives, General 11/25.

Chapter Four, French Exotics

1. Thomas Coryat, *Coryat's Crudities* (2 vols, Glasgow, James MacLehose & Sons, 1905), vol. 1. p. 171.

2. John Walter Stoye, *English Travellers Abroad*, revised edn (New Haven and London, Yale University Press, 1989), p. 19.

3. Coryat, *Coryat's Crudities*, pp. 158–9.

4. Quoted in *Encyclopedia Britannica* (2002).

5. Traveller Peter Mundy visited the Louvre in 1620 and describing the Long Gallery as '600 paces long, one side full of windowes, looking downe into the River and the Kings Gardens, full of curious knots and rare Inventions'. Peter Mundy, *The Travels of Peter Mundy*, vol. 1, ed. Lieut. Col. Sir Richard Carnac Temple (Cambridge, Hakluyt Society, 1907), 2nd series, no. 17, pp. 127–8.

6. Kenneth Woodbridge, *Princely Gardens* (London, Thames & Hudson, 1986), pp. 97–118.

7. Hatfield House Archives, Bills 58/31.

8. Historical Manuscripts Commission, *Downshire MS*, vol. 2 (1936), p. 299.

9. Hatfield House Archives, General 11/25.

10. According to Antoine Schnapper, the actual site is disputed – see *Le Géant, La Licorne et La Tulipe* (Paris, Flammarion, 1988). Marjorie Warner located the garden on the Ile Notre Dame. Another site given is west of the Ile de la Cité, now the Place Dauphine.

11. Marjorie F. Warner, 'Jean and Vespasien Robin', *The National Horticultural Magazine*, 35, 4 (October 1956), pp. 214–20.

12. See Guy de la Brosse, *Description du Jardin Royal des Plantes Medicinales* (Paris, 1636), p. 14.

13. John Gerard, *The Herball* (London, 1597), p. 122.

14. Ibid., p. 196.

15. Cartier made three journeys between 1534 and 1542.

16. Pierre Vallet, *Le Jardin du Roy Tres Chrestien Henry IV* (Paris, 1608).

17. Warner, 'Jean and Vespasien Robin', p. 220.

18. See Chapters 12 and 15.

19. MS Ashmole 824, Part XVI (fols 175–186v.).

20. Tradescant listed it in his 1634 plant catalogue as 'Locusta Virginia arbor'. See Warner, 'Jean and Vespasein Robin', p. 220.

21. Josephine Bacon, 'Oranges and Orangeries', *The Connoisseur*, October 1981, vol. 208, no. 836, pp. 101–3.

22. Parkinson, *Paradisi in Sole*, p. 584.

23. Ibid., p. 401.

24. Hatfield House Archives, General 11/25 and Bills 58/31.

25. Woodbridge, *Princely Gardens*, p. 114.

26. Mundy, *The Travels of Peter Mundy*, vol. 1, pp. xix–xx.

27. John Evelyn, *The Diary of John Evelyn*, ed. E. S. de Beer (6 vols, Oxford, Clarendon Press, 1955), vol. 2, pp. 122–4, 19 March 1644.

28. Ibid., vol. 2, p. 124.

29. Hatfield House Archives, Bills 59.

30. These would have been used for garden structures – see, for instance, Didymous Mountain, *The Gardeners Labyrinth* (London, 1577), p. 22: 'The Herber in a Garden may bee framed with Juniper poles, or the Willowe, eyther to stretch, or be bound togither with Osyers.'

31. Hatfield House Archives, The Building of Hatfield House, p. 165.

Chapter Five, Waterworks and Vines

1. Samuel de Sorbière, *A Voyage to England* (London, 1709), p. 65.

2. Jacques Androuet du Cerceau, *Les plus excellents bastiments de France* (Paris, 1576–79). See also Paula Henderson, 'A shared passion: the Cecils and their gardens', in Pauline Croft (ed.), *Patronage, Culture and Power* (New Haven and London, Yale University Press, 2002), pp. 99–120.

3. National Archives, SP 14/48.

4. British Library, Lansdowne MS 89, fols 92v.–93.

5. See Chapter 2.

6. Quoted in Henderson, 'A shared passion', p. 111.

7. Historical Manuscripts Commission, *Calendar of the Manuscripts of the Most Hon. The Marquis of Salisbury*, vol. 12 (Hereford, HMSO, 1910), p. 407, letter of 30 September 1602 from Roger Houghton to Sir Robert Cecil.

8. British Library, Additional MS 27,278, fols 24–25v.

9. Sir Francis Bacon, 'Of gardens', in *The Essayes or Counsels*, ed. Michael Kiernan (Oxford, Clarendon Press, 1985), pp. 139–45.

10. See Paula Henderson, 'Sir Francis Bacon's Water Gardens at Gorhambury', in *Garden History, The Journal of the Garden History Society*, 20, 2 (Autumn 1992), pp. 116–31.

11. British Library, Additional MS 27,278, fol. 25v.

12. Sir Francis Bacon, 'Of gardens', pp. 142–3.

13. See Chapter 24.

14. Both examples are quoted by Malcolm Airs in '"Pomp or glory": the influence of Theobalds', in Croft (ed.), *Patronage, Culture and Power*, p. 15.

15. Hatfield House Archives, The Building of Hatfield House, p. 78, provides estimates for pipework, besides Jennings' charges.

16. Hatfield House Archives, The Building of Hatfield House, p. 224, bill relating to January 1611. The 'Frenchman' is presumably Salomon de Caus.

17. Ibid., p. 78.

18. Ibid., pp. 79–82.

19. Hatfield House Archives, Hatfield House and Gardens, p. 155.

20. Hatfield House Archives, The Building of Hatfield House, p. 40, letter from Thomas Wilson to Lord Salisbury, 25 November 1611.

21. Ibid., p. 282.

22. Salomon de Caus, *Hortus Palatinus* (Frankfurt, 1620).

23. Salomon de Caus, *Les Raisons des forces mouvantes* (Paris, 1615).

24. De Sorbière, A Voyage to England, p. 65.

25. Hatfield House Archives, The Building of Hatfield House, p. 298.

26. Hatfield House Archives, CPM I/15.

27. Kenneth Woodbridge, *Princely Gardens* (London, Thames & Hudson, 1986), p. 110.

28. Hatfield House Archives, The Building of Hatfield House, p. 40, letter from Thomas Wilson to Lord Salisbury, 25 November 1611.

29. De Sorbière, A Voyage to England, p. 65.

30. John Evelyn, *The Diary of John Evelyn*, ed. E. S. de Beer (6 vols, Oxford, Clarendon Press, 2000), vol. 2, p. 80.

31. Samuel Pepys, *The Diary of Samuel Pepys*, ed. Robert Latham and William Matthews (11 vols, London, Bell & Hyman, 1970–83), vol. 2, pp. 138–9, 22 July 1661.

32. William Brenchley Rye, *England as seen by Foreigners* (London, 1865), p. 52, account by Jacob Rathgeb, private secretary to Frederick, Duke of Wirtemberg.

33. See E. M. Carus-Wilson, *Medieval Merchant Venturers* (London, Methuen & Co., 1954), pp. 267–9.

34. Hatfield House Archives, The Building of Hatfield House, p. 28, letter of 2 October 1609, Sir Michael Hicks to the Earl of Salisbury.

35. Hatfield House Archives, The Building of Hatfield House, p. 38, letter of 5 February 1610/11, Thomas Wilson to the Earl of Salisbury.

36. John Rose, *The English Vineyard Vindicated* (London, 1666).

37. This jibe at French fashions is a little puzzling from the man who translated Nicolas de Bonnefons's *The French Gardiner* (London, 1658).

38. Rose, *The English Vineyard Vindicated*, pp. 2–3.

39. Hatfield House Archives, The Building of Hatfield House, p. 233, bill for July 1612.

40. Ibid., p. 257.

41. Thomas Fuller, *The History of the Worthies of England* (4 vols, London, 1662), vol. 2, p. 17.

Chapter Six, Muck and Mystery

1. Hatfield House Archives, The Building of Hatfield House, p. 98.

2. John Parkinson, *Paradisi in Sole, Paradisus Terrestris* (London, 1629), pp. 461–2.

3. Sir Hugh Platt, *Floraes Paradise* (London, 1608), p. 95.

4. Ibid., p. 45.

5. Sir Hugh Platt, *The Jewell House of Art and Nature* (London, 1594), Part 2, p. 59.

6. Ralph Austen, *A Treatise of Fruit-Trees* (Oxford, 1653), p. 66.

7. Samuel Hartlib, *Samuel Hartlib his Legacie* (London, 1651), pp. 43–9.

8. Hatfield House Archives, Hatfield House & Gardens, p. 317.

9. John Evelyn (trans.), *The French Gardiner* (London, 1669), pp. 98–105.

10. Hatfield House Archives, The Building of Hatfield House, pp. 86–7, note dated 1 July 1611.

11. Hatfield House Archives, Bills 69, April 1612.

12. Parkinson, *Paradisi in Sole*, pp. 530–2.

13. Hatfield House Archives, Bills 69, May 1612.

14. Parkinson, *Paradisi in Sole*, p. 461.

15. See Chapter 2.

16. John Evelyn, *Directions for The Gardiner at Says-Court*, ed. Geoffrey Keynes (Nonesuch Press, 1932).

17. Ibid., p. 96.

18. Ibid., p. 100.

19. Ibid., pp. 101–3.

20. Ibid., p. 98.

21. Tradescant claimed for wages paid to these women weeders in August 1612: Mabell Colyer, Margret Rofe, Ellyn Loughton, Jone Davis, Jone Buk, Ellyn Renalls, paid 6d a day, with an unexplained additional 3d to their monthly wages.

22. Hatfield House Archives, The Building of Hatfield House, pp. 136–7.

23. Thomas Tusser, *Five Hundred Points of Good Husbandry*, ed. Geoffrey Grigson (Oxford University Press, 1984), p. 177. The text is that of the edition of 1580.

24. For details of his leases, see Prudence Leith-Ross, *The John Tradescants* (London, Peter Owen, 1984), p. 43.

25. Hatfield House Archives, General 7/13.

26. Hatfield House Archives, General 103/28.

27. Hatfield House Archives, Bills 71.

28. John Rose, *The English Vineyard Vindicated* (London, 1666).

29. Sir Francis Bacon, 'Of gardens', in *The Essayes or Counsels*, ed. Michael Kiernan (Oxford, Clarendon Press, 1985), pp 139–45.

30. Parkinson, *Paradisi in Sole*, taken from 'The Epistle to the Courteous Reader'.

31. Ralph Austen, *A Treatise of Fruit-Trees* (Oxford, 1653).

32. William Lawson, *A New Orchard and Garden with The Country Housewifes Garden* (1618), ed. Malcolm Thick (Totnes, Devon, Prospect Books, 2003), pp. 35–6. This edition is a facsimile of the 1656 printing.

33. See Rebecca Bushnell, *Green Desire* (Ithaca and London, Cornell University Press, 2003), pp. 55–9.

34. Platt, *Floraes Paradise*, pp. 1–16.

35. Ibid., pp. 174–5.

36. Sir Thomas Hanmer, *The Garden Book of Sir Thomas Hanmer Bart* (London, Gerald Howe, 1933), p. 13.

37. Sir Hugh Plat[sic], *The Garden of Eden* (London, 1653), p. 86.

38. Parkinson, *Paradisi in Sole*, pp. 23–5.

39. See Chapter 8.

40. Parkinson, *Paradisi in Sole*, pp. 23–5.

41. Nehemiah Grew, *The Anatomy of Plants* (London, 1682).

42. William Shakespeare, *The Winter's Tale*, Act IV, scene iv (London, The Arden Shakespeare, 1963), ed. H. P. Pafford, p. 94. Early in the eighteenth century, London nurseryman Thomas Fairchild produced the first deliberate hybrid plant (known as Fairchild's mule) by crossing a gillyflower and a sweet william. See Michael Leapman, *The Ingenious Mr Fairchild* (London, Headline Books, 2000).

43. See Chapter 18.

44. John Prest, *The Garden of Eden* (New Haven and London, Yale University Press, 1981), pp. 50–2.

Chapter Seven, Death of a Lord

1. John Nichols, *The Progresses and Public Processions of Queen Elizabeth* (London, 1788), vol. 2, p. 22 of 'The Queen's Progress, 1601'.

2. Lawrence Stone, *Family and Fortune* (Oxford, Clarendon Press, 1973), p. 93.

3. London County Council, *Survey of London*, vol. 18, *The Strand* (London, 1937), pp. 120–1.

4. J. B. Lingard, 'The Houses of Robert Cecil, First Earl of Salisbury, 1595–1612', unpublished MA dissertation, Courtauld Institute of Art, 1981.

5. Hatfield House Archives, Accounts 160/1, no. 42.

6. Hon. Alicia Amherst, *A History of Gardening in England* (London, 1895), p. 68.

7. Lingard, 'The Houses of Robert Cecil'.

8. Hatfield House Archives, Bills 59, 5 January 1611/1612.

9. Hatfield House Archives, Family Papers, Second Supplement, I/176.

10. Hatfield House Archives, Bills 59.

11. David Cecil, *The Cecils of Hatfield House* (London, Constable, 1973), p. 148.

12. Inigo Jones and William Davenant, *Britannia Triumphans: A Masque* (London, 1637); see also Lingard, 'The Houses of Robert Cecil', p. 42.

13. Lingard, 'The Houses of Robert Cecil', p. 39.

14. Hatfield House Archives, Accounts 160/1.

15. Map by John Norden of Cranborne Manor, Dorset, c.1610, Hatfield House, CPM Supp. 87.

16. Norman Egbert McClure (ed.), *The Letters of John Chamberlain* (2 vols, Philadelphia, American Philosophical Society, Memoirs 12, 1939), vol. 1, p. 338.

17. Ibid., vol. 1, pp. 341–2, letter to Sir Dudley Carleton of 25 March 1612.

18. Ibid., vol. 1, p. 346, letter to Sir Dudley Carleton of 29 April 1612.

19. Ibid., vol. 1, pp. 350–1, letter to Sir Dudley Carleton of 27 May, 1612.

20. Ibid., vol. 1, pp. 364–5, letter to Sir Dudley Carleton of 2 July 1612.

21. Cecil, *The Cecils of Hatfield House*, p. 118.

22. Hatfield House Archives, Bills 69/28.

23. Cecil, *The Cecils of Hatfield House*, p. 160.

24. See Pauline Croft, 'The Reputation of Robert Cecil', *Transactions of the Royal Historical Society* (6th series, vol. 1, 1991).

25. Lynn Hulse, in Pauline Croft (ed.), *Patronage, Culture and Power* (New Haven and London, Yale University Press, 2002), pp. 139–58.

26. *Calendar of State Papers, Domestic Series, Charles I, 1627–28* (Nendeln, Liechtenstein, Kraus Reprint, 1967), p. 556.

27. The Hatfield House wages bill records payments to John Tradescant of £5 15s for the quarters ending Christmas 1613 and Lady Day 1614. See Hatfield House Archives,

Accounts 13/18. Bills 57/2 showed that he received £12 10s for the quarter ending Christmas 1611.

28. Hatfield House Archives, Bills 77, 19 November 1613.

29. Hatfield House Archives, Bills 82.

30. Hatfield House Archives, Box G/14.

31. Ibid., p. 145.

Chapter Eight, Canterbury Belles

1. C. W. Chalklin, *Seventeenth-Century Kent* (London, Longmans, 1965), p. 50.

2. Norman Egbert McClure (ed.), *The Letters of John Chamberlain* (2 vols, Philadelphia, American Philosophical Society, Memoirs 12, 1939), vol. 1, p. 180.

3. Ibid., vol. 1, p. 614, letter to Sir Dudley Carleton at Venice of 15 September 1615.

4. Ibid., vol. 2, pp. 19–21, letter to Sir Dudley Carleton at The Hague of 24 August 1616.

5. Ibid., vol. 2, p. 24, letter to Sir Dudley Carleton of 12 October 1616.

6. John Parkinson, *Paradisi in Sole, Paradisus Terrestris* (London, 1629), p. 378.

7. Ibid., p. 141.

8. Ibid., p. 430.

9. N. F., *The Husbandman's fruitfull Orchard* (London, 1609).

10. In a letter to Sir Dudley Carleton, announcing Cecil's death, John Chamberlain also noted that Wotton had 'bought lately Canterbury Parke of [Cecil] for 12000l'. McClure (ed.), *The Letters of John Chamberlain*, vol. 1, p. 351.

11. Margaret Sparks, 'The Abbey site 1538–1997', in Richard Gem (ed.), *Book of St Augustine Abbey* (London, Batsford, 1997), pp. 143–61. See also Antony Charles Ryan, *The Abbey and Palace of St. Augustine Canterbury* (Canterbury, Old Manse Publications, 2nd edn, 2001).

12. Cobham's principal seat was Cobham Hall in Kent.

13. Canterbury Cathedral Archives, Map 123, Map of Canterbury c.1640.

14. Chalklin, *Seventeenth-Century Kent*, pp. 31–2. In the 1630s, there were 900 alien communicants at Canterbury.

15. L. G. Wickham Legg (ed.), 'A relation of a short survey of the western counties', *Camden Miscellany*, vol. 16 (London, Royal Historical Society, 1936).

16. Ibid., pp. 18–19.

17. See Chapter 12; and Margaret Toynbee, 'The Wedding Journey of King Charles I', *Archaeologia Cantiana* (Ashford, Kent Archaeological Society, 1956), vol. 69, pp. 75–83.

18. National Archives, State Papers Domestic 14/113, fol. 85, letter of 27 March 1620. See also *Calendar of State Papers Domestic Series, James I, 1619–1623* (London, HMSO, 1858), p. 133.

19. Christopher Thacker, *The Genius of Gardening* (London, Weidenfeld & Nicolson, 1994), p. 77.

20. T. F. T. Baker (ed.), A History of the County of Middlesex, vol. 10, Hackney Parish (London, Oxford University Press for the Institute of Historical Research, 1995), p. 11.

21. William Robinson, The History and Antiquities of the Parish of Hackney (2 vols, London, 1842–3), vol. 1, p. 131.

22. Sir Hugh Plat [sic], The Garden of Eden (London, 1653), pp. 143–4.

23. G. E. Manwaring (ed.), The Life and Works of Sir Henry Mainwaring (Navy Records Society, vol. 54, 1920), vol. 1.

24. Ibid., vol. 1, pp. 69–71.

25. Parkinson, Paradisi in Sole, pp. 465–6.

26. Ibid., p. 525.

27. John Evelyn (trans.), The French Gardiner (London, 1669), p. 138.

28. British Library, Eve.b.42, p. 466.

29. Evelyn (trans.), The French Gardiner, p. 152.

30. Parkinson, Paradisi in Sole, p. 466.

31. Bodleian Library, MS Ashmole 824, Part XXIV, fol. 254.

32. Ibid., fols 250–3.

33. I am indebted to Mike Webb, Head of Cataloguing, Western Manuscripts, at the Bodleian Library, Oxford, for examining the handwriting in the two manuscripts. Writers of the time would often mix 'gentlemanly' italic with the more businesslike secretary handwriting.

34. See appendix to Robert H. Jeffers (ed.), John Rose, The English Vineyard Vindicated (Falls Village, Connecticut, Herb Grower Press, 1965).

35. Bodleian Library, MS Ashmole 824, Part XXIV, fols 250–3.

36. Lord Braybrooke (ed.), The Private Correspondence of Jane Lady Cornwallis (Audley End, 1842), p. 164.

37. See Karen Hearn, 'Sir Nathaniel Bacon I, Horticulturalist and artist', and Barrie Juniper, 'Sir Nathaniel Bacon II, the vegetable world', The British Art Journal, 1, 2 (Spring, 2000), pp. 13–18.

38. John Tradescant, Musaeum Tradescantianum (London, 1656), p. 40.

39. Details of school life are taken from Thomas Hinde, Imps of Promise (London, James & James, 1990).

40. A claim made by historian Arthur Leach in a letter to The Times in 1896.

41. Canterbury Cathedral Archives, Dean and Chapter Canterbury Cathedral, signature of John Tradescant from Miscellaneous Accounts (DCc/MA/41).

42. Hinde, Imps of Promise, p. 12.

43. Information kindly supplied by Peter Pollack, Archivist at the King's School. Prize money of 13s 4d was recorded in the Dean and Chapter Accounts for 1626.

44. William Somner, The Antiquities of Canterbury (London, 1640).

Chapter Nine, A Virginian Adventure

1. John Prest, *The Garden of Eden* (New Haven and London, Yale University Press, 1981), p. 39.

2. John R. Hébert, 'The westward vision', in Richard W. Stephenson and Marianne M. McKee (eds), *Virginia in Maps* (Richmond, Virginia, Library of Virginia, 2000), p. 6.

3. For general background on colonization, see Kenneth R. Andrews, *Trade, Plunder and Settlement* (Cambridge University Press, 1984).

4. See David Beers Quinn (ed.), *The Roanoke Voyages, 1584–1590* (2 vols, London, 1955 Hakluyt Society, series 2, vols 104 and 105).

5. For much of the context to the English settlement of Virginia, I am indebted to a presentation by Dr John Appleby of Liverpool Hope University College at the National Maritime Museum, Greenwich, on 29 April 2004. Martha W. McCartney has provided one of the clearest histories of the Jamestown settlement in her three–volume work: *Documentary History of Jamestown Island* (Williamsburg, VA, Colonial Williamsburg Foundation and College of William and Mary, 2000).

6. Quoted in Hon. Alicia Amherst, *A History of Gardening in England* (London, 1895), p. 148. For details of individual investments, see Alexander Brown, *The Genesis of the United States* (2 vols, New York, Russell & Russell Inc., 1964), vol. 2, pp. 807–1068.

7. Robert H. Jeffers, *The Friends of John Gerard* (Falls Village, Connecticut, Herb Grower Press, 1967–9), pp. 14–15.

8. Brown, *The Genesis of the United States*, vol. 2, p. 858. The amount subscribed by the Company of Gardeners is blank.

9. For a discussion of the Company's financing and its three royal charters, see Wesley Frank Craven, *The Virginia Company of London, 1606–1624*, Jamestown 350th Anniversary Historical Booklets, no. 5 (Williamsburg, VA, 1957).

10. Philip L. Barbour (ed.), *The Jamestown Voyages*, Hakluyt Society, 2nd series, vols 136 and 137 (2 vols, Cambridge University Press for the Society, 1969), vol. 1, pp. 49–54.

11. The 'Other Sea' was the Pacific Ocean, which early maps continued to show just over the Appalachian Mountains.

12. Barbour (ed.), *The Jamestown Voyages*, vol. 1, p. 54.

13. *Dictionary of National Biography*, online edn, 2004, based largely on Smith's own account, 'which may be credited with a substratum of fact'.

14. Philip L. Barbour (ed.), *The Complete Works of Captain John Smith* (3 vols, Williamsburg, VA, University of North Carolina Press for the Institute of Early American History and Culture, 1986), vol. 3, pp. 382–4.

15. Bodleian Library, MS Ashmole 1758. See A. C. Mare, 'Manuscripts and printed books in the Bodleian Library', in Arthur MacGregor (ed.), *Tradescant's Rarites* (Oxford, Clarendon Press, 1983). p. 357.

16 Quoted in Barbour (ed), *The Jamestown Voyages*, vol. 1, pp. 133–4.

17. To appreciate how the native population felt about the alien invasion of their land, see Helen C. Rountree, *Pocahontas, Powhatan, Opechancanough* (Charlottesville and London, University of Virginia Press, 2005).

18. Barbour (ed.), *The Jamestown Voyages*, vol. 1, p. 136.

19. Ibid., vol. 1, p. 141.

20. Ibid., vol. 1, p. 139.

21. Barbour (ed.), *The Complete Works of Captain John Smith*, vol. 1, pp. 151–3.

22. Barbour (ed.), *The Jamestown Voyages*, vol. 1, pp. 143–4.

23. Charles E. Hatch Jnr, *The First Seventeen Years*, Jamestown 350th Anniversary Historical Booklets, no. 6 (Williamsburg, VA, 1957).

24. Barbour (ed.), *The Complete Works of Captain John Smith*, vol. 1, p. 143.

25. Rountree, *Pocahontas, Powhatan, Opechancanough*, p. 50; and William M. Kelso with Beverly Straube, *Jamestown Rediscovery 1994–2004* (Richmond, VA, Association for the Preservation of Virginia Antiquities, 2004), p. 28.

26. Barbour (ed.), *The Jamestown Voyages*, vol. 2, p. 322.

27. Barbour (ed.), *The Complete Works of Captain John Smith*, vol. 2, p. 151.

28. Ibid., vol. 1, p. 213.

29. Rountree, *Pocahontas, Powhatan, Opechancanough*, pp. 76–82.

30. William Strachey, *The Historie of Travell into Virginia Britania*, ed. Louis B. Wright and Virginia Freund (London, Hakluyt Society, 2nd series, no. 53, 1953), p. 72.

31. John Smith, *The Generall Historie of Virginia* (London, 1624), pp. 121–3.

32. Barbour (ed.), *The Jamestown Voyages*, vol. 2, pp. 369–72.

33. Gregory A. Waselkov, 'Indian maps of the colonial southeast', in Peter H. Wood, Gregory A. Waselkov and M. Thomas Hatley (eds), *Powhatan's Mantle* (Lincoln and London, University of Nebraska Press, c 1989) pp. 292–343.

34. Christian F. Feest in MacGregor (ed.), *Tradescant's Rarities*, p. 135.

35. John Tradescant, *Museum Tradescantianum* (London, 1656), p. 47.

36. Barbour (ed.), *The Jamestown Voyages*, vol. 2, pp. 413–14.

37. Ibid., vol. 2, p. 456.

38. Craven, *The Virginia Company of London*, p. 21.

39. McCartney, *Documentary History of Jamestown Island*, vol. 1, pp. 24–5.

40. *Dictionary of National Biography*, online edn, 2004.

41. A contemporary account of Pocahontas's seizure appeared in Ralph Hamor, *A True Discourse of the Present State of Virginia* (Richmond, VA, Virginia State Library Publications, no. 3, 1957, reprinted from the London edn, 1615), p. 4.

42. For Rolfe's letter to Sir Thomas Dale, see Hamor, *A True Discourse*, pp. 61–8.

43. Strachey, *The History of Travell*, p. 62; see also Rountree, *Pocahontas, Powhatan, Opechancanough*, pp. 156–67.

44. See McCartney, *Documentary History of Jamestown Island*, vol. 1, pp. 41–2, and Rountree, *Pocahontas, Powhatan, Opechancanough*, pp. 176–85.

45. Barbour (ed.), *The Complete Works of Captain John Smith*, vol. 2, pp. 258–62.

46. Norman Egbert McClure (ed.), *The Letters of John Chamberlain* (2 vols, Philadelphia, American Philosophical Society, Memoirs 12, 1939), vol. 2, pp. 49–50, letter to Sir Dudley Carlton at The Hague of 18 January 1617.

47. Later portraits would Europeanize her features but this is the only one taken from life.

48. McClure (ed.), *The Letters of John Chamberlain*, vol. 2, p. 50, letter to Sir Dudley Carleton at The Hague of 18 January 1617.

49. Ibid., vol 2, p. 66, letter to Sir Dudley Carleton at The Hague of 29 March 1617.

50. Barbour (ed.), *The Complete Works of Captain John Smith*, vol. 2, pp. 258–62.

51. Ibid., vol. 2, p. 262.

52. Barbour (ed.), *The Jamestown Voyages*, vol. 2, p. 459.

53. National Archives, CO 1/2, Part 2, fol.157, 12 February 1616/17. The associates in the plantation are: Sr Wm Lovelace Knt, Sr Antho, Aucher Knt, Mabell Lady Cullamore, John Argoll Esquire, John Tredescant, Capt. Sam Argall.

54. Craven, *The Virginia Company of London*, pp. 31–2.

55. For more on the headrights system, see Chapter 21.

56. David B. Quinn, 'A List of Books Purchased for the Virginia Company', *The Virginia Magazine of History and Biography*, 77, 3 (1969).

57. Charles Estienne and John Liebault, *Maison Rustique, or The Countrie Farme*, trans. Richard Surflet (London, 1600), pp. 280–92.

58 King James I, *A Counter-Blaste to Tobacco* (1604) in Edmund Goldsmid (ed.) *Bibliotheca Curiosa* (Edinburgh, 1884), p. 32. Tobacco was associated with the bawdy houses where it was commonly smoked.

59. John Gerard, *The Herball* (London, 1633), p. 359.

60. Barbour (ed.), *The Complete Works of Captain John Smith*, vol. 2, p. 262.

61. Craven, *The Virginia Company of London*, p. 34.

62. For a brief history of Argall's Town see McCartney, *Documentary History of Jamestown Island*, vol. 1, pp. 42–5, and Charles E. Hatch, *The First Seventeen Years*, pp. 36–7.

63. Quoted in Hatch, *The First Seventeen Years*, pp. 36–7.

64. McCartney, *Documentary History of Jamestown Island*, vol. 1, p. 45; see also Michael Jarvis and Jeroen van Driel, 'The Vingboons Chart of the James River', *William & Mary Quarterly*, 3rd series, vol. 54 (1997), pp. 377–94.

65. Martha W. McCartney, 'An Early Virginia Census Reprised', *Quarterly Bulletin, Archeological Society of Virginia*, 54, 4 (December 1999), p. 186.

66. 'Instructions to Governor Yeardley 1618', *The Virginia Magazine of History and Biography*, vol. 2 (year ending June 1895), p. 163.

NOTES TO PAGES 111–116

67. Quoted in Peter Wilson Coldham, 'The Voyage of the *Neptune* to Virginia, 1618–1619', *The Virginia Magazine of History and Biography*, vol. 87 (1979), p. 36.

68. Henry F. Waters, *Genealogical Gleanings in England* (2 vols, Boston, 1901), vol. 2, pp. 919–20.

69. S. M. Kingsbury (ed.), *The Records of the Virginia Company of London*, vol. 4 (4 vols, Washington, Library of Congress, 1906–35), p. 229.

70. *Calendar of State Papers, Colonial Series, 1574–1660*, ed. W. Noel Sainsbury (Vaduz, Kraus Reprint, 1964), vol. 1, p. 43; see also McCartney, *Documentary History of Jamestown Island*, vol. 3, pp. 313–15. Tradescant's predecessor at Oatlands Palace was John Bonnell or Bonoeil, who is credited with selecting the French vignerons who settled in Virginia to promote the culture of grapes. See *William & Mary Quarterly*, 1st series, vol. 12 (1903–4), p. 289.

71. John Parkinson, *Paradisi in Sole, Paradisus Terrestris* (London, 1629), p. 152.

72. John Gerard, *The Herball* (London, 1633), p. 49.

Chapter Ten, A Muscovy Rose

1. Bodleian Library, MS Ashmole 824, Part XVI, fols. 175r.–186v. A full transcript of the diary (with punctuation added) appears in Prudence Leith-Ross, *The John Tradescants* (London, Peter Owen, 1984), pp. 53–65.

2. W. H. Black, *A Descriptive, Analytical, and Critical Catalogue of the Manuscripts Bequeathed by Elias Ashmole* (Oxford University Press, 1845), p. 470.

3. Preface to Dr J. Hamel, *England and Russia*, trans. John Studdy Leigh (London, 1854), pp. iv–v.

4. G. S. Boulger, 'The First Russian Botanist', *The Journal of Botany, British and Foreign*, ed. James Britten, vol. 33 (London, 1895), pp. 33–8.

5. John Parkinson, *Paradisi in Sole, Paradisus Terrestris* (London, 1629), p. 346.

6. Hamel, *England and Russia*, pp. 254–5.

7. Tradescant did not continue to Moscow with the main part of the mission, and he did not list himself among the principal figures of the delegation.

8. See, for instance, Leith-Ross, *The John Tradescants*, p. 52.

9. Geraldine M. Phipps, *Sir John Merrick* (Newtonville, Mass., Oriental Research Partners, 1983), p. 5.

10. John Stoye, *English Travellers Abroad*, revised edn (New Haven and London, Yale University Press, 1989), p. 48.

11. Robert Brenner, *Merchants and Revolution* (Cambridge University Press, 1993), p. 13.

12. See Phipps, *Sir John Merrick*, pp. 134–51.

13. Ibid., p. 137.

14. The quotations from Tradescant's Russian diary are from Bodleian Library, MS

Ashmole 824, Part XVI, fols 175r.–186v., supplemented by Leith-Ross, *The John Tradescants*, pp. 53–65.

15. There is no good reason to accept Hamel's assertion that Tradescant gave himself the pseudonym of 'Jonns an Coplie'.

16. An equivalent journey today, travelling at a steady speed of twelve nautical miles an hour, would take just a little over seven days.

17. John Tradescant, *Musaeum Tradescantianum* (London, 1656), p. 4.

18. Ibid., p. 1.

19. Peter Mundy, *The Travels of Peter Mundy*, vol. 4, ed. Lieut. Col. Sir Richard Carnac Temple (London, Hakluyt Society, 1925), 2nd series, no. 55, p. 129.

20. E. D. Morgan and C. H. Coote (eds), *Early Voyages and Travels to Russia and Persia by Anthony Jenkinson*, vol. 1 (London, Hakluyt Society, 1886), p. 22.

21. Tradescant, *Musaeum Tradescantianum*, pp. 47–51.

22. Ibid., p. 54.

23. Mundy, *The Travels of Peter Mundy*, vol. 4, p. 134.

24. Hamel, *England and Russia*, p. 263.

25. Dr Hamel identified this functionary as Peter Perfirjeff, chief of the Strelitzes at Archangel. Ibid., p. 264.

26. William Shakespeare, *Othello*, Act I, Scene iii, verses 143–5 (London, The Arden Shakespeare, 3rd series, 1997), ed. A. J. Honigmann, p. 144.

27. Mundy, *The Travels of Peter Mundy*, vol. 4, p. 137.

28. Gerrit de Veer, *The Three Voyages of William Barents to the Arctic Regions*, 2nd edn, ed, Lieut. K. Beynen (London, Hakluyt Society, 1875), p. xii.

29. From Paul Hentzner's travels in England in 1598, quoted in William Brenchley Rye, *England as Seen by Foreigners* (London, 1865), p. 111.

30. Mundy, *The Travels of Peter Mundy*, vol. 4, p. 152. The bears were in the English court, 'some tied, some loose'.

31. Ibid., vol. 4, p. 135.

32. Ibid., vol. 4, p. 145.

33. Ibid., vol. 4, p. 142.

34. Quoted in Boulger, 'The First Russian Botanist', p. 34.

35. John Tradescant, *Plantarum in Horto Johannem Tradescanti* (1634).

36. *Catalogus Plantarum*, attached to Tradescant, *Musaeum Tradescantianum* (London, 1656).

37. Boulger, 'The First Russian Botanist', p. 37.

38. Ibid., p. 38.

39. John Parkinson, *Theatrum Botanicum* (London, 1640), p. 705.

40. Hamel, *England and Russia*, p. 272.

41. Mundy, *The Travels of Peter Mundy*, vol. 4, pp. 148–9.

42. Boulger, 'The First Russian Botanist', p. 38.

43. See Phipps, *Sir John Merrick*, pp. 149–51.

44. Bodleian Library, MS Tanner 74, fols 121–3, Digges to the Marquess of Buckingham, 31 July 1618.

Chapter Eleven, Pirates of the Mediterranean

1. John Parkinson, *Paradisi in Sole, Paradisus Terrestris* (London, 1629), p. 579.

2. John Evelyn, *The Diary of John Evelyn*, ed. E. S. de Beer, (6 vols, Oxford, Clarendon Press, 2000), vol. 2, p. 38, August 1641.

3. Bodleian Library, MS Ashmole 824, fol. 167v, lists 'John Tredescant' among the 'shott' (presumably gunners) on the *Mercury* (as opposed to the 'Rowers').

4. Much of the background to the Levant trade is from Kenneth R. Andrews, *Trade, Plunder and Settlement* (Cambridge University Press, 1984), pp. 87–100.

5. John Gerard, *The Herball* (London, 1597), p. 151.

6. Parkinson, *Paradisi in Sole*, p. 420.

7. John Gerard, *The Herball* (London, 1633), p. 754.

8. Gerard, *The Herball* (1597), p. 472.

9. Ibid., p. 753.

10. Ibid., p. 1304.

11. Ibid., pp. 1329–30.

12. John Parkinson, *Theatrum Botanicum* (London, 1640), pp. 1108–9. Parkinson complained that Boel gave many plants from his Spanish trip 'of love' to another plant collector, William Coys, who had a famous Essex garden called Stubbers (ibid., p. 1064).

13. Parkinson, *Paradisi in Sole*, p. 103.

14. Ibid., p. 236.

15. The main source used for Barbary pirates and the Algiers expedition was David Delison Hebb, *Piracy and the English Government* (Aldershot, Scolar Press, 1994). Also consulted were J. S. Corbett, *England in the Mediterranean* (London, 1904); Christopher Lloyd, *English Corsairs on the Barbary Coast* (London, Collins, 1981); and Daniel J. Vitkus, *Piracy, Slavery and Redemption* (New York, Columbia University Press, 2001).

16. Paul Hentzner in William Brenchley Rye, *England as Seen by Foreigners* (London, 1865), p. 110.

17. Hebb, *Piracy and the English Government*, p. 9.

18. James I, *His Majesties Poeticall Exercises at Vacant Houres* (Edinburgh, 1591).

19. Sir Henry Mainwaring, 'On the Beginnings, practices, and suppression of pirates', in G. E. Manwaring and W. G. Perrin (eds), *The Life and Works of Sir Henry Mainwaring*, vol. 2, (Navy Records Society, vol. 56, 1922), pp. 3–49.

20. For Mainwaring's 'Seaman's Dictionary' see Manwaring and Perrin (eds), *The Life and Works of Sir Henry Mainwaring*.

21. Ibid., pp. 29–30.

22. Bodleian Library, MS Ashmole 824, fols 149 and 150.

23. Lloyd, *English Corsairs on the Barbary Coast*, p. 66.

24. Ibid., pp. 67–8.

25. John Button, *Algiers Voyage* (1621).

26. Hebb, *Piracy and the English Government*, p. 84.

27. Pett built a miniature ship for Prince Henry, the young Prince of Wales; and carried Princess Elizabeth and her husband over to Flanders in 1613.

28. W. G. Perrin (ed.), *The Autobiography of Phineas Pett* (Navy Records Society, 1918), p. lxvi.

29. Ibid., pp. 122–3.

30. Button, *Algiers Voyage* (pages unnumbered).

31. Hebb, *Piracy and the English Government*, p. 90.

32. Perrin (ed.), *The Autobiography of Phineas Pett*, p. 121.

33. Button, *Algiers Voyage* [n.p.].

34. Ibid. The tonnages given here were twice those commissioned by the merchants. In his autobiography, Pett inflated them further to 300 tons and 200 tons respectively.

35. Gerard, *The Herball* (1633), p. 1208.

36. Bodleian Library, MS Ashmole 824, fol. 159v.

37. Parkinson, *Paradisi in Sole*, p. 430.

38. Ibid., pp. 189–90.

39. Ibid., p. 512.

40. Prudence Leith-Ross, *The John Tradescants* (London, Peter Owen, 1984), p. 71.

41. Button, *Algiers Voyage* [n.p.].

42. Ibid. [n.p.].

43. Norman Egbert McClure (ed.), *The Letters of John Chamberlain* (2 vols, Philadelphia, American Philosophical Society, Memoirs 12, 1939), vol. 2, p. 402, letter to Sir Dudley Carleton at The Hague of 20 October 1621.

44. Perrin (ed.), *The Autobiography of Phineas Pett*, pp. 123–4.

45. Samuel Purchas, *Purchas his Pilgrimes* (London, 1625), Book 2, p. 792.

46. Ibid., p. 779.

47. Ibid., pp. 813–14.

48. All these items are listed in John Tradescant, *Musaeum Tradescantianum* (London, 1656).

Chapter Twelve, Trunks and Treasures

1. British Library, Additional MS 12,528, fol. 12v. Crowe was made a baronet in 1627.

2. Roger Lockyer, *Buckingham* (London, Longman, 1981), pp. 10–11. Other biographical sources consulted include Hugh Ross Williamson, *George Villiers* (London, Duckworth, 1940), and Alan Stewart, *The Cradle King* (London, Chatto & Windus, 2003).

3. Sir Henry Wotton, *Reliquiae Wottonianae* (London, 1651), p. 75.

4. Stewart, *The Cradle King*, p. 113.

5. Ibid., p. 51.

6. Lockyer, *Buckingham*, p. 155.

7. Ibid., p. 463.

8. Thomas Platter and Horatio Busino, *The Journals of Two Travellers in Elizabethan and Early Stuart England* (London, Caliban Books, 1995), p. 142.

9. British Library, Harleian MS 6,987, fol. 231.

10. Lockyer, *Buckingham*, p. 63.

11. John Evelyn, *The Diary of John Evelyn*, ed. E. S. de Beer (6 vols, Oxford, Clarendon Press, 2000), vol. 3, p. 124, 14 August 1654.

12. Norman Egbert McClure (ed.), *The Letters of John Chamberlain* (2 vols, Philadelphia, American Philosophical Society, Memoirs 12, 1939), vol. 2, p. 421, letter to Sir Dudley Carleton at The Hague of 19 January 1622.

13. A revised draft of the Victoria County History of Middlesex is currently in preparation.

14. British Library, Additional MS 12,528, Sir Sackville Crowe's Account of expences of the Duke of Buckingham 1622–1628, fol. 30r.

15. Simon Thurley, 'All the King's Houses', *Country Life* (10 October 1991), p. 86.

16. McClure (ed.), *The Letters of John Chamberlain*, vol. 2, p. 452, letter from John Chamberlain to Sir Dudley Carleton at The Hague of 25 September 1622.

17. The tennis court is significant: from the evidence of Sackville Crowe's account book, betting at tennis was one of Buckingham's chief leisure occupations.

18. Evelyn, *The Diary of John Evelyn*, vol. 3, p. 180, 10 July 1656.

19. John Evelyn, *Sylva* (London, 1664) p. 115.

20. Prudence Leith-Ross, *The John Tradescants* (London, Peter Owen, 1984), pp. 74–5.

21. British Library, Additional MS 12,528, fol. 17r.

22. Leith-Ross, *The John Tradescants*, p. 75.

23. Quoted in Williamson, *George Villiers*, pp. 242–3. Buckingham signs his letter 'Your Majesties most humble Hare and doge' and adds a postscript for 'Babie Charle, I kiss thie wartie hands', British Library, Harleian MS 6,987, fols 225–6.

24. British Library Additional MS 12,528, fol. 17v.

25. British Library Additional MS 12,528, fol. 17r., fol. 17r. and v., fol. 18r.

26. When he accompanied the duke to the Ile de Ré in 1627, he was described as 'John Tradescant the Dukes gardiner now an Ingineere' – see Chapter 14.

27 Hugh Ross Williamson, *Four Stuart Portraits* (London, Evans, 1949), pp. 26–8.

28. Gerbier was naturalized on 27 January 1629 when he was described as 'Balthazar Gerbier, gent., his Majesty's servant, born in foreign parts'. William A. Shaw (ed.), *Letters of Denization and Acts of Naturalization* (Lymington, Huguenot Society of London, 1911), vol. 18, p. 43.

29. Williamson, *Four Stuart Portraits*, p. 26.

30. Balthazar Gerbier, *A Brief Discourse Concerning the Three Chief Principles of Magnificent Building* (London, 1662), pp. 27–8.

31. Balthazar Gerbier, *Counsel and Advise to all Builders* (London, 1663).

32. Letter from Gerbier to Buckingham of 2 December 1624, quoted in Dr Godfrey Goodman, *The Court of King James the First* (2 vols, London, 1839), vol. 2, p. 360.

33. Quoted in Williamson, *George Villiers*, p. 121.

34. G. S. Gordon (ed.), *Peacham's Compleat Gentleman* (Oxford, Clarendon Press, 1906), p. 108.

35. British Library, Harleian MS 1,576, fols 295 r.–v.

36. McClure (ed.), *Letters of John Chamberlain*, vol. 2, p. 347, letter to Sir Dudley Carleton of 9 April 1625.

37. Ibid., p. 616, letter to Sir Dudley Carleton at The Hague of 14 May 1625.

38. British Library, Additional MS 12,528. See fols 21v.–25r. for Buckingham's expenses on his Paris journey.

39. British Library, Harleian MS 1,576, fol. 295.

40. British Library, Additional MS 12,528, fol. 21v.

41. Ibid., fol. 24r.

42. Letter to Buckingham from Boulogne, 17 November 1624, included in Goodman, *The Court of King James the First*, vol. 2, p. 343.

43. British Library, Additional MS 12,528, fol. 23r.

44. Kenneth Woodbridge, *Princely Gardens* (London, Thames & Hudson, 1986), p. 104.

45. Antoine Schnapper, *Le Géant, La Licorne et la Tulipe*, vol. 1, *Histoire et histoire naturelle* (Paris, Flammarion, 1988), p. 215.

46. René Morin, *Catalogus plantarum* (Paris, 1621).

47. Marjorie F. Warner, 'The Morins', *The National Horticultural Magazine* (July 1954), pp. 168–76.

48. See Guy de la Brosse, *Description du Jardin Royal des Plantes Medicinales* (Paris, 1636).

49. Pierre Morin, *Catalogues de quelques plantes a fleures* (Paris, 1651).

50. Evelyn, *The Diary of John Evelyn*, vol. 2, pp. 132–3, April 1644.

51. Evelyn, *The Diary of John Evelyn*, vol. 3, p. 33, 23 May 1651.

52. British Library, Harleian MS 1,278, fols 81v. and 82. See also Mark Laird, 'Parterre, grove, and flower garden', in *John Evelyn's 'Elysium Britannicum' and European Gardening*, Dumbarton Oaks Colloquium on the History of Landscape Architecture, vol. 17 (Washington, 1998), pp 181–4.

53. John Parkinson, *Paradisi in Sole, Paradisus Terrestris* (London, 1629), Bodleian Library Antiq.c. E.1629.1.

54. British Library, Additional MS 12,528, fol. 23v.

55. The National Archives, SP Dom 16/4, fols 226–7, letter from John Tradescant to Edward Nicholas, Secretary to the Navy, 31 July 1625.

56. See Margaret Toynbee, 'The Wedding Journey of King Charles I', *Archaeologia Cantiana* (Ashford, Kent Archaeological Society, 1956), vol. 69 for 1955, pp. 75–83.

57. Ibid., p. 83, quoting *Calendar of State Papers, Venetian Series, 1625–6*, p. 81.

58. Ibid.

59. Charles I, *A True Discourse* (London, 1625), pp. 28–9.

60. National Archives, SP16/3, fol. 105.

61. Charles I, *A True Discourse*, p. 32.

62. British Library, Additional MS 12,528, fol. 28r.

63. Ibid., fol. 34v.; and Lockyer, *Buckingham*, p. 285.

64. British Library, Additional MS 12,528, fol. 28v.

65. Ibid.

66. Ibid., fols 32r.–v.

67. Ibid., fol. 21r.

68. *Calendar of State Papers, Domestic Series, Charles I, 1629–1631* (Nendeln, Liechtenstein, Kraus Reprint, 1967), p. 252.

69. *Calendar of State Papers, Domestic Series, Charles I, Addenda March 1625–January 1649* (London, HMSO, 1897), p. 353.

Chapter Thirteen, A Passion for Strangeness

1. Balthazar Gerbier to Buckingham from Boulogne, 17 November 1624, quoted in Dr Godfrey Goodman, *The Court of King James the First* (2 vols, London, 1839), vol. 2, pp. 326–45.

2. National Archives, State Papers Domestic 16/4, fols 226–7; and *Calendar of State Papers, Domestic Series, Charles I, 1625–1626* (London, 1858), p. 77.

3. Bodleian Library, MS Ashmole 1758, fol. 74.

4. See Roger Lockyer, *Buckingham* (London, Longman, 1981), p. 411.

5. Among the many studies of early collecting, see Marjorie Swann, *Curiosities and Texts* (Philadelphia, University of Pennsylvania Press, 2001); Oliver Impey and Arthur MacGregor (eds), *The Origins of Museums* (Oxford, Clarendon Press, 1985); Arthur MacGregor (ed.), *Tradescant's Rarities* (Oxford, Clarendon Press, 1983); Lisa Jardine, *Ingenious Pursuits* (London, Little, Brown, 1999); and Richard D. Altick, *The Shows of London* (Cambridge, Mass, and London, Belknap Press of Harvard University Press, 1978).

6. Quoted in Thomas Coryat, *Coryat's Crudities* (2 vols, Glasgow, James MacLehose & Sons, 1905), vol. 1, p. 114.

7. Thomas Platter and Horatio Busino, *The Journals of Two Travellers in Elizabethan and Early Stuart England* (London, Caliban Books, 1995), pp. 33–5.

8. Hatfield House Archives, Box B/S fol. 15v. '

9. A *Handstein* was a bizarrely shaped rock sample trimmed with tiny gold or

silver figurines, popular with collectors of the sixteenth and early seventeenth centuries.

10. Quoted in Alan Haynes, *Robert Cecil Earl of Salisbury, 1563–1612* (London, Owen, 1989), pp. 75–6.

11. Quoted in Swann, *Curiosities and Texts*, p. 23.

12. H. J. Witkam, *Catalogues of all the Chiefest Rarities* (Leiden, 1980), pp. iv–v.

13. Arthur MacGregor, 'Collectors and Collections of Rarities in the Sixteenth and Seventeenth Centuries', in MacGregor (ed.), *Tradescant's Rarities*, p. 78.

14. The examples are taken from Witkam, *Catalogues*.

15. Antoine Schnapper, *Le Géant, La Licorne et La Tulipe* (Paris, Flammarion, 1988), vol. 1, pp. 180–245.

16. Pierrre Borel, a French doctor and collector of plants and rarities, included the 'trois Messieurs de Morin' in his list of Parisian *cabinets de curiosités*. See Pierre Borel, *Les Antiquitez, Raretes, Plantes, Mineraux, & Autres Choses* (Castres, 1649), pp. 129–30.

17. John Evelyn, *The Diary of John Evelyn*, ed. E. S. de Beer (6 vols, Oxford, Clarendon Press, 2000), vol. 2, pp. 132–3, April 1644.

18. Ibid., vol. 3, p. 33, 23 May 1651.

19. *Calendar of State Papers, Domestic Series, Charles I, 1625–1626* (London, 1858), p. 251, relating to *State Papers Domestic* 16/20, no. 55, 8 February 1626.

20. *Buckingham*, p. 410.

21. MacGregor (ed.), *Tradescant's Rarities*, p. 148.

22. Kenneth R. Andrews, *Trade, Plunder and Settlement* (Cambridge University Press, 1984), pp. 101–15.

23. A rich mid-eighteenth-century anthology of English and translated travel writings (usually attributed to map-maker John Green) is *A New General Collection of Voyages and Travels* (4 vols, London, 1745–7). Vol. 2 (London, 1745) retells some of the pioneering trade ventures to West Africa.

24. Ibid., vol 2, p. 306. Apothecary Thomas Johnson was the first person to display a banana in the window of his shop on Snow Hill, London, in April 1633. John Gerard, *The Herball* (London, 1633), p. 1515.

25. *A New General Collection of Voyages and Travels*, vol. 2, p. 357.

26. Ibid., vol. 2, p. 360.

27. Ibid., vol. 2, p. 363.

28. Ibid., vol. 2, p. 364.

29. Ibid., vol. 2, p. 371.

30. See Prudence Leith-Ross, *The John Tradescants* (London, Peter Owen, 1984), p. 80.

31. Borel, *Les Antiquitez*, p. 128.

32. Borel included one of Europe's most famous collections belonging to the Dutch physician, Bernard Paludanus, dispersed after his death in 1633.

33. Lockyer, *Buckingham*, p. 462.

34. John Tradescant, *Musaeum Tradescantianum* (London, 1656), p. 179.

35. National Archives, PROB 11/167.

36. Tradescant, *Musaeum Tradescantium*, p. 2.

37. Benjamin Daydon Jackson, *A Catalogue of Plants Cultivated in the Garden of John Gerard* (London, 1876), pp. 14 and 46.

38. See S. H. Vines, *An Account of the Morisonian Herbarium* (Oxford, Clarendon Press, 1914), p. 261.

Chapter Fourteen, To the Aid of the Huguenots

1. On military engineering in French gardens, see Chandra Mukerji, 'Engineering and French formal gardens in the reign of Louis XIV', in John Dixon Hunt and Michael Conan (eds), *Tradition and Innovation in French Garden Art* (Philadelphia, University of Pennsylvania Press, 2002), pp. 22–43.

2. Sir Balthazar Gerbier Kt, *A Manifestation* (London, 1651), pp. 8–9.

3. Mukerji, ' Engineering and French formal gardens', p. 24.

4. For the background to Buckingham's expedition, I have relied mainly on Roger Lockyer, *Buckingham* (London and New York, Longman, 1981), pp. 356–418, supplemented by contemporary sources.

5. Lockyer, *Buckingham*, p. 372.

6. British Library, Additional MS 12,528, fols 35v.–38v.

7. Ibid., fols 35v.–36r.

8. Lockyer, *Buckingham*, p. 371.

9. British Library, Additional MS 12, 528, fol. 38v.

10. Lockyer, *Buckingham*, p. 374.

11 William Shakespeare, *Henry IV, Part 1*, Act IV, Scene ii (London, The Arden Shakespeare, 3rd series, 2002), ed. David Scott Kasten, p. 290–1.

12. British Library, Additional MS 26,051, fol. 16.

13. Lockyer, *Buckingham*, p. 382. Lord Herbert (see reference 14) quotes a defensive force of 4,000 quartered at the citadel.

14. Edward, Lord Herbert of Cherbury, *The Expedition to the Isle of Rhé* (London, Philobiblon Society, 1860), p. 30.

15. Lockyer, *Buckingham*, p. 385.

16. Herbert, *The Expedition*, p. 49.

17. Lockyer, *Buckingham*, p. 388.

18. Historical Manuscripts Commission, *The Manuscripts of the Earl Cowper K.G.*, vol. 1 (London, HMSO, 1888), 12th Report, Appendix, Part. 1, p. 310, letter from Buckingham to Mr Secretary Coke, 26 July 1627.

19. Herbert, *The Expedition*, pp. 108–9.

20. John Gerard, *The Herball* (London, 1633), p. 1099.

21. John Gerard, *The Herball* (London, 1597), pp. 940–1.

22. John Parkinson, *Theatrum Botanicum* (London, 1640), pp. 622–4. The Count of Soubise was one of the leading defenders of La Rochelle.

23. Herbert, *The Expedition*, pp. 93–4.

24. Bodleian Library, MS Ashmole 824, fol. 191, from A Journall of all the occurrences happening at and after our landing in the Isle of Ree.

25. Herbert, *The Expedition*, pp. 106–7.

26. Historical Manuscripts Commission, *The Manuscripts of the Earl Cowper*, pp. 319–20, letter from Sir Edward Conway to Sir John Coke, 6 September 1627.

27. *Calendar of State Papers, Domestic Series, Charles I, 1627–1628* (Nendeln, Liechtenstein, Kraus Reprint, 1967), p. 390, letter from William Bold to Edward Nicholas, 16 October 1627.

28. Herbert, *The Expedition*, pp. 155–6.

29. Ibid., pp. 203–4.

30. Ibid., p. 168.

31. Ibid., pp. 237–46.

32. Lockyer, *Buckingham*, p. 401.

33. *Calendar of State Papers, Domestic Series, Charles I, 1627–1628*, p. 454.

34. Gerard, *The Herball* (London, 1633), p. 998.

35. E. A. Bowles, *My Garden in Spring* (1914), pp. 186–7.

36. Lockyer, *Buckingham*, pp. 451–2.

37. Quoted in Lockyer, *Buckingham*, p. 454.

38. Gerbier, *A Manifestation*, p. 8.

39. Peter Mundy, *The Travels of Peter Mundy*, vol. 3 (London, Hakluyt Society, 1919), 2nd series, no. 45, pp. 1–3.

Chapter Fifteen, Lambeth Walks

1. Thomas Platter and Horatio Busino, *The Journals of Two Travellers in Elizabethan and Early Stuart England* (London, Caliban Books, 1995), p. 131.

2. London Survey Committee, *The Survey of London*, vol. 23, *South Bank & Vauxhall* (London, 1951), p. 1.

3. For Thomas Johnson's warning against the herbswoman of Cheapside, see John Gerard, *The Herball* (London, 1633), p. 1060.

4. John Gerard, *The Herball* (London, 1597), p. 192.

5. Ibid., pp. 15–16.

6. Ibid., p. 388.

7. Ibid., p. 902.

8. Samuel Hartlib, *Samuel Hartlib his Legacie* (London, 1651), p. 11.

9. See also Malcolm Thick, *The Neat House Gardens* (Totnes, Prospect Books, 1998), p. 23.

10. R.T. Gunther, *Early British Botanists and their Gardens* (Oxford University Press, 1922), pp. 309–10.

11. London Survey Committee, *The Survey of London*, vol. 23, pp. 146–7.

12. Platter and Busino, *The Journals of Two Travellers*, p. 177.

13. See also Ronald Webber, 'London's Market Gardens', *History Today*, 23, 12 (December 1973), pp. 871–8.

14. Quoted in Thick,*The Neat House Gardens*, pp. 101–2.

15. London Survey Committee,*The Survey of London*, vol 23, p. 118.

16. *The A to Z of Elizabethan London*, compiled by Adrian Prockter and Robert Taylor (Lympne Castle, Kent, 1979), p. x.

17. Platter and Busino, *The Journals of Two Travellers*, pp. 12–14.

18. Ibid., pp. 134–5.

19. The monarch could vary the terms of letters of denization, but in Caron's case the heirs he named were judged invalid.

20. For information on Sir Noel Caron and his Lambeth properties, see London Survey Committee, *The Survey of London*, vol. 26, *The Parish of St. Mary Lambeth, Part 2, The Southern Area* (London, 1956), p. 66.

21. William Brenchley Rye, *England as Seen by Foreigners* (London, 1865), pp. 60–1.

22. Two copies of this map exist: Canterbury Cathedral Archives, CCA–Map/18; and British Library, Additional MS 34,790.

23. Canterbury Cathedral Archives, DCc-ChAnt/F/63. The history of Tradescant's property (plot 29 on Thomas Hill's 1681 survey) survives as a single sheet of paper (undated), torn, dirty and rust-stained. For a summary history of Tradescant's Lambeth home, see London Survey Committee, *The Survey of London*, vol. 26, p. 74.

24. C. H. Josten, *Elias Ashmole (1617–1692)* (5 vols, Oxford, Clarendon Press, 1966), vol. 4, p. 1640.

25. David Sturdy, 'The Tradescants at Lambeth', *Journal of Garden History*, 2, 1 (1982), pp. 1–16.

26. Annual contributions made by parishioners of St Mary, Lambeth, are recorded in Minet Library, P2/35, Collectors for the Poor Accounts, 1618–51. No Tradescant appears in the lists up to 1624, then the records skip to 1632–3, when 'John Tredeskin' of South Lambeth is recorded as paying 8s 8d. According to subsidy returns for South Lambeth, Tradescant had not arrived by September 1628 and by the next surviving returns (March 1640) the property was in the hands of his son. National Archives, E 179/186/436 and 448.

27. London Survey Committee, *The Survey of London*, vol. 26, p. 73.

28. See 'Vauxhall and South Lambeth: an 18th-century lease', *Surrey Archaeological Collections*, vol. 28 (1915), pp. 173–8.

29. Sturdy, 'The Tradescants at Lambeth', p. 1.

30. Prudence Leith-Ross, *The John Tradescants* (London, Peter Owen, 1984), p. 88.

31. John Parkinson, *Paradisi in Sole, Paradisus Terrestris* (London, 1629), Bodleian Library Antiq.c. E.1629.1.

32. Gerard, *The Herball* (1633), p. 412.

33. Ibid., p. 260.

34. Ibid., p. 948.

35. Ibid., p. 848.

36. Ibid., p. 135. Other daffodils were named after Gerard, Robin and Parkinson.

37. Ibid., p. 443.

38. Ibid., p. 1427; Tradescant's 1634 catalogue lists *Laburnum maius* and L. *minus.*

39. Ibid., p. 998.

40. Ibid., p. 1489.

41. Ibid., p. 1443. Other plants Johnson saw in Tradescant's garden included a good range of alliums (p. 184), a Mediterranean sea lavender (p. 412), and a ladies smock (p. 260).

42. *The Hillier Manual of Trees and Shrubs*, 5th edn (Newton Abbot, David & Charles, 1981).

43. See John Harvey, *Early Nurserymen* (London and Chichester, Phillimore, 1974), pp. 42–4.

44. Gerard, *The Herball* (1633), p. 589.

45. Ibid., p. 489.

46. Ibid., p. 437.

47. Ibid., p. 785.

48. Magdalen College, Oxford, Old Library, John Tradescant, *Plantarum In Horto Johannem Tradescanti nascentium Catalogus* (London, 1634).

49. B. D. Jackson (ed.), *A Catalogue of Plants Cultivated in the Garden of John Gerard* (London, 1876).

50. Gerard, *The Herball* (1597), p. 389.

51. Ibid., p. 781.

52. Parkinson, *Paradisi in Sole* (London, 1629), p. 518.

53. To take just two examples, day lilies were then called hemerocallis, liliasphodelus, liliastrum and liliago, while 'Hyacinthus' included bluebells, harebells, grape hyacinths and today's hyacinths.

54. Gerard, *The Herball* (1597), p. 1330.

55. Ibid., p. 792.

56. Ibid., p. 1226.

57. Magdalen College, Oxford, MS 239. For Stonehouse's friendship with the Tradescants, see Chapter 21.

58. Gerard, *The Herball* (1633), pp. 1545–6.

Chapter Sixteen, Queen's Silk

1. National Archives, E404/153 part 2, fol. 29. A payment of £50 out of his annual allowance of £100 is recorded in *Calendar of State Papers, Domestic Series, Charles I 1635* (London, HMSO 1865), p. 507.

2. John Bonoeil, *A treatise of the Art of Making Silke* (London, 1622). See also Samuel Hartlib, *Samuel Hartlib his Legacie* (London, 1651), p. 29.

3. *Calendar of State Papers, Domestic Series, James I, 1611–1618*, (London, 1858), p. 592, 8 November 1618.

4. National Archives, E351/3269.

5. *Calendar of State Papers, Domestic Series, Charles I, 1625–1626* (London 1858), p. 267, February 1626. A wife's 'jointure' was the estate settled on her for any time she survived her husband as a widow.

6. For a brief (unreferenced) guide to the history of the palace, see J.W. Lindus Forge, *Oatlands Palace* (Walton and Weybridge Local History Society, 5th edn., 1982).

7. Quoted in Forge, *Oatlands Palace*, p. 12.

8. John Nichols *The Progresses, Processions, and Magnificent Festivities of King James I* (4 vols, London, 1828), vol. 1, pp. 203–4

9. *Calendar of State Papers, Domestic Series, James I, 1603–1610* (London, 1857), p. 493, 28 February 1609; and p. 547, 1 October 1609.

10. M. A. E. Green (ed.), *Letters of Queen Henrietta Maria* (London, 1857), p. 19n.

11. Ibid., pp. 18–19.

12. Pierre Vallet, *Le Jardin du Roy Tres Chrestien Henry IV* (Paris, 1608).

13. John Parkinson, *Theatrum Botanicum* (London, 1640).

14. Green (ed.), *Letters of Queen Henrietta Maria*, p. 19.

15. National Archives LR2/297, A Survey of ... Oatlands, fols 105–12.

16. See David Blayney Brown, *Catalogue of the Collection of Drawings in the Ashmolean Museum*, vol. 4 (Oxford, Clarendon Press, 1982), nos. 15–17.

17. National Archives, E351/3253. Tradescant may have already encountered de Critz through Robert Cecil.

18. National Archives, LR2/297, fols 105–12.

19. National Archives, AO 1/2487/356, fol. 1.

20 See John Harris, Stephen Orgel and Roy Strong, *The King's Arcadia* (London, Arts Council of Great Britain, 1973), pp. 95–8.

21. National Archives, AO 1/2485/344.

22. National Archives, AO 1/2487/356, accounts of the keeper of Oatlands, Sir John Trevor, who died before Tradescant took up his appointment there.

23. Olivier de Serres, *The perfect Use of Silk-wormes, and their benefit* (London, 1607).

24. *Calendar of State Papers, Domestic Series, James I, 1603–1610*, p. 344.

25. Ibid., pp. 344 and 398.

26. De Serres, *The perfect Use of Silk–wormes*, additional text by N. Geffe, p. 3.

27. *Calendar of State Papers, Domestic Series, James I, 1603–1610*, p. 540.

28. *Calendar of State Papers, Domestic Series, James I, 1611–1618*, p. 246.

29. Ibid., p. 555.

30. De Serres, *The perfect Use of Silk–wormes*, p. 21.

31. Ibid., p. 23.

32. John Parkinson, *Paradisi in Sole, Paradisus Terrestris* (London, 1629), p. 599.

33. Samuel Hartlib, *Samuel Hartlib his Legacie* (London, 1655), pp. 54–5; and John Evelyn, *The Diary of John Evelyn*, ed. E. S. de Beer (6 vols, Oxford, Clarendon Press, 2000), vol. 3, p. 33.

34. Charles Estienne, *Maison rustique, or, The countrey farme* (London, 1616), pp. 486–90.

35. De Serres, *The Perfect Use of Silk–wormes*, p. 60.

36. Ibid., p. 57.

37. Estienne, *Maison rustique*, pp. 489–90.

38. National Archives, LR2/297, fol. 109.

39. Harris, Orgel and Strong, *The King's Arcadia*; included in the list of works by Jones is a garden arbour for Oatlands park (1631).

40. National Archives, E351/3265.

41. The relevant accounts at the National Archives are E351/3264 (1 October 1630–30 September 1631) to E351/3271 (1 October 1637–30 September 1638).

42. National Archives, E403/2606, fol. 311.

43. Ibid., fol. 312.

44. National Archives, E351/3268.

45 But see Chapter 22. In spite of the high value assigned to Wimbledon's orange trees, 'severall Oring Trees' from Oatlands were included in the inventories of the king's goods after his execution and sold very cheaply.

46 National Archives E317/Surrey/72, A Survey of the Manor of Wymbledon.

47. National Archives, LR2/297, A Survey of the Manor of Richmond, fol. 169.

48 Ibid., fol. 172.

49 André Mollet, *Le Jardin de Plaisirs* (Stockholm, 1651), pages unnumbered.

50. National Archives, E351/3266.

51. National Archives, E351/3269.

52. National Archives, E351/3270.

Chapter Seventeen, Tradescant's Orchard

1. John Parkinson, *Paradisi in Sole, Paradisus Terrestris* (London 1629), p. 575.

2. N.F., *The Husbandman's fruitfull Orchard* (London, 1609).

3. John Gerard, *The Herball* (London, 1597), p. 1269. Gerard gave Pointer's first name as Richard but John Harvey corrects it to Vincent. See John Harvey, *Early Nurserymen* (London and Chichester, Phillimore, 1974), pp. 41–2.

4. Parkinson, *Paradisi in Sole*, p. 571

5. According to John Harvey, *Early Nurserymen* (pp. 44–5), John Millen the elder died in October 1635.

6. Parkinson, *Paradisi in Sole*, p. 582.

7. Samuel Hartlib, *Samuel Hartlib his Legacie* (London, 1651), pp. 22–3. Hartlib's informant was Surrey farmer Sir Richard Weston.

8. John Tradescant, *Plantarum in Horto Johannem Tradescanti* (1634), among the Goodyer papers in the library of Magdalen College, Oxford.

9. Parkinson, *Paradisi in Sole*, p. 582.

10. Ibid., p. 578. Diaper was a linen or cotton fabric woven with small diamond patterns.

11. Ibid., p. 564.

12. Ibid., p. 574.

13. Ibid., p. 563.

14. By mid-century, the distribution of orchards remained very uneven, plentiful in Kent, Gloucestershire, Hereford, Worcester and around London, but rare elsewhere. See Hartlib, *Samuel Hartlib his Legacie*, p. 19.

15. Parkinson, *Paradisi in Sole*, p. 593.

16. Ibid., p. 587.

17. Ibid., p. 588

18. Ibid., p. 588.

19. John Gerard, *The Herball* (London, 1633), p. 1506.

20. Ibid., p. 1456.

21. Harvey, *Early Nurserymen*, p. 145.

22. Bodleian Library, MS Ashmole 1461, 'Tradescant's Orchard'.

23. Bodleian Library, B.C. Barker-Benfield, MS. Ashmole 1461, Technical notes, including analysis of watermarks (June 2000). Barker-Benfield concludes that one of at least three papers used may have originated in Basel in the 1620s and the others in northern Europe in the first half of the seventeenth century.

24. A red pescod plum is missing from the table, and the folio numbers suggest that at least ten fruits were missing by the time the volume was bound.

25. Parkinson, *Paradisi in Sole*, p. 578.

26. Barker-Benfield, MS Ashmole 1461.

27. R. T. Gunther, *Early British Botanists and their Gardens* (Oxford University Press, 1922), p. 329.

28. Prudence Leith-Ross, *The Florilegium of Alexander Marshal* (London, Royal Collection Enterprises, 2000).

29. John Tradescant, *Musaeum Tradescantianum* (London, 1656), p. 41.

30. See for instance, Crispin de Passe, *Hortus Floridus* (London, Cresset Press, 1928).

31 'The first trade lists to have survived date from after the Restoration of 1660.' Harvey, *Early Nurserymen*, p. 145.

32. Parkinson, *Paradisi in Sole*, p. 575.

33. Tradescant, *Plantarum in Horto Johannem Tradescanti*.

34. Parkinson, *Paradisi in Sole*, pp. 573 and 577.

35. Ibid., p. 537. Parkinson devotes Part 3 of this work to the Orchard.

36. Ibid., pp. 537–8.

37. Ibid., pp. 542–6. Parkinson described five different propagation techniques: grafting, inarching, whipping or splicing, 'inoculating or grafting in the budde', and 'grafting in the scutcheon'.

38. Ibid., p. 549.

39. Ibid., p. 550.

40. Ibid., p. 550.

41. N. F., *The Husbandman's fruitfull Orchard*.

42. See James Turner, 'Ralph Austen, an Oxford Horticulturist of the Seventeenth Century', *Garden History: The Journal of the Garden History Society*, 6, 2 (Summer 1978), pp. 39–45.

43. Ralph Austen, *A Treatise of Fruit-Trees* (Oxford, 1653).

44. Ralph Austen, *The Spirituall use of an Orchard; or Garden of Frvit-Trees*, appended to Austen, *A Treatise of Fruit-Trees*, from the 'Preface to the Reader'.

45. Austen, *The Spirituall use of an Orchard*, p. 6.

46. Austen, *A Treatise of Fruit-Trees*, p. 40.

Chapter Eighteen, The Lambeth Ark

1. John Aubrey, *The Natural History and Antiquities of the County of Surrey* (5 vols, London, 1719), vol. 1, pp. 12–13.

2. Account by Georg Christoph Stirn who visited in July 1638, quoted in Arthur MacGregor, 'The Tradescants as collectors of rarities', in MacGregor (ed.), *Tradescant's Rarities* (Oxford, Clarendon Press, 1983) p. 21.

3. See Chapters 15 and 17.

4. For a detailed catalogue of the surviving early collections, see Arthur MacGregor (ed.), *Tradescant's Rarities* (Oxford, Clarendon Press, 1983).

5. Just such a free-standing building was recorded by London's first large-scale Ordnance Survey map of 1871. OS London Sheet XI.23, scale 5′ to one mile, surveyed 1871, published February 1874.

6. After the hearth tax was introduced in 1662, the younger Tradescant's widow Hester was assessed to pay for eleven hearths. See C. A. F. Meekings (ed.), *Surrey Hearth Tax 1664* (Surrey Record Society, vol. 17, nos. 41 and 42, 1940), pp. xci and 154.

7. National Archives, C33/221, fol. 744v.

8. Maurice Exwood and H. L. Lehmann (eds), *The Journal of William Schellinks' Travels* (London, Camden Society, 5th series, vol. 1, 1993), pp. 62–3.

9. See Jim Bennett and Scott Mandelbrote, *The Garden, the Ark, the Tower, the Temple* (Oxford, Museum of the History of Science in association with the Bodleian Library, 1998), pp. 86–7.

10. See *The Transproser Rehears'd: or the Fifth Act of Mr. Bayes's Play* (Oxford, 1673), p. 123.

11. Peter Mundy, *The Travels of Peter Mundy*, vol. 3, Part 1, ed. Lieut. Col. Sir Richard Carnac Temple (London, Hakluyt Society, 1919), 2nd series, no. 45, pp. 1–3.

12. These included what was surely an early camera obscura, ibid., vol. 3.

13. Historical Manuscripts Commission 9, *Calendar of the Manuscripts of the Most Honourable the Marquess of Salisbury, Part 22 (1612–1668)* (London, 1971), p. 271, Accounts, 23 October 1633 to 30 September 1634.

14. MacGregor (ed.),, *Tradescant's Rarities*, p. 21.

15. Also called a suckerfish, the remora is a parasitic fish that attaches itself to larger fish by a sucker on the top of its head.

16. John Gerard, *The Herball* (London, 1597), pp. 1391–2.

17. John Gerard, *The Herball* (London, 1633), pp. 1587–9.

18. John Tradescant, *Musaeum Tradescantianum* (London, 1656).

19. Robert Herrick, 'Upon Madam Ursly', an epigram in *Hesperides or, The Works Both Humane & Divine* (London, 1648), p. 273.

20. Thomas Moisan, 'Herrick, Hollar, and the Tradescants', *Criticism* (Detroit, Michigan, Wayne State University Press), 43, 3 (Summer 2001), pp. 309–24.

21. John Cleveland, 'Upon Sir Thomas Martin', in *Poems* (London, 1651), p. 6.

22. Thomas Powell, *Humane Industry* (London, 1661), p. 187.

23. Bennett and Mandelbrote, *The Garden, the Ark, the Tower, the Temple*, p. 74

24. Ibid., p. 8.

25. A. C. Ducarel, *A letter from Dr. Ducarel, F.R.S. and F.S.A. to William Watson, M.D. F.R.S.* (London, 1773), pp. 8–9.

26. G. S. Gordon (ed.), *Peacham's Compleat Gentleman* (Oxford, Clarendon Press, 1906), pp. 104–5.

27. See Marjorie Swann, *Curiosities and Texts* (Philadelphia, University of Pennsylvania Press, 2001), pp. 27–38.

28. William Bird, *The Magazine of Honour* (London, 1642), pp. 147–8.

29. See Prudence Leith-Ross, *The John Tradescants* (London, Peter Owen, 1984), p. 105.

30. National Archives, PROB 10/573.

31. Mundy, *The Travels of Peter Mundy*, vol. 3, p. 3. Mundy's editor traces the reference to a Mr Josias Best, son of East India Company employee, Thomas Best of Whitehouse Street, Ratcliffe.

32. Cumbria Record Office, Le Fleming MSS WD/Ry (492), (243), (260).

33. Jennifer Potter, 'Capturing the Spirit' (London, 1995), pp. 68–71, unpublished thesis for Architectural Association, Garden Conservation 2.

34. Tradescant, *Musaeum Tradescantianum*, p. 40.

35. Ducarel, A *letter from Dr. Ducarel*, p. 7.

36. National Archives, LC5/134, fols 79 (dated 13 November 1635) and 91.

37. Tradescant, *Musaeum Tradescantianum*, pp. 47 and 49.

38. Oliver Millar (ed.), *The Inventories and Valuations of the King's Goods 1649-1651*, vol. 43, Walpole Society (Glasgow, University Press, 1972), pp. 180–1.

39. British Library, India Office Records, B/16, fol. 191, court minutes of 27 November 1633.

40. *Calendar of State Papers, Colonial Series, East Indies and Persia, 1630–1634* (London, 1892), court minutes of 21 February 1634, p. 523.

41. Quoted in Oliver Millar (ed.), *Abraham van der Doort's Catalogue of the Collections of Charles I*, vol. 37, Walpole Society (Glasgow, Robert Maclehose & Co., University Press, 1960), p. xvi.

42. Ibid., p. 152.

Chapter Nineteen, Family Matters

1. The median age for first marriage among small landowners and labourers actually went up from the sixteenth to the seventeenth centuries, rising from twenty–six to thirty for men. See Lawrence Stone, *The Family, Sex and Marriage in England 1500-1800* (London, Weidenfeld & Nicolson, 1977), p. 50.

2. Guildhall Library, MS 10232, Parish of St. Gregory by St. Paul, marriages 1627–35.

3. London Metropolitan Archives, X038/001, Lambeth, St. Mary at Lambeth, composite registers March 1539–August 1670.

4. Guildhall Library, MS 21128 and MS 03389/1A, Worshipful Company of Gardeners.

5. Guildhall Library, MS 03390/2, Worshipful Company of Gardeners, fols 142 and 176.

6. For a general history of the Company, see Melvyn Barnes, *Root and Branch* (London, Worshipful Company of Gardeners, 1994).

7. Guildhall Library, MS 03390/2, fols 163 and 178.

8. Peter Ackroyd, *London: The Biography* (London, Chatto & Windus, 2000), p. 90.

9. See Caroline M. Barron, *London in the Later Middle Ages* (Oxford University Press, 2004), Chapter 9.

10. John Stow, *The Survey of London* (London, 1633), p. 637; and James Howell, *Londinopolis* (London, 1657).

11. The Gardeners had to wait until the twentieth century before the privileges of livery were fully granted – see Guildhall MS 03396, Worshipful Company of Gardeners. For

insights into the Company of Gardeners, I am indebted to David Marsh whose researches will appear in Ian Gadd and Patrick Wallis (eds), *Corporate Worlds* (London, Centre for Metropolitan History, forthcoming).

12. Guildhall Library, MS 28953, Worshipful Company of Gardeners.

13. Ibid., fol. 28v.

14. Guildhall Library, MS 03396, pp. 7–9.

15. Ibid., p. 3 of 'Royal Proclamation, 1634'.

16. Charles Drew (ed.), *Lambeth Churchwardens' Accounts*, vol. 2 (Surrey Record Society vol. 20, 1950), p. 98.

17. Guildhall Library, MS 03390/2, fols 142–3.

18. Stone, *The Family, Sex and Marriage*, p. 81. The expectation of life at birth in England in the 1640s was only thirty–two years.

Chapter Twenty, A Physick for the Dying

1. Edinburgh followed in 1670 and the Society of Apothecaries' garden at Chelsea in 1673.

2. John Prest, *The Garden of Eden* (New Haven and London, Yale University Press, 1981), p. 6.

3. Ibid., p. 9.

4. L. S. Sutherland and L.G. Mitchell, *The History of the University of Oxford*, vol. 5 (Oxford, Clarendon Press, 1986), pp. 711–12.

5. The history of Oxford's botanic garden is taken principally from Nicholas Tyacke (ed.), *The History of the University of Oxford*, vol. 4 (Oxford, Clarendon Press, 1997), pp. 169–70, supplemented by S. H. Vines and G. Claridge Druce, *An Account of the Morisonian Herbarium* (Oxford, Clarendon Press, 1914), and R. T. Gunther, *Oxford Gardens* (Oxford, 1912).

6. Quoted in Tyacke, *The History of the University of Oxford*, pp. 169–70.

7. See David Loggan's plan of the garden in Loggan, *Oxonia Illustrata* (Oxford, 1675).

8. Anthony Wood, *History and Antiquities of the University of Oxford*, vol. 2, Part. 2 (Oxford, 1796), pp. 897–8.

9. Magdalen College, Oxford, MS 367, fol. 76.

10. Quoted in Vines and Druce, *An Account of the Morisonian Herbarium*, p. xv.

11 Ibid.

12. University of Oxford Archives, Matriculation Register 1615–1647, SP 2, fol. 349v. Bayler's name appears among other servants at the back of the register.

13. National Archives, PROB 11/177. The original will is contained in PROB 10/573.

14. John Parkinson, *Paradisi in Sole, Paradisus Terrestris* (London, 1629), p. 610.

15. Ibid., p. 593.

16. In the Churchwardens' Accounts, Lardner appears variously as Learner, Leardner and

Lardner. See Charles Drew (ed.), *Lambeth Churchwardens' Accounts*, vol. 2 (Surrey Record Society, vol. 20, 1950), pp. 126 and 261.

17. T. C. Dale (ed.), *The Inhabitants of London in 1638* (London, Society of Genealogists, 1931), pp. 222–3.

18. The Hartlib Papers, Humanities Research Institute, University of Sheffield, Ephemerides, c. April 1651, E 28/2/13A.

19. Ashmolean Museum, *Complete Illustrated Catalogue of Paintings* (Oxford, 2004), p. 26.

20. London Metropolitan Archives, X038/001, Lambeth, St. Mary at Lambeth, composite registers March 1539–August 1670.

21 Drew (ed.), *Lambeth Churchwardens' Accounts*, p. 130.

22. William Coles, *The Art of Simpling* (London, 1656), pp. 64–5.

23. National Archives, E 403/2757, Orders for Michaelmas Terme 1638, fol. 44.

24. Quoted in Vines and Druce, *An Account of the Morisonian Herbarium*, p. xvii.

25. *Catalogus plantarum Horti Medici Oxoniensis* (Oxford, 1648).

26. John Evelyn, *The Diary of John Evelyn*, ed. E. S. de Beer (6 vols, Oxford, Clarendon Press, 2000) vol. 3, pp. 109–10, 12 July 1654. Evelyn seemed slightly more impressed at his next visit on 25 October 1664, ibid., vol. 3, p. 386.

Chapter Twenty-One, Sweet Virginia

1. John Tradescant, *Musaeum Tradescantianum* (London, 1656).

2. J.A.F. Bekkers, *Correspondence of John Morris* (Assen, Van Gorcum & Comp., NV, 1970), p. 3.

3. National Archives, CO 1/1, fol. 30r. The year '1637' then extended to the March quarter-day in 1638.

4. For the story of Harvey's two periods of governorship, see Martha W. McCartney, *Documentary History of Jamestown Island*, vol. 1 (Williamsburg VA, 2000), pp. 81–96.

5. Ibid., vol. 1, p. 84.

6. David de Vries, *Voyages from Holland to America* (New York, 1853), pp. 46–54 and 108–14.

7. Ibid., p. 50.

8. Ibid., p. 53.

9. George Calvert, 1st Lord Baltimore, was knighted by King James who later elevated him to the Irish peerage. After his first attempt to found a North American colony in Newfoundland failed he lobbied King Charles for a colony of his own but died before the charter of Maryland received the great seal on 20 June 1632. The 2nd Lord Baltimore appointed his half-brother, Leonard Calvert, to be the first governor of Maryland.

10. McCartney, *Documentary History of Jamestown Island*, vol. 3, pp. 80–1.

11. See A. J. Morrison, 'The Virginia Indian Trade to 1973', *William & Mary College Quarterly Historical Magazine*, series 2, vol. 1 (October 1921), pp. 217–36; and National Archives CO 1/1, fols 32v.–33r.

12. McCartney, *A Documentary History of Jamestown Island*, vol. 1, pp. 87–8.

13. *Calendar of State Papers, Colonial Series, 1574–1660*, vol. 1, p. 216.

14. Ibid., vol. 1, p. 241.

15. The only documented link between Harvey and Tradescant is the record referring to their presence in the colony in 1637.

16. *Calendar of State Papers, Colonial Series, 1574–1660*, vol. 1, p. 245. See also Wilcomb E. Washburn, *Virginia Under Charles I and Cromwell, 1625–1660*, Jamestown 350th Anniversary Historical Booklets, no. 7 (Williamsburg, VA, 1957); and *Calendar of State Papers, Colonial Series, 1574–1660*, vol. 1, p. 27.

17. Nell Marion Nugent, *Cavaliers and Pioneers*, vol. 1 (Baltimore, Genealogical Publishing Co. Inc., reprinted 1979), p. xix.

18. Washburn, *Virginia Under Charles I and Cromwell*, p. 2.

19. Nugent, *Cavaliers and Pioneers*, vol.1, p. xxi.

20. Anon., *A Perfect Description of Virginia* (London, 1649), p. 7.

21. Ibid., p. 5.

22. John Smith estimated the cost of freight for one man to be about £1 10s 10d for half a ton. See also E. W. Gent, 'Virginia' (London, 1650), p. 10, in Peter Force, *Tracts and other Papers*, vol. 3 (Washington, 1844).

23. Philip L. Barbour (ed.), *The Complete Works of Captain John Smith* (3 vols, Williamsburg, VA, University of North Carolina Press for the Institute of Early American History and Culture, 1986), vol. 2, pp. 321–2. A Monmouth cap was a flat cap worn by sailors; canvas was strong, unbleached cloth, such as that used for sails; 'frize' or 'frieze' was a coarse woollen cloth.

24. National Archives, CO 1/9, fol. 110, 30 March 1637.

25. Barbour (ed.), *The Complete Works of John Smith*, vol. 2, p. 316.

26. De Vries, *Voyages from Holland to America*, p. 54.

27. *Calendar of State Papers, Colonial Series, 1574–1660*, vol. 1, p. 281.

28. Comments of Thomas Yonge, who stayed with Harvey in 1634, quoted in McCartney, *A Documentary History of Jamestown Island*, vol. 1, p. 84.

29. National Archives, CO 1/6, fols 135–6, letter dated 27 May 1632.

30. *Calendar of State Papers, Colonial Series, 1574–1660*, vol. 1, p. 268

31. See William M. Kelso with Beverly Straube, *Jamestown Rediscovery 1994-2004* (Richmond, VA, Association for the Preservation of Virginia Antiquities, 2004).

32. For the Indians' experience of colonization, see Helen C. Rountree, *Pocahontas, Powhatan, Opechancanough* (Charlottesville VA, and London, University of Virginia Press, 2005).

33. See map of settlers' claims in the mid–seventeenth century drawn by Helen C. Rountree in *Pocahontas, Powhatan, Opechancanough,* p. 228.

34. McCartney, *Documentary History of Jamestown Island,* vol. 1, p. 89.

35. Thomas Hariot, A *briefe and true report* (New York, Dover Publications Inc., 1972), pp. 7–12.

36. William Kelso and Beverly Straube, *1996 Interim Report* (Richmond, VA, Association for the Preservation of Virginia Antiquities, October 1997), p. 19.

37. My thanks to Bly Straube for this reference, taken from Johannes Henrici Curadi, *Silesia Togata* (Legnica, Poland, 1706).

38. Information from Historic Jamestown.

39. See Chapter 15 for the elder Tradescant's many North American plants.

40. John Parkinson, *Theatrum Botanicum* (London, 1640), p. 133.

41. Margaret Pelling and Frances White, *Physicians and Irregular Medical Practitioners in London 1550–1640, database* (British History Online, Institute of Historical Research, 2004). Among the Goodyer papers at Magdalen College Oxford is a small list of plants 'to have from Mr Gibbes', Goodyer MS 11, fol. 23v.

42. The list (from the Goodyer papers at Magdalen College, Oxford, Goodyer MS 11, fol. 21) is printed in R.T. Gunther, *Early British Botanists and their Gardens* (Oxford University Press, 1922), pp. 370–1.

43. Magdalen College, Oxford, Goodyer MS 11, fol. 20.

44. Could this be *Lonicera sempervirens,* included in Tradescant's 1656 catalogue as 'Virginian Woodbine tree'?

45. John Smith, A *Map of Virginia* (Oxford, 1612), p. 3. It ends with the Indian words for 'Bid Pokahontas bring hither two little Baskets, & I wil give her white beads to make her a chaine'.

46. William Strachey, *The Historie of Travell into Virginia Britania (1612),* Louis B. Wright and Virginia Freund (eds), Hakluyt Society, 2nd series, no. 53 (London, 1953), pp. 174–207.

47. See Rountree, *Pocahontas, Powhatan, Opechancanough,* p. 101. Although Strachey remarked that the native women were willing, with their husbands' permission, to 'embrace the acquaintance of any stranger for nothing' both Smith and Strachey included an Indian word for 'cuckold'.

48. Bekkers, *Correspondence of John Morris,* p. 3.

49. John Parkinson, *Theatrum Botanicum* (London, 1640).

50. I am indebted to ethnohistorian Helen C. Rountree for relating Tradescant's plant introductions to their Virginian habitats.

51. Parkinson, *Theatrum Botanicum,* p. 1477.

52 Despite a suggestion that Tradescant once owned or leased this land, documentary proof is lacking.

53. The first land patent to mention a cypress swamp was granted to Charles Barcroft on

10 February 1637, for 350 acres in Isle of Wight County: Nugent, *Cavaliers and Pioneers*, p. 80. Later patents mentioned cypress swamps in Lower Norfolk County (site of the Great Dismal Swamp), Nancimond County, and Surry County. According to Helen C. Rountree, the species is also found in the Pamunkey River, the Piankatank River, in Battle Creek off the Patuxent River and in the upper reaches of the Pocomoke River.

54. Parkinson, *Theatrum Botanicum*, p. 1206.

55. Ibid., p. 1427.

56. Ibid., p. 1367.

57. Ibid., p. 1465.

58. Ibid., p. 1595.

59. Ibid., p. 1607.

60. Ibid., p. 1368.

61. Ibid., p. 1163.

62. Ibid., p. 1417.

63. Ibid., p. 1050.

64. Ibid., p. 1235.

65. James W. Herrick, *Iroquois Medical Botany* (Syracuse, NY., Syracuse University Press, 1995), p. 148. Reference kindly supplied by Helen C. Rountree.

66. Philip Miller, *The Gardeners Dictionary* (London, 1731, and Dublin, 1764).

67. John Evelyn, *Sylva* (London, 1679), p. 79.

68. Cerinda W. Evans, *Some Notes on Shipbuilding and Shipping in Colonial Virginia* (Williamsburg, VA, Virginia 350th Anniversary Historical Booklets, no. 22, 1957), p. 37.

69. Sarah P. Stetson, 'The Traffic in Seeds and Plants from England's Colonies in North America', *Agricultural History* (Berkeley, California, Agricultural History Society, 1949), vol. 23, pp. 45–56.

70. See William Byrd, *The Westover Manuscripts* (Petersburg, VA, 1841) and Stephen C. Ausband, *Byrd's Line* (Charlottesville, University of Virginia Press, 2002).

71. Quoted in Ausband, *Byrd's Line*, p. 41.

72. John Tradescant, *Musaeum Tradescantianum* (London, 1656).

73. 'A letter from Mr John Clayton' in Force, *Tracts and Other Papers*, vol. 3, p. 15.

74. For detailed descriptions of the mantle, see Christian F. Feest, in Arthur MacGregor (ed.), *Tradescant's Rarities* (Oxford, Clarendon Press, 1983), pp. 130–5 and Gregory A. Waselkov, 'Indian maps of the colonial southeast', in Peter H. Wood, Gregory A. Waselkov and M. Thomas Hatley (eds), *Powhatan's Mantle* (Lincoln and London, University of Nebraska Press, 1989).

75. Peter Mundy, *The Travels of Peter Mundy*, vol. 3, Part I, ed. Lieut. Col. Sir Richard Carnac Temple (London, Hakluyt Society, 1919), 2nd series, no. 45, pp. 1–3.

76. MacGregor (ed.), *Tradescant's Rarities*, p. 21.

77. Christian F. Feest in MacGregor (ed.), *Tradescant's Rarities*, p. 135.

78. Waselkov, 'Indian maps', in Wood et al. (eds), *Powhatan's Mantle*, p. 308.

79. Annual letter of the Jesuits for 1639, quoted in Clayton Colman Hall, *Narratives of Early Maryland* (New York, Charles Scribner's Sons, 1910), p. 125.

80. See MacGregor (ed.) *Tradescant's Rarities*, p. 134.

81. Bekkers, *Correspondence of John Morris*, pp. 2–3.

82. I am indebted to Dr Tom Davidson of Jamestown Settlement for these suggestions.

83. Colman Hall, *Narratives of Early Maryland*, p. 147.

84. National Archives, CO 1/9, fols 224–5 (4 April 1638); and an abstract of William Claiborne's case, dated 4 April 1638, in *The Virginia Magazine of History & Biography*, vol. X for 1902–3, pp. 269–71.

85. But see National Archives, CO 1/8, fol. 92. The inked date on the record of Claiborne's patent (16 May 1631) has been replaced by a pencilled date of 8 October 1634.

86. Tradescant, *Musaeum Tradescantianum*, p. 181.

87. Bekkers, *Correspondence of John Morris*, p. 3.

88. Parkinson, *Theatrum Botanicum*, p. 1477.

89. See Sir Thomas Hanmer, *The Garden Book of Sir Thomas Hanmer Bart* (London, Gerald Howe, 1933), p. 15.

90 For an explanation of the system and its abuses, see Nugent, *Cavaliers and Pioneers*, vol. 1, pp. xxiv–xxvi; and W. Stitt Robinson Jnr, *Mother Earth*, Jamestown 350th Anniversary Historical Booklets, no. 12 (Williamsburg, VA, 1957), pp. 32–43.

91. Nugent, *Cavaliers and Pioneers*, vol. 1, p. xxv.

92. Stitt Robinson Jnr, *Mother Earth*, p. 40.

93. Nugent, *Cavaliers and Pioneers*, vol. 1, p. 135.

94. Library of Virginia, Lancaster County Record Book No. 2, 1654–1666, p. 163. Although the deed of gift was dated 3 May 1640 (and witnessed by Indian trader Henry Fleet), it was not recorded until 11 July 1660.

95. See W. P. Palmer (ed.), *Calendar of Virginia State Papers and Other Manuscripts, 1652–1781*, vol. 1 (Richmond, VA, 1875), p. 3.

96. McCartney, *Documentary History of Jamestown*, vol. 1, pp. 93–6.

97. Ibid., vol. 1, pp. 93–6

98. See Bekkers, *Correspondence of John Morris*.

99. Letter of March 1645 from Dr Robert Child to John Winthrop Jnr in John Winthrop, *Winthrop Papers*, vol. 5, 1645–1649 (Boston, Massachusetts Historical Society, 1947), pp. 10–11. 'I received likewise some seeds,' wrote Dr Child, 'which I have delivered to the Gardiner of Yorke garden and Mr. Tredescham, who are very thankefull to you for them, and have returned diverse sorts which you shall Receive by the hands of Mr. Willoughby.' Dr Child sent Winthrop five or six sorts of vine in a cask, 'with some prun grafts, some pyrocanthus trees, and very many sor[ts] of our common plants, and seeds'.

100. Nugent, *Cavaliers and Pioneers*, vol. 1, p. 329.

101. Tradescant, *Musaeum Tradescantianum.*

102. Nugent, *Cavaliers and Pioneers*, vol. 1, p. 303.

103 Stitt Robinson Jnr, *Mother Earth*, p. 41.

104. Nugent, *Cavaliers and Pioneers*, p. 329. These were genuine settlers, see Nugent pp. 492 and 511.

Chapter Twenty-Two, Of Cabbages and Kings

1. Short biographies of John Morris and Johannes de Laet appear in J. A. F. Bekkers, *Correspondence of John Morris* (Assen, Van Gorcum & Comp. NV, 1970), pp. xii–xxvii.

2. Ibid., p. 36.

3. The manuscript found its way into the hands of Elias Ashmole and is now in the Bodleian Library, Oxford, MS Ashmole 823.

4. Parkinson credits to 'Monsieur John de Laet' information about the 'sensitive thorny shrubbe' from a Spanish book published in Mexico. John Parkinson, *Theatrum Botanicum* (London, 1640), p. 1617.

5. Bekkers, *Correspondence of John Morris*, p. 3, letter of 9 June 1638. I am indebted to J. B. Jonas for his translation of Morris's correspondence.

6. National Archives, SP 38/18, warrant dated 12 November 1639.

7. Bekkers, *Correspondence of John Morris*, p. 6.

8. Ibid., p. 7, letter of 24 October 1638.

9. *Allegations for Marriage Licences issued by the Bishop of London 1611 to 1828*, vol. 26 (London, Harleian Society, 1887), p. 237. The licence was granted on 29 September 1638 and they married two days later.

10. Ashmolean Museum, Oxford, F707. The date of the portrait is given as 1645 and Hester's age as thirty-seven, suggesting that she was born c.1608.

11. Guildhall Library, MS 5685, parish registers for St Nicholas Cole Abbey: 'John Tradescant of Lambeth in ye County of Surrey & Hester Pooks of St Brides London maiden were married October 1st by licence.'

12. John Stow, *The Survey of London* (London, 1633), p. 398.

13. Rachel Poole, 'An Outline of the History of the De Critz Family of Painters', *The Second Volume of the Walpole Society 1912–13* (Oxford, 1913), pp. 45–68.

14. See William Page, *Letters of Denization and Acts of Naturalization* (Lymington, Huguenot Society of London, vol. 8, 1893), p. xxiii.

15. This Hester Pooks was born between 1594 and 1597, and on 7 June 1618 married 'Jeames Stayneforth' at St Andrew Undershaft: Guildhall Library, MS 4107/1, parish registers 1558–1634.

16. Mary Edmond, 'Limners and Picturemakers', *The Forty-seventh Volume of the Walpole Society 1978–80* (London, Pitman Press, 1980), pp. 144–52.

17. Ashmolean Museum, F659, now attributed to Emanuel de Critz.

18. Poole, 'An Outline of the History of the De Critz Family of Painters', pp. 45–68. Old John de Critz was born before 1568 and possibly even before 1552. He died at a very advanced age in 1642.

19. See, for instance, National Archives, E351/3269.

20. Poole, 'An Outline of the History of the De Critz Family of Painters', pp. 65–6.

21. Bekkers, *Correspondence of John Morris*, p. 10, letter of 12 November 1638.

22. Ibid., p. 12, letter of 12 January 1639.

23. See Barry Coward, *Social Change and Continuity* (London, Longman, revised edn, 1997), p. 28.

24. Charles Drew (ed.), *Lambeth Churchwardens' Accounts 1504–1645 and Vestry Book 1610*, vol. 2 (Surrey Record Society, vol. 20, 1950), p. 136.

25. National Archives, SP28/194, Part 1. Tradescant contributed to the Protestants in Ireland via his South Lambeth parish, dated 3 July 1642.

26. Drew (ed.), *Lambeth Churchwardens' Accounts*, pp. 262 and 263.

27. National Archives, E351/3272.

28. Tim Buxbaum, *Icehouses* (Princes Risborough, Bucks, Shire Publications, 1992), p. 3.

29. According to Aubrey, the idea came to Bacon as he was travelling by coach through snow towards Highgate Hill with the king's Scottish physician. John Aubrey, *Brief Lives*, ed. Andrew Clark, vol. 1 (Oxford, Clarendon Press, 1898), pp. 75–6.

30. National Archives, E351/3272.

31. David Blayney Brown, *Catalogue of the Collection of Drawings in the Ashmolean Museum*, vol. 4, (Oxford, Clarendon Press, 1982), pp. 87–8, item 142.

32. Sir Thomas Herbert, *Memoirs of the Last Two Years of the Reign of King Charles I* (London, 1839), pp. 45–6.

33. Ibid., pp. 17–18.

34. Arthur MacGregor, *Tradescant's Rarities* (Oxford, Clarendon Press, 1983), p. 13, quoting the 'Book of Benefactors' at the Ashmolean Museum, AMS 2, enclosure 4.

35. Herbert, *Memoirs of the Last Two Years of the Reign of King Charles I*, p. 60.

36. For a political reading of Caroline masques, I am indebted to Dr Richard Cust's presentation on 'The Political Style of Charles I' at the National Maritime Museum on 20 May 2004.

37. Not everyone was convinced. In a rabid attack published in 1633 (*Histrio-Mastix*), Puritan lawyer William Prynne likened women actors to 'notorious whores', for which he had his ears cut off.

38. *Salmacida Spolia* (London, 1639).

39. Roy Strong, *Art and Power* (Bury St Edmunds, Boydell Press, 1984), pp. 169–70.

40. Ibid., p. 163.

41. In June 1639, for instance, the queen went there for ten days while Charles was in Scotland and her eldest son remained in Whitehall.

42. Bekkers, *Correspondence of John Morris*, p. 18, written in summer, 1639.

43. Ibid., pp. 20–1, letter of 13 August 1639.

44. *Calendar of State Papers, Domestic Series, Charles I, 1640* (London, 1880), p. 495.

45. *Calendar of State Papers, Venetian Series, 1640–42*, vol. 25 (London, 1924), p. 60, letter of 27 July 1640.

46. Bekkers, *Correspondence of John Morris*, p. 38, letter of 27 July 1640.

47. Ibid., pp. 42–4 and 37.

48. *Dictionary of National Biography*, online edition (2004); and Poole, 'An Outline of the History of the De Critz Family of Painters', p. 54.

49. H. W. Kew and H. E. Powell, *Thomas Johnson* (London, Longmans, Green & Co., 1932), p. 124.

50. *Calendar of State Papers, Domestic Series, Charles I, 1641–43* (London, 1887), p. 126, for 28 September 1641.

51. Letter of Alexander Marshal to Sir Justinian Isham, 9 September 1641, translated by Prudence Leith-Ross, in *The Florilegium of Alexander Marshal* (London, Royal Collection Enterprises, 2000), pp. 362–3.

52. John Tradescant, *Musaeum Tradescantianum* (London, 1656), p. 41.

53. See Leith-Ross, *The Florilegium of Alexander Marshal*, pp. 4–5.

54. The Hartlib Papers, Humanities Research Institute, University of Sheffield, Ephemerides, Notes on Inventors, undated, 31/23/17A.

55. *Calendar of State Papers, Domestic Series, Charles I, 1641–43*, p. 292.

56. See letter dated 7/17 March 1642 from Elizabeth, Queen of Bohemia, to Sir Thomas Rowe, *Calendar of State Papers, Domestic Series, Charles I, 1641–43*, p. 294.

57. National Archives LR2/297, A Survey of . . . Oatlands, fol. 109.

58. Bekkers, *Correspondence of John Morris*, p. 71, letter of 3 March 1642.

59. Ibid., p. 73, letter of 18 April 1642. I am indebted for this reference to J. B. Jonas.

60. Ibid., p. 80, letter of 20 October 1642.

61. Ibid., p. 81, letter of 23 November 1642.

62. William Lithgow, *The Present Surveigh of London* (London, 1643).

63. London Survey Committee, *The Survey of London*, vol. 23, *South Bank & Vauxhall* (London, 1951), p. 118.

64. Maps of the fortifications show four forts south of the river – see 'A Plan of the City and Environs of London', British Library maps *3480. (8.) and 3485. (138).

65. Thomas Allen, *The History and Antiquities of the Parish of Lambeth* (London, 1827), pp. 237–8.

66. Daniel Lysons, *The Environs of London*, vol. 1, *County of Surrey* (London, 1796), p. 259.

67. Allen, *The History and Antiquities of the Parish of Lambeth*, p. 21.

68. Dorcas Day had married cooper Leonard Chambers at St Katherine by the Tower on 20 June 1602: A. W. Hughes Clarke, *The Registers of St. Katherine by the Tower, Part 1* (London, Harleian Society, vol. 75, 1945), p. 78. Soon after Chambers' death, she married his fellow cooper, Alexander Norman, on 16 January 1621 at St Botolph without Aldgate, Guildhall Library, MS 9220.

69. Recorded in: W. H. Challen, *Marriages & Banns 1547–1837*, vol. 52, (1942), transcripts of parish registers for St Bartholomew the Less, London, 28 January 1645: 'Allexander Norman of St Buttophes Algate London & Franncis Trudescant, (fac)'.

70. *Allegations for Marriage Licences*, vol. 26, p. 275.

71. T. C. Dale (ed.), *The Inhabitants of London in 1638* (London, Society of Genealogists, 1931), p. 223.

72. See John Stow, *The Survey of London* (London, 1633), pp. 117–18.

73. For more information about Alexander Norman's business, see Prudence Leith-Ross, *The John Tradescants* (London, Peter Owen, 1984), pp. 111–13.

74. The year after his marriage to Dorcas Chambers *née* Day, he registered his mark with the Company of Coopers based on the initials of her previous husband, L(eonard) C(hambers). Guildhall Library, MS 05633 fol. 67v.

75. Guildhall Library, MS 05602/3, fols 73v., 104v., 127r., 145r.

76. Guildhall Library, MS 9222/2.

77. Parish registers for St James Clerkenwell record that a 'Franses Norman' married a 'Willia' Ranes' there on 17 May 1667, but was this Frances Tradescant? See Robert Hoveden (ed.), *A True Register of . . . St. James, Clerkenwell*, vol. 3, *Marriages 1551–1754* (London, Harleian Society, vol. 13, 1887), p. 131.

78. Ashmolean Museum, F707.

79. Poole, 'An Outline of the History of the De Critz Family of Painters', pp. 64–5.

80. Ashmolean Museum, F667.

81. Poole, 'An Outline of the History of the De Critz Family of Painters', pp. 64–5.

82. Bekkers, *Correspondence of John Morris*, p. 73, letter of 18 April 1642.

83. Ibid., p. 111, letter of 2 February 1646.

84. Ibid., p. 117, letter of 11 June 1646.

85. See Kenneth R. Andrews, *Trade, Plunder and Settlement* (Cambridge University Press, 1984).

86. Tradescant, *Musaeum Tradescantianum*, p. 35.

87. Quoted in Arthur MacGregor, 'The Tradescants as collectors of rarities', in MacGregor (ed.), *Tradescant's Rarities* (Oxford, Clarendon Press, 1983), p. 22.

88. Ibid., p. 21.

89. Bekkers, *Correspondence of John Morris*, pp. 151–2, letter of 18 February 1649.

90. Ibid., p. 153, letter of 17 April 1649.

91. John Evelyn, *The Diary of John Evelyn*, ed. E. S. de Beer (6 vols, Oxford, Clarendon Press, 2000), vol. 3, p. 217, 10 June 1658.

92. Bekkers, *Correspondence of John Morris*, p. 155, letter of 6 August 1649.

93. Ibid., pp. 165–7, letter of 26 December 1649. Timothy Cruzo was a wealthy Dutch merchant who lived in the Parish of St Helen's–within–Bishopsgate. De Laet's son Samuel had married his daughter Rebecca.

94. The Hartlib Papers, Humanities Research Institute, University of Sheffield, Ephemerides, 1649, Part 2, April–August, E 28/1/17A.

95. The Hartlib Papers, Ephemerides 1649, Part 3, July/August–December, E28/1/33A.

96. The Hartlib Papers, Ephemerides 1649, Part 3, July/August–December, E28/1/32A.

97. Archives of the Royal College of Physicians, Oxford Physic Garden, Envelope 362 ; see also Sir George Clark, A *History of the Royal College of Physicians of London* (3 vols, Oxford, Clarendon Press for the Royal College of Physicians, 1964), vol. 1, p. 256; and British Library, Sloane MS 55, fol. 4.

98. London Survey Committee, *Survey of London*, vol. 23, *South Bank & Vauxhall, Part 1* (London, 1951), pp. 25–7.

99. John Aubrey, *The Natural History and Antiquities of the County of Surrey* (5 vols, London, 1719), vol. 5, p. 282. See also London Survey Committe, *Survey of London*, vol. 23, pp. 25–7.

100. John Rose, *The English Vineyard Vindicated* (London, 1666). See Chapter 5.

101. National Archives, LR2/297, fols 106–7, 110, 113–15.

102. National Archives, E121/4/8, item 29.

103. See 'Inigo Jones' connection with Weybridge' at the Elmbridge Museum, Weybridge, Surrey.

104. Oliver Millar (ed.), *The Inventories and Valuations of the King's Goods 1649–1651*, vol. 43, Walpole Society (Glasgow, University Press, 1972), p. 250.

105 These can be viewed online at http://elmbridgemuseum.org.uk.

Chapter Twenty-Three, The Useful Gardener

1. Ashmolean Museum, F684.

2. Rachel Poole, 'An Outline of the History of the De Critz Family of Painters', in *The Second Volume of the Walpole Society 1912–1913* (Oxford, 1913), pp. 64–5.

3. Arthur MacGregor (ed.), *Tradescant's Rarities* (Oxford, Clarendon Press, 1983), p. 308.

4. See Eleanour Sinclair Rohde's introduction to Sir Thomas Hanmer, *The Garden Book of Sir Thomas Hanmer, Bart* (London, Gerald Howe, 1933).

5. Quoted in Anna Pavord, *The Tulip* (London, Bloomsbury, 1999), p. 117.

6. See Jim Bennett and Scott Mandelbrote, *The Garden, the Ark, the Tower, the Temple* (Oxford, Museum of the History of Science in association with the Bodleian Library, 1998), pp. 33–42 and 157–68.

7. Quoted in Bennett and Mandelbrote, *The Garden, the Ark, the Tower, the Temple*, p. 37.

8. Samuel Hartlib, *Samuel Hartlib his Legacie* (London, 1651).

9. The Hartlib Papers, Humanities Research Institute, University of Sheffield, Ephemerides, E 28/1/59B (1650, February–May).

10. Samuel Hartlib, *Universal Husbandry Improved* (London, 1670), pp.155–6.

11. John Tradescant, *Musaeum Tradescantianum* (London, 1656), pp. 73–178.

12. See Chapter 15.

13. P. J. Jarvis, 'The introduced trees and shrubs cultivated by the Tradescants at South Lambeth', *Journal of the Society for the Bibliography of Natural History*, 9, 3 (1979), pp. 223–64.

14. An edited version of this chapter first appeared in *The London Gardener*, Journal of the London Historic Parks and Gardens Trust, vol. 10 (2005), pp. 100–7.

15. Hanmer, *The Garden Book of Sir Thomas Hanmer Bart*, pp. 18–20.

16. Ibid., p. 9.

17. John Evelyn, *Elysium Britannicum, or The Royal Gardens*, ed. John E. Ingram (Philadelphia, University of Pennsylvania Press, 2001), pp. 328–9. In a margin note Evelyn has added: 'Cf: Mr Hook Exp: that ayre is burnt up too much by fire'.

18. Other plants described as 'Virginian' that had not appeared in his father's catalogue included: an aster (*Aster tradescantii*); a honeysuckle (*Lonicera sempervirens*); a morning glory (*Ipomoea*); a turtlehead (*Chelone glabra*); Virgininia creeper (*Parthenocissus quinquefolia*); a 'Virginian Nettle Tree' or hackberry (*Celtis occidentalis*); an evening primrose; the Jerusalem artichoke (*Helianthus tuberosus*); a bistort; a Virginian firethorn (*Pyracantha*), which was probably something else; bloodroot (*Sanguinaria canadensis*); the stag's horn sumach (*Rhus typhina*); a plant he identified as 'Virginian tree Nightshade' and two vines – the 'Virginia wilde Vine' and the 'Fox-Grape from Virginia'.

19. Tradescant's variety did at least have a double flower, R. *repens* 'Flore Pleno'.

20. Ashmole first went simpling in June 1648, becoming (according to Anthony Wood) an 'eminent Botanist' within just a few months. For his visits to Oxford Physic Garden see C. H. Josten, *Elias Ashmole (1617–1692)*, (5 vols, Oxford, Clarendon Press, 1966), vol. 1, pp. 57, 60 and 167–8.

21. William Coles, *The Art of Simpling* (London, 1656).

22. Ibid., p. 72.

23. Ibid., p. 12.

24. William Coles, *Adam in Eden: or, Natures Paradise* (London, 1657), p. 592.

25. Sir Hugh Platt, *Delightes for Ladies* (London, 1602), Secrets in Distillation no. 6.

26. The Hartlib Papers, Humanities Research Institute, University of Sheffield, Ephemerides, E 28/2/75B (2 September–31 December 1653).

27. Northampton Record Office, Finch–Hatton Manuscripts, MS FH 2423.

28. Northampton Record Office, Finch–Hatton Manuscripts, MS FH 2417, 2455, 2448, 2450, 2455.

29. Samuel Hartlib, *A Designe for Plentie* (London, 1652).

30. Ibid., p. 6.

31. Ibid., p. 10.

32. John Evelyn, *The Diary of John Evelyn*, ed. E. S. de Beer (6 vols, Oxford, Clarendon Press, 1955), vol. 3, pp. 198–9, entry for 17 September 1657.

33. For a discussion of the London nursery trade in the seventeenth century, see John Harvey, *Early Nurserymen* (London and Chichester, Philimore, 1974).

34. Guildhall Library, London, MS 3389/1A.

35. Thomas Platter and Horatio Busino, *The Journals of Two Travellers* (London, Caliban Books, 1995), p. 117.

36. Guildhall Library, London, MS 03396, Worshipful Company of Gardeners.

37. Ibid., 'Constitutions, 1 July 1606', p. 22.

38. Guildhall Library, London, MS 21129/1, Worshipful Company of Gardeners.

39. In his book *The English Gardener* (London, 1670), pp. 82–8, Leonard Meager included a fruit catalogue from Gurle's nursery. See also John H. Harvey, 'Leonard Gurle's Nurseries and Some Others', *Garden History*, 3, 3 (Summer 1975), pp. 42–9.

40. *Calendar of State Papers, Domestic Series, Charles II, 1660–61* (London, 1860) p. 369. John Rose was appointed keeper and gardener of the garden in St James's Park in November 1660, at an annual salary of £40.

Chapter Twenty-Four, A Snake in Eden

1. C. H. Josten (ed.), *Elias Ashmole (1617–1692)*, (5 vols, Oxford, Clarendon Press, 1966), vol. 2, p. 530. This account of relations between the Tradescants and Elias Ashmole relies heavily on Josten's five-volume work. Ashmole's own biographical notes (Bodleian Library, MS Ashmole 1136, fols 2–98) also provide a brief overview of his life.

2. John Evelyn, *The Diary of John Evelyn*, ed. E. S. de Beer (6 vols, Oxford, Clarendon Press, 2000), vol. 4, p. 138, 23 July 1678, and see Chapter 26.

3. Anthony Wood, *Athenae Oxonienses* (4 vols, London, 3rd edn, Philip Bliss, 1820), vol. 4, col. 363.

4. Josten, *Elias Ashmole*, vol. 2, p. 448.

5. Ibid., vol. 2, p. 474.

6. Ibid., vol. 1, p. 114.

7. Ibid., vol. 2, p. 534.

8. Ibid., vol. 1, p. 26.

9. Ashmole replaced a cornelian ring from his first wife's sister with a black enamelled one given to him by Lady Manwaring. Josten, *Elias Ashmole*, vol. 2, pp. 450 and 451.

10. Elias Ashmole, *Theatrum Chemicum Britannicum* (London, 1652).

11. Quoted in Josten, *Elias Ashmole*, vol. 1, pp. 84–5.

12. Ibid., vol. 2, p. 537.

13. The Hartlib Papers, Humanities Research Institute, University of Sheffield, Ephemerides, E 28/2/11B (January–c. April, 1651).

14. The Hartlib Papers, Ephemerides, E 28/2/27A (1 January–7 October 1652).

15. Josten, *Elias Ashmole*, vol. 2, p. 580.

16. Ibid., vol. 1, p. 93.

17. Ibid., vol. 1, p. 44.

18. Ibid., vol. 2, p. 606. In Ashmole's astrology, these are called 'horary questions'.

19. Ibid., vol. 2, p. 612.

20. Prudence Leith-Ross, *The Florilegium of Alexander Marshal* (London, Royal Collection Enterprises, 2000), p. 6.

21. Josten, *Elias Ashmole*, vol. 2, pp. 612–13.

22. The Hartlib Papers, Ephemerides, E 31/22/32B (June/July 1648).

23. John Tradescant, *Musaeum Tradescantianum* (London, 1656).

24. Izaak Walton, *The Universal Angler* (London, 5th edn, 1676), p. 251.

25. No other benefactor was linked to the natural history items, although 'Mr *Sandys*' (most probably the elder Tradescant's correspondent, George Sandys) was credited with various Egyptian 'idols'.

26. See Thomas Wharton, *Adenographia* (London, 1656).

27. From a list of curiosities in Ashmole's handwriting, it seems that Ashmole listed the rarities himself, leaving queries to discuss with Tradescant, including this letter from a printer's block. R. T. Gunther, *Early Science in Oxford* (13 vols, Oxford, 1920–1961), vol. 3, pp. 436–40.

28. Among the benefactors who have appeared already in the Tradescants' story are: Archbishop William Laud, Viscount Dorchester (Sir Dudley Carleton), Countess of Arundel (wife to Thomas Howard, Earl of Arundel), Sir Thomas Roe (ambassador to Turkey), Sir Christopher Hatton, Sir Henry Wotton, Sir Nathaniel Bacon, Sir John Trevor, Mr Nicholas (Secretary to the Navy), Phineas Pett, fruit-grower John Millen, merchant Mr Slany, possibly John Smith (listed as either Sir John Smith or Mr Smith), court artists/craftsmen such as Rowland Bucket and stonemason Nicholas Stone. See April London, 'Musaeum Tradescantianum and the benefactors to the Tradescants' museum', in Arthur MacGregor (ed.), *Tradescant's Rarities* (Oxford, Clarendon Press, 1983), pp. 24–39.

29. Quoted in Josten, *Elias Ashmole*, vol. 4, p. 1665.

30. H. E. Strickland and A. G. Melville, *The Dodo and its Kindred* (London, 1848), p. 23.

31. Dr Robert Plot, *The Natural History of Oxford-shire* (Oxford, 1677), pp. 236–7.

32. John Aubrey, *Brief Lives*, ed. Andrew Clark (Oxford, Clarendon Press, 1898), vol. 1, pp. 132–3.

33. Josten, *Elias Ashmole*, vol. 2, p. 618.

34. E. G., Gent. and H. F., Gent., *A Prodigious & Tragicall History of the Arraignment, Tryall, Confession, and Condemnation of Six Witches at Maidstone* (London, 1652), p. 4.

35. See also C. L'Estrange Ewen, *Witch Hunting and Witch Trials* (London, 1929), pp. 239–43. This gives the date of the Kent Summer Sessions at Maidstone as 27 July 1652.

36. Josten, *Elias Ashmole*, vol. 1, p. 114.

37. National Archives, PROB 10/954 (the younger Tradescant's original will).

38. A. C. Ducarel, 'Upon the Early Cultivation of Botany', in *Bibliotheca Topographica Britannica*, no. 39, *The History and Antiquities of the Parish of Lambeth in the County of Surrey* (London, 1786), vol. 2.2, Appendix, p. 97.

39. National Archives, PROB 10/1090 (Hester Tradescant's original will).

40. Sir Anthony Wagner, *English Genealogy* (Chichester, Phillimore & Co., 3rd edn, 1983), p. 127.

41. William Bird, *The Magazine of Honour* (London, 1642), p. 147. See also G. D. Squibb QC, *The High Court of Chivalry* (Oxford, Clarendon Press, 1959), p. 172.

42. College of Arms, *Visitation of Suffolk 1664–1668*, Harleian Society, vol. 61 (London, 1910), pp. 53 and 213–14.

43. Quoted in Josten, *Elias Ashmole*, vol. 2, p. 620, n. 6.

44. Tradescant, *Musaeum Tradescantianum*, introduction.

45. National Portrait Gallery, NPG 1089. For a full description, see David Piper, *Catalogue of Seventeenth-Century Portraits in the National Portrait Gallery, 1625–1714* (Cambridge University Press, 1963), pp. 350–1.

46. The portrait hung in the Waiting Room at Strawberry Hill: Horace Walpole, *The Works of Horatio Walpole, Earl of Orford* (5 vols, London, 1798), vol. 2, p. 405, 'Tradescant junior, with a skull covered with moss for the powder of sympathy'.

47. Peter Cooper, 'Medicinal Properties of Body Parts', *Pharmaceutical Journal*, 273, 7330 (18/25 December 2004), pp. 900–2; and Sarah Bakewell, 'Cooking with Mummy', *Fortean Times*, no. 124 (July 1999), pp. 34–8.

48. See *Pharmacopoeia Londinensis* (London, 1682), pp. 194–6 for a recipe for spirit of brains, made by adding the brians of a 'young man slain' to various flower essences including lily-of-the-valley, cowslips, lavender and black cherries.

49. Henry W. Robinson and Walter Adams (eds), *The Diary of Robert Hooke M.A., M.D., F.R.S. 1672–1680* (London, Taylor & Francis, 1935), p. 263.

50. Josten, *Elias Ashmole*, vol. 2, pp. 630–6.

51. Ibid., vol. 1, p. 108.

52. Tradescant, *Musaeum Tradescantianum*, introduction.

53. Born in Prague in 1607, Wenceslaus Hollar came to England with Thomas Howard, Earl of Arundel, whom he had met in 1635. On the royalist side during the civil war he was taken prisoner at the siege of Basing House, afterwards joining Arundel at Antwerp for eight years of self-imposed exile. He died in 1677.

54. Elias Ashmole, *The Institution, Laws & Ceremonies of the Most Noble Order of the Garter* (2 vols, London, 1672).

55. Aubrey, *Brief Lives*, vol. 1, p. 408.

56. The Hartlib Papers, Ephemerides, E 29/5/74A (May–June 1656).

57. Ashmolean Museum, F663.

58. Arthur MacGregor (ed.), *Tradescant's Rarities* (Oxford, Clarendon Press, 1983), p. 301.

59. Quoted in R. T. Gunther, *Early British Botanists and their Gardens* (Oxford University Press, 1922), p. 272.

60. Josten, *Elias Ashmole*, vol. 1, p. 168.

61. The Hartlib Papers, Ephemerides, E 29/6/6A (January–May 1657).

62. John Evelyn, *The Diary of John Evelyn*, ed. E. S. De Beer (6 vols, Oxford, Clarendon Press, 1955), vol. 3, p. 199.

63. National Archives, C7/454/1. As the original documents are badly damaged, this account relies heavily on C. H. Josten's summary of the case in *Elias Ashmole*, vol. 2, pp. 768–71; and vol. 3, pp. 853–4.

64. Charles Hoole, *A New Discovery of the old Art of Teaching Schoole* (London, 1660), pp. 284–5.

65. For a facsimile of the dedication, see Prudence Leith-Ross, *The John Tradescants* (London, Peter Owen, 1984), p. 123.

66. Josten, *Elias Ashmole*, vol. 1, p. 130.

67. Ibid., vol. 2, p. 795, entry for 12 October 1660. I am indebted to Malgosia Nowak-Kemp for showing me a pair of mummified twin girls at the Oxford University Museum of Natural History, quite possibly the ones that Ashmole showed to King Charles II.

68. J. Q. Adams (ed.), *The Dramatic Records of Sir Henry Herbert* (New Haven and London, Yale University Press, 1917), pp. 46–7.

69. National Archives, SP29/38, item 74, fol. 152. See also *Calendar of State Papers, Domestic Series, Charles II, 1661–2* (London, 1861), p. 27.

70. Ibid.

71. Hilary Jenkinson and Dorothy L. Powell (eds), *Surrey Quarter Sessions Records, The Order Book for 1659–1661* (Surrey Record Society, vol. 13, 1934).

72. Hilary Jenkinson and Dorothy L. Powell (eds), *Surrey Quarter Sessions Records, Order Book for 1661–1663* (Surrey Record Society, vol. 14, 1935), pp. 101–2. Tradescant was also named as a prospective juror for Quarter Sessions at Croydon, ibid., pp. 125 and 170.

73. National Archives, PROB 11/308, fols 152v.–153v.

74. Josten, *Elias Ashmole*, vol. 2, p. 771.

75. Charles Drew (ed.), *Lambeth Churchwardens' Accounts 1504–1645 and Vestry Book 1610*, vol. 2 (Surrey Record Society, vol. 20, 1950), pp. 261–3.

76. Cottle was also named as overseer in the will of Emanuel de Critz, son of old John de Critz, which was attested by the same notary public, Richard Hoare. See Rachel Poole, 'An Outline of the History of the De Critz Family of Painters', in *The Second Volume of the Walpole Society* (Oxford, 1913), pp. 45–69.

77. London Metropolitan Archives, X038/01, Lambeth, St Mary at Lambeth, Composite Register March 1539–August 1670: 'April the 25 Mr John Tradeskin from Southlambith'.
78. Guildhall Library, London, MS 03396, Worshipful Company of Gardeners, p. 19.
79. Guildhall Library, London, MS 21129/1, Worshipful Company of Gardeners.
80. Minet Library P3/A, Extracts from Collector for Poor Accounts, fol. 13.
81. Pepys Library, Magdalene College, Cambridge, PL 2972/226a and b. See also Samuel Pepys, *Private Correspondence and Miscellaneous Papers of Samuel Pepys 1679–1703*, ed. J. R. Tanner (2 vols, London, G. Bell & Sons, 1926), vol. 1, p. 166.

Chapter Twenty-Five, A Death by Drowning

1. Bodleian Library, MS Ashmole 1136, fol. 37; National Archives, Chancery Proceedings C7/454/1. The complaint was filed on 14 May.
2. C. H. Josten, *Elias Ashmole* (5 vols, Oxford, Clarendon Press, 1966), vol. 3, p. 987.
3. See the *Dictionary of National Biography* for a résumé of their legal careers.
4. Samuel Pepys, *The Diary of Samuel Pepys*, Robert Latham and William Matthews (eds) (11 vols, London, Bell & Hyman, 1970–83), vol. 2, pp. 87–8. Pepys drank so much on the night of the coronation that 'when I waked I found myself wet with my spewing.'
5. Josten, *Elias Ashmole*, vol. 1, p. 71.
6. Ibid., vol. 3, p. 982: 8 February 1664, 'My Picture drawne by Mr Le Neve, in my Heralds Coat'.
7. Lists of witnesses are given in National Archives, C37/70, C37/71 and C37/72. Hester's other witnesses were Richard Grimes and Mary Whetstone.
8. John Aubrey, *Brief Lives*, ed. Andrew Clark (2 vols, Oxford, Clarendon Press, 1898), vol. 1, p. 408.
9. The notes are contained in National Archives, C37/70, C37/71, C37/72. The book of judgments is C33/221, fols 744v.–745r.
10. Quoted in Arthur MacGregor, 'Two Early Migrations from Private to Public Sector', *The Private Collector and the Public Institution*, ed. Sheila D. Campbell (Toronto, 1998), pp. 64–81.
11. See Marjorie Swann, *Curiosities and Texts* (Philadelphia, University of Pennsylvania Press, 2001), p. 196.
12. British Library, Sloane MS 3988, fols 12v.–14.
13. Josten, *Elias Ashmole*, vol. 3, pp. 1070–1.
14. *Calendar of State Papers, Domestic Series, Charles II, 1666–7* (London, 1864), p. 99.
15. Bodleian Library, MS Ashmole 1136, fol. 41.
16. Josten, *Elias Ashmole*, vol. 4, p. 1635.
17. Minet Library, T41, Tradescant.
18. Josten, *Elias Ashmole*, vol. 3, p. 1140, entry for 15 April 1669.

19. 'A short Account of Several Gardens near London ... in December 1691', *Archaeologia: or, Miscellaneous Tracts Relating to Antiquity* (London, Society of Antiquaries of London, 1796), vol. 12, pp. 181–92.

20. Josten, *Elias Ashmole*, vol. 3, p. 1140.

21. Count Lorenzo Magalotti, *Travels of Cosmo the Third* (London, 1821), pp. 325–7.

22. Ibid., pp. 322–3.

23. Josten, *Elias Ashmole*, vol. 4, p. 1393, for 15 September 1674.

24. R. Parkinson (ed.), *The Autobiography of Henry Newcome* (Chetham Society, vol. 26, 1852), p. 165.

25. Josten, *Elias Ashmole*, vol. 4, p. 1397. The Ashmoles did not in fact move into the house until 28 August 1675, having spent the first night together there on 1 May 1675. The purchase was finalized on 26 September 1681.

26. National Archives, C7/541/2.

27. Bodleian Library, MS Rawl. D. 912, fol. 668; and Josten, *Elias Ashmole*, vol. 4, pp. 1450–2.

28. Josten, *Elias Ashmole*, vol. 4, p. 1402.

29. This is almost certainly a son of painter Emanuel de Critz.

30. Josten, *Elias Ashmole*, vol. 4, p. 1607.

31. Bodleian Library, MS Ashmole 1136, fol. 58. Her burial is recorded in the composite parish registers for St Mary at Lambeth, October 1669–May 1718, London Metropolitan Archives, X038/002.

32. National Archives, PROB 10/1090.

33. Josten, *Elias Ashmole*, vol. 4, p. 1608.

34. Mary Edmonds was by then married again, to Mathew Leigh or Lea, gentleman. Ashmole's record for 18 June 1678 notes that 'Mr: Lea & his wifes Release to me, of the 100£: I was to pay after Mrs: Tredescants death'. Josten, *Elias Ashmole*, vol. 4, p. 1617.

35. John Parkinson, *Paradisi in Sole, Paradisus Terrestris* (London, 1629). The plants are also listed in R. T. Gunther, *Early British Botanists and their Gardens* (Oxford University Press, 1922), p. 346.

36. See Chapter 21.

37. National Archives, C7/541/2.

Chapter Twenty-Six, The Ark Comes to Rest

1. John Evelyn, *The Diary of John Evelyn*, ed. E. S. de Beer (6 vols, Oxford, Clarendon Press, 2000), vol. 4, pp. 138–9, 23 July 1678.

2. John Evelyn, *The Life of Mrs Godolphin* (Oxford University Press, 1939), p. 72.

3. Izaak Walton, *The Universal Angler* (London, 5th edn, 1676), pp. 31–2.

4. Francis Willughby, *The Ornithology of Francis Willughby*, trans. and enlarged by John Ray (London, 1678).

5. Ibid., p. 154.

6. Ibid., p. 323.

7. Ibid., p. 193.

8. Ibid., p. 90.

9. C. H. Josten, *Elias Ashmole* (5 vols, Oxford, Clarendon Press, 1966), vol. 2, p. 804.

10. 28 April 1677, quoted in Josten, *Elias Ashmole*, vol. 4, p. 1477.

11. Marjorie Swann, *Curiosities and Texts* (Philadelphia, University of Pennsylvania Press, 2001), p. 4. The Royal Society may have acquired only part of the collection.

12. Robert Hubert, *A Catalogue of many Natural Rarities* (London, 1664).

13. Quoted in Swann, *Curiosities and Texts*, p. 4.

14. Josten, *Elias Ashmole*, vol. 1, p. 206.

15. Ibid., vol. 1, p. 218.

16. For the founding and early years of the museum, see L. S. Sutherland and L. G. Mitchell, *The History of the University of Oxford*, vol. 5 (Oxford, Clarendon Press, 1986), pp. 637–58.

17. Ibid., p. 641.

18. Nicholas Tyacke (ed.), *The History of the University of Oxford*, vol. 4, *The Seventeenth-Century* (Oxford, Clarendon Press, 1997), p. 437.

19. Josten, *Elias Ashmole*, vol. 1, p. 247.

20. Ibid., vol. 4, pp. 1707–10.

21. Ibid., vol. 4, pp. 1714–15.

22. Ibid., vol. 4, p. 1717.

23. Ibid., vol. 4, p. 1718.

24. Ibid., vol. 4, pp. 1721–2.

25. Ibid., vol. 4, pp. 1821–2.

26. Tyacke (ed.), *The History of the University of Oxford*, vol. 4, p. 438.

27. Quoted in Josten, *Elias Ashmole*, vol. 1, p. 255.

28. Tyacke (ed.), *The History of the University of Oxford*, vol. 4, pp. 438–9.

29. Ibid., vol. 4, p. 439.

30. Josten, *Elias Ashmole*, vol. 4, p. 1828.

31. Josten, *Elias Ashmole*, vol. 4, pp. 1441 and 1462.

32. Ibid., vol. 4, pp. 1715–16 and 1727.

33. London Survey Committee, *Survey of London*, vol. 26, (London, 1956), p. 74. For a history of the property, see David Sturdy, 'The Tradescants at Lambeth', *Journal of Garden History*, 2, 1 (1982), pp. 1–16.

34. Josten, *Elias Ashmole*, vol. 4, p. 1698.

35. Ibid., vol. 4, pp. 1865 and 1871.

36. Ibid., vol. 1, p. 258, and vol. 4, p. 1713, n. 2. Virgin earth is a *substantia arcana* frequently mentioned in alchemical texts. John Worlidge or Woolridge, author of *Systema Horti-culturae* (London, 1677), dedicated to Ashmole the third edition of his treatise on cider, *Vinetum Britannicum* (London, 1691).

37. Josten, *Elias Ashmole*, vol. 1, p. 273.

38. Letter of 26 September 1691 from Dr Martin Lister to Edward Lhuyd, quoted in Josten, *Elias Ashmole*, vol. 4, p. 1884. Also party to the attempted concealment was William Courten (alias Charleton).

39. The burial records for St Mary at Lambeth are missing for five years from October 1687.

40. Anthony Wood, *Athenae Oxonienses*, 2nd edn (2 vols, London, 1721), vol. 2, column 891.

41. Letter of 12 April 1694, quoted in Josten, *Elias Ashmole*, vol. 4, p. 1897.

42. John Aubrey, *The Natural History and Antiquities of the County of Surrey* (5 vols, London, 1719), vol. 1, pp. 12–13.

43. Victorian watercolours of Turret House by John Crowther can be seen in the Guildhall Library and by Edward Hull at the Ashmolean Museum, Oxford.

44. Royal Society, *Philosophical Transactions*, 46, 492 (April–June 1749), pp. 160–1.

45. *The Family Memoirs of the Rev. William Stukeley*, vol. 3 (Durham, Surtees Society, vol. 80, 1887), pp. 201–2.

46. Philip Miller, *The Gardeners Dictionary* (London, 1731, and Dublin, 1764), listed under 'Cupressus'.

47. A. C. Ducarel, *A Letter . . . to William Watson*, M.D., F.R.S., (London, 1773), p. 10.

48. Ibid., pp. 7–9.

49. British Library, Evelyn MS 45, see also John Evelyn, *Elysium Britannicum, or the Royal Gardens*, ed. John E. Ingram (Philadelphia, University of Pennsylvania Press, 2001), pp. 296 and 393.

50. Richard Pulteney, *Historical and Biographical sketches of the progress of botany in England* (London, 1790), pp. 175–9.

51. Rev. James Granger, *A Biographical History of England* (4 vols, London, 2nd edn, 1775), vol. 2, pp. 370–2. Gerbier also appeared in Class 5.

52. Ibid., vol. 2, p. 371.

53. John Parkinson, *Theatrum Botanicum* (London, 1640), pp. 1564–5.

54. Josten, *Elias Ashmole*, vol. 4, p. 1375.

55. Ibid., vol. 4, p. 1376, n. 2.

56. Ducarel, *A Letter to William Watson*, p. 10.

57. Restoration brochure preserved in cuttings folder at Minet Library, T41, Tradescant. See also report in *Illustrated London News* of 31 March 1855.

58. Graham Gibberd, *On Lambeth Marsh: The South Bank and Waterloo* (London, J. Gibberd, 1992), p. 9.

59. Guildhall Library, Sale cats. 36, ... to be sold by auction by Messrs. Driver & Co ... 22nd day of June 1880.

60. *Surrey Mirror*, 6 November 1942.

61. Ordnance Survey 5′ to 1 mile, London sheet X1.23; 1st edn 1871, 2nd edn revised 1893.

62. *Surrey Mirror*, 6 November 1942.

63. W. H. Quarrell and W. J. C. Quarrell, *Oxford in 1710* (Oxford, Basil Blackwell, 1928), pp. 26–31. See also Sutherland and Mitchell (eds), *The History of the University of Oxford*, vol. 5, pp. 639–58.

64. Josten, *Elias Ashmole*, vol. 4, p. 1823.

65. R. F. Ovenell, 'The Tradescant Dodo', *Archives of Natural History*, 19, 2 (June 1992), pp. 145–52.

66. Lewis Carroll, *Alice's Adventures in Wonderland* (London, Macmillan, 1866).

67. Arthur MacGregor, *Ark to Ashmolean* (Oxford, Ashmolean Museum in association with the Tradescant Trust, c. 1983), pp. 22–4.

68. Bodleian Library, MS Add, B67.

69. John Parkinson, *Paradisi in Sole, Paradisus Terrestris* (London, 1629), p. 6.

Selected Bibliography

Primary Sources

Adams, J. Q. (ed.), *The Dramatic Records of Sir Henry Herbert, Master of the Revels, 1623–1673* (New Haven and London, Yale University Press, 1917).

Allegations for Marriage Licences issued by the Bishop of London 1611 to 1828, vol. 26 (London, Harleian Society, 1887).

Anon., *A Perfect Description of Virginia* (London, 1649).

Aubrey, John, *Brief Lives, Chiefly of Contemporaries, set down by John Aubrey, between the years 1669 & 1696*, vol. 1, ed. Andrew Clark (Oxford, Clarendon Press, 1898).

Austen, Ralph, *A Treatise of Fruit-Trees Shewing the Manner of Grafting, Setting, Pruning, and Ordering of them in all respects: According to Divers New and Easy Rules of Experienc; gathered in ye space of Twenty Years* (Oxford, 1653).

Bacon, Sir Francis, 'Of gardens', in *The Essayes or Counsels, Civill and Morall*, ed. Michael Kiernan (Oxford, Clarendon Press, 1985).

Barbour, Philip L. (ed.), *The Complete Works of Captain John Smith (1580–1637)* (3 vols, Williamsburg, VA, University of North Carolina Press for the Institute of Early American History and Culture, 1986).

Barbour, Philip L. (ed.), *The Jamestown Voyages under the First Charter, 1606–1609*, Hakluyt Society, 2nd series, vols 136 and 137 (2 vols, Cambridge University Press for the Hakluyt Society, 1969).

Bekkers, J. A. F., *Correspondence of John Morris with Johannes de Laet, 1634–1649* (Assen, Van Gorcum & Comp., NV, 1970).

Bonnefons, Nicolas de, *The French Gardiner: Instructing How to Cultivate all sorts of Fruit-Trees and Herbs for the Garden*, trans. John Evelyn (London, 1658).

Bonoeil, John, *A treatise on the Art of Making Silke* (London, 1622).

Borel, Pierre, *Les Antiquitez, Raretes, Plantes, Mineraux, & Autres Choses Considerables de la Ville, & Comté de Castres d'Albigeois* (Castres, 1649).

Brereton, Sir William, *Travels in Holland the United Provinces England Scotland and Ireland*, ed. Edward Hawkins (Manchester, Chetham Society, vol. 1, 1844).

Busino, Horatio, and Platter, Thomas, *The Journals of Two Travellers in Elizabethan and Early Stuart England* (London, Caliban Books, 1995).

Button, John, *Algiers Voyage in a Journall or Briefe Reportary of all occurrents hapning in the fleet of ships sent out by the King his most excellent Majestie, as well against the Pirates of Algiers, as others* (1621).

Byrd, William, *The Westover Manuscripts: Containing the History of the Dividing Line Betwixt Virginia and North Carolina* (Petersburg, VA, 1841).

Calendar of State Papers, Colonial Series, 1574–1660, vol. 1, America and West Indies, ed. W. Noel Sainsbury (Vaduz, Kraus Reprint, 1964).

Calendar of State Papers, Colonial Series, East Indies and Persia, 1630–1634 (London, 1892).

Calendar of State Papers, Domestic Series, James I, 1603–1610, 1611–1618, 1619–1623, 1623–1625 (London, 1857–9).

Calendar of State Papers, Domestic Series, Charles I, 1625–1626, 1627–1628, 1629–1631, 1631–1633, 1635, 1639, 1640, 1641–1643 (London, 1858–87).

Calendar of State Papers, Domestic Series, Charles I, Addenda March 1625–January 1649 (London, 1897).

Calendar of State Papers, Domestic Series, Charles II, 1660–1661, 1661–1662, 1666–1667 (London, 1860–4).

Calendar of State Papers, Venetian Series, 1625–1626, 1640–42, vol. 25 (London, 1913 and 1924).

Catalogus plantarum Horti Medici Oxoniensis (Oxford, 1648).

Caus, Salomon de, *Les Raisons des forces mouvantes avec diverses Machines tant utilles que Plaisantes Ausquelles sont adjoints plusieurs desseings de grotes et fontaines* (Paris, 1615).

Caus, Salomon de, *Hortus Palatinus* (Frankfurt, 1620).

Chamberlain, John, *The Letters of John Chamberlain*, ed. Norman Egbert McClure (2 vols, Philadelphia, American Philosophical Society, Memoirs 12, 1939).

Charles I, *A True Discourse of all the Royal Passages, Tryumphs and Ceremonies, Observed at the Contract and Mariage of the High and Mighty Charles, King of Great Britaine, and the most Excellentest of ladies, the Lady Henrietta Maria of Burbon* (London, 1625).

Coles, William, *The Art of Simpling. An Introduction to the Knowledge and Gathering of Plants* (London, 1656).

Coles, William, *Adam in Eden: or, Natures Paradise* (London, 1657).

College of Arms, *Visitation of Suffolk 1664–1668* (London, Harleian Society, vol. 61, 1910).

Cooper, William Durrant (ed.), *Lists of Foreign Protestants and Aliens, Resident in England 1618–1688* (London, Camden Society, old series, vol. 82, 1862).

Coryat, Thomas, *Coryat's Crudities* (2 vols, Glasgow, James MacLehose & Sons, 1905).

Dale, T. C. (ed.), *The Inhabitants of London in 1638* (London, Society of Genealogists, 1931).

Digby, Sir Kenelm, *A late discourse . . . touching the cure of wounds by the powder of sympathy* (London, 1658).

Drew, Charles (ed.), *Lambeth Churchwardens' Accounts 1504–1645 and Vestry Book 1610*, vol. 2 (Surrey Record Society, vol. 20, 1950).

Ducarel, A. C., *A letter from Dr. Ducarel, F.R.S. and F.S.A. to William Watson, M.D F.R.S. Upon the Early Cultivation of Botany in England and some particulars about John Tradescant* (London, 1773).

Estienne, Charles, *Maison Rustique, or, The covntrey farme*, trans. Richard Surflet, ed. Gervase Markham (London, 1616).

Evelyn, John, *Sylva, or A Discourse of Forest-trees and the Propagation of Timber in his Majesties Dominions* (London, 1664 and 1679).

Evelyn, John, *Directions for the Gardiner at Says-Court*, ed. Geoffrey Keynes (Nonesuch Press, 1932).

Evelyn, John, *The Diary of John Evelyn*, ed. E. S. de Beer (6 vols, Oxford, Clarendon Press, 2000).

Evelyn, John, *Elysium Britannicum, or The Royal Gardens*, ed. John E. Ingram (Philadelphia, University of Pennsylvania Press, 2001).

F., N., *The Husbandman's fruitfull Orchard* (London, 1609).

Force, Peter, *Tracts and other Papers . . . collected by Peter Force*, vol. 3 (Washington, 1844).

Gage, John, *The History and Antiquities of Hengrave in Suffolk* (London, 1822).

G., E., Gent. and F,. H., Gent., *A Prodigious & Tragicall History of the Arraignment, Tryall, Confession, and Condemnation of Six Witches at Maidstone, in Kent, at the Assizes there held in July, Fryday 30. this present Year* (London, 1652).

Gerard, John, *The Herball or Generall historie of plantes* (London, 1597).

Gerard, John, *The Herball or General historie of plantes*, enlarged and amended by Thomas Johnson (London, 1633).

Gerbier, Sir Balthazar Kt, *A Manifestation* (London, 1651).

Gerbier, Balthazar, *A Brief Discourse Concerning the Three Chief Principles of Magnificent Building: viz. Solidity, Conveniency and Ornament* (London, 1662).

Gerbier, Balthazar, *Counsel and Advise to all Builders* (London, 1663).

Goodman, Dr Godfrey, *The Court of King James the First*, (2 vols, London, 1839).

[Green, John], *A New General Collection of Voyages and Travels*, vol. 2 (4 vols, London, 1745–7).

Green, M. A. E. (ed.), *Letters of Queen Henrietta Maria* (London. 1857).

Grew, Nehemiah, *The Anatomy of Plants With an Idea of a Philosophical History of Plants; and Several Other Lectures, Read Before the Royal Society* (London, 1682).

Hall, Clayton Colman, *Narratives of Early Maryland 1633–1684* (New York, Charles Scribner's Sons, 1910).

Hamor, Ralph, *A True Discourse of the Present State of Virginia* (Richmond, VA, Virginia State Library, 1957, reprinted from the London edn, 1615).

Hanmer, Sir Thomas, *The Garden Book of Sir Thomas Hanmer Bart* (London, Gerald Howe, 1933).

Hariot, Thomas, *A briefe and true report of the new found land of Virginia of the commodities and of the nature and manners of the naturall inhabitants*, the complete 1590 Theodor de Bry edn (New York, Dover Publications Inc., 1972).

Hartlib, Samuel, *Samuel Hartlib his Legacie: or an Enlargement of the Discourse of Husbandry used in Brabant and Flaunders; Wherein are bequeathed to the Common-wealth of England more Outlandish and Domestick Experiments and Secrets in Reference to Universal Husbandry* (London, 1651).

Hartlib, Samuel, *A Designe for Plentie, By an Universall Planting of Fruit-Trees* (London, 1652).

Hartlib, Samuel, *Samuel Hartlib his Legacy of Husbandry* (London, 1655).

Hartlib, Samuel, *Universal Husbandry Improved, or Divers Rare and Choice Experiments and Secrets Relating to all Kind of Husbandry gardning & planting* (London, 1670).

Harvey, W. J., *List of the Principal Inhabitants of the City of London, 1640, from returns made by the aldermen of the several wards* (London, Mitchell & Hughes, 1886).

Herbert of Cherbury, Edward, Lord, *The Expedition to the Isle of Rhe* (London, Philobiblon Society, 1860).

Herbert, Sir Henry, *The Dramatic Records of Sir Henry Herbert, Master of the Revels, 1623–1673*, ed. J. Q. Adams (New Haven & London, Yale University Press, 1917).

Herbert, Sir Thomas, *Memoirs of the Last Two Years of the Reign of King Charles I* (London, 1839).

Historical Manuscripts Commission, 12th Report, *The Manuscripts of the Earl Cowper K.G., preserved at Melbourne Hall, Derbyshire*, vol. 1 (London, HMSO, 1888).

Historical Manuscripts Commission, *Calendar of the Manuscripts of the Most Hon. The Marquis of Salisbury*, vol. 12 (Hereford, HMSO, 1910).

Historical Manuscripts Commission, *Report on the Manuscripts of the Marquess of Downshire preserved at Easthampstead Park Berks*, vols 2 and 3, *Papers of William Trumbull the Elder 1611–1612* (London, HMSO, 1936).

Historical Manuscripts Commission 9, *Calendar of the Manuscripts of the most honourable the Marquis of Salisbury*, Part 18 (London, HMSO, 1940).

Historical Manuscripts Commission 9, *Calendar of the Manuscripts of the Most Honourable The Marquess of Salisbury preserved at Hatfield House Hertfordshire*, Part 22 (1612–68), (London, 1971).

Hoole, Charles, *A New Discovery of the old Art of Teaching Schoole in four small Treatises* (London, 1660).

Howell, James, *Londinopolis, an historicall discourse, or Perlustration of the City of London* (London, 1657).

Hubert, Robert, *A Catalogue of many Natural Rarities ...collected by R. Hubert alias Forges* (London, 1664).

Jackson, B. D., *A Catalogue of Plants Cultivated in the Garden of John Gerard, in the years 1596–1599* (London, 1876).

Josten, C. H., *Elias Ashmole (1617–1692)*, (5 vols, Oxford, Clarendon Press, 1966).

King James I, *A Counter-Blaste to Tobacco* (1604).

Kingsbury, S. M. (ed.), *The Records of the Virginia Company of London* (4 vols, Washington, Library of Congress, 1906–35).

Lawson, William, *A New Orchard and Garden with The Country Housewifes Garden*, ed. Malcolm Thick (Devon, Prospect Books, 2003).

Legg, L. G. Wickham (ed.), 'A relation of a short survey of the western counties made by a Lieutenant of the Military Company in Norwich in 1635', *Camden Miscellany*, vol. 16 (London, Royal Historical Society, 1936).

Lithgow, William, *The Present Surveigh of London and Englands State* (London, 1643).

Loggan, David, *Oxonia Illustrata* (Oxford, 1675).

Lysons, Daniel, *The Environs of London*, vol. 1, *County of Surrey* (London, 1796).

McIlwaine, H. R., *Journals of the House of Burgesses of Virginia 1619–1659* (Richmond, VA, 1914).

McIlwaine, H. R., *Minutes of the Council and General Court of Colonial Virginia*, 2nd edn (Richmond, VA, Virginia State Library, 1979).

Magalotti, Count Lorenzo, *Travels of Cosmo the Third, Grand Duke of Tuscany through England during the Reign of King Charles the Second* (1669), (London, 1821).

Mainwaring, Sir Henry, *The Life and Works of Sir Henry Mainwaring*, vol. 1, ed. G. E. Manwaring (Navy Records Society, vol. 54, 1920).

Mainwaring, Sir Henry, *The Life and Works of Sir Henry Mainwaring*, vol. 2, ed. G. E. Manwaring and W.G. Perrin (Navy Records Society. vol. 56, 1922).

Meager, Leonard, *The English Gardener* (London, 1670).

Meekings, C. A. F. (ed.), *Surrey Hearth Tax 1664*, Surrey Record Society, vol. 17, nos. 41 and 42 (Frome and London, Surrey Record Society, 1940).

Millar, Oliver (ed.), *Abraham van der Doort's Catalogue of the Collections of Charles I*, vol. 37, Walpole Society (Glasgow, Robert Maclehose & Co, University Press, 1960).

Millar, Oliver (ed.), *The Inventories and Valuations of the King's Goods 1649–1651*, vol. 43, Walpole Society (Glasgow, University Press, 1972).

Miller, Philip, *The Gardeners Dictionary* (London, 1731, and Dublin, 1764).

Mollet, André, *Le Jardin de Plaisirs* (Stockholm, 1651).

Morin, Pierre, *Catalogues de quelques plantes a fleures, qui sont de present au jardin de Pierre Morin le jeune, did Trosiéme; Fleuriste* (Paris, 1651).

Morin, Pierre, *Remarques necessares pour la culture des flevrs* (Paris, 1658).

Morin, Pierre, *Nouveau Traite pour la Culture des Fleurs* (Paris, 1674).

Morin, Pierre, *Instruction facile pour connoistre toutes sortes d'orangers et citronniers* (Paris, 1689).

Morin, René, *Catalogus plantarum horti Renati Morini inscriptarum ordine alphabetico* (Paris, 1621).

Mountain, Didymous (Thomas Hill), *The Gardeners Labyrinth* (London, 1577).

Mundy, Peter, *The Travels of Peter Mundy, in Europe and Asia, 1608–1667*, vol. 1, *Travels in Europe 1608–1628*, ed. Lieut. Col. Sir Richard Carnac Temple (Cambridge, Hakluyt Society, 1907), 2nd series, no. 17.

Mundy, Peter, *The Travels of Peter Mundy*, vol. 3, *Travels in England, Western India, Achin, Macao, and the Canton River, Part I*, ed. Lieut.Col. Sir Richard Carnac Temple (London, Hakluyt Society, 1919), 2nd series, no. 45.

Mundy, Peter, *The Travels of Peter Mundy in Europe and Asia 1608–1667*, vol. 4, *Travels in Europe 1639–47*, ed. Lieut. Col. Sir Richard Carnac Temple (London, Hakluyt Society, 1925), 2nd series, no. 55.

Nichols, John, *The Progresses and Public Processions of Queen Elizabeth*, vol. 2 (London, 1788).

Nichols, John, *The Progresses, Processions, and Magnificent Festivities of King James the First, his Royal Consort, Family, and Court*, vol. 1 (4 vols, London, 1828).

Nugent, Nell Marion, *Cavaliers and Pioneers: Abstracts of Virginia Land Patents and Grants*, vol. 1, 1623–1666 (Baltimore, Genealogical Publishing Co. Inc., reprinted 1979).

Page, William, *Letters of Denization and Acts of Naturalization for Aliens in England, 1509–1603* (Lymington, Huguenot Society of London, vol. 8, 1893).

Palmer, W. P. (ed.), *Calendar of Virginia State Papers and Other Manuscripts, 1652–1781*, vol. 1 (Richmond, VA, 1875).

Parkinson, John, *Paradisi in Sole, Paradisus Terrestris* (London, 1629).

Parkinson, John, *Theatrum Botanicum: The Theatre of Plants* (London, 1640).

Parkinson, R, (ed.) *The Autobiography of Henry Newcome* (Chetham Society, vol. 26, 1852).

Passe, Crispin de, *Hortus Floridus* (Utrecht, 1614).

Peacham, Henry, *The Compleat Gentleman* (London, 1634), reprinted in *Peacham's Compleat Gentleman*, ed. G. S. Gordon (Oxford, Clarendon Press, 1906).

Pepys, Samuel, *The Diary of Samuel Pepys*, ed. Robert Latham and William Matthews (11 vols, London, Bell & Hyman, 1970–1983).

Pett, Phineas, *The Autobiography of Phineas Pett*, ed. W. G. Perrin (Navy Records Society, 1918).

Platt, Sir Hugh, *The Jewell House of Art and Nature* (London, 1594).

Platt, Sir Hugh, *Delightes for Ladies, to Adorne their Persons, Tables, Closets, and Distillatories* (London, 1602).

Platt, Sir Hugh, *Floraes Paradise, Beautified and Adorned with Sundry Sorts of Delicate Fruites and Flowers* (London, 1608).

Plat [sic], Sir Hugh, *The Garden of Eden* (London, 1653).

Powell, Thomas, *Humane Industry: or, a History of most manual arts* (London, 1661).

Pulteney, Richard, *Historical and Biographical sketches of the progress of botany in England* (London, 1790).

Purchas, Samuel, *Purchas his Pilgrimes in Five Bookes*, Book 2 (London, 1625).

Quarrell, W. H., and Quarrell, W. J. C., *Oxford in 1710 from the Travels of Zacharias Conrad von Uffenbach* (Oxford, Basil Blackwell, 1928).

Ray, John, *Observations Topographical, Moral, & Physiological; Made in a Journey Through Part of the Low-Countries, Germany, Italy, and France* (London, 1673).

Rose, John, *The English Vineyard Vindicated* (London, 1666).

Rye, William Brenchley, *England as Seen by Foreigners in the Days of Elizabeth and James the First* (London, 1865).

Schellinks, William, *The Journal of William Schellinks, Travels in England 1661–1663*, ed. Maurice Exwood and H. L. Lehmann (London, Camden Society, 5th series, vol. 1, 1993).

Serres, Olivier de, *The perfect Use of Silk-wormes, and their benefit* (London, 1607).

Shaw, William A., *Letters of Denization and Acts of Naturalization for Aliens in England and Ireland 1603–1700*, vol. 18 (Lymington, Huguenot Society of London, 1911).

Sorbière, Samuel de, *A Voyage to England, Containing Many Things Relating to the State of Learning, Religion, and other Curiosities of that Kingdom* (London, 1709).

Stow, John, *The Survey of London* (London, 1633).

Strachey, William, *The Historie of Travell into Virginia Britania* (1612), ed. Louis B. Wright and Virginia Freund (London, Hakluyt Society, 2nd series, no. 53, 1953).

Tradescant, John, *Plantarum in Horto Iohannem Tradescanti nascentium Catalogus* (1634).

Tradescant, John, *Musaeum Tradescantianum: or, A Collection of Rarities preserved at South-Lambeth neer London by John Tradescant* (London, 1656).

Tyler, Lyon Gardiner, *Narratives of Early Virginia, 1606–25* (New York, Charles Scribner's Sons, 1907).

Vallet, Pierre, *Le Jardin du Roy Tres Chrestien Henry IV* (Paris, 1608).

Vallet, Pierre, *Le Jardin du Roy Loys XIII* (Paris, 1623).

Vries, David de, *Voyages from Holland to America, A.D. 1632 to 1644*, trans. Henry C. Murphy (New York, 1853).

Walton, Izaak, *The Universal Angler, Made so, by Three Books of Fishing. The first written by Mr. Izaak Walton.; the second by Charles Cotton, Esq.; the third by Col. Robert. Venables* (London, 5th edn, 1676).

Willughby, Francis, *The Ornithology of Francis Willughby*, trans. and enlarged by John Ray (London, 1678).

Winthrop, John, *Winthrop Papers*, vol. 5, 1645–1649, ed. Allyn Bailey Forbes (Boston, Massachusetts Historical Society, 1947).

Wood, Anthony, *Athenae Oxonienses*, vol. 2 (Oxford, 2nd edn, 1721); and vol. 4 (London 3rd edn, 1820).

Wood, Anthony, *History and Antiquities of the University of Oxford*, vol. 2, part. 2 (Oxford, 1796).

Worm, Ole, *Museum Wormianum seu Historia Rerum Rariorum* (Leiden, 1655).

Wotton, Sir Henry, *Reliquiae Wottonianae* (London, 1651).

Wright, Louis B. (ed.), *Advice to a Son: Precepts of Lord Burghley, Sir Walter Raleigh, and Francis Osborne* (Ithaca, Cornell University Press for the Folger Shakespeare Library, 1962).

Secondary Sources

Allan, Mea, *The Tradescants: Their Plants, Gardens and Museums 1570–1662* (London, Michael Joseph, 1964).

Allen, Thomas, *The History and Antiquities of the Parish of Lambeth and the Archiepiscopal Palace in the County of Surrey* (London, 1826).

Altick, Richard D., *The Shows of London* (Cambridge, Mass, and London, Belknap Press of Harvard University Press, 1978).

Amherst, Hon. Alicia, *A History of Gardening in England* (London, 1895).

Andrews, Kenneth R., *Trade, Plunder and Settlement: Maritime Enterprise and the Genesis of the British Empire, 1480–1630* (Cambridge University Press, 1984).

Baker, T. F. T. (ed.), *A History of the County of Middlesex*, vol. 10, *Hackney Parish* (London, Oxford University Press for the Institute of Historical Research, 1995).

Barnes, Melvyn, *Root and Branch: A History of the Worshipful Company of Gardeners of London* (London, Worshipful Company of Gardeners, 1994).

Baron, Xavier (ed.), *London 1066–1914, literary sources and documents*, vol. 1 (Robertsbridge, Helm Information Ltd, 1997).

Bennett, Jim, and Mandelbrote, Scott, *The Garden, the Ark, the Tower, the Temple: Biblical Metaphors of Knowledge in Early Modern Europe* (Oxford, Museum of the History of Science in association with the Bodleian Library, 1998).

Boulger, G. S., 'The First Russian Botanist', in James Britten (ed.), *The Journal of Botany, British and Foreign*, vol. 33 (London, 1895).

Bowles, E. A., *My Garden in Spring* (London, 1914).

Brenner, Robert, *Merchants and Revolution: Commercial Change, Political Conflict, and London's Overseas Traders, 1550–1653* (Cambridge University Press, 1993).

Brett-James, Norman G., *The Growth of Stuart London* (London, London and Middlesex Archaeological Society, 1935).

Brown, Alexander, *The Genesis of the United States* (2 vols, New York, Russell & Russell Inc., 1964).

Burnby, Dr J., 'Some early London physic gardens', *Pharmaceutical Historian*, 24, 4 (December 1994).

Bushnell, Rebecca, *Green Desire: Imagining Early Modern English Gardens* (Ithaca and London, Cornell University Press, 2003).

Cecil, David, *The Cecils of Hatfield House* (London, Constable, 1973).

Chalklin, C. W., *Seventeenth-Century Kent: A Social and Economic History* (London, Longmans, 1965).

Chapman, Allan, *Gods in the Sky: Astronomy, Religion and Culture from the Ancients to the Renaissance* (London, Channel 4 Books, 2002).

Corner, G. R., 'Elias Ashmole, His House and Lands and South Lambeth', *Surrey Archaeological Collections*, vol. 2 (London, 1864).

Coward, Barry, *Social Change and Continuity: England 1550–1750* (London, Longman, revised edn, 1997).

Coward, Barry (ed.), *A Companion to Stuart Britain* (Oxford, Blackwell, 2003).

Craven, Wesley Frank, *The Virginia Company of London, 1606–1624*, Jamestown 350th Anniversary Historical Booklets, no. 5 (Williamsburg, VA, 1957).

Croft, Pauline, 'The Reputation of Robert Cecil: Libels, Political Opinion and Popular Awareness in the Early Seventeenth Century', *Transactions of the Royal Historical Society* (6th series, vol. 1, 1991).

Croft, Pauline (ed.), *Patronage, Culture and Power: The Early Cecils* (New Haven and London, Yale University Press, 2002).

Dash, Mike, *Tulipomania: The Story of the World's Most Coveted Flower and the Extraordinary Passions it Aroused* (London, Victor Gollancz, 1999).

Daston, Lorraine, and Park, Katharine, *Wonders and the Order of Nature, 1150–1750* (New York, Zone Books, 1998).

Daubeny, Charles, *Oxford Botanic Garden* (Oxford, 2nd edn, 1853).

Desmond, Ray, *Dictionary of British and Irish Botanists and Horticulturalists* (London, Taylor & Francis, 1994).

Dictionary of National Biography, online edition (2004).

Edmond, Mary, 'Limners and Picturemakers', *The Forty-Seventh Volume of the Walpole Society 1978–80* (London, Pitman Press, 1980).

Fairbrother, Nan, *Men and Gardens* (London, Hogarth Press, 1956).

Fat, L. Tjon Sie, and de Jong, E. (eds), *The Authentic Garden: A Symposium on Gardens* (Leiden, Clusius Foundation, 1991).

Finch, Pearl, *History of Burley-on-the-Hill Rutland*, vol. 1 (2 vols, London, 1901).

Forge, J. W. Lindus, *Oatlands Palace* (Walton and Weybridge Local History Society, 5th edn, 1982).

Foucault, Michel, *The Order of Things: An Archaeology of the Human Sciences* (London, Routledge, 2001).

Gem, Richard (ed.), *Book of St Augustine's Abbey* (London, Batsford, 1997).

Gibberd, Graham, *On Lambeth Marsh: The South Bank and Waterloo* (London, J. Gibberd, 1992).

Gunther, R. T., *Oxford Gardens. Based upon Daubeny's Popular Guide to the Physick Garden of Oxford* (Oxford, 1912).

Gunther, R. T., *Early British Botanists and their Gardens* (Oxford University Press, 1922).

Gunther, R. T., *Early Science in Oxford*, vol. 3 (Oxford, 1925).

Hamel, Dr J., *England and Russia; Comprising the Voyages of John Tradescant the Elder, Sir Hugh Willoughby, Richard Chancellor, Nelson, and others, to the White Sea etc.*, trans. John Studdy Leigh (London, 1854).

Harris, John, Orgel, Stephen, and Strong, Roy, *The King's Arcadia: Inigo Jones and the Stuart Court* (London, Arts Council of Great Britain, 1973).

Harvey, John, *Early Horticultural Catalogues* (Bath, University of Bath Library, 1972).

Harvey, John, *Early Nurserymen* (London and Chichester, Phillimore, 1974).

Hatch Jnr, Charles E., *The First Seventeen Years, Virginia 1607–1624*, Jamestown 350th Anniversary Historical Booklets, no. 6 (Williamsburg, VA, 1957).

Haynes, Alan, *Robert Cecil Earl of Salisbury, 1563–1612: Servant of Two Sovereigns* (London, Peter Owen, 1989).

Heard, Nigel, *Wool: East Anglia's Golden Fleece* (Lavenham, Suffolk, Terence Dalton Ltd, 1970).

Hebb, David Delison, *Piracy and the English Government, 1616–1642* (Aldershot, Scolar Press, 1994).

Henderson, Paula, *The Tudor House and Garden: Architecture and Landscape in the Sixteenth and Early Seventeenth Centuries* (New Haven and London, Yale University Press, 2005).

Hinde, Thomas, *Imps of Promise: A History of the King's School, Canterbury* (London, James & James, 1990).

Hulton, Paul, *America 1585: The Complete Drawings of John White* (University of Carolina Press/British Museum, 1984).

Hunter, M. C. W., *Science and Society in Restoration England* (Cambridge University Press, 1981).

Impey, Oliver, and MacGregor, Arthur (eds), *The Origins of Museums: The Cabinet of Curiosities in Sixteenth- and Seventeenth-Century Europe* (Oxford, Clarendon Press, 1985).

Jardine, Lisa, *Worldly Goods* (London, Macmillan, 1996).

Jardine, Lisa, *Ingenious Pursuits: Building the Scientific Revolution* (London, Little, Brown, 1999).

Jardine, Lisa, and Stewart, Alan, *Hostage to Fortune: The Troubled Life of Francis Bacon* (London, Gollancz, 1998).

Jardine, N., Secord, J. A., and Spary, E. C. (eds), *The Cultures of Natural History* (Cambridge University Press, 1995).

Jarvis, P. J., 'The Introduced Trees and Shrubs Cultivated by the Tradescants at South Lambeth', *Journal of the Society for the Bibliography of Natural History*, 9, 3 (1979).

Jeffers, Robert H. (ed.), *John Rose, The English Vineyard Vindicated* (Falls Village, Connecticut, Herb Grower Press, 1965).

Jeffers, Robert H., *The Friends of John Gerard (1545–1612), Surgeon and Botanist* (Falls Village, Connecticut, Herb Grower Press, 1967–9).

440 SELECTED BIBLIOGRAPHY

Kelso, William M., with Straube, Beverly, *Jamestown Rediscovery 1994–2004* (Richmond, VA, Association for the Preservation of Virginia Antiquities, 2004).

Kew, H. W., and Powell, H. E., *Thomas Johnson: Botanist & Royalist* (London, Longmans, Green & Co., 1932).

Kingsbury, Susan M., *An Introduction to the Records of the Virginia Company of London* (Washington, Library of Congress, 1905).

Leith-Ross, Prudence, *The John Tradescants: Gardeners to the Rose and Lily Queen* (London, Peter Owen, 1984).

Leith-Ross, Prudence, *The Florilegium of Alexander Marshal in the Collection of Her Majesty the Queen at Windsor Castle* (London, Royal Collection Enterprises, 2000).

Lloyd, Christopher, *English Corsairs on the Barbary Coast* (London, Collins, 1981).

Lockyer, Roger, *Buckingham: The Life and Political Career of George Villiers, First Duke of Buckingham 1592–1628* (London and New York, Longman, 1981).

London County Council, *Survey of London*, vol. 18, *The Strand (The Parish of St. Martin-in-the-Fields, Part 2)*, (London, 1937).

London Survey Committee, *The Survey of London*, vol. 23, *South Bank & Vauxhall, The Parish of St Mary Lambeth, Part 1* (London, 1951).

London Survey Committee, *The Survey of London*, vol. 26, *The Parish of St. Mary Lambeth, Part 2, The Southern Area* (London, 1956).

McCartney, Martha W., *Documentary History of Jamestown Island* (3 vols, Williamsburg, VA, Colonial Williamsburg Foundation and College of William and Mary, 2000).

Magrath, J. R., *The Flemings in Oxford*, vol. 1 (Oxford, 1904).

MacGregor, Arthur (ed.), *Tradescant's Rarities: essays on the foundation of the Ashmolean Museum, 1683, with a catalogue of the surviving early collections* (Oxford, Clarendon Press, 1983).

MacGregor, Arthur, *Ark to Ashmolean: The Story of the Tradescants, Ashmole and the Ashmolean Museum* (Oxford, Ashmolean Museum, c.1983).

MacGregor, Arthur, *The Ashmolean Museum: A Brief History of the Institution and its Collections* (Oxford, Ashmolean Museum, 2001).

Morgan, E. D., and Coote, C. H. (eds), *Early Voyages and Travels to Russia and Persia by Anthony Jenkinson and other Englishmen*, vol. 1 (London, Hakluyt Society, 1886).

Mukerji, Chandra, 'Engineering and French formal gardens in the reign of Louis XIV', in John Dixon Hunt and Michael Conan (eds), *Tradition and Innovation in French Garden Art* (Philadelphia, University of Pennsylvania Press, 2002).

Page, W., *The Victoria History of the County of Rutland*, vol. 1 (3 vols, 1908).

Pavord, Anna, *The Tulip* (London, Bloomsbury, 1999).

Perrin, W. G. (ed.), *The Autobiography of Phineas Pett* (Navy Records Society, 1918).

Phipps, Geraldine M., *Sir John Merrick: English Merchant-Diplomat in Seventeenth-century Russia* (Newtonville, Mass., Oriental Research Partners, 1983).

Poole, Rachel, 'An outline of the history of the De Critz family of painters', in *The Second Volume of the Walpole Society*, 1912–13 (Oxford, 1913).

Prest, John, *The Garden of Eden: The Botanic Garden and the Re-Creation of Paradise* (New Haven and London, Yale University Press, 1981).

Quinn, David Beers (ed.), *The Roanoke Voyages, 1584–1590* (2 vols, Hakluyt Society, 2nd series, vols 104 and 105, London, 1955).

Raven, Charles E. *English Naturalists from Neckam to Ray* (Cambridge University Press, 1947).

Robinson, William, *The History and Antiquities of the Parish of Hackney in the County of Middlesex* (2 vols, London, 1842–3).

Robinson Jnr, W. Stitt, *Mother Earth: Land Grants in Virginia 1607–1699*, Jamestown 350th Anniversary Historical Booklets, no. 12 (Williamsburg, VA, 1957).

Rountree, Helen C., *Pocahontas, Powhatan, Opechancanough: Three Indian Lives Changed by Jamestown* (Charlottesville and London, University of Virginia Press, 2005).

Ryan, Antony Charles, *The Abbey and Palace of St. Augustine Canterbury*, AD 597–1997 (Canterbury, Old Manse Publications, 2001).

Scarfe, Norman, *The Suffolk Landscape*, revised edn (Bury St Edmunds, Suffolk, Alastair Press, 1987).

Schama, Simon, *The Embarrassment of Riches: An Interpretation of Dutch Culture in the Golden Age* (London, Collins, 1987).

Schama, Simon, *Rembrandt's Eyes* (London, Allen Lane / Penguin Press, 1999).

Schnapper, Antoine, *Le Géant, La Licorne et la Tulipe: Collections et Collectionneurs dans La France du XVIIe siècle*, vol. 1, *Histoire et histoire naturelle* (Paris, Flammarion, 1988).

Sellers, Vanessa Bezemer, *Courtly Gardens in Holland 1600–1650: The House of Orange and the Hortus Batavus* (Woodbridge, Garden Art Press, 2001).

Smith, A. G. R. (ed.), *The 'Anonymous Life' of William Cecil, Lord Burghley*, Studies in British History, vol. 20 (Lewiston, NY, Lampeter, 1990).

Stephenson, Richard W., and McKee, Marianne M. (eds), *Virginia in Maps: Four Centuries of Settlement, Growth and Development* (Richmond, VA, Library of Virginia, 2000).

Stewart, Alan, *The Cradle King: A Life of James VI and I* (London, Chatto & Windus, 2003).

Stone, Lawrence, *Family and Fortune: Studies in Aristocratic Finance in the Sixteenth and Seventeenth Centuries* (Oxford, Clarendon Press, 1973).

Stone, Lawrence, *The Family, Sex and Marriage in England 1500–1800* (London, Weidenfeld & Nicolson, 1977).

Stoye, John Walter, *English Travellers Abroad 1604–1667: Their Influence in English Society and Politics*, revised edn (New Haven and London, Yale University Press, 1989).

Strickland, H. E., and Melville, A. G., *The Dodo and its Kindred* (London, 1848).

Strong, Roy C., *The Renaissance Garden in England* (London, Thames & Hudson, 1979).

Sturdy, David, 'The Tradescants at Lambeth', *Journal of Garden History*, 2, 1 (1982).

Surrey Archaeological Collections, 'Vauxhall and South Lambeth: an 18th-century lease', vol. 28 (1915).

Sutherland, L. S., and Mitchell, L. G. (eds), *The History of the University of Oxford*, vol. 5, *The Eighteenth Century* (Oxford, Clarendon Press, 1986).

Swann, Marjorie, *Curiosities and Texts: The Culture of Collecting in Early Modern England* (Philadelphia, University of Pennsylvania Press, 2001).

Thick, Malcolm, *The Neat House Gardens: Early Market Gardening around London* (Totnes, Prospect Books, 1998).

Tindall, Gillian, *The Man Who Drew London: Wenceslaus Hollar in Reality and Imagination* (London, Chatto & Windus, 2002).

Toynbee, Margaret, 'The Wedding Journey of King Charles I', *Archaeologia Cantiana*, vol. 69 for 1955 (Ashford, Kent Archaeological Society, 1956).

Turner, James, 'Ralph Austen, an Oxford horticulturist of the seventeenth century', *Garden History, The Journal of the Garden History Society*, 6, 2 (Summer 1978).

Tyacke, Nicholas (ed.), *The History of the University of Oxford*, vol. 4, *Seventeenth-Century Oxford* (Oxford, Clarendon Press, 1997).

Vigne, Randolph and Littleton, Charles (eds), *From Strangers to Citizens: The Integration of Immigrant Communities in Britain, Ireland and Colonial America, 1550–1750* (Brighton, Huguenot Society of Great Britain and Ireland and Sussex Academic Press, 2001).

Vines, S. H., and Claridge Druce, G., *An Account of the Morisonian Herbarium in the Possession of the University of Oxford* (Oxford, Clarendon Press, 1914).

Warner, Marjorie F., 'The Morins', *The National Horticultural Magazine* (July 1954).

Warner, Marjorie F., 'Jean and Vespasien Robin, "Royal Botanists," and North American Plants, 1601–1635', *The National Horticultural Magazine*, 35, 4 (October 1956).

Waselkov, Gregory A., 'Indian maps of the colonial southeast', in Peter H. Wood, Gregory A. Waselkov and M. Thomas Hatley (eds), *Powhatan's Mantle: Indians in the Colonial Southeast* (Lincoln and London, University of Nebraska Press, c.1989).

Washburn, Wilcomb E., *Virginia Under Charles I and Cromwell, 1625–1660*, Jamestown 350th Anniversary Historical Booklets, no. 7 (Williamsburg, VA, 1957).

Williamson, Hugh Ross, *George Villiers: First Duke of Buckingham, Study for a Biography* (London, Duckworth, 1940).

Williamson, Hugh Ross, *Four Stuart Portraits* (London, 1949).

Williamson, Tom, *Suffolk's Gardens & Parks* (Macclesfield, Windgather Press, 2000).

Witkam, H. J., *Catalogue of all the Chiefest Rarities in the Publick Theater and Anatomy Hall* (Leiden, 1980).

Woodbridge, Kenneth, *Princely Gardens: The Origins and Development of the French Formal Style* (London, Thames & Hudson, 1986).

Yungblut, Laura Hunt, *Strangers Settled Here amongst Us: Policies, Perceptions, and the Presence of Aliens in Elizabethan England* (London, Routledge, 1996).

Index

Tradescant, John (younger) (cont.):
  proposed sale of collection 298
  social status 324–5, 372
  as traveller, to North America xxvi–xxvii, 100, 103, 251, 253, 256, 259–78, 280
  see also Musaeum Tradescantianum
Tradescant, Nicholas (brother of elder Tradescant) 4
Tradescant, Robert 325, 333, 347
Tradescant, Thomas (?half-brother of elder Tradescant) 7
Tradescant, Thomas (father of elder Tradescant) 3
Tradescant collection 9, 195–6, 230–41
  Ashmole's claim to 230, 328–31, 336–42, 344–50
  Ashmole's ownership xxiii, 351–2, 354–5, 364, 372
  benefactors 91, 322–3
  cataloguing by Ashmole and Wharton xxvii, 328–9
  decline in popularity 342–3, 361
  entry charge 238–9, 283
  and fragment of True Cross xxv, 233, 365–6
  Hester Tradescant's claim to 230, 330, 336–42, 344–7

and Oxford University 329, 331, 334, 346, 349, 355–8
proposed sale 298
and Tradescant (elder) xxi–xxv, 36, 73, 119–20, 161, 165–76, 219
and Tradescant (younger) xxv-xxvii, 242–3, 246–7, 251, 303
visitors 238–9, 296; Ashmole 314, 316, 342; Coles 308; Hartlib 303; Johnson 199–201, 204–5, 223; Mundy 271; Rose 342–3; Schellinks 230–1; Stirn 271
  see also Ashmolean Museum; Powhatan's mantle
Tradescant family, possible Dutch origins 2–3, 4–5, 10
Tradescant Trust 370
'Tradescant's Orchard' 223–6, 229, 311
tragacantha 198
travel:
  by river 27, 195, 269
  by road 18–19, 39, 269
  by sea 27–8
'Tredeskins Ark' see Tradescant collection
tree fern (Cibotium barometz) 73
tree primerose, Tradescant's 254
trees 129; see also fruit trees; ash; beeches;

birches; limes; oaks; walnuts
trefoil 142, 198, 306
Tresham, Lady 20
Tresham, Sir Thomas 50
Trevor, Sir John 140, 146, 208, 211, 422 n.28
trifoliums 202
Triumph (Buckingham's flagship) 179, 180
Trumbull, William 1, 11–14, 38–9, 42, 58, 65, 374 n.9
Tufton, Sir John 20
Tuggie, Ralph 197, 201, 295
Tuileries gardens (Paris) 41–2, 47, 211
tulip tree (Liriodendron tulipifera) 268–9, 278, 305, 348
tulips 160, 198–9, 198, 202, 203, 304
  'Agate Hanmer' 302
  Beau 199
  growing 71, 130
  Tradescant's purchases 37, 38, 44
tulip fever 2, 29, 37
Turkey, plants from 134–5
turnips, long-rooted 254
turpentine tree (Pistacia terebinthus) 143, 308
turtlehead (Chelone glabra) 420 n.18
Tusser, Thomas, Five Hundred pointes of Good Husbandrie 67–8

United Provinces 26, see also Netherlands
urine, as fertilizer 62
Utrecht 30, 38

HOME FROM WAR

Home From War

How Love Conquered the Horrors of a Soldier's Afghan Nightmare

Martyn and Michelle Compton
with Marnie Summerfield Smith

Foreword by HRH Prince William of Wales

REAM
...HING
...ND LONDON

First published in Great Britain in 2009 by
MAINSTREAM PUBLISHING COMPANY
(EDINBURGH) LTD
7 Albany Street
Edinburgh EH1 3UG

ISBN 9781845964504

This book is a work of non-fiction. In some limited cases,
names of people have been changed to protect the privacy of others.
The author has stated to the publishers that, except in such
minor respects, the contents of this book are true

A catalogue record for this book is available
from the British Library

Typeset in Caslon and Requiem

Printed in Great Britain by
Clays Ltd, St Ives plc

*Dedicated to Ross, Ralph, Alex and Sean and all the lads
serving with the Household Cavalry, especially those
who have made the ultimate sacrifice*

*In memory of Jean Compton
8 July 1943 – 23 November 1986*

ACKNOWLEDGEMENTS

Martyn and Michelle are grateful to their literary agent, Robert Smith, Mainstream Publishing, especially Bill Campbell and Peter Mackenzie, and their co-writer, Marnie Summerfield Smith.

They would also like to express their heartfelt thanks to Andrew Radford, Mick Flynn, Paul Hamnett, Alex Dick and everyone in D Squadron; all the medical staff at Camp Bastion in Afghanistan, especially Lieutenant Colonel Duncan Parkhouse and those who flew Martyn home; Peter Dziewulski, his incredible team and everyone who worked with and supported Martyn and Michelle at Broomfield Hospital, Essex; the amazing team at Headley Court; and Luke Cox, Douglas Lawson, Fiona Bantock and Hugh Robertson MP. Thank you to everyone who was involved in making their wedding day and honeymoon so wonderful. A special thanks to Major Will Bartle-Jones and Alistair Galloway, who have gone above and beyond the call of duty. Thanks to every single well-wisher, whether known to them or not. And, finally, thanks to their family and friends, without whom they would not have made it through.

Useful Websites

- www.helpforheroes.org.uk
- www.britishlegion.org.uk
- William.Bartle-Jones133@mod.uk
  (Household Cavalry Operational Casualties Fund)

CONTENTS

Woe to the man whose heart has not learned while young
to hope, to love – and to put its trust in life

Joseph Conrad

Lance Corporal Martyn Compton has come to epitomise the bravery and self-sacrifice of the modern British soldier. The sheer courage and resilience which he has shown since that day in Afghanistan two and a half years ago, when he was so terribly badly wounded, has been an inspiration - not just to his fellow Household Cavalrymen or, for that matter, to other members of the Armed Forces, but to the Nation as a whole.

With his wife, Michelle, by his side every step of the way, he has fought seemingly insurmountable odds to reach the state of recovery he now has. There is still a way to go for Martyn, but we must be truly grateful that this remarkable man is now fit enough to inspire others with his story.

It is, for me, a huge honour to be asked to write the foreword to 'Home From War'. Even more so, it is a privilege to count Martyn Compton – a fellow member of D Squadron, The Household Cavalry Regiment – as a friend.

William

PART ONE

Try Not to Think of
Me Until I Get Back

7 AUGUST 2006

Woke up today wondering how you were. Went to the hospital with your dad. It's hard to know what to say to you. It's horrible that you aren't awake, but I know you can hear. I just spoke to you stupidly, as I always do. The only person I see laying there is my Martyn and no one else. It's hard to be strong, but I am for your sake, as I know you can hear how I am feeling in my voice.

Kevin and Katie came down today to keep me and your dad company while you spent all day in theatre. That's the horrible thing: knowing that you are going through all that and we can't help. If I could spend every minute with you, I would, but I can't.

This feels like a dream. Saw you after the operation, and you were covered from head to toe in bandages. But you're mine, and I still love you. Didn't want to leave you, and I just wanted to be with you, but I know you will fight all the way.

CHAPTER I

✧✧ . ✧✧

MARTYN – I WAS EXPOSED, AND
I WAS TERRIFIED

HELMAND PROVINCE, AFGHANISTAN – 1 AUGUST 2006

The Taliban fighter peered over the wall. I recognised the unmistakable warhead of his rocket-propelled grenade. He was close, and he was going to fire it right at me. I couldn't go anywhere. Stuck inside the ruined hulk of my wagon with my mates dead, I was a sitting duck.

All I could do was hope for the best. I'd survived the initial attack, so maybe my luck was in. I wasn't normally a driver, but I'd been assigned as one for about a month. The regular driver had gone down with heat exhaustion. If he'd been all right, I'd have been in my signalman post. If he'd been all right, I'd have been dead.

The heat gets to you. Nothing can prepare you for what it's like in Afghanistan. When I stepped off the plane in Kabul almost six weeks earlier, it was 6.30 a.m. But even that early in the morning, a wave of heat swept over me. It was relentless. I couldn't get used to it, and it was getting hotter every day.

Further south in Helmand, July temperatures reach 50 degrees Celsius.

At one point, someone stuck a thermometer in a wagon, and it went over 100 degrees Celsius. When you're driving, you can add fifteen degrees Celsius to that, because you're sitting in a small cab right next to the engine. Great weather for shirts, shades and lazing under a palm tree with a cold beer. Shit weather for desert combat gear, a helmet, body armour, and trying to negotiate the wasteland, the enemy and landmines in a cramped steel box.

The Household Cavalry is an armoured reconnaissance regiment. We explore and get information. We're the barrier that delays attacking forces, and we act as a screen, a diversion, to allow other troops to move and carry out operations. We go in ahead of infantry, then support them. We're the most deployed regiment in the army, and we're right in the enemy's face.

Our operation had started two days before on 30 July. We were moving from Now Zad to Musa Qala to help extract the Pathfinder Platoon and resupply Danish troops holed up there. They were being ambushed every time they went to collect their supplies. The Pathfinders are an elite forward reconnaissance element made up mainly of paratroopers. As the crow flies, from Now Zad to Musa Qala was only 40 kilometres. But we had to go round some mountains, which almost doubled the distance.

Before we headed off, I checked my wagon over. It was a Spartan, which is more of a support vehicle than the sort that would be the first into battle. A Spartan weighs 13.5 tonnes. It has an added layer of ballistic armour on the body and a cage to protect against rocket-propelled grenades as well as another reinforced layer of metal underneath to protect against mines. You feel pretty safe inside one.

I gave the Spartan the once over: gearbox oil, engine oil, coolant, air filter, hub oil and axle oil, the wheel rubbers, balancing horns, and pins on the tracks. I checked every seventh one, and they were at the right angle. I was relieved. If one was loose, I would have had to check the whole track. They often got loose out there – the vehicles really took a battering in the terrain. The check took five minutes, but it seemed like five hours in the heat.

My clothes were moist with sweat, but there was no chance of a shower. I needed to eat, too. I was desperate for a fry-up. I ate a boil-in-the-bag corned beef hash. There wasn't much to it, but it was that or nothing.

We'd left Camp Bastion a week earlier, having returned overnight after about two weeks of operations. There were three of us in the wagon – my mate Lance Corporal Ross Nicholls was on signals. He'd been moved over from another troop, and I was pleased to have him on board. He was a nice guy, hard-working and a good influence on me. Behind me to my right was Second Lieutenant Ralph Johnson. In Now Zad, we picked up the senior officer in the troop, Captain Alex Eida of the 7th (Parachute) Regiment Royal Horse Artillery. Alex worked as our forward observation officer.

The night of 31 July, we found ourselves in a minefield. One of the other Spartans hit an old Russian anti-tank mine. The vehicle shot up into the air and wheeled 180 degrees. It scared the shit out of me – until I saw the tank's commander jump out and on top of his wagon and do a comical war dance.

The vehicle was trashed. The tracks, decks, gearbox and chassis were all destroyed. But because of the mine shield, the crew escaped unharmed – apart from being a bit bruised and battered. After the explosion, the driver stood up, touched himself up and down to check everything was in place, put his body armour on and took a couple of painkillers.

News of explosions always get home, so the men involved were given the opportunity to use the satellite phone to let their families know that they were OK. One guy said he wasn't fussed about calling, so his troop leader did it. He was hoping to allay any fears the guy's wife might have; instead, she screamed down the phone, 'The liar. He told me he was in Knightsbridge on ceremonial duties for three months.' We laughed. It broke the tension we were all feeling.

Our job that night was to create a screen for some Canadian troops, so we spent some time destroying the vehicle, denying it to the enemy. We knew the Taliban would wonder what the racket was and would be watching us. It was the perfect diversionary tactic and gave the Canadians the freedom to complete their task. Of course, destroying our own vehicles, which cost thousands of pounds, isn't how we usually created a distraction, but we made the best of the situation. And we weren't going to let the Taliban strip it for parts.

We weren't moving any further because of fog, so we tucked down for the night. The ground was my bed. Kipping out with the army isn't as relaxed as camping with your mates. You can't light a fire, for obvious reasons. But there are moments when it comes close to feeling quite nice. There's a rota for people to be on watch, or on stag, and you feel pretty safe.

Because of the structure of the Household Cavalry, we're an especially close-knit regiment. We have small squadrons and small troops of men. You can do your training with someone then work for 22 years with that same bloke. Everyone knows everyone's stories.

I listened as soldiers shared their thoughts. There's something about the atmosphere created when you're sleeping out at night that makes you share more personal information than you normally would. Maybe being faced with your own mortality makes you want to talk. Or maybe it's because there's no TV, no pub, no car and no wife or kids to act as distractions. Whatever it is, really personal stuff gets shared. It's a different kind of relationship to the one you have with your mates at home, and it's good. Until the following morning, of course, when emotional intimacy seems slightly ridiculous in the light of day and that personal information is used against whoever was stupid enough to share it. And there are no secrets in the army. Gossip moves faster than bullets.

I stayed quiet that night and covered myself in a mosquito net while listening to the chat. I thought about Michelle back at home in England. I loved her so much and couldn't wait for her to be my wife. We'd be getting married in two summers' time. My mind drifted back to how we'd met seven months ago. Michelle had been doing shifts in a pub near her home in Frittenden, Kent. It was my dad's local, and they got chatting. He told her about his soldier son, and she asked to meet me.

I was attracted to her the first night I saw her. She was a few years older and had so much energy and confidence. I felt shy and quiet in comparison. I hoped it wouldn't put her off. It didn't. We got on so well, and I was gutted when I had to leave the pub. I'd promised to meet Dad and his mate at another pub. As I sat drinking with them, Michelle was all I could think about. I wanted to go back and see her, so I made an excuse and left.

It was the right decision. As I walked into the pub, she smiled at me. Everything felt right when she looked at me. She asked me why I'd come back. With a bit of Dutch courage inside me, I joked that the beer had been off in the other pub. She didn't believe me, and I didn't care. We were inseparable from that moment – until I went to Afghanistan.

The chat in the camp soon moved on to how lucky the Spartan crew had been. I filed thoughts of Michelle safely away and turned to my responsibilities. I'd be driving a Spartan the next day, so I hoped it was a good omen for us that the crew had survived.

We were back on the road at 5 a.m., and the heat was already building. I focused on the track ahead, negotiating the potholes and ditches. The heat can dull your concentration, so you have to focus harder when it's that hot. With my left foot, I continually pushed up and down through each of the seven gears, lifting us out of every hole, pushing us forward. Ralph, standing and looking through the cupola where the machine gun was mounted, could see more than I could. 'Left stick, left stick, right stick,' he called. I tried not to over-steer. We were averaging about ten to fifteen kilometres per hour.

I was wearing my Crewguard helmet, which was plugged into the tank's intercom system. Instructions and banter were constant. I chucked in a few sarcastic comments of my own. But I couldn't distract myself from the heat. I was sitting in a puddle of sweat. Rivers of it poured down my back, my arse, my legs and my arms. A pool gathered in the shell of my headset cupping my right ear. It poured down my face and into my mouth, and I could taste it – mixed with sand and dust kicked up by the vehicle in front.

I swigged from my water bottle. It was encased in a damp sock. It was never going to be cold refreshment, and the sock kept it lukewarm – but that was better than drinking hot water. Anyway, it didn't make it to my bladder. It seeped right out of my pores as my body desperately attempted to keep me cool.

We stopped once. I took off my shirt and wrung it out. Sweat oozed from the material – you'd have thought I'd been swimming in my clothes.

Back on the road, the landscape was strange: sand, rocks and not much else, except for a few trees here and there. Afghan tribes settled near vegetation because it marked the site of water. Unfortunately, I couldn't indulge my childhood hobby of climbing trees because groups of villagers could be sheltering Taliban fighters.

I kept my eyes peeled, driving through this pale and barren land, burned by sun, damaged by conflict. Something flapped in the distance. As we drew closer, I noticed that it was a piece of material fluttering in the breeze. It was attached to two sticks poking out of the parched earth. A man sat under the canopy with a bottle of water. He watched us as we drove by. I don't know who was more surprised, him or us. Was this flap of material and these two poles his home? If not, what was he doing there and from where did he get his water? For a moment, I thought I was hallucinating.

Eventually, we arrived at a high point – a hill overlooking a village, which consisted of about 12 buildings with high sandy-coloured walls and no windows. It looked pretty derelict.

We got into a defensive formation while the officers and troop leaders decided what to do. We were under pressure to get 'eyes-on' to Musa Qala. Getting eyes-on means being able to see what's happening. We needed to see where the Danes were being ambushed from, so the decision was taken to drive through the village. The only way down was along a *wadi*, a ditch that had once been a stream.

I closed the hatch above me, and we set off. I had a tiny window to look through and could only see ahead, not to the sides. I was the second vehicle down the *wadi*. Mick Flynn, who was a corporal of horse at the time, was in front in a Scimitar. I kept close enough to assist him if he got into trouble but far enough back so I wouldn't be caught up unnecessarily.

Rolling down the hill and into the village, we found ourselves corralled by high walls on either side. We pushed through, keeping an eye out for enemy fighters. But everything seemed quiet – only the rumble of the wagons rolling through the dust. It was 7 a.m.

Someone shouted over the radio. My heart leaped. It was Mick Flynn coming under attack from small arms. We were being ambushed. I heard fire pinging off our vehicle. Ralph returned fire and shouted, 'Compo. Reverse, reverse. Get us the fuck out of here.'

I pushed the reverse lever forwards as hard as I could and felt it click. We shot backwards. A massive explosion rocked the wagon, and it stopped dead in its tracks. Instinctively, I ducked then looked behind me.

The back of the tank had split open like a can. Fire and smoke were pouring out everywhere. The machine-gun turret had dropped into the tank. The roof was gone. The back door was gone. The floor was gone. And the crew was gone.

They were dead. I was alone. I was exposed, and I was terrified. I was pressed into the wreckage of my vehicle. I didn't know what to do. I had to get out of there.

And then I caught a movement from the corner of my eye.

The Taliban fighter tucked a rocket-propelled grenade launcher into the crook of his shoulder. He tilted his head and aimed it right at me. He fired. The grenade hurtled towards me, trailing a plume of smoke. It shot past my shoulder and hit the Spartan's engine. The engine exploded. The fireball swallowed me.

CHAPTER 2

※ ᴄ . ℆ ※

MICHELLE – PEOPLE TOLD ME, 'IT'S ONLY SIXTEEN WEEKS'

I watched Martyn playing in the garden with my parents' golden Labrador, Harvey. A few weeks before, the lawn that they were now fooling around on had been transformed into the 'Wedding Patch' for my brother Kevin's wedding reception. It had been a great day, and towards the end of the night, Martyn and I had sneaked away to sit by the cornfield. We listened to the distant music and talked about our own future, the life we hoped to lead.

We sat there for ages. The moon shone, and a warm breeze wafted through the fields. I heard a cheer from the marquee. 'Kevin and Katie must be leaving,' I said. 'Come on.'

We raced to the drive just in time to see the limousine pull away. We stood with the crowd, waving and clapping. People began thanking my parents and moving towards their cars, but the slow songs were still playing, so I pulled Martyn into the marquee and towards the dance floor. '(I've Had) The Time of

My Life' from *Dirty Dancing* started up, and I snuggled closer to Martyn. He buried his face in my hair, and I felt his strong arms hold me tighter. We were the only people dancing, and as far as I was concerned we could have been the only people in the world. We were in our own little bubble. I couldn't believe I was so happy.

The memory glittered in my mind as I watched my gorgeous man frolic with Harvey. The future looked bright for the two of us. I should have been the happiest woman in the world. But in a few hours I would leave Martyn at Combermere Barracks in Windsor to get ready for his four-month tour of Afghanistan.

The knot in my stomach that had appeared when Martyn had told me he was going was permanent. I did think about the danger he faced, but it wasn't a danger I could relate to. All I could really think about was the separation. People told me, 'It's only 16 weeks,' or, 'It's just over 100 days,' but nothing made it better. We'd only met in January, and now we were going to be forced apart for almost as long as we'd been a couple. We didn't even know how often we'd be able to speak to each other. But we pushed our sadness aside and enjoyed the three weeks' leave Martyn had been given prior to deployment.

I looked down at my engagement ring. Martyn had proposed to me the night before. He'd taken me and my parents out for a meal then asked me to marry him when we got home. I was so happy. I called everyone I knew. Mum, Dad, Martyn and I opened a bottle of champagne. It was the happiest night of my life.

Eventually, tired with all the excitement, we went to bed. As usual, I lay my head on Martyn's chest and rested my arm across his stomach. How would I sleep without my hunky soldier to cuddle?

'Night, darling,' I said.

'Night, Mrs Compton-to-be. Love you.'

'Love you, too, husband-to-be. Sweet dreams.'

I'm sure I fell asleep first. I always do. I didn't know what thoughts I'd left Martyn with as I drifted away.

Morning came too quickly, and we were ready to leave.

'Martyn,' I said. 'Come on, babe. We better get ready to go.'

Harvey bounded into the house, and Martyn ran after him. I thought how strong my man looked, how fit and handsome he was. He grinned at me and gave me a peck on the cheek as he scooted upstairs and into the shower. I felt very lucky.

Dad, Mum, Martyn, Harvey and I began the journey from Kent to Windsor. Stick us all in a car together and there would normally be heaps of banter, usually about football, because Dad supported Southampton and Martyn and I followed Spurs. But that Sunday, silence filled the vehicle.

Harvey, in his compartment in the back, knew something was wrong. He'd usually be bouncing about looking for someone to stroke him, but that day he rested his chin on the back of the seat. Can dogs sense sadness? I don't know. But that day, Harvey definitely picked up on something.

We stopped at Martyn's dad's house in Staplehurst. I waited in the car, watching Rob and Martyn. Martyn wasn't one for long goodbyes, and when his dad reached to hug him, he said, 'What are you doing, Dad? I'll be all right.'

Typical of him. But I did notice him squeeze his dad's hand. They are so close. I knew that simple gesture meant a lot to Rob. And they'd already had a very emotional goodbye two days previously when Martyn had reappeared in our local, The Bull in Sissinghurst, a week after everyone thought he had already left. His deployment had been postponed, and he asked me not to tell anyone so that he could surprise his mates and his dad. Everyone gawped when Martyn and I walked into the pub. Our friends and Rob were there. Father and son hugged for five minutes. There were quite a few tears that night, and Rob made Martyn promise that he would never do that again.

After leaving Rob's house, we headed for Windsor. The journey took about two hours. When we got there, the four of us and

Harvey walked along the river. The sun fell, reddening the sky with the promise of a fine day to come. Martyn and I drifted behind my parents. We held hands but didn't speak much. There was so much I wanted to say, but I couldn't find the words. We made small talk about the houseboats, and the ducks and swans. Other couples and families with dogs strolled past us. They looked so carefree, and I envied them.

When the time came, Martyn quickly said goodbye to my mum, dad and Harvey. They went to the car, and Martyn and I stood beside the barracks wall, away from the entrance. He put his arms around my shoulders and I reached around his waist. I looked up at him. Tears rolled down my cheeks. 'I love you lots,' I managed to say. 'Keep safe.'

'You keep safe, too,' said Martyn. He began to say something else, but his voice broke and tears began to run down his face. We hugged. It was bittersweet to be so close to him when soon we'd be so far apart.

We looked at each other. 'You can't walk in like that,' I said, indicating his tear-streaked face. I rummaged in my pocket for a packet of tissues. The only ones I had were imprinted with cartoon monkeys. 'Have these.'

He managed a giggle as he took them. We hugged again. 'I love you, babe,' he said quietly in my ear.

It was time to go, and I strode towards the car. Dad was under strict instructions to drive away slowly so I could wave. I got in the car and slid my hand under Harvey's collar for comfort.

Martyn composed himself, blew his nose and tucked the tissues in his pocket. He picked up his bag and turned towards me. He waved and blew kisses. I did the same. Then he trudged towards the barracks gate.

And he was gone.

CHAPTER 3

✺❬❨•❩❭✺

MARTYN – IT WAS THE TALLEST
TREE I HAD EVER SEEN

DEVON – 1986

My mother, Jean, died on my third birthday: 23 November 1986. She bled to death after giving birth to my sister, Lorraine, the day before. My mum had already chosen my birthday gifts, so my dad, a lorry driver, gave them to me. I don't remember what they were, and I don't remember my mum, but I do remember everyone laughing and chatting at my birthday party. Thinking back, that must have been so difficult for them. But they were being strong for me, for the little boy who'd lost his mum but who was full of joy on his birthday. My aunties were there, Trina and Anne, who I call Annie. They are my dad's sisters, and they wore smiles, I remember. I was so lucky to have them. Dad has two other sisters as well: Lynn and Claire. I am so fortunate to have so many strong female role models.

My birthday must be a sad reminder for Dad, but he's never let it show, and we have always celebrated it. He's never come to terms with losing my mum, though. It's been more than 20 years since she died, and he's still angry. More so, he's sad that he wasn't with her at the end. The hospital had told him to go home and take care of his son – me. He left at 6.30 a.m., and at 7 a.m. the phone rang. Dad says he knew before he answered it that his wife was dead.

It must have hit him more than 20 years later when, in the early morning, a number he didn't recognise appeared on his mobile phone. He'd already seen on the news that British soldiers had been killed and injured and was so terrified that he didn't take the call. A few hours later, he saw flashing blue lights in the rear-view mirror of his lorry. He pulled over, and the policemen walked towards him. Behind them were two army family liaison officers. They told him what had happened to me.

When my mum and dad met in their village pub in South Tawton, Devon, my mum was 35. She had two sons, Roy, 17, and Paul, 15, from a previous marriage, but they lived mostly with their dad. My mum and dad were married within a year. Trina and Annie really took to Mum, and they became great friends, really close.

Dad says that everyone loved my mum. She was a typical country girl like her mother: hard-working, down to earth, and a brilliant mum and homemaker. She baked cakes and made a cracking Sunday dinner. Maybe that's why I love my roasts so much. My mum was hands-on, practical and no-nonsense. She was always happy and smiling.

After Roy and Paul were born, Mum was sterilised. However, after marrying Dad, she wanted the process reversed so they could have kids of their own. Dad says he thought the operation was risky and that he was happy just to be married. But Mum was determined.

The reversal went ahead, and they began trying for a family. Mum suffered a miscarriage, and she and Dad grieved for their lost child. They were delighted when I was born, even though I was delivered by Caesarean section. Dad says that they thought of me as a special gift. They doted on me, and the first few years of my life were really happy for them.

My mum was 43 when she died. She and Annie had pledged to look after each other's children if anything should happen to either of them, so Annie adopted Lorraine, who was born prematurely. Dad, feeling he couldn't cope with working and caring for a toddler and a newborn, agreed to the arrangement. I stayed at Annie's in Bampton, Devon, while Mum was in hospital. After her death, I stayed there while Dad was away working, and I looked forward to when he came home.

Annie is the most fantastic person. When she adopted Lorraine and began caring for me, she was already on her own with her children Jared, Katie and Emily. It must have been tough for her being a single mum to four children, as well as taking care of me. But she loved us all and made time for each of us.

Annie and Trina made sure my mum was never forgotten. Her pictures adorned the walls in their homes, and they always talked about her. I would point up at the pictures and say, 'Is that "She"?', which is how I referred to her.

A few weeks after her death, it was Christmas. I asked Gran if Father Christmas could 'bring She back'. I think they might have explained to me then that She wouldn't be coming back. My dad and Auntie Annie sat me down and said that Mum had gone to heaven. I was quite accepting of it. Kids are, I suppose. I certainly didn't fully understand – I guess I was lucky, being so young – but it hit me later.

I don't know how my life would have been different if she hadn't died. Mum, Dad, Lorraine and I would have lived together in Devon, I suppose. One thing I do know is that I couldn't be closer to my dad than I am. Lorraine, too. She's Annie's daughter, but she's my sister. And even though we've not always been brought up together, we're really close. I love her so much. I still have a strong bond with my brother Paul as well.

I've had some wonderful, kind women in my life: Annie, Trina and, later, Dad's partner Wendy. But no one could ever replace

Mum. Some people are convinced she was looking out for me in Afghanistan. In those moments when my life drifted away, they say my mum spoke to me, told me I had to live. I think of it as my mum kicking my arse and telling me, 'Get back down there. It's not your time to go.'

I was content, and I loved my Auntie Annie, but I was good mates with my dad and was happiest when he was around so the two of us could play together. I inherited his love of the outdoors and especially loved climbing trees. I would clamber as high as my little legs could take me. And if there wasn't a tree, I'd climb what I could find. One morning, Mum had found me on the roof of Dad's car. She'd called for him, trying to sound cross. But when he'd arrived, they'd both collapsed in giggles. Dad lifted me down. He couldn't tell me off, though – him and his mates had once climbed an electricity pylon.

Annie and Trina were so kind to me, even though I must have driven them mad at times. I think Mum and Dad had spoiled me a bit. One time, Annie and Auntie Lynn took me, Lorraine, Katie and Emily to Paignton Zoo. But never again. I climbed trees, fences, walls – anything I could see: not ideal in a zoo where you don't know what child-eating animal lurks on the other side of a barrier.

Trina had also been very close to Mum and doted on me. Lorraine, being such a tiny baby, needed lots of extra-special care, so to give Annie a break, Trina would take me out to play. Almost every day I'd paddle in the river, and build bridges out of rocks. I seemed happy to play alone. Nature was my playground. I loved being outside, and I could amuse myself for hours. One of my favourite things to do was feed the ducks. But I don't know which element of this game pleased me – the feeding or the ducks, as Trina says that she had to stop me carrying the bread because by the time we got to the pond I'd eaten it. Trina would try and tell me off and say, 'You little toad! Your mum's watching you!'

My dad went through hell after Mum died. He was angry, and he was sad, but I never saw that at the time. Ten months after Mum died, he was invited to an engagement party. He went and got chatting to Elaine, the woman who was getting married. She was from New York. Before the night was over, she asked him to take her away, and he agreed.

Everyone in the family told him not to get involved. Even his own dad, who isn't known for sticking his nose in, shook his head when he met Elaine. But my dad's attitude is try anything once and live life to the full. I think he knew it wasn't going to last. But right then he had a desperate need to escape from his grief, and Elaine seemed to offer him a route.

We were going to Florida to start a new life. I didn't care where I went. I didn't belong to any particular place, just anywhere my dad was. We were a team.

FLORIDA – 1987–88

Dad went to Florida first and married Elaine. He found work and a place for the three of us to live, and then he came to the UK to get me. Dad told Elaine that wherever he went, I went – I'd lost my mum and wasn't going to lose my dad, too.

In Florida, we lived in a gated community filled with cycle paths and trees. It gave an outdoor-loving kid like me all the freedom I could wish for. A new, always-sunny world kept me busy. I was four and felt like I was roaming for miles. But Dad says wherever I was you could hear the bell on my bicycle, so I couldn't have been that far away.

Dad worked and Elaine did her bit, collecting me from school and feeding me before I raced out on my bike. Taking on someone else's child isn't always easy. She had enough money from a family optician business in New York to keep all three of us. Dad could've stayed at home to look after me, but he wanted his independence and went out to work.

Elaine would sometimes shoot off to New York for a few days to see friends. This meant I had to hang around the school after all the other kids had left because Elaine wasn't around to bring me home. I had to wait for my dad, who'd race from work to pick me up. But I didn't care. I'd charmed my teachers and would happily charge about the playground or sit and eat cookies. The only time I was still was when I was eating.

Of course, Dad and Elaine were doomed as everyone predicted. He admits he took his grief out on her, and she couldn't have been too thrilled with life if she took 3,000-mile round trips to New York. We'd been in Florida for about a year when the crunch came. The three of us had gone for a picnic in the park. I was bursting with excitement – the park was known for its tall fir trees, and I intended to climb one. But Elaine warned me against climbing. I don't know why she was so against it. Perhaps she was trying to get some control over the situation. I can understand that; it must have been frustrating for her. I didn't listen, of course, and wandered off to find a suitable tree, Dad's and Elaine's voices fading behind me.

Then I saw it. My fir tree. It was the tallest tree I had ever seen. I looked up through its branches. I could see the sun twinkling between the leaves, and I blinked against its glare. I was so excited. I couldn't wait to get to the top and touch the sun. I would call out for Dad and show him how clever I was.

I started my climb, reaching for the branches, using them first as levers to pull myself up, and then as steps for my feet as I reached for the next one up. It took a while, but I didn't care. I loved every moment of the challenge. There were weird insects to look at. They zipped past me in the branches. I could see other children playing below me. 'Ha!' I thought, this is my own secret world. You have no idea I'm here.

One more stretch, one final step, and I was there. Excitement pulsed through me. I was so high up. Surely this was my best climb ever. I didn't care about touching the sun any more. I only wanted to show Dad where I was. I looked about, but I must have circled the tree as I climbed because Dad wasn't where I thought he'd be. 'Daaddy, Daaddy,' I called. I began to edge around the tree, calling out, desperate to share my triumph. I wondered if it would be easier to see him if I had my back to the trunk, so I began to turn, fumbling behind me to keep hold of the tree.

I slipped. I grabbed for something – anything – but there was nothing there. I was falling. My T-shirt rucked up my back, leaving my skin at the mercy of the bark. I felt my back tearing. I grabbed for the tree, desperate to stop. I screamed for Dad to rescue me. I could hear him shouting my name. But I couldn't see anything apart from the ground hurtling towards me. I flapped my arms, but the branches tore at them as I plunged. I slammed into the ground.

For a moment, I was relieved that I'd come to a stop. But then the pain kicked in, and I began to shout.

Dad was right there. 'Don't worry, son, you're safe now – you'll be all right.' I knew I was safe – but I also knew I was far from all right. Blood soaked through my T-shirt. Dad bent to pick me up and got covered in it, too. I screeched as he scooped me up.

Cradling me, Dad made his way back to the picnic blanket. Elaine sat there waiting for us. She was angry with me, saying I shouldn't have climbed the tree after she'd warned me not to.

Dad strode towards the car, comforting me as I sobbed and wriggled trying to avoid the pain. I think, for whatever reason, he decided there and then that his relationship with Elaine was over. It wasn't meant to be.

It took a few weeks for my injuries to heal. I'd mostly scraped skin off my back. When I was better, Dad and I were on the next plane home.

I don't think Auntie Annie was surprised to see us back in the UK and to hear that Dad and Elaine were getting divorced.

Devon was too full of sad reminders, so when we got back to England, Dad and I moved to Maidstone, Kent. Mum's brother, Gilbert, and his wife, Sheila, offered us a place to stay. I was five and loved living with them and their kids Ricky, Robert, Mark and Debbie.

We stayed in Maidstone with them for a year before getting our own flat and then a house in the village of Staplehurst. During the summer holidays, I'd go back to Devon. It was a great life for me: Kent during the school term and Devon in summer. Dad would drive me to the Fleet services on the M3, where Auntie Annie would pick me up. One time Gran came too and took me to a Happy Eater, where I was allowed to eat as much ice cream as I liked. It was great. I was always spoiled rotten, and, when she was old enough, Lorraine would come in the car to meet me, too.

I loved seeing Lorraine, and I also loved Trina's daughters, Laura and Katherine, although they were younger than me. It was great to grow up with them, Katie and Emily. Annie's son, Jared, had moved out by then, but I do remember him being around.

I would often go to the park, and it was there that I played with some other children who would later become like family to me: Ben and Sophie, and later their little sister, Kas. Their mum, Wendy Scott, fell in love with my dad, and they moved into our home in Kent.

Summers in Devon will always be special to me. And, of course, my mum's buried down there. As I got older, I came to know more about her and felt closer to her. Each Mother's Day, I'd ask Auntie Trina to lay flowers on my mum's grave – yellow flowers, which she loved. Every Mother's Day, if I'm not in Devon, I'm with Trina in spirit as she places those flowers on the earth where my mother is laid. It's a special day for me.

Your mum is always your mum, and I know my mum loved me.

As I got older, into my early teens, Devon in summer got really exciting. And I got to be more of a handful. It was 1 a.m., and I'd been to a 'scuffle' – a four-wheel-drive event. I was a kid, but I'd maybe had a drink or two. I'd made my way home and had managed to coat myself, head to toe, in mud. I knocked on Trina's door. She opened it, her face stretched in shock. 'Who's that?' she said.

I grinned at her, showing my white teeth. I said, 'Grandma won't let me in.'

'Martyn,' she said, exasperation in her voice.

'She wouldn't let me in, Trina.'

'Come in, for heaven's sake.'

I was always on the go. I'd pop to Trina's for tea, then call on Annie and see what she was doing. If she was busy, I'd go to Gran's, have a chat with her and Granddad for ten minutes, then be on the move again: back to Annie's for a snack, round to a mate's, grab a Chinese takeaway and back to Trina's.

I had ants in my pants all right. I drove my family mad, appearing unexpectedly, seeing what was going on, checking if I was missing anything, then grabbing a sandwich, eating it as I hovered in the doorway and considered my next move. I had endless energy – couldn't sit still. A fidget-arse, that's what I was. And always hungry, always eating. 'We need to keep you fed and keep you busy,' Annie used to say. At Christmas, if anyone in the family had complicated toys that needed to be put together, they'd save them for me to do – to see if they could keep me occupied.

And I started getting into scrapes. I felt invincible, I guess – like all boys do at that age. And by that time, I'd met someone who was encouraging my mischief – a partner in crime, if you like. A mate for life who's stuck with me through everything and who'd be at my side on the most important day of my life.

CHAPTER 4

❧✿❧

MARTYN – 'LOOK AT THE VIEW.
WE'RE NEARLY AT THE TOP'

STAPLEHURST PRIMARY SCHOOL, KENT – 1992

I noticed that all the other boys were wearing shorts. Not only was I the new kid – again – but I was also the new kid in long trousers. It didn't bother me. I was only nine, but I already had a strong sense of individuality. I didn't need to be part of the group to feel good about myself.

'Me! Me! Me!' A kid with long brown hair had his hand up in response to the teacher's request for someone to show me around. That kid was Christopher Humphrey. He wasn't being kind in offering his time. He just saw it as a chance to get out of lessons. He showed me the classrooms, the hall, the canteen, the loos and the best places to hide if you got in trouble. By the end of the day, we were mates. The next day, he turned up in his long trousers and our friendship was sealed. We discovered our houses backed onto one another's, and that made our bond even stronger.

Unfortunately, Chris wasn't keen on my favourite activity – climbing trees. The fir-tree incident in Florida hadn't deterred me. And I was keen for my buddy to share my hobby. I knew he'd love it once he tried it.

One of my favourite places in Staplehurst was the Bull's Field. It had a massive oak tree in one corner, which I'd had to master after being chased by a bull. It was the perfect tree for climbing, and at the top there was a great spot to sit with a catapult.

'I'll show you how,' I told Chris. I reached up with both arms, jumped, grabbed, swung one leg over the branch, heaving myself up so that I was straddling it, and then hopped up into a standing position. 'See?'

'OK,' he said, unconvinced but keen not to look stupid. He lifted his arms and jumped. It was good enough.

'Come on, then,' I said. And I was off. I was soon at the top, and Chris was catching up. 'Look at the view,' I called. 'We're nearly at the top.' No response. 'Chris?' I looked down over my left shoulder. Chris looked up at me.

'I can't move,' he said.

'What do you mean? Have you hurt yourself?'

'No. I looked down and now . . . I just can't move.'

'You'll have to, you div,' I said, trying not to laugh. 'Unless you're planning to grow wings and fly down.' Chris shrugged. I said, 'So you can't climb up, and you can't climb down?'

'That's right. Have you got a ladder?'

'What?'

'A ladder.'

'Yes, up my T-shirt.'

'Don't be sarcastic, Martyn. I'm stuck.'

I tutted. 'I'll go and get one then, yeah?'

'Yes, please.'

'I'll have to climb past you, then. Stay still.'

'I can do that.'

It took me ten minutes to run home. I knew our neighbour had a ladder. I don't know whether he believed my explanation of why I needed to borrow it, but he agreed.

I lugged the ladder towards Bull's Field. It was heavy and

awkward, me being just a kid. I had to keep stopping and putting it down because I got knackered. The sun glared powerfully and sweat poured off me. It took more than 20 minutes to get back to Chris. I didn't know if it would be more annoying to see him still up the tree or sitting on the grass with an ice lolly. But when I arrived, the sight of him up in the branches in the same position, humming to himself, made me laugh.

I leaned the ladder up against the tree. The top rested just below Chris's trainers. I climbed up and encouraged each of his feet onto the top rung. We were both down again within moments.

Chris looked at me sheepishly. 'Cheers,' he said. 'I owe you one.'

'Yeah, you do,' I said. 'You can carry the ladder.'

That wasn't the last time I had to rescue Chris from trouble I'd got him into. But we remained friends, and went on to senior school together.

Angley School in Cranbrook had another pupil who'd become important in my life: a girl called Michelle Clifford. I didn't know that at the time, of course, and our paths wouldn't cross while we were at school. Lucky, really. She might have thought me a bit childish – a stupid, misbehaving kid.

In the second year, the headmaster called in my dad and Chris's parents. He wanted to discuss our behaviour. I was constantly in detention. I threw an apple once, and it landed rather close to a teacher. Another time, I was given detention for setting off the school's fire alarm. I smashed the library window with a football, as well. And I released the pigs from the school's farm. I pissed myself laughing as they trotted around the playground. It was obvious that Chris and I were trouble. One of us had to go, and Chris's parents moved him to Cornwallis School in Maidstone.

Our parents were pretty frantic. They banned us from seeing each other outside of school, but our houses backed onto each other's, so there was only so much they could do.

STAPLEHURST, KENT – 1997

Even my duvet sounded loud as I shuffled out from underneath it. I had to be quiet or I'd be in serious trouble with Dad.

I reached down under my bed and grabbed my torch. I crept up to the window and tucked my head under the curtain, leaning my elbows on the windowsill. I pressed the small button on my digital watch. Its tiny light flooded the screen. One minute before Chris was due at his bedroom window.

I caught my breath. Dad's footsteps clumped on the stairs.

'Martyn? You sleeping?'

My heart almost burst through my chest. I slid the torch under the pillow. Dad wouldn't be too mad if I was still awake – but if he thought I was communicating with Chris, I'd get a bollocking. He'd already confiscated our walkie-talkies.

Dad didn't come in. He seemed satisfied that I was sleeping. I heard the bathroom door open and close.

I clutched the torch again and fiddled for the switch. I had to risk doing it while Dad had his back to the garden and wouldn't see the beam of Chris's torch. If I waited until Dad had gone downstairs, Chris might have been and gone. He'd give up, thinking I'd failed to make it or that I'd been caught.

I pointed the torch straight out of the window and switched it on, held it for three seconds and switched it off. I scanned the darkness. A beam shot back from the direction of Chris's house. I bounced up and down in silent excitement. I made nine quick flashes with my torch to signal 'meeting tomorrow at 9 a.m.'. Again, a single flash came back – Chris understood and agreed. I made one long flash, followed by a quick one. That meant: 'Meet at Martin's newsagents on Staplehurst High Street.' The long flash indicated the long queues for penny sweets; the quick flash meant to be ready to leave the front of the shop quickly so no one saw us together. If we pedalled up to the shop quickly and then sped away in a matter of moments, we might look like any two lads – not Martyn and Chris, the two lads who were always up to something.

Chris flashed back. For a moment, I stared into the darkness. And then I jumped as a light came on downstairs in Chris's house. His mum or dad must have gone into the kitchen. A moment earlier and they'd have seen my torch. I jerked out from under the curtains. I rolled the torch under the bed and jumped under the duvet, clutching my knees into my chest and trying to breathe steadily. The plans were made, and I lay awake, excited at the thought of showing Chris what I'd found.

When I pulled up outside the newsagents, Chris's black-and-orange mountain bike leaned against the shop. I cursed. This wasn't the plan. I didn't want to go in and get him in case a customer spotted us, knowing we weren't supposed to be together. I froze for a second, unsure what to do. My gaze darted around the High Street, hoping no one was loitering nearby who knew my dad or Chris's parents. Chris strolled out of the shop, tucking into a bag of gobstoppers.

'Let's go,' I said with a hiss. And I was off. Chris powered after me, gaining with every rotation of his pedals. He was fast on that bike, even with a bag of sweets in one hand. A few minutes later, I swerved left through a rickety gate. I raced round the back of a derelict house and stopped dead. Chris screeched to a halt beside me.

'Sweet?' he offered, his mouth full of white sugar and spit.

'No, thanks.' I rolled my eyes. 'Let's go in.' I'd had my eye on the house for a while and was keen to see what was inside.

'Brilliant,' said Chris. 'You're sure it's empty?'

'Definite, mate,' I said.

The house wasn't boarded up, and the back door opened easily. Inside, we discovered it had been turned into three flats. We wandered about until we came across a mattress in a second-floor bedroom. I had a deodorant spray and some matches in my rucksack – and I wanted to know what would happen if I chucked the can into a fire.

'I don't think that's a good idea,' said Chris. 'How are we going to put it out?'

'I don't know,' I said. 'Let's just see what happens.'

As I rummaged in my rucksack, Chris tried to talk me out of my plan. But I was curious. I told him to stand back. I lit a match and sprayed the deodorant through it. It was like a dragon's breath. The flames licked at the mattress, and the battered old thing was spitting fire. I lobbed the can of deodorant into the flames.

Nothing happened for a few seconds. Then an almighty bang deafened me and the mattress leaped off the floor. Orange flames shot through the fabric, and thick black smoke filled the room.

'Shit!' I shouted, laughing. 'Bloody hell, mate, let's go.'

I grabbed my bag and raced past Chris, who muttered something about trying to put the fire out.

Whoosh! The can went crazy, jumping about in the flames. Outside on the landing, I leaned against the opposite wall, trying to catch my breath. What was taking Chris so long?

I shouted for him. Nothing. Panic spread a cold hand over my chest. For some reason, *London's Burning* popped into my head. I decided to follow tactics I'd seen on the show. I touched the door handle. Christ! It was burning hot.

I shouted for Chris again. I lay on my side and kicked at the door. It swung open, and a tunnel of flames gusted over my head. Backdraft. God knows what would have happened if I'd been standing up.

I peered into the smoke. The mattress gushed flames. Chris lay on the floor next to it. I crawled into the room and grabbed his T-shirt, dragging him back out onto the landing.

'Wake up, Chris.' I shook him. 'Wake up.'

I then heard the wail of sirens. I didn't know whether it was police or fire brigade, but I didn't want to be there when either arrived.

Chris wasn't waking up. I realised I couldn't drag him downstairs in case he banged his head on every step. There was a small window on the landing. I kicked it hard, and it smashed. I dragged Chris to the window, pushing his head through the gap.

'Come on, mate, breathe,' I said.

Chris began coughing and spluttering. His appearance scared me. The sirens grew louder. I kneeled down next to him and pulled him over my shoulder. Desperation must have given me the strength to lift someone who weighed about as much as I did. I struggled down the stairs with Chris on my back. I pulled the back door open.

'Chris, are you all right?' I let him stand.

'I think so.'

'Grab your bike, then. Let's get out of here.'

We were on our bikes and through the hedge and into Bull's Field within moments. We slumped next to the oak tree and listened to the commotion as the emergency services arrived. Sweat poured down my face.

'Sorry to panic you there, mate,' said Chris.

'S'all right,' I said. 'Sorry I nearly killed you. Mates?'

'Truce,' said Chris. 'As long as you can afford another can of deodorant, you sweaty bastard.'

CHAPTER 5

MICHELLE – 'CLIFFORD SLICES THROUGH THE DEFENCE . . .'

FRITTENDEN, KENT

'You're in goal,' my big brother Kevin shouted over his shoulder as he raced out of the back door.

'Again?' I said.

I was nine, Kev was eleven, and he always stuck me in goal so he could take pot shots at me. I got pretty good at throwing myself around, saving his free-kicks, his penalties. But I wanted to be more than just a target for him.

I took my place between the goalposts, which were wild cherry trees that our dad, Brian, had planted. They'd been left over from a planting job on the farm where he was foreman, so he'd brought them into the garden and planted them in front of the fence. Small cages encased the base of the trees to protect them – but they could barely withstand the constant battering they received from our ball. The trees were planted almost a goal-width apart, so as children we had to work very hard to cover the ground. It took a lot of diving to save some of Kevin's shots. Mum and

Dad gave up on having any flowers. There was plenty of shouting and telling off at the beginning – but they finally decided the football had ruined any hope they had of a pleasant garden. As my mum, Rosie, says: it was never a garden; it was a football pitch. The trees are still there today.

I hope that one day my children might play football together like Kev and I did. I hope that they love each other as much as Kevin and I did, too. My mum says that from the moment I was born, Kevin adored me. Dad brought Kevin in to see us in the hospital. Kevin was only two and a half when I was born, but he was instantly protective. As Mum changed my nappy and turned away from me to reach for something, Kevin said, 'Mummy – the baby!' as if she'd forgotten me.

I was a happy baby. I slept a lot, which was a relief to Mum after Kev. He wasn't much of a sleeper as a baby. And on the rare occasions that I did cry, Mum would run me a bath and let me splash around in it – it pacified me instantly. I loved it. To this day, nothing soothes and relaxes me better than a nice long bubble bath.

It took me longer to walk than Kevin, because I'd only have to point at something and he'd toddle off and get it for me. He was a doting big brother, and I realised that early on. He would do anything for me and looked after me. The bond between us was strong from the first, and it lasts to this day.

I might have taken advantage of the fact he'd run around and get things for me, but I also had my uses as far as Kevin was concerned. As soon as Kevin could walk, he played football. And as soon as I could walk, Kevin roped me in.

I stood between the cherry-tree goalposts. Kevin dribbled towards me saying, 'Clifford on the ball – beats one man, beats another . . .'

I raced out of goal and whipped the ball off his toes. Kevin stopped commentating and turned around to gawp at me, hands on hips. 'Hey,' he said. 'You can't do that.'

'Why not?' I played keep-it-up with the ball.

'You're the goalie.'

He ordered me back between the posts and took the ball up field, dribbling it towards me again. And again I raced out, tackled Kev and took the ball off him, leaving him on his backside.

'Why d'you keep tackling me?' he said.

'Because it's fun.'

He grunted and told me to go in goal, and we played the game again – Kev racing towards me, his eyes on the ball, saying, 'Clifford slices through the defence . . .'

I shuffled out of goal. Kevin said, 'Clifford's through on goal. Clifford's ready to shoot. Clifford . . .' Clifford's on his backside on the grass again.

I'd dispossessed my brother for a third time, and he wasn't pleased. But I was thrilled. I loved football, but he always put me in goal. I wanted more, and it seemed that the only way I'd get it was to take it. And I'd proved my point. For the rest of the afternoon, I stayed in goal, just in case Kev found himself another teammate. I didn't want that to happen. I loved hanging around with my brother. I looked up to him and wanted to do everything he did. I followed him on my bike and climbed the trees he climbed. I had to be fearless or he'd have left me behind.

Looking up to him and following him around made me a tomboy. But Mum always said to us, 'Believe in yourselves. It doesn't matter what anyone else thinks of you as long as you do things right. You don't have to follow the crowd. If you believe in something, then you do it. It takes more courage to do what you feel you should do than to follow the crowd.'

Mum encouraged me to try different things, such as gymnastics and playing the piano. They even bought me a piano. But I always came back to football, to spending time with my big brother. I might have been jumping ditches and climbing trees with Kevin – but I loved my girl's things, too. My bedroom was decorated with Care Bears. It was a very girly bedroom.

Christmas was always wonderful for us, like it is for every

child old enough to know what it means, yet young enough to still believe in Father Christmas. We'd wake up at 5 a.m., shaking with anticipation. We'd get up and creep about upstairs, looking to see if there had been a late-night delivery of toys. Kevin would use the light from his digital watch to guide us on our adventure. Our parents heard us get up, we know that now, but they let us get on with it – let us enjoy the thrill of Christmas.

I know I was a tomboy, but one year I was desperate for a doll that talked and cried. If you gave it a bottle, it would stop crying. I was very excited, as usual. We'd been sent to bed early and told to go to sleep or Father Christmas wouldn't be coming. Then I heard crying. It was the doll – I was sure of it. I drifted off to sleep and woke up early to find the doll waiting for me at the foot of my bed. I played with it all day but was still convinced that I'd heard the crying and talking toy the previous night – and I asked my dad about it. He denied it – although I know now that he was putting the batteries in the doll that Christmas Eve and checking to see if it worked. That's why I'd heard the crying. I accepted Dad's denial at the time. He had to be right, of course. Father Christmas wouldn't have delivered my present *that* early, would he?

Childhood is such an innocent time. It's when we believe miraculous things; it's when everything seems possible. A girl can be anything she wants to be. She can play football with her brother, and she can pretend-feed her crying doll. She can dream of meeting her prince and marrying him. She can dream of a happy-ever-after. You can still achieve all that in the real world, of course – it just takes a little more hard work and commitment than in the fairy tales of childhood.

I was born on 13 March 1980 and was brought up on a small farm in Frittenden in the Kent countryside. My brother and I spent every spare minute exploring the fields and woods. The freedom was wonderful.

Kev and I had some great mates who would join in our adventures. Such as Darren and Claire Beard. Darren was my age; Claire was a bit younger. They lived just down the lane, and their dad put a plank of wood over a ditch so that we wouldn't have to cross the road to get to their house. That lane and the surrounding farms and fields were our own little world.

Ponds dappled the farm's fields, and Kevin and I spent a lot of time fishing in them. Dad took us most of the time. When he came with us, we loved sitting there, the three of us. Kevin had a yellow rod, and I had a little blue one. One school holiday, Mum took us fishing instead. We caught a big tench but couldn't get the hook out of its jaw. Kev tried, I tried and Mum tried, but we failed. We brought it home in a bucket of water, and our next-door neighbour, Ian, got the hook out of the fish's mouth.

'Why didn't you just kill it?' he asked.

'Oh, I couldn't. Poor fish,' said Mum.

We put the tench back in the bucket of water and took it back to the pond. Mum didn't take us again after that.

Life was so much fun – just one big adventure. Everything we did was an activity. We'd play on the Beards' farm, making athletic tracks round the house and in the garden. We'd build jumps for our BMXs, and Kev would attach a skateboard to his bike then let me sit on it as he raced up and down hills. I loved it. I didn't mind falling off when my big brother was there to look after me. We didn't care where we went with the bikes, and we'd get in trouble now and again. As a farm foreman, Dad sometimes got mad with us when we flattened the cornfields.

Even the weather didn't affect our fun. Who cared if it rained when we had our imaginations? If it was wet outside, Kevin and I would turn the sofas in the front room upside down and make dens. We'd lay our mattresses at the top of the stairs, sit on them and toboggan down. Once at the bottom, giggling after bumping down the stairs, we'd clamber back up, dragging the mattresses behind us, and start all over again.

We always had dogs when we were growing up. First there was Laddie, the black Labrador. Then came Sweep, the Springer Spaniel, followed by Patch. And finally Harvey, who's still with my mum and dad now. They were working dogs, mostly off with Dad on the farm, but we loved them. And Harvey, in particular, became very important. He played with Martyn the day we were taking my husband-to-be to Windsor to join up with his regiment before going to Afghanistan. It's an image that will stay with me till the day I die – a picture of joy that makes my heart swell. The moment when Harvey and Martyn frolicked on the lawn was all about fun. It was a carefree few minutes when nothing else mattered. It was the calm before the storm that was sweeping in to meet us.

When I was ten, we changed from BMXs to motorbikes. Darren Beard was given a 50cc grass track bike. It was so thrilling. We thought it was a big, powerful motorbike. We raced around the fields on it, churning up the ground, much to our parents' annoyance, no doubt.

I was roaring around one day, not thinking about anything, when I felt a pain in my leg. The pain increased, and I had to stop. It was burning my leg. The engine had got hot and scalded my calf. I found it hard to walk. But who was there? Kevin, of course. He always looked out for me. He walked me home, forgoing his opportunity on the bike to make sure I was all right.

I loved him fiercely. He was the best big brother I could have had. But sometimes he was a bit too protective. When I was 13 and a pupil at Angley School in Cranbrook, I discovered another interest: boys.

They started to notice me, too. One boy would buy me birthday presents and say he was going to marry me. I wasn't struck on the idea. Others said they fancied me, but never to my face. Boys got together and talked about girls; girls did the same, gossiping about boys. It was all who-fancied-who type of conversations, whispered around the school. But when boys talked about me, there was somebody there who was listening. And if he heard something and didn't like the boy, my big brother would tell him – in the way big brothers do – to leave me alone. He had one lad up against a wall, threatening to kill him. He wouldn't have done, of course, but it was wonderful to have a brother who cared for me so much, who'd go to any lengths to protect me.

And not just lengths, but heights, too. A boy said he fancied me, and Kevin overheard. Kevin went for the lad, and my admirer had to climb a tree to escape. But Kevin's mate got to him and dangled the Romeo from a branch until Kevin clambered up there to have a word.

If this had continued, I would have had no boyfriends. They'd all have been scared off by Kevin. I had a chat with Mum, and she explained to Kevin that I had a life of my own. He couldn't tell me who I could or couldn't like. He understood. It was a boy thing. If he couldn't protect his sister, who could he protect? Kevin's still protective of me, of course, and I wouldn't have it any other way. It's different now; a different kind of caring – he doesn't put men who fancy me up against the wall any more.

Despite my love of Kevin and our adventures together, I always liked my own space. I'd wander off for a little daydream around the farm. Mum liked to have time to herself as well, or at least that's what she said. She never got it with us around. But I'm sure she would have liked to have a read by herself or a soak in the bath.

Kevin and I were always close as we grew up, but when he got a bit older, he liked to go off and play football with his mates. He wanted to go further afield, spread his wings a little – a typical teenage boy's reaction, I guess. He didn't want to be attached to his mum's apron strings.

I was gutted when Kevin took his cycling-proficiency test. It meant he was able to ride on the road. He started leaving me behind to go up to the playing fields, and I was upset. Mum would ask Kevin if I could go with him. But that meant he'd have to walk his bike, instead of ride it. He got fed up. He wanted to fly down the road. Finally, Mum had to take me to the playing fields by car so Kevin had the freedom to ride.

It wasn't that Kev minded me being with him. As little sisters go, he says I was a good one: up for anything, fearless and ready to give as good as I got in our playfights. He couldn't complain about my swift kicks to his shins. After all, it was he who'd taught me to kick so well during the hours we'd spent playing football. I can't remember what we argued about when I kicked him in the face with a roller boot. But it gave him a black eye. Dad threw the boots in the bin, but I retrieved them and hid them away.

Kevin started playing football for a team outside school when he was eight. He played in defence for Staplehurst Monarchs. Mum, Dad and I went to watch every Sunday. I would join in the pre-match kickabouts and loved it. Kevin was a very good player, especially talented.

At the age of 13, he joined a local team called Bearsted FC. A scout for Norwich City spotted him and invited him to train with them. He would travel to their centre of excellence in London. I was desperate to go with him, but the training was in the evenings. It was too late for me because I had to get up for school the following day. I was gutted.

Gillingham FC then approached Kevin, and he signed on schoolboy forms with them. That suited me better. It was much closer than London, and I could go and see him play. But I had to watch my step. I was always very vocal on the sidelines – I'm passionate about my football, so it was inevitable. During one match, I made it known that I wasn't too pleased about a tackle that had brought Kevin down. One of the other opposition players told me to shut up. Kevin took exception to this verbal assault on his sister. He ended up having a go at the player who mouthed off at me and got himself booked.

As an apprentice at Gillingham, Kevin had duties when the first team played. He had to make tea and collect the balls. It was the life of a football trainee. They all had to do this kind of work. It was part of the learning process. I'm sure a lot of big names today, the England stars, have all had to clean boots and sweep dressing-rooms in their time.

It was great to be at Gillingham when the FA Cup came round. If they'd made it through to the third round, when all the Premiership teams entered the competition, there was a chance they'd get a brilliant draw, one of the big-name clubs visiting Priestfield Stadium. One year, the Gills were drawn against Arsenal. Arsenal's striker at the time was Ian Wright. I loved him and wanted Kevin to get his autograph for me. But he didn't manage it. I was determined, however. At the end of the match, I squeezed through the crowd. I went up to Ian and, star struck, asked him to sign his name for me. It was amazing, meeting this famous England footballer.

I never thought at the time that a few years later I'd be meeting David Beckham, Wayne Rooney and Frank Lampard. I couldn't have imagined, back then, Joe Cole telling Martyn and me that he'd read about us in the paper. I wouldn't have believed it had you told me that one day I'd be known and people would want to hear my story.

I was always on the go.

At school there was netball and trampolining. I even had ballet lessons, but they fell by the wayside. It was football I loved best. My parents never seemed to mind that their little girl was a tomboy. I was, however, a conscientious and hard-working pupil. I enjoyed everything apart from science. I was especially good at home economics. My teacher said that my attitude and commitment were exemplary, and that I had the 'utmost diligence and lots of common sense'.

In year 11, when I was about 16, I was a prefect. My school report that year said I showed confidence, maturity and responsibility. I couldn't have been more different to a boy four years below me called Martyn Compton, who was constantly in detention. He was not so much my prince, back then, more of a pain in the backside. I think it was fortunate that our paths never crossed when we were at school.

In year 11, my home-economics success continued, especially the child-development element. My report said, 'Michelle, your enthusiasm for this subject has not waned this year. You had a very successful placement, and your playgroup leader spoke very highly of you. To quote, "Michelle is just lovely with children – sensible, kind and understanding."'

Looking back at those reports now, I think they show that teaching was always going to be my chosen career, although I didn't think so at the time. But I loved kids. When I was little, I wanted to be a midwife. I've always loved babies. I can't wait to be a mum. It'll be such an adventure for Martyn and me after the incredible beginning we've had to our life together.

I bet if I have a daughter, she'll be as unpredictable as I was: tomboy one minute, girly the next. My mum didn't expect this, I'm sure, but when I went out school-uniform shopping with her just before I started year 11, I said, 'I want a short skirt.' I don't know why I said it. We were wandering towards the trousers, as usual. I think the need for change swept through me at that moment.

'Michelle,' said Mum. 'You wouldn't wear a short skirt.'

'Please, Mum,' I said. 'I will wear it.'

We went over to the skirt rail. Mum turned over a label on the short black skirts. 'They're £15, Mich. If I buy it, you'll have to wear it. I mean it.'

'Mum, I will. I promise.'

'OK, then.' Mum was unconvinced. 'You better try some on.'

I felt brilliant zipping myself into my short skirt, and I wore it to death.

I left Angley School after GCSEs and went to Homewood Sixth Form College in Tenterden to do A levels in psychology, media studies and English literature. I had a little Fiesta at the time and had just started going out in the evenings with Kevin to the pub. I was starting to feel really independent. I was also playing football at the weekend, so I was forging my own way in life. I wanted to become a teacher, but after I'd done my A levels, I was desperate to get out of school and earn some money. I wasn't sure about going to university. I thought it would be a waste of my parents' money.

I got a job in telesales at a local frozen-food company called Shearway. It was down the road, which was handy. And I loved the job, too. The staff were great, the atmosphere was laid-back and the money was OK. I didn't have to do any cold calling. I took telephone orders. Then, after I'd settled in, I was given my own clients. Eventually, I wanted more money, so I got a job in sales at the *Kent Messenger*, the local newspaper. I had to do cold calling, and I didn't really like it. I got a salary, and you could earn bonuses on top. But it wasn't for me. The pressures and the deadlines didn't suit me.

I did another couple of jobs before I came across my old football manager at Crowborough, the girls' football team I played for. He suggested I become a PE teacher at Senacre School, Maidstone, where he was a teacher. I applied and was taken on as an unqualified PE and English teacher, and started doing my training in-house.

I taught football, of course, and made a special effort to encourage the girls. I did my Level 1 Coaching Certificate in football through Crowborough, which gave me more confidence to teach the sport. A year later, I moved to Aylesford School, Maidstone, as an unqualified PE teacher for year seven and cover supervisor, which meant I was a supply teacher for the school and would fill in when other staff members were off. I was there for six years. I got to know all the kids, and I really enjoyed it. I knew it was what I wanted to do. I enjoyed the work and enjoyed the salary. And my sense of self, my independent streak, grew.

That's when I got my beloved blue MG. It was my dream car. I wouldn't get rid of it for just anyone. It would take an incredible man to make me part with that symbol of my independence.

CHAPTER 6

MARTYN – AND HERE WE WERE, TRYING TO JOIN UP IN HAWAIIAN SHIRTS AND TRAINERS

I looked at my watch. A few minutes yet before my appointment. Traffic clogged the junction outside the army recruiting office in Chatham. The office, a large brick building, was right next to the road. I stood outside and watched the cars. My nerves jangled – not because I was joining the army, but because I was worried that they'd reject me. What would I do then? Not back to mucking about with Chris, behaving like kids, that was certain. The truth was, I had no idea.

I looked at my watch again. 'OK, now or never,' I thought and walked into the recruiting office. I was there to take the British Army Recruit Battery – or BARB – test. I'm not a fan of exams. I sat at a desk in front of a computer. I was on my own in the room, staring at this screen – no chance of asking for help if I got stuck. I swallowed and made a start. I soon realised I didn't need any help. The questions weren't like exams at school. They seemed to be testing my logic, trying to discover what skills I had. I raced through it in 20 minutes, and a shot of adrenalin went through me. I thought I'd done all right.

I wanted to join the Royal Electrical and Mechanical Engineers, known as the REME, because I could learn a trade. I would do my basic training then get attached to a battalion regiment.

Wendy had helped me find out how to join the army. And she'd brought me to my appointment and was waiting in a car park around the corner. I hadn't been that chuffed when Wendy and her daughters, Sophie and Kas, had moved in with Dad and me. Up until that point, our house in Staplehurst had been a boys' pad. Then, without warning, I was chucked out of my big bedroom and surrounded by girls.

Tipping up and down on the Bampton Park seesaw with Sophie was quite different to living with her, and we fought like cat and dog at first. I was nearly 14 when they moved in and Sophie was 12. Kas, being five years younger than me, didn't really figure on my radar. It might have been different, a bit more evenly balanced, if their elder brother Ben had lived with us, but he'd moved out of Wendy's home by then.

As far as I was concerned, it was girls versus boys in my house. I was outnumbered, especially when Dad was away working, but that didn't mean I couldn't win. Wendy had her own ideas, though. She saw that I needed rules. She made me do the dishes, which I considered to be women's work, and she taught me to iron. I was unimpressed and escaped with Chris Humphrey whenever I could.

Eventually, Sophie became my ally. She wasn't naughty like I was, but she was good fun. She began joining in some of my and Chris's tamer adventures. Like the time we found a sofa someone had thrown out. That was too much temptation for Chris and me. First, we stuck it on the side of a cricket pitch and sat there watching the game. Then, when we were asked to leave, we decided we'd have the coolest treehouse ever – one with its own sofa.

We hadn't worked out how we were going to get the sofa into a tree, and we never got a chance to try. The farmer whose field housed the tree saw us lugging it along and chucked us off his land. We didn't know what to do with the sofa, but it didn't take us long to come up with a ludicrous plan. To this day, I don't know if the residents of Staplehurst ever discovered who left a couch balancing precariously on top of a pillar box, but I suppose they could have made an educated guess.

Wendy saw my energy and realised that it needed to be channelled. She suggested I join Headcorn Army Cadets with Chris, who was already going with our mate, Lance Cooper. I loved cadets, especially the days out, camping and adventure training. I didn't mind the discipline too much if it meant I got to do all this great stuff. Chris, Lance and I went twice a week for two years, and as Dad was away a lot Wendy took it in turns with Chris and Lance's parents to drop us off. Wendy was good to me, but I didn't really appreciate it at the time. Perhaps I could pay her back and make her proud with a career in the army.

I waited after completing the test, daydreaming about my future career. 'Martyn Compton.' I turned towards the voice and followed the man. They told me I could join the REME. I was accepted there and then. I'd done it – the first stage completed successfully. It felt good to achieve something.

I received a letter a few days later inviting me for a two-day physical assessment at the training depot for phase-one recruits in Pirbright, Surrey. It's the army's biggest training camp and is in a rural part of the county. The Royal Anglians are also based there.

I was on a high and couldn't wait to get there. With two weeks to go, I made sure I was in the best condition of my life. I ran every day and went to the gym. I wanted to succeed.

The only jobs I'd had up until that point had been with Chris, and you couldn't really call what we did work. We rocked up at an egg farm just outside Staplehurst – just turned up one day in the summer after we finished school, threw our bikes on the ground and strolled in asking for employment. We were to oversee a machine that tested the eggs one by one. Chris and I soon twigged that if we loaded too many eggs into it, it blocked up and we'd get a half an hour break while the technician was called. The boss wised up to our game, and we were soon escorted from the premises.

Next, Chris got a job in an ice-cream factory. He probably wished he hadn't asked me along too when I shut him in the freezer one day. We were taking it in turns to strip off and see how long we could last. I took it too far, of course, and kept him in there a bit longer than planned. I'll never forget the sight of him when I opened the door, his teeth chattering, hands clutching his bollocks, his mouth desperately trying to thaw so he could call me some colourful expletive, both of us pissing ourselves laughing. We didn't work there long, either. Yep, my days farting about with Chris were definitely over. I was getting a real job.

The physical at Pirbright was straightforward and nothing I couldn't cope with after my preparations. I was fit, strong and ready. We ran and did press-ups, chin-ups and sit-ups. They tested our strength in various ways – including us holding an ammo box for a certain amount of time. It wasn't a breeze, but I coped. At the end of the physical, I sat through a formal interview. I felt really confident. It was well founded. They made me a formal job offer. I wanted to do somersaults.

The basic training took place at the Army Technical Foundation College in Arborfield, in Berkshire. It's where junior-entry recruits for the technical corps are trained. The technical corps is made up of the REME, of course, the Royal Engineers, the Royal Signals and the Royal Logistics Corps. I'd be there for forty weeks – and I wouldn't be going home for the first three months. I was only 16 and young to be away from home. It was a long stint away from my dad, but it was what I wanted to do, so I had to live with it – we both had to.

We drove up on 6 September 2000. Training started the next day. Butterflies swarmed in my stomach. My heart raced as we drove. I didn't know what to expect. I had no idea how I'd cope. I was already thinking about home and how much I'd miss my day-to-day life. It would be strange not to see Chris. He was surprised that I wanted to join the army and a bit down that we'd be separated. But he told me he was proud of me. We'd stuck together, been mates throughout, despite people trying to keep us apart. Now it was me – my choice of career – that finally stopped us being around each other.

My throat was dry, and my nerves fizzed. I took my suitcase and bag out of the car. I reined in my emotions as Dad said a quick goodbye. I wanted him to get going, or I was going to get upset. I watched the car move away, then turned my back. It felt like turning away from my old life and the frivolous, childish Martyn and stepping towards adulthood – towards something serious and life-altering. That was true. But, as I quickly learned, there'd be no shortage of laughs and monkey business. The kid in me still had room to manoeuvre.

We were taken to our rooms. I shared with some other lads. It was pretty basic. We had a single bed each, a wardrobe and a desk. I dumped my stuff and sat on the edge of the bed, waiting. I expected someone to come and tell me what would happen next. It was the army, after all. I sat there for a couple of hours without a clue what I was supposed to do.

A face popped round the wardrobe and greeted me. 'Tom Chaney,' he said.

'Martyn Compton,' I replied.

I relaxed. I'd made contact with another human being. It was like being lost at sea and suddenly discovering dry land. I felt good. That soon changed, though.

The bugle blared at 6 a.m.

The wake-up call is the reveille, traditionally used to get you out of bed at dawn in the military. Reveille's French for 'wake up', and it does what it says on the tin: jerks you out of sleep and makes it impossible to doze off again. You can't hit the snooze button on a reveille. You can't roll over and stick your head under the pillow. It woke us up every day. Yes, it was grating, tearing you from your dreams, but if the army was to be my chosen career, I'd have to put up with it. I'd have to put up with much more than that.

When the reveille got us up, we'd have to make our beds. They were dressed the old-fashioned way with sheets and blankets, which was a bit of a pain. Then we'd have a shave and a shower and get dressed. And we'd then get screamed at to go outside for first parade.

There was a lot of that screaming-in-your-face business, all that 'drop and give me 20' stuff. If someone didn't turn up, we did ten press-ups. If someone else didn't turn up, we did another ten press-ups. If someone did something wrong, we all had to run to a tree three miles away and back.

And it was blanket punishment. We were all in the shit if one guy did something wrong. If half a group mucked up a task, the other half would be punished for it. It made you get things right so you weren't dropping your mates in the shit. If someone didn't have their helmet on properly, we'd have to run 300 metres in our gas masks and NBC (nuclear, biological, chemical) suits.

I was nervous but excited. You never knew what was going to happen next. It was always tough, but I liked the challenge.

The first couple of weeks we walked around the camp, seeing what was what and where stuff was. There was a massive gym, a cookhouse, a cinema and a parade square. We were also told we'd have to iron. I never thought I'd have to do something so domestic in the army; I thought we were there to fight, not to do housework. But I soon realised how important it is. It's all about looking your best and maintaining standards. And thanks to Wendy, I was no stranger to the ironing board and passed that test with flying colours.

We went out on exercises, learning tactical approaches. We pretended to walk across the battlefield and learned hand signals and how to not be seen. We learned snap ambushes: we'd cut off from the path we were taking then wait to see if anyone was following us. We'd sit there for 15 minutes. If no one came, we'd get up quietly, one by one, and carry on. If someone did come along, we'd ambush them. Regulars who were having a day's jolly would come and play the enemy. You could tell they loved it and had the attitude, 'Let's go and scare some kids.'

We were given temporary combats, which are not what the regulars wear and are really thick and heavy. We wore them for four weeks. We also had PE kit, consisting of T-shirts and shorts. During the fifth week, we were given proper Combat 95 uniforms – the ones you have to iron. You had to earn the right to wear them. It's the style of clothing that real soldiers wear. It's what you wear on operations; it's what you wear in battle. They don't hand Combat 95s out to anyone. We also had to undertake an assessment to get our belts, then our berets.

We were taught the basics of using a gun. At that point, the emphasis was on using them safely – there was no fancy stuff. The weapon we learned to handle was the SA80. We didn't really practise our skills until we joined the regiment and they took us on range days, teaching us to shoot the enemy, not our mates.

In the evening, there was more work to do. We were taught how to polish our boots properly. We'd scrub the toilets and the showers. After all that, I'd lay my kit out ready for the morning and lay the locker out for locker inspection. By 10 p.m., I'd be knackered. We were always in bed by 10.30 p.m. at the latest. Fatigue overwhelmed me by the end of the day. I was desperate for my bed. To get a good night's sleep, ready for reveille at 6 a.m. the next morning, you had to get your head down early.

Campbell, the lad who had the bed opposite me, couldn't get his reading light to work. He was a great lad, Campbell. There was an inspection on the way, and he'd get a roasting if the light didn't work. Tom was trying to help him, but he wasn't having any luck. The bulb wasn't fused, but for some reason it just wouldn't come on.

I had no idea what the problem was, but I said, 'Let's have a look,' and took the bulb out. I peered into the socket. 'There's something stuck in there,' I said. I jammed my finger inside. I felt something crackle right through me and flew 12 metres across the room. I was sprawled on the floor, my hair spiked up on my head. So much for being an army electrical engineer. Everyone fell about laughing. No one helped me up; they were too busy pissing themselves.

There wasn't much time to make friends, but we did bond during those first few weeks. Getting myself electrocuted for my mates certainly helped. And the training made us depend on each other. We didn't want to make a mistake, or the other lads were going to get punished as well. We didn't know it at the time, but what we were learning was that in a war situation fucking up could cost your mate his life.

In those early days, all we concentrated on was getting things right. There was so much to learn, more than I thought. We even had to learn about the REME, which is pronounced 'Reemee'. The corps is responsible for inspecting, maintaining and servicing virtually everything electrical and mechanical in the army. That means everything from a kettle to a tank. While we were sat there learning this stuff, learning about the corps' history, they shouted questions at us when we didn't expect it. You really had to have your wits about you – or it might well have been 'get down and give me ten'.

Quite a few people left during those first few weeks. But I was doing well. I was athletic and fast, and I enjoyed the training. I was fit before I joined the army. Like my dad, I'd always been a fast runner. He'd run cross-country for Devon, and I'd also represented the county. I'd also done karate, a lot of weight training and had been in the cadets, of course. I was in good shape, so came out on top on the sports side. However, I didn't like being told what to do, and I was stubborn. But I had to stick with it; I had to bite my tongue and get on with things.

I missed my dad and rang home as often as I could.

'It's bloody hard,' I told him.

'Are you going to stick at it?' he asked.

'Damn right.'

I missed Chris, too. But I'd made good friends with Tom. You can tell when someone's your mate because they start taking the piss, and Tom pulled my leg because of my vanity. 'There aren't enough mirrors for you,' he'd say.

When we weren't polishing our boots or scrubbing toilets in the evenings, we did have a bit of time to ourselves. We talked about the work and the training. We never really mentioned what joining the army might ultimately mean. The mention of war, of fighting, never raised its head. I was there primarily to get a trade and keep myself on the straight and narrow.

I'd phone my dad in the evenings, too. If Dad wasn't home, I'd have a quick chat with Wendy, then ask to speak to Sophie. And when she came to speak to me, I'd put a different lad on the phone to her every time. It was a laugh, the boys stuttering their way through a conversation. She got on well with some of my mates, though. She never got put on the phone to Tom Chaney. I don't know why. But I'd make up for that later on. They'd meet, fall in love and get married.

This was all about bonding, too, I guess: taking the piss out of each other, putting your mates on the phone with your sister. The army's all about teamwork. I learned a lot during those first few weeks. And when we got to go home after 12 weeks, people said I was walking taller. Pride was something I'd not felt so much before. But now I recognised the feeling. It did make you feel taller; it made you stick out your chest, throw back your shoulders. I felt like a man.

The growing up I'd done during those three months in Arborfield changed me in the eyes of a few of my friends in Kent. But when I saw Chris again, it was like nothing had changed. I reverted to my old ways, and we shared a few capers, including one occasion where I smacked someone for having a go at Chris. I realised afterwards that it was pretty stupid and could reflect badly on my career, so I didn't do it again. I was probably showing off a bit, defending my mate. But we had a special bond, and if his best friend who was training to fight couldn't defend him, then who would?

Passing out parade in April 2001. Did I feel proud? Did I feel like a man, like a soldier? Adrenalin flushed through me as we marched into the square at the college.

My family was in the grandstand watching me. It was a cold day, so cold that the army staff passed out blankets to the spectators. I didn't think about it. I was on such a high as I entered the parade ground.

We were in three companies, each company made up of three platoons. We marched and turned. We showed our rifle drill, spinning the weapons about our heads, doing all that twirling with them. You had to be careful. They had bayonets on the end.

The demonstration lasted 50 minutes. The crowd stood up and applauded. My chest swelled, thinking about my family watching me, cheering me. I hoped I'd made them proud.

We marched past and saluted the training camp's commanding officer. We strode off the parade ground and were at ease. We were told to go and see our families, and that's when the nerves hit me. The strength drained out of my legs as I made my way back to the square. It was emotional. There were tears. I hugged them all, and they congratulated me.

Auntie Trina said, 'I'm so proud of you. Seeing you up there, a part of that team.' Their praise filled me with joy. I felt a sense of achievement. Their happiness made me happy. I hadn't gone through this just for me. It felt now that I'd done it for all of us.

The recruits cheered, and we tossed our hats into the air. Caps peppered the chilly April sky and then rained down on us. A weight had lifted. All the uncertainty about where my life would take me had gone. I had a sense of independence. As I showed my family around the college where I'd trained over the past few months, the grounds and the rooms where I'd gone from being a boy to being a man, I felt a calmness wash over me. I'd found my place.

But that was only the beginning. With phase one over, it was on to phase two. In September, we went to SEME, the School of Electrical and Mechanical Engineers in Borden, Sussex. The mechanic's course we were booked on at Borden was oversubscribed. They gave us two options: guard duty at SEME – which meant standing around the perimeter, not doing much – or going on adventure training. Tough choice.

However, before we had to make this difficult decision, some of us had to attend an intensive-driving course. We were 17 and had to learn to drive, so the army put us through the test in a few days. Tom and I started on the Monday, and by Wednesday we had our driving licences.

The adventure training took us to Dorney Lake near Windsor. The lake is a world-class rowing and canoeing centre set in 400 acres of parkland, and it's owned by Eton College. It'll host the rowing events at the 2012 London Olympics. We went there every day on a minibus from Borden. Tom and I spent six months learning to row at Dorney Lake.

Borden was a bit more grown up. We were allowed duvets and had televisions. We had freedoms that made basic training in Arborfield seem like a prison camp. If we had time off during the day, we could go to our rooms and sleep or play PlayStation. The bar opened at 5 p.m., so we'd usually get smashed and then try to get up for physical training in the mornings.

I suppose it wasn't really geared up for new recruits like us. It was more for troops who'd been serving for some years to come back and do some top-up courses. We had a sergeant who'd come round and tell us to empty our bins, but that was about it.

I could have done with more discipline. We got into a lot of scrapes – just the sort of stuff young lads do. It's pretty much what you do when you're 17 and 18, isn't it? All pretty harmless. We were probably out on the booze too much. Well, too much for the commanding officers' liking. They'd had enough of us, and we were told to transfer to another regiment.

Tom and I decided to stick together. We went to the army careers office to see if we could find a regiment that would take us. He went in first. Giving the advice that day was a corporal major from the Household Cavalry. Tom liked the sound of what they did, and as he came out, he whispered to me, 'Accept the Household Cavalry.'

I listened to the corporal major, already knowing what I was going to do. I'd stick with Tom.

Combermere Barracks in Windsor, home to the Household Cavalry, is a fully working regiment. Tom and I didn't realise it would be so formal.

We drove to Windsor in my pale-blue Ford Escort. We were wearing Hawaiian shirts, jeans and trainers. You can't get much more informal than that. We knocked on the door of the guard room. A uniformed man opened the door. I tried to check his insignia, but the Household Cavalry has different ranks to the rest of the army. He wore three chevrons pointing down, with a metal crown above them. They looked like sergeant's stripes. I later learned he was a corporal of horse, but I had no idea at the time.

I said, 'We're here for an interview with the commanding officer. We've come to see if we can join the Household Cavalry.'

The guy's face turned red. You could almost see steam coming out of his ears. He said, 'You two couple of dickheads look like you're going to a barbecue.' His voice was a high-pitch squeal. He chucked us off the camp, saying he wouldn't let us see the commanding officer dressed like that.

We drove round the corner and opened the boot of the car. We were in a sweaty. Not a good start to our career in the Household Cavalry. The regiment has a great reputation and is respected worldwide. Its members play a significant role on state occasions – you've seen them, gleaming in their uniforms, mounted on magnificent horses. They're the ones who do the changing of the guard at Buckingham Palace. The Household Cavalry is also a front-line unit in times of war. And here we were, trying to join up in Hawaiian shirts and trainers.

We tore open our bags and grabbed anything that looked half sensible. Tom found a jumper to put on over his shirt so you couldn't see how creased it was. I rubbed my shoes on some grass to make them shine.

Ten minutes later, we went back and had our interview. They told us we'd be an asset to the Household Cavalry and that we'd be needed in Bovington in Dorset on the following Monday for armour corps training. We signed on the line and drove back to Borden. We tossed our mattresses in the store, said, 'See you later,' and screeched out of the camp.

It was late Friday. We were due in Bovington at midday on Monday. 'What shall we do?' Tom said.

'Let's go to Devon and stay with my grandma,' I said. 'We can go to Bovington from there on Monday.' Tom agreed and off we went.

Sophie was in Devon that weekend, so I took Tom to the pub to meet her. They got on really well. Better than I could've hoped. Tom and I travelled from Bovington to Devon quite often after that. It was convenient that my aunts and gran lived there. We did abuse their hospitality now and again. Sometimes at Gran's I was so drunk that I threw up out of the bedroom window. She'd give me both barrels in the morning and send me out to wash up the puke. I had to hosepipe her flowers clean. She'd tell me off, but I'd defend myself, saying, 'At least I made sure I was sick out of the window.'

We went round to Auntie Trina, and luckily she was more

forgiving. We later paid back her hospitality by decorating her house. Sometimes Sophie would be in Devon, too. She and Tom were becoming close, and they started seeing each other.

We weren't allowed to have cars at Bovington. Most of the recruits were too young or had only just passed their tests. They tried to say that we'd get found out if we brought our cars, that they'd get spotted even if we hid them in the town. But I wasn't having any of that.

We turned up in my Escort and found a place to park in the railway station. It was free, so that's where we left the car. If any other recruits were getting off the train as we arrived after a weekend off, we'd switch the lights off and roll into the car park so they couldn't see us and grass us up. We'd then get a taxi to camp.

When we were strolling up to the station with the other lads at the weekend, we'd tell them that my auntie was coming to get us so they didn't think it was weird we weren't getting on the train. We got away with it, no bother.

Life at Bovington was structured again, and that was fine by me. I needed the discipline. It helped me focus on what I was there to do.

When we first arrived, Tom and I stood out like sore thumbs. We were still wearing our REME cap badges. No one from REME goes to do armoured corps phase-two training. Armoured corps is all about driving, and REME don't do driving. Despite being in the Household Cavalry now, the others referred to us as the REMEs. Tom and I were older than the other lads, and the commanding officers cut us some slack – and I might have abused that leeway a little too much at times.

There were four accommodation wings at Bovington, and everyone took it in turns to be the troop senior in their respective wings. That meant being in charge and keeping an eye on all the others in the wing. It was great when Tom or I were troop seniors: we were older and happy being top dogs. But if some kid was troop senior and he ordered me to do something, I'd tell him where to go.

Chris Finney was sixteen and troop senior one week. He ordered me out of bed and told me to empty the bin. 'Fuck off,' I said and stuck my head back under the duvet. I know I didn't show him much respect. That was wrong of me, but I was battling those demons of ill discipline that had troubled me all my life. I should've listened. But to me, Finney was just some kid giving me hassle when I wanted to sleep.

Today, Chris Finney is the youngest-ever recipient of the George Cross. The George Cross is a bravery award given to those who've shown courage in action that didn't involve the enemy. Finney, for example, received his award for an incident in Iraq in March 2003 that involved friendly fire. Iraq was Chris's first operational deployment. He was 18 when the incident happened.

Finney and his mates from D Squadron Household Cavalry Regiment were travelling along the Shatt al-Arab waterway, north of Basra. They were about 15 or 16 miles ahead of the main 16 Air Assault Brigade when a Coalition Forces ground-attack aircraft came from nowhere, striking the British soldiers. As Chris helped his comrades, the aircraft came back. They were lining up a second attack. The planes fired, and Finney was hit in the legs and backside. But he carried on helping others until he collapsed.

He showed incredible courage and received his George Cross – the equivalent to the Victoria Cross – from the Queen in February 2004, that lad whom I'd told to 'fuck off' for asking me to empty the bin.

There was a massive cross-country circuit at Bovington where we learned to drive Spartans. The first time I drove an armoured vehicle was amazing – to be in control of this incredible vehicle. I'd never done anything like it. I really felt like I was in the army then.

We did our basic mechanics: how to change an oil filter, how to put the tracks back on if they fell off and how to tow someone. Then, at the end of our training, we had to do a few weeks' guard duty, patrolling the perimeter fence at Bovington. It was boring and cold. You'd get woken up at shit o'clock in the morning, and I like my sleep. I would always pay others to do my stints for me. The lads got used to it, and if they needed extra cash, they'd ask me if I had any guard duty coming up.

It was coming up to Christmas, and I was due to be on standby for guard duty on Christmas Day. I couldn't leave camp, but I was desperate to go home and see my dad and family. Of course, I turned to my mate for help. Tom lived too far away to go home, and he was going to be in camp anyway, so he offered to do my guard-duty stint so I could get back home. I didn't have to pay Tom. What are friends for, after all?

Tom and I were fast-tracked through Bovington. We were out of there in ten weeks, compared to the raw recruits who were there for six months. The regiment was short-staffed and needed us. Tom and I were back in Windsor on 21 January 2002.

The regiment, apart from C Squadron, which was in Bosnia, was on Salisbury Plain on a Tactical Engagement Simulation Exercise – TESEX for short. This is basically pretend war with laser guns. Tom and I, having just got back, were stuck at Windsor virtually alone. We hadn't been issued with a weapon and couldn't be put on guard, so we were at least grateful for small mercies. But for three weeks, while everyone else was on TESEX, we were in the Officers' Mess cleaning silver. Bored isn't the word. Every night, we ventured into Windsor – but soon discovered that the beer was very expensive.

I was always one of the fittest soldiers, and I worked hard. After seven months, I was moved to Military Transport. I wanted to get all my driving licences.

We were constantly on exercise after that. The whole regiment went to Longmore in Hampshire. There's a derelict village there that has been bought by the Ministry of Defence for the army to practise in. We learned FIBUA, which is fighting in a built-up area, and I was there to do the transport, ferrying people about. We slept in bushes and hung upside down under vehicles, changing gearboxes in the rain with a torch between our teeth. Training was tough, but it was starting to feel real. We had to acclimatise ourselves to war-like conditions. We never knew when we'd be called on. And when Iraq started to heat up in 2003 and the regiment began to train for that campaign, we had to put our grown-up heads on.

In 2004, Tom went to Iraq for seven months. He was a dad by then. Sophie had given birth to Alicia almost a year before. She was living in Staplehurst, so each weekend I'd go home and help her. I helped her find a house and gave her a hand to decorate.

Dad and Wendy had broken up in 2002 but were still friends. Wendy was back in Devon, and we remained close. Sophie was not only like a sister to me, but she was also Tom's partner, so it was natural for me to support her and Alicia. I didn't know at the time, but a few years later I'd be asking for her help just before I headed out to Afghanistan.

CHAPTER 7

✤

MICHELLE – I'D KISSED A FEW FROGS BEFORE I MET HIM

I had an obsession. He was called Martyn, and we'd met on a Friday night in January a few weeks previously.

He seemed stuck in my mind. I just couldn't get him out of my head. He was just so gorgeous and fit. I'd met him through his dad, who was a regular at the pub where I worked evenings.

The night we met, we went back to my parents' house and chatted all night. When that happens, you know there's something there – something more than just physical. We nattered about family, friends, work.

Martyn was a soldier, so he wasn't around all the time. He told me that after the weekend he'd be heading to Bournemouth for training. The fact he'd be away all week suited me fine – I'm independent; I wanted my own space. And I liked the fact that Martyn was his own man with his own mind.

I'd kissed a few frogs before I met Martyn and some of them had been very clingy. Some of them had insisted on spending all my shifts sitting at the bar, ready to leap in if anyone chatted me up – very annoying. Drinkers flirt with barmaids. Big deal. I could handle these things myself.

I had my concerns about Martyn, too. I was 25, doing well in my teaching career and hoping I'd soon meet 'The One' so I could settle down and start a family. Something about Martyn was different. I felt very serious about him. But he was three years younger than I was.

Kevin had recently been reunited with his childhood sweetheart Katie, so I asked her advice. She suggested that I might not have considered this a problem if the age difference was reversed. 'Do you like him?' she asked.

'Loads.'

'Well, go for it then.'

My feelings for Martyn grew. I wanted to spend as much time with him as I could. Before I'd met him, Saturdays were shopping days with my best mate Sarah Terri. We'd met in the pub a few years earlier. Sarah and I would spend our Saturdays going to different towns in Kent. We'd wander around the shops and have pizza for lunch. We were often planning holidays and looking for the nicest summer clothes, especially bikinis. Shopping was our religion. I was obsessed with anything pink – clothes, shoes and handbags. On a teacher's salary, I couldn't always afford everything I wanted, but I loved window shopping almost as much as the real thing.

On Sundays, I played football. Like shopping, that was sacred, too. Just because I'd met a man I really liked, I wasn't going to let go of the things that were important to me. You can't do that. Martyn liked me because I was me, and I was me because of these things: my independence, the shopping sprees, Sunday football.

My Saturdays trawling the stores with Sarah continued. Not as often, maybe, but I still found time for my mates. And now I was shopping for clothes to wear out with Martyn on our precious Saturday nights.

Football continued. Strangely for a bloke, Martyn wasn't that into the game. So after my match, I would rush home, have a bath, then spend a few hours with him before he had to leave for Lulworth near Bournemouth, where the Household Cavalry had sent him on an Advanced Signals course.

My family noticed how happy I had been since meeting Martyn. I didn't always go to a big effort to introduce my boyfriends to my mum and dad, but with Martyn it was different. I was so proud of him. I took him home, then round to Kevin and Katie's. They had this cool penthouse flat in Ashford, and we had a great night there, me showing off my big brother to Martyn. They hit it off straight away, drinking beers and larking about.

I was really excited, but I felt calmer than I ever had before. I loved being with Martyn. I loved the way he made me laugh and the way he made me feel. He was so much fun to be with. He was happy-go-lucky and full of fun with me, but when Martyn meets new people, he's always quiet. And that's what struck my family when they met him. But he got to know them, and they got to know him, and he soon started to stay at our house before leaving for Lulworth at 5 a.m. on Monday mornings.

My mum would offer to make him a packed lunch – the same as she did for Dad. Martyn would always say no thank you. But I knew he was being polite, not wanting to put Mum to any trouble. I said to her, 'He'd really like a packed lunch. He just doesn't want to say.'

Mum made him one the following morning. He was really grateful. So grateful that he'd eaten it before arriving at Lulworth. But that was Martyn – he could eat for England; he had an enormous appetite.

Martyn often ate at our house. Mum noticed the amount he devoured, so she started peeling more potatoes for the Sunday roast. But Martyn still managed to eat two Sunday dinners – one at his dad's, then another at ours at teatime.

My dad had an especially large plate that Mum had bought for him. Mum thought Martyn could do with a similar-sized dish, so she bought one for him. She said to Martyn, 'I've got a present for you.'

'You didn't have to do that,' he said, unwrapping the plate, which was identical to Dad's. He was chuffed. I think he knew he was a part of the family when he got that plate.

I really knew Martyn liked me when he started sacrificing a roast dinner to come and watch me play football.

I was falling in love with him, and I couldn't bear to be parted from him. Sarah and I went on holiday to Cornwall, and all the way there Martyn and I were either chatting on the phone or texting. Sarah was very tolerant, and I think she showed a lot of restraint – I know a few people who would have snatched the mobile and tossed it out of the window.

Sarah and I enjoyed our holidays together. The first time we went away was a long weekend in Prague. It was one long party, starting with a BA upgrade that saw us drinking vodka with our breakfast and champagne on the plane.

I was always up for a party. I loved the pub and our little crowd that hung out there: Sarah, Nicky Jakeman, me and whoever we might have been going out with at the time. There was also James the chef and Rob, Martyn's dad, constantly talking about his son the soldier. I'd be there with my pint of Heineken swigged through a pink straw. I didn't drink through a straw to get drunk – it was just that pink obsession of mine.

Shopping on Saturdays, football on Sundays, bubble baths followed by nights out with the lads, my blue MG convertible and a pint through a pink straw – I suppose that summed me up. But despite my slightly laddish ways, marriage and babies were always on my mind. I wanted to be married by the time I was 25, with my first baby on the way soon after that. I love children, which is why I became a teacher.

I'm family orientated. Probably because my own family is so close, and we've had so many happy times together. And when Martyn came into my life, I thought I might have met the man who could make my dreams come true.

CHAPTER 8

MARTYN – 'I'VE NEVER LIKED GOLD'

I decided to propose to Michelle and wanted to do everything properly, old-fashioned like. I wanted to have the ring ready, and I'd pictured the perfect one in my mind. All I had to do was find it.

Michelle was at work, so I nipped into Maidstone. I looked in several shops, but there was nothing similar to what I had in mind. I was in the last shop for quite some time, peering into the glass cabinets. Then I saw it. It was beautiful. I'd wanted something a bit different for Michelle, something special. The ring was two slim bands of yellow gold and white gold. The two bands twisted to a point, where a diamond balanced.

I thought Michelle's ring finger was the size of my little finger. I explained this to the saleswoman, and she went to try and find the size I needed. While she was gone, my phone rang. It was Michelle. My nerves tightened, and I felt myself blush. I looked around the jewellers guiltily, as if I'd done something wrong.

'I've just finished work,' she said.

'I'm in town. Come and meet me,' I said. 'Call me when you're here.'

I only had 15 minutes until Michelle arrived, and the jeweller hadn't come back with the ring yet. When she came, I tried it on my little finger. It fitted.

'I'll just clean it,' the woman said. She polished away. Then we began sorting out insurance and payment.

I was panicking a bit by this time. The ring was my only purchase of the day. How could I hide a ring bag from Michelle? I needed to buy something else before she arrived. As I left the shop, I saw Michelle strolling down the street. I froze and held my breath. She hadn't seen me. I dashed into HMV and picked up the first thing I saw. It was an iPod case. I took it to the counter and paid for it.

'Have you got a bag, mate?' I said to the fella behind the till.

'Actually, I've run out,' he said. 'I'll just have to go and get some.'

He came back with the bag, thank God, and I strolled out of the shop, trying to look nonchalant – and walked straight into Michelle.

'Hello, babe. Coffee?' I asked, giving her a kiss.

We sat down in a nearby café. Michelle reached for my bag. 'What have you bought?' she said.

'Nothing. Just a case for my iPod.' I pulled the case half out of the bag to satisfy her. Sweat beaded my forehead. I hoped she wouldn't notice. The ring was under the case, right at the bottom of the bag. 'See?'

The confidence I'd had in the jewellery shop started to fade. I started having doubts. Was it the right ring? By the time we got home, I was rattled. I was convinced I'd buggered it up.

Michelle usually only wore silver jewellery, but I thought an engagement ring should be gold. I sounded her out during the adverts for *Coronation Street* that night, trying to make my enquiries sound casual. 'Have you only ever worn silver jewellery?' I said.

'Yes,' she said. 'I've never liked gold.'

My throat went dry. 'Oh.'

'Why's that?'

'Oh, no reason. Just that, you know, sometimes people change their mind – go through phases with which one they prefer.'

'No, I never have,' she said. 'I just like silver best.'

'That's great. Good job, Martyn,' I told myself sarcastically.

But it was too late. I'd bought it. It was a perfect engagement ring, in my mind. Just the wrong metal, that was all. I'd have to hope for the best. I decided that I would propose that coming Saturday night, and on the Sunday I'd be off to Combermere – and from there, Afghanistan. I was going to take Michelle, Rosie and Brian for a meal and propose at the restaurant.

Nerves shook me up all that week. I didn't know whether I was coming or going. I rang Sophie. 'I'm thinking of proposing to Michelle,' I said. I was excited. It felt good saying it – saying that I wanted to propose.

Sophie was straightforward and told me to go ahead and do it. She knew it was what I wanted to do. I needed someone to nudge me, that's all. And she was the right person to give me a shove in the right direction. She was there for me, like I'd been there for her when Tom went to Iraq.

That Saturday, Michelle, Rosie, Brian and I went to The Bull in Bethersden for a meal. I had meant to ask her to marry me there, but we got a bit tipsy, and I decided to wait till we got home. Rosie and Brian knew what I was up to. They kept eyeing me throughout the meal, waiting for me to go ahead and ask their daughter. I faffed about so much, they must've thought I'd had cold feet. No way. I wanted to marry Michelle. I wanted her to be my wife more than anything else. My nerves were frayed. I'd slugged back too much booze.

It was a great night, despite the fact I'd mucked up and failed to propose as I'd planned. When we got back to Frittenden, Rosie and Brian made themselves scarce. I think they felt for me and knew that I was bricking myself, so they gave me and Michelle some privacy.

I got the ring out and said, 'Will you marry me?'

It's not arrogance to know the answer's going to be yes, but when she said it, floods of adrenalin swept through me. It was like learning that she loved me all over again. We hugged and kissed. Rosie and Brian came in with a bottle of champagne, and we cracked it open. Michelle texted her friends. I watched her, saw the ring glisten, and sadness crept into my chest. I'd be going away, and to be apart from Michelle was the last thing I wanted. I didn't know how I'd get through the next few months without her. It had been one of the happiest nights of my life, and I was now facing gloomy nights. An endless stream of them, stuck out in the desert, thousands of miles away from my girl, pining for her. It was going to be tough. I just wanted to hang out with her all the time.

'Is the ring all right?' I said.

She studied it, smiled and said it was beautiful. Even though it was gold.

CHAPTER 9

※⤳ ‧ ⤳※

MARTYN – IT WAS BLEAK, AND THE HEAT SMACKED INTO ME

I walked away from Michelle and across Combermere Barracks. I could hardly see through my tears. I couldn't walk into the room I shared with my good mates Keeno and P.J. in that state. I had five minutes before I got there, so I spent that time trying to pull myself together. It was tough. The night before had been so happy. Michelle had agreed to marry me, and now we were going to be apart for months. It tore me up.

I was gutted when I was told I was going to Afghanistan. It sounds weird, but it was a shock when the reality of the job hit me. I didn't know what to expect, even though the preparation had been going on for months. It never crossed my mind that I might not be coming back.

Michelle had been very practical when I told her I was being deployed. 'Well, it's your job,' she said.

Originally, I was being deployed for six months with two weeks R & R in the middle, but then it was changed to four months straight. 'Let's look on the bright side. At least we'll only have to say goodbye once,' Michelle said.

P.J. and Keeno were in the room when I arrived. They knew me well, and they weren't fooled. I put my bag down, sat on my bed and had a bit of a cry. I'd known P.J. for four years. He's a very thoughtful bloke – friendly and chatty. He was in A Squadron, so he wasn't deploying with us. He said, 'Get it out your system, mate. It'll be all right. You'll soon be back.'

Deep down, I knew I wasn't alone. Everyone was probably shitting themselves. But outwardly there's very much an attitude of, 'Let's do this. Let's get back. Let's go on leave.'

Keeno had a different approach: humour. 'Remember the day at Windsor races?' he asked. I did remember. It was a squadron day out, when wives and girlfriends get invited along. We'd gone to the racecourse on a riverboat. After a couple of bets and a few drinks, Michelle, Keeno and I fancied fish and chips. We decided to make our way into town, which was just over a mile from the racecourse. The fish and chips went down a treat. Then we needed to get back to Combermere Barracks

'Bollocks. No cabs for an hour,' said Keeno, snapping his mobile phone shut.

'We'll walk it,' I said. 'I know a shortcut. Won't take long.'

'God help us. That'll be the long way round then,' said Keeno.

We'd been walking for about half an hour when we got to an allotment. 'Through here,' I said, opening the gate.

'Martyn,' said Michelle. 'I am in a dress.'

'Honestly,' I said. 'It'll be quicker. Mind the marrow.'

Eventually, we came to a big barbed-wire fence. I helped Michelle over, then jumped it. 'Come on, Keeno, you big lump,' I shouted.

Keeno isn't graceful at the best of times – less so when he's pissed. He tried to jump but cut his hands to ribbons and ripped his trousers. And they weren't even his.

We were soon laughing at the memory in our room at Combermere Barracks, and the weight in my chest at saying goodbye to Michelle had lifted. 'I helped Michelle over the fence, not you, Compo,' said Keeno. 'You'd have just left her there.'

'Bollocks,' I said. 'And, either way, you walked back to camp with your arse hanging out.'

Keeno's first impression of me was that I looked like 'a boring old fart'. He thought this because I was quiet and had a receding hairline. I put this early impression to rest with a few drunken escapades and general loudness.

We were always taking the piss out of each other. Like Tom Chaney, Keeno thought I was vain. He spread a ridiculous rumour that I got up an hour and a half earlier than needed for parade so that I could style my hair and apply moisturiser. 'How can I take that long over my hair if you reckon I haven't got any?' I asked.

'You and P.J. are a right couple of posers,' he said. 'Down that gym, building up your muscles, pretending to be working on your fitness.'

He might have been a joker, but Darren Keen had his uses. He was a Spurs fan, like Michelle. He knew everything there was to know about the team. I wasn't really into football, but I wanted to impress Michelle. Keeno was very useful, telling me about the club's triumphs and failures, what the players were like, what the manager was about, what was expected in upcoming games and which players the club had their eye on when the transfer window opened.

It was going to be fine. I'd soon be back to Michelle and messing about again. I found my small black diary. I usually made a few notes in there about finances. But I decided to keep a tally of how many days it would be until I was home again. Home to Michelle. I wrote, '119 days,' but not much more. I didn't want to think about things in detail. And anyway, there wasn't much time to think about stuff. We were soon on our way to RAF Brize Norton. And from there we'd fly to Afghanistan.

'Thank God we're on a TriStar,' I said to Keeno. 'At least they're a normal plane, not those bastard noisy Hercules.'

The Hercules C-130 is like flying in an enormous metal drum. You're in the back with all the gear. You're crammed together on these canvas benches, and you can't hear a bloody thing, the engines are so loud. There's no chance of a chat, and it can be pretty boring – most people read or fall asleep – so I thought the TriStar would be good. We could chat, banter, take the piss. But as soon as we took off, my mood changed. I didn't feel like nattering. My head brimmed with so many thoughts that I couldn't actually focus on anything. I couldn't get Michelle out of my mind, and I was already missing her. I was thinking about my dad, too. The next few months, and what they had in store, also weighed on me. I listened to the iPod Michelle had bought me, my head filling with the music. The songs sparked a memory.

Michelle and I had gone to Devon to visit my family a few weeks before. On the drive, Michelle got fed up with my music. It was all club anthems, R & B – nothing you could sing along to, nothing you could belt out. She made me stop at a garage and bought a cheesy album called *Happy Songs*, a compilation of stuff you could sing to.

At first I thought, 'What a load of crap,' but once the songs got going, we were both belting them out, singing at the top of our voices. We can't sing, but that didn't stop us. We were really going for it. 'Don't Stop Me Now' by Queen was our favourite track. We screeched out the words, about having a good time.

It came on my iPod when I was on the plane, and I smiled. Over the next few hours, as the TriStar crossed the continents, carrying me to the place that would change me for ever, I played it over and over again.

We arrived at Kabul International Airport at 6.30 a.m. local time on 20 June 2006. It was the middle of the night at home. I was desperate to ring Michelle to tell her I'd arrived and to hear her voice. But she was tucked up in bed.

I went to sit down a few seats away from Keeno. 'I'm getting my head down, mate,' I said to him. I laid down and leaned my head on my bag.

When I woke up a few hours later, it hit me that I was in another world – one that was so different to mine. Daylight didn't do the airport any favours. It was so basic and nothing like any airport I'd seen. There were no shops, information boards, automatic doors, cool lighting or sleek furniture. Dust covered everything, and it all seemed thrown together. There was nothing to do, but we were stuck there until 2.20 a.m. the following morning. Military transport moves at night to be more secure.

I wrote in my diary: '118 days.'

There were about 90 of us in the Household Cavalry's D Squadron, and we were all deploying. I was on the last flight out. Soldiers milled around the airport, reading, and playing cards and small board games, waiting to be told that we were on our way to Helmand – or 'Hell-land' as it was nicknamed. We were called. We got our gear. We flew to Helmand in a Hercules C-130.

Before going to Afghanistan, we'd done loads of training, naturally. We travelled down to the Lulworth Gunnery Ranges and went through all the various scenarios and role-playing exercises, testing our awareness, fighting while dismounting from vehicles, casualty treatment and evacuation, reactions to improvised explosive devices and shooting the retreating enemy. It was great training and all stuff the squadron ended up doing.

We went to the Land Warfare School in Warminster, where they have desert-simulation units, in which we practised vehicle drills and radio procedures. We also had loads of specialists in to lecture us about the history of Afghanistan and its cultural and tribal make-up. We knew that Afghanistan had sheltered the Taliban, who'd refused to surrender Osama bin Laden after the 9/11 attacks. We also learned some of the languages and dialects.

And the Coldstream Guards came in to teach us what they'd learned in Northern Ireland about patrolling and public order.

The families were invited to visit, but Dad didn't come. People are different, I guess. Some cope better by knowing what's going on. Others prefer not to know too much. Dad is one of the latter, which is fair enough.

Helmand's in the south of Afghanistan. It's twice the size of Belgium, and the population's about 740,000. Helmand's the largest producer of opium in the world, and it's also teeming with Taliban. They needed to either retreat or be got rid of so that Afghanistan could have a chance of standing on its own two feet. This was Operation Herrick IV – 'Take Down of the Taliban'.

I stepped down from the Herc and got my first good look at the country I'd come to defend. It was bleak, and the heat smacked into me, even at 4 a.m. 'Christ,' I said to Keeno. 'I've never been anywhere like this.'

'It's not the sort of place you go on holiday, is it?' he replied.

I walked across the camp. Someone handed me a bottle of water. I drank it in two seconds. We'd been told that it was going to be even hotter in Helmand than it was in Kabul. But it was unimaginably hot, and our introduction to it, wearing a helmet and body armour, and carrying a bergen, a holdall and a day sack, was vicious.

Captain Alex Greenwood of the Scots Dragoon Guards, who was attached as the squadron logistics officer, showed us to our tent, which slept six. 'The air con's broken,' he said. 'But at least you'll get used to the heat quicker.'

We got our heads down for a few hours. It was starting to get light.

There was a queue for the phones, but I wanted Michelle to know that I'd done the first bit safely, so I waited. She snatched up the phone after one ring. Before she could speak, I said, 'It's me, darlin'.'

'Hi, babe,' she said, and her voice made my heart swell. 'Where are you?'

'Bastion, babe,' I said. 'It's fucking weird being here. It's just a desert. Nothing here – just us. And you should have seen Kabul airport. It was basically just a field and building, like an old school canteen. I can't describe it. It's so hot. I'm sweating my arse off. Anyway, how are you?'

'I'm good, I'm good. I miss you already, babe. Is Keeno OK? Who's in your tent with you?'

'Yeah, Keeno's fine, babe. He's making me laugh. Paul Hamnett, the medic, is in with us, too. He's a great fella. I've showed him all your pictures. Told him we're getting married. Still can't believe it.'

'I know. Me, too. I'm going to start looking at venues next week. Anyway, I'm off to school soon. I'm making some toast. Do you want some?'

I laughed. 'Nah, give mine to Harvey,' I said. We chatted for a few minutes more, then a recorded voice told us we had a minute left. 'I've gotta go,' I said. 'Take care. I'll call you soon. Give my love to everyone. I love you.'

'I love you too, darlin',' she said. 'Take care. Call me when you can. Miss you, miss you, love you.' And she was gone. I felt as if we were a million miles apart. I trudged away from the phones, the queue of soldiers still there, everyone waiting to tell their loved ones they were safe.

Three thousand troops inhabit Camp Bastion, the British Army's desert base in Helmand. It is named after the HESCO bastion protective wall units we use to shield our bases. Bastion has its own helicopter airstrip for Chinooks, Lynxes and Apaches, and a runway for Hercules C-130s. It's amazing to think that the Royal Engineers, protected by the Royal Marines, built Bastion in a few months. Before it was constructed, there was nothing but desert.

It's like a small town. We had telephones, the Internet, a gym, a cookhouse, a hospital, running water, drainage and power. We had, in weeks, what most Afghans had never had. But that's why we were there: to help them get some of what we had. Or at least help them reach out for it. But it was not going to be easy.

When British forces arrived in Helmand in 2006, we were supposed to be there to keep things safe and secure so that reconstruction could take place. Not that we weren't ready to fight; we always are. And luckily so – the opening battle between 3 Para and the Taliban a few months before I arrived in the country was described as the most intense fighting since Korea. The Taliban were known to be well armed, persistent, tenacious and courageous – often to the point of insanity.

We were given a week to acclimatise to the heat and get our body clocks sorted out. But we were up between 5 a.m. and 6 a.m. each day for parade. The bosses would check we were all there and had our equipment. Sometimes they'd update us on what was going on. The rest of the time we maintained our personal kit, worked on the vehicles and equipment, and sweated it out in the gym. By the third day, we were working between 2 p.m. and 6 p.m., the hottest part of the day. People were dropping like flies from heat exhaustion.

We had loads of briefings – reminders of the rules of engagement, awareness of landmines and improvised-explosive devices, and basic medical training. There was a firing range built just outside the perimeter fence, and we went there to fire our weapons and ensure the journey hadn't damaged their accuracy.

I missed the newspapers. The ones we got in Bastion were a few days old, and I missed knowing what was going on back home. I also missed the soaps on telly.

On Sunday, 25 June, we had a day off. I wrote to Michelle: 'It's like being in nick out here, away from normal life. I can't see anything green, and I can't wait to get back to you.'

I got my PlayStation out and had a go on the boxing game. That made me more homesick, because I was used to my opponent being Michelle. I missed our banter. When we boxed, she'd turn and punch me in the arm every now and again, and we'd end up in a playfight. This time, I was fighting the game itself.

One hundred and thirteen days to go . . .

I lost count of how many bottles of water I drank each day. We never put our bottles down, really – kept swigging away, grabbing another bottle, then another. But weirdly, we barely peed, just sweated. The heat and sweat got so bad out there that we had to wash our clothes a lot – or we stank. Underwear was the worst. Pants got really bad, and they needed a good clean. We took our boxer shorts to the wash basins to rinse them and then we'd drape them on our beds. But it wasn't ideal. They didn't dry quickly enough hanging there in our rooms.

'Come on, Keeno,' I said. 'Let's make a washing line. I've nicked some gaffer tape from the signals room. We'll string it between two tents.'

'Our clothes'll stick to it,' said Keeno.

'Shit, yeah,' I said. 'No, we'll double it over, make it stronger as well.'

Ten minutes later, our line was up. Keeno and I dashed to the sinks with an armful of socks and boxers. 'This is a result, mate,' I said to Keeno. 'I'm fed up with having sweaty bollocks all the time.'

We went back to our washing line. A few blokes had gathered round to see what we were up to. 'Here come the washer women,' someone said.

I folded my boxers over the line. 'Calvin Klein? Get you, Compo,' said a voice from the crowd.

'Shit, they're not gonna get nicked, are they?' I said to Keeno.

'Behave, Compo. Who wants to wear some other fucker's underwear?' he said.

We stood back to admire our domestic skills. I felt chuffed. The heat was raging, so we sat inside our tent for a few minutes to escape from the sun.

I went outside to check progress. 'Bloody hell,' I called. 'They're nearly dry.' I was in high spirits; my washing line had worked. Then a truck swept by, showering the damp washing in sand. It coated the material, sticking to it.

I grimaced and trudged back to the tent to tell Keeno his pants might need washing all over again. I stuck my head round the tent flap. 'Bad news, mate,' I said and told him what had happened.

'Oh, for God's sake. This place is doing my head in,' said Keeno. 'Are we gonna wash them again?'

'Not much point if those trucks are gonna keep going past,' I said. 'When they're dry, we'll bang it off.'

We whacked the pants on the side of the tent, but we couldn't get rid of the sand completely. Those boxers probably ended up dirtier than they started. But we weren't going to admit defeat, and I lost count of the times Keeno laughed at me for scratching my balls and complaining. It was better than the other option, though, which was common in the army: to wear your pants once, then turn them inside out.

Keeno's bed was next to mine in the tent. I think I bored the arse off him talking about Michelle. To be fair, he didn't complain much. He knew she meant the world to me and understood how much I missed her.

I was on the phone to her every minute I could. I felt like part of me was missing. I spoke to my dad, too. I knew he was worried, so I kept it brief. I wasn't allowed to tell him about what we were doing, anyway. When he asked me how things were, I told him, 'It's bloody hot,' and left it at that. Even when we're thousands of miles away, in a strange country with a different culture, Brits end up talking about the weather.

I wasn't embarrassed to cover any space I could find in the tent with pictures of Michelle. Back home, two of the lads' mothers, Mrs Hanaford and Mrs Game, had raised money to provide all of us with fans and 'comfy boxes' to keep our home comforts in. We were all chuffed about it, and I had my comfy box next to my bed as a table. The pictures of Michelle were on top of the box and tucked into every crevice I could find, including the bottom shelf of a canvas cupboard a few feet away, so I could see her when I was in bed.

The cot beds weren't very comfortable. You could really only sleep on your back. But we fell into bed knackered each night and managed to sleep even though the air conditioning was broken. It did get us used to the heat more quickly, which was good, as we still had the hottest part of summer to come.

From time to time, reports came in of troop casualties. When they did, the satellite was shut down, which meant no phone calls. It pissed us off, but we had to think of the poor lad who was injured or dead. It wasn't fair for his family to hear about it on the news or from another family member.

The first time I heard that someone had died, reality kicked in. It dawned on me that there were guys out there in the desert who were going to be shooting at us, guys who wanted to kill us.

Not surprisingly, perhaps, when we got out to Afghanistan, we immediately started planning what we were going to do when we got back home. I wrote to Michelle:

Hi, babe, everything going OK? Probably by the time you get this I'm either out somewhere or maybe even back in. It'll take ages to get to you, which is a pain in the arse really. As long as I get loads from you, I'm just about happy to plod on through.

I hope you're looking for a house, babe. Can't wait to say we've got our own house. It's going to be the best. We're going to have a big playroom, though, so I can have my big TV and Xbox 360 plugged in and my pool table set up. Ha, ha! – only joking.

I love those photos I've got of you, babe. I look at them every night and when I wake up, I can't wait to see you again. I'm not going to recognise you, and you'll probably be the same with me.

We will be going on a big spending spree when I get back, babe. You can have whatever you want. We can even go on holiday when I get back, because it's sounding like we're getting a month off. Hopefully, anyway. Or we can just go at Christmas, or even do both. Can't wait, babe. I'll go anywhere as long as it's with you and we can spend lots of time together. Say hello to your parents for me and tell your dad I'm looking forward to one of his barbecues. And tell your mum I can't wait to be eating off that big plate of mine. We have to use plastic everything out here and it's shit. Anyway, babe, take care of yourself for me. Love you so much you wouldn't believe. There isn't a day I regret that I'm with you, babe. Can't wait to see you again.

All my love. Loads of big kisses and hugs.

And I finished it off with rows of kisses. I missed her so much.

When soldiers get to war zones, they immediately focus on home: I'm doing this when I get home; I'm doing that; we'll go here when I get back . . . I don't know why that is. Maybe it's a psychological brick wall that keeps our minds off the possibility that we might *not* be going home. It's keeping hope alive, I guess. And home and those we love are the hope that soldiers have.

In our second week, we were out on the runways in Bastion protecting the Royal Engineers who were repairing the ground. The signals equipment also needed checking. It arrived from Pakistan in shipping containers, and there were problems with stuff overheating.

Dust storms swept in from the desert while we were there. Visibility was down to about ten metres, and we had to wear goggles and a scarf over our faces if we needed to move about the camp. Keeno and I went out in a storm to see what it was like. Sand lashed us, and we had no idea where we were going. The sand covered me, and got into my ears and up my nose. At least I had an excuse to pick my nose. Keeno took some pictures of me to send to Michelle.

We got inside, and I went to email the photos to her, but the Internet and the phones were down. It gets you down: you're so far from home, and you're desperate to talk or message the ones you love, and then technology gets in the way. I sat down on my bed instead and wrote to her. I missed her badly by then. There was a hole in my chest, a void there because I was so far from Michelle. I had pictures of her, but it wasn't the same. You can't touch someone, you can't hear their voice, you can't smell their hair, their skin, you can't kiss them and hold them. It hurts, but I wasn't the only one hurting. Three thousand of us were, I guess. And all the other troops out in Afghanistan, as well.

In my letter, I wrote:

> I had a good dream last night. It was about me and you and how our life's going to be when we are married. We had a nice house, and in the dream I remember the kitchen was quite big. We had the family around, and we had a son who had his Tottenham kit on, and we were just so happy. I just can't wait for that dream to be real. That's how I picture it being like. Can't wait to see everyone again. It's going to feel like a lifetime being out here. Thinking of you every minute of the day, babe. Look after yourself. Love you so much you wouldn't believe. I'd do anything for you. You're a part of my life. Love you with all my heart.

And the kisses flowed again, all across the page. Criss-crossing them on the paper made me wish I could kiss her for real.

We had to change our formation when we got into theatre. The ninety of us in D Squadron were divided into three gun troops, each containing four vehicles – three Scimitars and a Spartan. The Spartan is a support vehicle and carries specialists such as forward observation officers. It was decided that each gun troop needed a Spartan. The threat of coming into contact with the enemy was high, so we needed an extra vehicle to carry interpreters, extra ammo and to be able to evacuate anyone who was injured. We weren't planning on taking any casualties, but you have to be prepared.

The other troop of vehicles is known as the squadron headquarters, or SHQ. This contains command vehicles, REME, signals – which are the communication side of things – a recovery vehicle and a Samaritan ambulance. Our admin troop remained in Bastion while we were out on ops.

Back in the UK, I was in motor transport, which is part of the HQ Squadron, but when we deployed, I was due to be a signaller in SHQ. Then, on 28 June, I was transferred to driving a Spartan that was supporting one of the troops. I was also given the Minimi machine gun to operate. I was shitting myself, because it was quite a responsibility, but I was also chuffed, as it was a new piece of kit for us. It's what we call 'Gucci'. You know, the opposite of Primark – a bit posh, top of the range, a luxury. Plus it fires a lot of ammo pretty rapid-like.

There were queues for the phones and the Internet. When your turn comes, and you get a terminal, you can't piss about looking at other websites – you get on your email and write your message or the blokes behind you get tetchy, and rightly so. Everyone's desperate to contact their loved ones, even though most people act a bit nonchalant about it. Inside, you're shivering, desperate to get on that keyboard. But you don't show it to your mates.

On 30 June, I emailed Michelle then quickly went on the Interflora website and sent her some flowers and a red balloon with 'I Love You' written on it. On the way back to my room, I bought her a small teddy bear from the Bastion shop. It wasn't unusual to see blokes walking around camp with soft toys they'd bought for their girlfriends or kids. Then I dropped by the post room and found a parcel from Rosie.

'Fantastic,' I thought. I started fantasising that it might contain one of her roast dinners, which I could have killed for, despite the fact I was as hot as it was possible to be. But a Rosie roast wasn't going to appear in Afghanistan. A man can dream, though.

I took the box back to my room. Keeno was there. 'What you got, Compo?' he asked.

'Something to eat, I hope,' I said. I ripped into the parcel. I could only recognise what was inside by its smell. The tiny yellow fragments inside the box had once been crisps. The bag had burst, spilling its contents all over the box, and the crisps were crushed. 'Bollocks,' I said. 'Bag of crisps – or *used* to be. Now a *box* of crisps crushed to fuck.'

'What flavour?' asked Keeno.

I licked my finger, dipped it into the shards and licked it again. 'Ready salted, I reckon. Want some?'

Keeno and I sat on the bed eating the tiny pieces of crisps. They tasted like home.

The next day, I had some time to myself so wrote to Michelle. I listened to 'Don't Stop Me Now' as I scribbled my thoughts:

> Got you a few things today. Sorry they're pretty shit. Hope you liked the flowers, babe. I'm going to get you some flowers every month. Then, the last month I'll be delivering them. Can't wait for then, babe.
>
> Sent you a box today. Lucky you. Thought it would make a change, you getting a box. Hopefully, you'll like some photos of me, just so you can remember what you're marrying.
>
> It's still really hot here, babe, but I'm getting used to it. The other night, though, it was freezing, and we had to put our winter jackets on. Crazy, innit. Not looking forward to the English weather. Just means you're going to have to warm me up, babe.
>
> OK, babe, looks like I've got to go now because the paper's come to an end. Will let you know what we've got to do in the future, but if I can't write or ring you, babe, just think, deep

down, I'm thinking of you always, even though I'm the other
side of the world. I still love you with all my heart.

I kissed her from thousands of miles away and imagined her
face as I fell asleep.

The World Cup was on when we were there. I'd always taken an
interest in England's games, but Michelle had got me more into
football. The lads gathered outside by some shipping containers
to watch England play Portugal in the quarter-finals on 1 July.
The match was beamed out to us on a big screen, and we took
our own chairs. That was a pretty rowdy night even though there
was no booze in Bastion. We lost on penalties – knocked out of
another tournament. We were all pissed off, and I wanted to be
home with Michelle. I knew she'd have been watching, too, and
I wished I could've shared my gloom with her.

We went out on our first patrol on 3 July. We were supposed
to be out for five days, practising our skills and drills, but we
only spent two days out in the desert in the end.

Before we went to Afghanistan, we were told that a large
part of our work would be to stick around and hope that
the Taliban would leave. We'd be out and about, showing a
presence and encouraging the locals to be on our side. The
first time we went out we ended up in some tiny village where
the people hadn't seen outsiders for decades. They thought we
were Russians, still there since the Soviet invasion more than
20 years before. I felt a bit of an idiot for writing to Michelle
to say I was missing *Coronation Street* after seeing that. These
people had nothing compared to what I had, compared to what
we had back in the UK.

We had an interpreter with each troop, but I was amazed at
how many people had a smattering of English. I got out of the
wagon and met the locals, making sure I chatted and was friendly.
It was an experience I'll never forget. How could people live like
that? With nothing?

It was seeing the kids that wrenched my heart. We handed out some boiled sweets, and the youngsters loved them. Then someone held up a pen. The kids were amazed, their faces lighting up, and they began to fight over it. Over a stupid pen. It made me appreciate what I had back home. And thinking about that brought about the familiar gnawing in my guts: I was homesick.

We were told to come back to Bastion for another op, which would start on 6 July. I was excited. It was a reconnaissance job, which is what we're trained for. It's what the Household Cavalry excels at. But the night before, fear gripped me. There's nothing you can do in that situation. You've got to accept that you get scared and crack on regardless.

I wanted to ring Michelle, but the phones were off the night before the op. That pissed me off. Hearing her voice would've done me the world of good. And when you're going on ops, you don't know what'll happen. You don't know if you're going to come under fire. You don't know if you're coming back. You don't know anything. At times like those, you need to hear the voice of the woman you love.

I wrote to her saying that the op we were going on the following day was in probably one of the worst places in Afghanistan. Sangin, a town in the Sangin district of north-western Helmand, was a Taliban stronghold. It was one of the most difficult letters I had to write. I welled up writing it, and I had to stop now and again to wipe my eyes:

> I've had to tell you this now, babe. Because I want you to know that I will always be thinking of you, whatever happens. I've had to tell Dad what I want to happen if worst comes to worst. It's reality now, babe. I hate to say it. You don't realise how hard this is to be telling you this, babe.
>
> I got your parcel, babe. Bless you. You bring a tear to my eye every time I get something off you. It just makes me really

want to be with you. I'm getting really upset writing this now
– it's happening to me tomorrow.

We were going to be out in the Sangin district for two weeks,
and I told Michelle that I'd try to ring her when I got back. It
was going to be tough going a fortnight without speaking to her.
I knew she was going to worry. It's natural; everyone worries.
But I had to at least *tell* her not to. I couldn't imagine her pain,
not hearing anything for two weeks. I imagined how I'd feel.
I'm not sure I'd have been able to hack it. It's sometimes easier
being on the front line than being back home waiting for your
loved ones.

I signed off with:

> I'll be thinking of you all the time, babe. I'm going to have to
> go now. Sorry to be putting you through this shit, babe. Not
> too long to push now and you'll be back in my arms. I love you
> so much, babe. Try not to think about me until I get back.

I'd asked the impossible, I know. But what can you do?

I thought we were going to be leaving early the next day, but in
the end we were delayed, which meant we had to travel in the
hottest part of the day.

First, we were travelling to Forward Operating Base Price,
which is in Gereshk, not far from Sangin. Forward operating
bases, or FOBs, are basically secured positions. They can be really
basic – just some barbed wire surrounding a camp – or they can
have airstrips and hospitals situated in them.

Our orders were that while we were on the way to FOB Price
we had to create a screen to protect Canadian troops while they
carried out an operation. A screen is basically what it says on
the box: we provide security; we 'screen' other troops from any
potential attack. We were also ordered to stop any Taliban fighters
from escaping the area.

Travelling in the worst of the heat caused problems. A few guys went down with heat exhaustion. One of them had an inner-core temperature of 41.7 degrees. Forty-two and you're gone. A couple of drivers burned their skin on the metal of the tanks. The air con in the Samaritan ambulance was knackered, which meant that the saline drips overheated, and the cases on the drip's needles melted, too. 'That's fucking reassuring,' I thought.

We moved up from FOB Price to insert the screen. While we were sorting ourselves out, someone yelled 'Contact!' over the net. I was ready to shoot. But we soon realised that it was a farmer warning us off his land. You're on edge in situations like that. You've got to be ready, but you can't go shooting angry farmers.

In the end, our screen was successful for the Canadians. They found what they were looking for and killed some Taliban, who would probably have escaped towards us – except, of course, they would have seen us and decided against it, which made it uneventful for us. I wrote 'Saw fuck all' in my little black diary.

We stayed at FOB Price, working on the vehicles. The fuel tanks were filthy, and the fuel-intake pipes were blocked. We were fortunate that we hadn't broken down while we'd been moving about or we would have been in serious danger.

If you were lucky, you got some post while you were out on operations. It was great for morale, which is why I think they brought it out to us if they could. One morning I heard a shout that cheered me up. 'Compo, mail.'

It was a letter from Michelle's brother, Kevin. 'Hurry home, mate,' he wrote. 'Michelle's round at ours talking about weddings non-stop with Katie. It's driving me mad. I need you here so we can go out for a beer and leave them to it.'

It was great to hear from Kevin. He's a good guy, honest and hard-working, and it was going to be great being his brother-in-law. I'd been an usher at Kev and Katie's wedding and planned to ask him to do the same at ours. I was really looking forward to marrying Michelle, and it cheered me up to hear that she was so excited.

I also got a letter from Michelle's mum, Rosie, and she signed it off with, 'Harvey says hello.' I loved that dog and couldn't wait to get one of my own, perhaps after Michelle and I were married. The thought of Harvey's yellow smiling face and wagging tail put a spring in my step.

I'd seen a few dogs in Afghanistan, but mostly I'd just heard them. At night, they roamed about in packs, completely wild. The Afghans used them as guard dogs, and they didn't have names. The locals would be shocked at the way we treat dogs back home, like they are part of the family. Out there they are just animals. People form no emotional bonds with them.

Life is tough in Afghanistan – even for the dogs.

'Ninety-five days to go,' I wrote in my diary on 13 July.

I was knackered and fell into bed. We had been crashed out at 2 a.m. A hundred and fifty Taliban were suspected of being in the area, but we didn't see anything.

We had the next day off, and I sunbathed. It's not very wise under the Afghan sun, but there wasn't much else to do. Then on Sunday, 15 July, we were in briefings all day ready to leave FOB Price at 5 a.m. the following day.

Sangin was our next destination. The Taliban had a lot of support in the town. A year before, in July 2005, Taliban fighters attacked a United Nations convoy south of the town. The UN personnel all got away OK. But it showed what a dangerous area it could be.

Soon after leaving Gereshk, the last vehicle in our convoy got hit by an improvised-explosive device. The vehicle was carrying four Afghan policemen. They were all killed, and another three bystanders were injured. The REME were just in front of them, but they were lucky, and none of them were hurt. It was a bit close for comfort, to be honest, but we carried on and arrived at FOB Robinson at 2 a.m., had breakfast and went to sleep.

The next day, I managed to speak to Michelle. We weren't expecting to speak to our loved ones. There weren't any phones, but the D Squadron leader, Major Alex Dick, had a satellite phone, and he lent it to the lads to keep morale up. He's left the army now, Major Dick. He was a good guy. It really lifted my spirits to hear Michelle's voice.

'Hi, babe, how are you?' I said.

'I'm good. I'm OK, darling. I've found somewhere gorgeous for us to get married. Port Lympne Wild Animal Park. It's amazing – so beautiful. Do you fancy that?'

'Sounds great,' I said.

'How're things with you?' she asked.

'Yeah, there's a few fucking wild animals out here, I can tell you,' I joked. 'It's not too bad, babe. Don't you worry. Everyone OK?'

Even in a hostile place, you can have a laugh. If you're talking over the radio and don't release the button, you're on 'permanent send'. Everyone can hear what you're saying, and they can't communicate. You're blocking the airwaves.

During the op in Sangin, one of the lieutenants was trying to get a hold of a colleague. He forgot to release the button and stayed on send for two minutes. We all listened in on his nattering, and in the military the language is sometimes colourful. The lieutenant was discussing a rendezvous point with a trooper, making sure the trooper knew where he was going. The lieutenant said, 'You better get this right, "Fruitilicious", or we're fucked.' Everyone pissed themselves laughing.

A few days later, we were making our way through Sangin town. A lance corporal of horse was directing his driver. It was bloody difficult driving through the town. The roads were so narrow, even more so when you were battened down due to the threat. You could only see directly in front of you. The driver relied on the lance corporal of horse completely. Except the driver was on permanent send, so everyone but him could hear the lance corporal of horse saying, 'Left stick. Left stick. Left stick, you fucking idiot. LEFT STICK! Oh, you've just knocked some poor twat's house down, you prick.'

We got to FOB Robinson, called FOB Rob for short, on 18 July. I was knackered. When I wasn't driving, I was on stag. And the kip you get, if you get any, isn't great. The beds – either the ground or inside a wagon – aren't very comfy. You can't relax, because you've no idea when it's going to kick off.

We thought we were going to be in FOB Rob for a couple of weeks, putting in various screens. But on 21 July, we were moved out into Sangin Valley. We didn't see much Taliban activity, just a couple of suspicious cars.

That day, we bought some watermelons from the locals. They tasted fantastic after the boil-in-the-bag shit we'd been eating. It was so hot, we didn't even have to boil the bags. We just opened them and there was our food, warm and sweaty.

Back at FOB Price on 23 July, I had my first shower in two weeks. I stank like a tramp by that time and looked like Robinson Crusoe. The shower was a hosepipe, and the water smelled dirty. But it was better than nothing.

'Never mind. At least Mich can't smell me,' I wrote in my diary. 'She wouldn't kiss me. Eight-five days to go . . .'

On 24 July, we left for Bastion. But on our way we had to give covering-fire support for aircraft that had come to drop off supplies. By the time we got in the wagons, we were sweating like pigs, and the journey to Bastion was going to take 16 hours. At least in the driver's cab the only sweat I could smell was my own.

I stared at the desert ahead. It was dull and made me feel so desolate for the people that were trying to survive here. The occasional poppy field punctuated the forlorn land. The lush green momentarily cheered me, and I thought of Chris and our carefree fun in the Kentish countryside. I also thought about our goodbye.

'Be careful, mate,' he'd said.

'I'll be fine,' I'd replied.

'No. I mean it. Be careful.'

My six years in the army hadn't taken the shine off our friendship. We were muckers and as close as ever. But the opium swathes of Afghanistan were so different to the garden of England. Their tragic story drenched me and dulled my senses. I'd see Chris soon enough. I snapped my mind back to the job at hand.

When I got back the next day, I was fucked and not amused to hear we'd be off to Now Zad within a few hours. There was a letter waiting for me from Michelle. Reading that perked me up no end.

I wrote back:

> I love getting your letters. It just makes me happier and the day brighter if I know you're OK. Things out here are dull and horrible. Don't really want to talk about it, but just want to say, if you do hear any news, please take it with a pinch of salt. I will try my hardest to call you at least every other day. Going to go to sleep now, babe. I need some sleep.
>
> Because I'm not there with you, I still don't think it's sunk in for me that I'm marrying you. But I am, and you've made me the happiest man alive. I can't wait for the day when I walk in and there you are. I think that day will be like our first day all over again. I've got a feeling I will cry, so you can't laugh. Love you so much, babe. Make sure you take care of yourself. Love you loads and loads. Big hugs and kisses from me. Mr and Mrs Compton – looks good, doesn't it!

I wasn't impressed with Now Zad. For a start, the ants were fucking huge. Then the wagon broke down, and to top it off we got the news that we might not be returning to the UK until the beginning of November. I decided not to tell Michelle this particularly shit piece of information and tried to look on the bright side: it would mean we'd be going straight onto Christmas leave.

Three days later, just when I thought I couldn't be any more fed up than I was, I got a letter – this time from Katie. 'Bless her!' I wrote in my diary.

Katie is one of the happiest people I know. She's like sunshine walking into a room. And having just returned from honeymoon in Antigua and about to move into her dream cottage with Kevin, she was extra perky.

The next day, 31 July, we started moving from Now Zad to Musa Qala to help extract the Pathfinder Platoon and resupply Danish troops holed up there. 'Hopefully it's over tonight,' I wrote in my diary. 'Might get to speak to Mich soon. Seventy-seven days . . .'

CHAPTER 10

MICHELLE – HEARING MARTYN'S VOICE WAS BETTER THAN ANY PARTY

'Sorry it's a bit crappy,' said the note.

I looked at the small teddy bear that had arrived in the post. Tears welled. How could Martyn think it was crappy? It was such a sweet gesture.

What a life this teddy'd had. Someone had gone to the trouble of buying him, flying him to Afghanistan, transferring him to Helmand, then putting him on the shelf in the tiny shop at Bastion – just so one of our soldiers, my Martyn in this case, could buy him and send him back again to show me that I was missed. The crappy little bear was a miracle as far as I was concerned. I put him by my bed.

Since Martyn had left, I'd felt empty and tearful. Fortunately, my mates, Sarah and Nicky and Katie, and Kevin and Mum and Dad had made sure I wasn't alone. Sarah and I had started going to the gym every night. I tried to exhaust myself, because I found I couldn't sleep for thinking about Martyn unless I was very tired.

I wrote him my first letter on Tuesday, 20 June, two days after he left:

Martyn, honey bun. Since you left, I haven't been doing very much apart from missing you. I went to the gym with Sarah tonight. We worked out on the treadmill, bikes and the stepper. Then we did sit-ups and went swimming. We relaxed afterwards in the sauna and steam room. Then I went to the pub to watch the first half of the football, then home to watch the second half with Mum and Dad. It was nice to spend time with them.

Last night, Sarah cooked me dinner. I'm really glad I have my family and friends around me, or I wouldn't be coping the way I am.

I know you are coping really well, too. Well done to you, darling. You keep being strong and don't worry about your dad and me. We will be here for you when you get back, and we both can't wait. You just concentrate on what you have to do.

I keep looking at my engagement ring. It is so, so nice and sparkly and pretty. You have made me the happiest woman alive by asking me to marry you. I want to spend the rest of my life with you and have your babies and live happily ever after. You will be glad to know that I have tidied my bedroom! It's very clean.

By the way, the fish and Harvey say hello and to look after yourself and to take care. You may ask how I know this? Well, each and every fish told me, and Harvey always tells me when he speaks to me. Say hello to Keeno for me.

Well, darling, this is where I am going to end the first letter of the four months. Can't wait until I hear from you or receive a letter.

I signed off with kisses and said that I missed him so much.

Fortunately, work kept me really busy. There's not much time to dwell on your thoughts when you're surrounded by teenagers. And if I wasn't with Sarah or down the pub, I popped round to see Katie and talk about the wedding. The first thing to do was find a venue. I ordered some brochures of places I thought Martyn would like. We both loved the outdoors, so it was important to me that where we married had a sense of space and freedom – somewhere green, with lots of trees and flowers.

Martyn's occasional phone calls were precious. I tried to picture him sitting in his room and chilling out with his mates. But, of course, it wasn't like that.

Because Martyn and I hadn't been together very long, I didn't know many of the wives and girlfriends of the guys he worked with. But I discovered an online chat room for army wives and girlfriends. Someone mentioned that the lads on tour liked powdered squash sent to them to make the water taste of something, so I popped out in my lunch break to buy some and put a parcel together to send on Tuesday, 27 June. Martyn was always on my mind.

The World Cup proved a good distraction, though being an England supporter didn't exactly cheer me up. I wrote to Martyn that it was all turning into a bit of a shambles.

Sarah was brilliant, keeping me company. We used to drive down to Hastings on Saturdays in my metallic blue MG with the top down, the wind whipping through our hair. I loved that car.

In Hastings, we'd play on the games machines to try and win a couple of naff teddies, something like that. It was fun, and I appreciated Sarah's friendship. But, of course, I missed Martyn. I wanted him home so we could chat about our wedding plans. It's not ideal discussing such things over letter or email, and it's not that easy on the phone, either. He didn't get much time on the landlines from Afghanistan, so it was simply a matter of me asking how he was, telling him I loved him and saying I couldn't wait to see him. You couldn't talk something through in detail.

In the six weeks before he came home, Martyn and I wrote dozens of letters, and I sent him countless parcels. It was difficult to know what to send. I had to be sure that things wouldn't melt or explode. I posted wine gums, pepperoni, chewing gum and baby wipes, which he could use while out on exercise when he couldn't wash. I sent some boxer shorts, too.

Martyn had advised me not to listen to or watch the news, so I didn't. I spoke to Rob every few days, just to see how he was, but I avoided the subject of Afghanistan.

At the weekends, I arranged my social life around the times I was expecting a call from Martyn. One Saturday, I knew he was going to call me at 8 p.m. on the home phone. It was better to call a landline, as we got more time together. I'd been at a barbecue all afternoon, and although I was having fun, I wasn't drinking, because I had to leave at 7.30 to drive home and take the call. I chatted to my friends, one eye on the time, then dashed out. Hearing Martyn's voice was better than any party. I got stuck behind a tractor on the way home. Unable to pass it on the tedious country lanes, I trundled along, getting more and more wound up, watching the clock and drumming on the steering wheel. I'd never forgive myself if I missed Martyn's call.

As I pulled onto the drive, the phone started to ring in the house. I slung the patio door aside and raced upstairs. 'It's for me. Dad, can you shut the gate?'

I lay on the bed and closed my eyes, trying to shut out everything in the world apart from Martyn's voice. But all too soon, he was gone again. Sadness washed over me. Martyn was thousands of miles away in a world I didn't understand. My friends were enjoying themselves at a party, but I wasn't in the mood to rejoin them.

I wandered downstairs. 'Martyn OK?' said Dad. I nodded.

'Good party?' said Mum. I nodded. 'Cup of tea?' I nodded. I felt a bit tearful. Harvey wandered over, settled at my feet and let out a big sigh. I reached down and patted his smooth head. 'I know how you feel,' I thought.

The following Monday, I went to the gym after school, then on to Sarah's for dinner. When I got home, there were several large brown envelopes on the kitchen table – wedding-venue brochures. I ripped the packages open and feasted my eyes.

I was drawn to Port Lympne Wild Animal Park, as I have always loved animals. I rang Katie to ask if she would come and check it out with me. She was really excited and brilliant at planning things, especially weddings, so I knew she'd be the perfect person to come with me. I planned to ask her to be one of my bridesmaids. I wanted Mum to come along, too, so the following weekend the three of us were shown round the venue. It was beautiful and looked wonderful in summer, with all the flowers blooming everywhere.

I looked out across the English Channel and tried to imagine Martyn all those thousands of miles away. I felt such a rush of joy as I imagined us standing there in two summers' time, promising to love each other for ever.

Then we had a look around the park. I was very excited to see the elephants, as they're my favourite animals.

I went home and wrote to Martyn:

Sunday, 16 July. Darling. Well, while I am writing this, you are out and about playing soldiers. You knew that there were four places I had chosen as potential wedding venues, but now this has changed. I would like to get married at Port Lympne. It's beautiful, and if you have your wedding there, the money you pay goes towards the care of the animals.

I would like to get married on 12 July, if it falls on a Saturday in 2008, because that is the day that Mum and Dad got married.

Next week, I'm going to Chessington World of Adventures for school activities week. I am going to go on all the rides even if no other teachers are. I really don't care. I am going, and that's a fact.

I am missing you loads and loads and can't wait until we are back together again. It will be like the first time we met. It's going to be great.

Well, I'm sure by now you are out in the desert, all smelly. But hey, I will still love you, however you smell. Love you loads, miss you loads. All my love, hugs and kisses, always, Mich.

CHAPTER 11

MARTYN – I WAS STIFF, LIKE
A PIECE OF BARK

HELMAND PROVINCE, 1 AUGUST 2006

I knew my face was on fire.

Flames tore into my torso and arms. Pain shot through me, agony like I'd never known. I had to move, so I threw the burning steel of the tank off me and jumped from my seat through the gap where the front of the wagon had been. I landed on my arm and thought I'd broken it.

Fire engulfed me. I thought, 'I'm going to get shot. I've got to get out of here.'

I stumbled round the front of the wagon behind a wall and began putting myself out. It was then that I thought, 'I'm really going to die here.' My dad, Michelle, and family and friends started flashing in my mind.

I had to survive. I had to get home.

I threw my body armour off. Half of it had melted into me. It was supposed to be fire retardant, but not at those temperatures, I guess. I rolled around on the floor and put the rest of the flames out. I had to get into cover. I half crawled and half ran about 80 metres towards a low wall. I threw myself down behind the wall and hoped for the best.

I felt totally alone. Fear swept through my veins. I'd never been so scared. I had no armour and no weapon.

I lay behind the wall and tried to be as still as possible. A shot came from the tree above me. The bullet ripped through my thigh. My right leg jerked out to the side. I felt nothing. I guess the nerves had been burned away.

'Shit. I'm going to die,' I thought.

All I could do was hope that nothing else would happen. Bullets were hitting the wall beside my head. I waited for one to hit me.

It seemed like ages before I saw a tank rumbling down the hill. I heard British voices and saw one of the troop leaders pointing towards me and shouting. I thought, 'Thank God for that,' and started to feel a little bit safer.

Troops started moving towards me. I recognised one of them as Andrew Radford. 'Radders, I could kiss you,' I said when he got to me.

Radford tossed me over his shoulder. I was hurting, the pain was terrible, but I now felt safe. Radford carried me all the way back up the hill. Some of the other lads were giving him cover, and they followed us.

Radford put me on the front of the wagon. Pain pulsed through me. It had really started to kick in, especially where I'd been shot in my right thigh. The agony made me shout. Voices began to shout back at me, 'You'll be all right, mate.' Relief washed over me despite the pain: I was alive.

I felt the wagon bounce over the terrain, heading towards the rest of the squadron.

Lance Sergeant Paul Hamnett's one of the guys who saved my life. He was 27, an army medic, and his skill and his remain-cool-under-pressure attitude made sure I got through those first few minutes.

While the Taliban's improvised-explosive device destroyed my wagon and killed my crew, Hamnett was up on the hill with the SHQ. He hung about smoking, not really expecting any trouble. But that changed when news of the contact came over the net. Hamnett jumped into the ambulance. He and the crew made their way down the hill but were ordered back. The firefight was still going on – the firefight I was in the middle of, my body burned, my leg shot and my mates putting their guts on the line to save my life.

I was going to be Hamnett's first casualty of the tour, so he started checking his equipment. He knew it was all there and working, but there's nothing you can do in those moments while you're waiting. All you can do is check your stuff and hope you can cope with whatever's coming your way. Well, I was coming his way.

Hamnett threw open the ambulance doors. The mortar rounds blasted around him. Mick Flynn, carrying me off the front of the wagon that had brought me up the hill, handed me to Hamnett, and he laid me on a stretcher. He'd never seen anything like it.

I was stiff, like a piece of bark – dark brown with two white eyes staring out. Hamnett didn't know if I was already dead. He didn't know if it was worth speaking to me. But then words came to him. He started talking about Michelle. He kipped next to me in the tent, so he'd seen the photos of her pinned up on the wall around my bed, heard me speaking about my wedding plans. 'You don't want to leave Michelle. You're going home, mate. You're getting married,' he said, not knowing if I could hear him or not. 'We're gonna get you back to Bastion. The Chinook's on its way. You're gonna be fine.' And then I heard him say, 'How far's the Chinook?'

Alex Dick signalled that it would be 20 minutes. Twenty minutes. It seemed like a lifetime. Hamnett looked at me. I was a mess. He said, 'Just a few minutes now, mate. Chinook's nearly here. We're gonna get you out of here.'

I knew he was lying, but what else was he supposed to do? He was giving me hope. But he was also giving me a chance to live.

I was so tired, drifting in and out of consciousness. I said, 'I need to get my head down . . . need to sleep . . .'

But Hamnett and the others were saying, 'No, stay with us! Stay with us!' If I'd gone to sleep, I might've died.

Hamnett needed to secure my airways. They'd swell up and choke me if something wasn't done. He put a tube down my throat, but it gagged me. Not pleasant for me, but at least he knew I was conscious. He also knew that the more awake I was, the more pain seared through my body. And it was agony.

Hamnett got a nasal tube instead. He needed some lubricant. He'd normally use spit. That sounds disgusting, but in the field, in situations like that one, it's just quicker. He tried to spit, but his mouth was dry. He was blowing dust. Finally, he got the tube down my nose and started cutting my clothes away. Most of them were stuck to my charred body, and Hamnett couldn't pull them off because they would've ripped more of my skin away.

I needed fluids, quick, but my skin was so hard and shrunken that he couldn't feel any veins. He called Leach and Minter over, and they ripped open bags of saline, pouring the contents over me to keep me cool and keep my wounds clean. I was hurting and tried to stop them, but they kept doing it. Now I know it was for my own good, but at the time it was unbearable.

Hamnett then saw the damage the bullet had done to my leg. But there was no blood. The heat had singed my blood vessels. Hamnett splinted my leg while the other two poured saline over me. They emptied bags of it over my lips, too, to try and keep my airways from swelling up.

I tried to speak, but all I could produce was a moan. I felt like I was melting. The pain was like wires slicing through me. At least they knew I was alive. Hamnett gave me morphine.

I don't know how long Hamnett treated me before the Chinook arrived – I don't think he knows – but he'd used all the oxygen he had: one bottle, which takes twenty-two minutes to finish. I don't know what he would have done for oxygen if the helicopter had been delayed or there had been more than one survivor.

The pain just didn't stop. It was like a blinding white light, a laser cutting through my body, searing my skin, my muscles, my organs. It felt like fire was tearing into every inch of me.

The last thing I remember was one of the Chinook crew telling me I'd be all right. Only just, but I was. And it was thanks to Paul Hamnett that I survived. He's told me since that he was worried he'd not done enough. He wondered if he could've got those fluids into me, instead of pouring them all over me.

He came to see me in Bastion, though I don't remember. The medics there told him that they'd not been able to get a drip into me, either. I guess that made him feel better about his efforts, as he should have done – without him, without so many others, I'd have died out there.

Thirty-six hours later, I was back in the UK, alive. Just.

PART TWO

The Driftwood and the Star

CHAPTER 12

※◌〰◌.〰◌※

MICHELLE – IN AN INSTANT, THE WORLD SHRANK TO NOTHING

FRITTENDEN, KENT – 1–2 AUGUST 2006

I felt a buzzing in my pocket and signalled to Ella, the hairdresser, to switch the dryer off. I pulled the phone out of my pocket and looked at the screen: Martyn's dad. I hesitated. Every time there was a news report about soldiers in Afghanistan being killed or injured, Rob phoned me. It was stressing me out. He was next of kin, and he would have been told first anyway. I did what Martyn told me: avoided the news. I didn't want to panic every time something happened. I'd asked Rob not to keep calling me, because the first time he'd done so I'd been teaching and had become absolutely fraught.

I answered the phone. 'Michelle, there's been an accident,' Rob said. I caught my breath. In an instant, the world shrank to nothing apart from Rob's voice. 'Martyn's seriously hurt.'

I asked Rob if I should go to his house to wait for the army family liaison officers. He told me I had time – they wouldn't arrive until 4 p.m. I hung up.

My hairdresser stared at me in the mirror. 'Martyn's been hurt,' I said. 'Badly.'

'Oh, my God,' she said. 'You'd better go.'

I was in shock. I heard myself say, 'No, it's OK. You can finish my hair.'

I called Sarah. She said, 'I'll meet you at Rob's at 4 p.m. Don't worry. Martyn's strong. Whatever it is, he'll get through it.'

When I arrived at Rob's, two officers were there – one in uniform and one guy in civvies. Rob sat in his armchair. Sarah stood behind him. Tom and Sophie Chaney had come over, too. They sat on the couch. I sat next to them, silent, still, intent.

'There was an ambush this morning. Three soldiers were killed and Martyn suffered serious burns. He's very seriously injured,' said the one in uniform.

I said, 'When can I see him?' That was the only thing that mattered: seeing my man. My nerves were wound tight like violin strings, and I thought they'd snap at any moment. But I kept myself together, tried to focus.

'We don't know any more than what we've told you,' said the man in uniform. 'Martyn will be flown into the UK as soon as he's stable. We'll keep in touch. Call us whenever you like.'

I had so many questions: where was Martyn? Was he frightened? Was he alone? Who was looking after him? Did he know that I was here, waiting for him? No one knew the answers, so there was no point asking.

When the officers had gone, Tom put his arm around me. 'You can cry if you want to,' he said. 'No point bottling things up.' I shed a few tears, then I thought of Martyn. What was he going through while I was sitting there crying?

I made a decision there and then: I would be strong for Martyn. I pulled myself together and decided I wouldn't cry again. I've no idea where that strength came from, but I was glad I had it in me. I needed to hold things together, for Martyn's sake.

I also realised that I had to start telling people. I called Chris Humphrey. He was still Martyn's best mate. It wasn't an easy call to make. They were like brothers. Chris was shocked and miserable. He wanted desperately to see Martyn, and I assured him that as soon as he could, he would be able to.

I called my parents. Kevin came to meet me. Kevin, Sarah, Rob, Tom, Sophie and I went to The Bull. There was nothing to talk about except Martyn. But we didn't know much, so there was nothing to say. We just scraped around for conversation, never finding anything decent to talk about. There was only Martyn now.

I wished the minutes and hours away. I tried to imagine what was happening. Seeing Martyn was all I cared about. 'At least I'll see him sooner than I would have done,' I said, trying to instil some optimism into my newly wrecked world.

He was still out there in Afghanistan, but I had no doubt he would get home to me. Later, I would discover that the first medic who had treated Martyn, Paul Hamnett, had seen my pictures by Martyn's bed. He'd encouraged Martyn to live, to get home to me and our future. And my soldier had somehow heard and was fighting for our life together.

I drank a few glasses of wine. It seemed like a good idea. I was in denial at that point. 'Martyn will be fine,' I repeated loudly. I walked round the pub, telling anyone who would listen.

I stayed at Sarah's in Staplehurst that night so I could be near Rob's house. I didn't sleep much, and in the morning I just hung around, waiting for news. Then the confirmation came that Martyn would arrive at the burns unit of Broomfield Hospital near Chelmsford that evening.

Rob came to collect me. We didn't smile at each other, just nodded our heads. We knew we had something dreadful to face. The journey to Chelmsford took a couple of hours. We didn't say much to each other. What could we say?

We pulled off the M25. Red signs with a large white letter 'H' and hospital written underneath began to appear. Every sign was like a knot in a rope. I used them to pull myself closer to Martyn. 'Left at the next roundabout,' I told Rob.

'Yup,' he said. But he was already indicating.

We turned into Hospital Approach, the road leading to Broomfield. A heavy gloom filled my chest. The sun shone yellow, but the tall buildings loomed grey. Had they swallowed my Martyn? How would I find him? Fear gripped my heart. I was barely breathing.

We parked and walked towards the hospital entrance. The blue sky vanished as we stepped into the shadows thrown onto the tarmac. People stood around, talking and waiting. They were busy with their own lives. Some of them smiled. I wanted to scream, 'Stop! For God's sake! Martyn's hurt!'

The automatic doors parted. We followed the signs to St Andrew's Burns Unit in a daze. There was a buzzer on the wall and a bottle of alcohol rub on a table. How could this be? I'd left Martyn at Combermere giggling about some stupid monkey tissues. How could he be coming back to a burns unit?

I considered throwing open the door and running and running until I found Martyn. I needed to grab him and shout in his face, 'I'm here. You're OK.'

Rob pressed the buzzer. A nurse opened the door and asked us to follow her. Silence filled the burns unit. Doors lined the walls, all of them closed. Pieces of equipment cluttered the corridors. Everything was alien. The walls were pale grey, and the air smelled fresh.

We stepped into the family room. Toys were piled in a box in the corner. For a moment, I hated their cheerful colours. I tried to smile at the nurse. 'Martyn will be arriving shortly,' she said. 'We'll need to assess him and prepare him, then you'll be able to see him, so it's more waiting, I'm afraid. You can stay in here. We can bring you a drink, or you can go and get one and use up a bit of time. We'll update you as soon as we can. Our desk is just around the corner if you need us.' The nurse left the room.

Our friends were holding vigil in the pub, waiting for my call. I texted Sarah: 'We're here. Martyn's on his way. Let you know more later.'

'Tea?' I said. I studied Rob. He looked awful, terrified. His skin was grey, and he was obviously tired, but his eyes were wide open, making him appear strangely awake. He didn't answer me. I didn't know what to say.

I got up and went for a walk. A while later, I shuffled back into the room with two teas and a couple of newspapers. We shifted in our chairs, barely drinking the tea or reading the news.

The door opened, and the nurse came in. 'Martyn's here now,' she said. 'He's stable. We're redressing his wounds, assessing him and making him comfortable. You'll be able to see him in a few hours.'

Time seemed to stretch, and every movement and noise became magnified. If Rob coughed, I looked at him expectantly. If I moved my head, he waited for me to speak. Mostly, we were silent: Rob with his head in his hands, me texting Sarah and waiting for her to respond. I wanted to be right there, near to Martyn, but I also wanted to be far, far away.

At 11.30 p.m., the moment came.

Rob was taken in first. I paced the floor, my heart beating loudly in my chest. Rob was only in with his son for a few moments, but to me it seemed like an hour. I didn't think he could look any worse than he had. He walked towards me. He looked as if someone had stolen his soul. He stood in front of me for a few seconds, struggling for words, then he said, 'Michelle, prepare yourself. He looks awful. You won't know it's Martyn.'

'I will,' I said.

'Michelle, you won't recognise him. I'm just preparing you. Telling you for your own good.'

'Rob, I will recognise Martyn.'

I was taken into a small space. It said 'Gowning Room' on the door. I was given a blue plastic gown and mask. Someone was there, a voice explaining how Martyn looked. I wasn't listening. I would see for myself.

Rob waited beside me. My hands shook as I tied the mask. I blinked several times. I tried to breathe deeply. My breath was warm on my face. I could feel my heart banging against my ribcage and hear my blood throbbing in my ears.

Everything went into slow motion as the door swung open, and there, amid a macabre nest of ominous wires and machinery, was Martyn. I stepped forward. Each move caused a rustling noise. The door closed quietly. He was bandaged from head to toe. His body was abnormally huge, and metal rods pierced his right thigh. All I could see was his face, which, although it was grotesquely swollen, I still recognised as Martyn's. There were two holes where his nose had been. A tube disappeared into each one. A large black nozzle plugged his lips, which were enormous. A breathing tube snaked from it across his chest. His eyebrows were black and singed, his cheeks were black and cracked, and his eyes were slightly open, staring but vacant. It was as though he'd been beaten. I shuddered at the violence. I then looked at his neck. It was as wide as his head and had a large gash in it, several inches long. Deep and red, it was absolutely horrific. I wanted to scream.

There were two chairs beside the bed. Rob and I sat down. We weren't allowed to touch Martyn, and I didn't speak because I couldn't trust myself not to cry. I wanted to sob and sob, but I knew Martyn wouldn't have liked to hear me upset. In my head, I said, 'I love you. Please live,' and hoped he would somehow hear me.

We weren't with Martyn long. Rob and I were taken into the family room in the unit. Peter Dziewulski, the clinical director of the burns unit, spoke honestly. 'We know a little bit about what happened to Martyn,' he said. 'He was in a tank that hit a roadside bomb and exploded. The other men died, but Martyn was thrown from the tank, still on fire, and was then shot in the leg. Another soldier rescued him.'

I grew cold. I was shaking with terror. It was like a nightmare.

The doctor continued: 'Martyn's been well looked after by military medics and arrived here in a good condition, but he has

75 per cent burns. That is to say that three-quarters of his body is burned. The burns are very severe, full-thickness, down to the bottom layer of skin. A major burn like this is the most severe injury the body can sustain and survive, but Martyn is very, very sick. All his organs are affected. The shot to his right thigh has shattered the bone. It's a very nasty break.'

My throat had locked up. I stared at the doctor.

He said, 'I can't make any promises. I can only promise you that we will do our best. But I have to tell you there's a big chance Martyn will not pull through.'

Rob broke down. It was more than I could take, and I ran outside. I got my phone out of my handbag and hit the green button. 'Mum?' I said. 'Can you come? I need you.'

I woke up, barely breathing, flattened by grief. For a moment, I didn't know where I was. But then my eyes adjusted to the dim light, and the hotel room took shape. The sunlight spilled under the curtains as I lay there, thinking about this new dawn, this new life. It was Thursday, 3 August, the day I was to begin a weird existence, living between Martyn's hospital room and a strange hotel.

The previous day had been terrible. The day to come wouldn't be much better. The horror of what Martyn faced would be revealed.

The truth slammed into me. I stumbled from my bed and pulled on my robe. Rob was in the room next to mine. I knocked on the door. 'I've just phoned the hospital. He's had a stable night,' he told me. 'Do you want breakfast?'

'I'm not fussed,' I said. 'Meet you downstairs in 15 minutes.'

I had a quick wash. I was desperate to get to the hospital. Mum would bring me clothes and more toiletries when she returned to Broomfield in a few hours. I'd sort myself out properly later. Fortunately, it was the school summer holidays, so I didn't have to worry about work.

'How are you feeling?' I said to Rob as we pulled into the hospital car park.

'I've been better,' he said. 'I haven't slept. I've got a million questions buzzing round in my head. Trouble is, I don't think I want to know the answers.' His voice broke. 'That's my boy in there.'

Tears welled in my eyes, but I fought them off. I tried to be strong. Rob's pain must have been searing. It *was* his boy in there, his son – the baby boy, the toddler, the child, the teenager, the youth . . . the man. Rob had lost his wife, and now he thought he was going to lose his son. But I was convinced that Martyn had to live. And that even if Martyn's physical appearance had altered, inside he was the same. Rob's son was still there; my fiancé was still there.

The burns unit was on the second floor. There were two sets of doors. On the left, a sign read 'Burns Unit Rehabilitation'; on the right, 'St Andrew's Intensive Care Unit'. I pressed the buzzer on the door of the intensive-care unit. It seemed as if the night before had been an awful dream. In one way, so much had changed. Martyn was home, and I'd seen him. But now we had to face whatever came next.

The bustle of the hospital corridors diminished to deathly silence as we stepped into the burns unit. Martyn's room was the second on the right. A few minutes later, I was in the room again, horrified at what I saw. I listened to the bleeping monitors. Their sounds transfixed me. Hypnotised, I stared at my man.

Peter Dziewulski eased so much of my burden in those first days. Not knowing what was happening to the man I loved was as bad as seeing his physical condition. Ignorance is *not* bliss; ignorance is terrifying, I can assure you.

But Mr Dziewulski had sat with us the night before. He and the night sister had told us the truth. They'd told us that Martyn might die. And it would be weeks before anyone would concede that he might live.

Mr Dziewulski explained what was happening to Martyn and what they planned to do. Truth can be painful, but at least you can deal with it. I was not going to kid myself about Martyn's condition or about his chances of survival. I wanted all the information. With that knowledge, I would know how to help him. It was very important to understand my husband-to-be's condition – I planned to spend the rest of my life with him, after all.

Mr Dziewulski said that Martyn would be heavily sedated for at least three weeks. He would be on a constant drip of anaesthetic. 'Initially, this is to keep him pain free,' he said. 'We'll be doing lots of procedures, such as dressing changes, which would be painful if he wasn't sedated. And he'll need lots of operations to graft skin. We don't want him moving about, as he could damage that new skin.'

He explained that they needed to monitor Martyn's heart because it wasn't pumping as effectively as it should after the trauma he had suffered. 'He's also on dialysis,' he continued, 'which means a machine is cleaning his blood, because his kidneys, which have been working overtime to clean his system, are going into shock. We're feeding him, too. He'll need double the calories he would normally, because his body has so much healing to do. But his gut might have been damaged and not able to absorb that, so we'll keep an eye on that.'

It was terrifying. I found it difficult to digest the information, but I held myself together, and Mr Dziewulski did give us a fragment of hope. He said, 'I know it sounds like a lot, and Martyn is very, very ill, but he's young and he's strong.'

I would hold on to that fragment like a woman lost at sea would hold on to a piece of driftwood. It would keep me afloat as this ocean of suffering tried to drag me under.

Rob asked, 'Why is he so swollen?' Martyn did appear bloated. His fingers were as wide as sausages.

Mr Dziewulski said, 'The body's response to injury is inflammation. Fluid is released from the blood vessels, and, of course, he's lost a lot of his natural moisture because his skin is burned. We're pumping litres and litres of fluid into him.'

'What about that cut on his neck?' I asked.

'That's an escharotomy,' he said. 'That was done by the medics in Afghanistan, and Martyn has them all over his upper body. Burned skin becomes like leather, very tough and tight. It squeezes the tissue underneath and stops blood getting through to the extremities. We make a cut through the burned tissue to release everything, otherwise his hands or arms could die. It's temporary, and you won't see those cuts when we've taken that skin away and grafted.'

Hope is a small thing, but sometimes it's the only thing. It's that piece of driftwood in the ocean, or a single shimmering star in the vast darkness of the night sky. I knew that to be strong for Martyn I'd have to be constantly scanning the darkness for that shimmering star. And I knew that I wouldn't always find it.

After Mr Dziewulski left, I sat with Martyn. There was a nurse there, too. I looked at her, wondering if she was going to give us time alone. But it transpired that there would always be someone in Martyn's room, a nurse who'd relentlessly be working on him, ensuring he was all right. It was something I'd get used to and something I appreciated. They were angels, those nurses.

I felt shy with her there, but I started speaking to Martyn. I tried to sound strong, as I knew he would sense if I was upset, although I had no idea if he could actually hear me. I knew that when someone dies, the hearing is the last sense to go – but Martyn wasn't dying . . . was he? My throat was dry. Would this be the last opportunity I had to speak to him? I grasped for that driftwood, looked for that star.

Martyn was a mass of tubes – almost a man-machine hybrid. Ventilation tubes were fed into his nose. Drugs and fluids were being piped into his arms. A gastric tube spooled out of his stomach. He was also on kidney dialysis, and he was plugged into a heart monitor.

Three physiotherapists came into the room and introduced themselves. They began moving around Martyn, and I asked them what they were doing. My thirst for knowledge was intense. I had an urgent need to know everything that was going on. How else was I going to help him through this?

They told me his chest needed assessing. Martyn's lungs had been damaged by smoke inhalation, they said. He needed suction to remove the debris. 'Martyn's also getting a build-up of phlegm because he's not upright and moving as he should be,' one of them explained while they busied themselves around my fiancé.

They also told me that the ventilator breathed for Martyn. It made sure he got enough air to prevent hypoxic brain injuries, which result from a lack of oxygen. One of the physios pointed to the tube coming out of Martyn's mouth and said, 'That's what this is for.'

The nurse said, 'Medically, Martyn's body has been taken over. If he was conscious, he'd try to breathe alongside the ventilator, which would cause problems with his oxygen and carbon-dioxide levels. Being ventilated, and the damage to his lungs, means he is at risk of developing pneumonia.' I looked at him, my heart racing. What else did my poor man have to face?

The physios also had to keep Martyn moving. This would keep his joints and muscles in good working order. They couldn't move his badly broken right leg, but his feet were undamaged. They flexed them up and down to maintain movement. I watched them do it.

They would return later to splint his feet so they remained at a 90-degree angle. Otherwise, they would've flopped forward, shortening his Achilles tendon. That would've made it difficult for him when he came to stand and, finally, to walk with me down the aisle as my husband.

I would watch the physios work at him over the next few days and weeks. When his dressings were being changed, they'd give him a really good move. Martyn, of course, was oblivious. He was

MARTYN – My second birthday party. Sitting on Mum's lap and eating, I couldn't have been happier.

MARTYN – Aged three, asking Father Christmas if he could bring "she" back, a reference to my mother who had died on my birthday, one month earlier.

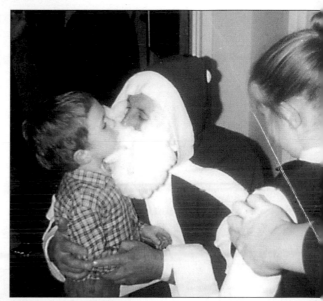

MICHELLE – My big brother Kevin and me. I'm aged seven here.

MARTYN – Here I am getting ready to row at Dorney Lake just after I joined the army.

MICHELLE – My first love, football. Here I am playing, aged 25.

MARTYN – Michelle and me just after we met in January 2006.

MICHELLE – Martyn and me at Kevin and Katie's wedding. We were so happy and had no idea what life was bringing our way.

MARTYN – Paul Hamnett and me in Afghanistan. A few weeks later, he'd be fighting to save my life.

MARTYN – Me and some of the lads working hard in the heat. Check out my tan.

MARTYN – The scene of the explosion that killed my three colleagues and set me on fire. When this was taken, I was back at Camp Bastion.

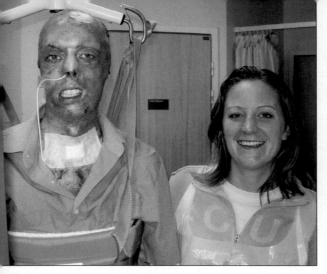

MICHELLE – The day Martyn stood up in the MasterVest. It was a breakthrough moment, and we were both ecstatic.

MARTYN – Dad and me in The Angel pub near Broomfield hospital. I was celebrating my 23rd birthday. Dad never thought I'd live to see this day.

MICHELLE – A big brother's hug from Kevin for Martyn and me. We all had straws that day. Martyn's was in a bottle of champagne given to him by his surgeon and the clinical director of the burns unit, Mr Peter Dziewulski.

MARTYN – The day I met Simon Weston at Headley Court in March 2007. He's been a great support to me. (© Anastasia Taylor-Lind)

MARTYN – Here I am on stage at the Britain's Best Awards in 2008, shaking Prime Minister Gordon Brown by the hand. It was an awesome moment and an awesome evening. (© Getty Images)

MARTYN – A typical pose by my best mate Chris Humphrey, who is always up for a laugh.

MICHELLE – Finally, our wedding day arrived. Here I am at home getting ready to leave. I felt like a princess. (© www.paulwardphotography.co.uk)

MARTYN – My sister, Lorraine. Her speech was one of the most moving moments of our wedding day.

MICHELLE – Martyn promised to stand beside me on our wedding day, and he did. How could I resist a kiss? (© www.paulwardphotography.co.uk)

MARTYN – Michelle took my breath away with how beautiful she looked on our wedding day.
(© www.paulwardphotography.co.uk)

MICHELLE – Everyone who was there had given us so much support. It was such an emotional day.
(© www.paulwardphotography.co.uk)

MARTYN – My ushers were, from left to right, Stevie (best man), Keeno, Chris (best man), Lance and P.J. Kevin is sitting with Joe Jackson, my godson.
(© www.paulwardphotography.co.uk)

MICHELLE – Here we are on honeymoon.

MARTYN – Me, Michelle and David Beckham, in case you didn't recognise him. We were invited to watch the England team in training through the charity Give Us A Sporting Chance. It was brilliant.

MICHELLE – Here we are doing Walk New York in aid of the Household Cavalry Operational Casualties Fund in November 2008. We'd come so far and were on top of the world that day. (© Stuart Griffith)

unconscious. His body would flinch, but he wouldn't remember the pain. It wouldn't be etched into his memory.

It dawned on me how much work was required to keep Martyn alive. But I didn't care if it took 24 hours a day; it had to be done. And if I had to do it without sleep, without food, I would.

He would live. He had to.

Later that Thursday, we met Mr Dziewulski again. He said, 'Tomorrow, Martyn will have an operation to debride, which means to cut away the dead skin ready for us to graft.' I shuddered. Something was happening. They'd moved so quickly. 'If we don't do that,' said Mr Dziewulski, 'Martyn could get an infection. The skin is donor skin. It's called allograft. Martyn's blood vessels will grow into it to encourage the healing of his own layers of skin.'

They were piecing him back together. It sounded astonishing to me – how it was possible to rebuild someone in this way.

'An orthopaedic surgeon will also re-pin Martyn's leg,' he continued. 'While we've got all his dressings off, we'll also give him a good clean. We have a special shower trolley that we'll lay him on.'

I hoped that everything would be all right. I knew Martyn was in a serious condition; it was touch and go. Surgery would put him at even greater risk. But it had to be done. It was how I'd get my Martyn back. These operations would help him recover, help him come alive again.

I also had practical considerations. After Mr Dziewulski spoke to us, I rang my school. I spoke to the secretary and explained everything. The headmaster, Douglas Lawson, was away, but the secretary said she'd pass a message on and told me not to worry about work.

Luke Cox arrived at the hospital on the Thursday, and he was there on and off throughout. He was our army liaison officer, and we couldn't have found someone more dedicated. He was amazing. Accommodation, food, expenses: he took care of everything and was on 24-hour call. Rob and I couldn't have coped without him.

My mum had arrived by that point. I said, 'I can see it's Martyn. Even though he's swollen, I can see it's my Martyn.'

They'd said that even if Martyn came round, his memory might be gone – and he wouldn't remember me or he'd have forgotten that he loved me. Mum also warned me, preparing me for the worst. But I shook my head and refused to accept any possibility that we couldn't be together. And the thought of him not remembering that he loved me was something I wouldn't consider. 'I'll just have to jog his memory,' I told Mum.

Sleep didn't come easy that night in the hotel. Worry gnawed at me all night. I slipped under at some stage and woke early again, the sun's rays edging into my room. But I felt cold – cold with fear. Martyn faced his first operation. But could I face waiting for the outcome? I didn't know. I sucked in a breath, trying to find strength from somewhere. I forced myself out of bed and got ready to leave for the hospital. I would look the difficult, uncertain day that lay in wait for me in the eye.

Mum arrived as I was leaving the burns unit. I'd spent a little time with Martyn before they wheeled him away to theatre. My nerves were frayed. I said, 'They've taken him down for the operation. But they did let me touch his hand. I touched his hand, Mum.' I burst into tears.

Mum took me outside and got me a cup of coffee. 'He'll be OK,' she said. 'You know Martyn.'

'You should have seen Rob, Mum. It broke my heart. The only part of Martyn he could see was his thumb. He kissed it and told him he loved him. He really thinks that Martyn's going to die.' Tears ran down my cheeks.

'Michelle, honestly, it'll be OK.'

But I couldn't be consoled. 'The injuries are so bad, Mum. They don't know if he's going to pull through. And it's going to be a long operation.'

Back in the hospital, Kevin arrived with Katie. Never had a girl wanted her big brother so badly. He held me and told me it would be all right. Kevin's as strong as granite and as gentle as feathers. If anyone could hold me up, it was him.

Then we waited. The hours dragged. I don't remember much about them. Martyn's Auntie Annie arrived from Devon. She's the mother hen in Martyn's family, and Rob relied on her support. He was really glad she'd been able to make it. But I don't think anything would've kept her away.

My mum, Kevin, Katie and Annie wouldn't have been able to see Martyn before the operation had they been there. There was a risk of infection, and Rob was sensitive about people seeing his son. I could understand how he felt, but I needed my family there for support.

Seven hours passed like seven years, and finally they came to tell us that Martyn had made it. I wanted to cry with joy, but I stayed calm. A silent elation filled me. I think that's how we all felt. We were quiet, the sense of relief washing through us. 'My hero,' I thought. 'My brave, strong hero.'

Martyn spent the weekend recovering, and I spent it trying to look ahead. I asked Mum to bring in photos of everyone so I could decorate Martyn's room. I pinned the pictures up on the wall. Most of them were in front of Martyn so that when he woke up, he would see the smiling faces of those who loved him. Even Harvey was up there. It comforted me, seeing those photographs. I talked to Martyn about them. I talked non-stop. It was exhausting, but I wouldn't stop when I was with him. If there was any chance at all that he could hear, I wanted him to know that I was there.

I had to leave his room now and again. The physios or the nurses had to do things to him, and I couldn't stay. So I sat outside and waited quietly. I wanted to be inside my own head, not speaking unless I spoke first. I didn't want to make small talk. Mum brought me some puzzle books: word searches and sudoku. I'd never done sudoku before, but I'd sit there, in my own world, doing these brainteasers. Mum also brought me some notebooks and pens.

Although I'd become insular during these first few days, I was aware of the kindness sweeping in from all sides. People are wonderful in times of pain; family and friends were so supportive. There were so many thoughtful gestures. Katie's parents, for example, bought a tape recorder. Martyn's friends and family recorded messages for him so he could constantly listen to the voices of those who loved him while he was in his coma. Kevin spoke about England's performance in the World Cup, which had come to an end a month previously. And there was even a message from Harvey. He gave a few barks of encouragement.

There was also a CD player in Martyn's room. I wondered what I could play for him. Then it jolted me. I ran outside and called Mum. I told her to go to my car and find the *Happy Songs* CD that we'd bought and played on the way to Devon with all those great tunes we'd sung along to at the top of our voices. I rushed back to Martyn's room, thinking about us belting out 'Don't Stop Me Now' as we drove along. I'd made a copy of the CD onto his iPod for him to play in Afghanistan – I hoped he'd got the chance to listen to it. Those songs were a link between us: him in Kabul, me in Frittenden. Mum brought the CD, and I put it on and started singing away, watching Martyn all the while. The nurses weren't too keen, I don't think. But I was willing to try anything to help Martyn. I smiled and carried on singing.

I began writing to Martyn each day, filling diaries, starting at the beginning with that dreadful call from Rob:

> Martyn, the day I got the call from your dad was the worst day of my life. I was shocked. I didn't know how to feel. When I saw you, it was scary. I really wanted to see you, and I saw you, and all I could see was my Martyn. Through everything that went on, I could still see you. I had to be strong for you

and your dad. Then I had the news that you might not make it, and I broke down. I could not be strong any more. I rang my mum, and she was there within the hour for me.

To be able to write to Martyn was a lifeline. It felt like I was talking to him, sharing my feelings. I knew he had no idea what I was saying, but I had to believe that he heard me. I had to have hope. I had to trust that somehow my voice was reaching him and that he knew how much I loved him.

CHAPTER 13

꒰ ꒱

MICHELLE – THAT WAS HIS BABY LYING THERE

BROOMFIELD HOSPITAL, ESSEX – AUGUST 2006

'No,' I told my mum. 'No, I can't leave Martyn.' I must have sounded desperate – as if someone had told me I had to go away and that I wouldn't be allowed to see Martyn for weeks or months. But Mum had only asked if I'd like to go to Chelmsford for a coffee – a break from sitting in the hospital all day. Chelmsford's only four miles away – a ten-minute journey from Broomfield Hospital – but to me it felt like a world away from the man I loved.

'There's nothing you can do here, Michelle,' said Mum. She was right. I stared at Martyn. It felt terrible to leave him. She said, 'Just come and get a bit of fresh air, a change of scene. We'll have a coffee and do a bit of shopping.'

Mum was trying to instil some normality back into my life. She and my dad were wonderful. I wouldn't have been able to make it through without them, without Kevin. I couldn't wish for better parents, for a better brother. But sometimes you lash out at the people you love.

I went through a roller coaster of emotions. I think anyone who grieves goes through similar feelings. At first, I was in denial, then anger filled me. I snapped at people, the smallest thing pushing me over the edge. I always wanted Mum to let me know when she'd got home safely. One evening, she forgot. I rang her in a rage. 'Are you home?'

'Yes, Michelle.'

'You didn't ring me.'

'Sorry, I forgot.'

I started having a go at her, and she began to cry. 'Don't cry,' I said. 'I've got enough on my plate.'

Mum said, 'Sorry,' and put the phone down.

The guilt chewed me up, and half an hour later I rang to apologise.

I agreed to go with her to Chelmsford. I don't think I was good company. I wanted to get back to the hospital. They'd operated on Martyn again that morning. It was relentless: he'd spent the weekend recovering from Friday's surgery, and then they wheeled him back into theatre on the Monday morning.

They debrided his skin again, and he had more skin grafts. These were called autografts, in which Martyn's own skin was used. They took layers from his lower legs and used them to cover his back and chest. Most of his body was damaged. It was only his calves and feet that the fire didn't get to. Surgeons shaved off a layer of skin from his legs, which left a graze. The skin would grow back, and a graft could be taken from the same spot up to ten times. Martyn needed grafts regularly because, without three-quarters of his skin, he was vulnerable to infections.

The priority was to keep him warm and clean after surgery. For a few days after a skin-graft operation, Martyn couldn't be moved. The grafts had to have time to settle. But then, once or twice a day, the physios would carry out some passive movements, gently lifting his limbs and his body to keep his circulation going.

Sometimes when the physios worked on him or nurses changed his dressings, I saw Martyn flinch. It would send a wave of panic through me. My throat would be dry, and my gaze would flicker all over his body. Was he in pain? He was in a coma so shouldn't have been able to feel anything. The nurses said that he wouldn't remember any of it and that it was only his body reacting to the obvious discomfort. I couldn't bear to think that he was suffering. After it was done, I'd sit next to him and speak to him, trying to comfort him. 'It'll be all right, darling,' I said.

Sometimes, I think he might have been flinching because he suffered nightmares. I was convinced that what happened in Afghanistan had been seared onto Martyn's subconscious. The experience would always be with him, physically and emotionally.

That night, back in my bleak hotel room, I wrote, 'Saw you after the operation today. You were covered head to toe in bandages. I didn't want to leave you tonight. I just wanted to be with you. But I know you will fight all the way.'

Rob was very quiet in those first few days. We didn't talk much. We had our own ways of dealing with the situation. We drove in together from the hotel every morning and drove back there at night, but words were difficult. You live mostly in your own head; you blank the rest of the world out.

We were both focused on Martyn, but our approach was different. And it was inevitable that we'd clash. We were in that tiny room together for 15 hours a day. The pressure on us was intense, and we occasionally took it out on one other.

I wanted to understand everything that was happening to Martyn. I peppered the nurses and the surgeons with questions. They were all fantastic, explaining in detail what was happening to him. However, Rob didn't want to know as much as I did. He couldn't bear it, I imagine. It was terrible, listening to what was happening to Martyn's body, but, at the end of the day, it was for the best. The experts at Broomfield were putting him through this for his own sake.

I always tried to look on the bright side, but Rob always saw the worst. He found it hard to trust the hospital staff. It was so difficult for him. That was his baby lying there.

Martyn told me early in our relationship about his mum dying. I think I'd asked about her because I'd seen a photograph of her in his bedroom. Sadness filled my heart when he told me. I couldn't imagine being without my mum. His mother's death made the relationship between Martyn and Rob even stronger. They were really close, and although they argued a lot, there was a strong bond there.

I think Rob was angry that this had happened to his boy. Seeing his son in the hospital made him think that he hadn't protected him – and that's what every parent wants to do for their child, whether that child is four or twenty-four. It doesn't matter – you're always someone's son or someone's daughter; you're always a child to your mum and your dad. I didn't share those feelings about Martyn, of course. He was a man to me; I'd met him as an adult. He was my equal, and I was looking forward to our future together as husband and wife.

FROM MICHELLE'S DIARY

TUESDAY, 8 AUGUST 2006

I am positive tonight that you were trying to talk to me, because your little lip was moving, and this was the first time I saw that. I'm sure you were telling me you loved me. There have been so many times tonight I have nearly cried. I nearly rang Chris to cry on his shoulder, but I managed not to do it. Bless him, he has been great, along with everyone else. Well, I had better go, as it is getting late, and I am getting tired. I will see you about 7.30 tomorrow morning. I love you loads and loads and nothing will drag me away from you. Sleep well. Have a good night.

Life lugged on. My days took on a routine: getting up, travelling to the hospital, sitting with Martyn, going back to the hotel, sleep . . .

And so it went on for those first couple of weeks. My comfort came from my family and friends. Mum was there almost every day. Kevin and Katie were there every time Martyn had an operation. They couldn't do anything, but they offered support. Kevin brought puzzles. We'd loved doing puzzles together when we were young. Katie brought me my favourite Chupa Chups lollies – strawberries-and-cream flavour. Annie was fantastic, too. I was learning about what sort of woman she was. She was strong and practical. This was tearing her apart, but she held herself together for Rob, for Martyn and for Lorraine.

I kept scribbling in my diary, writing as if to Martyn, telling him what was going on and how I felt about him. Within a week of him coming home, I wrote in my diary that I wanted to have children with him as soon as possible. I've heard that this might have been a reaction to all the talk of death. Maybe it was; maybe it wasn't. I don't know. I've always wanted a family, and seeing my future husband lying there, so very poorly, made me realise how important it was to me.

I'd always kept diaries. I'd loved my little books, with their pristine covers and tiny padlocks. One day, we'd read these diaries together and look back at this turbulent time. And we'd show them to our children when they were old enough to understand the trauma that the words contained. We'd show them how courageous their father had been; we'd show them what it means to love.

From Michelle's diary

Wednesday, 9 August

Hello, my angel. Well, in all fairness, you have had a quiet day. You have not given us any scares. At the moment, I am feeling quite useless, as I cannot do anything for you.

All I want to do is hug you so much, and I decided today that as soon as you are better you are going to give me babies before us getting married, and I told my mum that. Susan was your nurse tonight. My mum took me into Chelmsford just to give me a break from everything, which was really nice of her. I got you a teddy saying 'I Love You', a little wallet card with 'Especially For You' on it and an 'I Love You' card, which I hope you will like. I am sure you will.

I was telling Susan about buying you a toothbrush, and she asked me if I wanted to brush your teeth, so I said yes. That was the happiest I've felt. I actually did something to help you. You really don't know how that made me feel. I was walking on air. I was so happy that I rang Katie and Mum to tell them.

THURSDAY, 10 AUGUST

Today I woke up feeling quite happy, as I was still on a high from brushing your teeth last night. I know it may seem silly to you, but to me it was a great step. I'm still thinking that this is all a dream and you are going to call me from Afghanistan to tell me that everything is OK. But I never seem to wake from this dream, because it's real, and I'm not too sure if it has all sunk in yet. I am scaring myself at how strong I actually am. Every time I go into your room, it is getting easier and easier. All I know is that you are in the best place, and they are going to do the best possible job to look after you and make you better.

I keep thinking of the day we walk down the aisle together to be husband and wife.

I am gonna choose a book to start reading to you tomorrow so you can hear my voice a lot more. Night, night, babe. I love you so much.

FRIDAY, 11 AUGUST

I've been in quite a good mood recently, darling, due to the fact that you are holding your own. But then some bad news hit us when we met one of your surgeons today. You have picked up bugs, because your

139

whole body is basically an open wound. It's hard, because we were told rather than you going on a day-by-day basis, you are now going an hour-by-hour basis, and, to be honest, I am now very worried. They can give you antibiotics, but you need to keep fighting. If you give up, you are gone for ever. But you have shown us you are strong and will not give up this fight. At the end of the day, we are going to get married. Maybe not in July 2008, but we will get married. I love you to pieces – always remember that.

SATURDAY, 12 AUGUST

I keep worrying about the time when you wake up and realise what's going on. The only thing I hope for is that you realise and know that I am not going to go anywhere. I love Martyn, and you are still my Martyn. You have not changed at all.

Today, your right eye that was swollen has gone down and is nearly back to normal, which is good. But your left one is still very swollen, and it looks sore, which makes me think it is giving you pain, which hurts me. You are going to rise above all this, which makes everything worthwhile. I'm gonna be by your side every step of the way.

SUNDAY, 13 AUGUST

I'm writing this after seeing you tonight and then brushing your teeth. You responded to what we asked tonight. Susan asked you to open your mouth, and you did. You were so good and showed us you can hear us. You are beginning to respond so well.

I am looking forward to the day when I walk in and you are looking at me with those lovely eyes of yours. I think I will cry, but they will be tears of happiness.

Mum and Dad brought up a bluey [letter], which you obviously sent before all this happened. Your letter made me cry. Your last words were, 'Love you so much, babe. Miss you like mad. Can't wait to see you.' That was so nice, angel. I love you so much and can't wait for the day when I can hug you again. You just need to keep going, angel. You have far too much to live for.

MONDAY, 14 AUGUST

The good news today is that I spent a lot of time with you on my own, which was really nice. I was talking, chatting and singing to you. You have a big operation tomorrow, so we both need to get some sleep. Sleep well. I love you to pieces and always will, no matter what.

Martyn was back in surgery on Tuesday, 15 August. Again, I was on tenterhooks. Every time they operated, Martyn was at risk. There were so many times during those weeks that I could've lost him. I'd found his iPod with the *Happy Songs* CD on it, so I plugged it into my ears while I waited.

Martyn's bag had been sitting in the Gowning Room for nearly three weeks. It had come back from Afghanistan with him. Rob wouldn't go through it; he found it too emotional. I could understand that. Contained in the bag were the things that made Martyn, I guess: his belongings, his clothes. Martyn had changed physically for Rob, so the task of digging through his son's stuff was too much. The bag sat there, zipped up. I'd seen it and thought, 'Someone's going to have to open it one of these days.' It looked as if it had to be me.

I unzipped the bag and found a parcel my mum had sent him that was full of sweets. I bit my lip, trying to fight back the emotion. There was also a parcel I'd sent him. It contained pictures of me and Martyn, and a teddy bear I had sent him. Martyn's boxer shorts were also in there. And the iPod.

That became a comfort when I was left alone when Martyn was wheeled to surgery. Those songs were our songs, and when he was on the operating table, his life on the line, my head filled with tunes that had brought us so much happiness and fun.

Martyn was having a tracheostomy in which surgeons slice

a hole in the patient's throat to enable him or her to breathe. This allowed them to remove his ventilator tube. The tube would have eventually scarred his windpipe and caused pressure sores in his mouth. A tracheostomy is quite a common procedure for a patient who's suffered extensive facial injuries that need surgery, but it didn't stop me worrying.

Fear clawed at me when he was in theatre. And when Martyn went in for a procedure, it wasn't just the one thing they'd do – he'd have surgeons working on two or three different things. The day of the tracheostomy also saw him being debrided again. The surgeons placed an allograft on top of the debrided skin. An allograft is donor skin from a dead body. It covers a raw wound until the patient's own donor sites – his lower legs, in Martyn's case – could be reharvested. When an allograft starts to die, the patient's body rejects it. It is surgically removed and an autograft laid in its place. That day, they also inserted wires into Martyn's fingers to stop them from curling.

When he came back from theatre, I went to see him. I kept thinking about him being put back together, rebuilt from the pieces that the Taliban attack had left. That night, I wrote:

Today, darling, you have spent about eight hours in theatre. It's always scary, as there's that question in my mind: are you going to be OK? Today they have debrided your head, neck and face. They weren't too sure about doing your face, but they decided you were strong enough to go through with it. They have also stitched your eyelids together on both eyes, so you can close your eyes properly when you have healed. You have also had a tracheostomy, so you no longer have anything going into your mouth, which makes you look a lot more comfortable. Every time I look at you, all I see is you. In my eyes, you haven't changed one little bit. I can't wait until the day comes that you can open your eyes and see me there for you.

Martyn looked different without his ventilator tube. I was allowed to swab his mouth for him to keep it moist. It gave me a jolt of energy to be able to do something for him. I didn't want to be just sitting there all the time. I was going to be his wife, his partner for life; I wanted to learn how to take care of him. The nurse gave me some capsules. She said they were fake saliva tablets. She told me to put them in Martyn's mouth, so I did, gently slipping them between his burned lips.

These things I could do for him were the driftwood and the star, the hope I looked for in this situation. But there was a long way to go, and the road ahead was cluttered with obstacles. And the last thing I wanted was to crash headlong into one of those impediments.

A few days later, I was sitting with Martyn. I was chatting away to him, without thinking about the words spilling out. The nurse said, 'Michelle, quick – look at the heart monitor.'

My stomach lurched and cold fear shot through my veins.

CHAPTER 14

❦

MICHELLE – KEEP RUNNING, BABE

BROOMFIELD HOSPITAL, ESSEX – AUGUST 2006

The nurse's voice had panicked me: 'Look at the heart monitor.'

What had she seen? Was I losing my Martyn? I'd been chatting to him, unaware of what I was saying, then the nurse had called my name. I looked at Martyn, then frantically scanned the machines beside him. 'What?' I said. 'Is he OK?'

'Keep talking,' said the nurse. She was up on her feet now, standing next to me by Martyn's bed. 'He knows you're here. His heart beats faster every time you speak. He can hear you.'

The strength drained out of me, relief sweeping all the strain of the past few weeks away. Martyn had provided the first sign that he was coming back to me. I had to control myself. My emotions rose. I wanted to clutch him, to kiss him.

I said, 'I'm here, darling. I love you.' The beeps on the monitor quickened. The man I was marrying knew who I was. He was aware of my presence. The hope I'd only seen a glimmer of days before flared brightly. Joy swelled in my chest. I wanted to share this with someone.

I rushed out of the room and found Kevin. He hadn't seen Martyn yet – it was only Rob, Annie, Mum and me who'd been into his room. Kevin's eyes filled with tears as I told him the news. 'Mich, that's really brilliant,' he said, squeezing me tight. 'How long will Martyn be here?'

Mr Dziewulski had told me that patients stayed one day for each percentage they're burned. 'In Martyn's case, it'll be about seventy-five days – nearly three months,' I said.

'At least he'll be home for Christmas,' said Kevin.

He hugged me again and then turned to Rob, embracing him, too. It had been a positive few days: being able to help swab Martyn's mouth, hearing those beeps accelerate when I spoke to him. It all added up, in my mind, to Martyn coming back to me. There were still risks, of course; his life was on the line every time he went into surgery.

I started to help more and more with Martyn's care; only simple things, such as wiping his mouth, but they meant a lot to me. The more I was able to do things for him, the quicker he seemed to pull through infections – I could see that star shining brightly. I was with Martyn all the time and could see tiny improvements occurring every day: a new piece of skin, a little bit less swelling, an increased movement in his right arm.

The more questions I asked, the more I understood what was happening. I learned so many things. My conversations were infused with medical jargon. But the pressures of being there every day started to tell. I started to smoke. I had occasionally enjoyed a cigarette before, but now I became a chimney. Mum smoked now and again, so she offered me one. It must have been stressful for her to offer me a fag.

My image fell apart, as well. I'd always taken care of myself and was proud of the way I looked. But I trudged around the hospital and my hotel in tracksuits with my hair tied back, and I wasn't eating properly. I'd always loved my food. I could usually wolf it down. But in the hospital, it didn't seem as if I had the time to eat. I was always at Martyn's bedside. That seemed far more important than going to the canteen. Mum did bring me food, but I just didn't fancy it.

I was barely at the hotel. The army was wonderful, paying for Rob and me to stay there. But most of my time was spent with Martyn. I did try, though, to make my hotel room a bit more homely. Mum and Dad brought a grey bear over that Martyn had given me for my birthday. It was a large toy, with its arms spread out and a message on it saying 'I love you this much'. But in my bed at night, I lay awake. The day would replay itself in my mind. I would go over the events, one by one. I'd try and look on the bright side, find the little glimmers of hope – the single star in the darkness.

I started to find it difficult to sleep. Martyn was less calm at night than during the day, and it worried me. He would often jump in his sleep. We were told that he was dreaming, possibly because of the war but possibly because of all the drugs he was on. Rob would speak to him and say, 'You're OK, Martyn – you're safe,' and he would calm down.

If I couldn't sleep, I'd get up in the middle of the night and run myself a bath. My friend, Nicky, had bought me Ted Baker bubble bath – my favourite – so at least I could wallow in luxury for a while. However, even in the suds my thoughts dwelled on Martyn. We knew very little about what had actually happened to him. It wouldn't be until he was fully conscious that he'd tell us, bit by bit, about the incident.

We'd been told there was a possibility that Martyn's sight had been damaged by the fire. I was frightened, but because no one knew for sure, I decided to look on the bright side and assume that he was going to be able to see OK. He also had problems with his left arm. He had obviously landed badly on it when he was thrown from the tank. Now it was overhealing and extra bone was growing. The joint was very stiff.

All I wanted was for him to get better, and any healing, for me, was an improvement. And one sign of healing was pink skin. I loved to see pink skin. The nurses would leave a bit uncovered for me to see, if they could. I arrived at the hospital one day and the nurse smiled at me. She said, 'His bum's nearly healed.' For me, tiny steps such as these were giant leaps.

Still, there was sadness. How could there not be? Dark clouds hovered above me and Martyn, and although I did my best to waft them away, the gloom never really lifted. Friends and family kindly sent cards, and they swelled the hospital post bag. I tried to read them, but it was too much for me. There were days when I'd go outside for a little cry. I continued to wonder if Martyn was going to make it. I knew things had improved, but he was so vulnerable.

Sarah visited one day. I went out with her and had a cry. I told her how scared I was that he might not make it.

Sarah, strong as ever, said, 'He's made it this far. He won't go back now.'

FROM MICHELLE'S DIARY

WEDNESDAY, 16 AUGUST

Darling, I keep thinking to myself that you don't know where you are or what day it is. I think that you are thinking you are still in Afghanistan.

You had another long day in theatre yesterday, and you were expected to have a bad night, but you seemed to be stable throughout.

Well done, honey. You are one brave person. I left you at about half-past two today to come home for the evening, as I was going insane looking at the same four walls. It was nice to get back, but at the same time not nice knowing I wasn't going to be with you, as I like talking to you. I have to say, though, it was nice coming back to reality and seeing and talking to friends.

FRIDAY, 18 AUGUST

You had a five-hour operation today, from 3 p.m. until 8 p.m. The surgeon told us they cut more dead skin from your head and face because you had an infection. The surgeon said he is really pleased with how you are doing but says once you are healed there will be a lot of reconstructive surgery. But, hey, we can put up with that as long as you are here with us.

SATURDAY, 19 AUGUST

Your dad and I will move into our army house tomorrow, babe. We won't be at the hotel any more, which will be better. So tonight he went home, and I stayed here with you. There's a little room here for families, with two single beds. Katie came up to keep me company. We went to Pizza Hut, had a glass of wine, came back here and fell asleep. We planned to watch a video, but we couldn't keep our eyes open. I'm so tired – emotionally drained, I suppose. Two gorgeous young women like us, asleep by 11 p.m. on a Saturday night. What is the world coming to? Only joking. There's nothing I'd rather be doing than sleeping here with you.

MONDAY, 21 AUGUST

Today, you had another iodine shower. When I came back, you did look nice and clean. This time your legs were showing from the knees down, and it was great to see pink skin. I was chuffed. I could also see some on the tips of your fingers. Also, where they have grafted you on your neck and chest, it is looking great. I am going to bed now, because I am really tired, and you have a long day tomorrow. They are going to graft your arms and hands.

They took him away again. 'Bye, darling,' I said as they wheeled him out. 'I'll be here when you come back.'

I watched him go, fear returning to clutch at my breast.

Another operation, another few hours of worry for Rob and me, and all our friends and family.

Infection was a danger during surgery. They had to be careful and do all that they could to protect Martyn from any bugs. In the preparation room, each of his wounds was thoroughly cleaned and his drips changed.

It was 22 August, a Tuesday, and Martyn was due another debriding, this time on his arms. After doing this, they autografted skin from his legs and tummy onto his arms. They also planned an allograft on his hands, using skin from another donor. During every operation, up to six surgeons, three anaesthetists and five nurses worked on him. The grafting makes the skin look like a grid. This is because they make small holes in the skin to allow it to stretch over a larger area. The effect is similar to a string vest.

When they brought Martyn back, the physiotherapist taught me about scar management. It involves massage, and I had to rub a subaqueous cream into Martyn's skin. Scar management prevents the scars from thickening. If Martyn's scars thickened, the layers of skin could prevent the limbs from moving, like when a piece of paper is folded too many times. I had to massage Martyn's scars four times a day with the cream. It was very emotional for me – a physical link between Martyn and myself. The contact was so important. Helping him made me feel less frustrated. It made me happy to know that I was helping.

FROM MICHELLE'S DIARY

SATURDAY, 26 AUGUST

I stayed with you later tonight as I hadn't been with you much during the day. I now realise why you have unstable nights. I think you fall asleep, then start to dream and panic because you can't hear a familiar voice. When the nurse speaks to you, it takes you longer to calm down.

When you started to panic tonight, I put my hand on your chest and spoke to you, and you were fine. Goodnight, darling.

I spoke to Martyn all the time. Nonsense, really; words spilling out of me so he could hear my voice. Then, one day, I had some really exciting news for him. Katie was pregnant. 'Martyn, it's so exciting,' I told him. 'I'm going to be a proper auntie, and you're going to be a proper uncle.' Martyn waved his right arm a little bit, to show me that he'd heard. I went outside and texted Katie and Kevin.

I had other news, too. An 'e-bluey' had arrived from Afghanistan. Keeno had organised all the lads to send a message to Martyn. I was really touched. They hadn't forgotten him; of course they hadn't. Martyn's arm moved again when he heard it.

The more I chatted, the more the heart monitor quickened. My voice made life pulse through Martyn. My voice meant something to him, deep inside – deeper than skin and muscle; deeper than wounds and pain. My voice touched his core. My voice touched the real Martyn that lay beneath the red, raw surface.

I was with him for hours, and I noticed changes in him. As the swelling went down, I could see he was wasting away. His muscles had almost entirely withered. My strong man was shrivelling. He'd been fed a high-calorie diet over the past weeks, but his body had used up all the energy he'd taken on to repair itself. Mr Dziewulski said that Martyn was running the equivalent of a marathon every day in terms of the calories he was burning. 'His body is hypermetabolic,' he said, 'using energy from every possible source, including fat and protein from the muscles – hence the muscle loss. It's an enormous pressure on his system, because people who run a marathon then rest. There's no rest for Martyn. We're feeding him double the calories he would have in normal life.'

I went back into Martyn's room and told him this. 'Trust you to be eating twice the food of a normal person even when you're poorly,' I said. 'Even your super-size plate wouldn't be big enough for you these days!' I watched for a reaction. This time there was none apart from the increased beeps from the heart monitor when I spoke. I smiled at Martyn and said, 'No wonder you're sleeping all the time. Keep running, babe.'

Towards the end of the month, the surgeons grafted Integra onto Martyn's face. Integra is artificial skin developed by the Massachusetts Institute of Technology in the USA. It has two layers: the bottom one is collagen, and the upper layer is silicone, which is a type of plastic. The collagen is held together by a protein that comes from shark cartilage. Integra replaces the bottom layer of skin and improves the final look – that's why it's used on the face. A small piece of Integra costs about £1,000. Martyn has an expensive face.

When I first saw him after the operation, I flinched. The silicone made his face shiny, and he had staples in his skin. The surgeons explained how it would work. The blood vessels grow into the collagen before the silicone layer is peeled off and Martyn's own skin placed on top; the blood vessels then continue to grow into his skin. It didn't look nice, but it would heal. And he was now part shark.

During the operation, they had also debrided him again, scraping the skin off his scalp, forearms, chest and inner thigh, and then they carried out an autograft. Martyn's leg also needed to be fixed. The bullet had ripped through the muscle of his right thigh. I'd not seen the wound yet. A muscle sits in elastic tissue, which is like a sack. A damaged muscle can swell, and its blood supply can be cut off, resulting in it dying. It's called compartment syndrome. The surgeons carried out a procedure called a fasciotomy, a cut, which allowed continued blood flow to the muscle.

It was incredible to me that there were people who knew exactly what to do to save every little part of Martyn that they could. Martyn's leg had been saved, and every day the surgeons, the nurses and the physiotherapists battled to keep him alive. They were miracle workers. And they were fighting a war over Martyn's body against those who'd put him there.

Men make weapons that can inflict terrible damage on other human beings. It scares me to think about it. I don't know who made the bullet that fired through Martyn's leg, but when I saw the damage it had done, my heart grew cold.

I'd assumed that bullets go in and then out of the body, leaving a mark no bigger than a fingerprint. I now know different. And after seeing the wound on Martyn's leg, I learned quite a bit about bullets. Some are designed to explode on impact. Others are made to enter the body first, then explode. It makes me shudder. Why would anyone design something like that?

The entry wound on the outside of Martyn's right thigh was quite small. But the bullet erupted inside his leg. It ripped through the bone and tore away almost all of the flesh on the inside of his thigh. There is a crater there, and there always will be.

I stared at the wound and thought, 'Someone did that to him. They did that to my Martyn – a regular guy who likes a cup of tea, *Coronation Street* and a cuddle.' I couldn't get my head around that.

Rob found it hard to cope with the change in Martyn's appearance. But Martyn's his baby. Rob is protective of his son and always will be. He told me that Martyn was never going to look like Martyn again. But I wouldn't accept that. I knew that Martyn's appearance had changed dramatically, but to me nothing important had changed. I just saw Martyn. I did wonder if the change in his appearance would alter how he felt about me, about getting married.

But I couldn't dwell on that. I had to look ahead, grasp that driftwood. For example, his skin was improving all the time. He was changing, healing very quickly, and that filled me with hope.

I think it's the same as when old couples have been married for 40 years. I'm sure they don't look at their husband or wife and see an old person. They only see the person whom they love.

I knew that Martyn would have the same smile and the same eyes when he woke up, and those are the most important part of anyone's face. That's the part you really connect with. That's where the person truly lies. That's where they exist. I knew that Martyn was there, waiting for me, and I'd be there to see him come back to me.

CHAPTER 15

✧◝◟.◞◜✧

MICHELLE – ONE DRESS STOOD OUT. IT WAS PINK, OF COURSE

BROOMFIELD HOSPITAL, ESSEX – AUGUST 2006

I stared at the contents of the small brown envelope. I was looking at pictures of Port Lympne Wild Animal Park in Kent. It was where Martyn and I were due to be married. I'd visited the venue with my mum and Katie. It was perfect, so beautiful, with breathtaking views over the English Channel.

I'd sent the pictures to Martyn in Afghanistan, but they hadn't arrived before he'd been hurt. He'd never seen them. Now they were back, and so was he. But would he still want to marry me when he woke up?

I'd been dreaming of my wedding day for so long. I'd pictured the horse and carriage and the big pink dress. I took a deep breath. There was only one thing to do. I took some Blu-tack from the packet in my bag and pulled away some small pieces, rolling them into balls and pressing them onto the back of the pictures. Then I stuck the pictures on the wall.

'Martyn,' I said, my voice shaking, 'I know you can hear me, darling. I've just stuck some pictures on the wall. It's Port Lympne, where we're going to get married. It's lovely. You'll be able to see them when you wake up. So you better get well soon.'

I often thought of our wedding. Doubts crowded my mind. I wanted Martyn to be my husband more than anything, but would he be able to make it? I wondered if I should put it on hold and spoke about it with a nurse. She said, 'Go ahead and book it. It will give him something to work towards.'

The white dresses in the window caught my eye. I looked away. I didn't want to tempt fate. But Sarah had seen me look. 'Let's go in,' she said.

She'd taken me to nearby Braintree just to get me out of the hospital for a few hours. 'No, I don't think so,' I said, drawing my gaze away from the window. 'The wedding's ages away.'

'They've got a sale on,' said Sarah. 'Come on. It would be daft not to look.'

I felt intimidated, almost fraudulent, as I walked into the shop. Was it madness to be trying on wedding dresses when I didn't even know if my fiancé wanted to marry me? Was it right to be doing something so fun, so frivolous, while Martyn was so sick?

The women in the shop smiled at us and said good morning. The rows of pristine white dresses glinted in the sun. Their exotic fabrics, beading and sequins shone, sprinkling the air with promises of happiness. One dress stood out. It was pink, of course. I walked towards it. It was my size. I felt a rush of excitement. 'Shall I try it on?' I said to Sarah. She grinned.

Ten minutes later, I stepped out of the dressing-room and stood in front of the enormous mirror. I felt peaceful, grounded in the future again. I knew Martyn loved me. I knew we'd get married. What would he think if he saw me in this dress?

'Where are you getting married?' the sales assistant asked.

Reality slapped me in the face. 'Oh. Not near here,' I said. 'I'm from Kent. But my fiancé's in Broomfield Hospital at the moment. I'm just looking.' I felt a void in my stomach. Sarah smiled at me, giving me a jolt of hope.

'I suppose we better get back,' I said. I walked into the changing-room. As I stepped out of my dress and into my jeans, I felt myself being drawn back to Martyn, to what was happening to us now. I knew we'd get through it. I knew we'd stand together in nearly two years' time – me in a wedding dress, him in a suit – and declare to the world that we loved one another, that we were husband and wife.

I returned to Broomfield, called Port Lympne and booked the wedding. The date was set: 12 July 2008.

FROM MICHELLE'S DIARY

TUESDAY, 29 AUGUST

It has been good talking to you these last few days, now that you are awake enough to nod. I just can't wait for the day when you can talk to me again. You had another nine-hour operation today, and Sarah took me out shopping, which was nice of her, although I do always worry about your dad being on his own. Sarah's been an emotional prop to your dad, too. By the way, I booked our wedding today. It will be on the 12 July 2008. So you have something to aim for now. And I tried a wedding dress on. It was lovely.

August, the most dreadful month of my life, which began with Martyn being wounded, was slipping away. It had been up and down since then – mostly down. But at least he was still alive.

My brave man had come through the deadliest fight of his life – but there were still enemies to be defeated. He was still vulnerable to infections. He was fighting pneumonia, and although they pumped him with antibiotics, there was still a chance something else could get through. He was so fragile.

And then they discovered a patch of an Afghan infection on his cheek. He'd picked it up while rolling around in the dust, trying to put himself out after the attack. It had lain dormant there until now. And it came awake with a vengeance, going after Martyn.

The doctors had come to the point of having just one antibiotic left they could use. It was a matter of looking for that glimmering star. I prayed it would work. The bug launched itself at Martyn – but his willpower, I'm certain, and the efforts of the doctors beat off the infection. Martyn had made it through again.

I willed the month to end on a positive note so that we could enter September with hope. I would get my wish.

We were in intensive care. I sat next to Martyn after the doctors had closed his tracheostomy to see if he could breathe for himself. It had been a success. I watched his chest rise and fall, and listened to the air being drawn into him. I spoke to him, as usual, and then I asked him a question: 'Do you love me?'

Martyn slowly nodded his head

My nerves tightened. 'Can't you tell me?' I said.

Then he said it. A tiny, imperceptible breath that sparked a bonfire in my heart: 'I love you.'

FROM MICHELLE'S DIARY

FRIDAY, 1 SEPTEMBER

Hello, my darling. You have been running a high temperature for the last couple of days, since they did your face with the Integra. So today they decided that they would give you another full dressing change and see what the problem was. They found that you had an infection on your right cheek so they had to cut a lot away.

MONDAY, 4 SEPTEMBER

I went home yesterday, darling, to play the first game of the season – and we lost 2–0. In a way, I wish I hadn't gone. Today has been a good day for you. You have had a shower and a dressing change, and your temperature has gone down, which is nice.

When I got to see you today, you had lots of pink bits, and you had your eyes open. They decided to take the stitches out, which is good. I asked you earlier if you could see me, and you nodded yes. But I think you may be just seeing shadows.

CHAPTER 16

❧ ·⁓❧

MICHELLE – 'I COULDN'T DO IT FOR ANYONE ELSE'

BROOMFIELD HOSPITAL, ESSEX – SEPTEMBER 2006

I dipped my little fingers in the orange juice, placed them into the corners of Martyn's mouth and pulled his mouth open. I grimaced. I knew it hurt him, but that's scar management: if it's not hurting, it's not working.

Rob and I had moved into an army welfare house, a three-bedroom place in Colchester Garrison. It was a nice house, but I was barely there. I spent most of my time at the hospital. Martyn dragged himself further away from death's door every day, and I wanted to be there with him – I wanted to share every step. There was still danger, of course. He remained vulnerable. But he was getting better – slowly, slowly, he was getting better.

Although he wasn't fully conscious, Martyn seemed to be making attempts at communicating with us. But speaking was difficult. His mouth was painful. The scar tissue on a burns victim's mouth contracts. The mouth closes, and sometimes you can only get a straw in there. Martyn became the first patient at Broomfield Hospital to have mouth splints installed – it was hoped that these would ease the stress around his lips and his jaw. Joanna, the occupational therapist, had them made. The maxillofacial department took dental impressions of Martyn's mouth, and the splints were made to match: a bright-orange gum shield. They made Martyn look like he was sucking an orange.

He wore the splints when he slept. They improved the size of his mouth, but he managed to indicate to us that they were uncomfortable. The scars around his mouth contracted, and it was difficult to get the splints in. So once they'd been placed in his mouth, they became sore. We began mouth exercises with him instead, and again I was able to help. Being able to play a practical role in Martyn's recovery was important to me. I didn't want to be just sitting there, watching things happen to him. I wanted to learn how to care for him, how to lead him through this difficult process.

I dipped my fingers in the juice again, and stretched out his lips once more. 'If it's not hurting, it's not working,' I thought as I pulled his lips open. It did occur to me that I was doing things for my Martyn that I would expect to do for him at the end of his life, not now, in his 20s. But when you plan to take someone in sickness and health, there aren't any regulations on timing.

Rob couldn't bear to be in the room and see Martyn in any sort of discomfort. He told me once that I'd make a brilliant nurse. 'I couldn't do it for anyone else,' I said.

The operations continued. They wheeled him away from me, and I watched him go, a yearning in my heart. These were the fearful times for me: when I wasn't with him; when he was truly vulnerable. He'd already fought off so many infections, but there was only so much his body could do. But, time and again, he came back to me.

A few days after the graft operation, they took him for a shower. The nurses laid him on a trolley that had a plug at the bottom and was slightly tilted. It looked like a flat bath. The soap they used was an iodine solution – which would've stung if he were awake. The iodine helped keep him clean, keep those bugs at bay. I imagined the solution fighting off the infections. It gave me confidence that Martyn was getting stronger and that his body was arming itself to combat the germs that always lurked around him, ready to attack if his defences were down. I remembered the Afghan bug that almost got him, the doctors racing to find the antibiotic that would destroy the infection. It had been touch and go. He'd almost died. I didn't want to go through that again – we had far too many other things to worry about.

I started to feel confident, hope growing in me. I even found time to get a little of my life back. I'd started to play football again. My friends and family had encouraged me. They'd said I should try to get some normality back into my life. I'd been reluctant at first, but then I'd realised they were right. I'd been holed up in the hospital for weeks; I was becoming reclusive and insular. I needed to dust off my social skills. I didn't want to be dark-eyed and lank-haired when Martyn woke up. I wanted to have a spring in my step for him; I wanted rosy cheeks.

I went back to Kent for a game one Saturday and then stayed at my parents' house that weekend. It was a wrench to be away from Martyn, but I knew the change would do me good.

My confidence had bloomed by then; I knew Martyn was on his way back. It was a long way back, certainly, but he was heading in the right direction.

Then, on the Monday, Rob rang. He said, 'We've got some news, but I can't tell you what it is – you'll see when you get here.' A cold finger crept down my spine.

FROM MICHELLE'S DIARY

FRIDAY, 8 SEPTEMBER 2006

Well, darling, today you are going down to surgery, and you won't be in there too long, as they are just patching up a few bits and putting some stitches in your eyes again because you can't shut them properly. I was talking to the surgeon today, and he said that apart from your face they have done most of the skin grafting. They will start your face in a couple of weeks. Then, when it is grafted, it is just the reconstructive surgery to happen. I like seeing your pink bits, as it shows me that you are healing.

Tell you what, it was hard for me, but now it's getting easier, as I love coming to see you and talking to you now that you can respond. Just can't wait until I can have a conversation with you. I know it's gonna be hard for you, and it will be hard for me, but we have got to get through this together. We both love each other, and this will make us stronger together. We are going to get through this. I love you.

CHAPTER 17

﹨❦ . ❧﹡

MICHELLE – HE WAS MEANT
TO STAND TALL

BROOMFIELD HOSPITAL, ESSEX – 11 SEPTEMBER 2006

Panic clutched me as I raced back to the hospital. Rob's message had sent adrenalin pulsing through me.

'We've got some news.' If it was bad, he would've told me, or I would've been able to sense it in his voice. However, there was a lightness in his voice when he spoke to me. There was a smile. My heart raced as I parked up and strode into the hospital, then up to the burns unit. I was trying not to sprint, trying to control myself.

I held my breath and walked into Martyn's room. He said, 'Hello, babe. Are you all right?' Elation washed over me in waves. I reached out a hand to steady myself. Tears threatened to gush down my face – tears of euphoria. I couldn't believe the joy I was feeling. The gloom had lifted. The light poured in. That driftwood had got me to shore; that star was now the brightest one in the heavens.

It was amazing that Martyn was asking me how I was after

all he'd gone through. 'Yes, darling, I'm all right,' I said. 'You?'

His voice was like a treasure I'd been looking for all those weeks – and after finding it, I knew it had been worth the wait, worth the anguish. Being able to talk was a relief for Martyn, too – he was unstoppable. His voice was quiet, weak, but we chatted away as if we'd not seen each other for years and he was filling me in on all his adventures.

After Martyn had woken up, more people were allowed in to see him. While he was in a coma and vulnerable to infection, only a few of us could go into his room – me, Rob, Annie, my mum, Kevin and Katie. Katie had been very shocked and upset at the sight of Martyn. Kevin, too. Beforehand, I didn't know how he'd react to seeing Martyn. As we entered Martyn's room, I said to him, 'Please don't cry.'

Kevin thought the world of Martyn – regarded him as a brother. And Kevin's very emotional: a real man who's not afraid to show his tears. I was worried how he'd react. But Kevin made it through. He's strong. But he had a little cry outside afterwards.

Lorraine had visited, and it had really boosted Martyn to know that his little sister had been there. Now, everyone wanted to see him, to wish him well and to cry tears of joy at seeing him alive.

Martyn's brother Paul came with his wife Jill. He'd been keeping in touch and was desperate to support his brother. Chris Humphrey came, chatting away like nothing had changed. Wendy came. She and Rob were no longer together, but they were still friends, and Wendy loves Martyn. And Tom Chaney is her son-in-law now. Tom came, of course. Wearing his gown, he said to Martyn, 'Finally, you've got me in a dress.'

Sophie didn't come. Rob was protective of her and wanted her to wait until Martyn was a bit better.

The second time Tom came, he brought P.J. Martyn had written to him from Afghanistan, and P.J. had been halfway through writing a letter back when the news of the attack had arrived. P.J. had mistakenly been informed that Martyn was dead and had walked the streets for hours, dazed and distraught, until he'd heard that Martyn was alive. P.J. had then kept in touch with Rob and came as soon as he could.

Going into Martyn's room was difficult for P.J. Martyn managed to tell him 'I'm in clip, mate', which is an army term for being in a bad way. Hearing that, P.J. started to cry, but Rob, who was standing behind him, tapped him on the shoulder and told him to pull himself together. P.J. took Martyn's hand and told him he'd come again soon. And he did.

Martyn's strength amazed me, and my love for him seemed to grow impossibly. He showed so much courage, dealing with his terrible injuries. On one occasion, Sarah and Nicky visited, and Martyn said, 'Dad, Dad, show them my bullet wound.' I think that's quite an army thing, to see a bullet wound as a kind of trophy. I expect it's just a way of coping, a way of claiming that mark as their own, instead of it being something that someone did to them.

Nicky said that seeing Martyn was quite a shock. She'd stood outside the room and heard him speak and thought he sounded exactly the same. But, of course, once she was inside the room, she could see what had really happened to him. To me, that was a comfort. Martyn had changed on the outside, but inside he was the same. He was Martyn. He was drugged up and dopey, but he was my Martyn.

The nurses suggested that Martyn might enjoy an ice pole. He was still on various drips for food and fluid, but this would be a way of getting more fluid into him. Eating an ice pole would be easier for Martyn than sipping water. The nurses gave me an ice pole for him from the freezer, and he loved it. He said it was like heaven, the best thing ever, and I suppose having not drunk through his mouth for weeks, with a dried tongue and sore lips, it must have been wonderful. Everyone who came after that brought Martyn a box of ice poles. We stuffed every freezer we could find. Cola was his favourite flavour.

Just over a week after he woke up, Martyn had another operation. I was terrified – more scared than I'd been during the previous weeks, I think. I don't know why that was. I assume it was because he'd come back to me, and now he was going back to the state where he was most at risk – the state of unconsciousness, under anaesthetic.

Martyn was nervous, too. He didn't want to go down to theatre. I reassured him, but my stomach fluttered with apprehension. I went with him. I don't know how I made it, my legs weak with anxiety, light-headedness making me unsteady on my feet.

I said I loved him, biting my lip. They took him in, and the doors closed on him. I shut my eyes and grasped for that driftwood again. I felt as if I was being dragged out to sea, the waves hauling me into the turmoil once again.

I waited like I'd always waited. The minutes dragging into hours, the hours sluggish in their forward march. I wanted to spin the hands of the clock, push time forward, bring on the moment Martyn would come out of surgery.

They debrided his face again and carried out an autograft, laying it over the Integra. They took the skin from his leg, which had grown back by then.

Four hours that felt like four months went by, and they brought him up. He'd made it again, and I breathed out a long, heavy breath – it felt like I'd been holding it in for the past four hours.

I went in to see him, and my mouth opened. I stared at him for a long time. They'd taken a lot of the bandages off his head and face. He'd been swathed in them for seven weeks, and I'd got used to seeing him like that. Now, I could see most of his face again. He looked a bit like a patchwork quilt, with no left ear, half a right ear and his face stapled. But his skin looked smoother, not the grid that had previously covered his face. There were a couple of tiny holes in the graft, which allowed blood to ooze out – but nothing you'd notice after the face was healed.

I saw that his eyes were different, too. They'd carried out an upper-eyelid release, making the lids longer. Until then, when they weren't stitched, they'd always been slightly open, never shutting properly. Dust had been getting in and making Martyn's eyes sore. The operation had involved cutting a gap into his eyelids and slotting new pieces of skin in there to extend the lids.

It was, to me, an amazing transformation. I could see it was him, and it filled me with happiness.

'I feel strange. I feel sick,' Martyn said.

He looked strange, strapped to the tilt bed. I saw panic in his eyes. Emily the physio assured us it would be all right. But Martyn wasn't happy.

'I'm tipping forward,' he said, his voice showing concern. He was upright on the table, at a 90-degree angle. One of the physios said that he wasn't tipping forward, that he'd be fine. 'I'm going to fall. My face is going to smash into the floor,' he said through gritted teeth.

'Martyn, we won't let that happen,' I said.

'You feel disorientated because you've been lying flat for so long,' said Emily. 'Your balance system is askew.'

The physios are remarkable. They are completely confident in what they're doing. They should be. They've done it over and over, helping hundreds of people like Martyn. They know what works; they know how it works. But that didn't comfort Martyn. Not those first few times, anyway. But, typically, he adjusted. He got used to the tilt table, just like he got used to everything else in his turned-inside-out-never-the-same-again world. He was amazing, a remarkable human being, this ordinary man who was extraordinary.

I didn't like to see him in distress. A sweat broke out on the back of my neck, and my mouth felt dry. I wanted to leap in and rescue him, but I knew this was helping him, and I knew the physios were right.

Things moved rapidly. Broomfield tries to get its burns patients upright as soon as possible. It's vital for blood pressure and blood flow, so it would be good for Martyn's heart and bowels. The Achilles tendons and thigh muscles also start working again when the body's at 90 degrees. The human body is, after all, designed to be upright. We're not meant to be flat on our backs. Martyn certainly wasn't. My man was always meant to be up and about. He was a confident, strong soldier when I met him.

The tilt table helps patients regain confidence, and it also empowers them. They know they're getting better. I knew that when he got used to it, it would be a much-needed shot of assurance for him.

Every few days, the physios slid Martyn from his bed, shifted him onto a sheet and then over onto a large soft bed that was horizontal. His feet rested on foot plates, and the physios strapped him on the table.

Every time he went through this process, I flinched. I didn't want to think of him in pain. His body was so fragile that any movement could cause him anguish. But I knew it was good for him in the long run, so I cast away my fears.

And I loved to see Martyn upright. I know it sounds strange, but when you've watched the man you love lie on his back for weeks and weeks, it is a revelation to see him at 90 degrees. Like I said, we are meant to be upright. Martyn was meant to be upright. He was meant to stand tall.

It filled me with hope, seeing him like that. It's nothing to most people, I know, but for me at that time it was everything. The star shone brightly in the darkness. Surely we were now on our way.

The tilt table conquered, Martyn was able to see its benefits the more he used it. Once strapped on and tilted upright, he was able to do some simple exercises, such as having his arms lifted and turning his head. These might sound like nothing, but to Martyn, to us, it was like lifting the FA Cup and coming first in the Tour de France at the same time.

CHAPTER 18

⁂

MARTYN – LOVE WRECKS YOU AT THE BEST OF TIMES

BROOMFIELD HOSPITAL, ESSEX – SEPTEMBER TO OCTOBER 2006

I had an urgent question to ask someone. But it couldn't be just anyone. I waited until I was on my own with a male doctor.

'How are you today, Martyn?' he asked.

'Fine,' I said. I always said I was fine. 'Erm . . .' The doctor looked me in the eye. I tried to lift my head and look down. Then I said, 'Everything's all right, is it? Down there, I mean. I'm all there, am I? No damage? No bits missing?'

The doctor smiled. 'Everything's fine down there, Martyn. You've been lucky.'

I tried to smile back. 'Nice one,' I said.

But when Dad came in later, I said, 'Have a look under the sheet, will you?'

'No harm in checking twice,' I thought, and Dad always told me the truth.

'You're all right, son,' he said. 'You must have had them tucked away somewhere.'

It was a relief. I might have been badly hurt, I might have been scarred, but at least I was still in one piece down there. I wanted to marry Michelle, and I wanted to be a dad. I don't know what my reaction would've been if they'd told me I couldn't have kids. I'd been through so much – three-quarters of my body burned – the least fate could do was throw in a little bit of good fortune.

I wanted to share the news with everyone. My Auntie Trina came to visit and was allowed to come in and see me for the first time. She'd not been able to come before because she works in a school. They were worried she'd ferry in some infections picked up from the kids. It was devastating for her, not being able to be there at the beginning. She'd filled a book with poems she'd written for me in those early days. I haven't read them yet, but I'm sure I will one day.

But when I woke up and started to build my strength, Trina could come and visit – bugs and all. And I was really pleased she was able to. It's a long old trek from Devon, but both she and Annie were wonderful – they didn't let the travel concern them. They wanted to be there for me and Dad and Michelle. On four occasions, Annie and her husband, David, drove all the way back to Devon – two hundred and thirty miles, a four-hour drive. Each time, she went to bed but woke up in the middle of the night, convinced I was going to die, and told David that she wanted to return to Chelmsford. They got in the car and drove all the way back again. Amazing people. Amazing family. I couldn't have got through this without them. Where would I be?

Trina said, 'You look better than I thought you would.'

'Thanks. You don't look too bad yourself.'

We bantered, like we do. I said, 'I've got some big news. I've still got my bits.'

'That *is* big news,' she said. We laughed. 'I'm sure Michelle's pleased,' she added, giving me a wink.

I looked around the room at all the photos Michelle had

pinned up: friends and family, all grinning, all posing, everyone around me. And then I saw the photos of Port Lympne. I felt something churn in my guts. We were getting married there in a couple of years. But would Michelle want to marry me now? We'd talked about the wedding. Michelle had told me all about the venue, the date, what she had planned. But I still needed to know if she actually *wanted* to marry me. The question had plagued me, but I'd not asked it.

We'd told each other 'I love you', so at least that was a comfort to me. But I wondered what kind of bridegroom I'd be. I didn't know what I looked like, but I guessed I'd had a hell of a makeover since the last time I'd brushed my hair in the mirror. As it was, I couldn't even stand up properly to be next to her when we took our vows.

Out in Helmand, I worried about her not wanting to marry me. But I suppose that was only natural, because I was so far away. Love wrecks you at the best of times. But when you're separated, it's a hundred times worse. Throw a war and thousands of miles into that separation, and the pain and apprehension gets even worse. My fears were allayed when I heard her voice, when she told me she loved me. And I loved her so much.

I gazed at the images of Port Lympne. It was the ideal wedding venue. And Michelle would make the perfect bride. In my mind's eye, I imagined her looking beautiful in her dress. And then I imagined me next to her.

I made a decision. I didn't know how I was going to do it, but I'd die trying: I was going to walk Michelle down the aisle. I was going to be the best bridegroom I could be. And after that, I'd be the best husband.

TUESDAY, 19 SEPTEMBER

Darling, I haven't written for a while, as we're able to talk to each other. I'm writing today because you're in surgery. You were really nervous, but I followed you all the way, then I waited for you to come out. We will get through this and our love will be stronger. I love you so much.

On 25 September, I was transferred next door to the Burns Unit Rehab. It was a massive step. I had to stay in a side room – I couldn't be with other patients, because I still had a lot of infections. Most of them were Afghan bugs never before seen in the UK. They needed to be kept away from the other patients.

I had a meeting with a nurse, the physiotherapist, Joanna the occupational therapist, two social workers, a psychotherapist, Luke Cox, Dad, Michelle and Rosie to discuss my discharge. I was desperate to go home, and getting a date would give me something to work towards. Goals were important for me. I'd set a long-term one – walking Michelle down the aisle. It would take some doing, the state I was in. But I was determined. If I could've made fists and punched the air and said, 'I'm going to do it,' I would've done. But I couldn't make fists. I couldn't lift my arms. It was a long road.

I wanted to be home for Christmas. We settled on 11 December as a discharge date. It was a Monday – the beginning of a week. 'Good,' I thought. 'The beginning of something.' It would make me look forward to the following weekend. I'd make the most of the week, get my strength up.

'I've got 78 days to get ready for the rest of my life,' I said to Michelle.

However, rehab's tough. There's a strict regime, and they keep you busy. But, then, if you want to walk your girlfriend down the aisle, if you want to be home by Christmas, you can't be lying around staring at the wall all day. They also try to make life as normal as possible in there: you wear your own clothes, and you can eat your own food.

I had daily physio sessions and a variety of therapies. I'd get up and be washed, dressed and fed breakfast, and then I'd have an hour or so of physio or an occupational-therapy session. Often the two happened together, and there was always a purpose to what I was doing. It wasn't just 'Bend and stretch your arm, Martyn,' but 'Reach to the plate then back to your mouth. We're going to do this ten times, Martyn.' I could see the reason for everything, and that really helped. All my goals were written on the wall in my room, one of which was feeding myself with adapted cutlery.

After a session, I'd always have a nap. Then I'd eat lunch, have more physio and another nap. I was continually knackered. Everything was bloody hard work. I felt as if my body had packed up. It had certainly had enough. It just didn't want to do any more – it needed rest, rest, rest. But I kept pushing it. My body and I were at odds, but I was the boss.

In the afternoons, I always hoped for visitors, otherwise I was on my own with the nurses. They were lovely, and I got to know them well, but it wasn't the same as seeing friends and family. Trina would come and see me, and she'd feed me yoghurt. I could see it was hard for her. The last time she'd done that, I'd been a toddler. Perhaps that was when I realised that I was going to be dependent on a lot of people for a long time to come. But I had to get on with it. You can't let things get to you, however difficult it gets. You've got to keep fighting. You've got to have goals, and if that means being hand-fed by your auntie, then so be it.

There was a big clock in my room. It reminded me of a school classroom. I would watch the seconds tick by, one by one – tick, tick, tick. It drove me mad. It made me think about the time I had left to get this right, to reach my goal. I had the idea that I'd walk Michelle down the aisle planted in my head now. That was my big thing. But I had a bad break to my leg, and the physios didn't think I'd be walking alone by the time I went home at Christmas. Emily, the physio, said, 'We'll want to get you up and walking, but that won't be possible until your thigh bone is healed. That may take more time, because your body has been healing itself elsewhere. And it's a bad break. The bone shattered.'

I didn't want to hear how bad it was. I wanted to know how long it would take. They couldn't tell me that. I had to get on with it – grit my teeth and battle on. The stubbornness that had got me into trouble during my youth and my army days came in useful. The bolshie side of me – and it's a big side – wasn't having any of this 'It'll take a long time' nonsense.

That's not to say I didn't have down days. I did. But someone or something always came along to cheer me up. From time to time, someone would come onto the ward to do balloon modelling for the kids – to help them use their hands for something fun. Balloons were good because they were light. One day when I was really grumpy, Joanna asked the balloon guy to make something to amuse me. I nearly pissed myself when the door of my room opened and Joanna shoved a rude purple-and-green shape through the gap. It was even funnier because I was sitting having a serious discussion with the social worker at the time.

Michelle and I did have some chill-out time in rehab. We had a little TV and a DVD player. We watched *Deal or No Deal*, the TV show presented by Noel Edmonds, a lot. It had only just started. It was the one about contestants gambling on how much money was hidden in various boxes. I liked the risk element. I know they weren't risking much – only cash – but it appealed to my adventurous side. We also had a DVD version of the game that we played together. It was all part of getting back to normality, and I soon realised that watching telly and playing games was also part of my rehabilitation.

Michelle and I spoke about the incident. There was a

psychiatrist available to me, but I didn't feel I needed that. I had Michelle. I could talk to her. I've never been one for sitting down to chat or having heart-to-hearts – that's not me. But with Michelle, it was different. From the moment I met her, I could talk to her. I could open up and reveal all my feelings. I wanted to share everything with her. I never felt awkward with Michelle. It was difficult to talk about some things after I woke up, but I soon realised it was the same Michelle I'd fallen in love with, with whom I'd shared everything. Nothing had changed.

We had a little base there in burns rehab, Michelle and I. Rosie would bring us meals. I loved Rosie's food. Her shepherd's pie is like heaven in your mouth. It was lucky that she kept bringing me food, because I wasn't having much luck with the hospital grub. I just didn't like it. The nutritionist argued with me about it. She said I needed to put on weight, but I couldn't eat the stuff they were giving me. I knew that I needed to pile on the pounds, and I was happy to do that – but only on the Rosie diet or with takeaways. I was never going to get meat back on my bones eating what they were feeding me.

Michelle helped take care of me. She spent hours rubbing cream into my red, raw skin. It needed to be done four times a day, and I loved the fact that she was doing it. The touch thing was important to me. Having that physical contact with my fiancée was valuable. It made me love her even more, I think – if that was possible. I watched her as she did it and thought, 'What a brilliant woman – so strong, so determined, so beautiful. I couldn't bear it if I lost her now.' She'd get on the bed and snuggle up to me sometimes, and although it was occasionally painful for me, I'd put up with the agony just to be near her. It was excruciating, but it was also amazing.

She also helped me with my hand exercises. The grafts would tighten, so my skin had to be stretched. It was agony. The pain seared through me. Sometimes I couldn't stand it, but I went through it. It was going to be worth it in the end.

There was so much pain. Pain all over my body. Different kinds of pain; different levels of pain. I had scars on my hips, and after I'd been sitting up for a while, they would tighten. I'd lay back down. The skin felt like it was tearing, and I'd scream.

I wouldn't wish that pain on anyone.

CHAPTER 19

※⁀⁓ . ⁓⁀※

MICHELLE – HE WAS DISTRESSED,
AND I DIDN'T KNOW WHAT TO DO

The cocktail of drugs Martyn took was gradually reduced. He got stronger and was soon able to lift his right arm. As he grew in strength and resolve, the physios introduced new techniques that would help him recover.

Martyn's determination to stand saw him use a piece of equipment called the MasterVest. It was a frame with a vest that would support his weight and help him get out of bed. It was the only way he could stand to begin with, because the vest supported most of his weight. The orthopaedic surgeon warned him not to put any weight on his broken leg. The bone was taking a long time to heal because it was a nasty break and because Martyn's body had been busy healing other parts of itself. So the MasterVest was an ideal way for him to get upright. It was preferable to the tilt table. At least he was able to support some of his own weight with his good leg, and he wasn't strapped in, like he was on the table.

Martyn sat on the bed. The physios and I slid slings under his legs. The slings were like dungarees. They were attached to two hooks on a frame. The physio pressed a button. The MasterVest lifted Martyn, pulling him forward into a standing position. He put his hands on the bars in front of him to help him balance.

I watched, amazed. It was thrilling to see him stand. It filled me with confidence. I asked him how he felt.

'My leg hurts,' he said, 'but it's great – I'm standing up.' Emily, the physio, was excited. She rushed out. 'Where's she off to?' said Martyn.

Emily returned with a camera. She took a photo of Martyn, standing in the MasterVest, with me next to him. We grinned at each other. I felt my heart flutter. I looked Martyn in the eye, and he stared back. I could see the steel in him. I think he felt he was on the way. He could visualise himself walking me down the aisle – and I could picture it, too. It would be a difficult task – some would say impossible. But with his resolve, anything was possible. It really was. He'd always been stubborn, and in the past that had got him into trouble. But now it could well be the making of him.

I spoke to Peter Dziewulski. He said, 'Martyn is very, very fit, which has been a great help to him. He's extremely self-motivated – an undeniable factor in his rehabilitation. And the effect of having so much family support cannot be underestimated.'

He also said that Martyn wouldn't be where he was if it weren't for me. I felt like crying. I was so grateful to Mr Dziewulski and the rest of the staff at Broomfield. I thought, 'If it wasn't for *you*, he'd not be where he is.' I was only doing what any girlfriend, fiancée or wife would do. I loved Martyn. I wanted to marry him, to be with him for the rest of our lives. Why wouldn't I do all I could to help him? I thought being there for him, pushing him, encouraging him, was the most natural thing in the world for me to do.

I know that Mr Dziewulski had a lot of admiration for Martyn. 'He went out and risked his life,' he said, 'and whether you believe that's the right or the wrong thing to do, you have to respect that.'

❧ · ❧

On 12 October, a Thursday, Martyn had to undergo another operation. Those same feelings washed through me: fear, apprehension, uncertainty. It was like hanging off the edge of a cliff, hoping someone would come along and hoist you up before you lost your grip.

They grafted raw patches on his elbow, back and the back of his head. His scalp caused him difficulties. They don't heal very well at the best of times. Hair keeps growing and can get trapped under the skin, causing infections.

Martyn had started to feel impatient, especially since using the MasterVest. He was encouraged and wanted to plough forward, but it was a slow process, and this frustrated him. Naturally, he wanted solutions to everything. But there were so many testing times ahead.

For one thing, he couldn't lie on his right side because of the scaffolding of the X-Fix attached to his shattered leg. And he was also uncomfortable lying on his left side. He'd landed on his left arm when he jumped from the tank, so that made it painful. His body had also overhealed and had grown additional bone in the left elbow. Because of all these things, he was always on his back – which meant he was lying on his scalp wound.

He couldn't have a pillow. Scar tissue pulled his head down towards his neck, and having a pillow would exacerbate this because it would lift his head further forward. He found it impossible to relieve the pressure on his head and neck himself. He was too weak to lift his head, and the muscles in his neck had wasted away. He was distressed, and I didn't know what to do.

And things were about to get worse.

Martyn hadn't been awake after surgery before. He'd been sedated for weeks, so after they'd operated on him, he'd been wheeled back to his room still asleep. But now he woke up. And it was awful, so upsetting.

After the first operation Martyn had on awakening from his coma, he couldn't open his eyes, because he'd had surgery on them, which was distressing for him. The dressing on his head made him hot and uncomfortable. His hands were bandaged and balanced on two small tables either side of him to keep them up.

'I feel terrible,' he said, his voice barely a whisper. 'My hands are really painful. I'm scared someone'll bang into them because I can't see people coming.'

'It'll be all right,' I said. 'I'm here.' It was the best I could do. And it was the truth. He would be all right. In a few days, I was sure he'd be back to how he'd been, standing up in the MasterVest, laughing and joking.

Being awake, he was aware of the changes that had taken place to his body during the operation. I think the seriousness of surgery hit him. 'I was standing in the MasterVest yesterday,' he said. 'I feel like I've taken a massive step back. I don't want to be lying in bed.'

It was hard to see him like this, and I wanted to comfort him. I told him again that everything would be all right, that he'd get strong again. But determined people want things to happen straight away. They see themselves making progress, and when something, anything, hinders them, they feel they've regressed.

I said, 'You're doing so well, Martyn. But it'll take time.' He lay still. I couldn't tell what he was thinking or if his eyes were on me, because of the bandages. I kept talking to him, telling him that things would soon be back to how they were. 'We'll get you in the MasterVest again,' I said. 'And your leg will start healing. The bone will get better, and you'll soon be able to put both your feet on the ground. It'll be Christmas before long, you watch. We'll be back home, and you'll be on your feet.'

He wasn't moving. He was silent. He wasn't breathing.

I furrowed my brow and watched him carefully. Very often, Martyn would breathe and then stop for a few seconds. He still had his tracheostomy in, so the way he took on oxygen was hardly normal.

I waited. I wasn't too worried to begin with. But a few more seconds went by. He still hadn't breathed. I glanced at the oxygen monitor. It was usually constant, the green numbers reading between 85 and 90 units of oxygen in his bloodstream. But the numbers started dropping – rapidly. There was no oxygen in Martyn's body.

Panic flooded through me. We'd come so far. Was I now going to lose him when things had started to improve? I called his name. He'd just passed out in front of me while I was talking. I stuck my head out of the door and said, 'I don't mean to panic anyone, but I think Martyn's stopped breathing.'

Two doctors rushed into the room. They hit an emergency buzzer. Another 12 medics spilled through the doors. They were all talking, their voices slicing across each other. I couldn't make any of it out. I stared at Martyn, still and breathless on the bed. 'He's dying,' I thought. 'He's gone.'

They told me to leave, and I backed out of the room. My eyes fixed on Martyn until the last moment, until the door shut and I was left outside. The muffled sounds of their efforts to save Martyn came from his room. I was in a trance. My head filled with thoughts of him.

I remembered us meeting in the pub, Martyn coming in, my heart fluttering when I laid eyes on him. I remembered us together before the incident, the fun we had. I remembered his proposal, how I'd felt, his eyes showing he loved me. I remembered Rob's phone call telling me that Martyn had been hurt, and Rob and me driving to the hospital, saying nothing. I remembered Martyn lying on his bed in Broomfield, under sedation, his life on the line. I remembered him waking up, sitting up in bed asking me if I was all right. I remembered him in the MasterVest, grinning at me, Emily taking our picture. I remembered him lying there, not breathing. All these thoughts reeled through my mind like a film on fast forward.

I went out into the waiting room and sat down, putting my head in my hands. I didn't know what to do. I looked up, wondering what was going on in there, waiting for a doctor to step out into the room, his eyes fixed on the floor, bad news in his stooped shoulders. I started thinking about how the words would sound: 'I'm sorry, Michelle, but there was nothing we could do . . .'

'No,' I thought. 'No, I'm not thinking like that. He's going to make it. He's coming through this. He's come through everything, and he'll come through this, too.'

I don't know how long I waited. It felt like years. I thought I'd aged in the time they spent with him. But there was no news. No one came to tell me anything. Was no news good news? Or could they not face me to tell me he'd gone? I couldn't believe that. Medics tell people every day that their loved ones have died; they are used to it. It's not a nice thing to do, but they know how to do it.

What was going on? I'd made some calls, telling people what had happened and how scared I was. Everyone replied that he would be all right, but that's the normal response, isn't it? No one would tell me, 'Oh no, he's probably dead. He's got no chance if he's stopped breathing.'

A thousand thoughts raced through my brain. I looked up at the clock: two hours and no news. Emily, the physio, popped her head around the door. She appeared confused, her brow creased. 'Why aren't you with Martyn?' she said.

'No one's told me I can go back in,' I said.

Emily looked shocked. 'Oh, he's fine,' she said. 'Something had blocked his tracheostomy.'

I don't know what I said, or if it was just a noise that came out of my throat, but I raced back into Martyn's room.

CHAPTER 20

꿏ᐧᐧ꿏

MARTYN – NOTHING WAS GOING TO BE THE SAME AGAIN

BROOMFIELD HOSPITAL, ESSEX – 31 OCTOBER 2006

Michelle gripped my hand and stared towards the door. I stopped talking and followed her gaze. Joanna, my occupational therapist, had come in. She was carrying a mirror. It was pressed against her, the glass turned away from me.

Joanna closed the door and walked towards the end of the bed. She smiled and said, 'I know you want to go outside, Martyn.' My heart beat faster. 'And we've got a wheelchair ready,' she said. 'But before you do, you need to know what you look like. You need to know what other people are seeing.' Michelle's grip tightened on my hand. 'And we can't risk you catching a reflection of yourself unprepared.' Joanna paused. 'Are you ready?' Michelle and I looked at one other. I turned towards Joanna and nodded, not trusting myself to speak.

It was three months since the incident. I knew that 75 per cent burns meant I couldn't look good. But I had no idea what to expect. It didn't cross my mind that it was Halloween, but if it had, it might have lifted my mood. I'd always had a dark sense of humour and army life had sharpened it.

'I can stay, if you like,' said Joanna.

I swallowed hard. 'Just Michelle,' I said. It was Michelle who had promised to marry me. And it was Michelle who would spend the rest of her life looking at me. It would be like meeting her all over again – and I was nervous enough the first time.

Joanna gave me the mirror. She looked at me, and I stared back. She said, 'You look very different, but you are the same person underneath. Your mouth is tight, and you've lost the tip of your nose and your ears.'

I digested the information. I didn't know what to do with it. I wanted to spit it out and start again, but I couldn't – this was what I was like. I still couldn't picture it, though. Joanna was preparing me for the moment I'd see myself, that was all. They verbalise what burns victims look like to lessen the shock. I'm not sure if it worked because I shuddered.

She continued: 'Your eyelids are turned slightly inside out.'

'Inside out!' I thought. 'What does that look like?'

'The texture of your skin is red and wrinkled.' She looked at me, and I said nothing. 'Call me if you need me.'

The few seconds it took her to leave the room seemed like hours. Nothing was going to be the same again. Everything seemed to move in slow motion. I was so frightened. I watched Joanna leave. She shut the door gently behind her.

I moved my legs round to the side of the bed, and Michelle shifted so she was beside me. Slowly, I brought the mirror up and our faces appeared.

I knew it was me, but the Martyn I remembered had gone. My skin was red raw and scarred. The fire had sliced me open and given me a good kicking.

I said nothing. Shock washed over me. I began to cry, and so did Michelle.

Eventually, I spoke. 'I look horrible.'

'You won't always look like this,' said Michelle. 'You've got a lot of operations to go through yet.'

I barely heard her words. I asked her to move the mirror so I could see round my head. I felt shattered. Where was the Martyn who used moisturiser and checked his appearance in every mirror he passed? Where was the young man always up for a practical joke? Would I ever laugh again? Could Michelle really imagine a life with me? With this face?

'Are you sure,' I said, starting to ask the question without knowing if I could handle the answer, 'that you still want to be with me?'

'If the situation was reversed, would you still want to be with me?' said Michelle.

'Of course.'

'There's your answer. But I'm telling you straight: if you're going to become a recluse and stay in the house and hide, then I'll walk away – because that's not you. If you stay the same Martyn I fell in love with, then I'll be with you always.'

I looked at Michelle and cried again. I counted my blessings for about the millionth time; I felt so lucky she was mine. She'd shown such strength in standing beside me, and now she'd been strong enough to be completely honest with me. I would find it inside me to match her strength. I had to. And she was right – I was the same Martyn. The packaging was different, but the essence was the same.

We sat and chatted for a couple of hours. Joanna joined us and explained more about how my surgery and appearance would progress. 'Your reaction is totally normal, Martyn,' she said. 'But this isn't about one look in the mirror. It's a long process from this point forwards. Things are going to improve.' I felt determination rise up inside me. There was no turning back. This was how life would be from now on, and I was facing up to it.

As Michelle wheeled me out of the burns unit, I didn't think about the people around me – whether they were looking at me, what they might be saying. I felt such peace at being outside again. I breathed in the chilly autumn air and was grateful to be alive.

I looked at the trees. It had been five months since I had seen trees. They were scarce in Afghanistan. Autumn had arrived in the UK, and some of the trees had already shed their leaves. Their branches were bare and exposed. I could have compared my condition to their vulnerability. But I focused instead on the new beginning that was around the corner. They would grow leaves again. They would flourish once more – and so would I.

As Michelle pushed me along in my wheelchair, we chatted. I asked her if we could stop for a moment. I looked up at the trees again. In that moment, I realised I'd probably never climb one again. But inside I felt as if I had already conquered a mountain.

PART THREE

That's What Normal Feels Like

CHAPTER 21

✦❧·☙✦

MARTYN – THE CRISPY STRIPS
TASTED AMAZING

BROOMFIELD HOSPITAL, ESSEX – EARLY NOVEMBER 2006

I stared at the hospital food in front of me. I didn't know what my lunch had been originally, and it was still unrecognisable. Everything I ate was puréed, because I couldn't open my mouth properly. I also had to be careful of the hole where my tracheostomy had been. Rosie had been making me shepherd's pies. They were delicious and, more importantly, soft. But there were none about that day. I was stuck with hospital food.

I looked over at Michelle. 'I don't remember requesting puréed mush,' I said.

She grinned. 'There's sausages in there somewhere.'

'I could murder a KFC,' I said.

Michelle looked at my food. 'Come on, I'll help you eat it,' she said.

'No, I'm serious. I really fancy KFC.'

'OK,' she said. 'There's one nearby. Shall I go and get you one? I can mush it up for you.'

I grimaced. 'I'm sure I can squeeze a crispy strip in,' I said. 'Go and ask if I can go out. There's a drive-through. We can go there.'

Michelle helped me clean my teeth and put my little beanie hat on. I knew I looked very bad, but I still had standards.

I needed help getting from my bed into my wheelchair and from the wheelchair to the car. This was done on a banana board, and I slowly slid from one place to the next. I was quite patient as I was helped into the wheelchair and Michelle pushed me to the car. She'd had to get rid of her little MG because it was too low for me. I knew she'd been gutted about that, but she hadn't made a fuss. Typical of her, really.

I had a sudden urge to prove that I was OK, and before anyone could stop me, or help me, I pulled myself from the wheelchair and into the car. I was quick, but I managed to avoid whacking my broken leg with the mass of scaffolding around it – I could easily have slammed into the handbrake.

'Martyn,' said the nurse. 'Your leg.'

'Sorry,' I said, 'but KFC calls.'

The crispy strips tasted amazing. A . . . mazing.

And there was no stopping me after that. Puréed mush just wasn't going to cut it. Whenever I could get out for a little bit of fast food, I was as happy as a pig in muck. Burgers, chicken, pizza – it was like being back to my old self. Like. Not for real. But it was the best I could manage, and it tasted great.

'Thinner than that,' I said to Michelle.

'If I squash it any harder, the burger's going to fly out the side,' she said.

'Well, I can't get that in my mouth.'

'Yes, Martyn, I know.'

We were sitting in the car park outside McDonald's, and food was becoming a source of irritation between me and Michelle. I couldn't feed myself because the skin on my arms had melted. My elbows were taut, and I couldn't lift my hand to my mouth, so Michelle was feeding me. The pieces had to be small because I was unable to open my mouth wide enough for great big chunks of food. I couldn't stuff myself, and that frustrated me. But as Michelle fed me, her food was going cold. And if I waited for her to eat, my food would go cold. I was irritated. I wanted to eat as I always had done. Lots of food and quickly.

It was a bit of a nightmare, to be honest, and although I tried to be patient, I don't think I was. Two steps forward, one step back: going out for fast food but then not being able to eat it properly. Everything was a battle – even enjoying a burger. But I had to get used to it – no point getting annoyed, even though it was difficult not to. I wanted everything to be like it had been. But that wasn't an option. This was it now, and I had to adjust, had to accept, had to deal with all the difficulties life threw at me – whether they were serious or whether they were trivial.

And at that moment, eating a burger properly was pretty serious.

I needed to eat, there's no doubt about that. They'd been feeding me a high-calorie diet while I was sedated, but my body just devoured the energy. It was fighting hard to heal itself, so it needed all the calories it could get. When I woke up, I weighed seven and a half stone. I'd lost nearly half of my bodyweight. So bring on the burgers and the KFC, was the way I saw it.

I've always eaten loads. As a kid, I'd eat several times a day – a meal at Trina's, then a Chinese takeaway, and later I'd pop to Annie's for a sandwich and get a KFC on the way home. So, I was capable of devouring lots of calories. The question was: would my body then start using them all to heal itself? It was going to take a while to get my weight up again, if that was the case.

Being thin had a lot of drawbacks. I'd started going out in the days after I saw myself in the mirror – well, the world had to get used to me. There was a fireworks display near the hospital on 5 November, and Michelle drove me there. We arrived late, and couldn't get in because it was ticket only. 'We can watch them from out here,' Michelle said, parking up outside the venue.

It would've been better inside, but I got out of the car – and it was freezing. I didn't have any fat on me to keep me warm. Seven and a half stones of skin and bone – that was me.

'I've got to get back in the car, Mich.' She helped me back inside, worried that something was wrong. Then I explained, telling her that I was cold – cold because I had nothing to protect my bones.

We watched the fireworks from the car, and it was nice – good to be out of the hospital, doing something that seemed almost normal. 'I think I need feeding up,' I said.

'Yes, you do,' said Michelle. 'Are you hungry?'

'You know me.'

We went down to the chippy, and I had sausage and chips – it was bloody lovely.

I liked getting out of the ward, but I was still nervous about it. Like I said, the world had to get used to me. But that was easier said than done – for the world, and for me. I felt uncomfortable to begin with and hated people looking at me.

A few days after I saw myself in the mirror, I was taken down to the hospital car park to meet an old friend. Harvey recognised me and wagged his tail. It didn't matter to him what I looked like. But he didn't jump up. He must've sensed that I was poorly.

When I was wheeled around the hospital, I kept my head down, my gaze fixed on the floor to avoid eye contact with patients and visitors. Down in the canteen, I didn't like people seeing me being fed, so we'd collect my food and head back to the ward to eat in private.

But, in the end, I had to go for it. What was the worst that could happen? Things couldn't get much worse than I'd already experienced. Still, it wasn't the easiest thing to deal with. And it took some childish honesty to make me accept my situation and hold my head up high when I was out in public.

We were down in the canteen, Michelle and I, having something to eat. There were a lot of people, but I tried to avert my gaze as usual. A lady and her son were eating at the next table. The boy, about six or seven, was chirping away. He sounded very happy. Then he looked over at me. He stopped nattering. I could see him staring from the corner of my eye. I tried not to think about it, and I hoped the boy wasn't scared or upset.

Then he said, 'Mum, that man's got no ears.'

I looked up at Michelle. A grin broke out on her face. I couldn't help myself. I blurted out a laugh. I looked over at the lady and her son, and she smiled at us. I think she was pleased I wasn't upset by what her son said. But why should I be? He was right – I *didn't* have any ears.

However, it does take a while to deal with the fact that you don't look like everyone else. I saw someone was staring at me when I was down in the canteen with Auntie Annie one afternoon. I said, 'What's he looking at?'

Annie said, 'He's looking at you, darling. You look different to anyone he's seen before, I expect.'

Straight talking from Auntie Annie. That helped me, too. I've suffered third-degree burns to 75 per cent of my body. I *do* look different to what most people expect. And then I realised that it wasn't me who had to get used to it. It was everyone else.

CHAPTER 22

MICHELLE – 'MORNING, SWEETIE. HAPPY BIRTHDAY'

'Ooh!' Sarah jumped out of her skin as another balloon popped.

'Ssh!' I hissed. 'You'll wake him up.'

'Sorry,' she said. 'Another one bites the dust. Shall we put that banner up now?'

'Yes,' I said, lifting a chair and moving it into position, ready to stand on. 'OK?' I passed her the 'Happy Birthday' banner. Sarah stood on another chair. As she lifted her end of the banner, she pulled it. I jerked and nearly slipped off my chair, just avoiding falling by grabbing the door frame. I started to giggle.

'Ssh!' said Sarah, smiling at me.

Martyn was asleep. We were trying to decorate his room without waking him up. But we found it hard not to laugh. We had the giggles. We carried out our decorating with shuddering shoulders and the occasional snorting sound.

Lisa, one of the nurses, came in. 'Ready?' she asked.

'Yes,' I said.

'Martyn, time to wake up,' she said, tickling his feet. He opened his eyes.

'Morning, sweetie,' I said. 'Happy birthday.'

'Thanks, babe,' said Martyn.

We were going to take him out for a meal. He was wearing some tracksuit bottoms my mum had made for him. She'd cut a slit up the side to accommodate his X-Fix. There was Velcro attached so that he could close the gap to keep his leg warm. He wore extra-large shirts, which he could get on without moving his arms too much. My mum had bought him a few woolly hats to keep his head warm, and he was wearing one of those over his bandages.

I'd gone back to work earlier that month. It was only part-time, but I'd been encouraged to try and get some normality back into my life. I think it did me good. I hated leaving Martyn, but his dad was still with him, and he had regular visitors. I think it was good for him to see different faces, hear different voices. The children at school knew why I'd been away and asked a lot of questions. And when Martyn and I started appearing on news programmes, speaking about his injuries and our determination to marry, they were very impressed.

We got Martyn ready to go out and went to The Angel pub in Broomfield, which was five minutes away, in time for lunch. Friends and family were there to greet him. There was my mum and dad, Rob, Katie and Kevin, Sophie and her sister Kas, Wendy, Tom and Sophie's daughter Alicia, and nurses and physiotherapists from Broomfield's intensive-care unit. It was great, and Martyn loved it. The surgeon, Mr Dziewulski, bought us a bottle of champagne, and Martyn drank some through a straw.

Martyn's dad told him, 'You're on medication. You can't drink.'

'I bloody well can,' said Martyn. It was his birthday, and he was determined it would be as normal as possible. And on a normal birthday, he'd have a drink.

We sang 'Happy Birthday'. I know people were emotional, and they tried not to show it – but I think they found it difficult to stifle their tears. After all, this was a day many of us thought we'd never see.

There was another special friend there, too: Harvey. Martyn stroked him and said, 'That's wonderful. His fur's all soft. That's what normal feels like.' I smiled through my tears.

Martyn enjoyed his presents. Lisa had arranged for Spurs to send him a signed football, and Sarah bought him a display case for it. I wanted to buy him a watch, because before he'd left for Afghanistan, he'd said he wanted a nice one. But when I mentioned it again, he'd gone off the idea, as he hated looking at his arms, which were thin and scarred. I bought him a CD instead. The locals at The Bull sent him a pint glass with the message 'This one's on us when you get back' engraved on it. That made him smile. I bet he could've done with a pint. I looked forward to walking into the pub with him again, doing the things that all couples do.

We stayed at the pub for a good few hours then Martyn started getting tired, so we went back to Broomfield and settled Martyn back into bed. He looked at me and said, 'Thanks for decorating my room as well.'

I smiled at him. I was so pleased he'd enjoyed himself, so pleased he appreciated our efforts – and glad that it was a surprise.

'And babe,' he said.

'Yes?'

'I was awake the whole time.'

I'd had to get rid of my MG. I never thought the day would come. I loved that car; it was my pride and joy. I'd had it a few years, and it symbolised everything I felt about myself: independent, self-sufficient, forward-moving – a nifty little speedster.

But it had gone. It had to for Martyn's sake. Martyn would have found it difficult to get into the MG. It was too low for him. He couldn't have got from his wheelchair into the car. The MG went.

I suppose I wasn't going to be an independent woman much longer, so that symbol of my single life could be sold off. I was going to marry Martyn. I'd be his wife; he'd be my husband. We'd be a team, not individuals. Martyn had sacrificed so much. He'd been terribly wounded fighting for his country. The least I could do was sell my car. It was nothing in the greater scheme of things.

The Alfa Romeo that replaced the MG was far better suited to ferrying Martyn around. It was much easier for him to get in and out of.

We made a surprise visit to Rob's house in Staplehurst. He'd gone home for the day to have a break from the hospital routine and a night in his own bed. There was nothing wrong with the beds in the army house, but they weren't home.

It was a journey of more than an hour from Chelmsford to Staplehurst, a long time for Martyn to be away from the hospital and in a car. I was worried to begin with, but he was great. He didn't moan or complain, which he could've done. We chatted and joked, and looked forward to surprising Rob. He didn't expect us, because he didn't expect Martyn to travel so far from Broomfield.

'What the bloody hell are you doing here?' he said, a big smile on his face.

We stayed a while, had a cuppa and a chat. And I think Martyn benefited from being home. He looked around a lot, taking it all in. The smells and sights were familiar to him. He grew up there, and now he was back – but as a very different Martyn.

'Still mine, though,' I thought, studying him as he drank his tea and talked to his dad. 'Still my Martyn.'

CHAPTER 23

MARTYN – PHYSIO, FRIENDS
AND FAMILY

I needed to stand. My ambition to walk Michelle down the aisle would be under threat if I didn't get up on my feet. But it was a slow process. I had to learn to stand up all over again. My broken leg was still weak, but there was no way I was going to sit on my arse or lie on my back all day when I had a wedding to attend in less than two years. My own wedding. So I had to use one leg.

I had sessions with Emily, the physio – sessions where I practised standing, leaning on a frame. I sat on the edge of the bed, Emily hovering nearby. She said, 'All right, Martyn. Try to get up.'

And I did. The pain seared through me. It felt like I had a Spartan on my shoulders. My legs seemed like paper, and they were struggling to carry the weight they had to bear. All the muscles had wasted away – the muscles in my thighs; the muscles in my shins. I was standing on matchsticks, practically – and one of those was snapped. So, it was really only one matchstick. I grimaced, refusing to let the pain defeat me. And slowly I got up to a standing position. My body screamed at me to let it sit down. I lowered myself onto the bed, groaning because of the agony that was tearing through me.

'All right, that's enough,' said Emily.

'No, another one,' I said.

'Just do one today.'

'I'll do two.'

I stood again, all the pressure on my one half-good leg. My throat was dry. I wanted to cry with the pain, but I wasn't going to. I wasn't going to show weakness. I'd fight this to the end. If I was going to walk Michelle down the aisle, I'd have to suffer – and I'd do anything for her. I stood again. My head was spinning. I gasped for breath, and Emily helped me sit down on the edge of the bed again. I felt like I'd climbed Everest.

Every time I had a session with Emily, I always wanted to do more. If she told me to stand up three times, I'd want to stand up four times. And I'd moan and complain until she let me do that extra one. In my mind, that extra one was getting me closer to my goal.

Michelle had gone back to school by then – only three days a week, but I missed her. She'd been there with me when I was sedated, and she was there when I woke up, so it was strange when she went back to work. Her school had been incredibly supportive, sending cards and messages. I wanted her to go. It was good for her – we were both aiming for normality. But there were days when I didn't see her, and those were difficult to begin with. Then I pulled myself together and enjoyed the chats we had on the phone when she wasn't there.

I couldn't grip the phone because of my hands, so Emily would hold it for me. I'd be chatting away to Michelle with Emily sitting next to me on a chair, leaning on the bed, one arm stretched out to my ear. She'd watch TV, trying to pretend she wasn't there.

I can't find the words to describe how I feel about everyone at Broomfield, people such as Emily, the nurses, Mr Dziewulski. They put me back together. They did everything, from saving my life to rebuilding my body and holding the phone so I could chat to Michelle – sometimes for hours.

My days were filled with physio, friends and family. The physio was tough; the friends and family was great.

Not many people saw me while I was unconscious, except Dad and Michelle. To be honest, I gave Dad a lot of grief after I woke up. He's not always the calmest person, but he put up with my grumbling and moaning, never saying a word. I was taking my frustrations out on him, but he was patient with me.

Now that I was awake and getting better, I had a lot of visitors. I was worried about what they'd think of me, how they'd react. I didn't want them to be sad. If I see someone I care for cry, I'm likely to blub myself.

Brian, Michelle's dad, was great. He's a strong, solid, sound guy. I know where Kevin and Michelle get their strength. He came in and said, 'Christ, boy, you've been through some shit.'

'Yeah, just a bit.'

Brian looked me in the eye, and that's what I wanted people to do. It made me uncomfortable when their gaze flickered around, when they obviously couldn't lay their eyes on my raw face. But Brian was strong. He made me feel at ease. He spoke honestly about what I looked like. He didn't skip around saying I looked great. I knew I didn't at that time, and I didn't want people pretending otherwise. Deep down, I was still Martyn to him, and he was my future father-in-law – nothing had changed in our relationship.

One of the people I was always really happy to see was Lorraine. Geographically, we haven't always been near each other, but emotionally we're really close. We share a sadness about our mum that no one else could ever understand. We've never spoken about our mum, who Lorraine calls Mother Jean. Not for any particular reason, really; we've just never had a heart-to-heart about it.

I've always tried to be a good big brother to Lorraine. I remember the time Annie brought her to stay with me and Dad one Christmas. She was about six, I was nine and already good mates with Chris. It had snowed that year, and Chris, Lorraine and I were in the garden making a snowman. It wasn't long before Chris and I were flinging snow at each other. Lorraine joined in, but she was only little and wasn't prepared for Chris's snowballs, which were packed together and filled with ice. When one hit Lorraine, she burst into tears. I took her hand and led her indoors to Auntie Annie, leaving Chris in the cold. He'd hurt my little sister, and I wasn't laughing.

Before I was deployed to Afghanistan, Lorraine was on a gap year, travelling in South America. But we'd caught up with each other at Annie's wedding to David a few weeks before I left.

'It must be serious,' Lorraine whispered to me after the ceremony.

'What?' I whispered back.

Lorraine nodded towards Michelle. 'You've never brought a girlfriend to a family occasion before. It must be love.'

'It is,' I said. 'I'm serious about her.'

'I can see that. She's "The One", is she?'

'Yes. I'm going to ask her to marry me, before I go to Afghanistan.'

'Gosh, really? That's lovely news.'

'Ssh, she doesn't know.'

'You've come a long way since playing tonsil tennis with all those girls at school.'

'What?'

'I remember you telling me that you'd been playing tonsil tennis in the corridors at school. I had no idea what you were talking about. I thought it was some cool new sport.' I laughed.

Lorraine was desperate to see me after I was injured, but Dad thought it would be too much for her to take, so he refused to let her come. Auntie Annie was stuck in the middle between her frantic daughter and her stubborn brother. She could see both points of view. In the end, she decided to ask me what I thought. At the mention of Lorraine's name, I waved my arm really vigorously. Correctly, Annie took this as a sign that I wanted to see Lorraine, and she told Dad. He relented, of course. I'd made a decision.

When Lorraine came in the middle of September, it was wonderful to know that she was there. She kissed me and touched me. It must have been tough for her, seeing her big brother lying there, barely able to move, his skin burned away, his body thin and broken. But that's what I was like. And everyone who'd known me as a fit, strong bloke would have to get used to the new look.

Lorraine chatted away about her gap year, her hopes for university and her concerns about student finances. I couldn't speak, but I patted her hand. I wanted to reassure her that she'd be OK. I was so proud of her for going to university.

Annie told me later that Lorraine had considered postponing her place because she felt she couldn't go away to Liverpool with me being so ill. Annie encouraged her to go. She told her that she thought I'd be upset if I knew Lorraine hadn't gone, and she was right. What's the point in having a clever little sister if she's not using her brain?

I knew some of my mates, especially some of my army mates, found it hard to see me the way I was. Keeno found it especially tough. He was with me from the start. We travelled to Afghanistan in the TriStar together and expected to fly home in it together.

The day the Taliban blew me up, Keeno went down with heat stroke and ended up in Bastion with me. He later told me he'd seen me at camp hospital. James Leach had been sitting with me. 'You were covered in bandages,' Keeno said. 'And I still didn't believe it was you.'

There wasn't much of me to see back then, I guess. There was barely any of me left. I was a whisker away from death – I'd *been* dead, in fact. Touch and go doesn't tell the story. But they stabilised me at Camp Bastion and made sure I didn't die again.

One of the nurses who treated me out in the field in Afghanistan visited me at Broomfield. She told me that I'd died twice and been brought back to life. She couldn't believe I'd pulled through.

I am grateful to be alive, don't get me wrong, I truly am. And I would never disrespect my friends who died by believing otherwise. But if I had a choice about serious injury, I'd rather have lost a limb than been burned like this. Burns are so complicated and will cause me to have problems and operations for years to come. If I'd lost a leg, I could have worn a prosthetic leg. Prosthetics are excellent these days. I could have regained my fitness more quickly, covered it up and no one would have to know. I could have even gone back to work. But burns restrict me. They affect the way I move. I can't go out in the sun, and, of course, they've changed the way I look. This is tough for someone who's always taken pride in their appearance, for someone's who's been accused of being vain by his mates. I never thought I was vain. I just wasn't a scruffy git, that was all.

Everywhere I go, people look at me. I don't blame them. If I saw someone who looked like me, I'd look, too. I'd be saying, 'Bloody hell. I wonder what happened to him?' But it's the gawping I can't stand. Don't people realise when they're staring? It makes Michelle mad. She's very protective and ready to kick the arse of anyone who looks at me for too long. Adults should know better, she says.

I don't think about the way I look now. I've dealt with it, and I get on with it. I don't have a lot of choice. Before something like this happens, you have no idea how you're going to cope. You can't guess. Between us, me and Michelle, I'm surprised at how well we've handled it all. When she says she's proud of me and that I've done really well, I always answer, 'We're getting there.'

We are, you know. We always are. That's what every day's about for me and Michelle: getting there, wherever 'there' is. That's what it was about from the day I got back to the UK, burned and broken. It was about getting there. Everything – the operations, the pain, the physio, the days out, the frustration, the visits – has all been part of 'getting there'.

I got a visit from Lieutenant Colonel Edward Smyth-Osbourne in October. He's commanding officer of the Household Cavalry. He was very kind to me, and I liked him a lot. He told me my survival had been amazing and then said I was going to be promoted. I think I said the right thing at the time, which was 'Thank you very much.' But inside I was laughing and thinking, 'Christ, did I have to go through all this just to get a promotion?'

CHAPTER 24

✣⟨⟨⟩⟨·⟩⟩✣

MARTYN – 'TAKE THIS BLOODY THING OUT OF MY NOSE'

BROOMFIELD HOSPITAL, ESSEX – DECEMBER 2006

Auntie Annie and Lorraine were with me, and I said to them, 'I want to buy Michelle a Christmas present. Will you take me into Chelmsford?'

It was a big ask. I still had my nasal gastric tube and the X-Fix on my leg. I was in a wheelchair and not in great shape. I was going to be difficult to handle at the best of times – you had to be careful not to bump me into things, and I was still in pain – but it was going to be double the trouble taking me into Chelmsford at the height of the Christmas shopping frenzy.

But I was determined to buy Michelle some presents. The easy option would've been to ask someone else to go on my behalf. But to me, that wasn't rehabilitation. It wasn't living a normal life, and I was determined to live as close-to-normal a life as possible.

We drove into Chelmsford. The decorations were up. The day was crisp, and shoppers were wrapped up against the chill. Shops were festooned with festive images – Santa in his sleigh, reindeers, snow scenes. People scurried about carrying bags depicting Christmas scenery and greetings. I could smell Christmas, and it got me excited. I don't think Annie and Lorraine were so thrilled.

We crawled through traffic, making our way to a multi-storey car park. We found a parking space, but there were no lifts, so Annie had to push me down the slopes to street level.

I think they were both flustered. They tried not to show it, but it must've been stressful for them. Annie pushed me, and I kept saying 'Mind my leg! Mind my leg!' as we made our way through the crowds. I was worried someone would bump into me. I'd be in agony if a shopper whacked my leg. But my stubborn streak was on show that day. I was buying Michelle a present, and that was that.

We came to Boots. The store was choked with Christmas shoppers. It was like they'd been rammed in there, and now they couldn't move. I could see a lot of shoving in the store, people shouldering past other people. 'I want to go inside,' I said.

Annie said, 'You wait here with Lorraine, and I'll go inside for you.'

'No,' I said. 'I want to go in. I want to buy the present myself.'

I wanted everything to be normal. Why shouldn't I be able to buy my fiancée a Christmas present? They wheeled me through the doors. It was like going into glue. We trundled slowly through the crowds. My impatience grew. I don't like waiting at the best of times – I want things *now*. But Christmas shopping in a wheelchair with an X-Fix on your broken leg . . . that doesn't make for a fun day.

We inched through the crowds. People had to move for me. They bumped into one another. Annie and Lorraine kept their cool, but I don't know how. I got Michelle an electric toothbrush and then queued up to pay. The line was long. It was muggy in the store. People babbled all around me. I felt choked up in there. The gift rested in my lap. I waited for the line to shorten, savouring every foot we moved closer to the tills. Annie and Lorraine breathed sighs of relief when we got out.

'I want to get her a watch,' I said. We wheeled on. The crowds got thicker. Although it was stressful, I felt excitement rise in me. Christmas was coming. I loved Christmas. I loved opening my gifts and loved seeing others opening what I'd bought them. I might not have got what I asked for that first Christmas after my mum had died, but they've all been pretty good ones as far as I can remember. I made sure I enjoyed them. And I was determined to enjoy this one, too.

We got to the jewellers, and Annie said, 'Point out the one you want to get Michelle, and I'll go in and get it.'

I looked up at her. 'I want to go in and get it myself.' I could see their exasperation, but they understood. I could've perhaps chosen a quieter day to try out my 'normal shopping' routine. But if I could manage it during the Christmas frenzy, I could manage it at any time.

I had more shopping to do. I wanted to get toiletries for Michelle and an Eeyore cuddly toy. Lorraine had also recommended some Elizabeth Arden Eight Hour Cream for my sore lips, and I wanted to try it. I was willing to try anything that might help. Elizabeth Arden Eight Hour Cream is a bit of a cult product in the beauty world. Legendary, some might say. Liz Hurley uses it. What on earth would Keeno say?

I was done. Annie and Lorraine were pleased. We made our way back to the car . . . And discovered a host of new challenges. Annie couldn't push me back up the slope to where the car was. I was heavy, and she was wearing high heels. So we decided I'd wait with Lorraine, and Annie'd bring the car to us. Unfortunately, she didn't realise that the car park operated a one-way system, and she ended up at the barrier with a queue of cars behind her. I can't imagine what her stress levels were like as she drove into Chelmsford's one-way system, knowing she'd left me and Lorraine behind. I was only supposed to have gone out for an hour, but I'd been gone for three. I was getting cold, and I needed my medication.

Lorraine and I saw Annie drive off into the one-way system and had to try and guess what she'd do next. We plumped for making our way to a loading bay. Lorraine was terrified of pushing me, because she was worried that I'd fall out and injure myself further. But she reluctantly rolled me along. I shouted instructions, and at one point Lorraine threatened to leave me in the middle of the car park. She didn't mean it, but I was frustrated and taking it out on her. And I'm a terrible back-seat driver, always bossing people about.

We finally met up with Annie, who was red-faced and flustered. She looked at me and said, 'That's the last time I'm taking you Christmas shopping.'

You've got to laugh your way through hospital sometimes. I had an air bed in burns rehab that vibrated and gave me a lovely massage. Auntie Annie and Auntie Lynn were with me, and I wanted to chat to them. I couldn't really speak when the bed was vibrating, as it made my voice all wobbly. But I managed to ask Auntie Annie if she could find out how you switched it off.

The nurse came in, but she didn't know how to stop it. She pressed a few buttons, but that made the massage more violent. I started shouting, 'Stop this bloody thing!' I was in agony.

'Turn it off. He's in pain!' said Auntie Annie, but the nurse didn't know how, and she ran out of the room.

'Christ!' I shouted, my voice quivering.

I could see that Annie and Lynn were trying not to laugh. Then Auntie Annie had an idea and pulled the plug out of the wall. The bed stopped, and even though I'd been in pain, we all dissolved in hysterics.

Having my tracheostomy taken out was weird. It had been put in under anaesthetic, and the tube was attached to my neck with a couple of stitches. But when it came to be taken out, they said

I wouldn't feel a thing. They weren't going to sew it up, either. 'But there's a hole in my neck,' I said.

'It'll heal up by itself,' the nurse told me.

'Right-o,' I said. 'I believe you. You've done this more times than I have.' She was right, of course. I didn't even know when the procedure to remove it was over.

When the tracheostomy was in, it wasn't that secure. If I coughed or sneezed, it shot out. One time, I coughed and it flew out and hit Rosie on the side of the head. She'd never seen it do that before and had no idea what had hit her or why I suddenly couldn't speak. She went into a complete panic while I was waving my arms about, trying to indicate where it was on the floor. She was so flustered she ran out of the room to get help.

I knew Andrew Radford wanted to visit me when he came back to the UK in October 2006. I wanted to see him, too. If he hadn't rescued me, I wouldn't be alive. I felt emotional; perhaps he did as well. But all I managed to say was that I owed him a beer. He showed me pictures of my wagon on his laptop. I stared at the wreckage. I couldn't believe I'd survived. As Radders and I chatted, I learned for the first time exactly what had happened.

Radders was in the third vehicle of the convoy going into Musa Qala, right behind my Spartan. A rocket-propelled grenade struck Mick Flynn's vehicle, the first one in the convoy. Radders' wagon reversed out of the ambush area and waited round a corner. Then there was another explosion. It was like nothing he'd heard before. The back door of our Spartan landed in front of his Scimitar – a couple of tonnes of metal thrown like it was nothing. Fire roared and smoke filled the air.

Mick Flynn came over the radio and said that my Spartan had been hit. Radders was firing like mad, by then, switching between his machine gun and the Scimitar's main armament. It was suppressive fire in the direction he thought the Taliban were shooting from, not necessarily at anyone in particular. He was trying to keep the enemy quiet so the others could get out. It was chaos – noise and sulphur fumes. Then Radders' wagon crept around the corner, and he saw my Spartan. It was a fireball.

Above the noise of fire, his troop leader, Lieutenant Tom Long, asked if Radders could see someone. He pointed to something about 70 metres away. Radders saw someone lying on the floor, barely moving. He assumed it was a Taliban fighter because the figure's skin was very dark. He didn't think it couldn't be one of our boys, because the body was so far from the Spartan. But then he recognised the desert combats. *My* desert combats.

Radders's fourth child, his first daughter, had been born the night before he left for Afghanistan. He only got to hold her for a couple of hours before he left the UK. I don't know how I would've felt if I'd been forced to leave my newborn. Radders obviously wanted to get home to his baby, his three sons and his wife. When he spotted the desert combats, when he knew the figure lying in the distance was a British soldier, he knew what he had to do. And in that moment, he said he hoped it wasn't his time to go.

He said afterwards, 'It's a very personal moment, facing death. I didn't think about Afghanistan, the war, the British public or what the newspapers might say. I only thought about my family. I pushed my feelings aside, threw my kit on, jumped from the vehicle and ran.'

Radders kept firing, and the Taliban fired at him. But he kept his eyes on that injured soldier, on me. He was totally focused. And then he recognised me.

He ran into Leach and Minter making their way back from Mick Flynn's wagon. 'What are you doing?' they shouted.

'Compo's up there. I'm going to go and get him. Cover me,' Radders yelled over the firefight.

They came towards me and ran into Mick Flynn. Radders told him what was going on, and he changed direction as well and ran with Radders. When they got to me, Radders saw that I was a mess. He thought I was going to die. He said the heat coming off my body was immense, and my clothes were in bits and stuck to me. He said he didn't know how I'd mustered the strength to stay alive. I guess no one knows that, not even me. But I'm convinced it was Michelle who kept me going. And Auntie Trina says that it was my mum who came to me on the battlefield and told me it wasn't my time, that I had to live. I don't know. All I know is I'm still here, and if it weren't for Radders, I wouldn't be.

I said, 'Radders, help me,' before I faded.

Mick started checking me. Radders got his morphine out, but he decided against injecting me, because it can be risky – it could've finished me off.

Radders grabbed me and threw me over his shoulder. It hurt, but I was in so much pain anyway, it wouldn't have made a difference if he'd been gentle. And Radders knew he needed to get me out of there quickly. He ran as fast as he could with me over his shoulder. Mick and the others provided cover. They put me on the front of Radders's wagon and drove back to where everyone was waiting. It was crazy. The driver couldn't see where he was going, because they were holding me on the front of the wagon. Radders shouted instructions, telling the driver where to go to avoid the holes in the earth.

Radders thought I was dead when he helped Mick get me off the wagon. But my eyes flickered. They put me in the ambulance, and Paul Hamnett went to work on me.

Keeno was on stag. Someone had told him that CS40 had gone – he knew that CS40 was my vehicle. Radders saw him standing there, staring at me. My mate recognised me because of the tattoo on my arm. It was a Celtic band. I didn't like it. I was planning to have it changed, made bigger or adapted somehow. But it's not there any more. It must have gone when they cut away the burned flesh.

There was still a firefight going on. The Taliban could be seen driving into the village in trucks – partly to continue fighting but also to collect their dead. Chinook helicopters flew in the quick-response team, which consisted of Paras, medics and military police. Mick and the others returned to the scene of the incident to help. The medics and military police did their jobs, collecting the bodies and flying them out on Chinooks.

Radders and the rest stayed nearby that night and returned to Bastion the following day. I know Radders didn't think I'd make it. I'm not surprised, the mess I was in. He said later, 'I called my wife as soon as I could. It was very emotional. I told her what happened, and she sobbed at how close I'd come to dying.

'I'd never experienced anything as intense as that day. I had bad dreams, lots of the lads did. My wife tells me I still do. Fortunately, I don't remember them. The support is there from the army if I need it, but I haven't yet. I will go back to Afghanistan one day, I'm sure. It's part of my job. It's what I do.'

Mick Flynn's Scimitar entered the village first, and he knew something wasn't right. I later remembered that he'd told us to change formation so that we were closer together and better able to cover each other. A soldier with Mick's experience senses when something's going to happen. He served in the Falklands War in 1982, left the army for a while in the 1990s, then joined up again.

It wasn't long before Mick's suspicions were proved correct. As he pushed forward, he spotted holes in the high walls of the compound: man-made holes from where Taliban fighters would be watching us; holes that they could push their weapons through. In hindsight, it was the perfect ambush. It was our only way through, and they knew it.

Mick looked towards my vehicle and could see that I was rumbling towards him. He looked forward again, and that was when the first rocket-propelled grenade hit his wagon and the fighting began. 'Ambush – ambush – contact – RPG,' he shouted.

Machine-gun fire erupted. Mick had to decide what to do. He had three options: he could try and get out by going backwards; he could stay where he was and fight; or he could fight his way forward. He had the blink of an eye in which to make his choice. He chose option three – go forward, fighting.

Mick chose the last option because the Taliban wouldn't expect it. They thought he would retreat. He was right. That's why they let me go forward over the improvised-explosive device before watching me reverse back over it and blowing it up. They probably wanted to get as many vehicles in front of the improvised-explosive device as possible then destroy the last vehicle to block our path of retreat and create a killing zone.

At the end of the alley in front of Mick was a machine-gun position. Mick's crew took them out and killed several other Taliban. He then decided to try and get back towards the rest of us. It was a good decision. Ahead of him, the path split, and he discovered later that there was an ambush waiting whichever way he went. As he turned to look back down the alley, there was a dogleg in the road. He could see smoke and realised that no other vehicles had followed him.

One of the things many people remember about that day was that there was a problem with Mick's communications system. The button had got stuck on his radio – he was on permanent send. We could hear every word he was saying – mainly effing, blinding and abuse – but no one could say anything back to him.

Trooper James Leach was Mick's driver and Trooper Paul Minter his gunner. Not surprisingly, Leach wasn't keen to go back through the ambush site. He'd already had a close shave that day. Mick had told him to shut his hatch to be safe, and Leach had been reluctant. It was too hot, and he couldn't see that there was any immediate danger. A few seconds after he'd battened down, the rocket-propelled grenade hit the wagon two inches above where his head had been. If he hadn't done what Mick had said, it would have taken his head off.

The roar of that rocket-propelled grenade left Leach shaken and dazed. He could barely hear as Mick told him to turn around, and as they did so, the fourth rocket-propelled grenade hit them.

Mick, Leach and Minter reached my tank. It was on fire, and our ammunition was causing constant explosions. They could see a hole in the front of it where the rocket-propelled grenade had sliced through. Mick couldn't ram my wagon out of the way, but there was a ditch on his left, so he commanded Leach to run up to it at best speed and take the wagon through. The wagon got stuck. Mick, Leach and Minter abandoned it and, using their drills and skills, fought their way up the hill on foot, taking fire all the way. Mick did look in the back of my Scimitar but didn't imagine that anyone could have survived. Then he ran into Radders.

'There's somebody over there,' shouted Radders.

'Well, shoot him,' Mick yelled.

'I think he's one of ours.'

Radders was right. It was me.

I've had a lot of time to think about what Radders and Mick did. It's difficult to find the words – I still find it difficult to this day – to express my gratitude. Radders just ran for me. Through gunfire, through hell, he came.

Sometimes people are surprised when they hear that I joined the army in 2000 but didn't fight until 2006. They ask me what I was doing all that time. What I was doing was training. We do things over and over and over again, making sure that everyone's weaknesses get up to standard. I realise now that that's what the punishment in basic training is about. Doing 20 press-ups because your colleague fucked up isn't about being pissed off with him. It's about him realising that if he doesn't buck up, he's letting everyone down. It's not cruel because that's what saves our lives.

We're working hard. You might not realise it when you're getting up dead early to drive to Lulworth to do your Advanced Signals course or when you're driving people about at Longmore practice village. But all the time we're living, working and training. The saying goes that we train hard to fight easy. And whether we realise it or not, we're bonding. I believe it's that bond that makes our army what it is: the best in the world.

It's that bond that made Chris Finney GC do what he did in Iraq. It's that bond that made Andrew Radford run for me. It was that bond that brought me home from war.

FRITTENDEN, KENT – DECEMBER 2006

I left Broomfield Hospital on 11 December 2006. My dad tried to thank the nurses but couldn't find the words to express his gratitude. Sometimes thank you just doesn't seem adequate.

I moved into Rosie and Brian's, so I could be with Michelle. I was still in my wheelchair. My leg hadn't healed. Rosie and Brian adapted their home to accommodate me. They put in ramps so I could be wheeled in and out, widened doors and moved a bedroom downstairs so I didn't have to struggle upstairs. They were wonderful, welcoming me into their home. And, of course, Harvey was there, bouncing about, wagging his tail.

We'd been transferring stuff from the hospital to the Cliffords' house in Frittenden for a couple of days. Clothes, CDs, DVDs, books, letters – they all had to come with us. We'd lived in that hospital for nearly four months. It was like moving house. And there were Michelle's Christmas presents, too. Piles of them. Added to those I'd bought in Chelmsford with Annie and Lorraine – best forgotten, that day – were a few I'd purchased in Maidstone when Kevin and Katie had taken me to do some more shopping.

Being back at Rosie and Brian's was wonderful. I looked around for a while, not believing that I was finally out of hospital. It brought a lump to my throat, and I could feel the emotion rise up in me. This was a real home. This was normal. I was looking forward to being with Michelle, to spending time with her in another environment. I was looking forward to eating properly, to good home cooking. And there was no one better than Rosie at making sure I'd get fed decent grub.

I'd still been having tussles with the nutritionist at the hospital. We'd not been seeing eye to eye right up to my discharge date. She wasn't happy about the amount I was eating, but I argued that the portions coming out of the kitchen at Broomfield were too small. The kitchen manager did come to see me in the end and asked me what I liked. That was decent of him to do that. But I still wanted home cooking, and lots of it. I had a big appetite. Not everyone – particularly burns patients – can eat like I do. I was trying to get that across.

The nutritionist and I had a meeting a couple of weeks before I left hospital. We had to discuss what needed to be in place before I could leave – the kind of food I was going to eat to build myself up. The nutritionist was dubious about me going home, because I wasn't eating properly. And although I didn't think the portions were big enough for my eat-for-England cravings, the gastric tube that went up my nose and down into my stomach didn't help much, either. Every time the food touched it, it made me gag and cough.

The nutritionist said that I would have to be fed straight into my stomach if I didn't eat properly. I wasn't happy about that. It would have meant two more operations: one to put the stomach tube in and one to take it out at some point in the future. The surgeons weren't keen for me to have any more anaesthetics than necessary. But if the nutritionist insisted, I suppose they would've gone ahead.

Luckily for me, the nutritionist went on holiday. A day later, when I was on my own with a senior nurse, I said to her, 'Take this bloody thing out of my nose. I want to go home without it, and I know I'll be fine when I get back to Rosie's home cooking. I'll start eating more.'

The nurse knew I was right. She'd seen me enjoying Rosie's shepherd's pies. The nurse drew it out of my nose quickly so I didn't have time to think about it, but it felt really weird spooling out of me, and there was a void after it had been withdrawn. But it was out, and I could start to enjoy food without gagging.

By the time the nutritionist had come back from holiday, I was home – no tube. I'd soon start eating four meals a day and snacks on top of those.

That first evening at Rosie and Brian's, sitting round a table, eating a meal at home, was a great way to start my new eating regime, which basically meant scoffing anything put in front of me.

I was tired. It had been a long day. I looked across at Michelle. It was time I was in bed. Nerves fluttered in my belly. I'd not slept in a normal bed in five months. And I'd not shared a bed with Michelle in all that time, either. My heart thundered. I didn't know what it would be like. We said goodnight to Rosie and Brian and went into our bedroom. Lying next to her was wonderful. Feeling her body next to mine, for the first time since I'd left for Afghanistan, was a moment I treasure and keep in my heart. My skin was ravaged, and I couldn't move much or shift towards her, but the sensation of Michelle snuggling up to me was magical. It was everything. I closed my eyes and felt calmness wash over me. I was home. I was with Michelle. There was nothing else.

The Defence Medical Rehabilitation Centre Headley Court is in Epsom, Surrey. I'd be spending a lot of time there over the next couple of years. It sits in 85 acres of land and is used as a rehabilitation centre for injured Armed Forces personnel. Two hundred staff, including nurses, physiotherapists, social workers and occupational therapists, work there. There are up to sixty patients on the two main wards, where they help patients with disabilities, as well as those suffering post-traumatic stress disorder. In another accommodation block over the road, there are people needing less intense treatment – people who've picked up sports injuries and need to regain fitness to get back to work. There are hydrotherapy pools and gyms, but Headley Court still needs more facilities. In October 2007, the charity Help For Heroes was set up mainly to raise money to build new facilities there.

Headley was expecting me. Staff there had been in contact with staff at Broomfield to make sure that everyone knew what was best for me. The Headley wheelchair department had already provided Broomfield with a wheelchair that could accommodate my X-Fix.

I first went to Headley Court on 12 December, the day after I'd come home from Broomfield. I got to have a look round. I'd be a regular there from 20 February 2007 – just a couple of months away. It's in a great spot, rural and peaceful. It was going to play a vital part in my recovery, but I was fed up that I had to go back for treatment. It felt like a step back to me. I was already going to be returning to Broomfield three days a week as an outpatient. I just wanted to be at home, getting on with my life.

But looking around Headley Court, I thought that if I had to be somewhere, this place was as good as any. I wanted to get better. I wanted to walk Michelle down the aisle. If coming to Headley Court and going back and forth to Broomfield would get me there, then that's what I'd have to do.

The next day – 13 December – I was at Broomfield to start my life as an outpatient. A burn is for life, as Peter Dziewulski had told us. It's continually treated. I'd be going to Broomfield for that purpose. They'd bathe me and put clean dressings on my wounds, and I'd also be put through physio sessions.

There was a lot of me that needed building up again. I had one particularly nasty problem that might hinder my goal of walking Michelle down the aisle. Because my shin muscles had wasted away, I developed a condition called drop foot, which meant I couldn't lift my feet. It was vital to strengthen my lower legs. Getting over this condition would mean I'd have a better chance of achieving my wedding-day ambition. It was tough, it was painful, but when you're a stubborn sod, you can get through most things.

The Broomfield sessions lasted two hours, three times a week. Michelle drove me there, and when she was at school, Rosie took me. I could've transferred somewhere nearer to home, but I had confidence in the staff at Broomfield. I felt comfortable with them. They had me on the right track, and I wanted to stick with them. Going there three times a week was frustrating, but it was for the best.

Before I went home on 11 December, I had a shopping spree. I bought a bed, a TV, a computer and an Xbox 360. I'd always wanted an Xbox 360, but I feared I wouldn't be able to use it and enjoy it. Michelle persuaded me that it would be good rehabilitation for my hands. And it was, especially for my thumbs.

I loved being at home. I was like a big kid again. I wouldn't sit still. I was back to my former fidget-arse self. I wasn't quite so freewheeling now, but I was making a go of it – on the computer, on the Xbox, off out with Michelle, never stopping. And no one was telling me what to do. I could do what I wanted. I was a bit of a nightmare to start with, because there wasn't much that I could do for myself. I was very weak and depended on Michelle, Brian and Rosie to help me.

Rosie was fantastic. If Michelle was at work, she'd massage my neck, making sure my skin was supple. The skin grafts got very tight and sore if they weren't manipulated. 'Rosie, will you do my neck?' I'd say. She always did.

She did everything I asked of her, but I still had the cheek to have a laugh at her expense now and again. For example, she'd be washing or dressing me, and I'd yell, 'Mind the X-Fix,' giving her a start. It was probably quite annoying for her, since I'd been shooting around the garden on my mobility scooter the previous day, X-Fix and all, with not a care in the world.

If neither Michelle nor Rosie were around – Rosie was a carer, so had to work – someone came in to help me, because I couldn't go to the toilet or eat by myself. That was frustrating and really annoyed me. I was still as stubborn as hell. You can't paint that streak out of me, but it's done me good. I won't let anything get in my way if I want to do something – even if other people might get pissed off with me. But mostly people were wonderful.

Michelle and I were with Katie and Kevin at The Bull in Bethersden. Kev was taking the mick out of me and really making me laugh. The four of us were roaring and having a great time. A man came over, a shy smile on his face. For a second, I thought he was going to ask us to be quiet, but it was a pub, and he wasn't likely to do that. Looking at me, he said, 'I hope you don't mind, but I had to come over and say this: you sitting there, smiling and laughing, has inspired me.'

I thanked him. It was a nice thing for him to do and gave me a spurt of confidence. It's great to hear that you inspire someone. Katie and Michelle were welling up. It was emotional. The guy obviously thought I was overcoming my injuries, being positive despite what had happened to me. But what other way can you be?

We liked hanging out with Katie and Kevin. They lived in a cottage in Hurst Green, a village that's a half-hour drive from Frittenden. There's a narrow path and several steps before you get to their door. The first time I visited them, I struggled with my wheelchair, getting flustered and frustrated. Michelle was trying to push me, and Kev was trying to lift the front of the chair. They were practically carrying me down the path. When you get to the end of the path, there's a sharp left turn leading down some narrow stone steps. They heaved and lurched me round the corner and trundled me down the steps.

I turned the air blue after getting to the door, curses of relief shooting out of my mouth – but once inside, there was a sharp bend into the living room. They didn't design houses with me in mind. It was madness trying to get into the cottage, but I was determined. I wanted to pop round like I'd always done. But this was hardly 'popping round' – it was a military operation if I'd ever seen one.

Once inside, I was knackered, huffing and puffing. But with only my underarm sweat glands left because of my injuries, I couldn't sweat much. And with it being December, they had their wood-burning stove on. With a biting winter breeze in the air, they had to open the window to cool me down. It was a hassle but worth it to see Katie and Kevin again.

'So when are you coming round to help me decorate?' said Kev. I'd written to them from Afghanistan, promising to help. Not much chance of doing that now. But it didn't stop Kev joking about it – and I appreciated that. I like a laugh and can take a wind-up as well as I can give one. Having a laugh with mates such as Kev makes me feel normal. Some people are strange about it, but I don't care. Let me take the piss out of myself if I want to. Let my mates take the piss out of me. I'll take the piss out of them in return. Humour keeps you going – and the darker, the better.

I might've been pig-headed, wanting to do things and go places that were awkward and difficult for me, but I didn't have a 'sod it, let's do it' approach to everything.

Pain scared me. And if something that was meant to be good for me hurt, I was reluctant to do it. I was supposed to reach up to the top of my head to stop the skin under my arms tightening too much. But it was painful, so I didn't do it as much as I should have. And if I had an itch on my scalp, I would ask Michelle to scratch it for me. I should've done it myself – it would've done me good, not only getting rid of the itch, but also giving my skin a good stretch.

Eating became very stressful, too. I still couldn't easily bend my elbow to reach my mouth. I had an adapted spoon with a padded handle because I couldn't grip, but it took me ages to eat. When I'm hungry, I want to shovel in food as fast as I can. But I couldn't eat quickly, as I could only get little pieces on the spoon at a time. I wanted Michelle to feed me, even though I hated being fed – it made me feel so helpless – but she didn't want to. She wanted me to be more patient and get better at it myself. It became such an effort that I gave up and stopped eating for a while. It was bloody frustrating. But ultimately, if I carried on like that, I'd have to be fed for the rest of my life. And I didn't want that. It was so difficult. My elbow hurt when I tried to bend it to feed myself, so I gave up trying because of the pain and had to depend on other people to hoist food into my mouth. It was driving me crazy – catch-22, going round in circles.

I knew the answer. I just had to push through the pain. I gritted my teeth and forced myself to do it. What kind of bridegroom would I be if I walked Michelle down the aisle, then at the reception had to have her feed me because I couldn't bend my elbow?

So where would the big day take place? I knew about Port Lympne, of course. It's an animal park near Hythe in 600 acres of Kent countryside. They've got rhinos, tigers, elephants, lions, monkeys . . . it's a jungle out there.

The mansion, where we were to be married, was built in 1912. Inside, it is like a Roman villa, with marble pillars and a stone staircase, and the floor in the hallway is black-and-white marble. Troops were billeted there during the Second World War, so there was a military connection. The mansion's set in 15 acres of terraced gardens, and that's where we'd have the ceremony: outside on the terrace overlooking the English Channel.

I'd not seen the venue, and I wanted to have a nose. We drove over just before Christmas. The X-Fix was still attached, and I couldn't walk, so I took my mobility scooter. Areas of the park are quite steep, so it can be difficult for disabled people, but Port Lympne go out of their way to help.

We trundled around the park, me on the scooter, Michelle walking beside me. The animals were great. It was a wonderful experience. But a December chill hung in the air, and we were getting cold. 'Come on, Mich,' I said. 'Jump on and we'll fly around quickly.'

She hopped on the scooter, although she wasn't too comfortable. We chugged along the park's walkways. Reaching the end of the tour, we came to a slope. It was steep, and the scooter conked out halfway up. Michelle got off, and I told her she'd have to push me. She heaved, but neither me nor the scooter would budge.

'What does that switch on the back do?' I said.

What it did was release the gear. We realised that when Michelle pressed it and I started to roll down the slope. Michelle tried to stand in my way, pushing against the scooter. But her trainers slipped on the damp earth. She moved out of the way, shouting desperately.

I yelled as I rumbled down the slope. Michelle's face stretched in horror. I steered with no idea of where I was going or what was going to happen. If I crashed and landed on my leg, it could do me permanent damage – I might not have been able to walk Michelle down the aisle. I might not have been able to walk ever again. It was no joke.

I guided the scooter into the fence. I was jerked off the machine and tossed backwards. I was waiting for the pain when my leg smashed under me. Luckily, I got away with it, falling on my back. I yelled for Michelle. Pain still rifled through me, but at least I'd not crushed my leg.

Michelle raced towards me, asking me if I was hurt, panic in her voice. I told her I was OK and just to get me up. She was shaking with fear as she struggled to get me on the scooter again. 'I'm all right, babe,' I said, trying to calm her nerves. 'Honest, I'm fine.'

Christmas Day was magical. Michelle, Rosie, Brian, Katie, Kevin and I had lunch, with me eating off my big plate again – albeit food that someone else had cut up for me, which I ate with a knife and fork with padded handles.

I've had happy times in my life, but you can't measure them – there's no 'happy gauge'. But if there was, that day was a ten out of ten. The love I felt in that house was overwhelming.

I tried to express to Michelle how much I loved her in a Christmas card. We hadn't even known each other a year, and she'd shown me more dedication than many people experience in a lifetime. How do you put that into words? I didn't know, but I did my best in my huge, spidery writing. I'd been practising at Broomfield. Joanna had given me a board to write on. But I wrote one nice message to Michelle, then was so chuffed with it that I refused to remove it. 'It took me nearly an hour to do that,' I told Joanna when she encouraged me to wipe it off and start again. It looked as if a child had written my card to Michelle, because I couldn't grip the pen properly, but she was touched, and that was enough for me.

There was one dark cloud hovering over everything, though – I lost at Monopoly. It pissed me off. I can't bear losing. I went to my room and put my head down. I was tired by that time, so it wasn't all about being in a huff. It had been a long day, a long few weeks, a long few months.

Christmas was like being a kid again, and I was able to forget about a lot of the shit that had happened to me. I got a hoard of presents. Michelle bought me a shooting game. It looked like a Christmas tree. A ball balanced on each 'branch'. When you switched it on, the balls were blown upwards by a gust of air. There was a little gun that fired sponge pellets, and you had to shoot at the balls.

I loved it, and so did Kev. We played it for hours, until 'Monopolygate' spoiled the party. Michelle also bought me an Armani watch. The one I'd had in Afghanistan was a G-Shock. Miraculously, it had come back to the UK having survived the whole thing and is still going strong, despite a few scorch marks. But now I wanted something new. I was happy looking at my arms again. I'd put on weight and had started to feel better about myself.

This must have had something to do with being home. I wanted nothing more than a normal life, and doing stuff that normal blokes do made me happy. I went to The Bell and Jorrocks pub in Frittenden with my dad. He'd go on his bike, me on my mobility scooter. Chris Humphrey took me for a drink as well, to The Bull in Sissinghurst, and it was good to have him around. Chris was great, treating me as if nothing had changed. I even got to go and watch Michelle play football. It was pelting down with rain, and the fields were like swimming pools. Brian had to persuade the guys on the gate to let us drive through to another field, because there was no way my wheelchair would have made it through the mud. We parked up, and I watched the game from the car – best seat in the house.

The mobility scooter was a great help. It got me out and about and gave me some independence. I whizzed around the garden on it and scared Rosie half to death when we went out for a walk. I think I took a few too many risks for her liking, scooting up banks and jolting over mounds.

The day after Boxing Day, we went to Devon to see my family. Rosie and Brian came too, and the visit capped a wonderful Christmas for me. I was home with my Michelle, four months after having been blown up, set on fire and shot. Four months after dying. It felt like I'd put those months behind me, and now I could look forward to the future with Michelle.

But I got my feet under the table a little too quickly. Life tricked me into thinking everything was OK. It wasn't. I had mountains to climb before I'd be close to being where I wanted to be. And I had to be kicked up the arse before I risked the climb.

CHAPTER 25

⁂

MICHELLE – 'IF YOU DON'T GO SOON, YOU'LL NEVER GO'

FRITTENDEN, KENT – JANUARY 2007

'Pass me the remote control,' said Martyn.

I glanced at him. We were sitting in the living room watching television. The remote sat on the coffee table. I looked at the gadget for a second then said, 'Get it yourself.'

He grunted, looked at the remote and then leaned forward to reach for it. He got it, though it was a struggle for him. Leaning back on the couch, he made another noise then started channel hopping.

I didn't want to be Martyn's carer; I wanted to be his wife. I knew there were certain things I had to do for him. I was cleaning the pin sites in his X-Fix, for example. Those are the pieces that go into his leg, and they had to be kept sterile to avoid infection. That was obviously something he was unable to do, but such things were temporary – he wouldn't have that scaffolding around his leg for much longer. I also had to feed him, wash him, dress him, take him to the toilet, massage his scars – it was exhausting for me, and I know it was frustrating for him.

He wanted to get better. He had to get better. And to get better he had to do things for himself – such as reaching for the remote control. Such a simple act was beneficial to Martyn. It helped to keep his skin supple and aided his muscles. He was seriously injured and had terrible wounds, but he was getting better, and if he was going to walk me down the aisle, he'd have to push himself.

Martyn was determined, I knew that. And his stubborn streak, his strength, saw him recover quicker than the doctors expected. But his stubborn streak also extended to him not doing things if they caused him pain. It was difficult for me. I hated seeing him hurt, and I wanted to help him. But more than anything I wanted him better.

Having him come home was wonderful. Removing the pictures from the walls in Martyn's room at Broomfield felt like a considerable milestone to me, and his homecoming was thrilling. Months before, I'd seen him lying on a bed, his body wrecked, barely anything left of him. But thanks to the brilliance of all those people at Broomfield, and to Martyn's own pig-headedness, he pulled through. He came back to me to say he still loved me and still wanted to marry me. He came home. But I can't pretend that being his carer wasn't difficult, and I continually reminded myself that it wouldn't be for ever.

Christmas was wonderful. He was there with us, being the Martyn I adored: cracking jokes, eating off his big plate, sulking when he lost at Monopoly – he certainly hadn't lost his competitive streak. Presents filled the house; Martyn was the recipient of most of them. It was great to see him enjoying himself. I bought him a shooting game. He had one or two for the Xbox he'd bought, but this one was a bit different, a bit less violent. I did think it strange that he wasn't bothered about playing violent shooting games. After all, he'd been in the real thing and had came out of it badly. He'd seen men die – seen the effects of guns. But it didn't trouble him, and I was relieved that, psychologically at least, he remained strong.

There had been instances when watching violence caused him to react. When he came out of his coma and was able to watch TV in rehab, he didn't want to see anything with shooting in it. We had to be careful which films we chose, but occasionally we got it wrong. We were watching *The Hills Have Eyes*, the 2006 remake of Wes Craven's 1977 horror film. In one scene, a character is tied to a tree and set on fire. I chilled when I saw what was happening and glanced at Martyn. He couldn't watch. I hurriedly grabbed the remote and pressed fast-forward. My throat was dry, and I felt dreadful. I didn't know what to say, so we didn't mention it. That's for the best sometimes – say nothing.

Although Martyn had learned to cope with fictional violence by the time he came home, he still found news stories about the war difficult to sit through. He said he didn't want to think about it, and I wasn't about to force him to confront his fears when he'd been through so much. It was one thing to make him reach for a TV remote control, but I'd never make him sit through a news report about soldiers being killed or injured in action.

But he was getting better, physically and psychologically. And he had to continue to get better. Headley Court would help get him healthy. We'd been to Surrey to visit the rehabilitation centre just before Christmas, and although Martyn felt at peace being among army people again, he was ambivalent about going back there for rehabilitation.

Although he was undecided about it at Christmas, by the new year he was quite hostile to the idea. 'It feels like a step back,' he said. 'Like I'm going back to hospital.'

'If you don't go soon, you'll never go,' I said. 'You'll just keep putting it off.'

'I'm enjoying being at home.'

'You've got a lot of work to do to get back to full fitness. Headley Court can help you.' He said nothing. He knew I was right, but that didn't make me feel any better. A pit formed in my stomach. I didn't want to lose Martyn again, but I knew it was for the best. I could switch off emotionally from it, but it was hard for him after the months he'd lain in hospital, desperate to clutch again at a semblance of normality.

I said, 'It'll give us back our relationship. We'll be excited to see each other again.' He looked at me, and I saw in his eyes that he knew it was for the best. He knew that Headley Court would keep alive his hope of walking me down the aisle.

'It's like a part of me's been taken away,' said Martyn, looking down at his leg.

'Will they let you keep it?' I asked.

He shook his head. 'It's too expensive, they'll use it again.' He kept staring at his leg. It had been a long time since we'd seen it without the scaffolding attached to it.

They removed the X-Fix on 19 January. It was a big step for Martyn, for both of us. The hospital gave him a Zimmer frame but warned us he wasn't supposed to use it unless someone was with him. That's like warning a greyhound not to chase a rabbit. I went back to school, leaving Martyn at home with Mum. He couldn't resist using the Zimmer frame, sneaking up on her and giving her a scare.

Mum said, 'I try to put it out of his way, but he always manages to get to it.'

That's Martyn for you. I knew he was bored. Headley Court couldn't come soon enough.

CHAPTER 26

꧁ ꧂

MARTYN – I SAW A 50P COIN ON THE PILE OF RUBBISH

I was bored and a bit gloomy. Michelle was back at school, and I was putting off going to Headley Court. I cheered up when I received a call from Alistair Galloway, an officer from the regiment. I knew him well and was chuffed to hear he was coming to Frittenden and bringing some of my mates.

I'd got to know Alistair in 2003, when the Household Cavalry put together a ski team. If you were fit, young, determined and happy to go away for a couple of months, you got an invite. I was well up for what sounded like a great adventure. There were about a dozen of us and two officers, one of whom was Alistair.

We made our way across Norway. Alistair and I were in the truck with all the equipment. One day, we pulled over by a café, and I ran in to get some hot grub. I'd done most of the journey, and Alistair had volunteered to get behind the wheel to give me a break. You don't normally find yourself giving orders to an officer, but as I got back to the van, I turned to Alistair and said, 'And don't chuck it in the ditch.' He took it on the chin. It's an army joke that officers can't drive.

The countryside was beautiful, with thick snow everywhere, but the roads were lethal, slippery with ice. I'm not quite sure what happened next, but there was a screech and a looming lorry, and two minutes later we were in a ditch. I looked at Alistair. 'What happened there?' I asked. 'And how are we going to get out of this ditch?'

An artic truck was parked nearby. I was still munching on my burger, so I let Alistair do the international conversation bit. The guy had some spare snow chains, but it still took 40 minutes to get us out, and the guy nearly jack-knifed his vehicle. The rest of the team had gone on ahead. So much for no man left behind.

A couple of hours later and we were on our way. I took the wheel. Al and I really bonded after that. He was still my boss, and I had a lot of respect for him. But he was prepared to laugh at himself and, crucially, was willing to let me laugh at him, too.

We were doing Nordic skiing, the really hardcore stuff you see on Eurosport. It's like cross-country running, but you're on tiny skis. You ski uphill, pulling yourself up as quickly as you can with sticks and every muscle in your body. Then you ski down little tracks. It's incredibly demanding and quite an art. We were competing against other army teams in a biathlon. We would ski like maniacs then shoot targets, controlling our heart rates so we could aim straight.

I loved being fit. I would never say I was the fittest, because there's always going to be another soldier who's fitter than you, but I could run a mile in seven and half minutes. Nine minutes is considered very fit. It's expected in the army that you can run eight miles in two hours carrying thirty pounds. I had no problems with that.

An Olympic medallist was training us, and we were fitter than ever when it was over. So much so that some of the lads went on to SAS selection.

At the weekends, we'd do ordinary skiing for fun. I'd never done that before either. 'You'll be all right, you'll pick it up,' one of the other soldiers told me.

'All right, boys. I'll follow you,' I said. 'Where are we going? A black slope? Right, what do I do?'

'Hold tight,' someone suggested.

I watched everyone ski off one by one. It looked a bit more complicated then just 'holding tight'. They seemed to be steering, and they knew how to stop. I watched as they gathered in a group at the bottom. Eventually, they started shouting up at me. 'Come on, Compo. We're freezing our bollocks off down here!'

There was nothing for it but to fling myself down the slope. I shot past the team like a bullet, letting out a scream. I couldn't stop at the end. I finished in a crumpled heap. Everyone was in hysterics. I couldn't say I'd mastered the black run, but I suppose I'd at least gone down it.

All in all, it was a fantastic six weeks. We stayed in a chalet, took turns to cook, had a few drinks at the weekend and, most of all, had a great laugh. My turn to cook was on Fridays, but every Friday afternoon we'd go drinking. When it was nearly time to eat, I'd go back to the chalet while the lads went for a sauna. I always decided on pizza, because I thought they were foolproof to prepare. But I'd invariably burn them, because I'd fall asleep at the table while they were cooking.

Alistair and I became good friends, although he had to leave Norway early, as he was deploying to Iraq. That's the job, I suppose. But so was the trip, and, in my opinion, it was some of the very best of what life in the army offers: great activities, great friendships and great times. And, unbelievably, I was being paid to do it.

I'm not sure what my future in the army will be, but I won't be going Nordic skiing with the lads again. I didn't realise how great all those things were until someone took them from me.

Andrew Radford was coming to see me with Alistair. Before the visit, Alistair had given Andrew a 50p coin. The coin, commissioned to commemorate 150 years of the Victoria Cross, showed an injured soldier being carried by his comrade. Alistair thought the image would be significant to Radders.

The three of us had a great afternoon. They filled me in on the regiment gossip, then, as they left, Radders gave me the coin. I looked at the silver disc and the image depicted on it. Radders didn't know it, but it was a 50p coin that had made me join the army. My mind drifted back . . .

It was a summer's day – dead hot and brilliant. Chris and I, both about 15 at the time, were racing about on our bikes as usual. We decided to return to the derelict house on Staplehurst High Street. We raced over there and leaped off our bikes. The house had been boarded up since our last visit.

'One of these planks has got to be loose,' I said as we circled the house.

'Here's one,' he yelled.

'Keep your bloody voice down. We don't want the whole neighbourhood to know we're here.' I wiggled the board. It came away with just enough room to squeeze through.

'Best we take our bikes in so no one knows we're here,' said Chris.

'If you think you can get yours through that hole, mate, you go for it,' I told him. 'You first.'

Chris always went first on our escapades. He was up for anything, and I loved him for it. If it would make me laugh, Chris would do it; if it made him laugh, I'd be up for it.

I flung my bike in a bush. Chris followed suit. He squatted by the gap. It took him a few minutes and quite a bit of swearing to get through. Seconds later, he poked his head back through the hole and said, 'You coming?'

Chris and I stood blinking in the house, getting our eyes accustomed to the gloom and dust. We began roaming. I don't know what we were looking for – trouble, I suppose. And if we couldn't find any, we'd create our own.

We spotted two planks of wood on the floor. I grabbed one

and threw the other to Chris. We began to whack anything we could see – a bookshelf here, a windowsill there. We laughed as they splintered and cracked. The noises they made excited us. Demolishing stuff was fun.

We continued through the house, up the stairs and into the third-floor flat. A pile of rubble covered the floor. I looked up and saw it had spilled from a hole in the ceiling. I jumped up and started poking the hole with my plank. More stuff began to fall through. A heap of plaster rained down, bringing all kinds of rubble with it. We were both laughing. Dust swirled around the room. Then I saw a 50p coin on the pile of rubbish. I pounced on it.

We both heard the noise at the same time: sirens, very close. We froze. 'Shit,' said Chris. 'Police.' We crept to the doorway. Someone had obviously heard us and reported a break-in. The cops were in the house. Torch beams sliced the gloom. I slipped the 50p into my pocket, looked at Chris and gestured towards a door on the other side of the room. We started creeping towards it. But we were too late.

'What are you two up to?' We turned. Three coppers stood in the doorway of the flat.

I don't know why, but in that moment I decided looking for money was a more noble pursuit than smashing stuff up. I took the 50p from my pocket. 'We found some money,' I said, showing them my coin, 'and we wondered if there was more. I think it's coming through the ceiling.'

'Right,' said one copper, obviously not believing a word of it. 'Downstairs. We're taking you to the station.'

As Chris and I were handcuffed and put in the back of the police car, it all seemed like a bit of a laugh, and we grinned at each other. But by the next morning, it wasn't funny at all. The police had rung my dad, who'd suggested a night in the cells would do us good. 'That should sort the pair of them out,' he'd said, and the police had agreed.

Chris and I were put in separate cells and started our stay by tapping on the walls to one another. However, come the next morning, neither of us had slept. We were tired, fed up and reality was kicking in – our parents were on their way to collect us. The shit was going to hit the fan.

I sat in the back of the car between Chris and his mum. The dads were in front, surly-faced. Chris and I didn't dare look at each other. Not even my grand loot of 50p, still in my pocket, could cheer me up.

As we got indoors, Dad told me to sit down while he took his coat off. I went into the sitting room. I thought I was going to be shouted at, but when Dad came back into the room, he stood with his arms folded and looked at me. 'Well?' he asked. 'What have you got to say for yourself?'

'I didn't like it in that police cell, and I'm never going back. I know that.' But I didn't know how I was going to stop myself getting into trouble.

After a few weeks of thinking about my life and what I was going to do with it, I came to a decision. 'Dad,' I said, looking at him, then down at my shoes. 'I've made a decision. I'm going to behave myself from now on.' I looked up at my father. 'And, Dad, I've made another decision.'

'Yes?'

'I'm joining the army.'

It seemed like an obvious decision. I loved the outdoors, and I loved sport. I'd been in the cadets. It was the perfect career for me. And deep down I knew it was either that or spend the rest of my life getting into trouble. We didn't talk about it much, but Dad was pleased for me, so I finished school and joined up.

Staring at the coin, my thoughts returned to Radders. He risked his life to save mine. He ran through bullets without a moment's hesitation and carried me to safety. I hadn't been able to find the words to thank him – it was a bloke thing – but I hoped he knew I was more grateful than I could ever express.

I wondered if one day some kid – a little sod like I'd been

– would pick up this coin and think about the soldiers depicted on it and what the rescue shown on the coin meant. I hoped that if he did, he'd be a lucky kid. Lucky enough to have mates who'd stick by him through thick and thin. Mates he'd risk his life to rescue. Mates who'd have the courage to rescue him.

If you ever see me in the street, you might think I'm unlucky. You'd be so wrong. I'm actually very, very lucky. Because I had mates such as Radders, who put his life on the line to make sure I got home alive.

HEADLEY COURT – FEBRUARY 2007

The bloke on guard waved us through. 'That's it,' I said to Michelle, as she drove us through the gates. 'I'm back in the army now.'

It had been nearly seven months since my injury, and I was arriving at Headley Court. In one way, it felt so familiar – blokes in uniform purposefully striding about, giving and taking orders, saluting each other – but I was way out of my comfort zone and had no idea what the weeks ahead would bring.

The plan was that I'd arrive at Headley each Tuesday morning and leave on Friday evening. Michelle would come and visit me each Wednesday night. On Mondays, I'd go to Broomfield for a check-up and to change the dressing on my head, which was still an open wound.

I was going to get back to normal. I knew that. I was going to walk unaided: no stick; no Zimmer frame. But as Michelle helped me from the car into my wheelchair, I realised that the gap between where I was and where I had to get to was enormous. The gyms, the equipment – all the things that would have once excited me – now daunted me. I'd have to learn to use them in a new way, and it was going to be tough.

'I want to get into my room and get my head sorted,' I said to Michelle.

'You will, babe,' said Michelle. 'But first we're having that meeting with George and Joy.'

George Glew was my occupational therapist, and Joy Hill was my physiotherapist. I'd met them in December when they gave me the Headley Court tour. Joy welcomed me back to Headley Court. She told me that there were lots of ways the centre could help me, and she asked me what my main goal was. I took a deep breath and squeezed Michelle's hand. 'I want to be as fit as possible for my wedding in 17 months. I want to walk Michelle down the aisle.' Michelle squeezed my hand back. Joy and George nodded positively.

We chatted on about how this larger goal of fitness could be broken down into smaller challenges, such as dressing myself, eating with normal cutlery, writing and driving. A timetable was devised and written down. They warned me it was going to be hard work. 'Fine by me,' I said. 'I don't want to be sitting about thinking.'

George took me and Michelle to the Peter Long Unit. I was in a side room. That suited me. I didn't feel up to company. 'I'll put your pictures up,' said Michelle. We'd brought the same ones that I'd had on the walls at Broomfield. I watched Michelle roll pieces of Blu-tack into tiny balls. Even something as small as that was impossible for me to do. She put my clothes away and laid out my toiletries. I watched her place my electric toothbrush by the sink. I was so used to her looking after me, now it was going to be someone new, someone strange. The thought of it pissed me off.

And then it was time for Michelle to go. I hugged her. 'I'll come tomorrow night,' she told me. 'I can hear how you're getting on. And you'll be home on Friday. Love you loads.'

I've always hated being on my own, and after Michelle left, my mood blackened. I lay on the bed. I missed being at home. I missed being with Rosie, Brian and Harvey. Not even the photos of my family and friends could cheer me up. I looked at the pictures of Port Lympne. I wanted to be inspired, but I couldn't snap out of it. I waited for Michelle to text me and let me know she was safely home, and I went to sleep feeling very sorry for myself.

❧ ❧

I felt slightly better when I woke up. I could hear noises and people moving about. Everyone was busy, and I too would be getting busy soon.

There was a text from Michelle on my phone: 'Morning, sweetheart. Missed you last night. Have a good day. Look forward to hearing about it later.'

I was helped to wash and dress. I'd opted to eat breakfast in my room. I could eat with adapted cutlery, but I didn't like people watching me.

After breakfast, George arrived to work on my hands. He chatted away, telling me that as part of his training he'd worn a brace to understand how people who couldn't use their hands felt. 'Fair play,' I thought. It wasn't something I'd ever thought about. But I was discovering that there was an endless list of stuff I couldn't do – shoelaces, buttons, zips, even holding a cup of tea were all nearly impossible.

'If it hurts, just tell me and we can stop,' said George, bending and stretching my fingers.

'I thought it was supposed to be painful to do any good,' I said.

'It is. But we can take a break at any time.'

I looked at my tiny pink hands. 'Come on,' I thought, 'work harder.'

'Is there anyone here with burns as bad as mine?' I asked.

'No, it's mainly people who've lost limbs or have shrapnel or gunshot wounds, stuff like that.' I nodded. We chatted on, and when it hurt, I gritted my teeth. I made it through the half-hour session. It had to be done. End of.

Next, I was wheeled to the lift and down to the complex-trauma gym, where Joy was waiting for me. She helped me onto a plinth and took me through some stretches. These were dead important if I didn't want a build-up of hard scar tissue that would restrict my movement.

'I'm knackered,' I told her.

'Do you want to stop?' she asked.

'No, let's crack on,' I said. Michelle was coming to see me that night, and I didn't want to tell her that I'd given up.

'You've got a high pain threshold,' said Joy.

'Just as bloody well,' I thought. She was right. I only ever took painkillers if I was desperate. I don't like having any drugs in my system.

Joy pushed my wheelchair to the end of two hand-height parallel bars. This was how I was going to learn to walk without anything but my own strength holding me up – eventually. The X-Fix was gone, and I was finally allowed to crack on with weight-bearing.

I stood up, gripped the bars and got my balance. Joy moved the wheelchair, then hovered protectively behind me and asked me if I was ready. 'Now or never,' I thought.

I felt her hands move away from my hips. I lifted my hands a few inches and then lifted my left leg slightly and moved it forwards. Pain ripped through my right thigh. I hissed, and for a moment my hands touched the bars. I lifted them up again and then moved my right leg. It felt heavy and useless, but I pushed through, gritting my teeth. I lifted my left leg again, stepped onto it, then held the bars. It was too much. 'I need to sit down,' I said.

I couldn't wait to tell Michelle. Three faltering steps wasn't the same as striding up the stone stairway at Port Lympne, but it was a start. Every journey starts with a single step, so the saying goes.

The session lasted for two and a half hours. Then I ate lunch. I was starving. George came back to work on my hands some more, then that was my lot. I collapsed on the bed. The next thing I remember is Michelle kissing me on the forehead. 'Been working hard?' she said.

The routine continued. Every day, I worked on my hands, my stretches and those bars. My first stint at Headley lasted four weeks. That's the way they do it there: four weeks in, then a few weeks off. If you stayed at Headley all the time, you wouldn't get the confidence to use the skills you were learning there. I needed to get used to the real world.

In that first month, I managed to get myself dressed – T-shirts and jogging bottoms or shorts only, no buttons. A major turning point was getting my trainers on by myself. I was elated. Imagine something as daft as that being able to make me so happy. I've always loved trainers – white ones, especially when they're new. As soon as they get a mark on them, I chuck them and get a new pair. So, it felt a bit like I was getting back to being me – being able to put my precious trainers on by myself.

Michelle had been right about Headley. I hadn't wanted to go. Things were easy at home. I'd got too comfortable and had put the shutters up on what my body still needed. But once I got there, I realised how beneficial it was. It wasn't like being in hospital. It was like being back in the army – with a new set of challenges. In the same way I'd learned to march in 2000, I was now learning to walk.

Going home to Rosie and Brian's on the Friday was great. And the following Tuesday, I wouldn't say I was looking forward to going back to Headley exactly, but I wasn't frightened.

Simon Weston is probably Britain's most famous injured soldier. He suffered nearly 50 per cent burns in the Falklands War in the early 1980s. I'd never known anyone who'd been burned before this happened to me, and apart from seeing Simon on the telly a few times, I had no experience of such injuries.

I'm sure he would've found me eventually. If you were army or ex-army, you'd get to hear about a badly injured colleague. But it was Kevin who made the first contact with Simon.

The night I arrived in the UK, burned and close to death, Kevin did what we know Kevin does – he came to protect. He wanted to look out for Michelle and was initially at a loss as to how to help and support her. But after being told I had 75 per cent burns, he got on the Internet. He knew about Simon – well, he was such a popular figure, an example of someone who'd been badly injured but had got on with life.

The former Welsh Guardsman was on HMS *Sir Galahad* in Bluff Cove, just off the Falkland Islands, on 8 June 1982, when Argentinian Skyhawk fighters attacked. The ship carried phosphoric bombs and thousands of gallons of fuel – petrol and diesel. So, when those Skyhawks launched their missiles, the *Sir Galahad* went up. Twenty-two lads from Simon's thirty-strong platoon were killed, and he was badly burned. Altogether, the Welsh Guards lost 48 men and 97 were injured that day.

Back at home, Simon went through dozens of operations. It was tough for him, but he got through it and made something of his life. He's been a tireless charity worker, raising money for some organisations, being patron of others. He's such a well-known personality, not just in Wales, where he was named as one of the top 100 Welsh heroes in 2004, but throughout Britain. The Queen gave him an OBE in 1992.

Kevin visited his website and emailed his agent, asking if he could speak to Simon. I think that was great for Kev. He always wants to be getting on with things, getting things sorted, trying to help, and speaking to Simon made him feel like he was helping out, keeping busy on my and Michelle's behalf.

Simon was honest with him when they chatted. He told Kev how I'd be feeling: that I might feel guilty for surviving when my mates died and that I might feel sorry for myself. There'd be anger and frustration, he said, and I'd take it out on the people around me. Simon told him that all Kev and the rest of my family and my friends could do was be there for me.

It did Kev the world of good, I reckon. He took his time telling Michelle, though. He didn't want to be the one pointing out to her that, like Simon Weston, I'd be scarred for life. Michelle knew that in the back of her mind. She didn't need to be told. But I guess it was her big brother trying to protect her again.

Eventually, he plucked up the courage and told Michelle: 'I

hope you don't mind, but I've been in touch with Simon Weston. He said that you can call him any time.'

She didn't call Simon – I think Mich was in a tunnel at the time and was only able to focus on me. But he'd given Kev his mum's number, and Rosie had quite a few chats with her. Being able to speak to someone whose loved one had gone through what I was going through helped Rosie.

Simon says it was his mum who got him through those difficult early months after he was injured. She first saw him on his return to the UK when he was wheeled into the transit hospital at RAF Lyneham but didn't know that it was him. She just saw a lad who was terribly burned and said to his gran, 'Oh, Mam, look at that poor boy.'

Simon cried out, 'Mam, it's me,' and, according to him, her face turned to stone.

I finally met Simon at Headley Court in March. He'd come to do a radio interview and asked if he could meet me. There was no one else at Headley with burns, and I was very pleased to meet someone who knew exactly what I'd been through. I was still pretty ill at the time and in my wheelchair. My arms were thin, and I was quite weak. But I managed to stand for a few seconds to have my picture taken with him.

He gave me some good tips. Wear loose, cotton clothing, he said, and always apply factor 50 sun cream. My skin was very sensitive to the sun, so it needed as much protection as possible. Simon also told me about his experiences and how his relationship had broken down when he came back from the Falklands. He said I was lucky to have Michelle. Don't I know it. She was there, too, along with Rosie, Lorraine and her boyfriend Dan. Rosie had been eager to meet Simon after chatting to his mum.

He was really fierce with me, telling me not to feel sorry for myself. Lorraine was a bit shocked, I think. She didn't expect him to be so straight to the point. But I felt a connection to him – not just because we've suffered similar injuries, but because he also joined up at 16 after getting into bother. The army saved him, I suppose. It certainly saved me. He's an inspiration, proving you can turn your life around no matter how bad things get, and a remarkable guy. I'm really impressed by his work for charity, by his media profile and his commitment to injured troops.

That night, Michelle, Lorraine, Dan and I went out for a meal, and we asked Lorraine if she would be willing to do a speech at our wedding. She was touched to be asked, and it meant a lot to me that she said yes.

It was so frustrating to have so little energy when I'd always been such a fidget. But there it was. My body was working hard. When the evenings came at Headley, it was all I could do to hold the phone and speak to Michelle. But there was no way I'd have gone to sleep without saying goodnight – no matter how exhausted I was. It was the highlight of my day.

Before long, I had something to face that I wasn't looking forward to. The Royal Military Police were going to interview me about the incident on 1 August. When soldiers die, the RMP's job is to find out how and why. Evidence would be needed for an inquest, and people needed to learn more about the way the enemy operated. The information could help soldiers in the future. I understood the reasons for the interviews, but I was dreading them. I would have to relive every detail.

Alistair volunteered to sit in with me, and I was really grateful to him. He sensed when I'd had enough and asked for breaks or that the interviews be continued at a later date. I will always be thankful that he made something really tough a little bit easier.

I had a few nightmares after those interviews. The incident haunted me. I'd be falling asleep and memories, images and sounds would come to me. If they came at the weekend when I was home with Michelle, I would tell her about it in the morning. She always listened patiently.

❧⳩ . ⳩❧

Everyone at Headley was essentially young, fit and used to working hard. I worked hard, too, but I had to be careful not to overheat, because on my upper body I can only sweat from under my arms. I have sweat glands on only 30 per cent of my body. I had to have the windows open while everyone else was freezing, otherwise I would have overheated. There was a hydropool there that could have helped me stretch while my body was supported by the water, but it was too warm for me. I couldn't stand it.

My walking improved every time I took to the bars, and by the end of the second month, I could get to the end and stand unsupported. The scar massage also continued, with Joy and George working together to cover a greater area. We always chatted. We got to know each other really well, and I now feel close to them – two more amazing people in the incredible team that put me back together.

On 23 April, I went to the Queen Elizabeth's Foundation Mobility Centre for a driving assessment. I passed and felt wonderful, like the 17 year old who'd taken his test at Borden. It was a big relief to start getting my independence. I could drive myself to Headley Court and to Broomfield for my weekly appointments.

Sophie and Tom had moved to Essex, so I'd pop round there after I was done at Broomfield, and Sophie would make me a bacon sandwich – just like old times. Then, on 28 April, Kevin and Katie's first child was born – Joe Jackson Clifford. Michelle and I went to the hospital to see him, and the moment Katie put him in my arms . . . I can't describe it. The picture is on our wall. Joe looked so perfect. It's funny to think that he'll never know me looking any different to how I do now. A week later, Katie and Kevin rang me to ask if I would be one of Joe's godparents. I said yes. Instantly, of course. It was an honour. After that, I loved popping round to see Katie and Kevin even more.

In May 2007, the Queen presented medals to four soldiers from the Household Cavalry for acts of gallantry in Afghanistan in

2006. This included Radders for rescuing me and Mick for his part in that and other actions.

Andrew got the Conspicuous Gallantry Cross. It's the army's second-highest award. His citation read:

> Without hesitation or prompting from the officer commanding his vehicle and seeing the imminent danger that the injured soldier was in, Radford dismounted his vehicle and, under sustained enemy fire from the Taliban fighters and with total disregard for his own safety, ran into the ambush killing area towards a gravely injured man. A father of four young children, he deliberately put himself in harm's way to rescue a fellow soldier. He showed an almost superhuman effort to rescue Trooper Compton and extract him uphill the 70 metres back to his own armoured vehicle . . . all the more remarkable as he was still under fire from a mixture of AK-47s, machine guns and RPGs. At no point did he think of himself, utterly focused on saving his fellow comrade in trouble, who had suffered horrendous injuries. Without doubt, his immediate action saved Trooper Compton's life. It is this act of selflessness, conspicuous gallantry and bravery in the face of a well-coordinated and sustained enemy ambush that merits public recognition.

Hearing a citation like that makes you realise what heroes like Radders go through. He didn't think at the time; he just went for it. But, like he says, if he had been in the same situation as I was, someone would've run for him. It's what you do for your mates.

After Radders and Mick received their medals, there was a party for them, and two others from D Squadron who'd been honoured, at the Household Cavalry's Knightsbridge Barracks. Michelle and I were invited, and it was great to be with everyone again. It was the first time I'd seen Mick Flynn since he'd helped Radders rescue me. He's a no-nonsense bloke, Mick, something of a legend in D Squadron. The award he got for rescuing me and other actions made him the most decorated soldier for bravery in the British Army. Everyone admires him. I tried to thank him, but he wasn't having any of it, so we all had a few drinks instead.

CHAPTER 27

MARTYN – A PLACE WHERE IT
LOOKED DOWN OVER US

WESTFIELD, EAST SUSSEX – JUNE 2007

Michelle came downstairs. She said, 'Has your dad been round?'

I glanced up at her. 'No.'

'Who put that chest of drawers together, then?'

'I did.'

'You're joking. Martyn, you shouldn't have. Was it hard?'

'A bit . . .'

A bit? It was murder. But that's me and my pig-headedness again. Who'd've thought that putting together an IKEA five-drawer unit would be so difficult? I found it hard to grip things. My armpits were soaked. It's uncomfortable not being able to sweat – especially when you're doing a flatpack. But after I'd finished and saw the chest of drawers there in all its glory, I felt that it'd been rewarding.

'You should've got your dad to help,' said Michelle.

'It was all right. I managed.'

She looked at me. She knew me well but couldn't work out quite *how* I'd managed. Physically, at least. Mentally she could see I'd go for it, push myself. But handling the various slats and screws would've been nearly impossible for me – she knew that. I did it, though, and it felt good. To me, it was an achievement, a step forward. Getting help would've been too easy, a get-out. And anyway, this was my house, our home. It was down to me to sort things out. I couldn't depend on Dad, on Brian and Kev, on Chris, to do all the physical stuff.

We'd found the house on the Internet while we were holidaying in Devon with my family. We loved it straight off and booked a viewing when we came home. It was roomy, on a lovely modern estate – and Michelle and I could imagine raising kids there. Westfield's a nice little village in the countryside, although it's near the beach, too. It's not too far from Hastings and close to my dad, and to Michelle's mum and dad.

I was still at Headley from Tuesday till Fridays, and Michelle would come to visit me on Wednesdays. Moving house and travelling to Surrey, being away from Michelle while she got on with packing and unpacking, was stressful. Dad and Brian helped out. They painted the whole house. I gave it a go, but it proved too knackering. I was out of breath and in pain, my arms turning to feathers after a few sweeps of the brush. It was very frustrating. I had a plan for the bathroom. I wanted to paint it red, white and blue, but it would've done me in. Michelle did it for me. It looked great – a Union Jack bog.

But it still got me that I couldn't do it myself. It was almost a year since the incident, and I was still in a bad way. I had a year to go till the wedding, till I walked Michelle down the aisle. It felt like a long time, but the months shoot by when you've got a goal. And before you can say 'I do', you're facing your challenge, and you've got no excuses.

Michelle was still worried about the IKEA flatpack. I told her it was no problem, but in truth there'd been a lot of swearing, most of it directed at my limbs: 'Fucking arm, hurry up and work.'

I'd gone through hell to be with Michelle in our own home. I'd gone through hell to put an IKEA flatpack together. I gazed around the living room. Our home was coming together – IKEA flatpacks, Union Jack toilets, a flat-screen TV . . . My eyes rested on a figurine hanging above the bay window. A black cloud moved over me, and my heart felt heavy. The figure was a silver guardian angel, watching over me and Michelle and our home. The ornament itself, or what it was meant to represent, wasn't what saddened me at the moment. What made me sad was thinking about who gave us it and the pain she'd gone through.

It was a gift from Angela Nicholls, Ross Nicholls's widow – my friend Ross, who died that day in Musa Qala along with Ralph and Alex. We were so grateful to her for meeting us, so grateful she wanted to be our friend. It was incredible for me to meet her, and I admire her so much. We loved her gift, and we'd chosen a special place for it in our home – a place where it looked down over us. I felt tears welling in my eyes but kept my gaze fixed on it.

As I have said, some people say there was someone watching over me that day. My mum, says Auntie Trina. A guardian angel, say others. But why me? Why should a guardian angel watch out for me more than Ross, Ralph or Alex? Don't tell me it was their time. I don't believe that. Don't tell me that they were abandoned by their spiritual protectors. They were good men with good families. Why them more than me? Why?

If you ask that question, it can destroy you. It can drill into your brain and puncture your senses. You start thinking about guardian angels and the like, and you question why their sentinels weren't there that day. You can go on and on, and it can rot you.

The truth is: there is no reason. What happened, happened. I was lucky, that's all. Lucky to live. Some people might think that I wasn't lucky – that I would've been better off dying. Not me. I don't think that; Michelle and my family don't think that. I'm grateful every day.

Major Will Bartle-Jones gave me a gift from the squadron. It's a beautiful frame filled with images of D Squadron in Afghanistan and photos of Ross Nicholls, Ralph Johnson and Lance Corporal Sean Tansey. Sean died in an accident while repairing a vehicle on 12 August 2006. Will had five of these frames made. He sent one each to Ross, Ralph and Sean's families, gave one to me and the fifth belongs to the squadron. Mine hangs on the wall in the sitting room. It's a reminder of my friends, the lads who gave their lives. I'll live my life as best as I can, and I'll live it in honour of Ross and Ralph and Alex, and all the others who've been killed and who didn't come home to their guardian angels.

WEMBLEY STADIUM, LONDON – 1 JULY 2007

Prince William got us tickets for the Concert For Diana. The date would've been her 46th birthday. It was moving: William and Harry organising this massive gig in remembrance of their mum. The event was spectacular, and being so close to the stage added to the excitement.

It kicked off at 4 p.m., with Sir Elton John singing 'Your Song'. The atmosphere was great, and it really got going when Duran Duran came on next. It was a great day, and a host of stars took part. It was great for William that so many people turned out to support him and his brother. They're supportive of so many causes – injured soldiers most of all – so it's good that people, famous people, can lend their support.

Michelle really wanted to see Joss Stone, but she had to queue up when she went to the bar, so she missed her. At the end of the night, they played a video of Diana as a child to the soundtrack of Queen's 'These Are the Days of Our Lives'.

Going to the concert was another example of how our lives had changed since the incident. We'd have had to try and get tickets like everyone else before 1 August 2006. But now we were being treated like, well, royalty. Everyone was showing us kindness – from princes to people next door. Everyone wanted to meet us, to help us out. It was unreal.

A few weeks before, the picture of me and Simon Weston taken at Headley Court in February was published in *The Sun*. It was the day after our story had appeared in the paper. It was the first time what had happened to me and Michelle, my battle to survive, Michelle's strength in sticking with me all that time, had been made public. In the photo taken at Headley Court, I had my Spurs woolly hat on. Someone at the club saw the photo and got in touch to ask if me and Michelle would like to meet the team. We went to their training centre in August, just before the season started. We met everyone – although Robbie Keane, my favourite player, wasn't there. The manager, Martin Jol, was really nice and wished me well. All the guys were great. It's incredible meeting people you see on TV and in the papers, and then realising that they've heard about you, too. Michelle was made up. She's been a Spurs fan for much longer than me. She liked Paul Robinson, the team's goalkeeper at that time, and was over the moon to meet him and the others.

We're blessed, we really are. I know I harp on about it. I know something bad has happened to me, and I guess if I could go back, I would. But I can't. Thinking like that is no good, because it's not going to happen. You've got to make the best of what you've got. You've got to take every opportunity that comes your way. We counted ourselves lucky, going to places we would've never got to, meeting people we would've never met. It's strange to say it, but we were having the days of our lives.

HEADLEY COURT – AUGUST 2007

Six months down the line, I'd made incredible progress. For three months, I'd been able to eat with normal cutlery and had joined everyone else in the canteen at mealtimes. Of course, when I was finally brave enough to do that, I saw that lots of other people were struggling with their eating, and I realised that everyone was in the same boat.

I loved the atmosphere at Headley. There was plenty of army banter flying about. The first question everyone asked each other was 'What happened to you?', and it was therapeutic to keep speaking about what I'd been through.

I needed to build up my strength, so I'd started working with weights after four months. They probably didn't weigh a pound each. I felt slightly pathetic when I thought about the weights that P.J. and I used to throw about. He was a real gym monster, and I enjoyed trying to keep up with him.

I was walking quite well, and George had been taking me out in the grounds, getting me used to walking on different surfaces and up small slopes, things like that. But now I faced a new challenge: stairs. And the day I was due to tackle them was a day that Will and Alistair were coming to visit.

Will arrived in Afghanistan just after I left. He took over D Squadron from Major Alex Dick. Just after the handover, Will's father died, and he came back to the UK. While he was home, he came to Broomfield to see my dad and reassure him that after the tour he would be in touch and would do everything he could to help me. That was quite a gesture: to be thinking of my family when there was so much sadness in his own life. He was true to his word. There was certain equipment that I needed: a special mattress, an adapted car and other things. There was a budget for me to have some of these things, but it would have taken a long time for me to get them if the Household Cavalry had gone through the official channels. Will decided to set up a fund to get some money to help me in the short term. People were very generous, and I got everything I needed. In fact, there was more than I needed, so Will created the Household Cavalry Operational Casualties Fund. People have leaped on board to support it. And it has now attracted £250,000 in donations, grants and favours. Some of the money was spent in 2008 assisting the families of Trooper James Munday, who died on 15 October 2008, and Trooper Ratu Babakobau, who died on 2 May 2008.

I will always be grateful to Will. And I'm pleased that the fund was able to help other people and their families. Will says he would have done it for anyone. He says that what he did was nothing special. I believe that. Will thought nothing of it and just went ahead to help me. That is exactly what makes what he did and the sort of person he is very special indeed.

Three days after he got back from Afghanistan, Will came to see me at Rosie and Brian's. He returned to Afghanistan in 2008. He's now the officer commanding of the Household Cavalry Training Wing (Mounted Regiment).

The Household Cavalry has been with me through every single one of my highs and lows. So, it was quite appropriate that Alistair and Will were at Headley that day. The stairs were quite a way from my room, so Joy wheeled me there.

I made it up those seven steps, but it was bloody hard work. Having Will and Al there spurred me on. I felt like Rocky when I got to the top. Will and Alistair pushed me back to my room. If we'd had a bottle of champagne, I'd have cracked it open there and then. But I think we just had a cuppa instead.

CHAPTER 28

⁂

MICHELLE – YEAR'S END AND A NEW BEGINNING

'I don't want to go back there,' said Martyn.
'I know,' I said.
'I'm terrified.'
I nodded. So was I. He was going under anaesthetic again. That's when he was most vulnerable. How many times had I been terrified in hospital during the latter months of 2006, waiting for Martyn to come out of surgery? I didn't want him to go back into hospital, either, but he had to. It was always the same. I felt Martyn's pain, but I had to be strong. I had to be the one who said, 'You've got to do it. Everything will be fine.'

The scar tissue on Martyn's neck had thickened, making it difficult for him to turn his head. The operation would loosen the skin. It was essential work, but when it's you going under the knife, it doesn't feel essential. It feels like walking back to the hell you've only recently managed to escape from.

'I don't know why,' he said, 'but it just makes me nervous.'

'I know,' I said again, 'but it'll be all right.'

Going to hospital felt like a step back to him. It was a time in his life that he'd pretty much blanked out. It was part of his past, something he did when he was really ill, when he was close to death. Now he felt as though he was recovering, and having to return to Broomfield – however wonderful they were over there – brought back those days of pain and fear he suffered during late 2006.

But there was a positive side, of course. In addition to the neck release, Martyn was having his upper lip resurfaced. It was his first cosmetic operation to improve his appearance, which felt like a big step forward. When Peter Dziewulski first started rebuilding Martyn, I hardly dared dream of the day when they'd be moving on to that stage. It was a big psychological boost for Martyn, too. He'd be getting more movement in his face. But first he had to face his fears.

I went with him to Broomfield, and he made it through, like he always did. I sat by his bed again, thinking about the first Christmas in our new home. We'd decorated the tree together and made everything perfect. We were having my mum and dad round for dinner, to thank them for everything they'd done. The previous year, I'd had to cut Martyn's roast potatoes for him. This year, miraculously, Martyn would be helping to peel the roast potatoes. Maybe.

PART FOUR

We Climb a Step Every Day

CHAPTER 29

༺✥ · ✥༻

MICHELLE – I WAS, AS THE FOOTBALL CLICHÉ GOES, OVER THE MOON

LONDON – 23 FEBRUARY 2008

The Wembley roar went through me. It's like being lifted on a wave when a football crowd chants, when tens of thousands of voices chorus, the sound racing around the stadium. Chills went down my spine. My heart fluttered. I was at Wembley with the man I love, watching the team I adore – and it was thanks to Prince William that we had these seats. He'd been very kind to us since Martyn's accident. It's amazing to think of this man whom you read about, whom you see on telly, the man who'll be king one day, doing this for us. And when you meet him, he's so down to earth, so friendly – no airs and graces at all.

We first met the previous year at Windsor Barracks. Major Will Bartle-Jones had invited us over there so Martyn could see his friends again. He'd not been there since he deployed to Afghanistan, but when we arrived, it was as if he'd never left. The welcome was warm and generous – and there was plenty of banter thrown in. We'd gone to the mess for something to eat, and after the meal we were outside chatting. Keeno said, 'There's Prince William.'

'Where?' I said.

'Over there,' he said, pointing.

I gasped. The heir to the throne strolled by in a pair of shorts. I rang mum and said, 'I've just seen Prince William in his shorts.' I'm not sure she believed me. I'm not sure *I* believed me. But why shouldn't Prince William, a member of the Household Cavalry, be strolling around the barracks? He'd joined the regiment a few months earlier.

After I'd rung my mum and shared an excited phone call with her, Keeno and P.J. helped get Martyn into the car. We told them goodbye and said our thank yous, then started driving out of the barracks.

Keeno and P.J. waved frantically at us. I waved back. Martyn said, 'No, they're saying stop. Stop the car.' I pulled over and pressed the button to wind down Martyn's window.

Prince William stuck his head through. 'Nice to meet you, Lance Corporal Compton,' he said 'I've heard so much about you. Next time you're here, we'll have to have a proper chat.'

Before Martyn could say anything I reached across. 'And I'm Michelle,' I said, offering my hand.

'Hello,' he said, shaking my hand. He was lovely, really friendly, and offered to help Martyn in any way he could.

Before I could drive off, there was someone I had to call. 'Mum, I've just shaken Prince William's hand.'

Prince William is president of the Football Association and was able to get me and Martyn tickets for the Carling Cup final. I was, as the football cliché goes, over the moon. Tottenham Hotspur has been my team for years. Meeting them the previous August had been brilliant, a dream come true. Paul Robinson, the goalkeeper, was my favourite player, but all the stars were there – although sadly not Robbie Keane, one of Spurs' top players.

However, the previous weekend, a week before the final, we had a little surprise. Martyn and I were on holiday in Yorkshire.

Since we were up north, we travelled to Chester-le-Street near Newcastle to see Stevie Waugh and his wife, Gemma. Stevie was one of Martyn's closest mates in the army. He was a lovely Geordie whom Martyn had met just before his 21st birthday.

We were in a pub, where it was quite noisy. Martyn's phone rang, and he answered it. A voice said, 'It's Robbie Keane.'

Martyn thought it was one of his mates messing about and shouted 'Who?' into the phone.

'Robbie Keane.'

Martyn said, 'What?'

'Robbie Keane,' the man saying he was Robbie Keane said again. 'I heard about you.'

'What? *The* Robbie Keane? You're having a laugh.'

'I'm sorry I missed you at training in August. I wanted to say I hope we have a good game for you next week.'

Martyn realised that it was Robbie Keane – none of his mates could pull off an Irish accent as effectively as the man on the other end of the phone. 'Thanks very much,' Martyn said. He looked across at me and put the phone away. 'Bloody hell, Mich. Robbie Keane's just phoned me.'

'Are you sure?' I said.

'Yes, I'm sure.'

'You could've put him on the phone to me.'

We were thrilled – Robbie Keane phoning Martyn, hoping that the team could put on a good performance for my fiancé.

It would be tough. It hadn't been an illustrious few years for Spurs. We'd not won anything since the League Cup in 1999, and success before then had been sporadic. Our close neighbours and arch-rivals Arsenal were one of English football's so-called 'Big Four', along with Manchester United, Chelsea and Liverpool. We were desperate to join that club and make it a 'Big Five' – or, better still, oust Arsenal, the Gunners, from the top table.

We nearly always came out second best when we played Arsenal. But in the Carling Cup semi-final a few weeks before, we'd thrashed them 5–1 – in footballing terms, it doesn't get much better than scoring five times against your sporting nemesis. Five is a psychological figure in goal-scoring terms. It's the difference between a comprehensive win and a thrashing. Scoring five times is significant; it stays in the memory. Who can forget England's 5–1 win over Germany in Munich in 2001?

After the highs of the semi-final, Spurs now faced Chelsea, the favourites, in the final. Chelsea were desperate to win after their manager, José Mourinho, left a few months previously. They had their eyes on a unique quadruple that season: the Premier League, the FA Cup, the Champions League and the Carling Cup. All the pundits plumped for Chelsea to beat us. But I had a good feeling about Spurs that day. I was confident that we could do it. I know it was only football, but after what Martyn and I had been through, I knew anything was possible.

I'd supported Spurs for years. My friend Dean had got me into them. I'd met him through Kevin. They were mates and drank together at The Bull in Sissinghurst. Dean knew I was mad keen on football and asked if I wanted to go along to White Hart Lane with him and his pal, Spinner. I was 18 at the time and thought it would be fantastic. I'd always played football, and I'd seen games at Gillingham, but I thought it would be thrilling to go along to a Premiership ground. It was, and I got the Spurs habit. But my first visit to White Hart Lane was noteworthy for another reason. I'd bought a lottery ticket that day and fortunately won £100. I bought a pair of Patrick Cox shoes. They were cream wedges, priced at £135. I wore them to death, I loved them so much. Almost as much as I loved Spurs.

Dean and Spinner were Tottenham Hotspur club members – not quite season-ticket holders, but they had priority when it came to getting tickets. We went to White Hart Lane once a month. It was fantastic. Football meant a lot to me.

There at Wembley, my memory reeled back to those days in the garden, me in the cherry-trees goal, Kevin dribbling towards me, thinking he was going to score . . .

※〇ᘏ . ᘏ〇※

At primary school, I played for the netball team. But it was football I loved. The school's football coach had seen me play with Kevin while we waited for Mum to pick us up after school. And in my last year at primary, I got a great offer. 'You can either captain the netball team,' said the teacher, 'or you can join the boys' football team.'

It was difficult to choose. I was only ten. I wanted to be the netball captain, but I loved football. I made a choice. I joined the boys, making history in the process – I was the first girl to play for the school team. I don't know what the boys thought, especially as I was better than most of them.

When I moved to Angley School, I wasn't allowed to play football in the boys' team. I kept training and improving by playing with Kevin and Darren Beard. And in year ten – when I was fifteen – we had the option of doing mixed PE, which meant girls could participate in the boys' sports. I spoke to the PE teacher and asked if I could do football. I'd had a training session with Gillingham Ladies at around that time. Kevin was at Gillingham, so I went along. They asked me to sign up that very night after the first session, but I decided not to – I didn't feel I'd enjoy it there. But I was keen to continue and to improve.

The PE teacher said he was happy for me to do football. 'But you'll probably be the only girl,' he said.

'I don't have a problem with that,' I said. Although I was the only girl doing the PE option, there were others at the school who were interested in football, and we were soon playing for the school's girls' five-a-side team. I became captain. After a match against Senacre School, the opposition manager told me about the Crowborough women's team. He was one of the guys running the team and told me I should come along. Dad took me, and I settled in straight away. I loved it; in fact, I loved it so much that I'm still playing for Crowborough now. Twelve years I've been playing for them – the longest I've ever stuck at anything. I represented Sussex County from the age of sixteen to eighteen and was one of the five best players selected from my league to be a league rep. I did that for five years.

I really enjoyed my football during year ten. I was confident and felt no apprehension even when I played against the boys. My PE teacher wrote in my year-ten report, 'Michelle has good coordination and team-work skills, such as positioning, and these are best demonstrated in football. Michelle always gives 100 per cent effort to the activities she has selected.'

That's absolutely right: 100 per cent. I always gave my all to football. And at Wembley Stadium that day, I gave my all to supporting my team. I screamed and clapped my hands: 'Come on, Spurs!'

It was amazing to see the players I'd met a few months earlier trot out. The atmosphere was electric. Martyn bounced next to me, catching the mood. There had been so many incredible adventures since he'd come out of hospital. People had been so kind. But for me, this was one of the highlights. And the day would be perfect if Spurs could win.

It was an exciting game. After only a few seconds, Robbie Keane raced through and had a shot at goal. John Terry, the Chelsea captain, deflected the ball wide. An 'Ooh!' rifled through the 88,000-strong crowd. We almost took the lead again through Pascal Chimbonda, who hit the bar, and Dimitar Berbatov.

But then disaster. Chelsea scored five minutes before half-time when Didier Drogba lashed in a free-kick from 20 yards. Paul Robinson didn't move as the ball whipped past him into the bottom corner.

What I've learned over the past couple of years is to put things into context. I now know what's important in life – and, ultimately, football isn't. But when your team goes a goal down in a cup final, I can tell you that it feels like the end of the world. And when they go a goal down to high-flying Chelsea, it's doomsday. Chelsea are one of the best teams in the world at defending a lead, and they were doing a good job of it until halfway through the second half.

Wayne Bridge, one of the Chelsea defenders, gave away a penalty, slapping the ball away with his hand. I leaped to my feet with the rest of the Spurs fans in the crowd and shouted 'Penalty!' Berbatov stepped up and slotted the ball home. I threw my arms around Martyn and squealed in his ear.

The match went into extra time. It was biting-the-nails time. I couldn't believe the nerves fluttering about in my tummy. The excitement fizzed through me. And four minutes into the extra half-hour, Jonathan Woodgate headed the ball into Chelsea's net – we were 2–1 ahead. We went crazy, screaming and cheering.

When the final whistle went about 25 minutes later, the relief was incredible. I hugged Martyn and a tear ran down my cheek. The white-and-navy flags of the Tottenham supporters seemed to fill the stadium. Cheers rang around Wembley, and I felt the electricity pulse through me.

I looked at Martyn. Football was meaningless in comparison to what he'd gone through, to the life-and-death situations soldiers like him face every day. The footballers who'd be hailed heroes in the Sunday papers after winning this cup weren't really heroes – not like Andrew Radford, Mick Flynn and all the other troops who put their lives on the line. I knew that football wasn't as powerful as the love Martyn and I shared, the love that had got us through this nightmare. But today, just for one day, football was the world.

CHAPTER 30

꿏ᐵᑐꕥꕥᐳ꘍

MARTYN – A DUTY OF CARE

Some people say that soldiers know the risks involved when they join the army. They know that they might have to fight in a war some day and that it might end badly. Because of that, some people think that soldiers shouldn't be entitled to compensation. But I know that if I hadn't been blown up, I would've willingly fought for my country for the rest of my life. So now that I'm unable to do that, I hope that my country feels it's right to look after me. Me and all the injured soldiers.

There's something called the Military Covenant in Britain, which is the duty of care the nation has towards its armed personnel. The covenant says:

> Soldiers will be called upon to make personal sacrifices – including the ultimate sacrifice – in the service of the nation. In putting the needs of the nation and the army before their own, they forgo some of the rights enjoyed by those outside the armed forces. In return, British soldiers must always be able to expect fair treatment, to be valued and respected as individuals, and that they and their families will be sustained and rewarded by commensurate terms and conditions of service.

That's the pledge, and some people have argued that this is not being upheld.

The army has looked after me. It saved me from wasting my life away when I was a teenager, it gave me chances when I sometimes didn't behave as I should've behaved and it helped me grow up. I'm grateful to the countless individual members of the Armed Forces who saved my life, got me home and helped me heal. But I think that the covenant between soldier and state needs strengthening, and I can understand why soldiers and their families sometimes feel let down.

Now that I'm wounded, I've had to face the fact that my career might be over. There are probably jobs that the regiment could find for me, but I've always wanted a career, to progress through the ranks. That's what everyone who joins the army wants. But now, everything I've trained for has been taken away, and the future is very uncertain.

The army makes you who you are. Without it, you lose that identity. You've been forged into this certain person, trained to be a certain way. You've got mates, and your bond with them is deeper, sometimes, than with people you've known your whole life. It's tough coming to terms with losing all that. So the money you get, the compensation, it needs to be for more than just the physical injuries.

It's heartbreaking seeing ex-soldiers unable to cope with having to leave the army because of injuries. They find it hard to adjust to ordinary life, and some turn to drugs and drink. Some are homeless. And a few reach the end of their tether – suicide isn't uncommon among former military personnel.

In 2007, the Royal British Legion got nearly 1,500 calls from ex-service personnel who badly needed help. Why should that happen? Where's the covenant gone? It makes me sad. And it makes me realise how lucky I am. But it also makes me realise why we should be compensated decently for our service to our country.

Nowadays, you get a lump sum of compensation if you're

injured. If you can stay in the job, you carry on getting a salary alongside that lump sum. If you're medically discharged, you get a lump sum and a monthly payment based on the salary you had when you left. It's called a guaranteed-income payment and is tax free for life, but it's obviously not as much as you would have got if you'd stayed in and been promoted.

My award was £98,837.50 – for my three worst injuries. At that time, the Armed Forces Compensation Scheme only took into account the three most serious injuries. The worst injury was paid at 100 per cent, the second at 30 per cent and the third at 15 per cent – you didn't get paid for the rest of your injuries. That's how it was – but there was no reason not to try and change it, and Alistair Galloway said he would help me.

The eight other wounds I'd suffered counted for nothing. If all my injuries were paid in full, I would've got more than £366,000. So, we appealed the decision. Alistair knew some solicitors, who have been fantastic, and the award was upped to £163,000.

I told the prime minister about my situation when I met him at the Britain's Best Awards in May 2008. Gordon Brown knew I was fighting for compensation, and he asked me how it was going. I told him the truth – told him how I felt and said that my claim was complex because of all my injuries. He nodded and listened graciously. I hope he understood how important the issue was to me. I'm sure he did. I'm sure everyone does, including the Ministry of Defence. But sometimes red tape can get in the way of things. And if we can cut through that, then we can pay our injured soldiers the compensation they deserve.

I'm sure the public wants that. I've had a lot of support from people all over Britain and from across the world since I came home. I think the public's opinion of the Armed Forces is changing, which is great. People are learning more. They can't totally understand what's going on if they only watch and read the news, but thanks to programmes such as *Ross Kemp in Afghanistan* they're seeing the truth about our current conflicts, which is only right. They're seeing how talented soldiers are, how hard they work, the dangers they face and how they think and act as a team. It's amazing that I was part of that, and I'm gutted it's over. But you've got to go on. You've got to keep fighting.

Alistair has worked so hard, having meetings and involving important people at various levels. I wouldn't have known which way to turn without his help. This process has been so complicated, and I would have been totally lost without Alistair. He's left the army now, but the fact he's sticking up for me shows that you're still there for each other even when you're in civvy street.

I've had wonderful support, and it was amazing to hear that Simon Weston was backing my compensation claim. He gave it both barrels after my initial compensation payout. 'I'm disgusted but not surprised,' he said in the *Sunday Times* in February 2008. 'We're treating our people so badly.'

Later in 2008, the rules on multiple injuries changed, and I received an additional award. The lump-sum compensation payment for the most seriously injured now constitutes a full rate for all injuries in a single incident, up to £570,000. Then towards the end of the year, I was told that my lump sum had increased again – to almost four times what the original award was.

I was pleased, for myself and for all the soldiers who will doubtlessly, sadly, be injured in the future. Thanks to Alistair, I was able to help change the rules for them.

If I leave the army, I'm not sure what my guaranteed-income payment will be, so there's still stuff to sort out.

Compensation might be complicated, but my reasons for needing it are quite simple: I want to be able to look after Michelle and the family we plan to have. That's all I've ever wanted.

CHAPTER 31

MICHELLE – I DREAMED ABOUT MY DRESS

WESTFIELD, EAST SUSSEX – MARCH 2008

While Martyn was at Headley Court, my job kept me preoccupied – and I also had a wedding to organise.

I had plenty of support. Katie and Mum were wonderful, and my friends were supportive. It was going to be a wonderful occasion. I'd been dreaming about it since I was a little girl, and that dream had started to come true when I met Martyn. The Taliban almost turned my dream into a nightmare, but Martyn's stubborn streak, his strength, his determination, had sparked the dream to life again. It was going to happen. My Martyn's hardheaded. He'd promised to be at my side, to walk with me, and I knew that he would keep his promise.

It was February, a gloomy Thursday evening. I brought the box of paper, ribbons and sequins into the front room and sat down to make the wedding invitations. I'd decided to make them by hand to show everyone who was going to be there how special they were to us, what it meant to have them there to share our day.

On the front there would be a picture of Martyn and me before the accident. It was the most formal picture that we had of the two of us together, and I didn't give it any more thought than that, really. It had nothing to do with presenting an ideal image of him. He was ideal as he now was – still the perfect man. We just hadn't had a formal photo taken, that was all. He'd been laid up in hospital for months. Martyn was still the man I wanted to marry, no matter how his appearance might have changed.

As I put the invites together, I dreamed about my dress. After Martyn and I appeared in *The Sun* in June 2007, a dress shop called The Fitting Room in Eastbourne phoned me. Jan, the owner, offered to make my dress for no charge as a gift. Her kindness staggered me, and I couldn't believe I was so fortunate. After she rang, I put the phone down and raced into the sitting room to tell Martyn. I was breathless with excitement and the words tumbled out of my mouth as I explained what Jan was offering. 'It's what you deserve,' he said, his eyes filling with tears.

I knew my wedding dress would have to feature pink, my favourite colour. I went to see Jan at the shop, and that first day I fell in love with two dresses. I liked the bodice on one and the skirt on the other, so Jan said she would design something that combined the two.

Over the months, my dress took shape. The white panelled bodice had a sweetheart neckline with pale-pink lace trim at the top and waistline. The back was fastened with lengths of pink ribbon. The white skirt was large and voluminous. It drew to a bustle at the back, then opened to reveal pink tulle with a five-foot train. That was Jan's suggestion, and I absolutely loved it. The first time I tried the dress on, I knew it was everything I had ever wanted. It was such an amazing experience.

I trusted Jan implicitly, so I told her that she was free to create any sort of veil. I wouldn't see it until the morning of the wedding, months away. But I knew that I'd love it. I knew in my heart that Jan would do a wonderful job and produce something I'd be proud to wear.

I chose Katie to be my bridesmaid. She had been so supportive to us, and we'd become very close. I'd never seen Kev happier than when he was reunited with his childhood sweetheart. I also wanted Katie's niece, Honor Tress, who was two, to be my second bridesmaid. I love children and wanted a little girl as a bridesmaid on my wedding day. I couldn't think of anyone more perfect than Honor. She was so sweet-natured and beautiful with her bright blonde hair. She looked like an angel, and I knew she'd love to do it.

Katie and Honor's dresses were also made for them, as was my mum's. She deserved to feel special that day. She's been amazing through all of this and has treated Martyn like a son.

As the months counted down, we planned other elements of the wedding. We wanted something special for the place settings. We'd got ourselves a puppy by that time. Humphrey was a chocolate Labrador and was proving to be lots of fun, bouncing about all over the place. He got on well with Harvey, and Martyn and I loved to take him for walks in the fields behind our house. Humphrey also enjoyed going to Hastings beach. We collected stones off the beach, filling a rucksack. I know you're not supposed to do that, but if someone reads this now, I hope they forgive us. We asked Katie to write the guests' names on the stones and use them as name tags at every place setting. It was another personal touch, just like the invites. I wanted everything to be perfect.

Everything was coming together. The dress was going to be beautiful, the invites were handmade, the name tags were unique, the rings were spectacular. They were matching platinum-and-gold bands. Mine was set so that my engagement ring could sit alongside it, and it contained 11 diamonds. Martyn's had one diamond in it, too.

The months leading up to the wedding were thrilling. We'd gone through so much, and Martyn still had a lot of challenges to come. He had months of hard work ahead of him at Headley Court and years of rehabilitation to come. But our lives had changed dramatically. And in a few months' time, everything would culminate in the most life-changing and wonderful event of all.

Getting married, for most people, is a stressful, exciting, happy, crazy time, involving months of chaos, months of planning, months of spending for one marvellous day. But for Martyn and me, getting married was a matter of life and death. Getting married was a dream that was torn away from us, rebuilt, shredded again and then put back together. It was a goal that kept Martyn going, a goal that kept him alive.

Windsor Working Men's Club, London – April 2008

Prince William put his arm around me. The other women in the room looked daggers at me. He'd arrived late and obviously wanted to get to the bar. But everyone crowded round him, vying for his attention. Martyn and I watched as he made his way through the well-wishers. His smile was constant and genuine. I don't know how he maintains the patient air of a prince.

He was headed for the bar and spotted us. He smiled and came over, saying hello and draping an arm over my shoulder. Can you imagine how wonderful that felt? The future king embracing me like a friend, chatting away as if we'd known each other for years. I could smell the envy in the room. It eked out of every female pore.

We were at D Squadron's leaving do. The guys were headed out to Afghanistan, many of them Martyn's friends. People were asking William if they could have their photo taken with him, but he courteously refused every request. I imagine it's protocol. If he agreed to have his picture taken, they'd turn up everywhere – Facebook would be teeming with images of people hugging Prince William.

He chatted to us for a while, then drifted off to the bar. I saw him head off towards the toilet, and, although he'd not spotted

William move that way, Martyn said he needed to go, too. A few minutes later, Martyn came back brandishing his mobile phone. He said, 'I've got a photo of me and Wills.' He showed me, and there they were: my husband-to-be and Prince William outside the toilets together, like old mates.

'Martyn,' I said. 'I want to have my picture taken with William.'

Martyn, a few drinks down by then, went over to William and said, 'Hey, Wills. Michelle wants a photo.'

William said, 'I shouldn't really . . . but as it's you, Compo,' and he came over to pose with me while Martyn took the photo. I didn't have to be told to smile.

We also met Prince William a few weeks later at the City Salute, which is a tribute by the financial district of London to the Armed Forces. The event raises funds for Help For Heroes and the Soldiers, Sailors, Airmen and Families Association.

It was an incredible occasion, with hundreds of people gathered outside St Paul's Cathedral. It all began when three Eurofighter Typhoon jets blasted through the sky, sending a roar through the warm summer air. Jeremy Clarkson, the *Top Gear* presenter, hosted the event, and he said it was being held to thank servicemen and women for the work they do. It was wonderful to hear a popular presenter such as him speak about the Armed Forces. He has an influence, and people listen to what he says. Knowing that he and the hundreds of people there that night respected Martyn and his colleagues brought a lump to my throat.

They showed a film of Mark Ormond, a Royal Marine, on the big screen. Mark lost his legs and his right arm after stepping on a Taliban landmine in Afghanistan on Christmas Eve in 2007. He was at Headley Court, along with Martyn and so many others. 'It means a great deal to be here. It's an honour,' he told the crowds. 'It's a bit overwhelming. You don't realise until events like this how much support there is from civilians.'

Joss Stone performed at the event. She was a friend of William and Harry, and supported the cause. It was great to see her after missing her at the Diana concert. We met William afterwards. He always made time to chat to us and ask after Martyn. We often spoke about football, Martyn and me being followers of Spurs and William supporting Aston Villa.

William has so much respect for servicemen and women. He can't hide it. He and his brother recognise the courage and professionalism of everyone serving in the Armed Forces. I've looked at him with awe every time I've met him, thinking how all this came about – how I got to meet a man who would be king one day. All this, from that August day nearly two years before when I heard that Martyn had been injured to the City Salute and Prince William chatting about football, has been unreal in so many ways. It's gone from nightmare to dream to nightmare and back to dream. And sometimes I wonder if I'm actually still sleeping, and it is no more than my subconscious frantically spilling out the fragments of a rather stressful day.

CHAPTER 32

❧ ⬩ ❧

MARTYN – BEN WAS THE REAL HERO

SOUTH BANK, LONDON – 18 MAY 2008

I said to Michelle, 'Do you think we should ask Gordon Ramsay to bake our wedding cake?' It wasn't a stupid question. Gordon Ramsay was right there, so it would've been easy to stroll over and ask him. He might well have agreed. But, in the end, both Michelle and I were too star-struck.

What were we doing here on the red carpet, going into the Britain's Best Awards? It was amazing. The two of us and all these stars. We were both glancing around, and everywhere we looked there was a celebrity. The job was to find someone who *wasn't* one: Gordon Ramsay and his wife, Tana; Formula One driver Lewis Hamilton; actors James McAvoy and Jude Law; Bionic Woman Michelle Ryan; London Mayor Boris Johnson; *OC* star Mischa Barton. The whole thing was magical. It was almost like you name them, they were there.

As we walked in, the cameras flashed, the photographers called out, the celebs posed. My heart raced. Nerves made me shake. But it wasn't terror; it was excitement. And the whole event was being broadcast on ITV1. We were going to be on telly, at a do that seemed to me to be like the Oscars. It was one of the many incredible events I'd been invited to since my return to Britain, since my story was first published in *The Sun*.

I'd been invited along with Ben McBean to accept The Sun Global Recognition Award on behalf of the Armed Forces. It was such an honour, and I felt very emotional. The Armed Forces are such an incredible organisation, and Ben's a great guy. I've since met him at Headley Court a few times. He was 21 when he lost an arm and a leg in a landmine attack in Helmand in February 2008. He was wounded hours after the press revealed that Prince Harry was fighting in Afghanistan – something the government and Royal Family had rightly tried to keep quiet. You can't have the Taliban knowing the whereabouts of the third in line to the throne. Because the story broke, the prince had to come back to the UK.

Medics saved Ben's life like they'd saved mine. And then he was flown home with Harry. Ben's bravery moved the prince, and he refused to accept the 'hero' tag the media seems to pepper people with if they've done anything out of the ordinary. Instead, Harry said that Ben was the real hero, which was true. I was proud to be accepting the award alongside him. It was a brilliant recognition of what injured soldiers such as me and Ben face.

Moments before we went out on stage to accept the award, the organisers said who'd be presenting it to us: the prime minister, Gordon Brown. I was chuffed, as I wanted to meet him. It's not often you get to meet your country's leader.

Mr Brown said we had so much to be proud of in Britain and that he was honoured to be there. He said, 'Troops like Ben McBean remind us of the courage and bravery that our forces have, and despite everything they are so upbeat and determined to get on with things. It's very humbling meeting those chaps. I could talk to them all night.'

We were called out on stage. Mr Brown was waiting for us, along with the host, Piers Morgan, the rude judge from

Britain's Got Talent. Ben and I walked forward. The audience cheered, and it sent a tremble through me. Pride swelled up in my chest when I shook the prime minister's hand. It was surreal. When the Taliban blew me up, I thought I was going to die. Less than two years later, there I was, on TV, shaking hands with the prime minister. I couldn't believe it. I could see Michelle in the audience crying. It was very moving and an incredible moment for me, just an ordinary bloke in an extraordinary situation.

I had a chat with the prime minister afterwards. That's when I told him about my concerns for the future and the fight for decent compensation. He was aware of what was going on. He also congratulated me on my wedding plans and wished me and Michelle luck. He's a very genuine man. He wanted to know how I was getting on. I told him about Headley Court and how well I was doing there. It's just an incredible place, and I'm so grateful for the help they're still giving me. I don't want to think what life would've been like without that place, without the people who work there. We're lucky in so many ways to have been born in Britain. Afghanistan didn't have such a facility, that's for sure. And it reminded me again why we were over there – trying to help them get a fragment of what we had.

The PM and I also bantered about football. I told him I was a Spurs fan, but he seemed to suggest that Chelsea were the better team. I was having none of that. He might be prime minister, but he didn't know a thing about football, did he? We'd just beaten Chelsea in the Carling Cup final. But maybe he was just saying that because Avram Grant, who was Chelsea's manager at the time, was standing next to us. And why should the fact that Avram Grant was standing next to me be a surprise? By then, I was looking around at all these stars and not thinking anything of it – I'd been conditioned to celebrity.

But then we met Abi Titmuss, and I got excited again . . .

THE NAVAL AND MILITARY CLUB, ST JAMES'S SQUARE,
LONDON – 22 MAY 2008

I support the Help For Heroes charity, because without it, where would I be? It raises funds to improve facilities at Headley Court, where guys such as me, such as Ben McBean, get a chance at living.

Mich and I went to a fundraiser for the charity in London in May 2008. Alistair Galloway had helped to organise it. It was at The Naval and Military Club – nicknamed 'The In and Out Club' – which was opened almost 150 years ago by a bunch of officers looking for somewhere they could get together, somewhere that felt like home to them. It's a fancy place, and it was a fancy do to raise awareness and money for the charity. Simon Weston was there, so it was nice to see him again. We'd been keeping in touch by phone. Michelle and I also had our photo taken with Boris Johnson, who had recently been voted in as mayor of London. He was posh and had mad hair, but he was all right. The guy had a lot of respect for the Armed Forces.

The club had offered me and Michelle one of their rooms for the night. It spared us a trip back to Kent. It was the Colonial Room, their best suite. It had a four-poster bed, a lounge and a dining area. If I'd been paying, it would have set me back more than £300 for the night. I'd not stayed anywhere as grand as that, and I was definitely looking forward to the breakfast.

We came downstairs in our jeans, relaxed and ready to leave after fuelling up with a fry-up. The waiter, or maître d', I'm not sure what you'd call him, smiled and said we couldn't go in to the Coffee Room, where they served breakfast. He was very polite, of course, and very apologetic. Apparently, I had to be in a suit to go in for breakfast, and 'the lady has to be in a dress'.

Michelle and I had been dressed up for the fundraiser the previous day, and we didn't want to be dressed up now. I'd never heard of anyone having to wear a suit or a dress for breakfast before, and I didn't fancy putting my jacket and tie on again

– especially for eggs and bacon. It was a stand-off, with the guy being courteous but firm, insisting that we had to be dressed for breakfast, and me and Michelle trying to persuade him otherwise. Eventually, we won the day. We got to sit down in our jeans.

Who would've thought that anyone had to wear a suit or a dress for breakfast? Being dressed up posh after crawling out of bed didn't sound right to me. But it wouldn't be the last time that Michelle and I came down for breakfast in unsuitable clothes – I'd be eating my words, and my fry-up, in full morning suit in a couple of months' time.

CHAPTER 33

꧁ ꧂

MARTYN – THE KINDNESS OF STRANGERS

BLACKPOOL – 4–5 JULY 2008

I didn't buy a beer all night. It was great. The club was packed, and people kept coming up to me and asking if I'd like a drink. I said I would and thanked them.

You don't normally get that at a stag do. You don't get strangers coming up to the groom offering to buy him a drink. You go to these places, these clubs, and it's packed with stag nights – husbands-to-be having their 'last night of freedom', all of them in the same place. There's rarely ever any camaraderie. You get on with your own drinking with your own mates. But I was treated like a king. It might have been because of the way I looked, but I think it was down to the T-shirt I had on.

This was my second stag do. Why not have two? Why not have as many as I could manage? I'd been dead, after all. I should be celebrating being alive, celebrating getting married to my wonderful Michelle, the angel who'd got me through the worst time of my life. Why shouldn't I have fun?

My first do took us to London in June. Kev organised it, and in attendance were me, Kev, Brian, Chris, Lance Cooper, who'd come to cadets with us, Lee Hallam, who lived next door to Michelle, Kev's brother-in-law Justin (who drove the minibus) and two of Kev's friends, Tony and Miles. We were all suited and booted, and headed for The Colony Club, a flash casino in Mayfair. I'd never been to a casino before – well, not a fancy one like that, at least.

I was buzzing on the drive to London. I couldn't wait. The whole idea of going on a stag night excited me. It made me realise that I was finally getting married. It was really happening. Michelle and I would be husband and wife. I was going to spend the rest of my life with her, making that commitment. Stag nights can be wild and crazy, but they do make you think about what you're doing. They're like the opening of the door into the next room, if you like. You're stepping out of the room of being single into the room of being married.

The Colony Club treated us like royalty. They gave us a complimentary meal and paid for our drinks all night. It's amazing the way people have treated me since my injury. Before, I was never shown so much respect, despite the fact that I was a soldier, putting my life on the line. I want to make it clear: I'm not asking for respect, and I'm not asking for freebies, but it says a lot when people show you kindness. It shows they're grateful. It shows they have respect for the Armed Forces.

People have been amazing, no doubt. I know Michelle's been moved by the kindness of strangers. People do simple but sweet things. Like a girl in our local pub who kept all the newspaper cuttings and told us how moved she'd been by our story. And the couple in Hawkhurst who sent us money. There's The Fitting Room, of course, ringing up and offering to make Michelle's dress. Then there's the Household Cavalry giving me more than I could've wanted since I got hurt. And there's our family and friends. I could go on and on, but words don't always convey how grateful we are. We can only say thank you, and sometimes that doesn't seem enough.

Well, I said it anyway and told The Colony Club I was grateful for the food, which was amazing. I had duck, and I don't think I'd tasted food like it. After the meal, they brought out a cake. It had 'All The Best For The Future' written on it. All the lads agreed that they'd never eaten a cake like it. I'm a big fan of Rosie's legendary Victoria sponge, and I won't hear a word said against it. But that Colony Club sponge ran it close . . . and maybe it was a slice of icing better. Sorry, Rosie.

The gaming rooms were cool. I felt like I was in a James Bond film. It was modern and flash, with mirrors everywhere, so it was lucky I'd got used to seeing myself. Eighteen months before, I might have felt differently about being there, and it gave me a shot of confidence to know how far I'd come psychologically. People still looked at me, but I didn't mind so much by then. I just looked back. And I wasn't bothered about being reminded of my injuries. I'd steeled myself. I'd got used to it and had told myself, 'What's happened has happened. Get on with it.'

A few weeks before, I'd cut my finger slicing some bread. I'd made a mess – there was blood everywhere – so I went to hospital. It felt ridiculous, really – me with all my injuries waiting to be treated for what I'd consider a scratch. I'd been waiting a while, and I'm not that keen on hanging around. My impatience started to get the better of me. I told a nurse that I wasn't waiting any longer and was going home.

She looked at my finger, spouting blood, and said, 'You can't go home. You'll need to have that stitched or you'll have a nasty scar . . .' She stopped dead and gawped at me, her mouth open. She realised what she'd said. I had enough scars to contend with and wasn't worried about a nick on my finger. I haven't got any ears, for God's sake.

Embarrassment flushed her cheeks, but I smiled and showed her that I didn't mind. People have just got to get used to me. This is how I am. I'm at peace with it now. That nurse was worried she'd hurt my feelings. My feelings were the last thing I was worried about.

※◁・▷※

The guests at The Colony Club were sophisticated and rich-looking. We spotted James Caan from *Dragons' Den* having a little bet with some of his hard-earned cash, I guess. 'Good for him,' I thought.

The lads and I played blackjack. I guess it was beginner's luck, but at one point I was up £700. I decided to stop playing and moved over to the bar. I scanned the club, watching the players at the tables. My mates were having a great time. Some of them were still at the tables, but most of them were watching, like me. I couldn't believe I was there. Me, just a normal bloke who had been fighting in Afghanistan two years previously, in this posh Mayfair club, mixing with all these stylish people.

My gaze roved around the club. I could see people winning; I could see them losing. I started tapping my foot. 'With £700 in the bank, I should stay quit,' I thought. I'd already decided that I'd won enough. But boredom nudged me towards the table. It was telling me to have another go, just one more crack at the tables. I wanted the thrill of gambling again. I crossed over to the table, took my seat and started playing. The cards didn't go my way. I should've quit while I was ahead, trousered my £700 winnings and gone home. I ended up down £40, but so what. We had a fantastic night – one that I couldn't have imagined having before all this happened.

And a few weeks later, I was doing it all over again. Chris, Stevie, Lance, P.J. and I went to Blackpool. On the Friday night, we were in a club, and that's when the offers of free drinks flooded in. As I said, I think it was down to my T-shirt. The lads had it made for me. On the front, it said 'Blown Up, Set Alight And Shot By The Taliban', with a photo of me and Michelle, and on the back it read 'I Survived Death To Walk My Fiancée Michelle Down The Aisle'. I could see people looking at me in the club, their eyes flicking from my face to the T-shirt. They were reading it, hundreds of pairs of eyes gazing at me at the same time.

The first people to approach me said, 'We think you're amazing, and we want to buy you a drink.' That's pretty much what everyone else who came up to me said as well. It was funny, because I didn't think I was amazing at all. And, really, I'm not. Something extraordinary has happened to me, but I didn't ask for it. All I know is that it happened, and I have to get on with life. What else can you do? We're just ordinary, really, all of us. But inside us is the power to cope with anything if we want to. It's all about being pig-headed and stubborn.

I wasn't going to let this get the better of me. What's the point in giving up? While there's a breath in you, there's hope. While there's a heartbeat, there's life. I wanted to marry Michelle, to walk her down the aisle. The Taliban might have burned my skin away, but I was still me, and I could still muster enough determination to get through this. They weren't going to beat me. What they'd done to me wasn't going to stop me. That's not being amazing, I don't think – it's being human. And being human means we can have fun, and that night we had fun till 4 a.m. – it was a great night.

It didn't feel so great the next morning. My head thumped, and the others looked worse for wear, too. We went go-karting that Saturday morning, which isn't easy with the hangover from hell. I felt dizzy and sick whipping around the track, but my will to win hadn't been dulled. I was determined to get round first, but with my head in a spin and the hangover really kicking in, no one's clear to this day who came out on top. Anyway, winning doesn't matter, does it? Well, it does, which was why when we went out that night in fancy dress I was determined to have the best costume.

It was a *Star Wars* theme. Stevie went as Luke Skywalker, P.J. was Darth Vader and Lance came as Darth Maul. Chris made a lovely Princess Leia, and I went as Yoda. I think I looked great, the best of the lot. I was an authentic Jedi master. I had the Yoda head on, and the Yoda cloak. I was a bit too tall, maybe, but it was a great costume. And it was nice to have ears, although I wasn't sure about the green colour.

After 45 minutes, P.J. bravely said, 'Right. Stick your hand up if you feel like a dickhead.' Everyone raised their arm, and we went home and got changed.

We had another great night, and I felt happy about my life. A terrible thing had happened, but being out with my mates made me realise I had great friends, a great family and, within a week, I'd have a great wife.

WESTFIELD, EAST SUSSEX/FRITTENDEN, KENT – 6–11 JULY 2008

I had two best men. I wanted one from army life and one from civvy street. Chris was a no-brainer. He'd been there since I was a kid, my best mate, my partner in mischief. It's not often blokes say they've been friends with someone since they've been primary-school children. Girls stick together, I guess, but men don't seem to. But me and Chris had been thick as thieves since childhood.

My other best man was Stevie. We were both in the Household Cavalry, me in armoured, Stevie in mounted – that's the one with the horses. Then he got transferred to armoured. We were soon introduced, with me being referred to as Compo, as usual. Hearing my nickname before he met me, Stevie thought I was going to be like the character from *Last of the Summer Wine* – a scruffy wreck. I bet he was surprised to meet a suave, well-groomed, handsome bloke like me. We clicked immediately.

Stevie's laid-back and very kind. He's also wise and someone I go to if I need advice. He's a really good singer and performed at the wedding. If you described him to anyone, you'd say, 'He's really tall,' and before you'd finished the sentence, they'd say, 'and always singing.'

Stevie left the army in 2006 because of a foot injury, but we kept in touch, and he was horrified to learn I'd been injured. He kept up with my progress through my dad and P.J. He also kept trying to ring my mobile. It was off, of course, and Stevie thought it had been in the wagon with me and had been destroyed. It wasn't, so when I got it back, I was able to call him from burns rehab. I think he was a bit spooked when he saw my number come up on the screen of his phone.

I saw him at a Household Cavalry do in May 2007, and he gave me a big hug. In February 2008, his son Euan was born, and he asked me to be his guideparent. So I'm accountable for the moral guidance of two lads now: Euan and Joe Jackson. I'm very proud, and my eyes well up when I think about it. I'm not sure sometimes if I'm the best candidate for the job, but I take the responsibility seriously. I'll take them both out for their first pints when they're 18, that's for sure.

The week before the wedding, Michelle had to work. It was coming up to the end of term, so she was really busy. After work on the Monday night, she had her final dress fitting. After work on the Tuesday, we went to London to do two interviews about the wedding. They were for the *Mail on Sunday* and the *Sunday Mirror*. It was good to talk about everything again, right from the beginning, because it made me reflect on what we were doing at the weekend and why, and how special and significant it was for both of us.

On Wednesday, we went to Port Lympne for a wedding rehearsal. Chris, Dad, Rosie, Brian and Katie came along. It started to feel real as we talked through the running order where we would take our vows. My nerves were fizzing, and I wondered how I'd feel on the day. It was building up, an emotional volcano that would erupt on Saturday, on my wedding day. I hoped I could keep it together. It was incredibly poignant, all of it. Thinking of myself in that Afghan war zone, my body on fire, the Taliban shooting at me, I realised it was a miracle that I was there, days away from my wedding, rehearsing for the most wonderful event of my life.

On Thursday, I went shopping with Katie to get Michelle's wedding jewellery and gifts for the best men. Katie's brilliant at gifts. She has an instinct for what to buy, and I'd have been lost without her. She'd been wonderful throughout the difficult times and had been invaluable while we'd been organising the wedding.

It was a manic week, all in all, but I had loads of help from people such as Katie, Rosie and Brian, and Kevin. I had so much to do, and the week just got eaten up. The days were slipping away, and I could feel panic rise up in me, making me cold all over. I had to collect the champagne. I was arranging decorations – the balloons and pink- and chocolate-coloured serviettes. I had to sort out the favours, which were these gorgeous boxes of biscuits in shapes such as bouquets of flowers and diamond slippers from a company called Biscuiteers. I also had to finalise flowers, make sure people had their readings and deliver the rings to the right people. And I had to collect the cake from Windsor. It had been made by an army chef and was decorated with animal faces to keep with the Port Lympne theme.

On the Thursday night, we sorted out all the gifts we'd bought as thank-yous. The best men were getting watches. Our friend Sarah and Auntie Trina were getting angel figurines. We'd got engraved mirrors for Lorraine and Katie, and hip flasks for Brian and Rob. Rosie was getting a cuckoo clock. She'd always wanted a grandfather clock, but we couldn't afford one, so we went for something different. For Honor, we bought a Tinkerbell jewellery tree. It was a good feeling, seeing all the gifts.

I also had to collect all the suits, which were lent to us free by Etiquette, the suit-hire firm. The cravats and waistcoats had been made by Jan at The Fitting Room, and I had to get those as well. It was a full-on week. I'm not sure I'd worked so hard in years. Recovering after getting burned and shot was bad enough, but sorting a wedding out was something else altogether. My nerves were frayed. I was trying to keep cool, trying to sort everything out, running around here and there. Michelle had been at work all week, so she was going to be more knackered than I was. I didn't want her to be frazzled, so on the Friday I arranged for her and Rosie to be pampered at Pennyhill Park Hotel in Surrey, which has a spa and offers all kinds of treatments that girls seem to like. They went there for a massage and a manicure while I finished things off, collecting bits and bobs from here and there, making sure everyone had everything they needed, praying the day would go smoothly. Honestly, if I had sweat glands, I'd have been soaked.

I needed a drink come that Friday night. Michelle stayed at our house in Westfield, and Katie stayed with her. I was staying at Rosie and Brian's house in Frittenden. Stevie was staying at a hotel with his wife Gemma, but he came over that night. Chris, Stevie and I popped over to The Bell and Jorrocks pub for a drink and something to eat. We had a few beers. We had a few shots of tequila. We were pissed. We sat at the table and talked about the wedding. Stevie was worried that neither Chris nor I had written our speeches. Pissed in the pub the night before the wedding wasn't the ideal place to write them, but we had no choice.

I scribbled out mine while eating my meal. It was just trying to remember everyone, that was the task. Chris was having more trouble than me. How could it be difficult to find great things to say about me? I knew it would be easy to find mischievous things to say. He wouldn't tell me what he'd written; I'd have to wait. But Chris and Stevie liked my speech. I just hoped I wouldn't cry while making it. It was going to be difficult. It was more than an ordinary wedding speech.

We kept drinking, and we chatted, bantered and got bladdered. Thankfully, the landlord gave us a lift home. I wasn't able to walk very far anyway, but tanked up like I was, I'd only have managed a few steps. It was another act of kindness. There's a lot of good in this world. I know it's not a big thing, taking a drunk home, but to me it was a kindness.

I slumped into bed, not able to grasp that it was my last night as a single man. I'd definitely had a few jars too many. I slipped into sleep and woke up with my dreams forgotten and my head drumming. It was early, and I hauled myself out of bed. The nerves came at me again, making me anxious.

'How're you feeling, mate?' said Chris as I made us a fry-up.

'Shitting myself.'

I dished up the breakfast. Normally, I would've wolfed it down – me and a fry-up, we're on the same wavelength – but I just stared at the eggs, the bacon, the sausage. My stomach wasn't responding. It was fluttering when it should've been rumbling. I shifted the food around on my plate.

Chris said, 'Not hungry?'

'I am, but I can't eat. I'm too nervous.'

The food went to waste. I looked up at the clock. It was still early, but I was scared of being late. Chris calmed me down and told me not to worry. He left me to it and went home to Cranbrook, a couple of miles down the road, to get ready. I was on tenterhooks by then, so it was lucky that Stevie arrived to help me get sorted. He tied the black scarf around my head, the one that was made especially for me. I always wear a scarf or a hat, because my scalp's so raw and damaged, and it was nice to have a cool one made for my wedding day.

Stevie was fantastic: cool, calm, telling me it'd be fine. I was so glad he was there. We were lucky to have him at the venue, too, because it turned out that he was the only one who could knot cravats and arrange buttonholes and handkerchiefs. He sorted everyone out, making sure I was tidied up, helping the ushers get organised. I thanked him, and I meant it.

PORT LYMPNE – 12 JULY 2008

Dad, Stevie and I were in the car. It was a Jaguar, an army vehicle with 'no stop' plates. 'No stop' means exactly that – the car can't be stopped. No matter how fast it's going, cops can't pull it over. It was exhilarating. We pelted along at 140 mph, our trained army driver zooming along the roads. The speeds he was going at, we chewed up the 30 miles between Frittenden and the wedding venue. It was so quick, we were there before we left. Chris was following us in his car. Unfortunately – or fortunately for the safety of road users – Chris doesn't have no-stop plates on his car, and he's not a professional driver, either. We were flying, and he couldn't keep up. He lost us.

Luckily, he knew the way to Port Lympne – or I'd have been a best man down.

It all became real for me when we got there. Any strength I had in my legs – and for a long time, I didn't have much – had drained away. I was light-headed, my mouth dry, my heart racing.

My ushers were all there – except Keeno. He'd taken R & R from Afghanistan to be my usher and had stayed the previous night at a hotel in Ashford, a few miles away from the venue. He was supposed to have come to Port Lympne with us, but he'd not turned up at the house that morning. We bagged up his morning suit and left it outside the front door, so when he arrived he could change into it.

It was nail-biting. I'd be getting married in an hour or so. The guests arrived – my friends, my family. The Household Cavalry guys were there in uniform, ready to be a guard of honour for me and Michelle. It was great to see them, and I was very moved that they were doing this for us. The excitement was overwhelming. I tried to make small talk with people, chatting as they milled around the lawn outside Port Lympne's mansion house. We'd be getting married round the back on the terrace, which overlooked the English Channel. The photographers were there. They started taking pictures. One of them was the guy from the *Mail on Sunday*. There'd be a feature in the paper the following day.

The newspapers have loved our story. I don't know why, because for me it's just normal – I love this girl, and this girl loves me, then I got hurt doing my job, but we're still going to get married no matter what. It's simple. It's what everyone in our position would do. But the press like us, and that's nice. They've been on our tails since the first story appeared in *The Sun* in 2007. We've had a journalist sit outside Brian and Rosie's house all night wanting to speak to us. Brian made them a cup of coffee. They don't always take no for an answer, but most of them are OK. They're just doing their job, and it's nice that so many people want to read about me and Michelle. We've had so many messages of support after people have read about us in a newspaper or a magazine.

What was the time? It was getting closer to Michelle's arrival, but still no Keeno. At this rate, he'd be later than the bride. A cab pulled up, and out stepped Keeno – right at the last minute, because we were getting ready to wait on the terrace for Michelle.

Keeno, red-faced, greeted me. It was great to see him – really emotional. He'd been in Afghanistan up to a couple of days before. I asked him what had happened. 'I got a cab to Rosie and Brian's,' he said, 'and I found the suit and got changed in the garden.' Unfortunately, he'd sent the cab away. And after getting into his suit, he realised he was stuck in Frittenden. He had to book another cab, and the whole trek cost him £94.

The plan was that I'd be waiting on the terrace. The guests would wait outside on the lawn to see Michelle pull up. She'd dreamed of arriving at her wedding in a horse-drawn carriage. I was lucky that, being in the army, I could make that dream come true.

I waited on the terrace with Chris and Stevie, nervous as hell. I heard the 'oohs' and 'aahs' from around the building that signalled Michelle's arrival. By this time, I could barely stand. My stomach churned with anxiety.

The guests came through to the terrace, taking their seats overlooking the lawns and the fountain, the English Channel in the distance. I glanced over the faces. They looked so happy, so pleased for me.

The wait seemed like for ever. My mouth was dry. I could've done with a drink, but it was too late. The Household Cavalry trumpeters started playing the 'Knightsbridge Fanfare'. I turned round and waited. And there she was, gliding round the corner, the girl who meant everything to me . . .

My heart sang and tears came easy.

CHAPTER 34

❧ ⋅ ❧

MICHELLE – 'I NOW PRONOUNCE YOU HUSBAND AND WIFE'

PORT LYMPNE – 12 JULY 2008

I said, 'Dad, slow down.' I wanted to savour the moment. The two cavalrymen trumpeted their fanfare, and I looked up at them. It was amazing to have such a salute at my wedding. I couldn't heave dreamed of this. I looked over at the guests on the terrace, and my heart bounced. I was almost there. It had been a long, hard journey, and I was about to stand beside the man I loved, the man I had seen lying torn and broken and burned in a hospital bed less than two years before. The man who'd said he'd walk me down the aisle, despite some people doubting he'd ever stand up again, let alone lead me through a guard of honour on our wedding day.

'Slow down,' I told my dad again.

We came to the bottom of the terrace. The guard of honour lined the steps. I looked up at Martyn and held my breath. He looked handsome in his morning suit and his black headscarf. He smiled down at me, and my heart leaped. My dad led me through the guard of honour, and I felt a tug on my dress. 'Dad,' I said. 'Don't stand on my dress.'

I glanced up at Martyn, and he smiled. He'd heard me, and I think the troops forming my guard of honour had heard me as well, because one or two of them were trying to stifle grins.

I took a breath and held on tightly to my bouquet, a teardrop of lilies, pink ranunculus and pink roses. I was also carrying a horseshoe that my mum had given me – a symbol of good luck as Martyn and I prepared to make the biggest commitment of our lives. I felt like a princess in my beautiful dress, my make-up, my hair that had been done in tight curls down to my waist by my friend Ella. She'd been cutting my hair the day I'd got the call from Rob to tell me that Martyn had been wounded.

My dad walked me towards the guard of honour. It was magical – a princess ready to marry her prince. And I'd even arrived in a horse and carriage. A few minutes earlier, the Household Cavalry Coach Troop had brought Dad and me to the mansion in a Victoria coach led by two black Dutch Warmblood horses. They were called Neils and Marco. They were beautiful horses, so elegant and powerful, and they completed the fairy-tale atmosphere.

The guests gazed open-mouthed as I arrived, and dozens of cameras went up all at once as we trotted around the corner. Dad loved it, too, grinning all the while and waving at people as if he were royalty. It was only a brief ride in the horse-drawn coach, of course – it didn't bring us all they way from Frittenden. I'd enjoyed that part of the journey in a Daimler – and not just any Daimler, but the one that Princess Anne uses in her role as Gold Stick for the Household Cavalry. The car belongs to the Royal Logistic Corps. It was another fantastic thing that the regiment had arranged for us.

Stepping into the coach near Port Lympne's entrance felt wonderful, and in the few minutes it took us to trot down to the mansion, happiness flared in me.

I savoured every second of the walk through the guard of

honour – after telling Dad to slow down. My veil wasn't down over my face, so I could see everything and everyone clearly. It was a beautiful veil, though. I'd not seen it until that morning. Jan from The Fitting Room had brought it with her that morning. It was a double-layer white veil that flowed down to my waist. Tiny crystals embroidered it, and it was finished with a handmade tiara that contained dozens of pink crystals. Just right. You can see why I felt like a princess. And even better, the veil complemented a gift that Martyn had left for me at my parents' house that morning. The parcel contained a diamond necklace and earrings. I gasped when I saw them. They were beautiful, the perfect finishing touch to my outfit.

Along with the gift, Martyn sent a card depicting the teddy bear he'd bought me for my birthday a couple of years before. The bear had his arms stretched out, and the caption said 'I love you this much'. That bear was the only thing I had with me in the hotel room in Broomfield as I waited and waited and waited for my husband-to-be to survive his terrible ordeal.

My mum, Katie and everyone at the house in Westfield on the morning of the wedding said how wonderful the jewellery was and how perfectly they went with the veil. Everything was pink, everything was perfect. Even Katie and Honor, my lovely bridesmaids, were in pink. Katie complemented her dress with a chocolate-coloured sash, and Honor's sparkled with silver stars. Seeing all the pink, I smiled and remembered the pink limousine that had come to pick up me and my hens the previous week.

Katie organised my hen day. Katie did a great deal, actually, and without her the week before the wedding would've been very difficult. For my hen day, I'd requested that the limo – in my favourite colour, of course – take us to London, and I wanted everyone to wear matching T-shirts. I had no idea what would happen once we got there. 'Be at your mum's house at 1 p.m., Saturday, 5 July,' said Katie. She's brilliant at organising, so I knew to be there on time. Everything would be like clockwork.

My friends and family were there to greet me, as well as Martyn's aunts, Trina and Annie, and his sister, Lorraine, and Annie's daughter, also called Katie. My heart swelled, seeing them all. It moved me and made me realise I was a week away from being a married woman, a week away from being Martyn's wife. Hen days are fun, they're frivolous, but when you sit down and think, they're really symbolic. It dawns on you how close you are to making the most important commitment of your life – a commitment to another person, to the person you love most of all.

All the girls wore black T-shirts with the words 'Michelle's Hen Day – Pink Ladies' emblazoned on the front in cerise lettering. Mum handed me a glass of pink champagne, and Katie gave me my own T-shirt. We sat down for a meal, followed by a few slices of mum's wonderful Victoria cream sponge – topped with pink icing, of course.

The girls presented me with gifts, each tag containing a clue to the sender. I had to guess whose gift it was before I could open it. Then they presented me with a commemorative plate, signed by all my hens with messages of luck and love.

And then a car pulled up outside. The room buzzed with excitement. I didn't know what was going on until I stepped outside and opened my mouth. It was the pink limo, just as I'd hoped. I couldn't speak, I was so thrilled. We packed into the car and discovered that Katie had stocked it with my favourite lollies: strawberry-and-cream-flavoured Chupa Chups. She'd thought of everything. It's little touches, such as the lollies, that make Katie so special. I popped on a veil – not the glamorous, beautiful one I'd be wearing a week later at Port Lympne – and we drank more champagne as the limo took us to London.

We arrived at our destination, Bar Salsa, where we had a meal and a salsa lesson. I was paraded on the stage, because I was a hen, and then we danced and danced, and it was such a wonderful evening. It made me want to be with Martyn even more, if that was possible. I felt so happy, dancing with my family and friends and thinking ahead to my wedding.

When we got back to Frittenden, the mood was still high. Dad ferried everyone home, including me. Because there were so many people to take, I was packed into Harvey's compartment in the back of Dad's car. But even that didn't dampen my mood.

Dad walked me up the steps to where Martyn waited. When I got to his side, I held his hand and looked him in the eye. We smiled at each other, and I couldn't believe how lucky we were to be standing there. That terrible incident two years before that had almost taken Martyn from me had left three families without fathers, sons, husbands, brothers. It had been a long, hard battle for Martyn. But he had fulfilled his promise – he was standing next to me, and I knew that in a few minutes he'd achieve the goal he'd set himself when he'd woken up nearly two years previously, a goal that to many seemed impossible. He would walk me back down the aisle, or at least through our guard of honour.

The ceremony was magical, and we were both smiling throughout. There were tears, though, because there were some emotional moments. One of the most moving parts for us was Lorraine's speech. She was 21. She's a lovely, kind and thoughtful young woman. She choked back the tears as she spoke powerfully about her brother: 'Finding in yourself the ability to hope, love and trust in something often beyond your control changes your outlook. But finding these emotions during the toughest and most demanding times changes your life. In Michelle, among other things, it made her more devoted and steadfast that Martyn was her true love. In Martyn, it made him stronger and determined to meet Michelle at the altar on their wedding day.'

Her powerful words made me shudder. Their strength seeped through me, and I felt astonishingly close to Martyn – I felt a part of him, almost.

Lorraine said, 'When I sat down to write this speech, I came up against the infuriating writer's block. But when I began to think about my brother, Michelle and my family, with a little help from Joseph Conrad, I knew what to say.'

She then quoted Conrad, the novelist who wrote *Heart of Darkness*: 'Woe to the man whose heart has not learned while young to hope, to love – and to put its trust in life.'

Lorraine continued, 'I am teeming with pride that my big brother is getting married and more so because he chose Michelle as his future wife. It stands to reason that you will go on to spend the rest of your lives together, as your relationship is clearly built on rock-solid foundations. You are truly an inspiration to me, and I am sure to everyone here. Everybody who hears your story, whoever they are, cannot fail to gain perspective and enormous courage from it.'

Tears filled my eyes. Lorraine moved forward and touched Martyn's hand. I could see the emotion stream through both of them. It was a powerful, intimate moment, and Lorraine's words summed up how Martyn and I felt about one another. Martyn dabbed his eyes. I scanned the guests and saw tears there, too. Rob was clearly moved, proud of his son and of his daughter. My mum, beautiful in a bespoke golden bustier and skirt, had been crying, I could see from her eyes. All around the terrace, handkerchiefs were applied to cheeks that were damp with tears.

We couldn't actually get married on the terrace – you have to be inside – so we stepped into the mansion, just within the doors. The guests could still see us, but it seemed quieter in there, more intimate. Martyn and I looked into each other's eyes, held hands and made our vows. We offered to love, honour and respect one another, and promised to be best friends. Our voices were quiet and confident, and we smiled as we said the words.

We stepped outside again, and a hum went through the guests. I glanced over at the English Channel. It was blue. The sun shone. Martyn and I exchanged rings. A warm feeling spread through me. The registrar said, 'I now pronounce you husband and wife,' and told us we could kiss. We kissed and the guests clapped, and my dreams had come true.

Our witnesses were Keeno and Rachel, my good friend from football. Sarah gave a beautiful reading, and Trina read a message of celebration, wishing us a long and happy life, and then she hugged us both. It was done. We were married. Martyn and I had come through it triumphant.

Sitting next to his bed at Broomfield Hospital in August 2006, this day had seemed a long way away. Back then, I had been determined to get through. I was always optimistic, and I wouldn't let anything get me down. I constantly fought the demons that tried to tear at my happiness. But they kept coming, they kept threatening our future. Martyn's life had been in the balance so many times that I'd lost count. Death was always at the door, waiting to come in. But, luckily, we held the key and kept the door locked. I don't know how, but we managed it. Love kept us going, I know that. Friends and family, too. The doctors, the nurses, the Household Cavalry, they were invaluable in our battle to get through this. And strangers, people we'd never met, people we met only a few times. Public support has been remarkable, and it's increased my faith in humanity.

Martyn took me by the hand. He looked at me. His moment had come, the moment he'd fought for. He was going to walk his wife 'down the aisle', through the guard of honour made up of his comrades. The trumpeters played a fanfare called 'Merry-Go-Round', and my husband led me through the line of soldiers, their swords held high to form a corridor of steel. The guests cheered, and I felt ecstatic.

Martyn said later that although it had been his goal to be well and strong enough to walk me down the aisle, when the moment came he'd forgotten about that pledge. 'I wasn't Martyn the injured soldier,' he said. 'I was just Martyn. Martyn the husband who had married Michelle.'

The views at Port Lympne were great, but I didn't have time to do more than glance at the scenery – Martyn and I looked at each other most of the time. The day went nice and slowly; it wasn't rushed. People had time to enjoy the surroundings. Meanwhile, we had photos taken in the Victorian coach. Many were for us, our record of the day, some were for the *Mail on Sunday* and *Sunday Mirror* the following day.

The meal was in the Garden Room at Port Lympne. Floor to ceiling windows were covered in sheer drapes. Pink and chocolate balloons decorated the room. The tables were set beautifully, and our personalised name tags – those pebbles we'd collected on Hastings beach – welcomed each guest to his or her seat. Once seated, there were pink and chocolate serviettes at the settings.

My friend Sarah is addicted to mayonnaise, so we made sure she had a pot next to her roast. We wanted the people who'd supported us to know we cared about them. And the best way to do that for Sarah was to give her a pot of mayonnaise.

After eating, we had the speeches, and they were packed with emotion. Even the best-men speeches, which were like chalk and cheese, delivered sentiment. Chris, who'd got drunk with Martyn the night before and had written his speech in the pub, seemed worse for wear at the wedding as well. He'd been drinking to calm his nerves before his big moment, but when his big moment came, he was too drunk to make his speech. Pointing at Martyn, he said, 'I love that man. I love you, Martyn.'

It was probably the shortest best-man speech on record, but, in a strange way, it was meaningful and perfect. To Martyn, those slurred words summed up his and Chris's friendship. They loved each other, and that's what Chris had said. It was enough.

Stevie was less nervous and less drunk. He said, 'You might have heard my accent if you're familiar with *Auf Wiedersehn, Pet* or Ant and Dec, but if you can't understand me, then just laugh and nod your heads.'

He said that he'd known Martyn for more than four years when he transferred over to the armoured division of the Household Cavalry. 'We worked together for three or four weeks,' he continued. 'We'd been told to get this four-tonne wagon up to scratch, replace the canvas – the works. We did that, working our hardest to make it respectable. And then we found out it was going to be used as a bin wagon.'

We did understand Stevie, and we all laughed.

'One of my memories of Compo at that time was when we had to drive an eight-tonne vehicle into Windsor to pick up a load of lads that were on a run. Martyn couldn't turn this vehicle and managed to churn up most of the grass in the Queen's park.

'It's a cool idea to have your wedding in a safari park. That way if anyone misbehaves, you can just chuck them to the lions.

'But, on a serious note, I'm sure you'll all agree that the ceremony was fantastic. Michelle looks stunning. Thank you, Compo, for the privilege and honour of being one of your best men. Thank you, Chris, for making me look good.'

He then proposed a toast: 'To the most amazing couple you could ever wish to meet, whose love for one another is overwhelming and something we should all aspire to. To the bride and groom, Martyn and Michelle.'

It was amazing to hear someone speak about us in those terms. Just like Lorraine's speech earlier, hearing her say how inspirational Martyn was, it was something we didn't think about. Our effect on other people wasn't something we considered, and to hear that people had been moved by what we'd done was like having an out-of-body experience – we couldn't believe that they were talking about us. I just thought, 'Well, what have we done?' All we'd done was love each other and fight for each other. That was all.

Martyn gave a lovely speech, thanking everyone for their support. He'd wanted to mention his mum but had decided against it, as he knew it would be too emotional for his family. She was in his thoughts, though. We then had some drinks before going outside into the sun to enjoy the grounds.

A bit later, Stevie told us that he'd messed up. He said that he'd forgotten to take our overnight bags out of the army car, the one the police can't stop – and now that car was shooting its way back to Windsor, probably at 150 mph. Poor Stevie was distressed, but Martyn and I laughed. We didn't mind. This was the happiest day of our lives, and we wanted everyone else to share in it. The last thing we wanted was for Stevie, who'd spoken so wonderfully, to worry about missing bags.

If you listen to the lyrics of 'Up Where We Belong', sung by Joe Cocker and Jennifer Warnes, it perfectly conveys everything that we've been through and everything that we still have to face. They sing about not knowing what tomorrow brings and how there are always obstacles in life. Martyn and I know all about that. All about mountains and long roads and taking a step, day after day. That's why we chose it as our first dance.

I held him and all eyes fixed on us. The music filled the room, and I heard every word and understood their meaning. It was wonderful to be in Martyn's arms, dancing with him, listening to those words.

Later in the evening, Stevie came to the fore again and made a moving gesture. He's a singer-songwriter, and we'd asked him to compose a song for us, but he found it too difficult. I think Martyn's injuries had scarred him like they'd scarred so many other people. It was too emotionally raw for him to sit down and write something. But he didn't let us down. Stevie would never want to let Martyn down. He stood in front of our guests and sang Paul Weller's 'English Rose'.

He had such a gentle, sweet singing voice. The words about how nothing could keep us apart were perfect, and I think it was the best moment of the day for me and Martyn.

It was a remarkable night, with moments of high emotion, such as Stevie's performance, mixed with the usual drunken laughs and bad dancing you expect at a decent wedding party. I danced all night, but Martyn was tired. It had been a long week for him. And the day had been frantic, too. As anyone who has got married knows, you're the hosts, and you can't really relax all day.

At the end of the evening, when the guests drifted away, we were ready to unwind. We stayed at Chilston Manor in

Maidstone, and like most couples, I think, we fell asleep pretty much immediately. It had been the best day of our lives. It had been what we'd both dreamed about.

We woke up together as husband and wife, and it felt magical. People who suggest marriage is not as special if the couple have lived together beforehand are wrong. You feel the girders tighten in your relationship, you feel the concrete harden. You're held together by something more now that you've got those rings, now you've made that commitment.

We didn't have our overnight bags, so I had to go down for breakfast in my wedding dress, and Martyn wore his morning suit. I was probably the first bride to wear her wedding dress to breakfast the day after she got married. Everyone looked at us, but we didn't care. At least I got to wear my wedding dress twice. Not many brides get that opportunity. Not many brides get to sit at breakfast next to an amazing husband such as Martyn Compton, a man who's gone through hell, who died and lived again to be with me.

CHAPTER 35

MARTYN AND MICHELLE –
TOMORROW WILL KEEP COMING

NEW YORK – 10 NOVEMBER 2008

Life comes at you, and you can either turn your back and cower or face it head on. We faced it head on. It's not that we're braver than anyone else; it's just that we didn't know what else to do. It was the only option.

We've lived life on a roller coaster for the past two years. When it's been bad, it's been dreadful, but when it's been good, it's been spectacular. The worst of it was the incident and the months spent in hospital keeping death at bay. The best of it was the wedding, our greatest day. But we've had some other wonderful experiences. Meeting Prince William and Simon Weston have been highlights. Watching Spurs win the Carling Cup at Wembley was electrifying. Joining the stars on the red carpet at the Britain's Best Awards was unreal. And receiving the award from the prime minister was something that had you told us two years ago we'd be doing, we would've said you'd had enough to drink and should stop now.

We had a dazzling £10,000 honeymoon – another kindness, this time from Abercrombie and Kent, the travel firm. We went to Sri Lanka and the Maldives. We dived in clear blue seas and did other things we'd never dreamed of doing. Particularly special was visiting an elephant orphanage, as Michelle loves elephants. There was one little fella there with a missing foot. He'd stepped on a landmine. We felt a special affinity with him.

And days after we came home from honeymoon, we were treated to another dream come true: we got to meet the England football team at Arsenal's training ground in Hertfordshire. They were preparing for a match against the Czech Republic, which we'd been invited to. The charity Give Us a Sporting Chance set it up after the Household Cavalry nominated Martyn. They give disabled people the chance to fulfil their ambitions. Martyn gave them a list of wishes: to get involved in carrying the Olympic torch when it comes to London for the 2012 games, to climb a mountain with a famous climber and to climb the Sydney Harbour Bridge. Given the chance, he'll achieve these goals.

The England guys were great. John Terry spent a while with us, chatting and wishing us well. David Beckham wished us well, and David James and Frank Lampard were really friendly. Kevin played against Lampard and Rio Ferdinand when he was at Gillingham when they were all kids. Joe Cole was a lovely guy, warm and friendly. He seemed in awe of us. He said that he'd seen our story and that he hoped everything went well for us.

This all shows that you don't know what's around the corner. You've got to be prepared for everything, and even if you think you can't cope, you've got to dig your heels in and get on with it. What happened to us, happened. It can't be changed. It's too late to regret; it's too late to be angry. We've got scars, yes, but scars are wounds that have healed. They're the sign of getting better.

New York has scars. The city was attacked, its heart ripped out by hatred and ignorance. But now those scars are healing, too. The wounds are mending. Life's still moving forward. And the city's moving with it.

We went there in November 2008 to participate in Walk New York in aid of the Household Cavalry Operational Casualties Fund. Noreen Hamnett, the wife of Paul the medic, and Paula Anderton arranged it. They've really got behind the cause and worked so hard. Seventeen of us took part. We wanted to raise £10,000 for the fund, but we raised nearly £35,000 in the end. We were chuffed to contribute almost £6,000 from the public after the story about our wedding appeared in the papers. Our friends and family and people at the pub where we met gave money, too.

While we were there, we took part in the New York City Veterans' Day Parade. It was the same day as Remembrance Day back home, when we should all wear poppies and never forget the men and women who died so that we can be here today. It was the 90th Veterans' Day Parade. It all started back in 1919, a year after the First World War ended. It was New York showing its commitment to those who served in the US forces. It's not a celebration of war but of ordinary people doing extraordinary things. This is a patriotic city, proud of its heroes, and it was an honour to be among them. We felt at one with them, because we've known what they've known. We've endured pain and suffering; we've lost friends.

It was very moving to stare out over the busy roads that were packed with veterans. The streets were lined with well-wishers, all of them there to pay tribute to the veterans. They waved their American flags proudly and sang their anthem. We took it all in, overwhelmed.

We received hundreds of letters from strangers when our story started to appear in the newspapers. We've had people come up to us in the street to wish us well. We've had correspondence from all over the world – including from here in the United States of America. We still shake our heads and say, 'This is just us. How can all these people be interested in us?'

A week later, we were back home in East Sussex with our dog, Humphrey, and Bud, the parrot. Just us and our pets in our home. Nothing special; nothing out of the ordinary. And we looked forward to another Christmas together – lots of presents, lots of food and drink, lots of fun. And then another year in our journey together got under way.

We've still got challenges ahead, more operations, more rehabilitation – as Peter Dziewulski told us, 'A burn is for life.' But we'll take those challenges on like we've taken on everything that's gone before, and we'll come through. We don't know how to do anything else. Life's in your face all the time, and you can't back down. Tomorrow will keep coming, whether you like it or not – so you might as well face it.

FROM MICHELLE'S DIARY

TUESDAY, 29 AUGUST

While you were having your operation, Sarah took me out shopping in Braintree and we went to a bridal shop. I tried a dress on, and it was lovely. We are going to get married whether you like it or not. I love you, and always will.

FROM MARTYN'S DIARY

SATURDAY, 17 JUNE

Asked Mich to marry me!! Love her loads . . .